D1570168

The Christ of the Gospels

The Christ of the Gospels

An Exegetical Study

By
J. W. SHEPARD, M.A., Th.D.
Professor of New Testament Interpretation
in the
NEW ORLEANS BAPTIST THEOLOGICAL SEMINARY

WM. B. EERDMANS PUBLISHING COMPANY
Grand Rapids   1956   Michigan

Copyright 1939
by
J. W. Shepard

Eighth printing, August, 1956

PHOTOLITHOPRINTED BY CUSHING - MALLOY, INC.
ANN ARBOR, MICHIGAN, UNITED STATES OF AMERICA
1956

CONTENTS

FOREWORD

The object of the author in this work is to give an exegetical study of the life of Jesus Christ as depicted in the Gospels. The true interpretation of any life may be had from a correct exegesis of its recorded expression through which the character is reflected to the world. A complete biography of Christ cannot be written. The Gospels record only a selected few of the many expressions of that life. But there ought to be and is a progressive comprehension of the Word of God and the life of Jesus in its meaning to mankind. Every new interpretation of that many-sided life should add some new view of the truth in Jesus. Though the recorded words and acts of Jesus are but a selected few, their full interpretation has never been approximated. Every new advance in the better understanding of nature and wider knowledge of theology brings another and more complete opportunity for exploring the field of spiritual truth recorded in the Gospels.

There is need of a new interpretation of Jesus to every generation. His life is the greatest of all objects of human thought. He is the Light of the World and the hope of mankind. In Him all the perplexing problems of a growing civilization must find their solution. Economists are coming to sit more and more at His feet, though He never professed to teach economics or sociology. Theology must be centered more yet in Him who was the full revelation of God. Science with all its splendid accomplishments must ultimately become the handmaid of the religion taught by Jesus. In the realm of psychology, He must at some future time be exalted to supremacy. His conquest, some day, will be complete in the realm of the thought and life of mankind.

"Jesus shall reign where'er the sun,
Doth his successive journeys run."

Many books have been written about Jesus. Some have merely put the old theology in a new dress. Others have presented Him as a mere man. But He is the door through which man must pass to a deeper consciousness and understanding of the mystery of life. Our modern Christianity has laid much stress on service and especially on method. We have thus lost motive power and vision. Jesus can lead us into a deeper experience of the sublime. He will usher us into the presence of the living God, if we follow Him. The application of His principles and ideals to our modern problems is a field relatively unexplored as yet.

The plan followed in this treatise is different from the ordinary. It is not simply biographical, but more widely expository. It is an ambitious plan, but commends itself in that it follows the principle of grammatico-historical exposition, which has become in our modern era scientific in its methods of research. At the same time that it seeks to present a realistic picture of Jesus as reflected in the Gospel narratives, it would not forget to relate the life and principles of the Master to the present as well as to the past environment. This is the practical aim. The plan is too comprehensive for one volume and the expositions will have to be too brief in places to be satisfying. But such a plan, we trust, will commend itself to the reader, who shall be willing to follow with patience the longer way, which leads to the more glorious view.

For more than a quarter of a century the author has specialized in the study of the life of Christ, teaching in theological seminaries, and by constant and ever widening readings laying foundations for a more complete understanding of Jesus as a man, and of Christ as the Son of God and Savior of the world. The study of these years, coupled with a wide experience in the work of teacher and preacher, has brought certain settled convictions, the expressions of which may contribute somewhat to the better interpretation of the life of our Lord. If such may be the case, the labor of the years will be more than repaid, and the author will feel deeply grateful for the privilege of being so used.

In this pretentious undertaking the writer has drawn from a long list of authors, the bibliography of which would be too extensive for presentation in this volume. The Greek text has been the main emphasis, recognizing that few authors have attempted a work of this character with special emphasis on the grammatical exegesis and at the same time due attention to the historical background. It would be ungrateful not to mention the very patient and most helpful counsels and constructive criticism of Dr. W. O. Carver, Professor of Missions in the Southern Baptist Seminary, and the deeply Christian encouragement of Dr. Hight C. Moore of the Sunday School Board of the Southern Baptist Convention. Space forbids the mention of many others. Valuable assistance was rendered in the typing, proof-reading and other phases of the task, by members of my family. On my desk during the four summers of activity in writing, many of my favorite authors, such as A. T. Robertson, David Smith, Edersheim, Farrar, and many modern versions and general treatises of others have been my constant companions in seeking to arrive at the accurate knowledge (epignosis) of the gospel record. If there has been any useful success it must be attributed to the Great Helper, whose help was daily sought "to bring to mind the things of Jesus."

J. W. S.

HISTORICAL INTRODUCTION

Christianity is a historic religion because Christ, its founder, was a historic person. In the beginning of the Christian era there appeared in history One who changed its current from a downward to an upward trend. He was born in Bethlehem and reared in Nazareth a small town of Galilee, of an humble family of the Jews who were then subjected under the provincial Roman rule.[1]

He received His elementary training in a synagogue school in which the Jewish child studied from the ages of six to twelve. Although the people of Galilee enjoyed more liberality in religion than those of Judea, the Jewish religion everywhere was oppressed by a narrow, Rabbinical leadership which headed up in Jerusalem. The boy Jesus had no highly literary education but became well grounded in Aramaic, and in the knowledge of the Hebrew language and the Sacred Scriptures of the Jews. He mastered also Greek into which these Scriptures had been translated centuries before His time. While supporting as a carpenter the family of the deceased Joseph He "cut His way forward" in the mastery of the Rabbinical lore and the Hebrew prophets, becoming deeply learned in the true religion of Israel. At the age of thirty, He appeared at the Jordan, asking baptism of John, and soon after He initiated His ministry, which grew into a religious movement, that has reached today the uttermost confines of the world.

Jesus, different from any other teacher in history, called attention to His person rather than His doctrine. The religion of the Christ of the Gospels is an experienced relation between Him and His believer-disciple. His personality was unique, attracting vast throngs about Him, reminding some of Elijah in His denunciation of sin; others of the tender-hearted Jeremiah weeping over the sins of his people. His authoritative teaching, which threatened to supersede that of the Pharisees, and His assumption of the true Messianic role, which stirred deeply the enmity of the vested interests of the Annas Bazaars, aroused an antagonism which during three intense years waxed ever fiercer until it brought Him to the cross at Jerusalem.[2]

History confirms the testimony of the gospel traditions, first oral then written, to the fact of His incomparable claims, His sinless life, His vicarious death on the cross and His resurrection from the tomb. The influence of His life and teachings, substantiated by the actual transformation of the lives of those who believed on Him, swept on and surmounted the antagonism of the bigoted Jewish

1 Cf. F. L. Anderson, The Man of Nazareth, Ch. I.
2 Ibid.

i

rulers, met and defeated the subtle heathen philosophies of the Greeks and passed unscathed through the ruthless Roman persecutions, to emerge with victory at last. Saul of Tarsus equipped with the culture of the Tarsian University and the theology of Gamaliel, who became the chief and first persecutor of the Nazarenes, was miraculously converted on the Damascus road and sent forth as the apostle to the Gentiles, to bear the message and plant the banner of Christianity in the chief provincial capitals of the Roman Empire. In the mortal struggle of young Christianity with its heathen enemies, during the first three centuries, it gained a signal victory, when Constantine bowed to the Galilean Peasant.[1]

Both Christian history and experience testify that Jesus Christ is the Divine Saviour, from His supernatural manger-cradle.[2] Primitive Christians believed that He was the Son of God and not a mere prophet or apostle. He is the author of spiritual life and had no flaw in His character. He never prayed for forgiveness for Himself. Leeky says that in three short years Christ did more to elevate humanity than all the sages of all ages. He created a type of character never before seen, which no culture can produce apart from Him. He gives an ideal to be attained in life and furnishes the power to attain it. He is the Savior of mankind by His own testimony and goes on revealing ever His power to save everyone who comes to Him. He saves from sin and gives the power to overcome it. He is the Savior of the present life of man; He is also the Savior of our future life because He brought life and immortality to light. He came forth from the grave and liveth forevermore. The power of the Christianity of Christ, to leaven the mass of humanity, has been demonstrated in multiform ways and is destined to bring in a new era in which right must rule over might.

The great central figure and vital personality in this marvelous development of the centuries is to be studied in this volume from the standpoint of the manifestations of His life as recorded in the evangelical records. The stupendous task is far too vast for even many volumes and may only be approached with humble reliance on the great Helper whom He sent to guide us into all truth. No apology would be sufficient for even attempting such a work except the sincere desire to make Him better known to some students, pastors, teachers, and earnest seekers after the truth. The grammatico-historical method of exegesis naturally calls for a historical introduction which will in part furnish the setting for the gem, the background of the picture. This work is not an attempt

1 Ibid
2 Cf. D. W. Forrest. The Christ of History and of Experience, Lecture V.

at a biography but a brief exposition, the object of which is to unevil as far as may be possible the wonderful picture of the Divine Savior, the Lord Jesus—the Christ of the Gospels. The simple historical resume is an attempt to pave the way for that. A very brief reference to the physical, historical, intellectual, moral and religious world-environment into which He was born, is all that can be attempted, with a glance at the sources from which the factual details of His life have been obtained.

1. The physical environment.

Coarse materialism of our modern times has largely robbed the wonderful little country of Palestine of the idyllic charm it possessed when its people "saw a great light." Only a hundred and thirty-six miles long by sixty-nine broad at its widest extension, it was cast in the midst of, but separated from the nations, fit place for the training of the chosen people of Israel and Israel's Saviour whose life was lived mostly within the central plateau with but infrequent and brief excursions into the regions surrounding. He was born in the little town of Bethlehem, not far from Jerusalem the greatest center, and reared largely in the picturesque little village of Nazareth, nestled in the hills of Galilee, overlooking the historic plain of Esdraelon, scene of much of the drama of Israel's history.

His life was connected up in wonderful ways with the beautiful mountains which He loved and to which He frequently resorted for seasons of communion with the Father. From snowclad Hermon of the north where He was transfigured, to the Mount of Beatitudes—the Horns of Hattin by the sea, the Mount of Olives, Quarantania—the traditional site of the Temptations, and Calvary to the South, there cluster recollections of His wonderful career. Most of the years of His early life were passed in Nazareth, but the three years of His public ministry carried Him into the plains and cities with their teeming populations, and especially into the villages and towns which surrounded the beautiful little lake of Galilee, fed by the clear waters of the Jordan, a mountain stream, with its sources at the base of Hermon.

The Jordon, which is its only river of any size, is only a hundred and thirty miles long. It is a beautiful stream flowing through the Sea of Galilee, descending through a gorge and emptying into the phenomenal Dead Sea. Its greatest mark of distinction is that Jesus was baptized in it by John the Baptist, His forerunner.

Palestine presented within its bounds all types of climates, from the frigid to the tropical, and consequently all types of vegetation. The Bible bears the imagery of a universal race and has a cosmopolitan character found in no other book. More than two thousand varieties of flowers flourished in Palestine in the time of Jesus. This little country situated in the heart of the world's drama, isolated from the surrounding nations by deserts, mountains and sea, was yet traversed by four highways, arteries of the blood of ancient civilizations. This peculiar people received the impact of the life, customs, and literatures of the Babylonian, Persian, Greek, and Roman civilizations. Such a physical environment was the best the world had for the arena of the life of Jesus.

2. The historical background.

No subject is ever studied completely until it has been studied historically. The life of Jesus apart from its historical setting would be like a painting without perspective. At least a partial glance at the inter-biblical period of the history of the Jews from the time of Malachi, the last of the prophets, until the time of John the Baptist, is essential to constitute a background for the picture of Jesus, the Messiah. The principle sources for this study are Josephus, the Jewish historian, and the Apocryphal books of historical, legendary, apocalyptic, and didactic character, variously. Seven of these books were added to the Septuagint translation of the Hebrew Canonical Scriptures when that translation was made in Alexandria about 283 B. C.

Before the Persian rule (536-331 B. C.) the Jews were for fifty years under Babylonian influence, a great number having been led away into captivity during that time. Jerusalem lay in ruins. Cyrus, the Persian Monarch, in the early years of his reign permitted a large group of the Jews under the leadership of Zerubbabel to return and rebuild the Temple of Jerusalem, which was finished in 516 B. C. Under Ezra in 458 B. C., and Nehemiah in 445 B. C., other groups returned and rebuilt the walls of the city and reestablished the worship of Jehovah in their native land. At the death of Nehemiah, his functions of governor were vested in a High Priest. From 359 B. C. the office of High Priest, with civil and religious functions, became an object of envy. Through jealousies in the family of one of the High Priests Jonathan, Manasseh, his son, went to Samaria where he married the daughter of Sanballat, and afterwards established the worship of the Samaritans in Mt. Gerizim (cf Jno. 4:51-56).

The Persians exerted a powerful influence over the Jews, who during the reign of Cyrus, 536-529 B. C., enjoyed the favor of the dominant people and were thus rendered more susceptible to their influence, evidenced in the apocryphal book of Tobit, written by a Jew in Persia during that period. The Persians were monotheists, and the religious views of the subject people were thus contaminated gradually by those of the Persians. In the book of Tobit, which is a romance, there are many doctrines contradictory to those of the Hebrew Scriptures, such as salvation by alms, prayers, and other good works, to say nothing of the doctrine of demons, asceticism, and many others.

Under the Greeks (331-167 B. C.) the Jews of the Dispersion were yet more radically influenced. Alexander the Great, with an army of 35,000 men, crossed the Hellespont and defeated the Persians in Asia Minor. He soon pressed his campaign down to Tyre which after some time yielded. He then went further south to Jerusalem where he was met by the High Priest at the head of a procession and received peacefully into the city. The conqueror treated with reverence the religion of the Jews, and later, when he had conquered Egypt and built the city of Alexandria, invited the Jews to live there. His invitation was accepted and a large colony of Jews soon grew up in Egypt. In 323 B. C. Alexander, having conquered the whole world, died at the early age of thirty-two, and his vast kingdom was divided among four of his generals.

Under the Ptolemies of Egypt (321-198 B. C.) the Jews, for the most part, enjoyed great favor. Ptolemy Philadelphus (285-247 B. C.) was a great friend of the Jews and after founding the famous library of Alexandria had the Hebrew Scriptures translated into Greek to serve a generation of the Jews who had grown up in the Greek language. Thus Alexandria became a great center and the Hellenistic influence was strong, as we may verify in the apocryphal book of Ecclesiasticus, wholly different from those of the Hebrew canonical books.

The Jews' allegiance, during this period, passed back and forth frequently between the rival kingdoms of the Ptolemies of Egypt and the Syrian kings to the north of them. Under the Syrian regime (198-167 B. C.) they were treated sometimes well but most of the time cruelly by the rulers. The first ruler, Antiochus the Great, was favorable and the Hellenistic influence was powerful. It invaded the high-priesthood in Jerusalem and largely changed the thought of the Jews, so that when Antiochus visited Jerusalem in 172 B. C., he was welcomed with a torch-light procession. A strong party in Jerusalem led many Jews to abandon their sacrifices and rites in favor of the Greek religion. There arose, however, during this time an opposing party of the strict and orthodox Jews led by the Scribes. They founded synagogues and zealously guarded their traditions. Antiochus Epiphanes (175-170 B. C.) treated the Jews most cruelly. Jason, the Hellenistic high priest under the patronage of Antiochus, introduced into Jerusalem the Greek gymnasium, and abominable customs, subversive of the faith and morals of the people. He invaded Egypt and, being un-

successful, returned to Jerusalem to wreak vengeance on the Jews
who hated him, slaughtering 40,000 of the inhabitants of the
city and selling many others into slavery. He also desecrated
the Temple, sacrificing a hog on its altar. When he later again invaded Egypt, he was unable to take Alexandria because of the
strong party of Jews there who joined in the defense. On his
return through Palestine, taking advantage of the Jewish religious
scruples, he entered Jerusalem on the Sabbath and made of the
city a slaughter-house, killing all the men and taking the women
and children captive. The streets literally ran with blood, and
the city was utterly laid waste. The worship of the Jews disappeared, the remnant of the people being forced to sacrifice to
pagan idols. In a fourth invasion of Egypt later, Antiochus completed the destruction of the city, and the Temple was razed to the
ground. (1 Macc. 1:43) Antiochus raised a decree, making uniform
the religion of his kingdom and prohibiting the worship of the
Jews. He sent Atheneu of Antioch to Palestine to receive taxes
and enforce the regulation against worship. He also dedicated
the Temple in Jerusalem to Zeus and established pagan worship
in it, introducing the lascivious customs of the Greek worship.
The observance of the law of Moses was prohibited under the
threat of capital punishment. (I Macc. 1:54; cf. Dan. 11:31).

The Jews, under the Maccabean patriotic leaders (167-63
B. C.), recovered their independence from the Syrian rulers to
the North. When Antiochus attempted to enforce his regulation
relative to worship, an aged priest, Mattathias, led in revolt.
He slew an apostate Jew who was worshipping at the idol altar
in Modin, and gathering a group of patriots, fled to the mountains
of Judea, where he carried on a guerilla warfare for a time until
his death. He was succeeded in the leadership by his son, Judas.
who soon became famous on account of his patriotic fervor and
his signal victories over the armies of the Assyrians, sent to sub-
due the revolters. These victories were gained by Judas with
greatly inferior forces, due to his strategy and his religious enthusiasm, manifested in a fast and a national confession of sins proclaimed at Mispah, at the beginning of his campaign to rid the
country of the enemy. When he had carried through his campaign successfully almost to the end, he fell into the temptation of
making an alliance with the Romans, and thus lost his hold on the
Jewish patriots, who had supported his religious leadership. Only
eight hundred remained loyal to him, and, in the next battle at
Eleasa, he died fighting valiantly against great odds. He was succeeded in the leadership by a younger brother, Jonathan, very
different in character from Judas. His leadership was one of trying

to outwit the Syrian kings by treachery, but he was soon caught in a trap of the same kind and executed.

Simon, a third brother of the sons of Mattathias, next took the leadership, and succeeded in taking the fortresses of the Syrians at Gaza, Jamnia and Joppa. This brought about peace with the Syrians, who recognized the independence of the Jews. Arranging a treaty with the Romans, Simon devoted himself to internal improvements until his death by assassination through Syrian treachery in 137 B. C. His son, John Hyrcannus, led the Jews in defeating the invasion of the Syrians which followed, and after re-establishing peace, renewed the treaty with the Romans and the country enjoyed independence for twenty years. During this time there is noted the rise of the Jewish religious sects of the Sadducees and the Pharisees. At the death of Hyrcannus, his son, Alexander Janneus, succeeded to the throne. He was greatly disliked by the Pharisees, who rose in revolt against him. After six years of civil war, Janneus was victorious and crucified eight hundred of his Pharisee enemies. He died in 79 B. C., and his successors for sixteen years experienced a troubled reign, which terminated with the coming of the Romans under Pompey, who took the city in 63 B. C.

Under the Romans (63 B. C.-637 A. D.) Antipater, a wealthy Idumean officer, gained great prestige with the Roman Emperor and was made Procurator of Judea. He placed his sons in charge of Judea and Galilee. Herod, who was given Galilee, suppressed the robber bands with a strong hand and called down on himself the envy of Hyrcannus, the high priest in Jerusalem, who summoned Herod to appear before him. Herod did so, but came dressed in royal purple and bearing letters from Caesar. The Sanhedrin was terrorized, but when Herod was accused by Shammai, he was counselled by Antipater to flee. The history of the rise of Herod's Kingdom (40-4 B. C.) is a drama of extraordinary moves of political chicanery accompanied by a succession of atrocious crimes arising from jealousy mostly within Herod's own heart, and against his own family. With rare ability he gained and kept the favor of the succeeding Roman Emperors, sacrificing all scruples in order to do so. He allied himself with the powerful Asmonean family of the Jews by marrying the princess Mariamne, but later had her and her sons Alexander and Aristobulus executed through jealousy, on account of their popularity. His reign was one succession of monstrous crimes until his death in 5 B. C.

At his death the Romans asserted a fuller sovereignty and divided the country into three tetrarchies under Archelaus (Judea), Herod Atipas (Galilee and Perea), and Herod Philip (Trachonitis, Aurtanitis, and Batanea). Archelaus was disliked by the Jews and banished in 6 A. D. being succeeded by a Roman Procurator. The fifth of the succeeding Procurators was Pontius Pilate (25-36 A. D.). He was banished to Gaul and there committed suicide.

In 37 A. D. Caligula made Agrippa I king, at first of the tetrarchy of Philip and later, ir 41 A. D., of Galilee and Perea. In 44 A. D. the Emperor Claudius reverted to the system of Procurators, two of whom were Felix and Festus (Acts 23-27). In 53 A. D. the country was again united under King Agrippa II who beheaded James (Acts 12). The Jews were given a large measure of autonomy by the Romans through their Sanhedrin, but with certain restrictions. They could not, for example, execute a death sentence until passed upon by the Roman ruler. The land passed from the Romans to the Saracens in 637 A. D. and continued under them until the World War in 1914-18, when it came under the jurisdiction of the English government.

3. View of the intellectual environment.

In order to comprehend the doctrines of Jesus one must know the current thought of His times. Culture among the Greeks and Romans had reached its culmination before the birth of Christ. Alexander scattered the Greek language and literature everywhere, greatly affecting the Jews. The Romans dominated the peoples, built roads, establishing universal communication and commerce.

(1) The Greek philosophy.

Socrates called the attention of the thought world away from the physical universe to the study of the moral qualities. He believed in one supreme God and the immortality of the soul, though he was agnostic about the future life. He was condemned to death for teaching the youth of Athens the necessity of a democratic form of government under a wise philosopher. Counseled by friends to flee for his life, he preferred to remain in Athens and drink the cup of hemlock bravely.

Plato, his brilliant disciple, deeply impressed by the death of his great teacher, began to teach the same doctrines and was forced to flee. He journeyed in foreign countries for several years and then returned to begin his brilliant career as poet and philosopher. His *Republic* discusses problems of metaphysics, theology, ethics, psychology, pedagogy, politics and art. According to his theory the people should be divided into three categories, for an ideal society. The industrials should produce but not reign; the military men should protect but not govern; the philosophers were suited for guiding and governing. Education should be universal, by the state, and to be firm, based on religion. Democracy was equality of opportunity and all should have an equal chance at education and the other opportunities of life. Justice was the efficient co-ordination of the social classes. The redemption of the race was necessary and salvation was by means of instruction.

Aristotle was a deist in his theory of the universe. He had the very widest sweep in research and intellectual attainments. He elaborated the science of logic in essentially its present form, but gave little attention to religion.

The Epicurean philosophers made fun of religion. They said that the chief aim of life was pleasure and the soul was not immortal. This was the most popular philosophy when the Christian era began. The Stoics were pantheists. God was everything and everything was God. They worshipped various phases of material creation. The aim of life was virtue. Freedom from emotion and passion was the main characteristic of the perfect man. The circumstances of life, such as riches or poverty, were not important. The Eclectics emphasized Plato but fabricated a system of philosophy composed of elements from all philosophies.

(2) Jewish thought.

The Jews developed a literature of their own during their subjection to foreign peoples. They had their Old Testament Scriptures as a beginning. In spite of their exclusive nature, the Greek influence affected them greatly, due to the friendly treatment they received from Alexander and some of his successors. The strict party of the Jews put a ban on "Greek wisdom", but the Hellenists rapidly gained ground mainly in the West. The strict party of the Jews had its stronghold in the Trans-Euphratic regions. They constituted an influential community, preserved the Hebrew Scriptures, and from their theological centers sprang Ezra and other scribes who became the teachers of Israel and conservators of their traditions. They compiled the Mishna and elaborated the Halakkah (an application of the Old Testament Scriptures). The Haggadah which was made up of personal sayings of the Rabbis had no absolute authority, as did the Halakkah, but came to have great influence. Jesus taught not as the Scribes and Pharisees, but with the authority of an original interpreter of the Old Testament. The conservatism of the strict Jews of the Diaspora later made Peter's work of evangelization largely ineffectual in Babylon.

So, the exclusive tendencies on the one hand, and the Hellenistic influence and liberalizing tendencies on the other, brought about two parties among the Jews. The intelligent Jew was confronted constantly with many true and beautiful things in Greek thought and soon reasoned that these also must be from God. Greek rulers sought constantly to Grecianize Palestine, building cities of (cf. Decapolis) and planting colonies. The Babylonian Jews who returned under Zerubbabel, Ezra, and Nehemiah used currently the Aramaic. They had to use an interpreter in their synagogue worship when they employed the Hebrew Scriptures. In Alexandria the Septuagint translation had been made by Philadelphus for the Jews and that came to be used in Palestine as a kind of People's Bible. It is probable that it was also used in the synagogues.

The extra-canonical literature of the Jews was of apocryphal and also apocalyptic character. The seven apocryphal books written from 200 B. C. to the time of Christ and embodied in the LXX were of the nature of an apologetic, extolling the dignity of Israel and depreciating heathenism. There were some apocryphal books, however, of conciliatory character. "The Wisdom of Solomon" and Fourth Book of Maccabees sought a common rational basis for the theology of the Old Testament and the philosophy of Plato, and took for their ethics the self-abnegation of Stoicism. The Babylonian Jews later tabooed these books.

In Alexandria the Hellenistic Jews worked out a system for the rationalization of the Jewish Old Testament theology using the Greek philosophy as a basis. They made use of the allegorical method of interpretation, giving a "spiritual" of mystical meaning to everything — a convenient expedient. Aristobulus, an Alexandrian rationalist, said the Greeks had gotten their philosophy from Moses.

The apocalyptic literature abounded in visions, expressed in symbolic figures, beasts and mystic numbers. Some of the Old Testament prophecies are classed as apocalyptic, such as Daniel, Ezekiel, Zachariah, and Joel. Of the apocryphal books, Baruch and II Esdras partook of this character, as also Enoch, Jubilees, Psalms of Solomon, the Sibylline Oracles, and Assumption of Moses.

Philo, an Alexandrian Jew, reduced the allegorical method of interpretation to a system. He sought to explain God in terms of the Platonic and Stoic philosophies, and elaborated the doctrine of intermediary potencies, (dunameis) and words (logoi). He developed the logos doctrine, but his logos is shadowy, unreal, impersonal. The logos, in his conception, was the instrument of creation of the physical universe and acts as priestly intermediary between God and man. He regarded matter as eternal, the world being formed of existing matter. The soul was a direct creation of God, the aim of life being to get rid of the sensuous and rise to the spiritual. The change was to be wrought by study of the physical, the ordinary circle of knowledge, and of divine philosophy. The form of thought in the introduction to the fourth gospel is Alexandrian, the logos doctrine being the point of contact.

John presents, however, a personal Logos full of grace and truth. The incarnation of this Logos is set forth as a fact. The way out for the soul is not by study, discipline, inborn disposition, but by birth from above meditated through the Holy Spirit by means of faith in the Logos.

(3) Roman culture and literature reached its golden age before Christ. The great Roman writers, such as Virgil, Horace, Ovid, Sallust, and Nepos, lived and wrote about the time Jesus was born. Cicero, Seneca, and Epictetus occupied the stage as statesmen, orators, and philosophers.

The Jews were hated by the Romans because of their exclusiveness. Their commercial prosperity excited the envy and jealously of others. Their God was exclusive also, and would not fit into the Pantheon. Their scruples about swines' flesh and the Sabbath were ridiculed and they were criticized as being haters of other people. Cicero held their religion to be a barbarous superstition because they worshipped an unseen God. Tacitus accused them of teaching their proselytes to renounce their own countries and even their own families. Such people, the satirists said, deserved no pity.

In spite of this fact many of the Roman rulers were friendly to the Jews. Because of their peculiarity of customs, Jewish slaves were in many cases freed for a small ransom. Added immigration swelled this nucleus of freedmen to a colony in Rome of some sixty thousand. The ruins of seven synagogues show a wide distribution over the city.

Expressions on their tombs in cemeteries bespeak faith in the future life in sharp contrast to the hopelessness of their heathen neighbors. The rulers granted them freedom of worship and, in many cities, Roman citizenship. The Jewish colony in Rome grew in influence and came to wield great power in determining the conditions of their Jewish brethren in other parts, as in the case of the banishment of Archelaus. As a people, the Jews held to their exclusiveness. Palestine was divided into Jewish territory and Hellenic towns; as Decapolis and other cities. The Herods built various towns: Sabaste, Cesarea, Ebionitis, Bethsaida-Julius, Cesarea-Philippi and others, where Greek and Syrian worship prevailed. Jesus did not enter these towns for evangelization but limited His ministry to "the lost sheep of the house of Israel." The worship and customs of the Gentiles were an abomination to the Jews. Frequent revolts of the Jews were suppressed with cruelty and they in turn cultivated in their children bitter hatred and distrust toward the Romans.

4. Views of the religious and moral world.

The Jews were always a religious people and their chief contribution to civilization was their religion. They were monotheists and uncomprimising in their claim to have the only true religion. For times they were influenced by the idolatrous religions around them but while in captivity they learned the spiritual and universal character of their own religion. Unable to return to Jerusalem and their Temple, erstwhile center of their worship, they learned that God answered their prayers in a foreign land and founded the synagogue which came to prevail widely over the world until now. In every town where ten heads of Jewish families could be found, a synagogue was established, and Jerusalem later came to have four-hundred and sixty, besides the Temple. Services were held on Saturday, Monday and Thursday.

(1) Religious parties or sects.

There were two distinct elements in the religious circles of Palestine in the time of Christ: the formalists and those who "hoped for the consolation of Israel". During a period of great persecution under Antiochus Epiphanes, Simon the High Priest taught his people that the permanence of the Jewish race depended on separateness and works of righteousness. During the period of subjugation to the Selucidae, the Great Assembly disappeared, to be replaced later by the Sanhedrin. Contact with the liberalizing tendency of the Greeks gave rise to two sects or parties: the Pharisees or Separatists and the Sadducees.

(a) The Pharisees resisted foreign influence and were zealous for their traditions. Their zeal degenerated later into formalism which put the Oral Law in the place of the living God and the Scriptures. This party was patriotic, orthodox, and in the time of Christ numbered six thousand in Palestine. Christ met with the opposition of this party because He did not follow their traditional methods of teaching and emphasized heart religion rather than ceremonialism, formalism, and self-righteousness. He soon attacked their traditional rules of the Sabbath openly, discriminating between their Oral Law and the Scriptures.

The Scribes were the pharisaic representatives of the people, who everywhere served as the ultimate authorities in questions of faith and practice. They formulated the Halakkah, or "way in which the fathers walked" which was their interpretation of the Scriptures plus the Oral Law, covering every conceivable case of conduct public or private. The Haggadah or "Sayings of the Scribes (Rabbis)" was a hedge around the Law to insure exact observance. This was a yoke upon the neck of the people, heavy to be borne. At the end of the second century (A. D.) the compiled Halakkah and Haggadah constituted the Mishnah. Later the Jerusalem and Babylonian Talmuds or Commentaries on the

Mishnah completed the formulation of the traditions. These writings contained many germs of truth which were covered up in a mass of formalistic rules and are not to be compared to the New or Old Testament. The Rabbis started with external observance, to come to the inner life of the Spirit as a goal; Jesus started with the inner life of the regenerated heart to come to the right outward observance and conduct as a result, making the tree good that the fruit might be good. The Scribes covered up the Scriptures with their Oral Law and multiplied rules until they crushed out the spirit.

(b) The Sadducees were a wealthy, sacerdotal aristocracy who did not believe in the Oral Law or in the future life. They opposed Pharisaic rigor and were ready to abide by the established order of things. Their chief interest was in politics and not religion. Though they were not so numerous as the Pharisees they held the presidency of the Sanhedrin. They were not concerned with opposing Jesus until political complications led them to do so at the end of His ministry.

(c) The Essenes were a sect of communists who lived mostly in isolated communities west of the Dead Sea. Their purifications and reverence for the sun indicated Persian influence. They did not go to the Temple but sent their tribute, read the Scriptures, and had their worship. Bloody sacrifices had no part in their religion, though in many characteristics they were Jewish. In the time of Christ they numbered four thousand.

(d) The Herodians were supporters of the government of the Herods, holding that a foreign governor was a better guarantee for protection of life and property and so to be preferred. They were like the Pharisees in belief.

(e) The Zealots were also like the Pharisees in belief but insisted on war against Rome. Various revolts promoted by them, as that under Judas of Galilee, were unsuccessful and severely punished. The party at last broke up into robber bands but did not lose the sympathy of the people. The spirit nurtured by this party afterwards broke out in the war against the Romans which terminated in the destruction of Jerusalem in 70 A. D.

(2) The messianic hope.

(a) Israel's prophets had foretold from the beginning the coming of a Messiah who would bring in a new day. God promised to Eve that her seed should bruise the serpent's head (Gen. 3:15). From the lineage of Japhet (Gen. 9:27) and from the seed of Abraham would spring the Messiah. Jacob foretold that the Messiah would be of the tribe of Judah—a prophet like Moses (Deut.

18:18). Later it was made known that He would spring from Jesse and many Psalms described Him (Ps. 22, 110) telling of the nature of His Kingdom (Ps. 72). In Isaiah the Suffering Servant was described (Chapters 40-46) as one who would make propitiation for the sins of His people—the very God and a priest and intercessor for the people. Born in Bethlehem, He would have a forerunner, and appear suddenly in the Temple (Mal. 3:1; 4:5).

(b) We also find this messianic hope expressed in the common literature of the Jews. The apocryphal books speak of a national restoration (Tobit 13:18; 14:5-7), though they differ from the Old Testament in their conception of the Messiah. The Book of Enoch speaks of a majestic temporal king who would establish a kingdom of righteousness. God's power would be revealed from heaven, destroying all sinners in His wrath, delivering His people, and giving them a new Canaan on earth. The Sibylline Oracles speak of a Messiah who would be a temporal king and rebuild the Temple, restoring the dispersed. All nations would then bring their wealth to the House of God. Even the book of Jubilees, written more or less in the time of Christ, refers to the future glory of Israel, the gathering of the dispersed and the building of the Sanctuary. Baruch, written after Jesus' time, describes a hoped-for temporal king. Josephus thought that Vespasian was the fulfillment of the prophecy about the Messiah. The Zealots believed in a temporal king as did also the Pharisees. The Sadducees had lost that hope. The current messianic hope in Jesus' time was for a temporal king as Messiah. The book of Fourth Esdras was written after the Temple had been destroyed in 70 A. D. The sufferings of Israel had been terrible. But even in this book no other way of salvation is presented than works and personal righteousness. Through the book runs a minor note of sadness. The author attempts to solve through prophecy the problem of Israel's fate. The Highest will send His Son in the form of Man who will pronounce judgment and destroy His enemies. The Jews of the dispersion, including the Ten Tribes, will be gathered back to Palestine. Even in Philo, the Alexandrian, the same hope is cleared and strongly expressed. When the dispersed should return, the "barren land would be transformed into fruitfulness."

(3) Other religions.

(a) The religion of the Samaritans was a mixture of Paganism and Judaism. A priest who fled from Jerusalem established worship in Mt. Gerizim. The Samaritans accepted only the Pentateuch. They expected a Messiah-Teacher but did not look for a Messiah King. They were despised by the Jews who would not even pass through Samaria when on the way to their Feasts in Jerusalem.

(b) The pagan religions of ancient Greece and Rome were polytheistic. They had lost much of their prestige when Jesus came. Greek philosophy had largely undermined the faith of the people in their gods which were mere exaggerated human beings with all the human passions and vices or else imaginary embodiments of forces of nature. The philosophers laughed at the gods, who were occupied with their feasts and their quarrels in Mount Olympus. When Rome conquered Greece she placed the Greek gods in her Pantheon. In both the Greek and Roman systems religion and morals were completely divorced.

The Religion in the Roman world at the time of Christ was mostly a matter of form and ritualism. Scepticism was almost universal among the educated classes. The Pontifex Maximus supervised the religious affairs and religion was a mere matter of the state. Emperor worship prevailed. Augurs studied the flight of birds to determine the will of the gods. Religion was a hollow and vain thing. Many sought satisfaction in Judaism and oriental cults.

(4) The moral status.

The world was in a state of extraordinary moral degeneration. Two thousand lords in Rome had 1,300,000 slaves, which were treated with great cruelty. In the Empire there were 6,000,000 slaves. The rich lived in the utmost profligacy. Chastity and marriage were the exception while divorce and immorality were the rule. The priests preyed upon the masses of the ignorant. Many seductive cults exerted a degrading influence. The religion of the Romans had no power to cope with the degeneracy of the times. The philosophies of the Greeks failed. None of the philosophies could meet the deep moral needs of the times. The Emperors were monsters of crime. Thousands of lives were sacrificed in the arena to furnish entertainment for the Emperor and a bloodthirsty population. Luxury was beyond description. The horrible character of vice and crime is witnessed to by the excavated objects of Pompeii. Seneca testified that children were considered with great disfavor and infant exposure was prevalent. Tacitus said that the spirit of the times was "to corrupt and to be corrupted." Paul gives a picture in the Roman epistle of a people who had departed from the God revealed in nature and conscience, to set up for themselves, through vain independence, gods like unto creatures. From this idol worship they had gone on into moral degeneracy and crime until they were lost in a world of darkness and destruction. This was the condition of the world morally when Jesus came, who was to "overcome the world" with His Gospel.

SOURCES OF OUR KNOWLEDGE

SOURCES OF OUR KNOWLEDGE

The historic life of Jesus is better known today than in any previous epoch. Many study the life of the Lord in modern times from the standpoint of His self-consciousness; but in the following treatise we interpret His life mainly from the study of His recorded works and teachings. There are various sources from which we derive our knowledge of Jesus.

(1) *Pagan Literature.*

This is the least important of all our sources, from the paucity of its testimony, but still important because it comes from the outside. Four great Roman writers refer to Jesus or to Christianity, which is remarkable since Jesus belonged to a distant and despised province. Tacitus (115-17 A. D.) in his Annals says that "in order to suppress the rumor that the Emperor himself had set fire to Rome in 64 A. D., Nero falsely accused and punished with most acute torture persons, who already hated for their shameful deeds, were commonly called Christians. The founder of that name, Christus, had been put to death by the procurator Pontius Pilate, in the reign of Tiberius; but the deadly superstition, though suppressed for a time, broke out again, not only throughout Judea, where this evil had its origin, but also throughout the city, (Rome), whither all things horrible and vile from all quarters flow and are encouraged. Accordingly, first those were arrested who confessed; and then on their information, a great multitude was convicted, not so much of the crime of incendiarism as of hatred of the human race." Suetonius says that the Emperor Claudius expelled the Jews from Rome "because of constant tumults under the leadership of Christus." The younger Pliny (112 A. D.) speaks of Christians in Bithynia, as followers of one, Christ, who "bind themselves with an oath not to enter into any wickedness or commit thefts, robberies, or adulteries, or falsify their word, or repudiate trusts committed to them." The Satirist Lucian (165-170 A. D.) speaks of the founder of Christianity as "a man who had been fixed to a stake in Palestine and who was still worshipped for having introduced a new code of morals in life." He further testified that Christ had taught His disciples *that they were brothers* and that *they also believed they would live forever.* It is not strange that the contemporary historians did not refer to Jesus. But by the end of the first century the development of Christianity could not escape their mention.

1

(2) *Jewish writers.*

Josephus, speaking of the martydom of James, calls him "the brother of Jesus who is called the Christ." He was probably afraid to say more, since he could only say good things. He apologizes for the crucifixion and lays it to the harsh judgment of the Sadducees (Antiq. 29:9:1). He also refers to John the Baptist (Antiq. 18:5:2) in an appreciative way. He did not mention Jesus in this same way because to do so would be to condemn his own people before the Gentiles. Of course the Old Testament prophecies spoke of the Messiah, whose picture, drawn by the prophets, was realized in Jesus. In the Apocryphal and Apocalyptic books we have a source valuable for the teachings of Jesus. The Talmud refers to the family of Jesus in a slanderous way.

(3) *Christian sources.*

(a) Paul's testimony is the earliest record we have. He testified to Jesus' descent from Abraham and David, His life of obedience (Rom. 1:3; 9:5; 5:19; 15:3), His poverty (II Cor. 8:9), His humility (Phil. 2:5-11), His death, burial, resurrection and appearances (I Cor. 11:24; 15:3-8). Of course all of Paul's epistles are built around Christ as the center of his theology. His epistles were written just thirty years after the crucifixion, and constitute therefore one of the strongest of testimonies. There was no need when he wrote for a detailed account of the life of Jesus, since many eyewitnesses were yet living.

(b) Hebrews speaks of the experience of Christ in Gethsemane (2:17; 4:15; 5:17). (c) Peter speaks of Christ's sinlessness and transfiguration (I Peter 2:21; II Peter 1:16). Of course all of Peter's epistles, as those of Paul and Hebrews, are built on Christ. (d) There are more than twenty-five Apocryphal gospels which contain legends and fanciful tales about the infancy, youth, death and resurrection of Jesus, but their testimony is of no practical value. They were written after the canonical gospels. The Gospel of the Hebrews was quoted by the church fathers. It was the most important of all but its testimony is not to be relied upon. The existence of these books does reflect the thought of the times. Jesus was in the thought of many people. (e) More than ten thousand inscriptions and many symbolic pictures in the Catacombs of Rome, of which some date from the first century, reflect the religious thought and beliefs of the early Christians, of whom 174,000 found their last resting places there. The symbolic pictures, particularly those in the room of Domitilla of the Flavian family, illustrate the work of Christ as Saviour. These inscriptions and pictures also testify to the devotion of the early Christians.

(f) The "Sayings of Jesus," recently discovered in Egypt, were probably taken from the Apocryphal Gospel of the Egyptians. They seem to be related to the Gospel of John and based upon it. (g) The church Fathers add little information. Justin Martyr states that Jesus made ploughs and yokes in Nazareth. He also gives the descent of Mary from David and depicts the outward appearance of Jesus. Clement of Rome gives the names of the seventy disciples sent out by Christ on the evangelistic tour and testifies to the excitement produced by Jesus' ministry, reaching to Rome. Most of the sayings reported by the church Fathers are very similar to expressions in the Gospels. Other New Testament books supply little information in addition to that contained in the four Gospels and other books cited. In Acts there is one saying of Jesus: "It is more blessed to give than to receive" (Acts 20:35). The sermons of the apostles in Acts argue the Messiahship of Jesus and interpret His life and death in the light of the Old Testament Scriptures. The book of Revelation reflects the apocalyptic thought current in the first century, which must have influenced considerably the writers of the four Gospels. (Cf. Matt. 24, 25, and other parallel passages).

The life and character of Jesus, as well as a considerable part of His teachings, could have been known, even if the four canonical gospels had been lost. A great variety of witnesses, varying from the unsympathetic and sometimes antagonistic Roman historians to the devoted church Fathers and heroic martyrs for His cause, left their undying testimony, to the faith, the stainless life, the incomparable courage, friendliness, and devotion of the Master, as well as to His heroic death and glorious resurrection. But almost without exception, the sayings of Jesus and facts about Him recorded by these sources are contained in the four Gospels, showing that the writers of the gospels had gleaned the field of oral tradition and written records with incomparable thoroughness.

(4) *The four Gospels, by Matthew, Mark, Luke and John are our principal sources of information. We take them in chronological order.*

(a) Early written sources underlying the four gospels.

Comparison of the first three of the synoptic gospels shows that they agree in the general order of events as well as in content. Three fourths of the Gospel of Matthew is a duplicate of Mark and eleven twelfths of Mark is duplicated in Matthew, in the same or slightly different form. Three fourths of Mark is found also in Luke. Matter peculiar to Mark alone constitutes altogether less than one chapter, being the following passages: 4:26-

29; 14:51-52. Of 88 incidents the synoptic gospels have 71 in common. The general plan and order of events of the three is the same.
The resemblances together with verbal agreements and the identity of phrases and even of long paragraphs lead to the conclusion
that these writers drew from common sources and from each other
in part but not wholly. Luke, as a rule, recasts more freely than
Matthew, though the latter condenses and expands in quoting
from Mark. John paraphrases freely the stories he quotes, as for
example the feeding of the five thousand (6:1-13).

There are certain differences (1) in incidents (about seventeen), (2) slight differences in the narratives of the same event,
as the order of the temptations of Jesus, (3) not a few verbal
differences in parallel accounts. These may be explained on the
theory first of oral tradition, and second of the common use of
older documents, as Matthew's Logia and according to some modern writers, Mark's Ur-Markus, together with some other early
sources less extensive.

Certain conclusions from the above and like facts have been
reached in the study of the so-called synoptic problem which
doubtless will stand the test of time. Matthew and Luke used
practically all of Mark and followed his general order of events.
But these two writers had another common source from which
they both drew material not found in Mark. This source which
is called Quelle (Q) or Logia was a collection of the sayings of
Jesus. Matthew and Luke used the Logia, each after his peculiar
style, as in the case of Mark. We do know that the collection bears
the impress of one author and according to the testimony of Papias
was of the nature of "sayings" of the Lord. "Everyone interpreted
them as he was able" probably in different versions. Matthew
quotes both the Logia and Mark more fully than Luke. The zeal
of those writers, though they wrote for practical ends, would
lead them not to omit any important part of it.

Both Matthew and Luke may have had various other sources
and doubtless did. Luke cites the fact in the preface to his Gospel
that he had examined carefully many such sources both written
and oral. By the testimony of Papias, Matthew wrote the Logia
in Aramaic. This was very early, before 50 A. D. It was from this
source probably that Matthew and Luke got their narratives of the
work of John the Baptist, the baptism and temptations of Jesus
and much of their reports of the teachings of Jesus.

There is much evidence that Mark wrote under the influence
of Simon Peter, as is witnessed by the vividness of his descrip-
tions, such as could only come from an eyewitness. Papias, (130-
160 A. D.,) states that "Mark, who was Peter's interpreter, wrote

down accurately, though not in order, all that he recollected of what Christ had said or done. For he was not a hearer of the Lord nor a follower of His; he followed Peter, as I have said, on a later date, and Peter adapted his instructions to practical needs, without any attempt to give the Lord's words systematically. So that Mark was not wrong in writing down some things in this way, from memory, for his own concern was, not to omit or falsify anything he had heard." In addition to his contact with Peter, whose practical and graphic account of the powerful works of Jesus he faithfully chronicled, Mark seems to have had contact with the Logia. While he does not quote the "sayings" elaborately he shows familiarity with that source. Undoubtedly he was acquainted also with the doctrines of Paul, though he was mainly influenced by Peter and the early disciples.

(b) The gospel of Mark is recognized today as the oldest of the four Gospels, being written before 65 A. D. in Rome. Mark calls it "An Introduction to the Good News of Jesus Christ, God's Son." It probably represented most nearly the actual course and order in the incidents of the life of Jesus and served as a chronological framework for the writers of the other Gospels. It is the simplest and shortest of the Gospels, but rich in detail, dramatic in presentation, graphic and animated in style. He portrays vividly the powerful deeds, the looks and gestures of Jesus, in the common language of the people.

John Mark, who doubtless wrote the Gospel which bears his name, was the son of a man who bore the pitcher and of Mary in whose house the Jerusalem church met (Acts 12:12). He was probably the young man who fled from Gethsemane on the occasion of the arrest of Jesus (14:51-52). He accompanied Paul and Barnabas, who was his cousin or more probably his uncle, on the first missionary journey, as far as Perga, whence for some reason unknown, he turned back (Acts 13:5). On the second journey Barnabas wanted to take Mark again, but Paul dissented, apparently because of circumstances connected with his previous return. Paul took Silas with him and went to the north through Asia Minor to Europe and Barnabas accompanied by Mark returned to Crete and thence went to the South. After some years Mark won again the confidence and friendship of Paul and was useful to him (Col. 4:10; Philemon 24; II Tim. 5:13). Mark was more intimate with Peter than with Paul. He was with the apostle when he wrote his first epistle (I Peter 1:15). Justin Martyr calls Mark's Gospel "The Memoirs of Peter."

Mark's purpose in writing was preeminently practical. Hoping to impress his practical Roman readers, he depicted the marvelous works, rather than citing the words of Jesus. He described the activities of Jesus and opposition which He met from the beginning, which increased until the tragic end. Eleven times the Lord retired temporarily from the centers to escape the fury of the enemies. Mark tells also of the growing enthusiasm and faith of many in spite of this opposition. Vivid and graphic description of the works of Jesus and the effect on the people constitute the preeminent characteristics. The author gives but a few words of introduction, beginning his narrative with the active ministry of the Lord.

The plan of the gospel is chronological, geographical, and topical. Oral tradition did not give a sufficient basis for exact chronology. The topical method would lend itself to the practical end in view and the general divisions of the narrative would naturally correspond to the geography of the ministry. The following outline presents the general scheme:

Introduction: Summary of John's work and Jesus' baptism and temptation, 1:1-13.

A. His great Galilean ministry (1:14-6:29).

B. Jesus in retirement with His disciples (6:30-10:52).

C. Closing ministry in Jerusalem (11:1-16:8).

Epilogue: Resurrection, appearances, and ascension (16:9-20).

(c) The Gospel according to Matthew was the second of the four gospels to be written. Matthew seems to have written two books: the Logia or sayings of Jesus, written in Aramaic, and our gospel, written in Greek in Palestine, at a later date but before 70 A. D., since there is no reference in it to the destruction of Jerusalem. The gospel draws from the Logia as its primary source.

The *aim* of the author was apologetic. Writing mainly for the Jews, he sought to prove to them that Jesus was the Messiah foretold in the Hebrew Scriptures. This was hard for the Jews, who crucified Him, to receive. There are forty references to the messianic prophecies and Jesus' fulfillment of them. Jesus is presented as the Teacher and His prophetic and miraculous power is emphasized. The development of the ministry is depicted. The treatment is topical. The aim was thoroughly evangelistic. The messianic Kingdom is presented as spiritual and universal.

Matthew was by the statement of his gospel a publican (9:9 and 10:3). He became a disciple a little while before the ordination of the Twelve. On the occasion of his call, he made a feast for Jesus and invited his friends of the custom house. Tradition says that he worked fifteen years in Judea and afterwards in Parthia and Ethiopia.

The general plan of Matthew's gospel is in part parallel to that of Mark. At the same time his order is topical rather than chronological, as for example: discourses (5-7; 24-25), miracles (8, 9) and parables (13). The following outline presents the general scheme:

Introduction: Birth and childhood of Jesus. Preparation for the work of the Messiah. The work of John the Baptist, Jesus' baptism and temptations (1:1-4:11).

A. Jesus' great Galilean ministry (4:11-13:58).

B. Jesus in retirement with the Twelve. The crisis and rejection in Galilee and the founding of the church (Chapters 14-18).

C. Ministry in Perea on the way to Jerusalem (Chapters 19-20).

D. Closing ministry in Jerusalem (Chapters 21-25).

E. Crucifixion, resurrection, and appearances (Chapters 26-28).

(d) Luke wrote his gospel in two books, the third gospel and the Acts, which was the Gospel of the Holy Spirit. The third gospel was the narrative of "all that Jesus began both to do and to teach until the day in which he was received up." Renan said it was "the most beautiful book ever written." It was probably written in Cesarea about 60 A. D. while Paul was in prison. There are others who place the date as late as 75 A. D.

Luke was the "Beloved Physician" and companion of Paul during most of his ministry (Acts 16:10; 20:7; Col. 4:14). He seems to have resided originally in Antioch of Pisidia, being a Greek and the only Gentile writer of the Gospels. It is likely that Paul knew him on his first missionary journey. The "we" sections in Acts show that he joined Paul's party on the second missionary journey, going from Troas to Philippi (Acts 16:16-17), where he remained behind for six years. Later he is with Paul on the return to Jerusalem after the third missionary journey, in the period of imprisonment at Cesarea, and on the voyage to Rome (Acts 27, 28), where he remained with Paul until his liberation (Acts 20:28; Philemon 24). In the second imprisonment he remained faithfully with the apostle and possibly suffered with him (II Tim. 4:11).

The motive and method of Luke in writing is set forth in his preface (1:1-4). The motive was twofold. First, many had written out well and in a thorough way the oral traditions about the life and ministry of Jesus which had been brought to fulfillment among them. Eyewitnesses and ministers of the word had left these oral traditions and they were dependable. But the brief

narratives which had been written out were but partial. Luke
desired to write a *fuller account*, though he was complimentary to
those who had written. There is always room for one more book
about Jesus provided it is different and more complete. Second,
he desired to confirm the faith of his Greek friend Theophilus
and every God-lover or God-beloved man. His aim was therefore
intensely practical and evangelical.

His method was that of a true historian. In that respect
Luke has been compared to Thucydides and other great historians. He had full knowledge before he wrote, having made accurate examination of all the narratives previously written including the Logia and Mark. He made a comparison of these with
the oral traditions of the eyewitnesses and ministers of the Word.
He studied these facts out as a physican follows up his case for
times, to make a complete diagnosis. He arranged this matter in
order making a careful, thorough, and scholarly job of it.

It was written principally for the Gentiles but also for the
Jews. The topographical references, manner of calculating dates,
attitude toward the Roman government, and genealogy of Jesus
show adaptation to Gentile readers. The author had a finished
literary style, the quotations from Mark being recast in classic
Greek phrases. The sentences are well balanced, the vocabulary
is rich, and the style fluent, abounding in hyperbole, antithesis, and
other figures. It is the longest narrative of the four gospels, giving
the amplest account of the birth and infancy of Jesus, based on
information received doubtless by this "beloved physician" from
Mary who had treasured those things up in her heart from the
beginning. The narrative of the last six months of Jesus' ministry (in Perea) is a distinctive contribution of the industry
of this historian. The gospel is beautiful with references to children and to the devoted women won by the ministry of the Lord.
It is preeminently the gospel of universal and free salvation. Repentance, faith and forgiveness are charcteristic notes. The poor,
afflicted, and outcast classes find here a ready friend and sympathetic Saviour. It is a social gospel in the highest sense and at
the same time more nearly a biography than the other gospels.
The plan of the gospel is as follows:

Preface (1:1-4).
A. Birth and infancy of Jesus (1:5-2:52).
B. Preparation for His public ministry (3:1-4:13): ministry
   of John the Baptist (3:1-22), genealogy of Jesus (3:
   23-38), baptism and temptations of Jesus (4:1-13).
C. His great ministry in Galilee (4:14-9:50).

D. Journey to Jerusalem and ministry in Perea (9:51-19:28).
E. Closing ministry in Jerusalem (19:29-23:56).
F. Resurrection, appearances and ascension (24:1-53).
(e) The gospel of John.
The picture given of Jesus in the fourth gospel is quite a contrast to that presented in the synoptics. These narrate His works and teachings; John gives Jesus' revelation of Himself to the world and more intimately to His disciples. John's gospel is the complement of the other gospels also in that it emphasizes the ministry of Jesus in Judea and Jerusalem over against the much accentuated Galilean ministry of the other gospels.

The author of the fourth gospel was John, one of the sons of Zebedee and Salome, and brother of James the Elder. He became a disciple of Jesus at the Jordan after Jesus' return from the temptations. He was one of the Twelve, the disciple "whom Jesus loved," the author also of the Revelation and the three epistles which bear his name. When youthful he was "a son of thunder," full of spirit and ambition. He had the desire to occupy a high place in the Kingdom (Matthew 19:20), wanted to take vengeance on the Samaritan village when it refused hospitality to Jesus (Luke 19:54), reclined on Jesus' breast at the last paschal supper (Jno. 13:25), followed Jesus into the palace of Caiaphas after the arrest (Jno. 18:16), and received the mother of Jesus into his filial care at the foot of the cross (Jno. 19:26). After the resurrection he visited the sepulcher with Peter (Jno. 20:2), was with the disciples twice in the room where Jesus appeared to them, and later with six others and Jesus at the Sea of Galilee. He later worked and suffered with Peter in Jerusalem (Acts 3:4; 4:7), was present at the conference in Jerusalem when Paul brought up the great question of Gentile liberty, took part in the larger work of the world evangelization, being banished to the island of Patmos, and died about 100 A. D., in Ephesus, the last survivor of the apostolic group.

Through modesty John did not give, in the gospel, his name as the author of the book. But the claim is made in Jno. 21:20 that "the disciple whom Jesus loved" was the author. Obviously the author must have been a Palestinian Jew, an eyewitness of the ministry of the Lord, who claimed the most intimate relations with Him. Objection is made that the John of the Gospel is the apostle of love and could not have been the "son of thunder" which John the Apostle was declared to be. But the character of Jacob was changed from that of a deceptive supplanter to Israel the saint of God, in the process of years. Such a transformation doubtless took place in John. It is argued that the style in the gospel is not the same that we find in Revelation, but the extraordinary circumstances under which Revelation was written, the earlier date, the lack of friendly editorial help, the development in the thought and style of the writer himself during the years between the writing of the two books, would easily account for the differences in style. In the epistles the style is very much like that of the gospel. Many, though not all, of the critics who reject the Johanine authorship, are rationalists or unitarians, rejecting the deity of Christ. But the Jesus of the fourth gospel is not less Lord and Christ than the Jesus of the synoptics.

The aim of John in writing the gospel, he discloses in the words: "but these are written that ye may believe that Jesus is the Christ, the Son of God; and that believing ye may have life in his name" (John 20:30f). He laid down as his thesis in the introduction (1:1-18) *the divinity of Jesus*, whom he set forth as the eternal, preexistent Logos, who "became flesh and dwelt among us." Man's salvation he held to depend on belief in Jesus as the Messiah and Son of God. So the purpose of the book was to reveal the personality of Jesus in His works, character and discourses on the way of life, in such a way that all men might believe in Him. The aim of John was incidentally apologetic. When he wrote, near the end of the first century, the Jewish-Alexandrian philosophy of Philo and his school was current, and the Gnostic error was rampant. John was apologetic, with the purpose of evangelism. The semi-personal logos of Philo was inadequate and a dangerous delusion. The Gnostic view of the person of Jesus was subversive of faith. These false philosophies must be met squarely with the truth about the divine, personal Logos.

John selected eight miracles (signs) from the many he had beheld, and the discourses and experiences linked up with them, to prove his thesis. He took the imperfect conception of Philo's Logos and filled it up to complete personality. John selected fresh miracles with rare exception, which were supplementary to the synoptic narratives. The miracles selected illustrated the power of Jesus in its various phases and interpreted His work and mission. The diction is of the simplest, while the thought is profound. The vocabulary is limited but there is no dearth of ideas. The author is master in the use of parallelism and antithesis. The dramatic power of the book is tremendous. Many allegorical figures are used, as the bread of life, the living water, the vine and branches, to present the teachings about the Divine Word. The book is deeply spiritual, and obviously the product of mature meditation and a long, rich, and varied experience of the life in Christ. It is complementary to Mark, filling in the gaps in Mark's chronology, through the definite mention of three and possibly four passovers (2:23; 6:4; 12:1; possibly 5:1). John wrote when Paul's epistle and the three synoptic gospels were well known. According to Ireneus John lived "till the times of Trajan" (98-117 A. D.). The gospel must be assigned to 90-100 A. D.

The plan of the fourth gospel is argumentative and not primarily biographical. The narratives of miracles, incidents, and discourses are so arranged as to prove the thesis. The parallel development of faith and unbelief is traced. The following is the general scheme:

Prologue (1:1-18).

The Logos, eternal, preexistent and active in creation.

A. The self-revelation of Jesus Christ to the world (1:19-12:50).

1. Through the witness (1:19-4:54) of the Baptist (1:19-34), of the first disciples of Jesus (1:35-51), of the first miracle of Jesus (2:1-11), of the works of Jesus (2:12-4:54) in Judea, Samaria and Galilee.

2. Through conflict in which He was rejected (5-12) in His work (5, 6), in Jerusalem (5), in Galilee (6); through His conflict in controversy (7-12), in the feast of Tabernacles (7, 8), in the feast of Dedication (9, 10), in His last struggle in Judea (11, 12).

B. The more complete self-revelation of Jesus to His disciples (13-17): in the example of humble service (13:1-30), in the last discourses (13:31-16:33), in the intercessory prayer (17).

C. The self-revelation of Jesus through His victory (18-20): in the betrayal (18:1-11), in the double trial (18:12-19:16), in the crucifixion (19:17-42), and in the resurrection (20).

Epilogue (21).

All of the four gospels were written by those who were advocates of Christ. All four writers presented His life, works, and teachings with a purpose to meet the spiritual needs of mankind. All alike present Jesus as the Christ and Lord, recognizing His divine character and His full humanity but without sin. Each gospel is individual: Mark's is the practical gospel, presenting the mighty work of Jesus; Matthew's is the gospel of the "sayings" presenting the supreme Messiah-Teacher: Luke's is the social gospel, defining man's obligations to God and man; John's is the theological or doctrinal gospel, interpreting the ministry and life of Jesus from different angles, that the picture might be complete and the world might see Jesus.

PART I

THE ADVENT AND EARLY LIFE OF THE CHRIST

(Harm. §§ 1-19)

CHAPTER I
THE ADVENT OF THE MESSIAH
(Harm. §§ 1-3) *

The birth of Jesus Christ was an advent. His life did not begin, as that of other men, when he was born. He came into the world from a preexistent state on a special mission.

1. The preexistent state of the Christ and His incarnation. His divine relations. Jno. 1:1-18.

The mystery of God is in the eternal Word incarnated in the Christ. The how of the incarnation is inscrutable, the why is incomprehensible, the fact is undeniable. The roots of the life of Jesus reach back into eternity. In the prologue of John's Gospel (1:1-18) we have a description of the Logos (Word) who was revealed to men and revealed God the Father to men through His incarnation. John sets forth in these verses not only the deity of Jesus Christ in the flesh and His preexistence before the incarnation but also the relations of the preexistent Christ with God, the material world, and mankind.

(1) Description of the Word. (1:1-2).

John takes us back before the beginning of creation (Gen. 1:1) and assumes the Word in a continuous state of existence, in intimate communion and fellowship of equality with God, and in essence the very God. His idea of the Logos was not that of Marcus Aurelius, the generative principle in nature, nor that of Philo, the Divine Reason and Expression, nor merely that of the Hebrew memra, the manifestation of God as the Angel of Jehovah or the Wisdom of God; but the religious idea of the Divine Word, creating, revealing, redeeming. John seized upon the terminology of current Greek thought and filled it with a new content. His Logos is not the semi-personal Logos of Philo but a personal Logos; not a cosmic but a spiritual agent. He reproduces with new content various phases of the Platonic conception; the eternal existence of the Word, its relation to God as toward Him and yet distinct, its creative activity, its function in the illumination and deliverance of men. Philo's conception wavered between personification and personality; John's fills the Logos with personality. In the Kenosis of Paul (Phil. 2:1-11) the Word is conceived as depotentiating himself, divesting himself of divine attributes, reducing himself to the measure of humanity, in order to become man. Jesus prayed the Father to glorify Him with the glory which He had before the world was (Jno. 17). John the Baptist testified to his belief in the preexistence of the Christ (Jno. 1:30). Jesus himself said: "Before Abraham was I am," signifying that He existed before

Abraham was born. The continuity of the consciousness of Jesus may not be declared dogmatically; but the absoluteness of His religious consciousness assured Jesus of His special, eternal, filial relation to the Father. The life of Jesus has this eternal, Divine background, without which it would be unaccountable.

The phraseology of John is aptly apologetic in his description of the Word. John denied Sabellianism by not saying, "the God was the Word"; but rather, "the Word was God" (in essence). The Word was not all of God but a person of the Godhead. "God is Spirit" but not all spirit is God. Modern Unitarianism finds in this phrase an insuperable difficulty. Nor could ancient Arianism meet the inevitable doctrine of the persons of the Godhead in eternal fellowship of equality here set forth. The humanity of Jesus was real and Jesus shed human blood on the cross, in spite of the opinion of the Docetic Gnostics. Jesus and the Christ were one person and Christ was not a mere Aeon who came upon Jesus at His baptism as the Cerinthian Gnostic held. So John declares of the Logos that before the incarnation he had preexistence. personality, and deity. The Word was "of the same substance" and Christ was not a mere creature endowed with godlike qualities. God was incarnate in Jesus Christ. The Word, in the Trinity, is that Person of the Divine self-expression. Thus John declared the personal relations of the Word in the Godhead.

(2) The creative relation of the Word to the material world and His redemptive relation to mankind (1:3-5).

Every single thing and the whole material cosmos came into being through the creative activity of the Word (1:3). In this statement John is supported by Paul (Col. 1:16) and Hebrews (1:2). The Father is the primary source and the Son the intermediate agent. John adds for completion the negative statement: "Apart from Him was not made even one thing that stands made" (Perfect).

That which stands created, was, in the Logos, life. He is the source of the life in the material universe, and is immanent in His sustaining power. Spirit, intelligence, and power are behind the physical creation, as science is coming to recognize more today. John declares (1:4) the relation of the pre-incarnate Word to men as that of the source of their moral light and their life. Jesus declared Himself, that He was the Light of the World (Jno. 8:12). He is the light through the medium of life. The moral light (Logos) keeps on shining in the midst of the darkness (induced by sin), and in spite of the darkness, which antagonizes it but cannot overcome it.

(3) The pre-incarnate and historical manifestation of the Word (1:6-13). It was announced by prophecy, represented in

the person of John the Baptist (Vs. 6-8), a God-sent man, the
end of whose coming was to be a witness and by his experiential
testimony help men to see the genuine light. Men need such help
because they are so blinded by sin. They even mistook John for
the true light. The purpose of his testifying to them concerning the
light was that all might believe through his testimony. The true
Light (Logos) was already in continuous existence, lighting by conscience and special revelations in nature, every single man,
even before the incarnation. But the Logos carried His revelation
further now by coming into the World. He was immanent always
in the universe, which came into existence through His agency;
but the world failed to recognize Him. In the incarnation there
was a tragedy.

He came unto His own world which was His property; but
His own intimate "family" people, whom He had chosen for a
special mission and to whom He was sent, gave Him no welcome
(Vs. 10-11). But the sad tragedy of national rejection was relieved by individual faith (Vs. 13-13). To so many as definitely
received Him, He gave the privilege, right, and power to become the
own-begotten children of God. The new birth from above is implied here. Confidence in the incarnate Word (Logos) was the
condition for entering into this new sphere of filial relationship and
intimacy with God. It was given to all believers to enter into
this sonship. They were not begotten by physical generation, nor
through natural impulse, nor through the mere will of a human
father. Faith must be exercised but the new birth is from above.

(4) The realization of the incarnation as experienced by men in
history and the nature of the resulting revelation (Vs. 14-18).
The Word came in the flesh. The Virgin birth is the natural implication. He dwelt as a man, in our midst, in the tabernacle of the
flesh. The Shekinah-glory of God was visible in Him. John and
other men were spectators of that never-to-be-forgotten glory of
the Transfiguration and other hours of the incarnate Word. It
was such a glory as could only be ascribed to the eternally begotten, only-born of the Father. He was full of grace and truth. Men
received the grace or unmerited favor of God through Him in
fullest measure. Jesus was loving and full of love. In Him also
was experienced the deepest passion for the truth or reality. He
was alert, intuitive, concrete, positive, constructive in His search
for and presentation of the truth. He was the truth incarnate.

John the Baptist bore witness to His eternal preexistence and
eminence. Even before he saw Him, the Christ stood preeminent
(Perfect). All of the attributes of God were summed up in the
incarnate Logos (v 6). The Gnostic heresy (Col. 2:9) had attributed the creative work to the Aeons. John meets this false phi-

losophy with the declaration that the Logos is the fullness (pleroma) of God. He himself and others had definitely received this fulness of grace, time after time, like the manna of each day. From the ocean of this fulness we receive wave after wave, beating on our shores. The law which was given through the instrumentality of Moses set forth preeminently the holiness and justice of God; but grace (love of God shown to those who do not merit) and truth, with the passion for reality, came through Jesus Christ, with whom John identifies the Logos (v 17). No one ever has seen God with the physical eyes. The only begotten God, the Logos (Reason, and the Word of God), the incarnate God, who is in the intimate fellowship of the Father, has made Him known. By the incarnation, Jesus made God comprehensible to man.

2. The lineage of the promised Messiah, His human relations. (Matt. 1:1-17; Luke 3:23-38). The object in introducing the genealogy of Jesus into the brief gospel narratives was to show His royal descent from David, as the Messiah of the Hebrew prophecies and His wider human relation with the whole race, going back to the beginning. During the entire history of the race God was preparing providentially for the coming of the Divine Son and Messiah into the world. Matthew, writing for the Jews, was naturally interested in pointing out the fact that Jesus was of royal line, and so traces the family tree down through David to Joseph from Abraham the father of the Hebrew race. Luke showed Jesus to belong to the whole human race. He is a member of the brotherhood of man, whose origin is one and divine. He was the reputed but not real son of Joseph, so Luke traces the genealogy through Mary. Matthew traced it through Joseph because regal descent was through the father's side always. Luke, writing for the Gentiles, pointed out that Jesus was the ideal man, a son of Adam, created by God.

Matthew's genealogy stands at the beginning of his Gospel, to establish the fact of Jesus' royal Hebrew origin before any other facts about His life are introduced; Luke's comes in as an interlude after the account of the birth and infancy of Jesus and John's ministry, to introduce the saving ministry of the Lord.

Matthew gives the official family record of the successive births as they came; Luke starts out fixing attention on Jesus, the person of supreme importance in the narrative and Saviour of the whole race, with which He is identified by the genealogy thus extracted, in the reverse order from the public records. Matthew's is the genealogy of the kingly; Luke's that of natural descent. In Matthew's genealogy the names are divided for convenience into three groups of fourteen each, corresponding to the three periods of the national history: from Abraham to David the theocracy, from David to the Babylonian exile the monarchy, and from the exile to the time of Christ the hierarchy. Such a division was wholly in accord with the Jewish custom.

There are certain discrepancies between the lists. Only forty-one names appear in Matthew's list, while it was customary for the Jews to divide into three divisions of fourteen each. But Matthew mentions David in two lists. He omits several names in the line, but he was only seeking to show the direct descent. He gives the names of four women in the list, contrary to Jewish custom. Three of these were also guilty of gross sin and two were foreigners. Matthew did not merely copy the records but selected the names with a purpose. The names of these women identified Christ with the sex and national divisions of the race and with sinful humanity as its Saviour. Some of the men of the line were also notorious sinners. There, heredity of Jesus is a bond of hope for the sinful race. He lived without sin in spite of His hereditary handicaps. He had to struggle against evil hereditary tendencies like every other man, and He overcame. Matthew punctures the pride of his Jewish brethren, by inserting the names which they in their hypo-critical self-righteousness would have repudiated, some sug-gestive of disgrace, others of apostasy and covenant-breaking. These proud Pharisaic brethren had recently rejected Jesus as unworthy and meriting death. But He was superior to the best of the forefathers even of the royal line.

The Virgin-birth of Jesus is safe-guarded in the genealogies. The word *begat* is used in the successive stages of the descent down to Joseph (Matt. 1:16), but there the statement is altered. "And Jacob begat Joseph the husband of Mary, of whom was born Jesus who is called the Christ." This is in harmony with Luke's statement (3:23): "Jesus being the son (as was supposed) of Joseph." Jesus was thought by the people to be the son of Joseph by physical descent. But He was genetically the son of God, begotten of the Holy Ghost.

Mark did not attach great importance to the family tree. He was concerned mainly with the practical outcome of the life of Jesus. The Roman readers would not think this important. The great works of Jesus would show Him to be the Son of God, and that was the main issue. Matthew defines His place in the Hebrew race and the wider Messianic hope. John dealt with the philosophic world and must define the place of Jesus in the cosmic scheme. So he goes back into the eternities and relates Him to God, the created physical universe, and all the world of intelligencies. Of mankind in particular, He was Creator and Redeemer. Luke ties Him up with the whole race without regard to racial, national, sexual, or social division.

CHAPTER II

THE ANNUNCIATION

(Harm. §§ 4-9)

An aureole of the supernatural surrounds the manger-cradle of Bethlehem. No other birth in all human history was ever heralded by angels and attended by such manifestations of interest on the part of heaven and earth. It was natural that Matthew who wrote the "Gospel of the King," should give Joseph's account of his own intimate experience—his consternation, misgivings, and the assurance which the message of the angel brought announcing the birth of Jesus. It was not less so that Luke the "beloved physician" whose gospel is one of tender human interest, should have received from the modest mother, who had kept all those things in her heart and pondered them for long, the delicate and reserved narrative of the angel Gabriel's visit to her in her home in Nazareth, announcing the birth of her son, as well as the account of other events, which accompanied it. There were three announcements which heralded the coming of the Messiah-King.

1. The annunciation to Zacharias of the birth of John the Forerunner (Luke 1:5-25).

The annunciation to Zacharias took place in the time of Herod the Great, who died in 4 B. C. The political status of the people was then deplorable as also their spiritual decline. Herod, a monster of crime, oppressed them, and their religion under the Scribes had become a mere empty form and system of ceremonies and rites.

But in the midst of the spiritual dearth, God had reserved unto himself a group of the devout, who "waited for the consolation of Israel" and prayed for the appearance of the long expected Messiah. Zacharias the aged priest and his wife the daughter of a priest, belonged to this group. They were both "righteous before God" and without reproach before men, observing the standards and requirements of both moral and ceremonial laws. They had "gone far in their days" and come to old age. In their hearts they bore a deep silent sorrow, for among the Jews it was a reproach and interpreted as a sign of divine displeasure to be childless. They had prayed much about this and not selfishly. Every Jewish family hoped for a son who would prove to be the Deliverer, the Messiah-King.

Twice each year Zacharias went up from his home in the hill country of Judea, probably near Hebron, to take part for a week in the sacred tasks of the service in the Temple. The priesthood had been well organized after the return from Babylon. At this time there were 20,000 priests, divided into twenty-four courses.

Zacharias belonged to that of Abijah which was the eighth. Each course did duty for eight days, all joining in on the Sabbath. About fifty were engaged every day, the duty of each being determined by the white-stone "lot," that there might be no contention in the house of the Lord. The offering of incense was considered the highest duty and could be exercised only once in a lifetime. The lot had fallen at last on Zacharias for this high task.

It was the time of the morning sacrifice (9 A. M.). The ponderous Temple gates swung open and three blasts of the silver trumpets of the Priests summoned the people of the city to a spirit of worship. The priests on the pinnacle of the Temple gave the signal for the beginning of the services of the day. One of the assistants of Zacharias reverently cleaned the altar and retired. A second as reverently placed the live coals taken from the burnt offering on the altar and, worshipping, retired. The organ sounded through the Temple. Zacharias entered the Holy Place, lit by the sheen of the seven-branched candle-stick on the right, bearing in his hand the golden censer. On his left was the table of shew-bread. In front of him beyond the altar was the thick curtain which separated the Holy of Holies. The people outside were prostrate in silent worship. Zacharias alone in the Holy Place awaited the kindling of the incense on the altar, when he too would bow in worship and then withdraw in reverence.

At that instant of intense expectation, the supreme hour of all his priestly life, as the cloud of incense symbol of accepted prayer began to rise, the angel Gabriel appeared, not where Jewish angelology would place him—on the left of the throne of glory— but on the right of the altar. Zacharias was agitated and terrified. By Jewish tradition one might not see God and live.

The aged priest had been praying at that hour, as long years before, for the Messiah, and at the same time for a son. The angel quieted his fear and declared that his prayer had been answered. The son of many prayers should be called John (the Lord is gracious). There would be gladness and joy in that quiet home of piety and hope, and many would rejoice at the birth of the child.

The angel then delineated the character and work of the son (Vs. 15-17). He would be great before the Lord, a life-Nazarite as Samuel had been, dedicated to a life of temperance and filled with the Holy Spirit from birth. He would bring about a great religious revival, turning many of the sons of Israel to the Lord their God as did Samuel. He would be the Forerunner of the Messiah, going forth not as Elijah himself, but "in the spirit and power of Elijah," to turn the hearts of the fathers to their children in a revival of love and religion in the home. He would save the home as well as the church until the children might grow up in a religious atmosphere. The rebellious sinners he would lead out by persuasion to lives of right conduct, thus preparing a people for the salvation the Messiah would bring.

It is almost incredible that Zacharias after years of praying for a son should doubt, when the angel Gabriel definitely promised and described him. He could not believe in the miracle. For his doubt in asking for a sign, he received a rebuke involving the supernatural power. The punishment of dumbness inflicted would be a blessing through which his faith would grow stronger. The people were impressed with his delay in the Sanctuary and yet more with his dumbness when he appeared for the closing benediction on the outside. He nodded and beckoned back and forth but could not utter a word. The people were convinced that he had seen a vision and went away wondering. When the week of his worship (liturgy) was filled out he departed for his home to the South. According to the prophecy of the angel, after these days Elizabeth his wife conceived, and kept herself thoroughly secluded for five months. Her reproach, the Lord had taken away.

John was born of pious parents. They had sought for long years in prayer a child. The prayer was answered in a way against nature. What would this supernatural gift of God's graciousness mean to the future of the Messiah's Kingdom? The angel predicted great things of John the Forerunner. Greater things still would come through the Messiah.

2. The annunciation to the Virgin Mary of the birth of Jesus (Luke 1:26-38).

This is a most important record as it reveals the nature of the incarnation. It is presented by Luke with all the delicacy and reserve with which he must have received the account from Mary herself.

Six months had elapsed after the vision of Zacharias in the Temple. The setting of this scene was the beautiful little town of Nazareth, nestled in the hills of Galilee, overlooking the fertile, cultivated, and densely populated plain of Esdraelon to the South, arena of many of the acts of Israel's historic drama. The angelic visit this time was not in the sanctuary of a great Temple but in the quiet seclusion of an humble home; not to a priest appareled in his sacerdotal vesture, but to a charming, beautiful girl, just eighteen years of age, daughter of poor parents, according to a Jewish tradition. She was betrothed (made sacred) to an humble carpenter, Joseph. After a year at most they would be married but in the meantime their contract was sacred and of complete reserve. Both were of royal lineage.

The salutation of Gabriel, "Rejoice, highly favoured one, the Lord is with thee!" has been made the basis of pagan misinterpretation constituting Mary a fountain of grace to be dispensed to others by her. "Hail, Mary! Thou art full of grace." She was highly favoured above all women in being permitted to be the mother of the Lord and Saviour. But the Gospel narratives attribute to her none of the special titles ascribed to her by later so-called Christianity. The *worship* of Mary is not warranted by the simple salutation of the angel here recorded. The "Ave Maria," which is the daily prayer of millions has no basis in the gospels. Much as we may admire and honor the Virgin-Mother, we may not pray to her or worship her in any way. Mariolatry is but one form of idolatry. The mother merits all honor but her Son our worship.

Mary was much disturbed and startled by this angelic visitation. Perplexed, she was reasoning in her mind what this wonderful salutation could mean. Gabriel quieted her fears, assuring her that she had found favor with God. She had lived a pious active life for God in her humble home. He then announced the conception and birth of a son, whom she must call Jesus (Jehovah-Hoshea or Jehovah-Saviour). Joshua (Jehoshua) had saved Israel from her enemies; Jesus would save them from their sins as a victorious leader and conqueror.

Gabriel proceeded to describe the character of the promised child. He was to be great in character and deeds and acknowledged as the Son of God. In Him was to be fulfilled the Messianic hope, and He would succeed in the throne of David, ruling over the house of Jacob forever. There would be no limit nationally or end temporally to His Kingdom. In this prediction and in the name of Jesus were bound up as the petals in the unopened bud of the rose, the flower of His wonderful life, His divinity. and His glorious mission as the spiritual Messiah in fulfillment of ancient prophecy (cf Ps. 72). But Mary did not understand all these things; for her the promised son could be only the temporal Messiah-King whom the Jews awaited.

Mary did not doubt as Zacharias, but was only perplexed as to how this could be. She expressed her astonishment and humbly asked for an explanation. There is no ground for the doctrine of perpetual virginity in this verb *know* (v 34). Mary simply meant that she was not married yet to Joseph her betrothed.

The reply of the angel is a clear statement of the virgin birth and the reality of the incarnation. The conception was of the Holy Spirit, though Mary and the Jews did not fully know the person of the Holy Spirit yet. The creative power of the Most High would overshadow her, as the cloud of Shekinah-glory had rested on the Tabernacle of Israel in the desert. The child would

be called "holy, the Son of God." To her inquiry, Gabriel added
to his declaration of the how, another proof. Elizabeth had conceived against nature six months ago. Mary might easily verify
the reality of this miracle. No promise of God would ever fail.

Mary did not need proof. In simple, beautiful faith and submission, she presented herself to the Lord, His slave, to do with her
according to His will, whatever might be the disgrace, slander,
ill-repute, or even death to her. Unfaithfulness in the betrothed
was punished with the mutilating death by stoning. But she was
willing to give up Joseph and even suffer the mutilation of a horrible death if need be. Such a faith was of the rarest. As quickly
as he had come, the heavenly messenger vanished from her sight.

3. The Visit of Mary and Song of Elizabeth. (Luke 1:39:45).

Mary hastened to visit her kinswoman Elizabeth who lived in
the far away hill-country of Judea near Hebron. It would be a comfort to talk to someone of her own sex about this wonder-visita-
tion. About ninety-seven miles to the south, Elizabeth's home was
four or five days' journey, according to their mode of travel.

Immediately upon Mary's arrival and salutation, Elizabeth
was filled with the Holy Spirit and with a loud voice in spiritual
ecstacy, pronounced a blessing upon her visitor and the promised
child. The Holy Spirit revealed to her the honor that had been
conferred on Mary. She was to be the mother of the Lord-Mes-
siah. There is no ground for the title "Mother of God," ascribed
to Mary centuries later. This visit of the mother of the promised
Messiah Elizabeth considered an honor. She praised Mary for her
faith, and assured her of the fulfillment of the promise of the angel-
messenger. She humbled herself, being the elder and daughter of
a priest, before the young girl destined to be the mother of her
Lord. This song of Elizabeth is real poetry, the first of the New
Testament hymns.

4. The Magnificat of Mary (Luke 1:46-56).

Mary hearing this confirmation of the word of the angel, was
filled with joy, which she expressed in one of the most beautiful
hymns of all the centuries. It was modeled on that of Hannah
(I Sam. 2:1-10), spoken when her heart was rejoicing also in the
promise of a son. Mary praises God for His great goodness to her
individually in permitting her to become the mother of the
Messiah (Vs. 46-49). But the hymn widens out later in its praise
of God for fulfilling to His people the ancient prophecies (Vs. 50-
55).

It is divided into four stanzas of four lines each, except the
third which has six. In the first stanza, she magnifies the Lord and

rejoices in God as her Saviour for His blessings on her lowly estate, raising her to the position of eternal praise. The second stanza praises God for His power, holiness, and mercy, in bringing blessings to untold generations (Vs. 49, 50). In the third stanza the proud and rebellious are scattered and the oppressed exalted; the rich are sent away empty while the poor are filled (vs. 51-53). In the last, she praises God for fulfilling His promises to His people Israel, made to Abraham and the forefathers, by sending the Messiah (Vs. 54, 55). Christianity was born in a burst of sacred song. It was fitting that the two women, who were to be mothers of the Christ and His Forerunner, should be the first of the soloists.

5. The birth of John and Song of Zacharias (Luke 1:57-80).

Mary remained at the home of Elizabeth about three months, probably until the birth of John, a part of the annunciation of the Christ. She would be interested to see the child of her kinswoman, the destined Forerunner of the Lord. According to the promise of the angel, when the time was fulfilled, Elizabeth gave birth to her son. The neighbors and kinfolk recognized that it was a miraculous conception. The Lord had magnified His mercy toward Elizabeth in giving her a miracle-child against the very laws of nature. They kept on rejoicing with her over and over.*

Eight days passed and the hour for the joyous ceremony of the circumcision arrived. On this occasion of domestic solemnity, the child would receive his name. Abram had suffered the change of his name to Abraham, when he was circumcised. It was customary to give the first born the name of the father. When the customary benediction had been spoken and the circumcision performed, came the final pronunciation of grace over the cup of wine: "Our God and the God of our fathers, raise up this child to his father and mother, and let his name be called in Israel Zacharias, the son of Zacharias." But this grace was interrupted by Elizabeth: "Not so" she said, "but he shall be called John." The neighbors and kinsmen in their turn dissented and were trying to name him Zacharias. "There is none of thy kindred that is called by this name'" they said. But she made no explanation. Then they turned to the aged priest-father and after their oriental emotional fashion were making over and over to him signs. "What would he have him called" if he could speak? Surely the aged father ought to be honored and his name perpetuated in the son. Then Zacharias showed his complete faith in the fullfillment of the word of the angel and asking for the wax-covered writing tablet he wrote: "John is his name." And all who witnessed this wondered.

*Imperfect tense, denoting repeated action.

At that moment the tongue of Zacharias was loosed and he burst into a hymn of praise of the name of the Lord, which has been sung for hundreds of years since daily in Christian worship— the *Benedictus*. His last words in the Temple had been words of doubt; his first words after the lesson of his dumbness had been learned, were words of faith and a hymn of praise. The Benedictus was modeled on the sacerdotal hymns of the Old Testament. It follows closely and spiritualizes the most ancient Jewish prayer— the Eighteen Benedictions. It is praise for the realization of those prayers. This is seen particularly in the fifteenth benediction: "Speedily make to shoot forth the Branch of David thy servant, and exalt thou his horn by thy salvation, for in thy salvation we trust all the day long." The piety of the aged priest is seen in the fact that he had treasured up in his heart these prayers and prophecies. Faith now loosed his tongue and he praises God for fulfilling in the coming Messiah the promises made before to his people.

The hymn was named Benedictus from the first word in the Latin version. It is divided into five stanzas of four lines each. Only one stanza of the five refers to the birth of John; the others refer with thanksgiving and praise to the approaching birth of Jesus and the salvation He would bring.

The first stanza (vs 68, 69) speaks of the redemption as already accomplished in the gift of Christ. In Him the power of salvation would be manifest. The second (vs 70-72) remembers the promise of salvation from their enemies, according to the ancient covenant. The third stanza (vs 73-75) describes the deliverance from political oppression, promised to Abraham, with a view to priestly service in righteousness, as a nation. The fourth (vs 76, 77), delineates the work of John, who is to be recognized as a prophet and to be a Forerunner, to make ready the way for the Messiah-King: announcing His coming, instructing the people as to the salvation He would bring, calling the nation to repentance for their sins, as a reformer. Moral reform and religious revival would accompany political liberation. The fifth and last stanza describes the mission of the Christ (vs 78, 79). In the tender mercy of God the Messias is to come. His coming would be like the Dawn with its new birth of hope and prophecy of the full-orbed day. Not like the birth of the Sun, this Day Star would come near from on high and visit men. Those that had sat in darkness helpless and paralyzed, unable to do ought but wait for the coming light, sitting and waiting as the shadows of life's day lengthen and the deeper shadows of the night of death approach, to them the new day now dawns in Christ. The Greeks poetically attributed the beauty of the dawn to the goddess Aurora. In Christ were the beauty and freshness of hope heralding a new day and new era. This light would lead the benighted into the paths of peace. The hymn of Zacharias was the "last prophecy of the Old and the first of the New Dispensation." It foretold political liberation in the popular conception but spiritual redemption through the moral and religious reformation under John, and spiritual regeneration in the salvation through Christ. He like many a prophet, speaking under the inspiration of the Holy Spirit, said more than he then fully comprehended. John kept growing physically and getting stronger spiritually and remained living in the deserts even after the death of his aged parents, until the day of his manifestation in his public ministry which began thirty years later. There he could study, close to the heart of nature and nature's God and develop a strong pure character for the service of the Lord.

6. The Annunciation to Joseph (Matt. 1:18-25).

The genealogy both of Matthew and Luke had intimated that Jesus was merely supposed to be and was not the physical son of Joseph. The supernatural character of His birth is now declared explicitly and in such a way as to leave no doubt. Mary was betrothed to Joseph and living doubtless in the home of her parents. Probably on returning from the visit of three months at the home of Elizabeth in Judea and before she was united in marriage with Joseph, she was found to be with child. The narrative makes it plain that Mary had not told Joseph, who was shocked and greatly grieved and perplexed by the discovery. Naturally he knew nothing of the announcement made to Mary by the angel. He could not have accepted any explanation of the grievous fact. Anyway, her modesty would prevent any explanation. There was a great struggle in his heart, for he loved Mary, and according to tradition he was much her elder. Exposure of her condition might result in a violent death for her. Though Joseph was conscientious with reference to the observance of the law, he did not wish to brand her with public disgrace, but rather avoid all the scandal possible. He resolved to release her secretly from the betrothal, which was considered as binding as marriage among the Jews. It was a relief that he could legally divorce her privately. It was possible for him to give her a bill of divorcement—the *gert* of the Mishnah— without a public trial. Such a plan he was contemplating when the Lord intervened.

The annunciation to Joseph was a necessity. There was no other way out of the difficulty. The Angel of the Lord appeared to him in a dream, which was considered a mark of God's favor. "Do not fear, Joseph son of David, to take to your home Mary your wife, for she is with child through the Holy Spirit." Here is a plain statement of the miraculous conception. Mary was innocent of sin. He was to take her and shield her, bearing her reproach. The angel further added that she would give birth to a son and Joseph should call His name Jesus (Jehovah-Saviour) because he would deliver His people from their sins. From the failure to hit the mark* and come up to the standard set by God, men would be saved by Jesus.

The virgin birth of Christ has always been a difficult problem for the belief of some. But when we admit the Incarnation and the supernatural element in His life and resurrection, we should not balk at the miraculous conception and virgin birth. Jesus had no human father. He did have a human mother. Only thus could He be the God-Man. This is the most natural and easiest explanation of the incarnation. Matthew and Luke agree in their accounts of the miraculous conception and John seems to refer to it (1:14), while Mark assumes His divine nature and His miraculous works.

Matthew interprets both the birth and name of Jesus as fulfillment of the purpose of God expressed in the prophecy of Isaiah (7:14). Possibly Isaiah did not understand by his prophecy a virgin birth. But it was Matthew's understanding that the virgin birth of Jesus was the fulfillment of the prophecy of Isaiah, as God purposed. Jesus was not a mere pledge of divine deliverance, promised in the prophecy, but was in reality a divine Saviour. The name Immanuel (God with us) was realized in a fuller sense in Jesus than Isaiah possibly comprehended. The real significance of the birth of Jesus is that He was the incarnate Son of God—the Divine Word becomes flesh, the God-Man.

Joseph quietly arranged the nuptials and took Mary his wife home in faith and obedience to the command of the angel, and lived in continence with her until she brought forth her first-born Son; and he called His name Jesus.

* Hamartia, Sin.

CHAPTER III

THE BIRTH AND INFANCY OF JESUS

(Harm. §§ 10-16)

The stories which cluster around the nativity of Jesus are full of idyllic charm. Mark was more interested in the personality and works of the Lord than in the place and manner of His birth. Luke desired to give a more complete account of His life and so added the beautiful narrative of his lineage; His birth, and announcement to the humble Judean shepherds. Matthew desiring to link the person of the Messiah up with the ancient prophecy gave his own independent account. Luke narrates in simplicity and brevity, with consummate art the circumstances of the birth, and adds the testimony of various divinely chosen witnesses, who give the interpretation and world-wide significance of the event. Matthew adds to this testimony of universal interest, introducing the narrative of the Magi, the providential flight into Egypt, and return to Nazareth in fulfillment of God's plan revealed in prophecy. But these narratives are supplementary and in perfect harmony. They agree in the Davidic descent, in the account of His humble origin, and in the profound and universal interest in the event on the part of Jew and Gentile, the royal Idumean ruler and the humble peasant class, the wise scientists and the ignorant shepherds.

1. The wondrous virgin birth. (Luke 2:1-7).

It is difficult to fix with more than approximate accuracy the exact date of the birth of Jesus. That, after all, is not fundamentally important. It was providential that the date was concealed, such is the tendency to emphasize holy days and places. But modern research has corroborated the testimony of Luke as to the two enrollments by Quirinius: one in 6 A. D. (Acts 5:37) and the other in 8 B. C. The Roman Emperors were proud of their power which was coextensive with the known world. In this period of comparative peace, Augustus busied himself in the registration of the subject peoples, and issued an edict "that all the world should be taxed." A universal census was to be taken and Quirinius was to superintend this work under the legate in Syria. Herod was always ready to fall in with the plans of the Emperor, but was politic in seeking to please the Jews whenever it did not conflict with his own interests. The census which was scheduled for 746 A. U. C. or 8 B. C., was likely delayed a couple of years or more in Palestine. A census in Egypt is recorded in 6 B. C. and the one in Palestine must have taken place the following year. There are a number of evidences that Jesus was born in 5 B. C. The death of Herod occured in 4 B. C., a short time after an eclipse of the moon, and Jesus was born while he was living (Matt. 2:1-6). This eclipse occured on March 12, 750 A. U. C. (Jos. 17:6, 4). Furthermore, John began his ministry in the fifteenth year of Tiberius at the age of thirty, making his birth fall in the early Spring of 749 and that of Jesus in the Fall of the same year or 5 B. C. The date may also be computed from Herod's building of the Temple (Jno. 2:20) which was forty-six years in construction. He began to build in the eighteenth year of his reign (Schürer's Hist. of Jewish People: Dv I, Vol. I, p. 410). This would give us 26 A. D. as the beginning of Christ's ministry and 5 B. C. as the date of His birth. The month and day of the month are uncertain fortunately, though it most probably occurred between April, the Passover time, and October, the usual period for having the flocks in the open pasture. The 25th of December was the date of the Roman pagan feast of Saturnalia, when they gave themselves up to revelry and also debauchery, albeit a season of good will when it was not pious to engage in war, when no criminal was executed and friends gave gifts to one another. For a whole day slaves enjoyed their freedom. The Christians, many of whom belonged to the oppressed and lowly classes, seized upon this day to celebrate in holy festival of goodwill the birth of their Lord. Custom did the rest and Christendom continues to hold this Christmas Day.

The plan that seemed best for the Jews in taking the census was that each one should be enrolled in his native place. Joseph and Mary were both of Davidic descent, whose native city was Bethlehem (I Sam. 17:12). This town was beautifully situated, six miles south of Jerusalem, on the eastern slope of a limestone ridge, with terraces covered with vines and fruit trees.

Schneller says that Joseph's home had been in Bethlehem and that he was a constructor or house-builder and not a mere carpenter, who went at seasons to other places for work as do the builders of Bethlehem yet. On such a visit to Nazareth he met Mary. He was betrothed to her, and after the marriage planned to take her to Bethlehem to live. The execution of this resolution was precipitated by the census and they went with the purpose of remaining. Such an explanation seems to be sustained by their intention to return to Bethlehem after the flight to Egypt. But there might have been other reasons for not returning to the north, such as, for example, the whisperings and backbitings in Nazareth. If Joseph had ever lived in Bethlehem he must have moved to Nazareth permanently before his betrothal to Mary. Else if he had a home in Bethlehem, when they arrived there for the census, why did he not go to his house immediately instead of stopping at the Caravanserai (inn) by the way? In any case, Joseph would not want to leave Mary in Nazareth under the circumstances amid curious and ill-judging people. So she came under difficult circumstances of travel with her husband on the three days journey. She was not obliged by the law to be present for the census. The country through which the travelers passed was full of idyllic sweetness and pastoral charm. Coming in view of Bethlehem, the typical Syrian town with its grey cluster of houses, they would pass the tomb of Rachel—pathetic memorial of a woman's travail and untimely death. This would impress Mary, as wearily she approached the end of her long journey and anxiously thought of her own condition. Or perhaps she would the rather reflect on Ruth the Moabitess, who came in loneliness to this little town, an utter stranger, to become the mother of a race of kings. And had not Micah said that from the little town of Bethlehem should come the "Ruler of Israel, whose goings forth have been of old from everlasting"? Had not the angels said she was to be the mother of this promised king?

The exact place in Bethlehem where Jesus was born cannot be known but He was born in Bethlehem. The last thing which a mother would be likely to forget is the birth-place of her child. Especially would this be true of this mother and her miracle-born Son. It must have been just as they were getting into the town at the eventide, to find it crowded now with the many who had come from various parts of the densely populated land also for the purpose of enrollment, that they were obliged to seek shelter for the tired, suffering, and anxious wife. So they turned into a Caravanserai or kind of oriental inn, somewhat after the nature of a tourist camp except with accommodations in the open court for the animals. There was no room in these compartments, crowded now to their capacity, and the tired travelers were obliged to content themselves with such protection as the open courtyard of the inn would furnish. In the Orient it was not uncommon to find the family and animals housed under the same roof.

There in the open court, Mary brought forth her Wonder-child and cradled Him in a manger. Such is the simple gospel declaration of the greatest of all historical events. An apocryphal gospel would have filled out the story with many details; but our gospel narrative, which was not a biography of Jesus, presents in the fewest traces this simple picture of earthly humility in circumstances and heavenly fitness in character.

Old Testament prophecy and Rabbinic traditon alike had pointed to Bethlehem as the birth-place of the Messiah (Micah). The finger of providence is seen in the historic circumstances, bringing this humble pair to their native city at this time. Jesus was truly the Messiah of the Jews. History has demonstrated that. He broke down the wall of national prejudice and made the monotheistic religion of the Jews the common heritage of all nations. He was the one Ideal Man and example for all men. His doctrine has penetrated the thought of all humanity. Born in the humblest circumstances and using the most unlikely means and methods, He has become the greatest factor in the spiritual uplift of humanity through all subsequent times.

No convincing evidence against the Virgin birth of Jesus here realized can be found in the New Testament. The difficulty of accounting for His life on any other ground is greater than the difficulty of accepting the Virgin birth as a fact. We are not obliged by the acceptance of it to believe in the immaculate conception or in the perpetual virginity of Mary. By the most natural interpretation of the expression "first born," Mary had other children, which were born from the wedlock of Joseph. The Gospel narratives speak of four such younger brothers and at least two sisters.

2. The praise of angels and homage of the shepherds (Luke 2:8-20).

The extraordinary character of the infancy of Jesus is attested not only by the manifestation of the supernatural in angelic visitation and earthly miracle, but by the most trustworthy human witnesses. Such were the humble Judean shepherds, who watched their flocks by night on the plains east of Bethlehem near the watch-tower of Migdal Eder. There was a popular belief that the Messiah was to be revealed from this "tower of the flock." According to the Mishna, flocks pastured there were destined for the Temple-sacrifices. Those shepherds were humble and devout but not of the most ignorant and lowest class. They were not under the ban of Rabbinism, as most of the shepherd class.

As they kept watch over their flocks, suddenly an angel stood before them and an intense light shone out round about them. They were stricken with a great fear. The angel calmed their fears with a word, as in the case of Zacharias. "I bring you a glad message of great joy, which shall be for all peoples," he said. "There is born to you today in the city of David a Saviour which is Christ the Lord." This was the brief but wonderful message from heaven. They would find the child wrapped in swaddling clothes and lying in a manger.

Then, suddenly, a multiude of the army of heaven burst on their vision in a great chorus, ascribing glory to God and peace to men of goodwill.

"Glory to God in the highest
Peace on earth among men of goodwill."

Only a part of the heavenly host was visible. The incarnation of Christ would bring glory to God by revealing Him to the world. It would bring peace internal and external to men whom God "wishes well." They will have this peace if they will learn good will toward God and men. Peace can only come through the creation in men of the contagious goodwill of God.

While the angels were yet going away from them into the heaven, the shepherds began to speak to one another in eagerness repeatedly: "Let us go even now to Bethlehem and see this thing that has taken place, which the Lord has made known unto us." Hastening, they came and found Mary and Joseph, with the new-born babe lying in the manger, just as the angel had said. In the hour of her supreme need Mary had been ministered unto by no loving tender hands of a woman. She herself had wrapped the child in swaddling clothes and laid it in the manger. When the shepherds verified all they had been told by the angel, they made known what had been spoken to them about the child, not only to Joseph and Mary but to everybody. This produced a profound impression. All were astonished at the things the shepherds told them.

But Mary treasured up all these things in her heart, going over them, meditating on them many times. The shepherds returned to their humbler tasks full of gratitude and praise to God for all they had been privileged to hear and see. To the humblest and most pious, God had revealed the best and the highest. They had lived the simple shepherd life in the fields, which reminded them constantly of Jacob, who years before kept his flocks here, of the beautiful romance of Boaz and Ruth, and of David, who in these very fields had kept watch over his flocks, studied God's nature, and meditated on nature's God. They were thus prepared by a devout life of prayer and meditation to be the recipients of the most glorious message the world would ever hear.

3. Circumcision and presentation in the Temple and homage of Simeon and Anna (Luke 2:21-38).

The law of Moses was zealously honored and scrupulously observed in the life of the infant Jesus (Matt. 3:15). When eight days passed He was circumcised according to the Covenant (Gen. 17:12; Lev. 12:3). At that time, after the prevailing custom, He was named, becoming thereafter "a son of the law" (Gal. 4:4). Thus every male child among the Jews accepted the conditions, obligations, and privileges of the Covenant between God and Abraham and his need, inscribing his name in his own blood in the roll of the nation. The parents usually selected the names of their children but God through Gabriel named Jesus (Jehovah-Saviour).

The purification (2:22-32) of the parents and redemption of the first born son took place according to the Law forty-one days after the birth (Lev. 12:6). The mother was not obliged to be present in the Temple but could send her offering by another. However it was then customary for devout women who lived near Jerusalem to be present personally for this impressive ceremony. Israel was at a low ebb in spiritual religion in those days, through the traditionalism and formalism of her Sadducean priests and Pharasaic teachers. But there was a remnant of the devout who "waited for the consolation of Israel." Joseph and Mary belonged to this group. They came from Bethlehem, where they were residing now with their new-born Son.

The presentation in the Temple had the double purpose of purification of the parents from legal and ceremonial uncleanness, and the redeeming of the first born son from priestly service. For the former, a lamb was brought for the sacrifice by the rich and two doves or two young pigeons if poor. The gift of Mary would indicate their humble circumstances. The first born son of every Israelite was to be consecrated for the special service of the priesthood (Ex. 13:2). But after the setting apart of the tribe of Levi (Num. 8), the first born son in other tribes was redeemed from this obligation by the payment of five shekels (about $4.00).

Two offerings were made in the purification of the mother: the offering for Levitical defilement attached to the beginning of life, and burnt offering for restoration of communion with God. The price of the two turtle doves or pigeons was dropped in the third of the thirteen trumpet-shaped collection boxes in the Court of the Women. The sacrifices were supplied by the Temple venders. The ministrants arranged those women who had presented themselves, in the designated place beside the Nacanor gate, where they would be nearest the Sanctuary and Court of Israel and could accompany the acts of sacrifice and see the cloud of incense — symbol especially of their prayers — rise from the golden altar.

Only after the purification ceremony was ended and Mary was Levitically clean could she participate in the ceremony of the redemption of her son. This simple ceremony consisted, first in the simple presentation of the child to the priest in recognition of God's ownership, and second in the payment of the five shekels. The priest on receiving the child pronounced two blessings: one in thanksgiving for the law of redemption and another for the gift of the first born son. Thus the pious parents of Jesus observed to the full all the requirements of the Law.

There was in Jerusalem when Jesus was presented a pious man named Simeon (Vs. 25-35). He was just in conduct toward God; reverent in contrast to the self-righteous Pharisee; expectant of the coming of the Messiah. Some think that Simeon was the son of the great Rabbi Hillel, founder of a theological school in Jerusalem, father of Gamaliel, Paul's teacher, and president of the Sanhedrin in 13 B. C. But it is more probable that he was one of those humble, circumspect, pious, unknown persons — found sometimes in the midst of unfavorable circumstances — who awaited with patience the coming of the Messianic kingdom. To this aged man it had been revealed by the Holy Spirit, that he would not die until he should have seen the Lord's Anointed. Under the influence of the Spirit, he came into the Court of the Gentiles just as Joseph and Mary entered to present Jesus to the priest. He took the infant tenderly into his paternal arms and blessed God. From the mountain height of prophetic vision, as one who stood on the borderland of the Spirit-world and beheld the first rays of the sunrise on the distant shores of the Gentile world, growing into glorious radiance over his own beloved people, Simeon gave utterance to his praise to God in the poetic prophecy — the Nunc Dimittis, the most solemn and sweetest song of the Nativity. The years of his prayers and patient waiting were at last rewarded. His years of earnest study of the Messianic prophecies had given him spiritual eyes to see the suffering Redeemer, where others sought a temporal Messiah-King.

"Now Thou art setting thy servant free, Sovereign Lord,
According to thy word in peace.
For mine eyes have seen thy salvation,
Which Thou hast made ready in sight of all peoples,
A Light to shine on the nations,
And a glory of thy people Israel."

The prophetic hymn of Simeon may be divided into three stanzas. In the first (Vs. 29-30) the faithful watchman greets the hour of his joyful dismissal by his Sovereign Lord. His eyes at last behold the promised salvation in the infant Saviour, who is to be a universal Light for all nations and the true glory of the chosen people Israel. In Him Israel's mission must be fulfilled in the gift of the true religion to the world.

The parents were filled with wonder. The aged Simeon paused a moment to pronounce on them a blessing; then addressing Mary, to whom he had returned the child, added in the third and last stanza, a dark and difficult prophecy:

"Behold He is set for the falling and rising of many in Israel.

And for a sign which is spoken against.
Yea, a sword shall pierce through thy soul, a long
   Thracian Javelin,
That the reasonings in many hearts may be revealed."

How truly that prophecy was fulfilled a few years later. Jesus' ministry was a stone of stumbling to many in Israel who rejected Him; but a foundation and corner-stone on which to build up a lasting life, to those who accepted Him. He was for a sign like Jonah, for a token-communication, an important message. Contradiction to this sign culminated on the cross (Acts 28:22). His high mission of privilege must be accompanied by great suffering. Such is ever the case. It would be so in the personal experience of Mary. So it was when she stood at the foot of the cross and looked on her Son. A great sorrow transfixed her soul, like a long, cruel, Thracian javelin. But the affliction and opposition which Jesus was destined to meet, would tear open the veil of externalism in the religion of Israel, revealing the thoughts of many. Men would be compelled to take a stand for Christ or against Him. The varnish of hypocrisy would be scraped away and the truth of the religious destitution of Israel would be revealed to all. Many would be awakened to recognize the futility of a sacramental religion and hopelessness of a salvation by mere religious rites. They would come to see the necessity of spiritual regeneration.

Another interesting figure presents herself at this juncture. It was the prophetess Anna, of the tribe of Aser, and of a distinguished family. She had been a widow for eighty-four years, after being seven years' married, bringing her age up to above a hundred. She literally lived in the Temple never missing a service. Her constant occupation was in fasting and prayers. Deeply moved by the words of Simeon doubtless, she burst out into thanks to God, and spoke in oracular strain to the company of the devout over and over* about the Child. Every day she kept on talking to those who had waited for the redemption of Israel.

4. The visit of the Magi to the new-born King. (Matt. 2:1-12).

It was probably after the presentation in the Temple and the return to Bethlehem, where Joseph and Mary seem to have decided to remain instead of returning to Nazareth now, for the same reason that Joseph did not wish to leave Mary behind when he came down for the census. Matthew records such incidents of the infancy as would sustain his thesis that Jesus was the promised Messiah. At first blush it would seem that he was getting out of the proper sphere of his argument, by introducing the visit of the Eastern priest-sages, from the Gentile world. Further examina-

*Imperfect, repeated action.

tion reveals, however, that one of the strongest proofs of His Messiahship, was the homage of the Gentiles and the universal expectation which prevailed, not only in Palestine, but on the outside at the time of His birth. There were premonitions of this greatest event of world history.

Matthew's narrative does not dwell at length on the circumstances of the birth, which were not important to the purpose. He identifies the place of Jesus' birth in Bethlehem, the "house of bread," so called because of the fruitfulness of the surrounding district Ephratah of Judea. This beautiful country was the home of David, who was born in Bethlehem. The Magi were priest-sages, students of science, especially of astrology and religion, but also philosophy and medical science. Their researches, mysterious and mostly unknown to us, embraced deep knowledge not unmixed with some superstition. They came from the East, probably from Persia, Arabia, or Babylonia. At that time there was a sacerdotal caste of the Medes and Persians scattered over the East, and also many Jews of the Dispersion through whom the priest-sages may have received some knowledge of Israel's Hope. Perhaps they may have received knowledge through the prophecies of Balaam of the promise of a King who would arise in Judea, who would reign universally. Tacitus, Suetonius, and Josephus bear testimony that such a hope existed at that time in the East.

The Magi naturally came to Jerusalem inquiring where the king had been born, because the current belief in their country pointed to Judea for the Deliverer from the night of despair which reigned universally when Jesus came.

The idea that the Magi or Wizards were kings, probably arose from a vague interpretation of Isa. 60:3, and Rev. 21:24. That they were three, is an inference from the three gifts offered, of gold, frankincense, and myrrh. There is no ground for assigning to them certain names, to say that they were three, or that they were representatives of Shem, Ham, and Japhet, coming from Greece, India, and Egypt. Much less ground is there for the supposition that their bones were discovered in the fourth century and their skulls are yet preserved in the Cathedral of Cologne.

There was a current belief among the Orientals, at that time as now, that a star could be the counterpart or angel of a great man. The Magi said they had seen the star of the new born King "at its rising." They represented the countless hungry hearts of the heathen world in all times, who seeing the light of nature, yearn for the Light of the World. They had come from afar to bow their knees in homage. Their visit was a prophecy, of how in the future the Gentile world would seek His salvation and bring to Him their gifts of wealth and talents.

In the next scene of the wonderful drama appears the savage murderous face of the monster Herod. He was greatly troubled and filled with alarm when he heard the report of the Magi. The "whole city was disturbed with him." The reason for this agitation of the people was not far to seek. Only a little while before this, filled with rage of family rivalries and jealous of anyone who might supplant him on the throne of Palestine which he an Idumean had usurped, he had secured the murder of his own beautiful princess of the Asmonean line and his two favorite sons Alexander and Aristobulus. Though he had sought by every means to secure the favor of the Roman Emperor, Augustus about this time had said he would prefer to be Herod's hog (hṽs) than to be his son (huios), for he would then have a better chance of life. The city feared now the revenge of this cruel and cunning king, who had in the beginning of his reign destroyed the Sanhedrin, and now in the last years of his bloody reign, might seize and execute the chief Jews.

It is no wonder that, when he called together the High Priests and Scribes of the people and asked one and another of them repeatedly about where the Messiah was to be born, that they hastened to reply: "In Bethlehem of Judea: for so it stands written through the prophet." These men who busied themselves copying the Hebrew Scriptures knew at once the definite prophecy (Micah 5:2) which expressed the common belief among the Jews (Jno. 7:42), that the Messiah was to be born of the seed of David, in Bethlehem. The prophecy was targummed in paraphrase according to the prevailing method, rather than quoted literally:

"And thou Bethlehem in the land of Judah,
Art in nowise least among the princely cities in Judea.
For from thee shall go forth a Prince
Who shall shepherd my people Israel."

Herod had swallowed a good deal of his pride in appealing to the Priests, whom he depised, and who hated him. But he must find out by any means whatever where the Messiah was to be born and avert every possible chance of a successor. Astutely, he avoided asking about whether the birth had already taken place or when it was expected, lest he unduly arouse their hatred and fail in his malignant purpose to slay the infant King. The High Priests showed no interest in the possibility of their Messiah's birth. They had more fear of Herod and for their own lives than courage or wisdom in protecting Him whom they expected and for whom the Wizards now sought. Herod did not call the Magi together with the princes of the Jews, but afterward secretly, and to inquire of them "accurately" the time that had elapsed since the star appeared. He was already meditating a thorough search in Bethlehem, among the male children whose age fell within the period since the star appeared, that he might carry out his sinister design. The subsequent incidents would indicate that the Magi informed him that it had been two years since they saw the star "at its rising." With the pretense of being himself desirous of paying the recent-born King homage, he made the Magi the unconscious instruments of his bloody plan, directing them to go and seek out accurate information concerning the Child and bring back a report to him. The deceit of Herod seemed complete and humanly speaking the Child's life was doomed. But all human strategy fails when the God of providence intervenes.

Having received this information about the place of the birth and the friendly request of Herod, the sages resumed their journey: and behold the star — which they saw at its rising and seem not to have seen for some time again — appeared once more and kept on going in front of them, until coming it stood over where the child was, probably a house to which Joseph and Mary had moved soon after the birth. The Magi rejoiced with exceeding joy when they saw the star.

There is a difference of opinion as to the character of the star. The atmosphere of oriental astrology would lend itself to the support of a naturalistic interpretation. Certain facts of astronomical history, together with expressions of the Magi, would tend also to confirm this opinion. The great astronomer Kepler observed in 1603 A. D. an unusual conjunction of stars, and found by diligent search that in 747 A. U. C. (or 7 B. C.) there was a similar conjunction three times, of Jupiter and Saturn in Pisces. In 748 A. U. C. (or 6 B. C.) Mars joined the conjunction. Consequently Kepler placed the Nativity in 748 A. U. C. Furthermore, trustworthy astronomical tables of the Chinese testify to the appearance of an evanescent star, probably a comet, in February 750 A. U. C. This would agree with the date approximately of the birth. The Magi probably placed the date of the rising of the star at two years before their appearance in Jerusalem. This would agree roughly with the time of the conjunction of Jupiter and Saturn. The fact that they rejoiced at the reappearance of the star when they left Jerusalem would syncronize with the appearance of the comet or evanescent star.

Over against these facts and arguments and in favor of the miraculous, stands the expression "his star" and the further declaration that the star was "going before them and coming stood above the place where the child lay." The Greek word for star was also not that which would be used of a group of stars. The whole supernatural atmosphere of the birth of Christ would favor the opinion that the star was miraculous and in keeping with the significant mission of the Magi. It would be called "his star" because of the prophecy foretelling the coming of the Messiah. On the whole the evidence seems to point to special supernatural guidance, at least from Jerusalem to the house of Joseph in Bethlehem. The tradition would direct them to Jerusalem.

The Wise Men entered the house, and when they saw the babe with His mother, they fell down and worshipped Him. Then opening their treasure-chests they offered to Him gifts, gold, and costly spices: both frankincense, a bitter and odorous gum, and myrrh, a species of gum used in the orient as perfume and also as spice, medicine, and for embalming. These were doubtless the most appropriate products of their own country, which they could present as offerings symbolic of the tribute of the nations. Heaven intervened to protect the life of the Infant Jesus, and these Wise Men were admonished by an angel in a dream not to return to the murderous Herod in Jerusalem but to depart by another way to their own country.

5. The flight to Egypt and the return to Nazareth (Matt. 2:13-23; Luke 2:31).

Matthew records one other incident omitted by Luke, the flight into Egypt, and finds in it the fulfillment of two prophecies. The Wise Men probably departed from Bethlehem within twenty-four hours after they were in Jerusalem. It is likely that Joseph and Mary, warned by the angel in a dream, also left Bethlehem by night to escape the vigilance of the crafty Herod, whom the angel said was about to make a search for the infant boy with the purpose of destroying Him. This wily Idumean King, now decrepit with seventy years of age and thirty-seven of cruel reign, had bathed his hands in the blood of three of his sons, his own wife, and many other kinsmen even, who happened to raise his suspicion and jealousy. He would spare no effort to destroy the infant Jesus.

The nearest place of safety to which Joseph could flee with his family was Egypt, to the nearest borders of which was a distance of seventy-five miles. Tradition says they penetrated more than a hundred miles within the country and abode for a year in a Jewish colony, in the village of Motorea near Leviantapolis, the site of a great Jewish Temple built in 150 B. C. There were more than a million Jews in Egypt at this time, and the colony was highly respectable and influential in the country. Thus the infant Saviour was snatched from the savage fury of the wicked tyrant.

Matthew found in this experience of Jesus the fulfillment of the prophecy (Hosea 11:1):

"Out of Egypt I called my Son."

While the prophet referred primarily to the people of Israel in their deliverance from Egypt, the deeper meaning of the prophecy was filled out in the deliverance of the infant Messiah in whom the mission of Israel was fulfilled.

Tradition, and the apocryphal gospels written many years later, tell many absurd and fanciful things about the flight of the family and their entrance into Egypt. The flowers were said to spring up in their steps as they entered the land; the palm trees to bow down in homage, and wild animals to come near in friendly approach.

When the crafty Herod knew that the Magi had departed from Bethlehem by another route and his wicked plan had been foiled, his fury burst all bounds in a violent fit of temper, and he issued the cruel and irrational edict to have all the male children in Bethlehem under two years of age destroyed. He felt insulted that he had thus been lightly mocked by the Magi and would wreak vengeance on the helpless infants of a defenseless population. There is some ground for supposing that he fixed the age limit at two years, because of the report of the Magi as to the siderial appearance, but no conclusive proof. The ruthless decree was immediately put in execution. A traditon says that fourteen thousand children were slain. But the real fact would seem. to be that about twenty children met a bloody death. Josephus made no record of the event, as he likely would have done had there been so large a number. Matthew finds in this gruesome incident the fulfillment of another prophecy:

"A voice was heard in Ramah!
Wailing and much lamentation!
Rachel bewailing her children,
And she would not be comforted because they are not."
(Jer. 31:15)

This quotation from the Septuagint version referred to the incident. when Nebuchadnezzar assembled the heads of the chief Jewish families at Ramah, before they were borne away in captivity. Complete destruction threatened the nation. There was bitter grief, which the prophet described by representing Rachel, who was long since deceased and buried near Ramah and Bethlehem, as having come to life and bewailing — as the mother of the tribe in whose territory the exiles had been assembled — the unhappy and hopeless lot of her people. In the slaughter of the Innocents of Bethlehem also, the future of the people of God had been threatened. All depended upon the infant Messiah; if He should be slain the future of His people would be hopeless. But Jeremiah comforted Rachel with the hope for the future througn providential restoration; and it was God's hand that intervened also in the deliverance of the infant King.

Herod died of a loathsome disease in 4 B. C., a short time after the perpetration of this terrible crime. He had sought relief for a little while in the mineral baths of Callirhoe. There he attempted suicide which was prevented. At the same time, he ordered thousands of the most prominent Jews to be shut up in the circus of Jericho, to be executed at the hour of his death, that there might be no lack of lamentation in the land. But Salome to whom he intrusted the bloody order, when his death was announced set the prisoners free.

Again, the Angel of the Lord of special providence appeared to Joseph in a dream in Egypt, bidding him to rise up and taking the child and his mother to return to the Land of Israel. The information was added that all those who had been seeking the life of the child Jesus were surely dead, both Herod and his accomplices. Joseph obeyed at once, but on the way back to his native land heard that Archelaus, Herod's worst son, was reigning in Judea, whence they were wending their way.

In his last hours Herod had changed his will and appointed Archelaus instead of Antipas the oldest son over Judea, Idumea, and Samaria, with the title of King. To Antipas he gave the tetrarchy of Galilee and Perea and to Philip the other tetrarchy to the east and north. Archelaus possessed all of the vices and weaknesses of his father and none of his redeeming characteristics. Augustus did not permit him to bear the title of king but that of ethnarch. He was not liked by the Jews, and immediately on his accession slew 3000 Jews in the Temple at the Passover and later killed many Samaritans also. In 6 A. D., through a complaint of the Jews backed by the testimony of Antipas and Philip his brothers, he was banished, and Judea passed under the Roman Procurators.

Once more Providence intervened and Joseph's fears were allayed. He was admonished not to go back to Bethlehem to live, but to withdraw into a section of Galilee. Thus under divine direction Joseph returned to Nazareth and lived there. Matthew finds in this circumstance a third prophecy fulfilled:

"He shall be called a Nazarene."

This prophecy is less definite than the other two. Probably it refers to Ps. 22 and Isa. 53. To be called a Nazarene was a reproach, and prophecy had foretold that He would be "despised and rejected of men." Joseph and Mary had lived in Nazareth before the census and their change of residence to Bethlehem. They had been a year in Egypt and now returned to Galilee, as Luke says: "to their own city of Nazareth."

CHAPTER IV
THE SILENT YEARS IN NAZARETH
(Harm. §§ 17-19)

Almost all the years of the life of Jesus were passed in obscurity. After the first year of the nativity and infancy, the curtain on the scene of His life falls, and the evangelical narrative passes over twenty-six years, with the sole exception of one brief incident, when the boy at the age of twelve visited the city of Jerusalem with His parents on the occasion of the Passover.

One significant statement is made by Luke about the childhood, pointing to His normal physical, intellectual, and spiritual growth. He "increased in size and waxed strong," developing a robust physique. His intellectual life kept pace through the natural acquisition of experience. Wisdom is experiential knowledge. This does not refer to formal but to natural education. His moral and spiritual development was just as real as the physical and intellectual. The favor of God was upon Him. This was the first time in human history that growth was perfectly normal, unimpeded by acquired defects and evil habits. That He had to conquer hereditary tendencies toward evil was inevitable. He was a human child, subject to all its conditions yet perfect in them. The Saviour of the world was to be the Ideal Man.

We would give much to know all about the childhood days of Jesus, His words and actions such as are recorded in the memory of a fond mother, His daily companions, His childish feats and traits. The Apocryphal Gospels profess to tell much about His school days, His teachers, playmates, and many incidents almost blasphemously absurd. They relate how in a fit of temper He would strike down His companions with death, curse His accusers with blindness, and mock His teachers (Pseudo-Matthew 30, 31). His miraculous power, He would use also foolishly, in making clay birds on the Sabbath and causing them to fly when He was corrected for naughtiness. Such stories are revolting and wholly foreign to the character of the child who could become the man Jesus.

There is much that we may know indirectly of His childhood days, by a close examination of the environmental conditions under which He grew. He was reared in Nazareth, a town in Galilee, and in a religious home of the middle class socially. We know that certain educational conditions existed peculiar to the Jews of that time, and we have also the character and works of the Man to point us back to the days of the silent preparation in the seclusion of the Nazareth home.

Galilee was the most beautiful and fertile section of Palestine. A land of green hills and fertile valleys, it was beautiful and

wonderful for agriculture. Corn, grapes, olives, and fruits of
various kinds grew in abundance. A great profusion of flowers
were to be found everywhere. In this land "flowing with milk
and honey," animals domestic and wild, a great variety of birds,
green pastures and numerous springs and brooks, made up a
picture of life, happiness, and abundance. A population estimated
as high as three millions inhabited numerous villages and towns.
Various industries flourished.

The people were generous, impulsive, simple in manners, full
of intense nationalism, free, and independent of the traditionalism
of Judea. The Rabbinic circles of Jerusalem held the Galilean in
contempt, because of his manner of speech, colloquialisms, and
lack of a certain type of culture characteristic of the Jerusalemite.
They were accused of neglecting the traditions and preferred the
Haggadah to the Halakkah. Judea claimed to be the proud deposi-
tory of orthodoxy and perpetuator of Jewish institutions. The
contempt with which the Judeans looked on the Galileans was unjust and due in large measure to envy, since their own barren
land could not be compared to the fruitful and beautiful country
of Galilee. The Judeans were accustomed to say that no prophet
ever arose from Galilee. But such was not the case, since Jonah
and probably Nahum were born there and the ministry of both
Elijah and Elisha was cast in that section though Elijah was born in
Tisbeli of Gilead and Elisha in Abel-Meholah. Jesus had to
overcome much local prejudice due to these conditions in His
ministry in Jerusalem and Judea. It is said that Rabbi Jose, a
Galilean of great ability, labored long before his extraordinary
talents and learning were recognized, due to this local prejudice.
The Jerusalem Rabbis said with a sneer, of Jesus: "How could
this man know letters, having never learned." They said that the
Galileans knew no grammar and could not even speak correctly.
They were, for the Jerusalemite, the *Patios or Amhaarretz*.

There were many Gentiles in Galilee in the time of Jesus,
although the majority of the population was Jewish; and while
there were general contacts, the Gentiles dwelt apart in exclusive
colonies and the patriotism of the Galilean Jews was intense.

It was in the midst of this vigorous, rustic, liberty-loving
Galilean people that Jesus grew up. Nor is it strange that the
greater part of His active ministry was cast by preference there,
in the midst of the teeming populations which thronged this productive and beautiful land. There, great throngs of people gathered
about Him as from village to village He went in His blessed
ministries material and spiritual. There the people had open hearts
to hear and accept His message.

The little town of Nazareth was one of the loveliest spots in

Galilee. Situated on the southeast slope of a hollow pear-shaped basin, which descends gradually from the elevated plateau 1500 feet above sea level and opens out through a steep winding way — the stem of the pear — into the plain of Esdraelon, a thousand feet lower, it commanded a prospect truly pleasing. On the hill five hundred feet above the town, a most wonderful panorama opens to view of the beauties and historic scenes of the land. To the north one sees the plateaus of Zebulun and Naphtali and mountains of Lebanon with snow-covered Hermon towering above them all; to the west the coast of Tyre and the blue waters of the Mediterranean, with Mt. Carmel, historic scene of the struggle of Elijah with the prophets of Baal, jutting out into the plain of Esdraelon; to the south across that historic plain, scene of many of the most memorable battles of Israel, rise the hills of Gilboa where Saul and Jonathan lost their lives, with Mt. Ebal and the land of Shechem in the background; and to the east, across the sea of Galilee and the Jordan Valley, the headlands of Gilead and Jaulan, with the conical-shaped Mt. Tabor figuring prominently in the landscape. On this hilltop, the boy Jesus must have spent many an hour thinking "the long, long thoughts of youth," and meditating on the picturesque and historic world laid out before Him. At the foot of the hill passed the Roman road, "the Way of the Sea," connecting the ancient city of Damascus with the Mediterranean sea-ports. Southward ran another road to Egypt, and circling round the base of Tabor a mile and a half away, was the caravan route to Jerusalem along which Jesus must have passed many times in the days of His youth as well as in His later pilgrimages to that far-famed city.

The town itself was built of the white limestone from the quarries of the calcerous mountains which encircle the basin. Most of the houses were of one characteristic type. Wide disparity between the rich and poor was not known in Nazareth in those days. A copious spring furnished the water supply for the whole population and was a favorite rendezvous for men, women, and children, who doubtless gathered in groups as today in familiar conversation; for the town which today numbers a population of ten thousand was much smaller in the days of Jesus. Nazareth did not have the best of reputations even in Galilee. Nathaniel of Cana was but echoing a common opinion when he said: "Can aught good come out of Nazareth?" The passionate and lawless character of the people is reflected in the violent reception of Jesus when He preached there in the beginning of His ministry. Jesus bore the reproach of this evil reputation later when He was called a Nazarene (Nostri). Matthew said this was in accord with the prophecy of Isaiah (Ch. 53) which pictures the coming Messiah as

a "root springing up out of the dry ground." The best known of
the names for the Messiah among the Jews was Isemach or Branch,
based on Isaiah's prophecy (Isa. 11:1). The word Netzer is the
exact equivalent. The title Nazarene not only thus stood for the
reproach which Jesus bore, but was a fulfillment of Messianic prophecy. He was a Branch (Netzer) sprung out of David's roots.

In this small town were the good and the bad alike. Here
Jesus would have a splendid opportunity to study not only nature
but human nature also in all its variety. Every phase of life: the
common domestic and familiar experiences of the home, weddings
with their torch-light processions and glad festivities, funerals
with their sad laments, the daily contacts in the shop of His
father with the work and with people of all types and classes,
the frequent and regular services in the synagogue, all alike
were impressed indelibly on His boyish mind. So it was that He
"increased" in experience, waxed strong in physique, and was
filled with the experiential knowledge of human nature and the
common affairs of human life. Here He came to know men and
"what was in man," of ambitions, hopes, ways good and bad, and
character. Educators say that the child learns more in the first
three or four years than in all the rest of life. The teachings of
Jesus, years afterwards, drew from the inexhaustible store of
common experiences of His childhood days innumerable illustrations, such as the leaven hid in three measures of meal, women
grinding at the mill, sowing and reaping, the sparrow and the
lily, the children in the market place playing at *wedding* and
funeral, and many others, those mentioned as well as those unmen-
tioned by the gospels. Jesus knew the life of the poor and the
rich, the ignorant and the learned alike. Out of the great store of
common experiences He was to frame the highest philosophy of
life the world has ever known.

Nazareth was secluded by its natural location but it was not
cut off from the outside world. Sepphoris, the capital of Herod Antipas and strongest military center in Galilee, was only five miles
to the northwest across the rolling hills. Tiberias, Capernaum,
Bethsaida and other towns were a few miles away on the margin of
the Sea of Galilee; and even Jerusalem itself was not a great
distance from His Nazareth home. A branch of the great caravan
route to Damascus passed through the town. Many traders, soldiers, and emissaries of the Roman government, and not a few
scholars and philosophers, were to be found in the stream of
travelers going back and forth along this artery of the Roman Empire. From these daily pilgrim-visitors, the alert mind of the
growing boy would glean many an idea and seed thought of truth

from the philosophies and religions of the world. At the age of twelve the precocious child revealed a marked development and insight, which warrant the supposition that during these tender years His mind was gathering from many sources — and one that of the pilgrim groups in the market-place of Nazareth — an incomparable fund of facts, in later years organized into a system of thought which has been the admiration and the despair of great thinkers of all subsequent times. He was "filled with wisdom" as the years of childhood progressed, by reason on the one side, of His natural impressibility, and on the other of the many contacts His town and country environment furnished.

Jesus grew up in an exceptional home. His foster-father Joseph was known for his saintliness of character and integrity of conduct (Matt. 7:11). He belonged to the middle industrial class, being an architect-builder and woodworkman. He planned and constructed houses and manufactured domestic furniture and agricultural instruments. In Nazareth he seems to have attained by his character and industry to a special place of esteem and usefulness, and was called by the title "the carpenter" which included all these phases of activity. He seems not to have lived long (Mark 3:32) and to have left a considerable family when he died to the care and responsibility of Jesus, the oldest son.

Mary, His mother, is known to us as the most highly favored of all women. She was a woman of beautiful humility, pure, saintly, loving character and disposition, an intelligent student of the Scriptures, of fervent, poetic and patriotic idealism; deeply religious and loyal in her convictions; a capable wife and a fond and careful mother. Doubtless Jesus learned from the lips of His wonderful young mother many tender caressing words in the Aramiac language, such as Talitha, "My lamb," which He used at the bedside of the little daughter of Jairus as He took her by the hand and raised her up to new life (Mark 5:41).

In the family of Joseph, there were four half-brothers younger than Jesus and at least two half-sisters. The names of the brothers were James, Joses, Judas, and Simeon (Mark 6:3), two of whom we know in the epistles of James and Jude. They did not become disciples of Jesus during His ministry but only after His resurrection. They were not sympathetic with His work. Once when He had gained great popularity in Galilee and was working with such intensity that He scarcely took time to eat, they persuaded His mother to come with them and take Him home, saying that He had gone crazy. On another occasion later on, they cast in His face the sneering accusation of being a "Secret Messiah," because He would not manifest Himself in Jerusalem. From the picture we thus piece together, we can reasonably conclude

that they were rather severe and unsympathetic with Jesus. There
is doubtless some ground for saying that His pathetic expression:
"A prophet is not without honor save in his own country and in
his own household," had its basis in part in experiences which He
suffered for many years before His public ministry began.

There was no luxury in the home of Jesus. While the gift of
the two turtle-doves as the offering for purification in the Temple
does not betoken poverty, it does signify that the family was one
of moderate means. The house was doubtless similar to those
found in Nazareth today: square, built of stone or brick, with a
single door, few if any windows, and a dirt or tile floor on which
mats were spread for sleeping. The flat housetop, reached by a
stairway on the outside, was a place for gathering the family and
visitors, especially in the evening hours of the hot summer nights.

The Jewish child's education began in his home. In every
Jewish household the child was taught a sort of elementary cate-
chism, the Shema (Deut. 6:4, 9; Num. 11:13-21; 15:37-41), by
his mother as soon as he could speak. The rule of minute religious
instruction in a Jewish home was well organized, constituting a
vital element in the child's education. The Mezuzah attached to the
doorpost, with the name of the Most High on the outside of the
little folded parchment, which was reverently touched by everyone
who entered or went out followed by kissing the fingers which
had touched the name, was considered a divine guard over the
home. The private and united prayers and domestic rites were
impressive; the festive illumination of the house during a week in
mid-winter, in commemoration of the Dedication of the Temple by
Judas the Maccabee; the feast of Purim in celebration of the deliverance through Esther; the Feast of the Passover setting forth the
visit of the Death Angel and Israel's going out from Egypt; followed
by the Fast of the Day of Atonement and the Feast of Tabernacles
with its strange leafy booth; all were calculated to impress the childish mind in a most extraordinary fashion. Thus from the tender
years of infancy the child was under the influence of religion in
a very impressive way. Nor was the responsibility of instruction
solely that of the mother; but the father was bound to teach his son
the Torah. It is not improbable that Joseph possessed rolls of the
law and the prophets. Passages from the Old Testament, especially
the whole book of Psalms, short prayers, and select sayings of the
sages were memorized. We may be sure that Joseph and Mary were
diligent in following out this system of home training in the religion
of Jehovah.

The formal education in the synagogue school was begun at

the age of six under the Chazzan, who kept the building and guarded the rolls of the law, the prophets, and other sacred writtings. In this synagogue school there was further instruction in the law and in the rudiments of a primary education. Cross-legged, the children sat on the floor about their teacher. These schools existed in all the synagogues scattered through the land; and attendance was compulsory. The moral and religious purpose was placed as the ultimate object of all instruction. The office of teacher was esteemed in Israel and the work was generally done with patience, earnestness, and discipline. From six to ten years of age the child studied the Old Testament as his chief text-book; from ten to fifteen the Mishnah or traditional law; and after fifteen in the Academy the theology of the Gemaras. In the study of the Bible the child began with the book of Leviticus; then came the rest of the Pentateuch; and after that the Prophets and Hagiographa. The inference from the evangelical narratives of Matthew (5:18) and Luke (16:17) is, that Jesus read the Scriptures in the original Hebrew, written in the square Assyrian characters. The familiarity of the Lord with the text both of the Hebrew and the Greek, would lead us to believe that the Nazareth home possessed a copy of the Sacred Volume in both Hebrew and in Greek. In any case, He would have access to the rolls in the Synagogue. Jesus spoke the Aramaic in His home, and the Greek which was commonly spoken especially in the larger cities of Galilee and Judea. The likelihood is that He was master of all three of these languages, since frequent quotations show His use of the Hebrew Scriptures, references to the Septuagint testify to His familiarity with the Greek, and expressions such as that on the cross: "Eloi, Eloi lama Sabacthani," evidence His common use of the Aramaic branch of the Semitic tongue, in which He must have done all His teaching and preaching currently.

In addition to the formal instruction of the synagogue school, every Jewish father was required to teach his son some honest craft. Saul of Tarsus learned tent-making. We know that Jesus learned the trade of His foster-father and was after the death of Joseph called in Nazareth *the carpenter*. He never studied in the Jewish Academies. Only once do we find Him in the House of the Midrash in Jerusalem, the Theological Academy of the Doctors of the Law. That was when He was in attendance on the feast of the Passover at the age of twelve.

Once only was the curtain lifted on the twenty-six silent years in Nazareth. Luke gives us one wonderful glimpse of the splendid boy Jesus, at the age of twelve, on a visit with His parents in

Jerusalem at the time of the Passover. That was a critical age in the life of the boy, just turning to adolescense with the quickened growth physical and intellectual, and the expanding vision and idealism. It was exactly at this age that the Jewish boy became "the son of the law," and entered on the privileges and responsibilities of an Israelite, including attendance annually on the three most important Feasts (Ex. 34:22, 23). Jesus had been presented to the elders in the home synagogue, who examined Him as to His religious education and pronounced a blessing on Him declaring Him a son of the law. It is a great event in the life of a boy, when he is first brought from the quiet hamlet or country place to see the many new and strange sights of the city. This fact is greatly re-enforced when we remember that Jesus was reared in a Jewish home and this city was the beloved Jerusalem, center of the very life and affection of every Jew. Great had been the past of this city and her future was to be glorious. "Great things were spoken of Zion, the City of God." For her the golden age was thought to be in the future; little did they know how distant a future.

It was the custom of Joseph and Mary, devout Jews as they were, to attend the Feast of the Passover, the most important of all the religious festivals of the Jews, every year (Deut. 16:1-8). It was not obligatory on the women to be present; but Mary was devoted to the worship of Jehovah and was accustomed to attend with her husband on this occasion. We do not know if Jesus had ever before been with them on this annual pilgrimage. Even if He had, this visit was the one of outstanding importance to Him as He now came into full religious privilege as a son of the law.

There were three possible routes to Jerusalem: one by the plains of Esdraelon and Sharon and the pass of Bethhoron; one through Samaria, which the Jews usually avoided; and a third along the plain of Jesreel, passing the Greek city Scythopolis and along the western side of the Jordan Valley. This last was the usual route and the one Jesus and His parents and fellow-pilgrims would likely travel. It was a journey of four days of wonderful experience for the growing boy. Many places of historical importance, sites of the struggles, victories, and defeats of ancient Israel, they would pass, bringing to remembrance glorious feats of the great heroes about whom He had been taught from His earliest years. From Jericho, they must climb four thousand feet from the lower tropical level of the Jordan Valley up through the narrow robber-infested passes to Bethany and the Mt. of Olives, where they would get the first glorious view of the Holy City across the Kedron Valley.

On their arrival they would find the city filled with the

teeming multitude of those who had come up as they for the Passover. More than a million Jews from the outside annually poured into this city from all parts of the land to participate in this solemn and memorable Feast.

Just before this time, the very atmosphere had been vibrant with aroused nationalism. The old Maccabean spirit, which had broken out in Galilee in the beginning of Herod's reign in guerrilla warfare under the leadership of Ezekias and had been quelled ruthlessly by Herod, growing up later once again in the party of Zealots, and flaring out under Judas in unsuccessful revolt, was smouldering yet in the hearts of this people. It had been the cause but recently of the banishment of Archelaus to Gaul and the substitution of a Roman Procurator in his stead. Quirinius had just been appointed governor of Syria and had ordered another census like the one he made in 5 B. C. Such a census the Jews regarded as a badge of servitude. In order to curb the nationalistic spirit, Herod the Great years before had almost exterminated the Sanhedrists and placed the Sadducees and non-Palestinan High-Priests in power. Under these renegade Jews the party of Herodians sprang up. Coponius the first of the Procurators was now in power, Annas, a crafty poltician, had just been made High Priest.

The Temple was easily the first and central attraction among all the strange new sights to Jesus. It covered an area of twenty acres and could accommodate within its area 210,000 persons. It was a mass of snowy marble and glittering gold, standing out from the common level of the city, like an island from the surrounding billows of the sea. Entering the Temple area from the east or north, these pilgrims would pass first into the Court of the Gentiles, with its medley of races, its money changers, and those who sold the animals for the sacrifices. Then they would pass into the Court of Woman on a higher level, and finally Joseph and Jesus would enter the Court of Israel where the sacrifices were offered. How wonderful and impressive all this would be to that awakened boyish mind!

Friday evening, the family, either separately or with friends, would celebrate the Passover meal, with prayers, formulas, and dramatic representation of the events of the memorable hour of departure from Egypt. "When they had fulfilled the days," does not necessarily mean that Joseph remained with his family through the remaining days of the week of the Passover in Jerusalem. The facts seem to indicate that they remained only the two days required by the law. These days were a wondrous dream to the boy Jesus. Many of the pilgrims would want to return to their distant homes as soon as the two days were fulfilled, and in

company with many friends, the women in one group in front and
the men in another group behind, Joseph and Mary journeyed
joyfully. They had no anxious thought about the boy whom they
confided to be capable of caring for himself.

When the caravan halted for the night after the first day's
journey, these confiding parents made the discovery that Jesus
was not to be found. Hastening back anxiously to Jerusalem,
they found Him on the morning of the third day sitting at the
feet of the Doctors of the Law on the Temple Terrace. There the
Midrash or Academy of Jerusalem established popular sessions
on feast days and sabbaths, allowing all classes of Jews to sit
as learners and propound questions.

Jesus had never had an opportunity to attend the theological
academy and now availed Himself of the privilege of hearing the
explanations of the learned Doctors. As the discussion went
forward, we may well imagine how engrossed must have become
His attention in the deep theological questions as to the Passover
and other related themes. So intent did He become that time
ceased to be important and the hours sped past while He listened
spellbound.

Jewish tradition gives other instances of precocious students
who became masters of the law at the age of twelve. It was not
strange that Jesus should ask questions; but it was extraordinary
that His questions should show such insight as to attract the
special attention of the learned doctors; and that He should manifest such facility in answering the questions which were put to
Him. Zeal for knowledge was strong in Jesus. He had made good
use of the years of His childhood and stored up much knowledge
of the Old Testament in a retentive memory. Apocryphal gospels
have attributed to Him unearthly intelligence. Wondrous things
had come into His experience, to be sure, during these days of the
Passover season. His soul had blossomed out in this religious
atmosphere as the bud at the magic touch of a warm spring day.
God was speaking in His soul through the word treasured up
during years. Did He in the Midrash, stirred by the discussions
of historical events and their symbolic expressions, catch the deeper
meaning of the Passover Lamb sacrificed before the foundations
of the World? Did He become conscious in those hours of His
own fulfillment of the symbolism of this Feast? It is more than
likely that His great mother had told Him of another day, when
He was borne as an infant into the Temple to be presented to the
priests; and how the aged Simeon taking Him into his arms
had pronounced a hymn of prophecy about Him. Did Jesus
link up those predictions with Himself now in a vital, conscious
way? Such would seem to be the case from His first recorded

words, spoken on this occasion, words which sounded the depth of a religious consciousenss as broad as humanity and as deep as eternity.

His parents were astonished when they found their twelve year old boy in the Temple in the midst of the Doctors of the Law. Their eyes fairly bulged in surprise. Mary forgot all else when she found Him, in her joyful relief. Gently chiding Him she said: "Child, why did you treat us thus? Behold your father and I with sorrow were seeking thee." "How is it that you sought Me?" said He, "Did you not know that I must be in my Father's house?" (Gen. 41:51). This rather crisp reply would seem to savour of a gentle and delicate rebuke. They should have understood, by sympathetic observation of His life during the years of His boyhood, what His deepest interest was. But they understood not the words which He spoke to them, nor have we ever fully comprehended them to this day.

Theologians have speculated as to when Jesus first became conscious of the fact that He was God's son in a peculiar sense and of his Messianic mission. We turn to these words as the sole clear self-revelation of Jesus in His boyhood years. In them we find His feeling of a distinct disappointment, that His parents did not understand Him better. He reveals in them the consciousness of a unique relationship to His Father. He expressed in them a clear sense of His primary obligations to God, which for the time had so engrossed His attention, that He almost lost sight of time and His human filial relationships. The imperative "must" was deeply felt in His soul. There is no doubt that the awakened soul of the boy was dreaming of the great "things" of God. They were dealing with subjects related to those things of His Father in the Temple, which was His Father's house. Jesus had gone beyond all the intimacy of the prophets and servants of God in history, in assuming relationship of special nearness to God as His own Father in a special and unique sense.

But Jesus returned to Nazareth and continued subject unto Mary and to Joseph also in a simple and duteous life (Ex. 20:12). He was a gentle, obedient, affectionate boy. During the next eighteen years He remained there. After Joseph's death He succeeded in the office of Joseph, becoming *the carpenter* (Matt. 13: 55). No later mention of Joseph in the Gospels leads us to believe that he did not live many years after this time. Mary guarded carefully all these last words of His in her heart. How full her heart was now with the many wonderful things. While the young Master-builder went about His daily occupation making architectural plans, and superintending the work of constructions in and around Nazareth, His thought was upon greater plans of the "things of His Father." Many a practical lesson He derived from this training for the greater task out ahead. Luke, with scholarly and scientific precision, describes in the most graphic way the progress the youth made in His development from day to day. He "kept cutting His way forward" as a pioneer cuts his way through the undergrowth of a jungle. He kept growing in stature or physical size and robustness and in wisdom or experiential knowledge. But He also kept growing spiritually or in favor with God and He became a favorite with men. He was successful socially.

Much has been said about the normal growth of Jesus; more should be said as to His perfect development. The Gospel narratives present Jesus as the Ideal Man as well as the Son of God. His humanity was as perfect as His Deity was complete.

Jesus was perfect in physique. This is indicated in the reference to His natural physical growth in boyhood days. Hoffman has put into his celebrated picture of the youth Jesus, as far as art can express it, the Gospel conception of the beauty and strength which must have marked every stage of His physical development. He had no flaw or defect in His body. His obedience of the laws of nature was perfect. We read in the Gospels of where He got tired, but not that He was ever sick. The tremendous work which He carried on through His strenuous ministry is indicative of a robustness which was unknown. He was subject to all the human limitations of our nature, but He was the first normal man. No sin had invaded the holy temple of His body and left the marks of its ravages. From the records we may easily infer: His aspect was that of gentleness and power; His expression in reproof or threatening, terrible; in teaching and exhortation, full of grace and majesty. We would give much to have a picture of the only perfect man. But to have had it would have meant idolatry.

The mind of the Master was a master mind. His intellect had to grow gradually like that of any man, "cutting its way through" many a mental problem. But it developed normally and perfectly, in spite of the fact that He could not study in the Midrash at Jerusalem. The intelligence of Jesus was unclouded. Nature to Him was the purposeful creation of the Father. We can well imagine that as the youth Jesus went about His work in the carpenter's shop, He laid nearby a roll of the Hebrew Scriptures, and ever and anon, as He went on making yokes and ploughs, He would stop for a moment and read and then go on turning over in His mind the words of revelation. From the well-springs of these studies, He later drew forth the living waters to slake the thirst of the multitudes. Other men have thought and given utterances, partial glimpses of the full-orbed truth. But when Jesus spoke, His words recorded eternal verities and laws. Men have taken His words and written volumes in commentary upon them without exhausting their meaning. He wrote nothing; but the world is full of books about what He spoke. The ideas, thoughts, ideals, principles of the Nazarene Teacher have penetrated and inter-penetrated the thought fabric of the entire world today; and continue to advance across the centuries in repeated conquests and ever more complete victories. This is true because the consciousness of Jesus was a perfect consciousness. He was at all times perfectly conscious of God and the "things of the Father."

The emotional nature of Jesus was perfect. His was a unified soul. There was no disharmony between His emotions. The great controlling sentiment of love dominated all other sentiments in a perfect microcosm.

His will was in perfect harmony with the will of God. There were no warring desires in His soul. From the beginning, every desire had become subservient to the will of God in a life of active obedience. While He was tempted in all points like other men it was always without sin.

The spiritual development of Jesus also kept pace with His physical and mental growth. Hours of meditation and communion with the Father, followed by days of obedient and loyal service, brought Him into the experiential understanding of spiritual things. This spiritual discernment manifested itself in His intuitive understanding of men, in His intimate knowledge of human life and experience, in His clear perception of sin and its awful effects, and in His full knowledge of the remedies necessary for all individual cases. The grace of God was poured out upon Him as He went about His daily tasks, in special guidance, full power, beautiful graciousness of personality. He grew in favor with men because the grace of God was upon Him.

PART II
THE BEGINNING OF THE MINISTRY
(Harm. §§ 20-36)

The paucity of the records of the silent years in Nazareth stands over in sharp contrast to the high state of physical, mental, and spiritual development which we find in Jesus as His public ministry bursts with intensity and brilliance upon us when He reached the age of thirty years. We are left largely to conjecture as to how He must *have exercised His talents of teaching and preaching during the years of His youth.* The ultimacy of His thought obliges us to conclude, that He not only had wide contacts with the current ideas of His times, but that He had given long hours of meditation to the great theme which became the core of His message in His public ministry. Many a time, He must have climbed the stony path that led to the hill-top above Nazareth, and remained for hours in meditation and prayer. When He emerges on our horizon in His public ministry, it is in the full-orbed splendor of spiritual power.

CHAPTER V

JOHN THE BAPTIST

(Mark 1:1-7; Matt. 3:1-12; Luke 3:1-18)

(Harm. §§ 20-23)

The ministry of Jesus was preceded and ushered in by John the Baptizer, who was His Herald or Forerunner. One of the most palpable evidences of the greatness of Jesus is the extraordinary character and lasting impression of the personality and work of John, who prepared the way before Him. Mark introduces his narrative with the title: "Beginning of the Gospel of Jesus Christ, Son of God." He thus registered, not only his own but the current belief of the early church, in the Messiahship and Deity of Jesus. The ministry of John is the first theme of his gospel, introducing immediately the divine activities of Jesus, the Messiah and Son of God.

Luke was particularly careful to fix the exact date historically of the first appearance of John. No prophet had appeared in Israel for four hundred years. As an accurate historian, he identifies John as the son of Zacharias, to whom the annunciation was made of John's birth thirty years before. He also states definitely, that "the word of God came to John," just as it came to Elijah in the prophetic period, and he like Elijah was "in the wilderness," during the years of his preparation.

John's ministry began in the fifteenth year of the reign of the Emperor Tiberius, who was associated with Augustus from 12 A. D., on the throne. The times were ripe. The crisis had been reached in the history of the Roman Empire, which held absolute sway over the whole known world. Rome had reached her highest pinnacle of development under Augustus and was now on the downward road of decline. Two philosophies, Epicureanism and Stoicism, contended for the supremacy; but the former led to sensuality, the latter to pride, and both to despair; and in the end Atheism prevailed largely among the philosophers. All religions of all the subject peoples were tolerated in Rome, but none satisfied the deeply felt needs of the times. Slavery abounded, and indescribable cruelty everywhere marked the treatment accorded the slave. The sacredness of marriage had disappeared and nameless abominations remained instead. Oriental religions with the vilest of rites were substituted in the place of the ancient religion of Rome. Worship of the Emperors led to promiscuous deification accompanied with the vilest lusts. Might was substituted in the place of right and justice fled from the land. The degenerated tastes of the people ran to unlawful public

58

amusements, in which the emperor would butcher thousands in the arena to make a Roman holiday. Charity disappeared and honest manual labor was looked on with contempt. The current philosophies offered no relief but only led to deeper degeneracy. The conditions in the provinces were somewhat more favorable, but it was the policy of Rome to absorb and Grecianize all subject nationalities. But the Jews held to their monotheistic religion and exclusiveness of race in considerable measure. They had undergone such trials in the exile as would cure them of tendencies toward the surrounding idolatries. But they were under the sway of the mighty Roman power. Judea, with Samaria and Idumea, was subject to a Procurator Pontious Pilate, subordinate to the Governor of the Roman province of Syria; Herod Antipas was tetrarch of Galilee and Perea; Philip, another son of Herod, was tetrarch of Iturea and Trachonites; and Lysanias, by the testimony of Luke, confirmed by modern excavation, was tetrarch of Abilene. Roman soldiers garrisoned Jerusalem, Roman flags waved over the strongholds, and Roman officers received the taxes.

Harshness characterized the administration of Palestine in the reign of Tiberius. In Rome the Jews suffered severe persecution. The procurators in Judea had changed the High Priest four times, although it was supposed to be an office of life tenure; until they found and appointed Caiaphas, who was willing to be a puppet of the Roman Tyranny. Violence, robbery, insults, venality, murders without trial, and cruelty, were charged against the administration of Pontious Pilate. Annas was deposed from the office of High Priest after nine years, and various successors were tried out, until Caiaphas, his son-in-law, succeeded to the office. Annas through his astuteness and political influence, remained the power behind the throne still, and continued to preside over the Sanhedrin (Acts 4:6).

The religious conditions in Palestine were low. There was much religiosity but little sincere religion. The externals had been multiplied and the spirit had been quenched. The Pharisees emphasized separateness but not true holiness. They filled themselves with self-satisfaction, depending on their hereditary relationships with Abraham and losing sight of the necessity of personal character. The Scribes professed great devotion to the Scriptures, but emphasized traditionalism and sought selfish aggrandizment. They multiplied regulations for every detail of life, until these became a burden too heavy to be borne. The ceremonial was elevated to the same rank with the moral law, with the result that the latter was soon lost to view. The Sadducees ridiculed Pharisaic separateness and scrupulosity, but were themselves indifferent and disbelieved in the future life. They praised morality but themselves preferred lives of comfort and self-indulgence. They were favored by the Roman authorities and in turn submitted to their tyranny without protestation.

1. The messenger and his message.

"In those days" which Luke points out historically, John comes on the scene, preaching in the wild wilderness of Judea near the mouth of the Jordan river. Not many details are given in the picture which the gospels present of this rugged son of the deserts. He was a true successor in the prophetic line. His message was like that of Amos, who lived and preached in that same region eight hundred years earlier. But his appearance and demeanor were yet more suggestive of the old prophet of judgment on national infidelity, Elijah the Tishbite, who came out from the desert of Gilead, to reprove kings and call the people to repentance (I Kings 17:1; II Kings 1:8). In his prophecy of a new era, John reminds one of Isaiah. Ancient prophecy had foretold the coming of a Forerunner of the Messiah. Jesus identified John as the fulfillment of that prophecy. John thus served as a link with all that was best in Israel's past, was a protest against the evils of that present generation, and a herald of a glorious new era in the future when the Messiah would come.

Matthew and Luke give a vivid picture of that prophetic figure, dressed in the rough sack-cloth customarily used by the poor, made of camel's hair and bound about his loins with a leathern girdle. His food which was the simple diet of the ascetic, learned perhaps through contact with the Essenes or more probably after the example of Elijah, was of locusts, a kind of insect, and wild honey taken from the clefts of the rocks in this rugged wild desert country.

He was a bold and fearless spirit, calling the people to repentance. He held aloof from the common life and was a dweller in the desert where he had been reared. But he knew the needs of his times, which he may have learned through his father Zacharias the Priest and his own observation, on visits he surely must have made to Jerusalem to the Feasts. There is no record of such visits or of any incident of his youthful days; but that he had an intimate knowledge of the evils of his generation, the hypocrisy of the religious parties and the corruption of the masses, is beyond question. Along with a vigorous physique, of one who had been a Nazarite from his birth, went a virility and acuteness of intellect which is seen not only in his keen discernment of the needs of various classes but his prompt expression of the way to deal with those needs. His bugle call of repentance was sounded out to all classes including the haughty religious leaders of Jerusalem. This was an exhibition of courage which was further attested in his rebuke of wickedness in the rulers, and which eventually caused his premature death in the prison of Machaerus. His robustness was linked up with the most beautiful humility and self-effacement. John, when asked by the Pharisees who he was, replied in the language of the prophet Isaiah (40:3). He was the mere "voice of a herald," sent ahead of the king to bid the people prepare (Jno. 1:23). Indeed, he was a voice, but such a voice as yet rings down across the centuries! Isaiah had told the Israelites in Babylonian captivity of the coming of such a herald.

John had no patience with the popular opinion which would make him a Messiah, nor with the astute committee of the religious leaders of Jerusalem who sought to extract from him some confession of aspiration toward the Messiahship. If they could get such a confession from him, it would be easy to bring him to face the Roman authorities as a successor of Judas, leader of the ill-fated revolt of the Zealots. Indeed, Josephus tells us that Herod Antipas gave out to the public as his reason for executing John months after this, that he was afraid that the great influence John had over the people might lead to some rebellion, for the people seemed likely to do anything he would advise. He thought it would be better not to spare the man rather than run the risk of a revolt (Antiq. 18:5, 2). John had no sympathy with the violent methods of the Zealots, but was zealous rather for the higher type of patriotism which would bring Israel to her true spiritual mission in the world. John's replies to the publicans and soldiers show that he differed radically not only in his methods but in his aspirations, also, from many of the narrowly nationalistic views of the Zealots.

No doubt, the apocalyptic writings of his times stimulated the thought of John on the subject of the coming Messiah and the judgment He would bring. But the message of the Forerunner was intensely practical, bearing rebuke and warning for sinners of all classes, a denunciation of dependence on any hereditary claims for salvation, and an unsparing cutting up by the roots of all fictitious shams either in individual or national life.

The message of John was one which electrified the people from one end of the land to the other. His coming was a fulfill-ment of Isaiah's prophecy and marked the initiation of a new era. In the Orient, a herald went before the king, calling the people together to repair the roads which were usually very poor, that the royal equipage might pass safely. John was such a herald, calling the people to repent, changing their mental attitude, purpose and conduct. It was not mere sorrow for sin that he required, but a turning away from their sins to a new life.

John's mission, according to Luke, was to summon the people to make ready the way for the triumphal march of the Lord. Every deep ravine must be filled in and every hill leveled down; the curved places in the road must be made straight and the rough places smooth, so that the King might pass in full view of all (Isa. 40:4-5). The salvation of the Lord was to be universal. Luke, writing especially for the Gentiles, cites the whole prophetic passage presenting the universal message and mission of the Messiah.

The part of John's message, which was as a spark in the tow in Palestine, was the announcement that "the Kingdom of God, the heavenly Kingdom, was right at hand." The phrase, "Kingdom of Heaven," was variously interpreted by the Jews of his day. Heaven was used as a synonym for God to avoid familiarizing the ear with the name Jehovah. The current apocalyptic idea was, that there would be a supernatural overthrow of existing conditions, by which the pious would be exalted, and a new political era inaugurated with Israel supreme. The people must repent. It was currently taught and believed among the Jews, that "if Israel repented but one day, the Son of David would immediately come."

Over against this popular conception, stood the idea of the "rule of heaven and Kingship of Jehovah," as the central theme of the Old Testament and object of the calling and mission of Israel. The fulfillment of the mission of Israel would be realized in the Messiah. The prophecies described the kingdom as universal, heavenly, and permanent (Ps. 72). But there was misinterpretation of the prophecies; and the Jews commonly looked for a temporal kingdom such as the nationalists (Zealots) hoped to establish. The kingdom of God, in the teachings of the New Testament, by the analysis of 119 passages is "the rule of God which is manifested in and through Christ." The visible church is but an outward expression of the kingdom. Moreover the kingdom is present in the world now in the hearts of believers, "gradually develops amid hindrances, will be triumphant in the end at the second coming of Christ and perfected in the world to come." This view of the Kingdom John grasped only partially. His mission was that of a Forerunner of the Messiah. We may be sure that John recognized the spiritual nature of the kingdom. The coming of the Messiah was to be a triumph of righteousness. The kind of preparation he sought to make was deeply ethical according to the conception of the ancient Hebrew prophets.

Another part of the message of John was the baptism of repentance. This was a different baptism from any the Jews had
known. The idea of a baptism was not new, however, for Jehovah
had said through His prophet Isaiah: "Wash you, make yourself
clean." Furthermore the Jews used washing to remove various
types of ceremonial pollution (Ex. 19:10; Lev. 15). The proselytes were initiated into the Jewish communion by a baptism.

John immersed the entire man in the water in the Jordan
river. This mode of baptism symbolized a complete moral cleansing. It was a public confession of sin and of the need of a
Saviour-Messiah. The one receiving this rite had to first give
evidence of genuine repentance, a sorrow for sin and a determination to turn away from it. It was a declaration also of allegiance
to the coming Messiah, when He should appear. John's new rite
was not a means to secure the remission of sins. It was a baptism
on the basis of repentance and a confession of sin which accompanied the rite, being related thus to the remission of sins (Mark
1:4; Luke 3:3). It was humiliating for a Jew to be considered a
pagan and submit himself to this rite publicly, thus making confession of his sins. It was this to which Nicodemus objected.

But the distinct prophetic note which had not been heard
for centuries, calling the people to repentance, stirred the whole
land. The deep-felt need of the times, coupled with the long
smouldering Messianiac hope, prompted an eager response to the
preaching of this austere prophet of the desert. Sin, judgment, repentance, forgiveness, and the hope of a glorious new era, preached with a note of authority, and accompanied by a definite demand
and rite, brought eager and expectant multitudes from all the
region of the Jordan Valley where he was preaching, from all
Judea, and even from Jerusalem. They kept pouring out to
hear this very remarkable desert preacher and every day there
were crowds being baptized. What a wonderful sight these bap
tisms must have been in the beautiful Jordan!

2. A specimen of John's preaching.

Matthew and Luke give us an example of the preaching of
John, taken doubtless from the Logia of Jesus, (Matt. 3:7-10; Luke
3:7-9), and Luke further adds a sample of John's examination of
the candidates for baptism, making his account ample, as his preface promised.

When John saw, in the midst of the thousands of those who
were coming out to his baptism, many of the Pharisees and Sadducees, he recognized that they came with some ulterior and
wrong motive. The Pharisees were curious perhaps about the Messianic news and even the cold Sadducees had their attention and

possibly their ambition drawn to this popular movement. They were saying outside that John had a devil. John denounced these bland hypocrites in no uncertain or euphemistic terms. "Offspring of vipers," he said, "who has warned you to flee the wrath to come? You are like the snakes which rush from their lair, when the brush-wood catches on fire in the desert, as they scuttle away across the stones to their dens." This scene, which John had doubtless witnessed many times in the desert country of Judea, he employs to bring home to his auditors the venom of Pharisaic hypocrisy and the terrible judgment of the approaching Messianic era. "Who warned you to flee the wrath of that coming judgment?"

With acute irony, he reminded them of their dependence on their boasted descent from the loins of Abraham. They thought "all Israel had part in the world to come" (Sanh. 10:1), because of their connection with Abraham. In their conception, Abraham sat at the gates of Gehenna to deliver any Israelite, who otherwise might have been consigned to its terrors. The mixed multitude which was hearing this denunciation, knew that these hypocritical leaders from Jerusalem considered the Israelites "nobles infinitely higher than any proselyte. For Abraham's sake, Jehovah allowed Moses to ascend into heaven to receive the law, and Daniel also for his sake had been heard." Pointing to the stones on the river bank and possibly to those used by Joshua to make a monument, where Israel rested after passing miraculously the Jordan, he declared solemnly to them, that God could raise up of those same hard lumps children unto Abraham. From stony-hearted Gentiles, he did make spiritual sons of Israel in the Messianic kingdom. They must learn that one is a son of Abraham, only when he has the spirit of that great servant in his heart. Mere flesh and blood relationship avails not in the kingdom of the Messiah. He warns them that the axe of judgment of the Messiah is laid in readiness already at the root of the tree, whether individual or national, and the unproductive would be hewn down and cast into the fire. Thus, his moral indignation flamed forth in violent and vivid images, stirring that oriental population to the point almost of hysterics.

In his audience there were many publicans and sinners, with Gentiles, Samaritans, soldier-police, and people of all classes. His message was democratic and deep; conviction gripped the hearts of many through this earnest preaching with the result that multitudes were asking earnestly and repeatedly: "What then are we to do?"

As the crowds pressed forward for confession and baptism, John put his finger on the besetting sin of each in turn, besides laying down certain broad principles of reformed conduct. Those who were able, must be charitable in a definite way, sharing the necessary clothing and food with those who had need. John had pointed out the sin of the Pharisaic class to be that of a self-righteous dependence on their hereditary and class privilege. The Pharisees had not even inquired what they must do. To the Publicans, (tax-buyers) the despised class of those who bought up from the Roman authorities the privilege of collecting the taxes and then made use of extortion exceeding the established tariffs, John gave the instruction: "not to *do* the public by extorting more than the appointed." The police-soldiers, probably Samaritans, also asked what they should do. "Have done with bullying and rough handling, extorting money along with the publicans by intimidation, false accusations, and calumnies," said John. "Be not mere mercenary soldiers complaining of your wages and mutineering." Thus in turn each individual and class was instructed as to the reform of manners and correction of abuses in conduct, revealing a genuine repentance. The prophecy of the angel of the annunciation was now being fulfilled in religious revival and moral reform.

3. The Forerunner's picture of the coming Messiah.

The revival grew apace. John's preaching about the kingdom had made the people yet more expectant than they were before of the Messiah's coming. They were reasoning in their hearts whether John himself might not be the Christ. The Pharisees in Jerusalem were uneasy because of his resemblance to the hoped-for Messiah. Had not his popularity proven his Messiahship? None had ever attracted such crowds and won so many and so devoted disciples. We know that the influence of John's preaching had a powerful influence over the masses of the people. Even a quarter of a century later, Paul found a body of John's disciples in distant Ephesus, who yet believed and followed his teachings (Acts 19:1-7). It is true, he had offended the Pharisees by his severe arraignment of them before the public. He had demanded that they should put away the sham of dependence upon mere hereditary relationships with Abraham and the traditions of the past, in favor of a vital contact with the living God in a sincere life of faith and true benevolence. The Pharisees had resented this deeply. But, on the other hand, John had gripped the great masses of the people with the magnetism of his personality and the extraordinary character of his message, reminding them vividly of Elijah, whose name was yet a terror in the East. Vast throngs attended his ministry and great numbers were submitting themselves eagerly to the strange and impressive new rite of baptism in the river Jordan. Even some of the Pharisees were content to rejoice in his light for a season. Others were slow to take any open stand against so popular a preacher.

But in the midst of all this popularity and fever of excitement, John never wavered an instant in his loyalty to the Christ. He was convinced wholly that he was only the Forerunner. As the friend of the Bridegroom he rejoiced. Not only was he sure of his part as Forerunner but he gave others to understand that he was not the Messiah.

In order to clarify the atmosphere of any misunderstanding about his relationship, he drew a vivid picture of the Messiah whom he had never seen. We cannot understand in these days of facile communication, why John should not have had an opportunity to know personally his kinsman Jesus. It is probable that both Zacharias and Joseph died when John and Jesus were quite young, and if so that might account in part for their separation during a large part of the thirty years. Then, too, ninety miles was not a short journey in those days and the responsibility of a large family such as that Mary reared, would make difficult a visit to the aged Elizabeth, which in her youthful days Mary had considered easy enough. Neither do we know if Elizabeth lived for many years, since her name disappears from the gospel record after the birth of John. His picture of the Messiah was therefore depicted after the prophetic style. John was doubtless an ardent student of the prophets and he himself was by the declaration of Jesus more than a prophet. This appears in his very testimony itself to the Messiah, in which there is the most complete self-effacement and humility. "There is coming one stronger than I, after me" he said, "whose sandal-strap I am not worthy to stoop down and unfasten, and, as a slave, bear his sandals." The people had been particularly impressed with the beautiful baptism *in the clear water of the Jordan river.* A baptismal scene in a river, typifying complete moral cleansing, always attracts and fascinates. But the baptism which the Messiah would institute would be *in the Holy Spirit* and also *in the fire* of Messianic judgment. By this judgment, those who believe shall be purified and those who disbelieve shall be separated and destroyed. John saw the Messiah's coming as one to be attended by judgment. He would separate between the good and bad, like the man on the threshing floor, who, with his shovel, tossed up the wheat that the chaff might be blown away. The wheat was thus saved in the garner and the chaff was separated and burned. When the fire gets into the chaff it flares up and in an instant devours all of it completely. So will the judgment be in the midst of the wicked. John thus vividly pictures the coming Messiah as one who would bring a great moral cleansing of the people. What a tremendous impression sermons filled with these vivid images must have made on the crowds gathered in the open places of the wild rugged country. Josephus bears testimony to the impression John made on his race: "He was a good man and commanded the Jews to exercise virtue, both as justice toward one another and piety toward God, and so to come to baptism; for baptism would be acceptable to God, if they made use of it; not in order to expiate some sin, but for the purification of the body, provided that the soul was thoroughly purified beforehand by righteousness" (Antiq. 18:5, 2). This is the opinion of an observer, who would not allow himself, later, to refer to Jesus and His work, because he would, thus, through acknowledgement of Jesus, condemn the Jews. It does not even approximate the popular conception of John's character and work, for the people looked upon John as a prophet.

CHAPTER VI
THE INITIATION
(Harm. §§ 24-25)

The initiation refers not only to the beginning of the ministry by Jesus but to the ushering of Jesus into His life mission. In the initiation, Jesus was Himself active and purposeful, taking positive steps and initiative in the inauguration of His ministry. On the other hand, He was also passive, being led by the Spirit and obeying the divine plan for His life.

The baptism was a definite step which Jesus took on His own initiative. At the same time it served as an initiatory rite. The temptations were in a peculiar sense a test to which Jesus was submitted, but which He fearlessly met. They served in a special way to prepare Him for the struggles that were before Him. In the baptism He committed Himself in a definite way to His life mission; in the temptations He won the first decisive battle of that life struggle, issuing in a successful carrying out of His mission.

1. The Baptism (Mark 1:9-11; Matt. 3:13-17; Luke 3:21-23; Jno. 1:32-34).

News of the great revival in the Jordan Valley had filled the land. A vast concourse had surrounded the fascinating figure of John the Baptist, the desert preacher, for six months. The rugged old preacher-prophet was not a "reed shaken by the winds" but a man of settled convictions; he was not ambitious and self-seeking but humble and self-effacing; he was not dressed in the rich Pharisaic garb with wide fringes but wore the poor prophet's garb bound around with a leathern girdle.

His call to repentance and announcement of the near approach of the Messianic Kingdom stirred the people, and from all parts individuals and groups were seen gathering in, to the new center of his activities further up the valley at Bethabara (house of passage), one of the best known fords of the Jordan.

Every day, pilgrims to and from this center discussed in the market place in Nazareth the chief topic of the day, the revival meetings: the extraordinary character and mannerisms of the preacher, the fundamental notes of his thrilling sermons, the peculiar fascination of the baptisms in the river Jordan, the unprecedented crowds, which grew as the weeks elapsed, and the marvelous results in religious decisions and moral change which were witnessed.

During the eighteen "silent years" in Nazareth, the life

68

purpose of Jesus, hinted at in the Temple, when He made the reply to the query of His mother: "Did you not know that I must be about my Father's business?", had been steadily deepening. Even at the age of twelve, He had thus revealed the consciousness of a special relationship to God and a distinct sense of a life mission, in His Father's business. His instruction in the home and studies in the synagogue school had given Him a firm basis on which to continue His studies of the Hebrew Scriptures and other fundamental and practical branches of His education. That He made good use of the spare hours, as He pursued the daily program of *the carpenter*, dipping into the rolls of the Law, the Prophets, and the Hagiographa, we may well imagine. Then too, each day's program was preceded by an earnest seeking after God in prayer. His daily contacts bore in upon Him constantly the sad estate of sinful humanity and its need of a spiritual salvation. More and more keenly, He came to feel the responsibility of His mission as its Saviour. His observation drove home this conviction no less than His study of the Messianic prophecies of the Old Testament. He felt in His soul each day more strongly the call of His life mission. He had not made haste but awaited the clear indication of Providence before He should launch out. But the purpose had grown steadily and was now clamoring for expression.

At last He had come to the parting of the ways. Those years of patient, dutiful service to the family, after the death of Joseph, were now complete, and He must leave His wonderful mother to the care of the younger half-brothers, the oldest of whom had already come to responsible age. How much the companionship of this mother, now mature in her wisdom and experience of fifty years, and this son, strong, and manly, yet tender and thoughtful, wise for every emergency and problem of the family program and careful for every need, meant to each of them! How she could, secretly in her heart, wish that He might remain at home and go on with His ordinary tasks of *the carpenter*, while He exercised His splendid talents of teaching in the local synagogue and in personal ministration among His countrymen in Nazareth! But something told her that His mission was not to be accomplished thus. And when the day came for Him to lay down the homely task of the carpenter and take up the more serious work of life, she was ready to give Him up for His wider mission.

Now the call comes clear and unmistakable, in the preaching of John. The gospel of the Hebrews tells how Jesus was induced by His half-brothers to go and listen to the stirring sermons of the wilderness preacher. The heretical gospels also put in the mouth of Mary, an invitation to go to that baptism; to which Jesus declared that He was sinless so far as He knew (Gosp. according to Hebrews p. 38, 92, 93). There might be some basis in tradition for such declarations, but certainly the answer He gave does not harmonize with His character, in the Gospels, and only serves to show the heretical nature of such narratives. John was proclaiming the presence of the *Messiah*, in the midst of the people. For six months his message had rung out through the land and had reached the ears of Him who *was* the Messiah. In that message was the echo of Isaiah's words (61:1-2) and those of the Psalmist which He had conned so well: "Then said I, Lo I am come: In the roll of the Book it is prescribed for me, I delight to do thy will, O my God" (Ps. 42:6-11). His heart leaped to respond to the ringing challenge of John's ministry. He recognized in John one who saw through the hollowness and sham of Phariseeism and penetrated to the deep ethical meaning of the Hebrew prophets. John's sermons found a deep echo in the heart of Jesus and turning over the carpenter's shop to the younger brothers with a deeply understanding farewell to His mother, He strode forth from the Nazareth home to meet the issues of His life career.

So Jesus comes one of "those days" to John at the Jordan, for the purpose of being baptized by him. His decision had been made before He started from home. He needed not to hear the sermon or to be exhorted. When the crowd was baptized Jesus presented Himself. It was John's custom to examine the candidates before baptism. Usually the penitents came with humble confession of their sins and the manifestation of deep contrition. Jesus made no such confession of guilt nor showed any sorrow. Such an attitude in itself would disqualify the candidate for the baptism. But here was a singular exception. There was a majesty, purity, and peace written in that visage, which caused John to draw back with a feeling of unworthiness and sin. There are various opinions as to whether John knew Jesus personally. Even though he might know this kinsman of his as a man, he did not know Him as the Messiah (Jno. 1:31).

John recognized and confessed, now, his subordination to Jesus, whom he must follow and obey. Jesus assumed His superiority over John, whom He now directs and will lead. Nor was this assumption vain.

John kept trying to prevent Jesus from being baptized. "I have need to be baptized of thee," he said "and comest thou to me?" He had called the people to repentance for sin but here was One, who, examined, was not conscious of any sin. He had proclaimed the coming Messiah. Could this be the Messiah?

"Suffer me now" said Jesus, "for it is fitting thus, that we fulfill all righteousness." With these words Jesus satisfied the Baptizer and he proceeded with the rite.

From earliest times, it has always been a question why Jesus went and was baptized. There have been many explanations, as to why He took His place among the penitents and submitted to the rite, which symbolized the cleansing away of sin. The true reason is in the reply of Jesus: "Suffer it now; it is becoming for us to fulfill all (vicarious) righteousness." Jesus was born under the Law, and in His infancy was circumcised and redeemed. At the age of twelve He became a son of the Law. He later paid the Temple tax, though as the Son of God He should have been exempt. It was fitting that He should fill out all the ordinances of the Abrahamic covenant to completion. From a later deliverance, we know that He came not to abrogate the Mosaic Law but to fill it out, giving it a deeper meaning (Matt. 5:17). Throughout His life He fulfilled the Law that He might redeem them that were under the Law (Gal. 4:4-5).

Among the many explanations offered for why Jesus sought baptism at John's hands, some are mere opinions, while others have basis in reason and Scripture. That He came because He felt Himself sinful is contradictory to the Gospel narrative. The supposition of mere collusion with John is unthinkable. That He did come with the purpose formed in His heart to dedicate Himself to His life-mission is beyond doubt. It was an act of self-consecration. His view of life was not that of merely being a good man of righteous conduct. He had started out from His Nazareth home with the purpose of committing Himself to a mission, which embraced "every aspect of righteousness," in carrying out God's plan for His life and for the race through Him. The burial and resurrection in the rite of baptism, meant for Him the raising of man from the death of sin into a new and glorious life. This would be accomplished at the cost of His own physical death and resurrection at the end of His earthly career. He accepted the mission in the full consciousness of its price. In coming He also put His seal of approval on the ministry of John. He could only fulfill all righteousness by bringing Himself to the observance of the Law. In the act of baptism He would receive the seal of the Heavenly Father on His mission and the gift of the Holy Spirit qualifying Him for it. But this was not His purpose in coming. John's baptism was for other men a "baptism of repentance," but it held a wider significance for John's ministry and Christ's mission. It was the initiatory rite for the New Covenant of the kingdom. The baptism of John "was from heaven," and Jesus' motive in it was to fulfill all righteousness in the perfect accomplishment of the will of God.

All of the synoptic gospels record the baptismal vision. When Jesus came up out of the water and was praying, He and John saw the heavens being rent asunder, and the Holy Spirit in bodily form as a dove descending upon Him. John in the fourth Gospel adds that it "abode upon Him." The records and subsequent events lead us to believe that only Jesus and John saw the vision. The revelation was designed for them alone: for Jesus, in confirmation of His special enduement for His work; for John, in preparation for his testimony to Jesus. It was here that Isaiah's prophecy was fulfilled and Jesus received the Holy Spirit for His Messianic work (Isaiah 42:1; 61:1, 2; 48:16). It crowned and reenforced His peculiar powers. The physical being of Jesus was dependent on the Holy Spirit from conception. But His human nature had to be endowed with gifts and sustained in their exercise. His miracles, teaching, preaching, all His supernatural activities are attributed in the Gospels to the Holy Spirit. His human was thus made the servant of His divine nature.

The Spirit came upon the ancient prophets for special inspiration and guidance in the beginning of their prophetic ministries. Upon Jesus He came without measure. By spiritual baptism, Jesus was able to communicate the Spirit to others and His own natural gifts and powers were raised to the highest pitch of usefulness and service. Entrance of Jesus upon His Messianic work called for this experience of the super-empirical, substantiated by the entire record of His subsequent life. The form of the dove would recall the Spirit, creatively brooding over the waters in the Genesis. The Rabbis spoke of the Spirit as a dove.

All the persons of the Trinity are, for the first time in the New Testament, seen together at the baptism. The voice of the Father is added as a separate seal of His ministry, after the descent of the Holy Spirit. "Thou art my beloved Son in whom I am well pleased." Jesus enters upon His career with the express approval and blessing of the Father. His deity is here presented in unmistakable terms. John saw the Spirit, heard the voice, and bore permanent witness to the Divine Sonship or Deity of the Christ. This voice was not the *Bath Kol* of Jewish traditon, but the real voice of the Father, expressing His eternal pleasure in Jesus as He enters upon the work of human redemption.

2. The Temptations. (Mar. 1:12-13; Matt. 4:1-11; Luke 4:1-13).

It was immediately after the baptism that Jesus met with the extraordinary period of testing, which in common terminology is known as the Temptations. It is what we would expect to find in the narrative following the response of Jesus to the call of His life mission. Psychologically, a period of struggle was inevitable after the moments of spiritual elevation and decision. The testing of

Jesus had been going on during the thirty years of silent preparation. He had overcome always and now the supreme trial of His character must be faced. It has been so in the life of other great servants of God and humanity; and victory has ever been the road to spiritual greatness. Jesus must start His career with a decisive victory over sin. Naturally, at the very beginning of His ministry, Jesus would meet the hour of decision as to plans and methods for His work. Satan sought at this opportune time and critical moment to secure the defeat of that life. He tried out in the previous life of Jesus and now especially in these forty days every device he commanded.

The place of the temptations was in the wilderness. The first Adam met his temptation in the garden of beauty and plenty; the last Adam in the barren, flowerless waste, with poverty, hunger, and the wild beasts. Tradition locates the temptations in Quarantania, a mountain which rises out of the Judean plain, fifteen hundred feet above the Jordan Valley. It is six or eight miles from the traditional place of the baptism, to the west of the Jordan and Jericho, agreeing with Luke's expression, "returned from the Jordan." The mountain is barren, scarred by numerous artificial caves made by monks of the period of the Crusades and other times. There is little ground for the assertion that the wild animals, "lost their ferocity" and were in confederacy with Jesus, recognizing in Him God's millenial man. The steep road leading up from Jericho to Jerusalem was called Ascent of Blood, because it was infested with robbers. Along this road Jesus would travel to reach the mountain, the heights of which commanded a vast prospect, reaching to Jerusalem on the West, to the Jordan Valley and the plains of Moab on the East, and to Hermon on the North. Highways also were visible, leading to "all the kingdoms of the world."

The purpose of the temptations is clearly implied. Jesus was led by the Spirit into the wilderness for the purpose of being tempted. He did not go into the wilderness to imitate John's ascetic mode of life. A divine plan was being wrought out. Mark is graphic and says: "The Spirit driveth Him forth into the wilderness." The word tempt means to try or test character with the purpose of good or evil. God tried Abraham when He commanded him to sacrifice his son Isaac. The temptations from the devil are always for the purpose of inducing men to do evil. Men tempt God by putting His patience to the test in some improper manner (Matt. 4:7). Luke makes clear the divine plan, by declaring that Jesus "was led by the Spirit in the wilderness during forty days, being tempted." His temptations were not limited to the time after the forty days' fast, but only culminated at that time and extended through the whole period. Christ was submitted to temptation, first for His own sake as a test of His character (Heb. 5:7-9), and second for our sakes that He might become a sympathizing High Priest. (Heb. 4:15-16), and our example.

The personality of the tempter is made explicit. The Hebrew word Satan, used by Mark, is translated *devil* by Matthew and Luke. It means a *slanderer* or *false accuser*. The real existence of the devil is fully sustained by the Scriptures. He is called the prince of the power of the air. Any attempt to explain his existence away is unavailing. Various devices and schemes have been suggested to explain away the visible appearance, such as that of an internal vision or dream, evil thoughts suggested by Satan as in our own temptations, or some person, perhaps a Jewish priest, used by Satan to bear the suggestion. None of these schemes satisfy the plain language of the gospel narratives of the temptations or the fundamental character and philosophy of Christianity. There is no instance of ecstatic state or vision in the life of Jesus. During the forty-day period, Jesus doubtless suffered from mental suggestions coming from Satan and leading to the wrong. But the statement is too explicit that Satan appeared in bodily form to allow of any other interpretation than the natural and obvious one. We do not lessen the difficulties of interpretation by eliminating the idea of the personal appearance of the devil in the three temptations, which Jesus himself must have narrated to His disciples later in His ministry for their edification. He was tempted in all points as we are, but He went beyond us in meeting the arch-enemy in all his power. These temptations were a real conflict with a real personal devil. They were not a mere inward vision, dream, or mental suggestion; nor were the methods of Satan limited to the merely outward and visible. Satan was present in visible form, making use of all his methods both inward and outward, subjective and objective, to gain the ascendancy over Jesus.

The problem of how Jesus could be tempted has always vexed the theologian. That He might have yielded to the temptations is definitely implied in the narrative. That He was in reality tempted in all points like as we are is declared explicitly in Scripture. Christ was a real human being and His unfallen nature was capable of sinning. Temptation was felt and overcome. At the same time, in virtue of His divine nature and the indwelling Spirit, it was morally impossible that He should sin. Jesus was tempted both to commit positive evil and to shrink from doing the right. The first Adam had a nature "capable of not sinning" but not "incapable of sinning." If he had followed the line of obedience he would have attained the state of being "incapable of sinning." The last Adam had an unfallen nature like the first, capable of not sinning, and obedience to the will of God was His unswerving line of action, because He was the Son of God and led by the Spirit. He had a real human nature in all points like ours but without sin. He was not able to sin. After saying all this we must confess that there are depths unfathomable here and we must be content to face the reality of temptation and seek to follow Jesus in overcoming it in our experience. The practical and not the metaphysical problem is what should chiefly concern us.

The great thought that occupied the mind of Jesus during the forty days of fasting and prayer was that of the messianic Kingdom and how to establish it. The current messianic ideal would naturally present itself before Him. That His Kingdom was to be spiritual He had no doubt. But how should He go about the work of its establishment? This was His chief concern.

(1) The first temptation (Matt. 4:3, 4; Luke 4:3, 4). The first temptation was in the sphere of the physical appetites. After forty days of fasting, Jesus was hungry. For Him, the temptations to the gratification of physical appetites were far less strong than others, though He certainly did suffer such. This temptation as the others is a type. Mankind is tempted in the realm of physical appetites and passions. Appetite is not sinful but its wrong use and gratification is sin. The use of our God-given power to satisfy and gratify ourselves defeats God's purpose in us.

Satan subtly seeks to destroy the faith of Jesus in God's work of approval and sanction at the baptism — "Thou art my Son in whom I am well pleased." He comes to Jesus with the affirmation that He is *a* son but does not say *the* son. So there is an if* and the devil seeks to instill into the mind of Jesus that the Father who had expressed His approval was now leaving Him to care for Himself. Had He not been impelled by the Spirit to come out into these desert wastes? Should not God provide bread for His hungry body that He might continue in His intense study of the plans of the kingdom? If God was not willing to do that in a miraculous way, was Jesus more than a mere son, just as any other creature? Why should not He use His miraculous power to change "these stones," lying at His feet, into loaves? Thus subtly did Satan tempt Jesus to be disloyal to God and distrust His providence. Did he believe that Jesus would distrust His Father because He was hungry? Would not the act of turning the stones into

* There was no doubt in Satan's mind as to the deity of Jesus. Cf. First class conditional sentence.

bread be a means in itself of glorifying Jesus and promoting the kingdom? All of these suggestions and many others, Satan must have brought to bear in this first supreme temptation. Jesus was tempted to doubt God, to satisfy His selfish physical need by the improper use of supernatural power given for the service of God and mankind, to put material bread above the spiritual. Jesus meets it by assertion of full confidence in God's providential care over Him as a man, a refusal to use His God-given miraculous power to serve self, and by putting the spiritual above the material.

If Jesus had yielded, He would have put Himself outside the circle of common human experience. He now met the temptation to use His power of Son to satify His needs as man. Other men could never do that and so Jesus yielding could no more serve as their proper example nor their understanding High Priest subject to all their conditions and trials. "Man shall not live by bread alone," He said.

It is interesting that Jesus chose as His weapon of defense in these temptations the Word of God, which is the sword of the Spirit. In this He serves as our example. In the Word there are cases and examples to suit every situation. Jesus chose the experience of Israel in the wilderness when God fed the people with manna, that they might learn that "man shall not live by bread alone but by every word that proceeds out of the mouth of God" (Deut. 8:3). The Father could sustain the life of Jesus Christ, His Son, in the ordinary or the extraordinary way. The Son should not distrust either His Father's ability or desire to do what was best for Him. It has ever been a device of Satan to make man believe that bread, in that which it represents of material sustenance and prosperity, is the supreme thing in life. Man shall not live by bread *alone* nor by bread principally. There are many other things more important than bread for man's life. Man should seek to make a life and not a mere living. Jesus might have chosen the example of Job, whom Satan slandered by saying that he served God just because he was hedged in by material prosperity. But man will not give all that he hath for his physical life. The man Jesus stood against such a slander and was victorious over Satan.

(2)   The second temptation (Matt. 4:5-7; Luke 4:9-12).

In the first temptation, Satan had sought to lead Jesus into distrust and Jesus had asserted perfect confidence and loyalty toward the Father. In the second, he suggests a measure of daring and heroic confidence, and seeks to involve Jesus in presumption, by suggesting His jumping from the pinnacle of the Temple and depending on the Father to bear Him up. How astutely too the devil takes the weapon of the Word from the hands of Jesus and assails Him with, "It stands written," citing but misapplying the expression from the Psalmist (Ps. 91:11, 12).

"He shall give His Angels charge concerning thee, on their hands they shall bear thee up, lest haply thou dash thy foot against a stone." Satan misinterprets with a bald literalism, involving supernatural fulfillment of these words, where they refer only to providential protection.

Did the devil take Jesus, actually, from the desert mountain to Jerusalem and up into the Temple? From the heights of Quarantania the pinnacle of the Temple was visible. Some hold that Christ was put at the disposition of Satan during the temptations, as Job in other days. If so he might conduct Him into Jerusalem, the Holy City, and place Him on the wing (pinua) of Herod's royal portico, which overhung the Kedron valley, four hundred and fifty feet below (Jos. Ant. 15:11, 5). From here James, the Lord's brother, was thrown down thirty-eight years later and killed. This wing was the watch-post, where the white-robed priests customarily called the people to the early worship and the priests to the morning-sacrifice, as the massive Temple gates swung open ere sunrise. The word of command to Jesus: "Cast thyself down from here," would gain great force, if Jesus were actually standing on those dizzy heights. But the temptation would be just as real, if Satan had transported Jesus mentally to the well known *pinnacle*. There are difficulties to either interpretation, and after all that is not the essential point. The real ascent to the pinnacle seems more in accord with the phrases of the text.

In the background of the second temptation, constituting its main force, was the popular apocalyptic, messianic expectation of a splendid political kingdom to be established in a spectacular way. This kingdom was to be world-wide, with Jerusalem as its center. The Jews did not give the moral and spiritual elements precedence in the messianic ideal but rather the material and political. If Jesus would ally Himself to these messianic hopes He would at once receive the popular acclaim and leadership of Israel. It was expected that the Messiah would suddenly appear in the Temple in a spectacular way. The Jews loved signs and portents and expected that the Messiah would show such in attestation of his claims (Jno. 6:30).

Once again Satan assails the sonship of Jesus. In the first temptation he had suggested that He show if He was *a son of God*, in fact, by turning the stones into loaves. In the second he urges that if He is a son of God He has the right to presume on God's special providence and insists that He put providence to the test.

The great objective of Jesus was the establishment of His messianic kingdom. If He will now cast Himself down from the pinnacle of the Temple, the people will know at once that He is the Messiah. He can then proceed by such ethical and spiritual methods as He may choose, once the leadership is secured. This was the temptation to yield to the lure of selfish vanity and attain quick popularity and success by improper means, a common test to which many yield today. Jesus is tempted to take into His own hands the work of His ministry and make God responsible for His success. Satan would put Jesus outside the circle of human methods through His use of supernatural means, and thus nullify His example as a human Messiah and Saviour.

Jesus takes the sword of the Spirit once more. "Again it stands written," He said, "thou shalt not put to the test the Lord thy God." (Deut. 6:16). He declared by this reference to Israel at Massah that testing is not trusting. The man Jesus will not use the Divine Son's power or supernatural resources to establish by improper means His kingdom, but will follow God's plan of a long period of development and His ideal of a spiritual kingdom, to the end. If we trust God completely, we will not doubt in the least or seek to put His work to the test. It is our privilege as children of God to meet calmly whatever comes to us in His providence. Jesus was no wonder-worker and desired not the homage of the gaping multitude.

(3)   The third temptation (Matt. 4:8-10; Luke 4:5-8).

Satan had failed to ruin the man Jesus, tempting Him through His physical appetites, because He put material sustenance in a secondary place and spiritual bread first. He had also failed to ruin His spiritual nature through vanity and presumptuous trust. He now tries to deceive Him by presenting a quick way to become in reality the King of the world. Had not a messianic Psalm (Ps. 2) promised to the Son the kingship over the kings of the earth and had not God announced from heaven at the baptism that Jesus was His Son?

Satan employs now, in this last supreme test, his most subtle and powerful wiles. Taking Jesus with him up into a "very high mountain," he causes to pass before Him in panorama all the kingdoms of the known world and the glory of them in a moment of time. It is impossible to eliminate here the idea of a mental vision of some kind. Otherwise it could not have embraced all the kingdoms of the inhabited world nor been in the brief scope of a moment of time. From the heights of Quarantania, the highways were visible leading away to Damascus, Egypt, Arabia, Persia and the ports communicating with Greece, Rome, and other places He had visited, and others about which the travelers had talked many an evening in the fountain-square of Nazareth in His boyhood days.

Once again the worldly messianic ideal of the Jew obtrudes itself. The embers of messianic expectation were smouldering in the hearts of the Jews and if fanned but a little would burst into an unquenchable conflagration. Had not the Sanhedrin sent to John to know if he were the Messiah? And if He, with His conscious possession of supernatural power, should but ally Himself with the Jewish rulers, who would welcome any successful messianic leader, could He not conquer the world?

Satan avails himself of the vantage ground of current ideals and offers to Jesus all these kingdoms and all the glory of them, if only He will for a moment fall down and worship in his presence. Of course to have done so would be to recognize the sovereignty of the devil. There is no doubt that the world lies in darkness and the dominion of the devil. He has been called the Prince of darkness of this world but he is a usurper. It does not rightly belong to him. But if Jesus would ally Himself with the injustice, irreverence, rebellion of sinful humanity, He would have the sanction and help of Satan and could win the place of world-ruler, as a vassal of his Satanic majesty. Would this not be better than to fret out His days within the bars of His limited mission "to the lost sheep of the house of Israel?" Could He not, after the political supremacy was gained, turn the world of darkness into light? He must win the world, and here was a quick and easy way.

If Jesus will not follow this way, there is but one other left to His choice. That will be the way of suffering and the cross. He will have no political prestige or powerful friends to help Him. It will be a slow process of centuries of time and infinite cost. Millions will go down in wreck and ruin, while the mill of God grinds on. Such a vision of the future must have come to Jesus as He thought of the Kingdom. The spiritual way was a hard and long way.

Jesus meets this last temptation with a positive command: "Get thee hence, Satan!" The Prince of Light had won the ascendency over the Prince of Darkness. Jesus would have to face the allies of Satan at every turn of His ministry and would come to the cross by their wicked devices but He has gained the decisive victory over the world-ruler and will win out in the end over all his allies.

Every time the Sword of the Spirit is whipped out it proves the means of victory for Jesus and defeat for Satan. "For it stands written, thou shalt worship the Lord thy God and Him only shalt thou serve" (Deut. 6:13). Jesus would receive from God, the heathen for His inheritance and the uttermost parts of the earth for His possession, and not from Satan. He would follow God's method of winning the world's loyalty to Him and not take some short and easy route to that goal. As a man, Jesus would by choice worship and serve God and not do honor or homage even for an instant to Satan. Instead of receiving from Satan the power over humanity He would wrest it from him in mighty mortal conflict, ending in final and complete victory.

CHAPTER VII

THE MANIFESTATION OF THE CHRIST

(Harm. §§ 26-31)

The manifestation of the Messiah to Israel was through the twofold testimony of John (Jno. 1:19-34), the testimony of the first disciples (Jno. 1:35-51), through the first miracle (Jno. 2:1-11), and the first cleansing of the Temple (Jno. 1:13-22). In the terminology of the Jews Christ was the title meaning Messiah, though it has become in our thought linked with *Jesus* in the full name Jesus Christ or Christ Jesus. In these opening scenes, not only the character of the Messiah is revealed but also the programme of His future work.

1. The testimony of prophecy (Jno. 1:19-28).

The first part of the twofold testimony of John was called forth by a committee of Sadducees sent by the Sanhedrin of Jerusalem at the suggestion of the Pharisees to ascertain what he claimed to be. Both the Pharisees and Sadducees had been scathingly rebuked by John for their hypocrisy and warned of the hollowness of their hereditary claims (Matt. 3:7-10). They were rejected, when they presented themselves for the baptismal examination, until they should show forth fruits in their lives in harmony with the requirements of his baptism of repentance and confession. Hypocritically now, the Pharisees hide behind a committee of Priests and Levites whom they send to tempt or trap John. The fame of the Baptist had filled the land and these Jewish rulers must call his authority in question. They came to Bethany beyond the Jordan where he continued baptizing.

"Who art thou?" they sharply asked him. In the background of their question was the messianic expectation, now fanned to white heat by the popular ministry of the Baptist and especially his message about the "Kingdom at hand." Could they get him to confess to being the Messiah? Many people already nurtured the hope that he was the promised One.

John received the committee courteously but frankly. He did not refuse to say who he was but confessed at once and clearly that he was not the Messiah. They had been uneasy about this. It was indeed a real temptation into which John might fall, to declare himself the Christ. He understood the thought of the deputation from Jerusalem. If he should confess that he was the Messiah, counting on his wide popularity, he might even elicit the support of the deputation for his claims. But John stands out as a great example of unswerving loyalty. He must have realized that when he denied being the Messiah, he would have to face immediately the question as to just what his function and authority might be. With sincerity and conviction, in spite of what the consequences might be, he responds immediately: "I am not the Christ." "What then?" they asked, "Are you Elijah?" The Jews expected Elijah to return in person as a herald of the Messiah. This John denies. "I am not," he said. Jesus afterwards asserted that John was the Elijah of Malachi's prophecy (Mal. 4:5) "in spirit" (Mar. 9:11). John was not the Elijah of the popular Jewish expectation, returned to life. He might get prestige by confessing to being Elijah, in truth he was the real Elijah of prophecy; but again he resists temptation. "Are you the prophet?" they add. Moses had predicted the coming of a prophet like unto himself (Deut. 18:15). The Jews thought this prophet would be another forerunner of the Messiah (Jno. 7:40). Even John in prison later on seems to have been in doubt whether Jesus were not just one of the forerunners of the Messiah (Luke 7:19). To this inquiry he gave the shortest possible reply — "No."

Now, the committee has his frank declaration. No longer are they filled with fear of his popularity. He has divested himself of his power. He cannot go back on his own public declaration. They will proceed now to make quick work of this bold preacher who dares to rebuke them publicly. But they will do it astutely. "Who are you," they add with bland hypocrisy, "that we may take an answer back to those who sent us. What account do you give of yourself?" The Pharisees who had sent them felt very deeply offended by the baptism of John, which they considered to be an invasion of their exclusive ceremonial domain and privileges. To the Sadducees themselves this baptism was of little concern. But to the Pharisees, John had no right to baptize. The proselytes were baptized by the Pharisees because they were considered unclean. But these Jews thought it a great presumption in John to impose his baptism of repentance and confession on all the people alike. The Pharisees were not unclean and needed no such baptism! In reply to their question as to who he was, John cited the prophecy of Isaiah — "I am the voice of one crying in the wilderness" (Isa. 40:3) — and applied it to himself, thus identifying himself with the real spiritual forerunner of the Messiah. He claimed to be nothing more than a voice. But his mission was to prepare the way before the Messiah. He was conscious now of this mission as never before, since he beheld the Messiah in His baptism. The days since that memorable event had burned into his soul that conviction.

The deputation did not, however, understand the deep meaning of the claim of John. This confession to being a mere voice did not give sufficient authority, they felt, for the assumption of the right

to baptize. He was thus treating the Jews as if they were Gentiles
— a very deep offense to the Pharisees. So the committee raises
the question with him as to his baptism? "Why then do you baptize if you are not the Christ, neither Elijah, neither the prophet?"
With great meekness, and compassion for them in their blindness,
he replied: "I baptize with water only but in your midst stands the
unrecognized Messiah who is to be my successor, and whose sandal-strap I am not worthy to unfasten. I am merely making preparation for Him, though unworthy of doing Him the humblest
service." About *Him* the deputation did not even make inquiry.

The second part of the twofold testimony of John (Jno. 1:29-
34) identifies the Messiah, to those who are with him, publicly.
He had spoken to the Jerusalem deputation about the Messiah
being in their midst unrecognized. Now on the following day, he
points Jesus out, as he is looking on Him approaching. The forty
days which had elapsed since Jesus was baptized had served to
deepen John's convictions about the character of the Messiah. The
same forty days had also marked a great victory for Jesus in the
struggle with Satan and He had attained full certainty as to the
path to be pursued. Conviction and resolve were written in His
countenance. Looking on Him John cried out: "Behold the Lamb
of God who is taking away the sin of the world."[1]

John was a great student of the Old Testament. His father
was a priest. He had lived in the solitude of the desert for thirty
years. The vision of the baptism had borne him in thought to
sublimer heights, and this last prophet of the old and first of the
new dispensation saw in Jesus the fulfillment of Isaiah 53, in the
suffering servant. He was not dominated by the current messianic
conception of a magnificent temporal king. His idea was that of a
sin-bearer led like a lamb to the slaughter. Both Isaiah and Jeremiah had prophesied of a Messiah who would be an eternal sacrifice for the people, taking away the sin and corruption of humanity. The Jews sacrificed the Paschal Lamb at the time of the
Passover and also in the daily sacrifice embodying the ideas of
redemption and fellowship. The daily morning and evening sac-
rifes were intended to atone for the sins of the night and the
day. Even in the schools of the Rabbis Hillel and Shammai, there
was symbolic import of the washing away and suppressing of sins
in the sacrifice of lambs. John saw more deeply than the Rabbis
and understood Jesus to be the Paschal Lamb of Isaiah's prophecy.
He views sin as a totality, constituting a barrier between God and
humanity. Jesus was taking away the collective sin of the world
of mankind. The only way He could as the Paschal Lamb take away
the sin of the world was by being sacrificed. John saw in Jesus the

1 Present tense of progressive action.

vicarious sacrifice pictured in Isaiah 53. In this he might, as other prophets, have spoken under the inspiration some things, the import of which he did not completely understand. His hearers certainly did not understand all the meaning of his words, at any rate. Jesus was the Lamb of God for the whole world, not just for the Jews. His mission was to be universal.

John goes on to explain the purpose of his own mission to Israel. He points out definitely, now, that Jesus was the one about whom he spoke before the baptism. "After me is to come One who has been put before me, for He was before me in time and rank. And I did not know Him." We cannot say positively that John was not acquainted with Jesus, his kinsman, but he certainly did not know Him, as the Messiah, previous to His baptism. But the very purpose of his own preaching and baptism was to manifest the Messiah to Israel.

He now adds his second word of clear testimony: "I have seen the Spirit coming down like a dove out of heaven; and it remained upon Him. I did not yet know Him as the Messiah, but He who sent me to baptize in water said to me, 'The one on whom you see the Spirit coming down and remaining, He it is who baptizes in the Holy Spirit.'" Then John adds his concluding testimony to the deity of Jesus: "This I have seen and have become a witness that He is the Son of God." In these words he pointed out the unique, divine personality, the preexistent Messiah, who being the Son of God is to baptize "in the Holy Spirit." John had baptized in water but Jesus will give a true penitent, inner, spiritual renewal, of which the water baptism is but a symbol. Calculating back from the marriage in Cana, which according to Rabbinical law was on Wednesday, John's interview with the Jerusalem deputation was on Thursday, and his first testimony to Jesus as the Lamb of God on Friday corresponding with the other Friday of His sacrifice. The last personal testimony of John the Baptist in the presence of Andrew and John, who followed Jesus, was on the Sabbath closing properly the ministry of John; and the bringing of Peter and James to Jesus was on Sunday opening the ministry of Jesus. The whole testimony of John had headed up in the declaration of the deity of Jesus. This was the reason the author of the fourth gospel cited it.

2. The testimony of the first disciples (Jno. 1:35-51). The testimony of John issued in the faith of the first disciples and their birth into spiritual life. So the work of the Baptist passed naturally into the work of Jesus. The manifestation of the new life in the disciples took the form of a new witness to the Messiah.

During the last day of the official ministry of John, his per-

sonal witness to Jesus repeated in the presence of two of his disciples led them to follow Jesus. Standing with the two, he saw
Jesus walking around and filled with rapture exclaimed: "Look!
There is the Lamb of God!" The two disciples, Andrew and John,
who afterwards recorded the happy experiences of that day, took
their teacher at his word and followed Jesus. They understood that
he was pointing them to Jesus and bidding them farewell. Suddenly Jesus turned around and looked straight and gladly into
their wondering faces with a direct and searching question: "What
are you seeking?" He said. Abashed lest they were intruding they
replied: "Teacher, where are you lodging?" "Come and you shall
see," said Jesus kindly. They had followed, unconscious of a
definite purpose at first. Jesus helped them to define their aim
by a question. They were seeking "whom" and not "what," a
person and not some *thing.* This is the essence of true religion.
It is a personal relationship with Jesus. John remembered years
later that the hour of this first personal encounter with Jesus was
ten o'clock in the morning. They accepted His gracious and typical
invitation and went with Him to the place of His lodging, perhaps some secluded spot in the near-by wilderness where He dwelt
in meditation and poverty; but a place made glorious by His royal
presence. They met there the fact of His poverty, which they must
share if they would become His followers. But they were charmed
with their new Master and spent the whole day, the first of many
wonderful days with Him. We are not told of anything said or
done during the day; but the next day revealed the fact of their
deep and certain conviction that Jesus was indeed the Messiah of
prophecy.

It was during this memorable day that these two disciples,
Andrew and John, sought their brothers Peter and James. Andrew
was the first to find his own brother, Simon. The natural inference
is that John afterwards found his brother James, though he modestly
withheld his own name. This was in harmony with his customary
attitude of humility and self-effacement. Andrew seems to have
had some trouble in "leading" Simon to the Saviour. "We have
found the Messiah-Christ," he said, and conducted him face to
face with Jesus. The evangelist tells us what then transpired. Jesus
"looked upon Simon and said, 'You are Simon, son of John, you
shall be called Cephas, that is Peter (or rock).'" Simon never
forgot that look and another Jesus gave him three years later in
the court of the palace of Caiaphas. Jesus read the character of
Simon with one intuitive glance. "He needed not that anyone
should testify concerning man for He knew what was in man."
He prophesied what grace would make out of the vacillating and
impetuous Simon — a rock of strength and a foundation stone in

the church. The new name Cephas or Peter which He gave Simon would be a constant reminder of what the Lord expected him to become. The confidence of the Master gripped the soul of Simon then and there and through the years transformed him. It was there a power in his conversion; it was later a mighty force in his development. Peter was destined to become one of the greatest pillars in the church. He was brought to the Saviour by Andrew, who is hardly known in Christian history, except through this one wonderful act which immortalized him.

The second day (Sunday) of His public ministry, Jesus wished to leave Bethany to go up to Galilee. That was the best region in which to begin His work. He might have already had also an invitation to the wedding to take place at Cana on the following Wednesday. He would want to tell His mother of the marvelous experiences of the baptism and temptations. She would sympathetically treasure them up in her heart and ponder them. And now the Master begins his own active initiative in soul-saving. He had heard from Andrew and Simon, doubtless, about Philip, one of their fellow-townsmen from the western Bethsaida, perhaps near Capernaum. Jesus, doubtless with their help, looks around until He finds him.

"Follow me," He said to Philip and that was sufficient. The appeal met with immediate response. Philip had been attending the revival at Bethany and without doubt had heard the testimony of John. His two fellow-townsmen had attached themselves to the new Teacher pointed out by the desert preacher. He too had desired to follow but held back. Only the invitation was needed and he eagerly became a disciple. John's preparation was ripe in Philip.

At once this new disciple begins to work for others, seeking for his friend, Nathanael, until he found him (Jno. 1:43-51). "We have found Him about whom Moses in the Law wrote and also the prophets," he said, "Jesus the son of Joseph from Nazareth." But Nathanael was skeptical and cautious. "Can any good thing come out of Nazareth?" he replied. There was some clan spirit and scorn in this resident of Cana, perhaps. It never pays to argue in such a case and Philip did the only sensible thing and invited the cautious Nathanael to investigate for himself. "Come and see," said Philip. This was a challenge which Nathanael could not refuse. It had seemed like an anticlimax, when Philip linked up the messianic idea with a poor carpenter of Nazareth, a town of no enviable reputation. But Philip was sure that once in the presence of Jesus, Nathanael's doubts would vanish like a fog before the rising sun. And such was the case, for even while Nathanael was approaching, Jesus said of him:

"Look, this is truly an Israelite in whom there is no deceit!"
Nathanael had been in the revival also and was thinking much of
what he had heard there. He was a devout student of the Scriptures
which declared that the Messiah would be born in Bethlehem. He
would like to beleive that the Messiah had come. Under the wide-
spreading fig tree by the way, Nathanael had stopped for prayer
and meditation as he journeyed toward his home in Cana.

"How do you know me?" Nathanael asked.

"Before Philip called you, while you were under the fig tree,
I saw you," said Jesus, with a discerning look. The surprising insight of Jesus fathomed the very thoughts of Nathanael, while under the fig tree. He had been thinking of the age to come when
Jacob would become Israel indeed. He was now won completely to
Jesus and cried out: "Teacher, you are the Son of God, you are
the King of Israel!" John had just testified that Jesus was the Son
of God and Messiah. His testimony was bearing fruit already in the
living faith of these who became the first disciples of Jesus. At
once Jesus commended and blessed this initial faith of Nathanael
and promised him a vision of greater things in the future.

"Because I said to you that I saw you beneath the fig tree, do
you believe?" said Jesus, "You shall see greater things than these."

They were not far distant even now from the exact place where
Jacob had seen the wonderful vision of the ladder connecting heaven
and earth. On the ladder angels had ascended and descended.

"Verily, verily, I say unto you all," said Jesus to the group,
"you shall see the heaven opened wide and the angels of God
ascending and descending on the Son of Man." Intimate communion would be established between heaven and earth by Jesus who
now for the first time assumed the half-veiled title of Daniel's
prophecy, "Son of Man," thus identifying Himself completely with
humanity as the Representative Man and at the same time declaring His Messiahship in veiled language. He would thus avoid
the antagonism and legal complications in the assertion of His
messianic claims. He declared His function of Mediator between
God and man, as the "Jacob's ladder" between heaven and earth;
He asserted His universal relation to the race as its representative; and He approved the testimony of Nathanael and of John the
Baptist to His deity. The Jews were looking for a glorious Messiah, a Son of God; they would heap upon Jesus soon the contemptuous epithet, *a son of man*. Jesus would now assume the
veiled Messianic title, *the Son of Man*, under cover of an opprobrious nickname. He now approved the title given Him by John and

Nathanael, "Son of God," and would soon declare Himself to be *the Son of God* in a peculiar and separate sense. The first two days of the ministry of Jesus were filled with joyous soul-saving, a prophecy of the arduous but glorious work of His life during the next three years. The campaign to win the world had begun.

3. The testimony of miracles (signs).

The first miracle is typical of many other signs which manifested the glory of the Messiah and produced or strengthened faith in the people (Jno. 2:1-11). The character of Jesus was set forth not only by the witness of others but also and mainly by His own works.

It was on the third day after His conversation with Nathanael that the wedding-feast in Cana, where Jesus worked this first miracle, took place. Cana (Kefr Kenna) was about four miles northeast of Nazareth. It was situated on the slope of a hill looking north and west over the plain of Batlauf and south upon a valley, and it was on the road to Capernaum. Today it is a dilapidated village almost without inhabitants. Near the village is a spring of good water, around which in other days must have clustered gardens and orchards. It was here that Nathanael lived, and most probably Jesus and the small band of six disciples were guests in his home, when the invitation came to bring the others with Him to the wedding feast. The mother of Jesus was already there, and was either a very intimate friend or a kinswoman of the virgin whose marriage was to be celebrated, after the custom, on Wednesday. She probably had something to do with the invitation sent to Jesus and His six disciples, just returned from the revival in Bethany. The omission of any mention of Joseph in the narrative would lead us to think that he was already deceased. It is probable that the other members of Mary's family were there, including four half-brothers and at least two half-sisters of Jesus (Jno. 2:12).

The marriage feast among the Jews was an occasion of great gladness and festivity but also of serious import. It was preceded by fasts in pious families. The betrothal of twelve months' duration or less before the marriage, was effected through legal proceedings, and was considered as sacred and binding as the marriage ceremony itself. On the evening of the marriage, the bride was led from her paternal home to that of her husband, accompanied by music with the distribution of oil and wine among friends and nuts among the children, and led by the "friends of the bridegroom, who bore torches and lamps, myrtle branches and chaplets of flowers." The veiled bride on arrival was led to the bridegroom, the marriage formula pronounced, and the legal documents signed. This was followed by the washing of the hands, and finally the marriage feast, which might last a day and sometimes a week.

During this feast the wine gave out. Evidently the resources of the family were limited. The coming in of seven previously un-expected guests might have had something to do with the em-barrassing situation which arose. If so, Mary would feel some responsibility for the lack of wine which she reported to Jesus.

Why did she appeal to Jesus? The long years of experience with this wise son in the Nazareth home had taught her to confide in His resourcefulness. But this was not the only idea she had in her appeal. In her heart she had treasured up for years the won-derful incidents which clustered around His birth (Luke 2:19, 51). To these were added those strangely significant words of the twelve year old boy, in the Temple: "Why is it that you have been searching for me? Did you not know that I must be engaged in my Father's business?" On through the years of His patient wait-ing, faithful work, and earnest study in Nazareth, she had watched His symmetrical growth in physique and spirit. The recent happen-ings at Bethany when He was baptized, and in the wilderness when He was tempted, about which He must have told her, stirred her deeply. Had not the Baptist called Him the "Lamb of God" and testified that He was the Messiah and Son of God? And He had just returned now from Bethany with a group of disciples, who told her many wonderful things about their experiences with Him and His remarkable understanding of them. Mary was certainly under the spell of the current Jewish idea of the Messiah. Would not such a Messiah-King come with signs as Moses did? Was not the time opportune for His manifestation unto Israel? It seems that she did not merely ask Him for counsel as to how to meet the embarrassing problem of the wedding feast but requested on His part supernatural providence. What more opportune time could there be for His manifestation through some "sign," than here before sympathetic and understanding friends?

The reply of Jesus shows His mother that her maternal au-thority did not extend into the realm of His messianic work. There was no lack of respect and affection in the terms He employed. He used the same term, "woman," when, hanging on the cross, He turned her over to the care of John, the beloved disciple.

"Woman, what is there to thee and to me?" He must be guided from now on by the messianic intuition of the Son of God. Her maternal suggestions must henceforth be subordinated to His superior and divine relationship. She would like to see Him mani-fested as the Messiah and King of the Jews? Well, "His hour of manifestation had not yet come." He was to be no mere worker of miracles. Human kinship must be subordinated now to spiritual relationships. He had been the dutiful son of Mary; He must now be the World's Redeemer (Matt. 12:46-55). The Romish church asserts the supreme intercession and intervention of Mary; it was this that Jesus denied.

If we might have any idea of harshness in this apparent rebuke of His mother by Jesus, it would be removed by the fact that He denied her not the request. He told her that the hour of His greater manifestation as Messiah had *not yet come*. This was a confirmation of her hope for Him and a promise for the future. She gives direction simply to the "attendants" to obey His behests, confident that He will supply the need and meet the embarrassing emergency. She knew her wonderful Son.

The circumstances of the miracle were simple. Six large water jars containing the water for the numerous ablutions of such a feast, stood in the gallery which opened upon the great reception room. Purification was one of the main points of Rabbinic sanctity. The largest of the six books of the Mishnah was devoted to the subject of purifications, and their neglect was attributed to gross ignorance or rank impiety. The six large water jars would hold, by the measure of the near-by capital, Sepphoris, 120 gallons.

"Fill up the jars," said Jesus to the attendants, and they filled them full up to the brim. There was no collusion or delusion here. The jars which had been drained for the ablutions as the guests came in were refilled with water.

"Draw out now and bear to the ruler of the feast," He directed and they obeyed. The result was clearly attested by the President of the feast. It was his duty of office to superintend the feast, examine and taste everything before it was served, see that all were served promptly, guide the conversation, repress undue excitement, and preserve order and decorum by breaking a glass when any guest might be disorderly, without naming him. It is useless to speculate as to when or how the miracle took place. Real water was placed in the pots by attendants; real wine was taken out and borne to the President of the feast by them. He knew not whence it came, but pronounced it the best that had been served. He even expressed his surprise that the bridegroom should save the best wine for the last, contrary to the general custom in such feasts. Usually the best was served first, and when the guests were satisfied the inferior quality was brought forth. The witnesses to the reality of this historical event are unimpeachable.

Jesus made real wine out of the water. But there was a great difference between the Palestinian wine of that time and the alcoholic mixtures which today go under the name of wine. Their simple vintage was taken with three parts of water and would correspond more or less to our grape juice. It would be worse than blasphemy to suppose, because Jesus made wine, that He justifies the drinking usages of modern society with its bars, strong drinks, and resulting evils.

It was clearly a wonderful miracle; but with Augustine, "not incredible to one who recognizes the divinity of Jesus." If Jesus was God, we need not deny Him the power of God, who is personal and supreme over all His natural laws.

John points out that the purpose of Jesus in the miracle was not merely to meet the embarrassing need of the wedding feast. By it He made plain His glory, the glory of the preexistent Word and only begotten Son of God (Jno. 1:14). For the first time His divinity broke through the veil of the flesh and shone out in the midst of men. In the narrative of the fourth gospel, John made use of various miracles to set forth the divinity of Jesus. But it was not just the supernatural power that was manifested. It was such power with the highest moral purpose behind it. The glory of the personality of Jesus was made plain. He was no ascetic, but a friend of men who dwelt in their midst sharing their joys and sorrows. He did not frown on joyful mirth but ennobled their common life by participation and gracious fellowship with men. The glory of the purpose of Jesus was made manifest. He would make use of His power only as a help to bring men to faith, and establish a spiritual kingdom. The glory of His work was revealed. He came to do good to mankind by ministering to their needs and raising them up by His fellowship. He would cleanse society by contact with it; not by fleeing away from it to the solitude of deserts or a cloister. Jesus was successful in His aim; His newly made disciples were confirmed in their faith in Him.

After the wedding-feast at Cana Jesus went immediately for a brief visit of a few days in Capernaum, probably situated eighteen miles northeast of Cana on the shores of the Sea of Galilee and on the great Roman road to Damascus (Jno. 2:12). Its site is contested, but evidence favors the ruins Tell Hum as the probable place of the town, which became the main center of the activities of Christ's ministry. There was a Roman garrison and custom house there and at least one synagogue. Andrew, Peter, James, and John lived near there and Bethsaida the native place of Philip, Andrew, and Peter was near (Mar. 1:19, 20; Jno. 1:44). Jesus was accompanied by His mother and His brethren on this visit. The brothers of Jesus here mentioned, were, by the most natural interpretation, the children born to Joseph and Mary after the birth of Jesus. In the narrative of the Gospels, Jesus is called the first born, naturally implying the birth of other children later. Jesus took the family down to Carpernaum at this time, probably in view of changing their residence from Nazareth. He was also planning doubtless to join the caravan at Capernaum, destined for the Passover in Jerusalem, just a few days ahead.

4. The first cleansing of the Temple (Jno. 2:13-22). The early disclosure of the Messiah culminated in the assumption of the Messianic authority by Jesus in the first cleansing of the Temple. This is entirely in accord with the argument of the gospel of John. Following the manifestation of the Messiah, through the testimony of John the Baptist, the first disciples, and the first miracle, comes His self-disclosure also, in half-veiled form, in the assumption of the function of Prophet-Messiah in this act of authority. He began His public ministry in Jerusalem, the great center of Jewish life, as a prophet-reformer.

It was proper that Jesus should go up to Jerusalem to attend the Passover. It had been His custom doubtless to go up annually, since His first recorded visit to the Temple at the age of twelve. John notes two other Passovers and possibly three, after this one within the ministry (Jno. 6:4; 5:1), thus making it at least two years and a half in duration.

Jesus cleansed the Temple twice during His public ministry: the first time, recorded by John's gospel, being at the beginning, and the second mentioned by the synoptics, being at the close of the ministry, the day after the Triumphal Entry (Mar. 11:15-17; Matt. 21:12f; Luke 19:45f). There is no incompatibility in two cleansings. The first was an indignant protest of the Christ at the initiation of His public work in Jerusalem, against the corruption in religion; the other was a final outcry against the desecration of the Father's house, which by their nefarious traffic the corrupted priests had made *their own house*, and would soon bring it to destruction. The first cleansing, as understood by John, is no anticlimax in His life, but an understanding acceptance by Jesus of His Messianic mission with all that it involved of antagonism on the part of the religious authorities in Jerusalem, which would increase from this, His first encounter with them, until it should result in His death on the cross. Jesus had in His mind from the beginning the consciousness of His course leading up to Calvary, and went to meet "His hour" with transcendent heroism. He is master of His life and comes suddenly into the Temple as the Prophet-reformer predicted by Malachi (Mal. 3:1f). He was to be Israel's refiner and purifier.

When Jesus arrived in Jerusalem, He repaired at once to the Temple, where He found "those who sold oxen, sheep, and doves, and the money-changers." A month before the Passover, which took place in April, the booths of the money-changers were opened in every town. All the Jews including proselytes must pay the Temple tribute of the half-shekel. After ten days the stalls in the towns were closed and the pilgrims began to pour into the city of Jerusalem. From that time, the money-changers sat within the precincts of the Temple. They charged about twelve per cent for the exchange of Jewish coins required in payments in the Temple for various foreign coins common in currency. The annual revenue to the Temple from these sources was about seventy-five thousand pounds, and in the final spoliation of the Temple the Romans found in the treasury two and a half millions sterling which had accrued from this source.

A great system of graft had grown up in the Temple under the astute management of Annas, the ex-High Priest. Making use of the exaction by their traditional religion, of victims of certain type for the purifications and thank-offerings, the corrupted priests established in the Temple a market for the sale of sheep, oxen, and doves or pigeons, as well as a money market. Payment of the tax must be made under penalty of restraint of property.

The animals for sacrifices and offerings had to be examined by persons qualified to do so and duly appointed. For such inspection there were exorbitant charges. Improper transactions were carried on and undue advantage taken. Sometimes a dove or lamb was sold for five or six times the just price. The whole traffic was a terrible desecration of religion. The profits were all supposed to flow into the Temple treasury; but the fact is that they went mainly to the money-changers and to superintending priests to whom they in turn paid a percentage or rentals. This market in the times of Jesus was what Rabbinic literature called the "Bazaars of the sons of Annas." He was the infamous politician who dominated the High Priesthood for many years even after his deposition. These Bazaars were noted for the greed of their owners and were hated and feared by the common people. Popular indignation, three years before the destruction of Jerusalem (70 A. D.), swept them away, because of their injustices and greed. Here was the very seat of corruption in the religion of the Jews and Jesus knew it. He dared to "beard the lion in his den" now in the beginning of His work; later He would pay for it with His life when He should stand before Annas and Caiaphas in trial at the end of three years' ministry.

When Jesus entered the court of the Gentiles, it was reeking with the stench of the cattle and resounding with the lowing and bleating of the oxen and sheep and the clamor of the buyers and sellers, bartering after the fashion of an Oriental market. The quarreling and wrangling of the money-changers added to the disgusting scene. What emotions filled the breast of Jesus as He stood and looked upon this awful desecration of the Temple! This market was not a temporary arrangement for convenience of the pilgrims but an established system of graft. It was plainly an abomination to the house of the Father.

Assuming the role of prophet, and asserting symbolically His Messianic authority, Jesus snatched up in His wrathful indignation some pieces of cast-away cords lying about the court, and plaiting them together with dexterous hands into a whip — symbol of authority — He flourished it and drove the sheep and oxen forth from the Temple court. Then quick as a flash He turned upon the money-changers, poured their money into their receptacles, and overthrew their tables. None dared oppose Him. The popular crowd looked on awe-struck and with a desire to applaud. Turning to those who sold the doves and pigeons shut up in cages, He said: "Take these things hence! Stop making my Father's house a market-house!" Jerome said, "A certain fury and starry light shone from His eyes and the majesty of Godhead gleamed in His face."

Is it not strange that the traders should have given away before Jesus, who had assailed them single-handed? Is it not still stranger that the priests who owned the business, when summoned should not have interfered? Back of this paralysis of their activity there were reasons. First, they recognized in Jesus a very extraordinary personality. His whole aspect and mien, when filled with righteous and wrathful indignation, swept them like a scourge. None but a prophet or the Messiah Himself would attempt such an audacious act. Could He perchance be the Messiah? John had announced a Coming One when they had sent a deputation to him. Then too, the purging of the Temple of this nefarious market of greed was a popular act. In His audacity Jesus had championed the rights of the people and won their approval if not their applause. Such approval would be easily read in the very looks of the spectators. The rulers did not resort to violence against Jesus because they feared a tumult among the people, with the possible intervention of the Roman garrison stationed in the near-by tower of Antony. Moreover their "consciences made cowards of them all." They were engaged in illicit graft and rank injustice.

This was a scene worth witnessing by all true Israelites! The greed-filled priests quailed before His presence and yielded in confusion at His approach. They dared not lay violent hands upon Him! His enemies were stricken with terror and anger while His disciples who witnessed the scene remembered that it had been written: "The zeal for thy house is eating me up" (Ps. 69:9). This was the greatest exhibition of burning jealousy for the holiness of the house of God and His people they had ever witnessed. The over-powering energy and absolute fearlessness of this act of Jesus deeply impressed them. They knew that it cost Him much!

It was not to be expected that this assumption of authority in the Temple would go long unchallenged. With extraordinary astuteness and infinite cunning, the enemies rally outside the Temple and return with a counter-offensive. They will play safe and enlist if possible the popular sympathy. At least they will not antagonize openly the popular mind. They *assume* hypocritically before the public that He is the Messiah and simply ask that He work some wonder before them as a token of His authority. "What sign shewest thou to us, seeing thou doest these things?" they ask. They appeal as it were to the multitude. Surely He should not deny the people a *sign* if He were the Messiah or some prophet. They do not waive their own authority in the Temple. He is asked to show *them* a sign. Here again is the temptation Satan brought to bear in the wilderness. If He should perform some great miracle would not the multitude now acclaim Him as the Messiah? Had He not just demonstrated in Cana His supremacy in the realm of nature? Did someone tell these wicked priests of that *sign*? But these men were not sincere. They were of the darkness; He was of the light. Mortal enmity must inevitably surge up more and more, and the contest begun now would go on to the tragic end. This purging act of Jesus defined His attitude toward them and forced them to define their position toward Him.

He discerned clearly the whole situation, and in His response to their veiled demand for a sign made them an enigmatic reply, which in the people would provoke reflection but which by the enemies would be misinterpreted and used at the last to His hurt.

"You destroy this temple (sanctuary) and in three days I will raise it up," He said. He met their demand for a sign by the challenge of a sign which they did not understand. Not even His disciples understood this parabolic reference to His death and resurrection until after they took place. His enemies perverted these words in His final trial and quoted Him as saying: "I will destroy" (Mar. 14:58) or "I can destroy" (Matt. 26:61), neither of which He said. With a sneer His enemies at once retorted: "Forty-six years this temple was abuilding and will you raise it up in three days?" Evidently they understood not the dark saying of Jesus. Many years after this, John's interpretation was that Jesus had spoken of the Temple of His body. (Jno. 2:19).

In these sign words Jesus laid out a challenge and solemn warning before these religious authorities. They had challenged the right of any man outside the privileged and exclusive caste of the

priesthood to interfere with the control of the religious affairs of
the nation. Jesus had so interfered and was now challenged to
prove His authority. He could not do so by working some miracle,
without on the one hand bowing to their assumed direction of
Himself in His Messianic activities, a thing just denied His own
mother; or on the other hand precipitating a popular movement
in the direction of a temporal Messiahship. He could not at the
same time refuse to meet the challenge. He adopted the enigmatical
form of answer, which while misunderstood by them, expressed
His vision of the change to come about in the future through His
Messianic work. Jesus "had crossed the Rubicon" and precipitated
in the very beginning of His ministry a conflict which would only
terminate at His death. But let them apparently defeat Him and
He would triumph; let them crucify Him as they would and
He in three days would rise again! Behind this was a yet wider application of His words. They would be permitted to go on destroying the national religion of which that building was the sanctuary.
For the sake of gain they were polluting the Temple, of which
they had been constituted the guardians. They would destroy the
religious life of the nation until the Temple itself would be razed to
the ground. But when the old order should have been destroyed,
out of His Messianic work would spring up a new order, a better
and more enduring Temple in the church which is His body.

CHAPTER VIII
BRIEF EARLY JUDEAN MINISTRY
(Harm. §§ 32, 33)

The audacious, deliberate act of Jesus in cleansing the Temple immediately before the Passover, when the Temple court was fullest of animals and money-changers in anticipation of the Feast which was "at hand," called forth from the political lobbyists and owners of the Annas Bazaars the demand for a "sign." Jesus wisely gave them an enigma to puzzle their brains over while He went on with His work. They wished to force Him into obeying their demands but He wisely avoided their trap, into which they themselves fell.

1. Jesus performed many unrecorded miracles in Jerusalem during the week of the Passover (Jno. 2:23-25). He did no *sign* at the behest of the priestly caste but granted to the people what He had refused the rulers. These miracles produced a profound impression. Many believed on His name or title as the Messiah, according to John's announcement, seeing the signs which He was repeatedly doing day after day. But their belief was superficial in most cases and Jesus did not trust Himself to these "milk-faith" believers. Theirs was a faith built on mere mental impulse stirred by strange *signs*, and did not reach down to the heart. Jesus had granted to them the signs to produce incipient faith in them, which might in some at least be later deepened. Thus far He condescended to their level. But He distrusted their professions of faith, knowing that there was not the clarity of perception and depth of conviction about the kingdom, necessary. He read intuitively the heart of man on all occasions. He knew now what was in their thoughts. They were dreaming of a victorious king who should deliver Israel from subjection to alien nations and set up again in greater splendor the throne of David subjecting in turn the heathen people round about. He did not "trust Himself" to Satan for such a program in the wilderness temptation, neither would He now be led into such a plan. These were typical "rice Christians," a "bread and butter brigade" such as Jesus met later in His popular days in Galilee (Jno. 6).

2. The interview of Jesus by Nicodemus and other work in Jerusalem. (Jno. 3:1-15).

John selected this outstanding case to illustrate the work of Jesus with individuals in the Jerusalem campaign during the eight days of the Passover and Feast of unleavened bread. His record is a mere summary of the conversation which took place. Jesus gave much personal attention and sympathy to individual inquirers. He made much use of the Socratic method in His teaching. Three-fourths of His wise sayings reported by the Gospels were spoken to individuals, in reply to seekers or in personal approach to those whom He would reach. Nicodemus was a man of culture and social position. Culture inevitably breeds intellectual reserve, but Nicodemus had not failed to notice the extraordinary character of the signs and teachings also of this Rabbi from Galilee. No man had ever attempted the audacious act of cleansing the Temple of its deep-seated corruption and the desecrating graft of the vested interests. The tremendous courage necessary for such an act, coupled with the whole character of the strangely humble and unostentatious Teacher, did not fail to impress a man of reflective mind like Nicodemus. Even the signs, to Nicodemus, were a strong proof of the divine origin of this Teacher. The Jews approached the spiritual and moral through the miraculous; our scientific age comes to the miraculous through the moral and spiritual. By a true interpretation both hang together and mutually support each other.

Nicodemus sought Jesus secretly by night. If he came as a kind of private representative of the rulers who had failed in their demand of a sign, the fact is not divulged. When they sent a deputation to John to inquire if he was the Messiah, the fact was known. The character of Nicodemus, as we know, would not harmonize with the idea of his being such a secret emissary of the Jewish rulers. He was a Pharisee and member of the Great Sanhedrin in Jerusalem. As such he would need to proceed with caution and avoid needless talk of his associates. It is probable that he came at night, seeking to know for himself the secret of the miracles, and especially to ask Jesus about the coming kingdom, which constituted one of the main themes of the preaching both of John and of Jesus. He would be censured by his colleagues of the Sanhedrin who had been so deeply offended by Jesus in the purification of the Temple, if they knew about his coming. Why not avoid that by coming at night? Then too, Jesus would be more accessible at night after the multitude which usually surrounded Him had dispersed. Though he did not come as a committee of one from the Sanhedrin, he did represent in sentiment a small group of the more cultivated class. It is not improbable that Joseph of Arimathea dated his interest in Jesus from this time, also. It took years to break down completely the prejudice, so that these two Sanhedrists should become bold to confess their faith and identify themselves openly with the new faith. They knew full well the deadly character of the enmity raised by Jesus in purging the Temple.

Where the interview took place we cannot with certainty declare. It might have been in the home of John in the city of Jerusalem itself. It seems that John did own a home in the capital (Jno. 19:27), and he would hardly have purchased property there after his call to discipleship. It might have been on the slopes of Olivet, where many a time Jesus bivouacked beneath the star-lit canopy of the heavens with His disciples after the strenuous labors of the day. It might have been in the home of Lazarus and his two sisters, who probably came to know and accept Jesus in this first appeal in Jerusalem. Many times later in His ministry, at least, Jesus repaired to this lovely home of sympathetic friends for rest at night after His day's work in the city.

Nicodemus opened the conversation in a tactful and even complimentary way, by remarking on the obvious evidences of Jesus' divine authority, the very thing which the Temple authorities had questioned. He wanted Jesus to discuss with him the character of the Messianic Kingdom so much talked about now in the city.

"Master," said he, "We know that thou hast come from God as a Teacher, for no man can go on doing these signs which thou art doing except God be with him." That was a great concession for Nicodemus as a Pharisee to make. Jesus was looked upon with scorn by most of them. Here was a man different from Simon or Nathanael, a scholar hedged about by custom and social barriers, seeking truth through the maze of a ceremonial system. He was courteous in his approach but he was ready to submit every argument of Jesus to his legalistic test. Jesus seeks the point of contact in His reply to this indirect question about His miracles and His Messianic origin. He understood the defects of Pharisaic theology. He knew that Nicodemus was immersed in the current conceptions concerning the Messiah and the Messianic Kingdom. He also recognized that Nicodemus had come, because of the preaching of the new doctrine of repentance and the coming kingdom. Many were believing in this new doctrine and the popularity of Jesus was growing rapidly. What Nicodemus had in mind, was to ascertain from Jesus for himself and others of his inner circle of friends, whether or not the temporal kingdom was going to be established now.

Jesus replies by brushing aside the question of when the kingdom is to be established, and penetrates to the very heart of the subject, by declaring the character of the kingdom and the conditions which must be met to *even perceive* it. He explained what was necessary to enter it. "Verily, verily, I say unto thee, except a man be born from above he cannot see the kingdom of

God." He thus declares solemnly, that the messianic kingdom is a spiritual order, invisible to the eye and not perceived by the senses. This declaration almost stunned Nicodemus. He did know about the proselytes, who, when baptized from heathenism, were said to be "as a child newly born." Did Jesus mean that the Jews must enter, by that door of humiliation, the kingdom? Such seemed to be the doctrine and requirement of John's baptism. To this all the Pharisees would object. The proselyte, on baptism into Judaism, entered into a new relation to God and man just as if he had been newly born. But his *second birth* was a consequence of his taking upon himself the kingdom. On the other hand, Jesus makes the new birth the direct and immediate cause of perceiving the kingdom. The Jew understood that a proselyte must become a member of the kingdom in order to be a "new-born child;" Christ said one must be born anew in order to become a member of the kingdom. Nicodemus could not understand this teaching. He was familiar with the idea of the new birth, by the ceremony of baptism for the proselytes; but such a ceremony was not for the Jews even though John should require it. The sons of Abraham would never submit to such a requirement! The very idea of such a thing was an insult to the Pharisee!

What then did Jesus mean? One thing was clear to Nicodemus. Evidently one must by the new birth become "as a child." But how could this come about? Another question he ventured: "How can a man be born when he is old? Can he enter a second time into his mother's womb and be born?" Participation in the messianic kingdom, for the Jew, meant conformity to a moral code and ritual system. It was his interest to know duty in order to escape penalty and secure reward. Duty was defined by a complex code of observances and restriction. It was not conceived as an inward personal disposition. For obedience, participation in the kingdom was the reward. By their own merits and hereditary claims as children of Abraham, the Pharisees believed the kingdom was theirs.

Jesus was trying to bring Nicodemus to the idea that the kingdom was one of the heart and inner life. There must be a new birth of thought, emotion, and volition. Like the earth is renewed, by the benignant magic of the spring, so the soul of man when renewed is dominated by new thoughts, sentiments, and purposes.

It was hard for Nicodemus to come to this idea of the spiritual kingdom. Jesus seeks to make the way plainer for this inquirer, who never had any real experience of the spiritual life and kingdom. The Jews understood the significance of an ablution

and Nicodemus knew that John was requiring a baptism of repentance and confession on the part of all.

"Verily, verily I say unto thee," said Jesus, "Except a man
be born of water and of the spirit, he cannot enter into the kingdom of God." Nicodemus had failed to grasp the idea of the spiritual birth and the spiritual kingdom. He, like the rest of the Jews,
expected that all Gentiles would come into the Jewish fold through
the door of proselytism. There are various interpretations which
have been offered by these words of Jesus. Some have made them
mean baptismal regeneration, which is contrary to the general
teachings of the New Testament. Some have declared that both
baptisms mentioned refer to one act—the cleansing work of the
spirit. The mention of the water baptism in that case would seem
superfluous. Others would understand contrast between the natural birth and the spiritual birth, since Nicodemus had just inquired on that point, as to whether a second natural birth was
possible. That is nearer the truth and a possible interpretation.
In favor of that interpretation is the statement of Jesus immediately following: "That which stands born of the flesh is flesh; and
that which stands born of the Spirit is spirit. Do not wonder that
I said unto you, It is necessary that you be born from above"
(spiritually).

One of the greatest difficulties in interpretation, always, is in
the neglect of the historical setting of the text in its context; and
also the reading of our own present-day system of theology into
the isolated text. We should remember in this case, that Nicodemus was a slave of the ceremonial system. The Jews had a great
zeal for God but not according to knowledge of the spiritual way
of salvation. To them the kingdom must come as a reward of
meritorious obedience to the requirements of the moral and ceremonial codes. Jesus gives Nicodemus to understand that he must
come through the door of John's baptism of repentance and confession, and also experience the baptism of the Holy Spirit to
which John had referred in picturing the coming Messiah. "I baptize you in water," John had said, "but He that cometh after me
shall baptize you in the Holy Spirit." We must remember also that
Christian baptism had not yet been instituted and the passage under consideration is not speaking of Christian baptism at all. The
meaning to us in the plan of salvation today would be "you must
repent, Nicodemus, and confess your sins and also experience
the baptismal birth of the Holy Spirit."

Still Nicodemus was puzzled, and Jesus added an explanation
as to the unseen mystery of the spiritual birth—which he need
not understand—and the effects growing out of it which he might

easily perceive. They sat under the open canopy of the heavens at this evening hour; the gentle breeze fanned their cheeks and made the leaves on the near-by tree flutter. "See, Nicodemus, the effects of the wind which comes mysteriously from whence you know not and goes whither you cannot understand? So is the mystery of the new birth which you need not know. There are visible and tangible results in the life of the spirit-born man which you easily perceive." The new birth is not so strange. The spring wind passes over the earth and in a night's time the whole of nature is renewed. Human hearts breathed upon by the Spirit of God leap into new life. He who is thus renewed becomes as a little child, which lives more by intuition and simple faith than by reason.

It was difficult for Nicodemus to empty his mind of all his traditional belief in the system, which taught *becoming* as a means of *being* and accept the plan of salvation of first *being* in order to *becoming*.* "How is it possible for these things to come about?" he asked again.

"You are the well-known and accepted teacher of Israel," said Jesus, "and do you not recognize these things?" The trouble with Nicodemus was that he was "in the rote, rut, and rot of traditionalism." He insisted on knowing the how of the new birth about which Jesus spoke. To this Jesus simply asserts that He is speaking out of the experience of Himself and others in the kingdom. His small band of disciples there with Him could testify to the truth of His declarations from their experience. Jesus had told Nicodemus of the things which take place on earth — the spiritual birth and the spiritual kingdom and its work, and Nicodemus had not believed His testimony. What advantage would there be in testifying about the things in heaven, such as the how of the new birth, the springs of being, and the deep purposes and plan of God in redemption. There was no man who had ascended up to heaven and could therefore know of those things, except the One who had descended out of heaven, even the Son of Man. Here the continuity of the personality and consciousness of Jesus is set forth. He was the pre-existent Son and knew the things which took place in heaven before the incarnation. His was a timeless existence and He was conscious of His pre-existent state. The Jews had a tradition that Moses went up to heaven to bring down the "table of the ten words." But Moses, a mere man, had not been able to ascend into heaven, the realm of absolute reality, and so bring the people to the springs of being. Only the ideal man (Son of Man) who had descended from His pre-incarnate state in heaven could be the true and complete Teacher.

* Edersheim's Life and Times of Jesus.

Jesus now comes to the practical point of how Nicodemus or anyone might experience the new birth. As the final and authoritative Teacher, He reveals the conditions of the birth from above. The Jews had not heeded the teachings of Moses which came down to him from heaven, about the things related to their earthly life. He had pointed them to the way of faith in God. But they had murmured after being fed with the manna from above, and had fallen back into sin. God sent their punishment in the form of fiery serpents. When they were dying, as a consequence of this inflicted judgment, God made a way of escape for them in the lifting up of a brazen serpent in their midst, which He commanded Moses to make. There was no virtue in a look at a mere metallic serpent. But there was life in the obedient look of a repentant faith which raised the eyes of the dying man to the merciful and loving God. Jesus made use of this historic miracle in which thousands were restored to life and health, to illustrate the way of life through a look of faith at the Son of Man, who would of necessity because of the conflict between the world's darkness and His light be lifted up on the Cross. Indeed, it was by a law of the divine nature that He would be lifted up by the Cross, not to an earthly throne such as Nicodemus and others hoped for, but to the spiritual throne of the Universe. The atoning death of Christ must be the corner-stone of the Kingdom, which would be composed of twice-born men, who looked in faith to the Crucified One. The very purpose of the "lifting up" was that everyone who is believing may keep on having the endless and infinitely expanded life in the saving sphere of Jesus.* The sin-bitten one, who looks up in faith to the once dead but now living and life-giving Saviour, will feel the thrill of new life surging through his veins, with a new birth of his thoughts, emotions, purposes, and desires. Jesus thus revealed in these last recorded words of His conversation with Nicodemus the how of the new birth which was the vital point for him and for all men to know.

How well Nicodemus made use of this life-giving knowledge, we are not able to say. The Gospel record seems to warrant the conclusion, that if Christ did not make an instant convert of Nicodemus yet He made a real one in the end. Much later in Christ's ministry, when the hostility of His enemies broke out in violence and would have swept Him away, perhaps, but for certain restraining influences, Nicodemus appears on the scene again. Jerusalem was ringing with the popularity of Jesus. The Sanhedrin wanted to do away with Him. But Nicodemus stepped forth in the face of ridicule and asked: "Doth our law judge any man before it hear him and knows what he has done?" (Jno. 7:50).

* Progressive action of Greek tenses and locative case of sphere within which.

Even though the prophet were from Galilee, contrary to their traditions, He should at any rate have a fair deal before the law. Once more Nicodemus appears at the end, (Jno. 19:39), and this time as a professed and bereaved disciple of the Master, begging His body that he may give it a decent burial and spare it the indignity of a felon's grave.

The past tenses of the verses which follow (3:16-21), would indicate that they are not the words of Christ, who would have used present tenses in His conversation, but of John who in these verses recapitulates in summary and comments on the teaching of Christ to Nicodemus. These seasoned reflections of John on the interview, reannounce Jesus as the only-begotten Son of God sent into the world to be its Teacher and Saviour. The purpose of the Mission of Jesus, set forth in "Luther's little Bible" (v. 16) in its positive, and in the following verse in its negative, aspect, is that of salvation for believing men, flowing out of the great love of God, and not that of purposed condemnation of men. The actual result, however, growing out of the coming of Jesus into the world, is the justification of those who believe, and the condemnation of those who reject Him growing out of their deliberate choice of the darkness rather than the light in accord with their evil life (vs. 18, 19). John terminates his comment with a statement of the fundamental cause of the apparent failure of the mission of Jesus, in His almost universal rejection by the Jews. Judgment was coming upon unbelieving men because darkness has no affinity for light. Those who are full of darkness flee from the light; but the one doing the truth comes to the light. Trust in Christ and identification with Him prevents our condemnation, because He stands in our place and has paid the penalty for our sins. But judgment on the unbelieving has been passed already, and He merely awaits the day of its execution.

3. The ministry in the province of Judea (Jno. 3:22-36). We do not know how long Jesus tarried in Jerusalem. It is probable, from various circumstances, that His ministry in the city was not very extended. He began His work in the Temple, but was soon confronted by the Temple authorities who antagonized Him at every turn. Finding it impossible to continue there with profit and without violent consequences, He went out into the city and set His work up there. It was during this time probably that Nicodemus came and interviewed Him.

After a brief ministry in the Holy City, He transferred the seat of His work out into the interior of the province of Judea, and "was tarrying" there for some time. The early Judean minitsry probably covered about six months. Only the narrative of John

(1:19-4:43) records this part of the ministry of Jesus. The synoptics begin with His ministry in Galilee where Jesus met with a warmer welcome and greater success. But it was fitting that His work should be initiated in Jerusalem and in the province of Judea. For some time the ministries of the two ran parallel in the southern region. John moved up to Enon near Salim, located by Robinson four miles east of Shechem. Enon was a "place of springs." John had doubtless withdrawn to this place to avoid the intrigues of the Pharisees. It is not improbable that they were pushing him up in that direction, near to the seat of the government of Herod Antipas. They afterwards tried to work a similar scheme with Jesus, just before the end of His ministry. They were keen enough to foresee that John, the fearless wilderness preacher, would denounce the sins of the wicked ruler, as he did later and with what results we know. There were "many waters" in Enon for John's baptismal purposes and even in the summer time "immersion could be continued" (Marcus Dods). The exact place where Jesus established the seat of His evangelistic campaign is unknown. Some have supposed that He simply attached Himself temporarily to the work of John, though that is hardly probable. He may have begun His work east of the Jordan near where He had been baptized. There would be nothing against such a plan and it was far enough from the place of John's work not to seriously interfere. There was yet a stream of people pouring out from various places, and now likely many from Galilee, to hear the wilderness preacher's stirring messages; and many were being baptized by him constantly. His revival had gone on now for more than six months with unabated interest. This was an unprecedented spiritual experience in the history of Israel. The opposition of the Pharisees to John's work had waxed stronger as his messages against sin in high places had grown more vigorous. They were closing in on him now with their political intrigues, but he "had not yet been thrown into prison."

There was no rivalry between John and Jesus. Indeed, we may well think, that one of the chief purposes of Jesus in establishing His ministry in Judea at this time was to put His entire seal of approval on the work of John. The Lord could easily foresee that John was fast driving toward inevitable martyrdom out ahead. No man could denounce sin as he did without suffering the reaction on the part of the high vested interests of Jerusalem, and the wicked Herodian family represented now mainly by Herod Antipas. Jesus had, associated with Him in His evangelistic campaign, the six disciples whom He had won in the first days of His ministry, and probably others. These disciples had been trained at the feet of John, and not only loved him but understood thoroughly his ministry of preparation for the Messiah, his baptism of repentance and confession in securing that preparation, and his testimony definitely pointing away from himself and to the coming Christ. Jesus understood all of these things even better than His disciples. There was therefore no cause for jealousy on His part, which would be inconceivable in Him, nor on their part, since His ministry was just in its beginning and was rapidly growing. Indeed, it is a reasonable inference, that Jesus was conducting this evangelistic campaign in Judea in order to take up the work just where John was forced to lay it down a little later, when he was snatched from his activities and borne away secretly to the dungeon of Machaerus.

Jealousy arose on the part of some of the disciples of John, when they saw the growing crowds which attended the ministry of Jesus and the waning popularity of John, their master. This jealous feeling was fanned to a white heat by the intriguing Pharisees, who considered the baptismal cleansing or ablutions their own special privilege and province. Both John's invasion of this field, and now that of Jesus through the baptisms which His disciples were administering, were hateful to them, and in the form and manner in which the baptism was being administered, an insult to their Jewish pride. If they could bring about friction between the two preachers and their disciple groups, it would defeat the work of these "interlopers" and secure to the Pharisees their monopoly of baptismal cleansings. So they probably sent one of their most astute representatives into the midst of the disciples of John to raise the discussion as to the relative merits of the baptism as administered by John and that used by Jesus' disciples. It is always easy to raise a discussion, and what could be more natural than a comparison of methods now in these two revival meetings. This is the first recorded controversy about baptism. In what better way could Jesus show His approval of John's ministry than to allow His disciples to adopt the same form of baptism as that practiced by their former master. But Jesus must undoubtedly have explained, as John did, that the water baptism was merely a precursor of that baptism which He was to originate, the real spiritual baptism. He must have explained to the candidates for baptism, as He did to Nicodemus, the necessity of the second or spiritual birth. These added elements would naturally give rise to a comparison between the work of the Baptist and that of Jesus, to the evident disadvantage of the former. The discussion of the baptismal question was a mere entering wedge to bring about dissension between the two revivalists. The Pharisees had calculated well. The disciples of John, moved with envy, came to him addressing him as the "Rabbi," or master. They even half-way reproached him, for the witness he had borne to Jesus, when he was preaching over at Bethany beyond the Jordan. John had never retracted that testimony but had stood by it firmly.

"Behold," said they, "this one is baptizing and all are coming to Him." This was the real seat of the trouble. It was a clear case of jealousy, for the ministry of their leader John.

In his answer John gives one of the most beautiful examples of loyalty recorded in human history. "The revelation to Jesus on the true meaning and character of baptism had been received by Him from heaven," said John. Once again he reminds them that his own mission was that of a mere forerunner. He had said to them repeatedly as they would remember: "I am not the Messiah but the one sent before that one." He is content to be a "friend of the Bridegroom" and to rejoice with exceeding great joy at hearing the voice of the Bridegroom. Like the true paranymph or friend of the Bridegroom, he has brought the bride and the Bridegroom together. With tenderness and almost sadness, John recognizes that his own ministry is rapidly waning. Jesus' word must increase and his own diminish. Already this was taking place. In these last recorded words of John his testimony rings true. His loyalty is invariable. His joy stands complete in the full-blown ministry of Jesus.

In the last verses of this chapter (3:31-36) are recorded the comments of John, the author of the fourth Gospel, on the words of John, the *baptizer*. The Baptist had testified that the teaching of Jesus came from heaven. For this reason His teaching was superior to that of all merely human teachers. He possessed the knowledge and was endowed with the experience of both the earthly and heavenly spheres of existence. A teacher can only draw from the sphere of his own experience in his teaching. The superiority of the teaching of Jesus was in the fact of His experience in the realm of absolute truth. It was true that great crowds were attending on the ministry of Jesus, as John's disciples had said, but few of them accepted the testimony of Jesus. He had been rejected by the masses of the people always, even to the last days of the apostle John. But those individuals who did come to accept Him, became firmly convinced that God was fulfilling His promises in Jesus. They accepted firmly and permanently the words of Jesus, even as the words of God, recognizing that God put no limit on the relation of the Spirit to Jesus. More than this, the Father loves the Son and gave over permanently into His management all things. The outcome of this situation was that everyone who is believing on the Son is in continuous and conscious possession of eternal life, here and now.[1] On the contrary

1 See Greek tenses.

the one who is disobedient to the Son shall not even have the capacity to see life or have a true conception of it. Upon such an unbelieving and disobedient one the wrath of God is already abiding and in fuller revelation will be worked out in his experience in the future.

CHAPTER IX
SUCCESS IN SAMARIA
(Harm. §§ 34-36)

The brief ministry of Jesus in Samaria, where He stopped just two days on His return to Galilee, is peculiarly significant, in that He then defined His attitude toward that people. His work there is also a fine example of missionary method and policy. He won first an individual and thus gained a hearing in the city of Sychar.

1. Reasons why Jesus departed from Judea. (Mar. 1:14; Matt. 4:12; Luke 3:19, 20; 4:14; Jno. 4:1-7). Jesus did not leave Judea because His ministry there was a failure but because it was too popular and successful. He was making and baptizing more disciples than John, though He Himself never baptized anyone throughout His whole ministry and Christian baptism was not yet instituted. The miracles of the Lord in Jerusalem had attracted wide attention, and multitudes thronged Him as He preached, near the place where He had been baptized down across the Jordan not far from Bethany. The fundamental reason which led Jesus at first to decide to move the seat of His work to Galilee, was that the Pharisees were intriguing to bring about misunderstanding and friction between His own disciples and those of John. Jesus realized that these enemies would never cease until they brought about serious trouble, and He had come here not for the purpose of bringing confusion or detracting in any measure from John's ministry but rather to place His approval on it. He also recognized that the Pharisees would soon be sending a deputation to Him and would thus precipitate a crisis, forcing Him to withdraw from regions adjacent to Jerusalem or to enter into prolonged conflict, for which the hour had not yet come. While He was yet in the midst of the execution of this plan, news came of the arrest of John by Herod Antipas, the crafty, cruel, licentious son of the wicked Herod—so-called the Great. The trap of the Pharisees had proved effective. John had been pushed up to the proximity of the seat of Herod's government, and his denunciation of the conduct of that wicked ruler—which was a natural result—led to his imprisonment. Antipas had put away his wife, the daughter of Aretas, King of Arabia, and taken the wife of his half-brother Herod Philip, whose hospitality he had enjoyed while in Rome. Added to this was the fact that this guilty woman Herodias was the daughter of his half-brother Aristobulus, and the crime involved disloyalty, adultery, and incest. John denounced sin wherever he found it among the high and low, and it was sufficient

that this notorious crime should fall under his observation to call forth his just disapproval. Herodias was jealously vindictive, and soon succeeded in having John arrested and dragged in chains to the dungeon of Machaerus in the fortified royal palace to the east of the Dead Sea. Later Jesus defied this crafty ruler, when His ministry was coming to a close. Now, He avoids a trap, similar to the one into which John had been led, by withdrawing through Samaria to Galilee. There He would escape in part at least the vigilance of the Pharisees of Jerusalem. It is probable that John was taken down the way east of the Jordan. Jesus would avoid a needless encounter with the soldiery and heartless officers of Herod as they dragged their prisoner toward the dungeon of Machaerus. No intervention of His on behalf of John would avail, other than the miraculous which was not warranted. So, for this and other reasons He chose the route through Samaria.

2. The conversation with the Samaritan woman at Jacob's well (Jno. 4:5-26). Jesus probably started out for Galilee from Bethany, across the Jordan. This was about twenty miles from Jacob's well where several roads met, one of which led up through the gorge of Wady Farah which empties into the Jordan. It was at least twenty miles, over a rather rough and in places steep road that Jesus traveled. It must have been in January or February, as the harvest was about four months later. Jesus was accompanied by His band of six disciples.

When they emerged into the rich plain of Samaria it was late in the afternoon, and Jesus being tired out with his journey sat down on the curb stone of the well to rest.

Jacob's well, which was located a mile to the south of Sychar and at the junction of several ancient Roman roads, was the traditional well dug by Jacob (Genesis 33:18, 19). The patriarch bought from the people of the land a parcel of ground and sunk the well through the limestone rock, avoiding thus the strife with Amorite herdsmen around. Later he gave this parcel of ground to his son Joseph. The well remained as a memorial of Jacob's first symbolic taking possession of the land. It was originally 150 feet deep. In the neighborhood there were springs like that of El Eskor at the foot of Mt. Ebal, but their waters were calcerous and unpalatable. On the other hand the water of the well was a fresh, running, cool stream, palatable and healthful. Today that well is changed partly with time, but remains the most certified ancient landmark of all to be found in Palestine. Over against the well rose Mt. Gerizim, 880 feet high, with the Samaritan temple upon it in full view. As Jesus looked up at this temple, He must have reflected on the fall of the northern kingdom of Israel

when the Israelites were carried into captivity by Shalmanezer in
721 B. C. It was then that the mixed Samaritan people had their
origin, when the heathen king brought in immigrants from Cutham,
Avra, Hamath and Sepharvaim, and placed them in the cities of
Samaria with the remnants of the children of Israel left behind
in the deportation. Out of the amalgamation of these elements
sprang the Samaritans.

Left by the disciples, with the possible exception of John who
seems to have reported the incidents which followed as an eyewitness, Jesus sat resting on the curb of the well, which today is
several feet below the present surface of the ground. Various
churches have been erected at different times successively over the
well, the last one having been destroyed at the time of the Crusades. Today the curb is approached by a stairway leading down
into a vaulted chamber fifteen feet square.

As He sat thus resting and rehearsing in memory things of
history connected with this landmark, a woman of the nearby
town of Sychar came to draw water. Then took place one of the
most interesting conversations recorded in literature, in which
Jesus led the Samaritan woman, who was a sinner, out of a life
of shame into acceptance of the life of faith.

A simple and courteous request of Jesus, a Jewish Rabbi, for
a drink of water from her, a Samaritan woman, surprised her with
its unconventionality. "Give me to drink," He said. "How do you,
a Jew, ask drink of me, a Samaritan?" she replied. Since 536 B. C.,
when the Samaritans offered to help rebuild the Temple and walls
of Jerusalem and were refused by the Jews due to the fact that
they were a mixed race, there had been constant enmity between
the two peoples. The Jews called the Samaritans Cuthim in contempt. Spurious Judaism had been introduced into Samaria by
Manasseh, an apostate Jewish priest, who refused to divorce the
daughter of Sanballat whom he had married. There were various
expressions of contempt heaped upon the Samaritans by the
Jews, such as: "May I never set eyes upon a Samaritan." To partake of their bread was said to be like "eating swine's flesh."
But the extravagance of these expressions of the earlier periods
had been greatly modified by the time of Jesus. In His time all
their food was declared lawful. So it was that the disciples had
gone to buy bread in the Samaritan town. It was not lawful
however for a Jewish Rabbi to speak with a woman publicly.
Jesus broke over all the rules of tradition in order to save this poor
woman. She insulted Him impudently in her reply, but He stood
the affront patiently. "If you only knew the gift of God," He said,
"and who is the one saying to you: 'Give me to drink.' you would
have asked of him and he would have given you living water."

Thus, He met her *objection of race difference*, by asserting that all races are on equal footing before God's great love, which gave the Saviour to the world.

She wholly misunderstood His reference to the *living water*, thinking that He referred to the stream of flowing water in Jacob's draw-well. Usually there was at a well a skin bucket, held open at the top by three intersecting sticks and attached to a camel's-hair rope. But Jesus had no such bucket. How could He get the water from the well? So reasoned the woman. Once again Jesus clarifies. "But this water will only quench the thirst of anyone for a time; later he will thirst again. The one who drinks of the water that I will give him shall never thirst again; but the water which I give him will become in him a spring of water bubbling up unto eternal life." With mocking insolence she replies: "Sir, give me some of this water that I thirst not neither come hither to draw."

The arrogant woman was doubtless turning away to go back to the city, when Jesus arrests her attention, and this time with a positive command. "Go call your husband," said He, "and come hither." She winced under the command. "I have no husband," she replied blandly. "You said well that you have no husband, for you have had five men and the one you have now is not your husband. In this," said Jesus, "you have spoken the truth." The woman was taken aback. How did He, a perfect stranger and a Rabbi, know her shameful past? Could He be some prophet? Then she bethought her of another subterfuge and quickly she turns the conversation in yet another direction. "I perceive, Sir, that you are a prophet." And pointing to Gerizim nearby she said, "Our fathers worshipped in this mountain!" The ruins of the ancient temple were plainly visible from where they were. "And you Jews say that in Jerusalem is the place where men ought to worship." Jesus caught her idea immediately. She was flatteringly invoking His opinion on the *theological question*, which had been a bone of contention between the two peoples for ages. She was at the same time getting away from facing the problem of her sinful life. Quick as a flash, Jesus sweeps aside this quibble and brings her to face the spiritual realities again. "Believe me, woman, the hour is coming and even now is here, when neither in this mountain nor in Jerusalem—as the only or specially predilect places—you shall worship the Father. You worship what you know not; we know what we worship because salvation comes from the Jews. But the hour cometh and now is, when the true worshippers shall worship the Father in spirit and in truth, for the Father is also seeking such worshippers. God is spirit and it is necessary that those who worship Him should worship in spirit and in truth." Jesus had solved her theological question in one sweeping statement. He had revealed a few minutes ago the unity of the race, before the love-gift of God leveling all barriers of race. He now reveals the spirituality and consequent universality of the true religion. True worship does not depend on holy days and places but upon whether the worshipper is sincere and the God he worships be the true God. The Samaritans had a worship mixed with the idolatrous cults of Cutha and Sepharvaim. They did not know what they worshipped, just as the heathen, who today fall down before idols.

The woman was convinced now, but she sought to stave off the question of her personal salvation. When that hour about which He spoke arrived, it would be time. Such is the tendency of the human soul to procrastinate. "I know that the Messiah is coming, the one who is called Christ. Whenever He comes He will tell us everything," she said. "I am He" said Jesus, " the one now speaking to you." Her soul bowed at last in worshipful recognition, and forgetting the water jar in her haste she ran away to the city to break the joyful news.

3. The evangelization of Sychar. (Jno. 4:27-42). The first step had been taken and the door was soon wide open for the gospel to enter the Samaritan town of Sychar. The simple testimony of the woman, known as a notorious sinner in the city but now marvelously changed, was sufficient, added to the message of John the Baptist, to attract the attention of many. "Come" she said, "and see a man who has told me everything I have ever done. Is not this the expected Messiah?" Many left the town and were going forth to see Him.

Meanwhile the disciples, who had gone to buy victuals, were urging Jesus repeatedly saying, "Master, eat something." "I have food to eat" said He, "about which you do not know." And as they inquired privately among themselves whether someone had brought Him food to eat He continued: "My food is to do the will of Him that sent me and to finish His work completely."

Now they saw the multitude of people coming out from the city. Jesus was deeply moved by this sight. For Him it was a foretoken of how crowds from outside of Israel would later come to Him. "You say it is yet four months before the harvest?" said Jesus. "Behold! Lift up your eyes and look on the fields, white to the harvest." These Samaritan people were just ready to be garnered in for God. "Already the one reaping is receiving wages and gathering in fruit unto eternal life." Jesus was in the very beginning of His ministry but He was reaping already a rich harvest of souls. One of the finest evidences of true conversion is a real zeal in the converted one to lead others to the Saviour. Judged by this standard the Samaritan woman was a bright convert. She was leading a crowd of her people out to see Jesus. In this blessed work of soul-saving both the sowers and reapers rejoice together. In the nature of the case, many times, one sows and another reaps. But whether one sows or reaps, he is engaged in the same great common task and gathers the fruit of souls into eternal life. So Jesus was now sending His disciples to reap where He Himself and others had sown. But all were permitted to enter into the joy of the harvesting, just the same.

Such was the change wrought in the woman, that her testimony became powerful in convincing many that Jesus was the Messiah. He had read her whole past life with such startling exactness, that she was convinced of the fact that He was a prophet. Then He had revealed to her in plain terms—what He could only make known in half-concealed and enigmatic language to His own people—that He was the Messiah. The Samaritans besought Jesus repeatedly on every side to remain over with them, and He abode two days in Sychar evangelizing and ministering in many cures of their sick. During this time a far greater number believed because of His own words and not simply because of the testimony of the woman. They had verified what she told them, and their conclusion in the end was: "We have heard and we know that this man is really the Saviour of the world."

Jesus had left Judea because of His over-popularity (Jno. 4:1-3). Such had been His popularity that it was becoming a source of envy to the disciples of John. Jesus would seek another place of labor, where His popularity would not impede His own work and that of His forerunner. There was a proverb current among the Jews — "A prophet is not without honor (popularity) save in his own country." Some commentators seem to think that Jesus considered Judea "His own country"; but the more natural view would be, that Galilee would be thought of popularly as His country and that Jesus was running from too much popularity into His own country where He would not be over-popular. The preacher's over-popularity frequently gets in the way of his work. This interpretation accords with the reason assigned for His leaving Judea (3:1-3) and explains why Jesus Himself cited the proverb. This view further explains the statement immediately following by the evangelist, that the Galileans were receiving Him with a hearty welcome because He had done many miracles in Jerusalem at the feast and they had witnessed His popularity there. For the time at least they were proud of this son, who had received great honor outside His own country and now returned with the laurels on His brow. Not many preachers run from over-popularity. In this also Jesus was exceptional. But how about Nazareth?

PART III

THE GREAT GALILEAN MINISTRY

(Harm. §§ 37-71)

The ministry of Jesus in Judea followed the Passover Feast in April 26 A. D. and lasted probably until about the following December. This would accord with the expression Jesus used when speaking to His disciples at Jacob's well — "Say not ye, there are yet four months and then cometh the harvest" — since the harvest in these regions was from April to May. It seems that the small disciple band returned for a while to their old occupation, and the Galilean ministry, beginning sometime in the autumn of 27 A. D., lasted about a year and a half or until the spring of 29 A. D.

Prophecy had pointed to Galilee as the place of dawn for a new era of hope. The people that "sat in darkness" would see a new day of liberty, peace, and prosperity. That prophecy was uttered by Isaiah eight centuries before the coming of Jesus, while the Israelites were under the yoke of Assyria.

It was fitting that the ministry proper of Jesus should find its greatest expression in Galilee. It was the most beautiful, productive and populous district of Palestine. The bright sunny sea of Galilee with its sturdy fisher-folk, surrounded by a beautiful country, was a fit place, if there could be any, to serve as a setting for His wonderful life and activity. Galilee of the Gentiles was a choice cradle for the universal gospel. Jesus liked to mingle in the crowd. He loved human beings and here He found a dense population made up of heterogeneous elements of all types and nationalities. The mixture of various races tends to the lowering of standards of moral life. In the corruption everywhere prevalent, Jesus found a challenge for His work of regeneration, individual and social. He came on the horizon of this benighted people, as a brilliant sun of intense heart sympathy and yearning hopeful love. His great wisdom as a teacher flared up as a great light in the midst of their darkness.

CHAPTER X

THE BEGINNING OF THE GALILEAN MINISTRY

(Harm. §§ 37-43)

John had been arrested and was being taken down the road east of the Jordan, when Jesus made His way north from Judea to Galilee by way of Samaria. Herod Antipas had divorced his wife, the daughter of Aretas, King of Arabia, to·marry Herodias, his half-brother Philip's wife. John denounced this adulterous union, and was arrested and thrown in prison in Machaerus through the influence of Herodias, and afterwards beheaded in January, 28 A. D.

Mark says Jesus came into Galilee preaching the gospel or good news, sent by God to men. Repent was the central note of the stern wilderness preacher John; *good news* the keynote of the ministry of Jesus. The new evangelist repeated John's message of repentance and proclaimed the fact that the heavenly Kingdom had already arrived and was to be permanent. But He adds that the crisis hour of opportunity has struck and commands men to change their minds, purposes and desires, and believe in the message of good news He brings. The heavenly King was the messenger of this good news; men must dwell, by belief in Him, in the sphere of His good message. A little later Jesus removed His mother's family from Nazareth to Capernaum and from that strategic center began His work of heralding (preaching). Jesus was a *preacher* and His theme was repentance and the Kingdom of the heavens. He was very careful to explain that His Kingdom was not earthly, because of the current expectation with reference to the coming Messiah. In other places Jesus is called a *teacher* also, as every minister should be.

Luke gives no account of the earthly Judean ministry, but leaps at once from the temptations of Jesus to the work in Galilee. He summarizes briefly three things in general which characterized this ministry in Galilee. First, it was a ministry in the power of the Holy Spirit. There is no word in English to set forth the tremendous explosive force of this spiritual power[1] and its ability to shake up and change things, except dynamite. The ministry of Jesus was full of dynamite-power. A second thing which characterized this work in Galilee was the rapidity with which the fame of these activities spread abroad. The third element in the ministry was that of the repeated, customary, and habitual teaching of Jesus Himself in their synagogues. He found there an open door

1 Greek, dunamis.

116

everywhere. The reason was that He was greatly admired by all in His wonderful ministry of teaching.

1. The second visit of Jesus to Cana (Jno. 4:46-54).

The first visit was on the occasion of the wedding feast soon after the baptism and temptations of Jesus. On that occasion He had performed His first miracle, turning the water into wine. Now more than a year later He returns, probably in the winter of 27-28 A. D. He had spent some time teaching in the synagogues of Galilee with great acceptance, and His disciples, meantime, had gone back to their old trades.

Now He initiates His work of healing in a signal way in Cana, the little town which was the birth-place of Nathanael. Cana was located on a hill in the little plain of El Battauf. The "reedy place," which is the site of the ancient village, is now desolate, a hunting ground where leopards are encountered among the broken ruins of the modern village. A short distance from the place is to be seen the prosperous village of Sefurigeh, which stands where the ancient capital of Galilee, "Sepphoris," was located.[1]

Jesus went first to Cana instead of Nazareth. His first miracle would serve as a preparation for His ministry there, now. He would find a lodging place in the home of Nathanael. His disciples were not with Him when He visited Nazareth and so gave just a summary account of the happenings of that sad visit.

An officer in the service of Herod Antipas had a little boy, who had been wasting away with a continued fever in Capernaum. It is impossible to know if this officer was either Chuza, Herod's steward, or Manaen, his foster-brother (Luke 8:3; Acts 13:1). He heard that Jesus was already come out of Judea into Galilee. In his desperation he came to Him and began to beg Him and continued begging that He might come down at once and heal his little boy. He expressed a hope that this Rabbi might be able to heal his son, basing his faith on the current idea that Rabbis had healed some aggravated cases of sickness through prayer. He reported that the child was desperately ill — just about to die.

The request was not granted at first by Jesus. He was no mere Rabbi or benevolent physician to work local cures at the beck and call of any sufferer. Many were wondering at His miracles done in His Judean ministry. The fame of His cures had come before Him to Galilee, but few were giving thought to His message of salvation. He must guard against this materialistic tendency. He would have those who were not sick seek Him also; not merely those who were in desperate illness. Jesus repulses the request with the frank statement that "unless the nobleman should see

1 Life of Christ, Geikie. Ch. XXIX

signs or wonders" his feeble faith would not stand the test. He was like those Jews who stubbornly refused to believe in Jesus unless they should first see some miracle. But the request of the nobleman was in itself an expression of faith, though an imperfect one.

"Lord" cried the anguish-stricken father, "come down before my little boy dies." This agonized entreaty showed that the officer was not a mere sign seeker, but bore a great sorrow in his heart, which he now brought in hope to the Lord. Such a prayer never met with refusal when offered to Jesus. But in granting his request the Lord would further test and strengthen the nobleman's incipient faith.

"Go on your way," said Jesus, "your son is living." He had believed Jesus could cure the child if He would come down to Capernaum; will he believe that the cure can be effected in the distance? His faith stood the test. He started on his way instantly, "believing in the word of Jesus."

This eager father would be anxious to confirm his hope in verifying the cure but it was more than twenty miles from Cana (Kefr Kenna) to Capernaum. It was the seventh hour when Jesus spoke the word of cure. Soothed by his faith in the word of Jesus, the nobleman doubtless spent the night at some intermediate point, since a Jew would not pursue such a journey after dusk. On the journey homeward the next morning he was met by his servants. They reported that the little boy was living. Eagerly the father received this glad news and inquired the hour when he began to mend. The servants were not certain just exactly what time, but it was during the seventh hour[1] that the fever had left him. Then the father remembered that it was just at the seventh hour, that Jesus had said: "Thy son is living."

At once this nobleman rose to the height of a saving faith in Jesus, and in this led his whole household into a vital union with Christ. John adds that this was the second miracle performed by Jesus in Galilee; though He had wrought many in Jerusalem (Jno. 3:23).

2. The first rejection in Nazareth (Luke 4:16-31).

After preaching for some time and in various places in Galilee, Jesus came to His home town, Nazareth. He had probably moved His mother's family to Capernaum before this visit, as the statement of Luke, that He "had been reared there," would seem to indicate. Jesus would want to give Nazareth a good opportunity to receive the gospel after His reputation had been well established

---

1 Accusative case, duration of time.

in the surrounding regions and in Judea. Later on in His ministry He came back again, in spite of His being rejected on the first visit (Mark 6:1-6).

Jesus came into the synagogue on the sabbath day according to the habit He had formed in early life. If the boy does not form the habit of going to church the man will not follow that custom. In the worship of the synagogues, which since the restoration from Babylonian captivity had played so large a part in Jewish life, there were three persons who participated: the reader, the interpreter, and the expounder or preacher. On the sabbath and certain festive occasions there were several readers. Two lessons were read: one the *parashah* was from the Law and the other called the *haphtorah* from the prophets. Two prayers preceded the first reading. When the selection from the Law had been read, Jesus, invited by the chief of the ten leading elders, took His place to read the lesson from the prophets. The Chazzan, or school-master clerk of the synagogue, took from the ark of painted wood the roll of the prophet Isaiah, and handed it to Him. In the chief seats before Him were the ten leading elders, and behind them ranged the congregation, the men on one side and the women on the other of a lattice division in the middle of the synagogue.

When Jesus rose to read, the congregation stood to listen. The selection might be from three to twenty-one verses. He unrolled the parchment, rolling up the other side, and continued until He found the place of His choice. Instead of reading twenty-one verses or even three, He read part of the first verse and a part of the second of chapter 61 and interpolated in the midst a phrase from verse 6 of chapter 58.

> *"The Spirit of the Lord Jehovah is upon me;*
> *Because he anointed me to evangelize the poor;*
> *He hath sent me to herald release to the captives;*
> *And recovering of sight to the blind;*
> *To set at liberty them that are bruised,*
> *To proclaim the acceptable year of the Lord."*

What a remarkable selection of Messianic scripture! We may well imagine the grandeur and solemnity of the words, as they were read by the Messiah Himself. He had read in the Hebrew, translated into the Aramaic, and now closed the book and sat down in the elevated seat of the preacher to deliver His sermon, according to the custom among the Jews. The eyes of all in the synagogue were gazing fixedly upon Him, with their necks craned to see Him and not lose a word. They were spell-bound with eager attention. He began to speak to them.

The last words of the scripture read suggested the subject for
His expository sermon: "The year of Jehovah's favor." Luke gives
this sermon the prominence, in his gospel, that Matthew ascribes
to the Sermon on the Mount (Matt. 5-7). The first words of the
sermon expressed a daring claim to His Messiahship, in veiled
form. "The real year of Jubilee had come," the preacher said, "and
this messianic prophecy was fulfilled already in their ears." He
spoke with an inspiration, eloquence, and felicity which was irresistible. The new era of the Messiah had come, manifesting
Jehovah's tender love for the poor (meek), heralding liberty for
those taken captive in war, bringing the recovery of sight to the
blind, and setting at liberty those broken in body and spirit. Individual as well as social ills were to be cared for by the Messiah,
who was a spiritual, and not merely a temporal Deliverer. Just
such work Jesus had been doing in Galilee. Of this His hearers
were not ignorant. The fame of His cure of the nobleman's little
boy in Capernaum had reached them a short while before this,
along with reports of His signs and wonders done in Jerusalem
and Judea. The acceptable year of the Lord was to be an era of
grace to all classes and conditions of mankind! In the mouth of
Jesus the words of grace were gracious words which thrilled His
audience. According to the Jews the synagogue preacher ought
to be a man of good figure, pleasant expression, and melodious
voice. Without doubt Jesus fulfilled all these requirements.

What was to be the outcome of His wonderful discourse? They
all began to bear witness. At first there was admiration and
wonder at the gracious words which fell as music on their ears
and balm upon their wounded and hungry hearts. As He proceeded
with His discourse, a life-giving stream of these words poured out
continuously from His lips. It was customary for the Jews to give
vent to their feelings in the synagogue worship. Here was the
fulfillment of the promises, the realization of hopes, the satisfaction
of heart-hunger. So there were expressions in the after-sermon
hour, of admiration at first, which were soon mingled with expressions of doubt and then open criticism.

"Is not this the son of Joseph?" they said. Jesus had passed
in Nazareth for the son of Joseph. For Him to present Himself now
in His home town as the Messiah was too much for the credulity
of the people. So their mood of wonder and praise soon turned to
whispers and nods of doubt and hostility. How could this young
carpenter reared in their town make such claims for Himself. Even
some of His own family did not believe in Him. Let Him prove His
reputation, if He would, by doing some sign!

Jesus read their thoughts intuitively. You will be saying to

Me this proverb: "Physician, heal thyself!" Many people cannot see their friends and neighbors succeed! "What we heard was done in Capernaum," they said, "do here in your own country now." They were curious to see some of the miracles such as He was reputed to have performed in Capernaum, but He would not satisfy their idle curiosity. Again He solemnly cites the proverb He had already used before in slightly different form: "No prophet is received in his own country." But it was not the fault of Jesus, who was a prophet and more than a prophet.

It was customary for the preacher to answer questions and exchange ideas with his auditors at the conclusion of his discourse. Jesus perceiving their unspiritual comments and hostile attitude, made application of His sermon citing two illustrations from the ministries of Elijah and Elisha. Nazareth was no better than Tyre or Sidon, nor Galilee than Syria, before the sovereignty of God. His miracles were not just for them. He was no mere Nazarene. If they rejected His message they were not as good as the widow woman of Sarepta to whom God sent Elijah, when for Israel's sins the drouth held the land for three and a half years! In Elisha's time Naaman the Syrian was cleansed, while many lepers in Israel perished. The illustrations were pointed and the application was severe. God's grace which was so wonderful for the individual was also universal. He had pierced to the heart of their local pride and narrow patriotism, and laid bare their unbelief and the just consequences which would follow.

They were filled with wrath and their fury burst out into a flame. This strange, violent, impassioned people rose up and thrust Him forth outside the town, and were jostling and pushing Him along toward the brow of the hill whereon the town had been built. Their purpose was to crowd Him and push Him over the precipice forty feet high, which is pointed out today by travelers as the probable site of this incident. They hoped thus to escape the technical guilt. Murder was in their hearts. But He, doubtless with a commanding look of majesty, stood the mob off before they carried out their wicked design, and passing through their midst proceeded on His solitary way to Capernaum. This incident was typical of the whole gracious ministry of Jesus, beginning with the proclamation of God's favor and ending for Him in death-perils.

3. The new home in Capernaum (Matt. 4:13-17).

It was Matthew who recorded the coming of Jesus to Capernaum to live. Rejected in His own city of Nazareth now, He had before, perhaps in anticipation, brought His mother and the younger children, except the half-sisters, and established their home in this principal city of Galilee. This was the most strategic center He could have chosen for His ministry just begun. Here He was in a prosperous and busy city in the heart of a populous district, around the beautiful sea of Chinnereth where there were ten other towns, and also on the great international highway connecting Damascus and the Levant.

The exact site of Capernaum is disputed, but the arguments are in favor of Tell Hum four miles southwest of the entrance of the Jordan into the lake, as against Khan Minjeh four miles further down. This is the traditonal burial place of the ancient prophet Nahum. Beautifully located just to the north of the fertile plain of Gennesaret, the richest spot in Palestine, which was watered by five streamlets and was prolific in the production of a great variety of fruits and vegetables, it was a beehive of indus-tries, principal of which was that of fishing. The ruins of Tell Hum just to the east of the spring Tabighah, Josephus called Capernaum, because all the land from this fountain east to the Jordan belonged to this city. The Rabbis praised greatly this fair region giving it the name of "Gardens of the Princes." From the agriculture and horticulture surrounding the town, Jesus derived many of His beautiful illustrations and parables. The town must have covered an area a half mile in length running north and south and a quarter in breadth, as indicated by the ruins. At the end nearest the lake are found great blocks of carved white lime-stone which likely constituted the frieze, architrave, and cornices of the synagogue, built by one of the foreign officers, doubtless a proselyte to the Jewish faith. Being a boundary town between the tetrarchies of Antipas and Philip, there was a custom house located there as well as a Roman garrison.

The people, made up of various classes, were possessed of plenty and were generous in their entertainment even to the point of being called "gluttonous and winebibbers." There were many travelers passing through by the caravan route *Via Maris*. In this accessible center of a teeming population Jesus found a large opportunity. He had already healed the courtier's son in this town, while He was in Cana, and five of His disciples, Peter, Andrew, James, John, and Philip lived here. They had doubtless told many of their fellow-townsmen about the wonderful young Rabbi of Nazareth. When He brought His mother and the younger children, except the sisters who were likely married, He established their home probably in a house furnished by Peter. The family would not want to live in Nazareth, after Jesus was thus treated by the people there, even if they might not share in the persecution. These disciples lived in the fisher-town suburb of Capernaum called Bethsaida. In this quiet suburb it is likely that Jesus "made His home," for the permanent abode of His mother's family. Near by was the spring Tabighah and above it a vantage point commanding a beautiful view of the lake and surrounding regions, where Jesus may have spent many an hour of prayerful meditation alone or with His small disciple band.

Matthew found in the coming of Jesus, to live in Capernaum and work in this city and the surrounding regions, the fulfillment of the prophecy of Isaiah (9:1f).

"The land of Zebulun and the land of Naphtali,
The way of the sea, beyond the Jordan,
Galilee of the Nations,
The people which sat in darkness
Saw a great light,
And to them which sat in the region and the shadow
of death,
To them a light sprang up."

Capernaum was situated on the "road of the sea or Via Maris." Israel had first come to the east of the Jordan and all the country west was the region "beyond the Jordan." There were many foreigners in Galilee. Owing to this fact this region was spoken of as "Galilee of the Gentiles." Matthew applies the words about the deliverer from Assyrian bondage, to the Messiah. A new era dawned for that region which lay in spiritual darkness, when the Great Deliverer came to Capernaum. Matthew had been one who had sat in the region and shadow cast by death (personified). There at the receipt of custom he had sat and had seen Jesus passing by and heard sometimes His words, until that wonderful day, when with a love-look that thrilled his whole being, Jesus had said to him, the despised publican: "Follow me." When Jesus came, the promise to the early exiles was fulfilled. The great Reality had come when the Orient-Sun appeared in the preaching and teaching of the Christ!

The work of Jesus in Galilee, He now began in earnest. His message reenforced that of John the Baptist, taking up where he left off. "Repent for the Kingdom of Heaven has drawn nigh," He heralded. He had not come to destroy or replace the work of John but to fulfill and carry forward what His forerunner had begun. To John's message reiterated, He added a new element of His own: "Believe in the gospel, the Good Tidings of God." He had brought the good tidings of pardon and peace, forgiveness and joy, redemption and righteousness, justification, sanctification and glorification. There is no wonder that the multitudes soon hung upon the words of such a message of grace and of such a gracious Messenger!

4. The call of four fishermen to become fishers of men (Mark 1:16-20; Matt. 4:18-22; Luke 5:1-11).

When Jesus returned from Judea through Samaria to Galilee, the six disciples who had been with Him seem to have returned to their own homes and occupations. They had been convinced of His Messiahship and had spent some time with Him in the brief ministry of six months in Judea. But we do not find them with Him on the occasion of His rejection in Nazareth.

Jesus views now His new field of action in Galilee from the vantage point of Capernaum, its most strategic center. He must begin to widen the activities of His ministry and build solidly the new society of His Kingdom. In doing this, He must have regard for the deepening in individual lives of His influence as well as the broadening of the Kingdom by teaching large numbers.

Already His name and fame had preceded Him in Capernaum. It may have been a day or two after His arrival, that as He was passing along by the sea a crowd gathered about Him, and while He was standing by the lake the crowd "grew into a multitude," which in its eagerness to hear the word of God "pressed upon Him."

It is not strange that Jesus saw two boats of Simon's standing by the lake. He had doubtless come down to this very place, knowing that here He would find the fishermen-acquaintances who had already professed their faith in Him. Jesus went after people definitely and followed up work already begun in other days. These fishermen were not in the boats but had gone out after a night of fishing and were washing and mending their nets to hang them out to dry.

With the informality and confidence of understanding friendship, He entered into Simon's boat, and asked him to put out a little from the land. Then sitting down, He was teaching the multitudes using the boat as His pulpit, while the whole beautiful scene was lit up by the early morning sun reflected in the mirrored surface of the lake. Jesus had been watching these fishermen partners casting their round throw-nets first over the shoulder of one side then over the other to the other side. Now, He casts the gospel net from their boat, that they may understand the work better, to which He will shortly call them.

When He ceased speaking, He turned and addressed Simon as master of the craft: "Put out into the deep," He said, "and let down your large net for a catch." His tones were those of authority and Peter who was a master-craftsman recognized them as such. Peter was an experienced fisherman but he had just exhausted his resources in a vain night of *toil* and had caught nothing.

Now, the Carpenter-Rabbi tells them with assurance to let down the big net for a catch. Jesus had commanded and though Peter had no faith in the outcome, he obeyed. "Superintendent, on the basis of your word!" he said, and let down the net.

When they did this, they shut together in the folds of the net a great multitude of fish. Marvel of marvels, the nets were actually tearing in two and their Zebedee partners were far away near the shore! They beckoned to them to come and take hold, with them, of the tearing nets. They in turn hastened to assist, and all working together filled both the boats up to the point that they were just about to sink. Once again their eyes beheld a miracle over nature and they remembered the conversion of water into wine in the marriage feast of Cana.

The effect on the impulsive Peter was instantaneous. He fell down at Jesus' knees. Like young Isaiah who cried out in the temple-vision the confession of his sins, Peter besought with great reverence and awe the "Lord" of the moral realm, to "depart from his unworthy presence," "for," said he, "I am a sinful man." Wonder held Peter fast as it did all his fishermen-partners because of the draught of fish which they had taken. So great was the spell of awe cast over them that it amounted almost to fear.

"Do not fear," said Jesus, addressing Peter again, "from now on you shall be catching men alive and to life." They understood that this was a definite call to accompany Him, leaving behind their occupations and their relatives — a call to discipleship and service. When they came to the land He added to Peter and Andrew: "Hither, after me and I will make you fishers of men." Going forward a little to where Zebedee and his two sons, James and John, were, He repeated the call with a slight alteration in the words: "I will make you to become fishers of men." They had already professed belief in Him; now they are called to leave their lucrative business and become learners in the school of Christ, that they may later become apostles in His service. Jesus definitely undertakes the task of making fishers of men out of these humble fishermen. They did not question the outcome now, as they had when He told them to let down their large nets. They simply confided in His power. Leaving Zebedee their father with the hired men to carry on the fishing business, they joined the other pair of brothers, Peter and Andrew, and followed Jesus.

The significance of the call of these four humble fishermen to become fishers of men is tremendous. It was not the mere act of a Jewish Rabbi calling around him a small group of neophytes — a common procedure. No Rabbi or even ancient prophet of Israel

had ever used this same appeal or set before the world the same
ideal. "Follow me," said Jesus, "and I will make you fishers of
living men." He proposed to found a new Kingdom society around
His own person. Other great teachers of Israel and philosophers
of the world, had called attention to their own doctrines, appealing
to the loyalty of men; but Jesus makes loyalty to His own person
and example the basis of the new social order. Personal affection
and attachment to Him was to be the transforming and impelling
motive power. Love of truth and enthusiasm for humanity might
fail, but personal love and loyalty to Him would take the fisherman
from his nets, the farmer from his fields, the artisan from his
trade, and transform them by the alchemy of personal influence
into discerning disciples and able apostles of the new Kingdom
ideal and its King. Such an appeal would be universal, reaching
the high and the low alike. The friendship of Jesus was extended
to the pariahs of society and to the respectable sinner too. He began
at the lowest strata of society and lifted man by His sympathetic
association into a new environment. He was to give the world the
spectacle of a new society composed of men freed from worldly
aims, animated by the same motives of unselfishness, reconciled to
poverty and hardship, and employed in altruistic tasks.

5. In the synagogue in Capernaum Jesus teaches with authority
and expels a demon (Mark 1:21-28; Luke 4:31-37).

Mark vividly portrays the incidents of this period. Using the
historic present he says: "And they are going into Capernaum."
Jesus and the four disciples had been in the fisher-town suburb
Bethsaida when the call of the four occurred. It must have been
Friday when Jesus came into Capernaum. At the setting of the
sun, the beginning of the Sabbath was announced by three blasts of
a trumpet from the roof of the synagogue, the sign that all secular
work must cease, the sabbath light be kindled in every home and
kept burning till the sabbath ended.

The synagogue services would begin at nine o'clock the next
morning. The people knew that the young Nazarene Rabbi would
be there, since there was only one synagogue in the town — the
one built for them by the wealthy proselyte centurion.

The synagogue was one of the most democratic of all institutions among the Jews. It was controlled by the people through
certain rulers chosen from among ten elders. Its twofold purpose
was for worship and the study of the Scriptures, corresponding
roughly to our prayer meetings, Sunday Schools, and preaching
services combined. The service embraced prayer, praise, reading
of the Scripture, and exposition by any rabbi or other competent

person. The people took part in reciting the shema or public confession of faith, and in certain prayers which preceded and followed the reading of the passages from the law. The reading from
the prophets was next followed by an address by any itinerant
scribe or rabbi, who also allowed questions and discussion by the
auditors. The Ruler of the synagogue had charge of the service.
Three out of the ten elders of the synagogue had jurisdiction over
civil cases within their districts, including those of theft, debt, loss,
restitution, seduction, the admission of proselytes, and elections.
Three deacons cared for the poor, collecting alms for this purpose.
There were two services on the Sabbath, in the forenoon and evening, and two during the week, on Monday and Thursday.

There was a synagogue in every important town. The ruins
of the synagogue in Capernaum (Tell Hum) are yet in such a
state of preservation that there has been talk of restoring the
building. A great crowd gathered on this Sabbath, doubtless, expecting possibly to hear the new rabbi whose family had just
moved to their town. And they were not disappointed; for straight-
way coming into the synagogue Jesus *was teaching them.*

The effect of His teaching was remarkable. They were deeply
and strangely moved, with the contending emotions of wonder,
joy, almost fear at times. He spoke with a startling independence
and the charming originality of a teacher whose appeal was to
spiritual truth or reality. This was a new note to them. They
had been accustomed to hearing the rabbis quote extensively the
opinions of their predecessors, claiming no authority to say a
word of their own. Their sermons were a tiresome reiteration of
traditional rabbinical rules and ceremonial details, which hung
as a burdensome yoke on the necks of the people. The preaching
of Jesus was different. His fervid words stirred their hearts and
brought a great new light and relief to their jaded and burdened
spirits. The Scribes had neglected spiritual religion in favor of
the punctilious etiquette of ceremonialism. Here was a preacher
who made His appeal direct to the Scriptures and to God. At the
conclusion of His sermon a hum of comment ran through the
audience. Both Mark and Luke explain the reason for the continued amazement that held the people. All the way through His
sermon, the preacher was teaching them as one who held in His
own possession the authority and right to speak the final words
to their hungry hearts. His discourse was cast evidently within
the sphere of authority and divine prerogative. It was in complete contrast to the dull droning out of rabbinical rules by the
Scribes. The authority of this preacher, expressed in words, man-

ner, character, in His whole personality, was in His deep understanding of their spiritual needs, their soul hunger, and in His
ability to meet those needs. The mixed multitude that crowded
the synagogue to its utmost capacity was in great exictement.
"What is this," they said, "a new teaching?"

Just at this juncture came an incident which added to their
excitement. In the midst of the crowded synagogue was a man
who had a spirit of an unclean demon. The devil was in the man
and Mark adds that the man was in the sphere or grip of the
unclean spirit. This demon-possessing and possessed man, in his
confused dual personality, cried out with a loud voice, interrupting
the service and sending a chill of horror through the half superstitious audience. "Ah, what have we to do with thee, thou Jesus
of Nazareth. Art thou come to destroy us? I know thee who thou
art, the Saint of God." In contemperaneous phraseology this man
was a degenerate, victim of his own evil acts and habits, revealing
themselves in a deranged mental condition as well as in his physical appearance, words, and actions. There was a duality of consciousness revealed in the words addressed to Jesus. The powers
of the man were intermittently under the full domination of the
demon. He was convulsed and driven hither and thither involun-
tarily by the devil. At the same time it was by his own will that
he was possessing or having the demon within.

Demon possession is a difficult subject. The Jews believed
that many different kinds of diseases were attributable to demons,
which according to Josephus were the souls of departed evil men.
This popular belief in demons was shared by the Egyptians and
other ancient peoples. The idea of demoniacal possession originated in Persia. Physical distempers, especially epilepsy and mental derangement, were attributed to the influence of demons, despite
the contrary opinion of physicians. Not all the people ascribed
all diseases to demons, but there was a popular superstition "that
the backbone of a person who did not bow down to worship God
became a Shed or demon."

There were men professing to be able by the black art to
expel demons. They lived apart as ascetics, "mascerating themselves, and fasting to secure the fuller aid and inspiration of such
evil spirits." The Jews were not supposed to practice magic; but
in this their theory did not accord with their practice. Josephus
describes the wisdom, learning, and achievements of Solomon, referring especially to his skill in expelling demons, who caused various
diseases (Antiq. 3:2-5). Under certain circumstances the repetition
of magical formulas was declared lawful even on the Sabbath day.
According to Josephus, Eleazar, a Jewish exorcist, in the presence

of Vespasian, his sons, and his officers, applied to the nostrils of a demoniac a ring which had under its seal one of the roots prescribed by Solomon, and drew out the demon, who overturned a basin of water nearby, as he departed in obedience to the orders of the exorcist. There was an elaborate system of superstitious demonology current in the popular beliefs of the Jews, and as elaborate a system of the magic art of exorcism.

Jesus did not share in the superstitious beliefs. He never mingled His teachings with current superstitions. He never made a statement which has been discredited by the progress of human knowledge.[1] Moreover, He did not practice any kind of exorcism. Exorcists practiced on the credulity and superstition of the people, using mesmeric and sleight-of-hand methods. It would be wholly contrary to the character of Jesus and His method to suppose that He would have recourse to any phase of the black art of magic.

How then are we to interpret the phenomenon of demon-possession? Evidently the narratives of Mark and Luke are to be received at face value. Both represent the man as speaking of himself in the plural. "What have *we* in common with thee, thou Jesus of Nazareth?" "Didst thou come to destroy *us?*" Both the narratives clearly represent Jesus as addressing the demon: "Hold your peace" (be muzzled like an ox) "and come out of him." This language conveys the idea of two persons — that of the man and that of the demon. Furthermore, Jesus was not willing to receive the testimony of identification from such a reproachful source. "I know who you are, the Holy One of God." Here the demon is speaking of himself alone, not of the man, though he made use of the physical powers of the man in so doing. On other occasions, demons called Jesus the Son of God (Matt. 8:29). The demon was fearful in the presence of Jesus and gave forth a horrible scream that sent a shiver through the multitude. Jesus addressed the demon calmly, commanding him to come out of the man, thus treating the demon as a real spirit, in the domination of the man. He manifested in these words at the same time His power over the demon world.

The result proved the power of Jesus. Instantly, the demon threw the man down in a paroxysm in the midst, tearing him violently, and with another blood-curdling screech came out of him. Luke the physician notes that the demon did the man no permanent injury. This was not a mere case of epilepsy, though that disease might have accompanied demoniacal possession. Here

1 Romanes: Thoughts on Religion p. 157.

was an evident case of dual personality no less credible than that of the "indwelling of the Holy Spirit" in the theology of Paul. The effect of this evident miracle was to reenforce the wonder of the people. They were fairly swept from their feet. His teaching had amazed them. It was a "new teaching" with authority behind it. The buzz of excited comment filled the synagogue. He is even "commanding the unclean spirits with power and authority, and they are obeying him and coming out," they said. It is no wonder that rumor took wings and flew into every place of the whole region of Galilee round about. He had rung the bell of the universe. The fame of this day's sermon and of His power over demons would soon draw great multitudes from all the surrounding country about Him.

6.   Jesus heals Peter's wife's mother and many others (Mark 1:29-34; Matt. 8:14-17; Luke 4:38-41).

Jesus rose up from the seat of the speaker, and immediately when they had come out of the synagogue, He went home with Peter and Andrew, who also took along with them as their guests James and John. Peter was married before he became a disciple of Jesus, and had moved with his family from Bethsaida near the Jordan to a suburb of Capernaum not far from the synagogue. Clement of Alexandria says that Peter's wife helped him later in ministering to the women. He also says that Peter and Philip had children. On entering the house, they tell Jesus of Peter's mother-in-law who was sick. When Jesus came in He saw her and they besought Him for her.

Matthew says she was lying there bedridden, *stretched out.* Mark adds graphically, that she was *prostrate* with a burning fever. Luke the physician noted, that it was a *continued* fever, and adds the current medical discrimination of a *great* in contrast with a *small* fever (Galen).

One prayerful request from the afflicted family of friends was sufficient. Jesus stood over her as a kindly sympathetic physician, tenderly touched her hand to awaken her faith and expectation, rebuked the raging fever as He rebuked the boisterous waves in the storm on Galilee, and taking her by the hand raised her up. The raging fever, like the boisterous waves, obeyed His will. It left her at once. Immediately her full strength came without convalescence, in spite of the high fever with which she had suffered, and she arose from her bed and went about the domestic activities, ministering to Him and those with Him. What better way could she express her gratitude to Him. And she continued, we must believe, to minster to Him in this same way at intervals during the

whole period of His ministry; for it seems that the home of Peter
became the lodging place for Jesus whenever He was in Capernaum.
Peter was well-to-do and Jesus found there an open-handed and
insistent hospitality, from this very day. He could not desire
to burden His widowed mother with His disciple band. Doubtless
Peter's wife's mother had great joy in the domestic ministrations,
when Jesus and His disciples were the guests. She was the first
deaconess of the new Christian society, in the humble domestic
role, which has down through the centuries of Christian hospitality
been graced by many a grateful and beautiful spirit, in service unrecognized by the Master.

After the hospitable repast, Jesus would rest a while in the
joyful fellowship of this home, while rumor flew on the wings
of the wind to every quarter of the town and surrounding country,
about this additional wonder of supernatural cure in the home
of Simon.

A frenzy of hope seized the multitudes of those who had sick
ones in their houses or among their friends, and they hastily prepared to bring them to the new prophet who was performing such
astounding miracles in cure. Some even made use of the special
permission given to bear the sick at the end of the Sabbath day
(Vincent), and started early on their way bringing them to Jesus.
It is to be noted here that no objection was raised to these cures
on the Sabbath. The opposition of the Scribes and Pharisees had
not yet arisen. When the evening wore on they began to appear
and when the sun was just setting, crowds poured in from every
quarter of the town and adjacent places.

And now the sun has set behind the hills to the west of
Galilee. Its last rays, yet reflected from the summits of the mountains to the east, light up the waters of the lake, touching its
mirrored surface into a thousand hues. Small groups of eager men
and women, bearing those with every variety of disease, press
in around the home where Jesus was being entertained. So great
was the multitude, that "all the city," apparently, was gathered
together in front of Simon's house. The sick embraced all varieties
of diseases, including chronic maladies. These poor sick folk had
been having a bad time of it.[1]

What a beautiful scene, as Jesus comes forth to the door of
the house to minister to these diseased and suffering ones! The
vividness of Mark's description reminds us that Peter must have
looked upon this memorable scene with pride and gratitude. One
by one they brought the sick ones and He was laying His hands

1 Greek text, having it badly

on every one of them and healing them. There was one exception to this regular process. They brought those possessed of demons. These, Jesus cast out with His word of authority one after another. There were many of them. They cried out in fear: "Thou art the Son of God"; but Jesus kept on forbidding them to repeat their testimony. They knew that He was the Messiah, and their testimony would not help His cause but rather bring complications.

Matthew found in this wonderful day of cures in Capernaum a fulfillment of the prophecy of Isaiah (Isa. 53:4): "Himself took our infirmities and bare our diseases." He removed their sufferings from the sufferers. Jesus sympathized with the sufferers to the point of feeling their weaknesses and pains. The great passage in the prophecy of Isaiah (ch. 53) undoubtedly refers to Christ's suffering for men as their substitute. He took upon Himself our sin and so brings relief for all the distresses produced by sin. Christians must suffer, for their discipline, but they will not suffer punishment. By the blood of Christ, the believer is relieved, to some extent in this life and completely in eternity, of the results of his sins. Jesus suffered with those whom He saw suffer. He became weary and exhausted through His work of healing. He bore the burden of the world on His heart.

CHAPTER XI

THE FIRST PREACHING TOUR IN GALILEE

(Harm. §§ 44-48)

The work of Jesus in Galilee was now fully begun. He had tested out the situation in Nazareth and verified His expectation that His home town would not be the proper center for His headquarters in the Galilean ministry. He had given that city a chance and His fellow-townsmen had rejected Him decisively. After that decision His choice of the new and at the same time the most strategic center of the whole province for His work was fully justified. The curing of the Courtier's son helped prepare the way for a glad reception and His first-won disciple friends had moved there from Bethsaida. So His mother's family, for which He felt a large responsibility, finding Nazareth an inhospitable place in which to live, had moved to this town, whose name would be forever linked up with that of the Master. Very soon after Jesus came there, the four disciples had been definitely called to lay down their secular occupations and accompany the new Teacher. The first great Sabbath day's experiences had sent the name and fame of the new Teacher out into every place in the region round about. His preaching was the talk of the town and the like of His miracles had never been seen.

1. Jesus makes His first tour of Galilee with the four fishermen-disciples (Mark 1:35-39; Matt. 4:23-25; Luke 4:42-44).

This is the first of the three tours made by Jesus in Galilee. The second time He took the twelve with Him and the third He sent the twelve ahead by twos and followed after them.

The Sabbath day's great activity in Capernaum brought on such a popular movement as to render impossible the temporary stay of Jesus in the city. He foresaw such a crisis, and despite the apparent need of long hours of repose after such a full day, He rose in the early part of the fourth watch of the night and quietly passed out from the home and town into a solitary place for prayer. He fled from popularity and the complications it would bring, to the secret place of prayer. Temptation came to Him to follow the path of ease and public favor rather than the difficult way of duty. He "was praying there" through the dark hours. And when it was day He went yet further into the desert place. He understood clearly that He must leave the miracle-seeking multitude and go to other places, where His preaching could be carried on without interruption.

It was not long until Simon and those with him discovered that the Master had disappeared. He had lingered long, and the

133

multitudes were gathering again with their sick to be cured. So Simon and the others went in search and literally "hunted Him down" (Vulgate, perecutus est) until they found Him in His favorite place of prayer.

"All are seeking thee!" they said. To these disciples Jesus seemed to be losing splendid opportunities to minister to the needs of the multitudes and receive the glory of men. His reply was a surprise and disappointment to them.

"Let us go elsewhere into the neighboring village-cities or country-towns that I may preach there." A misplaced over-emphasis on institutional, eleemosynary and educational endeavor has often swamped the progress of world evangelization. Jesus put the preaching of the good tidings of the Kingdom of God in the first place. More important still is the clear understanding Jesus had of the nature of the *Kingdom of God.* His was not the Kingdom of the current Messianic hope. The Messiah of Jewish legend and tradition would not have left the open door of popularity in Capernaum as Jesus did. Miracles were a necessity, when the God-Man came in contact with disease and misery, from the very nature of the case.[1] But miracles often impeded the progress of the more important and fundamental work of His ministry as in this case. Jesus did not conceive of the "Kingdom of God" as a temporal Kingdom. It was not His purpose to become the center of an admiring populace by working miracles. On the other hand, His miracles were but a secondary consideration and means to the greater end of bringing men into the Kingdom of God, as are modern medical missions. Another important consideration was His clear expression of His recognition of a divine mission. He was conscious of a great purpose in His life and ministry; that "He came forth," from God for world evangelization. He "was sent forth," the Apostle of God to men. And His mission was an impartial one, as the sequel shows. The influence and activities of His ministry alike reached the people of Syria to the north, all Galilee including the Gentile elements, Decapolis, to the east of the sea, Jerusalem and Judea to the south, and Perea, the region beyond the Jordan river. Following out His announced plan, Jesus went about preaching in every part of Galilee. There is very little told us about this great preaching tour. It was begun in prolonged prayer. Jesus took the four fishermen with Him. His first point of attack was in the synagogue, though He often preached also in the open air in towns which had no synagogues. His glad message everywhere centered around the subject of the "Kingdom of God." Another phase of His synagogue ministrations was that of teaching. Jesus was the greatest of all teachers. Many

1 Edersheim. "Life and Times of Jesus" Ch. XV.

times. He was addressed by His disciples and others as teacher
(didaskalos). He emphasized the importance of the work of
religious education and education in true religion of the Kingdom.
The other phrase of the work of Christ was that of *healing.* He laid
the foundation for all true humanitarian effort for the healing of
the body and the physical betterment of mankind. Mental instruction, spiritual redemption, and physical restoration and development constituted His full-orbed program.

Mark, in his brief account, only refers to the casting out of
demons, the most aggravated malady of all. But Matthew refers to
the fact that they brought even from Syria all those who were held
in the grasp of various diseases, which the doctors could not cure
—the difficult chronic cases. He mentions three of these tortuous
maladies: demon possession, lunacy or "moonstruck" epilepsy, and
paralysis. Jesus was continually healing[1] these difficult cases.
The result as might be expected was that great crowds coming
from all the regions round about, even to Syria, Decapolis, Jerusalem, and Perea, followed Him wherever He went.

2. The astounding cure of a leper causes great excitement (Mark
1:40-45; Matt. 8:2-4; Luke 5:12-16).

Only one miracle from the first tour of Galilee is recorded
definitely. Up to this time in His ministry He had not healed a
leper so far as the gospel record goes. This case was reported,
perhaps, because of its extraordinary character. Even then the
narrative does not give the place where it took place, further
than to say it was "while he was in one of the cities."

Leprosy was a terrible and loathsome disease, believed among
the Jews to be a "stroke of God as a punishment for special sin."
It began with little specks on the eyelids and palms of the hands,
and gradually spread first over the surface of the body, and afterwards ate its way through all the tissues rotting the whole body
piecemeal. Death came as a welcome deliverance when the disease finally attacked the vital organs. It was considered by the
Jews to be highly infectious and hereditary to the fourth generation. According to the Talmud, "the blind, the leper, the poor
and the childless were accounted as dead." According to the Old
Testament, eleven principal kinds of defilement are listed which
are capable of communicating other defilements. In all Scripture
there are thirty-two to which Rabbinic tradition added twenty-
nine more. According to Scripture, defilements affected only in
two degrees but the Rabbis added three other degrees. So the
Mishnic section about "clean and unclean" was the largest in
the code. In the list of defilements, leprosy stood second in order,
next to defilement from the dead. The very entrance of a leper

1 See imperfect of the Greek verb.

defiled a habitation. Rabbinism traced this disease variously to
eleven different sins.

Segregation and social ostracism were applied heartlessly in
the treatment of the leper. He was not suffered to enter a walled
town. This is doubtless the explanation of why no lepers were
among those cured on that memorable first Sabbath in Capernaum
when so many sick folks came to Him. The ritual restrictions
were that the leper should warn the passers-by not to come near
him, by rending his outer garment and crying out Unclean!
Unclean! There was not so much fear of physical infection as of
ceremonial pollution by contact with one under the punishment
of God. The leper was obliged to go bareheaded and cover his
mouth, hiding his beard as a mourner in lamentation for the
dead. In later times he was permitted to enter the synagogue, if
he had a part specially partitioned off for himself, which he
would enter before the crowd came and leave after all were out.
If he entered a walled town it was at the peril of the penalty of
forty stripes.

The Rabbis were peculiarly cruel in their treatment of the
leper. According to their regulations no one might salute a leper
or come nearer than six feet to him. If the wind were from that
direction, a hundred feet was too near. Even to eat eggs from a
street where there was a leper was considered by one rabbi to be
dangerous; and others were known to hide out or else to pelt the
approaching leper with stones.

The treatment of Jesus was in utter contrast to that of the
rabbis. His whole attitude and mien laid open the way for this
poor leper who "was full of leprosy" to make his way into the
town and the house to Jesus, first kneeling and then in supplication in continued worshipful attitude, prostrating himself upon
his face and crying out his impassioned prayer: "Lord if thou wilt
thou canst cleanse me." Jesus was deeply moved with compassion
at the sight of the misery of this man, hopelessly covered with the
open sores of this loathsome and incurable disease. He was also
strongly impressed with the extraordinary faith of the man in His
ability to cure one full of leprosy.[1] Immediately He responded to
this call of anguish; and stretching forth His hand touched the
leper saying: "I will; be thou made clean!" To touch a leper was
a violation of the ceremonial law resulting in pollution. It was also
accompanied in the popular conception with the peril of infection.
Jesus passed over the boundaries of all current tradition and ran
all risks in order to minister to dire human need. This was
wholly unlike the rabbis and would also incur for Him their
displeasure and disgust.

1 Third class of conditional sentence, his cure depended on the will of Jesus solely.

The effect was marvelous. Instantly the leprosy departed from him and his flesh became sound. The hand of Jesus was not polluted but the body of the leper became clean.

It was a daring and perilous thing Jesus had done. Only the priest in the temple in Jerusalem was permitted to pronounce a leper clean. There was an elaborate ceremony after a lengthened examination before it could be done. This required much time and called for various rites, sacrifices, and offerings, as well as many ablutions and days of waiting. If this cure were noised abroad it would at once cause trouble. Jesus would be proclaimed as a revolutionist and disloyal to the Law. It was necessary to forestall any such difficulty if possible. So He privately charged the man strictly, with looks, gestures, and tones of uncompromising insistence and earnestness, that he *should tell no man*. Then He sent him out literally "pushing him forth" from the house, with the injunction: "Go and show thyself to the priest and bear the gift that Moses commanded for a testimony to them." All the details of the elaborate ceremony of cleansing must be complied with at once with the utmost secrecy. Otherwise the priest receiving the news first in Jerusalem might refuse to accept him as cured, and Jesus might suffer an interruption in His ministerial activities because of the popular conception of ceremonial pollution. It is likely that the miracle had been performed in the house where only a small circle of the disciples of Jesus were present. There was another peril also. The publishing of so wonderful a cure would inevitably be followed by the same kind of popularity from which Jesus had fled in Capernaum. This would be the main reason for enjoining the utmost secrecy.

But it happened this time, as so often in Jesus' ministry of cures, that when He requested secrecy His desires were not understood or honored. One of the best ways to scatter a thing is to request people not to tell it. No sooner was the man out in the streets of the town than he began "so much the more" to scatter the report everywhere. Perhaps he was moved by gratitude. He might have thought that he knew better than Jesus what should be done. He made a grievous mistake by being disobedient.

The result was just as Jesus had foreseen. Great crowds of curiosity-seekers and sick folk soon thronged Him. He was obliged to withdraw to the desert places of the uplands. He could no longer enter the cities. Even thus, the crowds of miracle-mongers kept coming to Him from every quarter. His fame more and more kept spreading abroad, the multitude continued to pour in, and Jesus went on preaching, healing, and praying. He had broken through the deadly externalism to cure the leper and the people did not object. Still, His campaign through the cities was seriously interrupted for a time by the unreflected disobedience of the man upon whom He had bestowed so great a blessing.

3. Returning from the first tour, Jesus heals a paralytic in Capernaum and encounters opposition (Mark 2:1-12; Matt. 9:1-8; Luke 5:17-26).

It was from the desert places in the uplands across the lake that Jesus, taking a boat, crossed over to Capernaum, now His own city by adoption, and headquarters for His ministry in Galilee. It was some days, we do not know how long, since He had come back from His first tour. News spread abroad that He was at home and great crowds came seeking Him. We don't know how many days this kept up before the cure of the paralytic took place. Luke states that it was "one of those days" while He was engaged in teaching, and when the doctors of the law were in the audience, that this incident of such extraordinary significance transpired.

This is the first account of the organized opposition of the Scribes and Pharisees in Galilee. It was the first definite and determined expression of that antagonism of His enemies, which was destined to increase as a gathering storm, until it should break in fury upon His head at Jerusalem two years later and bring Him to the cross. He had left Judea months ago because of the intrigues of the Jerusalem Pharisees, who sought to bring His disciples and those of John the Baptist into mutual conflict of envy and jealousy. These same enemies had doubtless watched with jealous care this rival, as His popularity waxed greater and greater in Galilee. Recent developments in His campaign in all the cities of that province made it imperative that His movements be watched at close hand by their emissaries. The popularity of Jesus was attracting people from all parts, even from Phoenicia\ on the north to Idumea on the south. They must, as the responsible guardians of the orthodoxy and civil authorities of their nation, curb this insane popular enthusiasm. Their own power was unquestioned in Jerusalem and Judea. Already, they had forced Him to leave those parts. Even in Galilee, despite its spirit of greater tolerance and liberty of thought the influence of their Pharisaic order was great. They were the theologians, the school men, the jurists and legislators. He would not be able to withstand their opposition. The people venerated their law; and were they not themselves the authoritative interpreters of that law?

The character of Jesus was in complete contrast to that of the members of this all-powerful order. He was sincere, while they were full of hypocrisy and religious cant, making a great show of their pretended piety, with their broad phylacteries and long robes with sacred tassels. He was real and intense, pure and elevated, human and sympathetic, open and accessible; while they were ostentatious and vain, corrupt and groveling, exclusive and full of bigotry. His light must needs be in conflict with their darkness, from the very nature of the case. And this was the first sharp hand-to-hand encounter. They had been watching Him closely with cold suspicion; they now resolved to draw their cordon of influence about Him, and to undermine and dispel His popularity and thwart His purposes.

Once again, the great crowd filled the house of Peter and the court-yard, until there was no access even to the door. Peter's house could not have been one of the smallest type, usually occupied by the very poor people. It was one of the better dwellings of the well-to-do classes, built with one story and a flat roof reached by a stairway from the yard or open court. The door opened out into the street and doubtless Jesus was standing where He could be heard by the crowd outside as well as those in the great chamber. The house was packed, so that there were no more places to squeeze into, such was the eagerness of the crowd to see the wonder-working prophet, who had been creating such a sensation throughout Galilee. Even now, He was preaching in the house, and the people craned their necks to get a glimpse of Him. He was preaching the doctrine of the Messianic Kingdom, the great theme which John had preached, but now with certain additions. Would He perform miracles today? They would not have long to wait. Yes, the power of Jehovah was on Him to perform miracles of healing!

Suddenly, there was a stir in the crowd outside. Four men, bearing a poor paralytic on a kind of pallet or hammock, elbow their way into the crowd seeking to effect an entrance. The jam is too great, but they are resolved to get at the Healer. Unable to thread their way through the throng the bearers go around to the side of the house, and making use of the ladder-like steps, succeed in getting their suffering burden on the roof. What next shall they do? There is no inside stairway; so they proceed to "uncover the covering," by removing first the earth and mortar, then the layer of brushwood and short sticks, leaving, between the logs three feet apart which traversed the room from wall to wall, an aperture. This was long enough to lower through it the sick man, by the four corners of his pallet, into the presence of Jesus in the chamber below.

The poor paralytic was stricken not only in body but also in spirit. His blanched lips were unable to utter even his petition.

But his physical malady was not his worst trouble. Looking on his calamity as a punishment of God visited upon him for the sin of a vicious life, he was fearful and troubled. His fear was depicted in his very countenance as he piteously looked up at the Healer. His eyes told the story of his fear, and Jesus divined his repentant thoughts and fearful forebodings. But He also recognized his faith and that of the four men, who had given ample demonstration of their belief in His power and willingness to heal this desperate case.

"Child, be of good cheer," said Jesus, tenderly, "thy sins are already forgiven." There was a current belief among the Jews that physical recovery would not be granted to the sick unless his sins had first been forgiven him. Jesus removed this inward paralysis of guilt before affecting the physical cure. The spell of fear was broken. A new look of hope spread over the countenance of the bed-ridden sufferer, even though his body was yet prostrate on his couch.

Instantly a murmur of disapproval ran through the back of the room. It was depicted on the countenance of the doctors of the law who had been sitting by, coldly and critically watching everything. Now, they were exchanging nods, glances, and whispered comments. They thought Jesus had delivered Himself into their hands. "He is speaking blasphemies," they were saying among themselves with satisfaction, "Who can forgive sins but the *one* God?" These enemies had come up here from all the villages and cities in Galilee, and from Jerusalem and Judea, determined to stay until they could find fault with Jesus and trap Him. He proved to be an easier prey than they had thought. Right here He had assumed the *divine prerogative of forgiving sins.* They whispered, half audibly, among themselves—"He is blaspheming." With hypocrisy, they added, so that they might be heard now by those immediately about them: "Why does this man speak thus? He is blaspheming!" These expressions—yet in subdued tones— created a hostile atmosphere which Jesus immediately sensed. These enemies of Jesus were right in saying that no one but God could forgive sins. This all the Jews understood. Their major premise was true and their logical reasoning sound. But their conclusion was faulty because their minor premise was not true. "Who is this fellow?" They did not know Jesus to be the God-man. "He had laid Himself liable to the penalty of the law for blasphemy. Now, they would put an end to this impostor."

They did not, however, reckon with the resourcefulness of the Nazarene prophet. He immediately perceived by His own spiritual intuition their inmost thoughts and their reasoning among themselves, and said: "Why are you reasoning these evil things in your hearts?" He then laid bare frankly the evil thoughts of their hearts and their calumnious comments whispered against Him. He meets their challenge of His authority to forgive sins with a counter challenge.

"Which is easier to say to the sick of the palsy: 'Thy sins are forgiven thee' or to say, 'Take up thy bed and walk'?" He left them to puzzle over this afterwards for a few moments. They treated His unanswerable question with silence and sullen obstinancy.

Then He adds: "But in order that you may know that the Son of Man has authority and power on earth to take away sins (he says to the sick of the palsy): I say unto thee, Arise, take up thy bed and go unto thy house."

The performance of the physical miracle of cure substantiated the claim of Jesus to possess the authority to forgive sins. Such a declaration involved a claim of His own sinlessness. He added under that assumption the assertion of His Messiahship, making use for that purpose of the half-veiled prophecy of Daniel, under the title "Son of Man." Furthermore, pardon of the sins of another would be contradictory to the consciousness of one's own guilt. Again had He cured the man first and afterwards pronounced his sins forgiven, there would have been room to doubt His authority to take away sin. But when He addresses the doctors of the law, He puts the case clearly to them. "You are calling in question my authority to forgive sins and my power to take them away. Will you believe I have such authority, if I perform an instantaneous miracle in curing the incurable paralysis in the man?" Such a cure had never been witnessed. They could not refuse before the people such evidence. They were caught in their own trap. For immediately the man arose, took up his little couch whereon he had been lying[1] and went forth before all of them. So the power to forgive sins was upon earth, contrary to their idea that it was in heaven alone. The people concluded that God had "given this power unto man." Jesus had frankly declared by the assumption of His words and the reality of His deeds, that He was *divine*, exercising the function of the deity in the forgiveness of sins. The Scribes had hoped to catch Him and He gave them the occasion at once. But their accusation of blaspheming had only served to emphasize the justification of Jesus of His right to forgive sins and His consequent declaration of His divinity. It had been incidentally the purpose of His performing the cure, to substantiate His claim of the right and

1 Imperfect of the verb, signifying customary action.

power to exercise the divine prerogative. But He had been careful to use the title "Son of Man" to declare His Messiahship, so that they would not be able to attack Him. His miracle made it unnecessary for Him to refute the Scribes further. He had now met His enemies and had gained over them a signal victory. But they would later dog His steps to the end.

The effect of this incident on the people was remarkable. They were filled with fear and were almost beside themselves with amazement. And they kept on glorifying God and saying: "We never saw anything like this. We have indeed seen strange things today!"

4. The call of Matthew (Levi) and his reception in honor of Jesus (Mark 2:13-17; Matt. 9:9-13; Luke 5:27-37).

Jesus went out from the house of Peter to walk by the seaside. He needed a brief rest after the sharp conflict with His astute and stubborn enemies. This walk on the beach was a favorite haunt of His. There was place for physical recuperation in the salt-laden breezes and for quiet meditation and prayer after the heated debate. Soon the crowd was gathering about Him again. We do not know how many days of strenuous activity He had in the ministry by the sea before the call of Levi. It may have been many days; but possibly it was on that same day that He passed by and "saw the son of Alpheus," who may have been the father of James the Less, also later of the Apostolic group.

Levi was a custom-house official. The Talmud distinguishes between the *tax collector* and the *custom house official*. The *Gabbai* collected the regular real estate and income taxes and the poll tax; the *Mockhes*, the duty on imports, exports, toll on roads, bridges, the harbour, the town tax, and a great multiplicity of other variable taxes on an unlimited variety of things, admitting of much abuse and graft. The very word Mockhes was associated with the idea of oppression and injustice. The taxes in Judea were levied by publicans, who were Jews, and therefore hated the more as direct officials of the heathen Roman power. Levi occupied the detestable position of a publican of the worst type—a little Mockhes, who himself stood in the Roman custom-house on the highway connecting Damascus and Ptolemais, and by the sea where all boats plied between the domains of Antipas and Philip. The name "publican," which applied to these officials, is derived from the Latin word *publicanus*—a man who did public duty. The Jews detested these publicans not only on account of their frequent abuses and tyrannical spirit, but because the very taxes they were forced to collect by the Roman government were a badge of servitude and a constant reminder that God had forsaken

His people and land in spite of the Messianic hope, founded on
many promises of the ancient prophets. The publicans were classed
by the people with harlots, usurers, gamblers, thieves, and dishonest herdsmen, who lived hard, lawless lives. They were just
"licensed robbers" and "beasts in human shape."

According to Rabbinism there was no hope for a man like
Levi. He was excluded from all religious fellowship. His money
was considered tainted and defiled anyone who accepted it. He
could not serve as a witness. The Rabbis had no word of help for
the publican, because they expected him by external conformity
to the law to be justified before God.[1]

The attitude of Jesus toward the publican was in complete
contrast to that of the Rabbis. He had come to seek and save the
lost. The Pharisees were separatists, and did not deign to have
anything to do with a publican, who was to them no better than
a Gentile. But Jesus came not to condemn a whole class or any
individuals, but to save every sinner to a better life. He refused to
admit that there was anything inherently wrong with paying
tribute to the Roman Government, while that continued supreme
and maintained order in the land. Why was it wrong to collect
the tax? Even though Levi and his colleagues of the custom-house
had been extortioners, Jesus would fling open the door of repentance and salvation to them. He despaired of none, not even
the worst.

Jesus made himself a friend of men, even of the publicans and
the worst of sinners. By doing this, He "made Himself of no
reputation" so far as the *elite* society was concerned. But He was
a friend of all classes, the rich and the poor, the learned and the
illiterate, the good and the bad.

Capernaum, being located on the Via Maris and being a
busy populous center, had a large custom-house with a correspondingly large number of tax-gatherers. It was located at the
landing-place for the ships which traversed the lake to various
towns on the other shore. The flow of commerce along the highway
was also great. From the midst of this group of men engaged in
a lawful occupation but likely unlawful abuse, Jesus would
win some to eternal life. He was accustomed to pass by that way
and doubtless made use of His opportunities to evangelize them.
Levi, may have heard Jesus preach by the seaside. He would
not feel free to enter the synagogue. The great Teacher frequently taught the humble fisher-folk and others in the open
air by the sea and so reached many in this way with His message who would be inaccessible in the synagogues. The sudden

1 David Smith, In the Days of His Flesh, page 124.

response to the call of Jesus would indicate that Levi had heard Him preach. Perhaps he had pondered long, as he sat at the receipt of custom recording the import and export duties, the words of some message on the Kingdom, and had secretly decided in his heart that he would be some day a disciple of the new prophet. He was strangely drawn to Jesus, recognizing in Him the helper of all men, even sinners. *He* did not require the hard rabbinic type of self-righteous religion, to be wrought out by the observance of an insupportable mass of rules and rites.

It is not strange, therefore, that when Jesus passed that way He should see Levi, whose other name was Matthew (the Gift of God) sitting at the receipt of custom. Nor was it sudden or un-natural that the Teacher should step up and speak to this officer, and after a friendly conversation leading up to the great subject, invite this man whose confidence He had won to become His disciple. Jesus was a student of men. He may have noted this man among His hearers more than once and perceived that he was deeply impressed with His message. Now, the opportunity was ripe for clinching matters with him and Jesus does not fail to make use of it. He saw in this man great possibilities for a demon-stration of the powers of God's gospel to transform a veritable outcast of society—a man now filled, through the coldness and lack of sympathy on the part of those who were looked upon by the world as religious, with a deep-seated resentment of the religion of the Rabbis, and helplessly lost in the corruptions of his detestable office—into a very saint and "a Gift of God," which Mattitijah, his name, signified. This would forever silence every argument against carrying the gospel to the most wretched and depraved sinners of humanity. It would always be an unanswerable argument for world-evangelization.

"Follow me," said Jesus, as He looked into the eyes of the officer sitting before Him with a deep yearning sympathy. At once, Matthew saw that Jesus loved him, and wished to make him a chosen instrument for spreading the good tidings of the Kingdom. The vision of a new world flashed upon his understanding soul and he sprang to embrace the new life it held for him. It was as the Teacher had said in His sermons about the Kingdom. He had come to establish a new social order, in which the democratic brotherly principle was to be the basis. All would be admitted to this new brotherhood, irrespective of class or caste, upon the fulfillment of the conditions of true repentance, faith, and loyalty toward Himself. Matthew arose at once and followed Him, leaving his books, his money box, and his old life behind. All of his powers and natural gifts or acquired training in any line, he freely dedicated to Jesus, casting himself in confidence upon the Lord for his cleansing, preserving, and saving power. He was to be an outstanding type of the work of Jesus with individuals, — and he was a publican!

We know with what momentous consequences that decision was wrought. He was from this time to be called by his second name, Matthew—"the Gift of God." His fine talents would soon be brought into play in recording the great sermons of Jesus. A few months later, he would set down the best and fullest outline of the greatest sermon the world had ever heard.[1] Later, his Logia would be treasured by scholars, and his gospel would become one of the four incomparable records of the teachings and deeds of Jesus.

It could not have been long after this that Matthew made for Jesus a "great feast" in his house. It was a feast worthy of his financial conditions, an adequate expression of whole-hearted appreciation of his Master. He invited the four fishermen disciples of Jesus, with Nathanael and Philip, and a great crowd of his old associates in the business world (publicans). The Pharisees, with their scribes or students, felt free to attend without invitation as on-lookers, according to the custom of the day. They were too keen in their endeavor to trap Jesus to let so opportune an occasion pass, though they would have scorned an invitation. Among the publicans, there were some others who had already become followers of Jesus, following the example of Matthew.[2] The twofold purpose of Matthew in giving this feast was to honor Jesus by this fitting confession of Him before all men, and to furnish an opportunity for those social outcasts like himself to come in contact with this new prophet, who had broken up every barrier of caste, and opened up to him a new life. He could and would do the same for them. Jesus frankly and gladly accepted the invitation leading His half-reluctant disciples to do the same. He saw in this occasion an opportunity to impress His new principle of democratic brotherhood on the people.

These Pharisees, with their young theological students, had come for the purpose of criticism, and the occasion was not long lacking. As they stood beside the wall of the long banquet hall, these lynx-eyed, long-bearded hypocrites affected to be horrified that Jesus and His disciples should be eating with publicans and sinners—the pariahs of society!

They directed their expressions of criticism to the disciples of Jesus, perhaps because they were afraid to risk themselves

1 The sermon on the mount.
2 Mark 2:15.

in debate with the Teacher who had bested them in that recent encounter. Perhaps they thought, as Chrysostom suggests, that they might instill disloyalty in the disciples, and discredit Jesus before them. At first, they began with remarks on the side to the disciples: "Just look at him; he is eating with publicans and sinners." While this remark was not addressed to Jesus, it was heard by Him. Next, they defined their criticism in the form of a direct question; "Why is your Teacher eating with publicans and sinners," they asked. The disciples were already doubtful about the propriety of such an act. Would it not discredit Jesus before the public of Capernaum? Emboldened by this timid, half-hearted, doubting attitude of the disciples, the enemies advance to the attack. They press upon the disciples with a combined movement. With their young students, they began to make a disturbing noise on the outside of the banquet hall. A "buzzing murmur" of disapproval arose on the outside of the crowd. Again, they bring their complaint to the disciples, laying this time the responsibility at the door of the disciples as well as upon Jesus. "Why do you go on eating and drinking with the publicans and sinners," they repeated. They assumed that the disciples were now convinced of the impropriety and the mistake of their new and inexperienced teacher. "He has ruined his prospects now surely before the self-respecting public." What a mistake! To sit down at the same table with this trash was to put themselves on the social plane with them. To even touch their very clothes would defile a Pharisee!

Jesus had overheard the hissing criticism, and before His timid and embarrassed disciples could respond, turned upon the critics with a terse answer which completely shattered the bulwarks of their Pharisaic exclusiveness and at the same time justified His attitude toward the outcasts of society. Accepting their caste classification of men into righteous and sinners, He said:

"They that are strong and sound in body do not need a physician but those who are sick ('have it badly'). I did not come to call the righteous, but the sinners to repentance." "You are the *righteous* in your own esteem" was the ironical implication. "These whom you classify as sinners recognize their need and are ready to receive a physician. It was for this reason that I came to minister to their needs." According to their idea of repentance, such a sinner as Matthew could not repent; but according to His, the door to a new life of restored favor of God was open to all, through a sincere change of mind and faith in the saving power of God. The welcome to God was always open. Jesus offered not only pardon, guaranteeing against punishment for sin, but forgiveness or restoration to the circle of divine favor and fellowship. The call of grace preceded repentance.

This was a new idea to the Pharisees with their legalistic views. Only sinners could be called to repentance, which was free and unconditional to all alike. "Go ye and start learning[1] what this means," He said to those doctors of theology and their students and scribes: "I desire mercy and not sacrifice." They had never learned what Hosea meant by those words, which were the very rudiments of their literature and prophecy. The real service of mercy and kindness rendered to poor humanity in its lost state was what Jehovah wanted and not the mere offerings of sacrifices and performance of ritual. He had come to show divine sympathy to lost sinners rather than an empty show of outward worship, to call men to a new spiritual life and so "into repentance."[2] Like a true Physician, He would look sympathetically into all the conditions and needs of sin-sick souls, and then minister the remedy necessary. This new conception was destined to bring a revolution in the religious history of mankind.

5. Jesus defends His disciples for feasting instead of fasting (Mark 2:18-22; Matt. 9:14-17; Luke 5:33-39).

Once again, the Pharisees had been worsted in another attempt to bring Him into disfavor with the people and with His own disciples. But they were not to be defeated, and brought to bear again all their ingenuity to entrap Him if possible. Even while they were in the midst of the second accusation, they conceived a third plot. This time, they tried again the old scheme of bringing Jesus and His disciples into conflict with the disciples of John. While John was yet free and preaching at Enon, they had incited his disciples to jealousy, by pointing out the growing popularity of Jesus and the decreasing crowds of John. This had been the main cause of the departure of Jesus from Judea, terminating His first short ministry of six months in those parts. John had been a popular teacher and had many disciples scattered all over Galilee, though he lay in the prison of Machaerus.

Would the Pharisees be able to stir up anew that jealousy, and bring about a final separation from Him of that element which had been trained in loyalty to Jesus by His forerunner? John was in prison, and if anything should happen to him, these disciples of his would naturally turn to the new prophet to whom John had directed them. Many of them had already declared their allegiance to Jesus and constituted an important element of the crowds of followers that waited on His ministry in Galilee. Some,

1 Ingressive imperative, begin to learn.
2 Luke 5:32.

it is true, had wondered why Jesus did not do something to help their master, who had languished for many weeks in prison. A little fuel added to the sleeping embers of resentment might flame out into hatred for the new teacher, who had now taken the place of their erstwhile popular leader.

The new plot grew directly out of the dispute at the feast which Matthew had made for Jesus. The young theological students of the Pharisees had maliciously invited (as it seems) some of the disciples of John to attend the feast in Matthew's house; or at least called their attention to the fact that Jesus had not taught His disciples to fast and pray according to the established custom among the Jews. It was not improbable that the feast fell on Thursday or Monday, the days of stated fasts to commemorate the going up of Moses to the Mount to receive the tables of the Commandments and his descent afterwards. It was true that the Law had appointed only one fast in the year, the Day of Atonement; but the Rabbis had added a great number both national and private. Strict Pharisees fasted for religious merit. They also thought thus to raise the soul by depressing the body. The disciples of John, following their ascetic leader, had adopted his regimen, much like that of the Pharisees in its severity. This was the popular usage sanctioned by tradition. Jesus did not follow this custom and the unscrupulous Rabbis saw in this their opportunity to embroil Him with John's disciples and thus deprive Him of this important accession to His cause, and also denounce Him as an innovator.[1]

The well-meaning, but simple minded disciples of John, not suspecting that they were but tools of the wily and astute Pharisees, come to Jesus with the question: "Why are we and the Pharisees fasting, and your disciples are not fasting?"

If they had but reflected a moment, they would have remembered how their old Teacher had denounced these men as a "brood of vipers," and the part they in turn had played in his arrest and incarceration later. But John would not have attended the feast at Matthew's house on a fast day, or on any other day, for that matter! Jesus and these disciples were not orthodox! Had not they themselves and the Pharisees, with all the leading Jews, been accustomed to fast on the second and fifth days of every week? Why should Jesus and His disciples go against this custom? The Pharisees had pushed these disciples of John to the front in this question, while they remained behind inciting them secretly. Now, their students come forward with an added suggestion of difference: "The disciples of John fast often and make supplications; likewise, also the disciples of the Pharisees. But thine,"

1 David Smith, In the Days of His Flesh.

they added coldly, "are eating and drinking." It was not a question merely of disregarding the custom of fasting, but also neglect of the stated system of prayers, which the Rabbis had invented as "the hedge of the law."

In His answer, Jesus omitted any reference to the objection respecting prayer and dealt with the question of fasting only. He addressed Himself to the disciples of John. He reminds them of the beautiful way that John had spoken of Him as the Bridegroom and himself as the friend of the Bridegroom. This was just before their Master had been borne away to prison. The Pharisees were stirring them to envy then as now. "The friend of the Bridegroom that standeth and heareth him, rejoiceth much by reason of the Bridegroom's voice. This then is my joy, which hath been fulfilled." Reminding them of that situation back just a few weeks ago, Jesus graciously called these friends to reflect upon the fact, that they were in peril of lining up with the enemies of their old Master. At the same time, He clearly set before them the true genius of His Kingdom doctrine over against the one of Judaism.

"Can the children of the bridechamber mourn, so long as the Bridegroom is with them?" He said. Jesus would have them understand that He was the Bridegroom just as John had declared. The "children of the bridechamber" were not only the groomsmen that accompanied the bridegroom when he conducted the bride to his home but included the guests also. Jesus characterized the fasts of the Pharisees as acts of mournful dreariness. By mortification and self-infliction they sought to secure religious merit. The fast also nurtured spiritual pride and was a mere hypocritical pretense of piety.

Jesus chose the figure of the Bridegroom as used by John, as the most apt illustration of the difference between the religion of the new regime and that of Judaism. If the Pharisees wished to accuse Him of being an innovator He would give them a chance. But His main motive was to explain clearly to the disciples of John the true character of His religion. His disciples were a wedding party. To put on mourning while the Bridegroom was present was out of keeping. Joy, mirth, and feasting were fitting while He was there, not mourning and fasting.

John had preached a severe message of repentance. "The Messiah," he said, "will come as a great Separator, with his winnowing shovel in his hand." As Luther thought to reform Catholicism, so John would reform Judaism. But he, like Luther, did not get away from all the traditional elements of the old system. His disciples still clung to the habit of fasting and praying very much as the Pharisees. These astute enemies were glad to cite the fact now, that John's disciples were accustomed to fast often. But the religion of Jesus was something more than a reformed Judaism, even if the reformation might be radical.

His religion was full of joy. The gospel of the Kingdom was a glad message. It was the announcement of God as a Father, ready to bestow His grace upon all men, even publicans and sinners. It was no wonder that Matthew and his publican friends should be full of joy and make a feast for Jesus. That was the true and natural response to such a glad message. The religion of Jesus is one of laughter and song, not one of melancholy dreariness, of penance and masceration. The disciples followed the example of Jesus in their joyful attitude toward life. There was a real sense of joy in the freedom from the slavery of Rabbinic tradition. There was genuine joy in the fellowship of the new service of the Kingdom.

Beneath the surface in the stream of Jesus' life, there was a more serious view of sorrow for the world's needs and pity for the distresses of men. Even now He reminds the disciples of John, sympathetically, that the day will come when His disciples will also feel the pains of injustice, loneliness, and sorrow, "when the bridegroom shall be taken away." "In that day," when *He* shall be seized away—as John had been suddenly taken—they will lose all desire for food, and in their intense sorrow and concern, fast. Their fasting will not be a self-imposed act to produce a mental state of concern for the Kingdom, but a natural result growing out of mental anxiety. True religion is internal, manifesting itself externally as the life-sap of the tree puts forth buds and leaves.

Jesus makes use of two homely and apt illustrations to set forth the difference between His religion and Judaism, even the Judaism of John. He approached the subject from both sides. It would not be well to take His new Kingdom regime and stitch it like a new patch of unshrunken cloth on the old tunic of Judaism. The result would not be salutary either for the old system of Judaism or for the new regime of Jesus. The incompatibility of the new and old would lead to the rupture of the old and to consequent waste and disaster. Then, the new would not harmonize with the old. The appearance of the new patch would be different from that of the old garment. Violence would be done to the new regime, as Luke shows, by tearing out a piece from a new garment and clapping it upon the old. The joy of Matthew's feast could not be patched on the old garment of Pharisaic fasting. It would be incongruous for the disciples of Jesus to fast in the midst of the hilarity of a wedding feast. The disciples of John needed to come

out from Pharisaism. John had tried to patch up the old torn robe
of Judaism, but he had also pointed them to the Bridegroom.
His effort to patch up the old theocracy but served as a work of
preparation for the new regime. The disciples of John should now
leave off their fasting and join in His feasting.

The other illustration, of the new wine being put in the old
dry skin bottles brittle with age and use, with the consequence of
rupture and loss, reenforces the first with added elements. These
bottles were made of the whole skin of the kid properly tanned and
treated. But when dry from age, with the fermentation of the new
wine in them, they would burst. In both illustrations it is the new
that rends the old. The new teaching and practice of Jesus and
His disciples must not be put into the old bottles of Judaism.
Else the old forms of stated fasts and prayers would burst with
the joyful spirit of the new message.

Christianity was spirit and Judaism was form. It was impossible to graft Christianity into Judaism. There was an effort
to do this in Paul's day by the Judaisers. It almost ruined Christianity in spite of Paul's valiant and heroic effort to the contrary.
Putting the new teaching of Christ into the old bottles of ceremonial Judaism wrecked for the most part historic Christianity
in the Middle Ages. The new garment was spoiled by tearing a
piece out of it and clapping it on an old cloak of form. On the other
hand, He would have them understand that to clap an old patch
of Judaistic fasts and formal prayers on new Christianity would
completely mar and destroy its beautiful spirit. It would be to
perpetuate the ancient bondage and annul the new liberty. Jesus
wound up His apologetic defense of the divergence of His new
regime from that of Judaism by a beautiful observation, full of
kindly tolerance for those who would cleave to the old and of
rare wisdom in appealing for the new. For those who clung to the
true Judaism of Moses, He had the greatest sympathy and patience. He recognized the value of conserving all that was true.
He honored the spirit of conservation, which refuses to cast in
the junk heap all traditions, the good and bad, in an insane desire
for the new and novel. The old is not true because it is old nor
the new because it is new.

"No man," said Jesus, "having drunk old wine desireth new,
for the old is good." There was a touch of humor and tolerance
in this, but no compromise.

CHAPTER XII
THE GREAT SABBATH CONTROVERSY
(Harm. §§ 49-51)

Jesus had now come to the end of the first year of His public ministry. The first six months of that year had been spent in Jerusalem and Judea, terminating in a frictional situation between the disciples of John and His own disciples brought about by intriguing Pharisees. The following months were occupied mainly by the first tour through Galilee, with His small group of the first disciples, recently called into special service. His fame had grown rapidly in Galilee and the jealousy of the Pharisees was already thoroughly aroused now in all parts of the country north and south.

The second year of His ministry, upon which Jesus now entered, was to be a year of great public favor. His activity during this year would be intense and His fame was destined to ring through all the land. Nearly all the year was spent in Galilee, but there was a feast, presumably the Feast of the Passover in Jerusalem, which He attended before entering on His greater activities in the Galilean province. There is difference of opinion as to which this unnamed feast was, but the circumstances of His ministry as a whole seem to favor strongly the supposition of its being the Passover.

It was on the occasion of this Feast that Jesus encountered His enemies, now thoroughly aroused, in a growing hostility of bitter antagonism in controversy about the proper observance of the Sabbath. They had attacked Him covertly at first in Galilee and afterwards more openly at Matthew's supper. They were awaiting now their chance to renew the attack in the Jerusalem feast.

There was no institution among the Jew regarded with more veneration and scrupulosity than that of the Sabbath. It was a divinely ordained and beneficent part of the Mosaic economy, designed for the rest of man and for his worship and service to God. Its purpose was to protect the underlings and oppressed in a nation afflicted with greed. Beginning with sunset on Friday, announced by three trumpet blasts from the Temple and synagogue, it ended at sunset on Saturday. All food must be prepared, all vessels washed, all lights kindled, and all tools laid aside. There were restrictions laid down in the Mosaic law; but the Rabbis had elaborated from these a vast array of injunctions and prohibitions, making of the Sabbath law a veritable bondage. Moses said: "Thou shalt not do any work." The Rabbis made out a system of thirty-nine works, which done rendered the offender subject to death by stoning. Derived from these "father-works" were numerous "descendant-works." One of the "father-works" was ploughing; a son of this was "digging." Wearing false teeth was a "descendant" of "carrying a burden." Among the descendants of "reaping" were the "plucking of a head of wheat" or the "pulling out of a grey hair" from one's head. Lengthy rules were formulated about what kinds of knots one might tie on the Sabbath. The camel-driver's and sailor's knots might not be tied or unloosed. Two letters of the alphabet might not be written together. To kindle or extinguish a fire was a great desecration, not being justified even in case of the emergency of sickness. The Sabbath had become a grievous burden by the thousands of such restrictions and rules too numerous to mention.

The excessive strictness and multiplicity of exactions heaped up by the Rabbis made the observance wholly impossible even for themselves. So they had recourse to casuistry and thought out many ways of evading the rules which they themselves had made. Two thousand cubits was the length of a Sabbath day's journey, but they would deposit on Friday evening their Sabbath food-supply at that distance from home and then double their journey, on the fiction that where the food was deposited was a part of the common dwelling. The Jesuitic idea of "intention" was made an effectual method of evading the precepts. It was unlawful to eat an egg on the Sabbath but if the hen that laid the egg was intended for the table, it might be eaten. The multiplicity and childishness of these casuistries reduced the Sabbath to the ridiculous. At the same time, while the Pharisees and Sadducees evaded these burdensome restrictions, they were uncompromising toward others who did not observe them.

Excessive formalism and pedantic scrupulosity had thus gendered religious indifference and quenched the spirit and enthusiasm of the Jewish faith. Its poets had ceased to sing and its prophets to prophesy. The priesthood was corrupted and aimed mainly at political power. The maintenance of traditions and zeal for scrupulous observance of rites and ceremonies had crowded out sympathy for the poor and diseased and all altruistic service.

1. Jesus heals a man at the pool of Bethsaida and defending Himself against the charge of Sabbath-breaking claims equality with God (Jno. 5:1-47).

The author of the fourth gospel, desiring to prove the divinity of Jesus, chose a number of outstanding miracles, this and two others of which (Chaps. 9, 11) the Lord performed in the midst of the conflict with His enemies.

(1) The narrative of this miracle presents three difficulties: the identification of what feast is meant, which cannot be settled

wholly, and second the location of the site of the pool of Bethesda, supposed by some to be the modern Birket Israel, by others identified with the Fountain of the Virgin, but by the Palestine Exploration Society a locality lying in the northeast angle of Jerusalem just inside the east wall. The Fountain of the Virgin, called the Gusher, periodically bubbles over, fed by an intermittent spring. This fountain was outside the wall in the valley of Kedron. The bubbling was probably due to volcanic forces and the water had a reddish tinge from chalybeate admixture, possibly. A third difficulty is with the text, most of the original manuscripts not including part of the third or any of the fourth verse. This part was probably an interpolation by some copyist to explain verse seven, which contains the words of the paralytic himself. He was but expressing the popular and legendary belief, that an angel came down at certain times and disturbed the waters. The Jews, like some other poeple of antiquity, ascribed the unexplained phenomena of nature to supernatural beings and in this case to angels. It is probable that the water contained curative mineral powers and popular imagination had woven legends about it.

Jesus went out to this pool on the Sabbath, doubtless aware that He would find there a crowd of sick folk. Bethesda means the House of Mercy, and there He would perform some work of mercy on the diseased ones. He was also aware that His enemies would have their eyes upon Him. He seems to have chosen the time, place, and person for this cure, that He might break up the false traditions of the Jews, which had made the Sabbath a burden instead of a day of true rest, worship and service. He thus carried the war into the territory of His enemies without needlessly provoking them.

There was a multitude of the sick, blind, halt, and withered, lying around on the five porches, waiting for the waters to be troubled. Jesus fixed His attention on one in their midst whom He recognized as being a long-time sufferer. Sympathetically He addressed him.

"Do you wish to be made whole?" He said. The man seems not to have caught any idea, beyond the possibility of a kindly act of someone, in helping him to get into the water first when it should be disturbed. So he recounted to this stranger, who seemed sympathetic and interested, how he had no friend to help him at the opportune time, and so before he could drag his paralytic limbs down the stairs of the pool and into the water, others less afflicted preceded him. His hopes had thus been long frustrated.

"Get up," said Jesus, "take your sleeping-mat and walk around."

For thirty-eight years the man had been held prostrate by this sin-conceived disease, but now he felt a thrill of new life pulsating in his withered limbs, as in instant[1] obedience to those words of unmistakable command, he "rose up, took his pallet, and went walking around."

(2) The scene then changed (vs. 10-14). Jesus passed into the midst of the large crowd and the man lost sight of Him. The man himself soon attracted the attention of the Jewish purists, who seeing him walking along with his pallet, at once approach him with the warning that it is not lawful for him to be carrying his couch on the Sabbath (Ex. 20:10; Deut. 5:14). His reply to them was conclusive.

"He who made me whole, said to me, 'take up your pallet and go walking around.' "

"Who is the fellow that said to you take it up and walk around?" they asked. But surprised and filled with wonder the man had not asked Jesus who He was, and now had lost sight of Him in the midst of the crowd. What could he do? He had violated the law of the Sabbath (Ex. 23:12; Neh. 13:19; Jer. 17:21). He put up the best defense he could when confronted by the authorities by laying the responsibility on the one who had cured him. But not knowing who the man was he was left in a poor case. He had consciously violated the law to all appearances, and was subject to the penalty of stoning. These Jews were not concerned that the man should be cured; they were angry because of the violation of the Sabbath law. They probably suspected that it was Jesus who cured him but they had failed to be present when it occurred. At any rate the man was allowed to go to the Temple to make amends for his fault on the plea that he did it unwittingly. This was permissible through their casuistry in dealing with such offenses. After all, the one they wished to catch in their trap was Jesus.

Some time later in the day, Jesus who had stepped to one side in the crowd to avoid the excitement after the miracle, found the man in the Temple. The Jewish purists had made the man come to the Temple, probably to atone for his Sabbath-breaking by sacrifices. He had either been so enfeebled by sin and disease or was so dull mentally, that he did not even recognize his benefactor when he met Him in the Temple. Jesus finds him and speaks to him.

"See," He said, "you have been made whole. No longer go

1 Aorist tense.

on sinning, in order that a worse thing may not happen to you."
Jesus had dealt mercifully with the impotent sinner at the pool.
He had not exposed him to shame by calling attention to the sin
which was the cause of his miserable condition. Here apart in the
Temple He reminds the man of the fact that he had been permanently cured.[1] He should be grateful for this, but instead, the man
had already shielded himself at the expense of his unknown benefactor.

We are not surprised that one from whom no expression of
gratitude is recorded, should have hastened back to the Jewish
authorities and reported the name of the one who had "commanded
him to take up his couch and walk around." This was contemptible
self-protection revealing a spirit of base ingratitude. In his case
the healing of the body did not mean the healing of the soul.
He did not heed the warning of Jesus against sin and "a worse
thing did befall him." This must be our conclusion or else the man
was a slow-witted dullard. In either case he had served as a
tool in the hands of the enemies of Jesus, who now precipitate a
determined movement against Him. "They *began to persecute Jesus*
because He was doing these things on the Sabbath" and thus becoming an *habitual Sabbath-breaker.*

(3)   It seems that Jesus was summoned to give account before
the Sanhedrin authorities, either formally or informally, for His
conduct in constantly breaking the rules of the Sabbath (vs. 16-
18). If formally, we may picture Him standing in the center of
the semi-circle of the assembled legal Sanhedral court. They
thought to over-awe Him into conformity to their legalistic system of Sabbatic rules. The accusers brought the charge of His
activities on this and previous occasions here and in Galilee. Jesus
answered the charge calmly in terse unmistakable terms.

"My Father keeps on working[2] until now and I am going on
working." He justified His continued activities for the good of
men on the Sabbath on the ground that God, His Father, had
done this from the beginning. The Sanhedrin was thrown into a
paroxysm of religious furor. They could not deny that God's
beneficent activities continued every day, in spite of its being
in the period of God's Sabbatic rest from the work of creation.
"As God His Father continued to work on the Sabbath in redemptive work for humanity, so He, Jesus, was going on working habitually on the Sabbath in the same kind of work." He had firmly
confessed, that He disregarded habitually their traditional rules
of the Sabbath, by continuing His beneficent activities every day
in the service of mankind. But He had added to His Sabbath

1 Perf. tense in Greek.
2 Linear present middle indicative.

desecration the worse crime of blasphemously putting Himself on equality with God in prerogative and privilege and of calling Him *specially* His own Father.

We may well imagine that the excitement ran high for a time. It is not improbable that official action was taken to kill Jesus if He should be found in Judea later. They could not carry out their designs during the Feast, likely, due to the presence of many of His Galilean friends.

(4) Jesus makes use of His opportunity to discuss before the people more fully His statement as to His relationship to the Father (vs. 19-23) and adds an explanation as to His consequent relation to mankind (vs. 24-29).

The Jews understood well what Jesus meant by "my Father" and went about in continued seeking to kill Him, all the more because He was not only a Sabbath-breaker by habit but called God "his own Father," making Himself thus equal with God. Continuing now His explanation of the statement before the Sanhedrin authorities in answer to the charge of Sabbath-breaking, He reenforces his claim to divine sonship. "What the Son does is identical with what the Father does." He had not healed the impotent man "from Himself." The Father had acted with Him in this. He did nothing that He did not see the Father doing. On the other hand whatever the Father would go on doing the Son "is going on doing" likewise. The act and reason behind this *modus vivendi* was that there was an intimate love of friendship existing between the Father and Son, leading the Father to keep on showing to the Son all the things that He Himself was doing. Intimate love led to revelation in perfect knowledge. The final motive impelling the Father to go on revealing even greater things than these present ones to the Son was, that "they might wonder" and be led to search more deeply into these things. So He and the Father were one in the intimate love of personal friendship, in the knowledge of their mutual activities, and in their beneficent purposes for mankind.

Jesus now adds to this reenforced statement of divine sonship, His claim to the power and prerogative of *Life* and *Judgment* (vs. 21, 22). These are some of the "greater works" being revealed. Just as the Father raises the dead and quickens into spiritual life whom He will, even so the Son makes alive spiritually whom He wishes. He would soon raise the daughter of Jairus (Matt. 9:18) and the son of the widow of Nain (Luke 7:11-17). He had power to "make alive" the soul and raise from the dead the body. Moreover the Father gave over permanently to the Son all *judgment* of men spiritually (Jno. 3:17). This He did

that all men might "keep on honoring the Son just as they honor
the Father." Jesus claims the same right to the worship of men
that they give to the Father. The one who does not honor the
Son does not honor the Father. The critic who denies the deity
of Jesus dishonors the Father.

Jesus next passes to define more exactly His relationship to
mankind (vs. 24-30). He claims the power to dispense the "life of
the ages," spiritual, divine, and eternal, to any one who hears
obediently and believes on the one who sent Him on this divine
mission. This spiritual life is a present possession.[1] He shall not
come into judgment, but has already passed over once and for all,
being separated out of spiritual death into spiritual life.

To this claim of power over the realm of death, life, and
judgment, Jesus next adds a declaration as to the present and
future exercise of this power. They will have an opportunity to
witness the calling forth of the dead from the tomb (Jno. 11) by
the word of this power. He will soon substantiate this claim before
their eyes. This is another evidence of His oneness and equality
with the Father because the Father gave to the Son to have this
source of life in Himself, just as He the Father had this life-
giving power in Himself.

The reason why the Father gave to the Son the prerogative of
judgment, was because He was the Son of Man, and so being
identified with humanity, fulfilled the condition of being judge. He
was touched with all our infirmities. This prerogative of judgment would extend, He declared, to the final and general judgment
and bodily resurrection of the good and the bad (Matt. 25:46).
He will make use of this power then and all will come forth
from their tombs on hearing His voice. That will be a resurrection to life for those doing good but a resurrection of judgment
for those practicing foul things. Jesus winds up His claim to the
prerogatives of deity, by assigning the basic principles for a true
exercise of the function of judge, that He was not seeking His
own will but the will of the Father who sent Him on this divine
mission. He had asserted His divine sonship and covertly under the
title Son of Man, His Messiahship. His declaration of the former
was clear and unmistakable to the understanding of His enemies —
and should be to the critics today — of His claim to deity. Certainly
His enemies there so interpreted His claim and went about to
make their plans to destroy Him. They could not carry out their
plans then; they would succeed with them later.

Jesus did not finish His defense before the people against the
charge of Sabbath breaking, before He had presented witnesses

1 Present tense, progressive action.

for all His claims to a right to do His proper work on the Sabbath
(vs. 31-47). He knows His own witness to Himself will not be
accepted as true (v. 31). So He dismisses for a time any claim
based on His own witness and presents the testimony of others.

He presents first the witness of John the Baptist (vs. 32-35).
The Sanhedrin had sent an embassy to John who bore *permanent*
witness to the truth (Jno. 1:19-28). His testimony was never
retracted and was abiding in the mind of the people. Jesus did
not need the witness of a mere man. The light needs no witness
to itself. He presented the witness of John for their sakes that they
might be saved. John who was now in prison, had been a burning
lamp shining in the darkness; and they had become willing to
rejoice for a little while in the sphere of his light. But they had
soon turned against Him. Their interest in him was short-lived and
superficial.

The second witness Jesus presents to His extraordinary claims
is that of the *works of Jesus,* upon whom the Father thus set
His approval (vs. 36). This testimony was more substantial than
that of John, much as the people had esteemed that prophet. The
works which the Father had given Him to complete and which
He was then doing before their very eyes, "are bearing witness"
concerning Him that the Father had definitely sent Him on a mission unto the world.

Furthermore, the Father who sent Him on this mission, Himself gave an abiding testimony to the Son. He "also" had borne
witness in the hearts of the believers. But these hostile Jews
had failed always and forever to hear His voice. That voice had
been heard at the baptism of Jesus by John (Mar. 1:11). These
unbelievers had not seen the Father's form and did not have His
word abiding in them because they were not believers in Jesus
whom the Father had sent.

He next cites the testimony of the Scriptures, and particularly
the writings of Moses in the Scriptures, which both Pharisees and
Sadducees claimed to accept (vs. 39). They professed to search the
Scriptures, because they thought they had in them the "life of the
age." "Even those very Scriptures," said Jesus, "are witnesses of
mine." But their stubborn unbelief blinded their eyes and paralyzed
their wills.

Jesus closes His apologetic address by assigning the reason
for their rejection of the witnesses to the Son. "They were not
willing to come to Him in order that they might have life." They
had no real love for God in their hearts. They would be willing[1]
to accept some false Messiah who might come in his own name

---

1 Ingressive aorist indicative.

receiving glory from men. But they would not receive Jesus who came in the Father's name, not receiving glory from men. Motivated by the desire to receive glory from one another they would never be able to believe. They sought not glory from God. Jesus would not be their accuser; but Moses upon whom they placed their hopes. Moses had written of Jesus and if they would not receive his written testimony how would they believe now the oral words of Jesus!

2. Jesus defends His disciples against the charge of Sabbath-breaking and asserts His supreme authority (Mar. 2:23-28; Matt. 12:1-8; Luke 6:1-5).

Jesus could not remain in Jerusalem after the unnamed Feast (Jno. 5:1). It was no longer safe for Him there. He had defeated His antagonists in debate over the Sabbath question. He was their prisoner virtually; but they were afraid of His numerous friends and allowed Him to depart to Galilee undeterred. But they would watch His every step from this time on, seeking to entrap Him.

They did not have to wait long for an occasion. It was probably on the very next Sabbath after the cure of the impotent man, or the second Sabbath perhaps, that He and His disciples were passing along a path skirting a field of grain of wheat or rye, probably the latter. At places the path led through the grain. They could travel a distance of only two thousand cubits on the Sabbath. This would render more difficult their coming to some place where food might be obtained.

It was permissible according to the law for one traveling to pluck enough heads of grain or grapes from a vine to satisfy himself;[1] and the disciples as they went along parting the stalks of grain to make a way[2] so as not to crush them down, began to pluck some of the heads, and kept on plucking and eating, rubbing them in their hands to remove the chaff. This custom was perfectly in accord with Mosaic law (Deut. 23:25) but according to the Pharisaic tradition could not be done on the Sabbath.

The scrupulous Pharisees were on the alert, probably, to see if Jesus would exceed the distance of the Sabbath day's journey. They arranged something better still. The disciples committed even in their sight an offense which rendered them liable to death by stoning. Jesus had not participated in the act but the approval of His silence was upon it. It was not far from Capernaum likely and the Pharisaic spies were anxious to forestall

1 The Land and the Book, page 684.
2 Mark 2:22.

further activities in Galilee. The disciples had been guilty of a double offense — reaping and threshing. The Mishna says: "He that reapeth corn on the Sabbath to the quantity of a fig is guilty; and plucking corn is reaping." Rubbing the grain out was threshing. Even to walk on the grass on the Sabbath was forbidden because it was a species of threshing.[1] Another Talmudic passage says: "In case a woman rolls wheat to remove the husks, it is considered sifting; if she rubs the head of wheat, it is regarded as threshing; if she cleans off the side-adherences, it is sifting out fruit; if she throws them up in her hand, it is winnowing."[2] The scrupulosity of these Jews about the Sabbath was ridiculously extreme. A Jewish sailor caught in a storm after sunset on Friday refused to touch the helm though threatened with death. Thousands had suffered themselves to be butchered in the streets of Jerusalem by Antiochus Epiphanes rather than lift a weapon in self-defense on the Sabbath! To these purists, the act of the disciples was a gross desecration of the Sabbath law. The worst of all was that Jesus permitted and approved it. If this daring innovator were not checked He would destroy all respect for their most cherished institution, the Sabbath.

At first the Pharisees excitedly call the attention of the disciples: "Why are you doing that which it is not lawful to do on the Sabbath?" they said. But these disciples had not been conscious of having done any wrong. The fine hair-splitting distinctions of these purists were far beyond the ken of the common people. These humble fishermen were nonplussed. Their enemies come next to Jesus. "Look" they say, "your disciples are doing that which is not lawful."

Jesus was alert with the defense. He did not hesitate a moment but with depth of insight and readiness of understanding He responded to the charge against the disciples, laying down the very principles which would in time undermine all their elaborate system of burdensome traditions about the Sabbath and restore the day to its original use. It is necessary to remember that the Sabbath was a divine institution in which God embodied an eternal principle. Far from transgressing the Sabbath law, Jesus appealed to the law now in His defense of the conduct of the disciples. He would discriminate between the spiritual principles of rest and the worship and service of God for which the day was dedicated, and the useless junk of endless hair-splitting distinctions and prohibitions imposed by Rabbinism.

His first argument in the defense, He took from the historical example of David. their favorite hero (I Sam. 21:6). He

1 Cf. Farrar.   2 Jer. Shabt, page 10a.

ironically chides the Pharisees for their ignorance of these historical Scriptures.

"Did you never read," He said sarcastically, "what David did when he had need and was hungry, he and they that were with him. How he entered into the house of God (at Nob) and ate the shew-bread."[1] This was the principle of *Necessity*. It was perhaps the Sabbath when David committed the double offense of entering—being a mere layman—the house of God, and ate the shew-bread consecrated for priests only. Saul was in pursuit. David and his soldiers were hungry. The priest Abimelech had only the "loaves of presentation"—a dozen loaves placed on the table in the Sanctuary and at the end of the week substituted by fresh ones, the stale being used by the priests. Jesus wisely made use of this example first, which had justification in the precepts of the Rabbis, that "danger to life superseded the Sabbath law and all other obligations" (Cf. Lev. 18:5).[2]

The second argument Jesus took from the Law (Num. 28:9, 10, 18, 19). He thus cites the law in justification of the setting aside of the ceremonial law under certain conditions.

"Have you not read in the law," said He, "how that on the Sabbath day the priests in the temple profane the Sabbath and are guiltless?" The priests worked in the Temple on the Sabbath preparing the sacrifices and caring for the Temple. This work was justified because it was the work of the Temple and for *worship*. Again, the Rabbis had laid down the principle that there was "no Sabbatism in the Temple." They could violate all the Soperium or rules about the Sabbath and be blameless. The Sabbath law not merely secured *rest* but also *worship and service*. The service of the priests was thus justified in being the service of the Temple. How much more should His disciples be justified now in His service who was greater than the Temple. He had cleansed the Temple a few months ago. Work necessary for the service and worship of God was justifiable. This was the principle to which Jesus appealed and in so doing incidentally made a claim for Himself of superiority to the Temple and therefore to the Sabbath, since the Temple service superseded the Sabbath law.[3]

The third point in the defense was drawn from the *prophets*. Matthew writing especially for the Jews cited the arguments from the law and the prophets. This argument was a direct thrust at the harsh and critical spirit of the Pharisees in the accusation they had brought against His disciples. Again He chides them for their lack of spiritual understanding of the Scriptures. If they had

1 Abimelech was priest but he and Abiathar, his father, probably bore double names.
2 Maimonides Hilkla Shabt II:I.   3 Broadus Commentary, page 258.

properly interpreted the words of Hosea (6:6) they would not have condemned His innocent disciples. God desires kindness and good will in men rather than punctilious observance of traditional rules. It was in their lack of mercy that they harshly demanded compliance with their exacting rules. The spirit and not the letter was important. The Sabbath was for the works of benevolence and good will and these Pharisees were not fulfilling the spirit of this prophecy. They began by accusing the disciples; they wound up by being themselves condemned before the spirit of prophecy.

The fourth point in the defense was based on the original idea of God in maknig the Sabbath and on the superiority of man to that institution. God made man and adapted the Sabbath to His use. It is a human necessity met by divine mercy. Man is more than any institution, whatever it may be. The state was made to serve man. Every institution of the church divinely founded is for the proper service of mankind. The Sabbath should serve man's body, mind, and spirit. It should not be a day of pain, sorrow, and burdensome fear; but one of refreshment, peace, and joy.

The fifth and last argument in defense on this occasion was based on the authority of Jesus as the representative of humanity and the Spiritual Messiah. "The Son of Man is Lord also of the Sabbath," He said. In these words He claimed not only Messiahship but final authority to change their Sabbath and rid it of the onerous burdens of their numberless traditions. As the representative of mankind He would make the Sabbath a universal catholic institution for man both for Jew and Gentile. He is Lord of the Sabbath and should be served and worshipped on the Sabbath. This was a proclamation of spiritual freedom.

Again they were worsted in their encounter with Jesus. His disciples had a champion. They stood vindicated before the Scriptures completely. At the same time the true character and end of the Sabbath as an institution had been explained. The rubbish of rabbinical tradition had been cleared away and the beauty and use of the Sabbath revealed. In His defense, Jesus had not abrogated the law but established it. He did not throw open the door to Sabbath desecration but stripped the Sabbath of its shackles and freed the disciples for greater activity in true worship and service on the Lord's day. This work of Jesus would lead later to the further separation from the bondage of Jewish traditions, when the day should be exchanged in honor of the resurrection of the Lord of the Sabbath.

3. Jesus heals a man with a withered hand on the Sabbath and the Pharisees combine with the Herodians to destroy Him (Mark 3:1-6; Matt. 12:9-14; Luke 6:6-11).

On another Sabbath, the one following perhaps, Jesus crossed over and went into their synagogue. Just where the previous event, of the disciples' plucking the grain, took place is uncertain. He was returning to Galilee, and if He went by the usual route it was east of the Jordan. This seems to fit in with the idea of *going over* in Matthew's narrative. This would bring Him somewhere in Galilee in the vicinity of Tiberias, the capital of Herod Antipas.

The synagogues were yet open to Him, and Jesus according to His custom went and taught on the Sabbath. It might have been in Capernaum but was more likely in some other town. We are not told what Jesus taught on this occasion but only what He did.

Luke, the physician, tells us that there was a man there whose right hand was withered.[1] A physician would more likely notice the details in such a case. The man's hand was in this state as a result of accident or disease. Tradition says that he was a stone-mason and had appealed to Jesus to heal his atrophied hand, in order that he might win a livelihood and not be forced to beg.[2]

The Scribes and Pharisees were sitting "on the side-lines"[3] spying on Him and kept on watching[4] to see if He would heal the man. It is not improbable that they arranged for this man to be present, in order that they might lead Jesus into their trap of Sabbath violation. If the man's life were in danger, the law would permit healing on the Sabbath; but evidently this was not the case. It would be a breach of the law, they judged, if He should heal him. They watched with the purpose of arranging an accusation against Jesus.

Indeed there was danger of Christ involving Himself in a serious situation, since all *external applications* were forbidden, though there was much discussion as to what would constitute an external application. A person having a toothache might not gargle vinegar unless he afterwards swallowed it. He might however dip his tooth-brush in vinegar. Casuistry had elaborated endless rules like this for the treatment of all maladies on the Sabbath.

These enemies sought to lead Jesus to do something, so that they might accuse Him. They asked, "Is it lawful to heal on the Sabbath day?" If He should take up the question one way or the other, He might involve Himself in an endless debate over the hair-splitting distinctions of their casuistry. If He should heal the man He would probably do something which would furnish a basis of accusation.

1 Mark 3:1. Perfect passive participle cf. adjective in Matthew and Luke.
2 The Gospel of the Hebrews.   3 Greek verb compounded with preposition.
4 Imperfect tense of continued action.

But in the face of this situation Jesus did not hesitate. No thought of Himself or any peril He might incur for Himself would deter Him from doing what was right.

"Rise up and stand forth in the midst!" said Jesus to the man with the withered hand. The man had been sitting on the floor like the rest of the congregation. Jesus was cognizant of the thought of the scowling Pharisees and turning to them said: "*I ask you:* Is it lawful on the Sabbath day to do good or to do harm? to save life (as I am doing) or to kill (as you wish to do)?" He echoed their whispered suggestion in a direct and frank question before the people. But to His question they made no reply. They were fearful lest they should give Him the lead and advantage in the debate. So they kept a stolid and sullen silence. They could not have answered otherwise than in the affirmative, since they themselves taught that it was lawful to save life or prevent death on the Sabbath. If they on the other hand should say it was lawful to do good they would thus give consent to the miracle. They were caught in the trap of giving consent by their silence at least. They were speechless and felt themselves outwitted.

When Jesus saw their obstinate silence, He cited a concrete case from their own Rabbinical teaching and practice. The Rabbis had said, if a beast fell into a pit on the Sabbath, its owner should find out if it was injured. If not, he should provide food and facilities for sleeping and let it remain until the end of the Sabbath. If it was seriously injured he ought to take it out and kill it. Casuistry had nullified this requirement as many others, and he might take it out with the *intention* of killing it even if he did not put this intention into practice. They were very merciful when their own property was at stake. But when their fellowmen were concerned they abated not the rigour of the Sabbath rules. Citing this familiar case He added:

"How much then is a man better than a sheep!" Still they kept their fierce and unbroken silence. Jesus was filled with a mingled emotion of anger and grief. His eyes blazed for an instant on "all of them" with a flash of unforgetable anger as their hard upturned faces scowled upon Him. His anger was momentary,[1] but it glowed on His countenance[2] and burned into the conscience of each rabbinical hypocrite there. Murder was in their hearts and Jesus knew it. But His anger was tempered by grief which was continuous,[2] being motivated by the hardening of their hearts. Their previous conceptions had so calloused their hearts that this new truth about the Sabbath could not find an entrance. He was grieved too by their selfishness, which would rescue a beast of their own, while their inhumanity would permit a fellow-creature to suffer and die without help.

1 Aorist tense of verb.   2 Present participle of continuous and progressive action.

Jesus faced the issue now of a more complete break with these ecclesiastical authorities than at any previous time. He had come to found a kingdom of pure spiritual religion. The veil of Sabbatic traditions, sacrifices, priestly meditations, rites, and rabbinical casuistries must be rent in twain; and the hollowness, cant, and hypocrisy of these long-bearded hypocrites of broad phylacteries must be exposed and their willful perversity put to shame. He knew the significance of the moment. Henceforth, He must face absolute separation and count on their relentless antagonism. Their sullen obstinate silence revealed hearts impervious to all spiritual truth. He must face the issue of their determined opposition and He did not hesitate.

"Stretch forth[1] your hand," He said, and the man stretched it forth and "it was restored whole as the other." Probably the arm was not withered, though nothing is said about that in the narrative.

The effect was electric. His enemies had been defeated again in argument and shamed into silence, when they had come confidently hoping to find some basis of accusation. Jesus had not done anything in the cure which would serve even as a pretext for accusation. He had made no "external application," had not even touched the man. They could get no ground of accusation even on the basis of their rabbinical rules. They bolted out of the synagogue filled with insane rage[2] and were taking counsel together excitedly[3] how they might destroy Him through some plot to kill Him. They remembered the way they had disposed of John the Baptist; and were not the Herodians nearby? Hitherto they had been enemies of the Herodians, considering them half-apostate Jews. The Herodians were supporters of the Roman domination, followed the heathen customs, and had held that Herod the Great was the Messiah. But they could be used as tools to destroy Jesus and so the Pharisees secretly establish a combination with them against Him, plotting together with them as to what would be the best method to kill Him. What they could not do by law they would effect through these unscrupulous court-adulators of Herod Antipas. The rift between Jesus and these champions of patriotism and orthodoxy was deep and final; and now there was added the designing political intrigue of the court of Herod in Galilee. This enmity was destined to grow until it would finally bring Him to the cross. He would be beset by these intrigues in Galilee henceforth. But it was inevitable that it should be so. He had come to establish a universal spiritual theocracy; the Pharisees stood for an exclusive Jewish intolerance.

1 Stretch it clean out full length.
2 A privative and nous mind, foolishness bordering on insanity.
3 Imperfect of repeated action.

CHAPTER XIII
THE ORGANIZATION OF THE KINGDOM
(Harm. §§ 52-54)

Jesus now enters upon the second period of His Galilean ministry. He had been in Jerusalem and in the Feast had precipitated the great Sabbath controversy, which gave opportunity for Him to break with the whole system of Rabbinic traditions, proclaiming once again His principles of religious liberty and this time in relation to the law of the Sabbath. He had laid down the principle about fasting, that men may fast or not as they are disposed. He said that ceremonial ablutions were mere types of inward purity, and as used by the Pharisees had only served to cover up spiritual purity by putting the emphasis where it should not be. The acts of Sabbath-breaking which they had attributed to Him, were not transgressions of the true Sabbath law, rightly understood. He rejected their explanation of the law and gave the people a new interpretation, appealing to the great fundamental principles of the Sabbath and rejecting their pedantic code of innumerable and ridiculous regulations.

1. Jesus withdraws to the sea and teaches great multitudes (Mar. 3:7-12; Matt. 12:15-21).

All of this filled these enemies of Jesus with an unutterable and insane rage against Him, and when He perceived their madness and their combination of a plot with the Herodians to kill Him, He prudently withdrew from interior places where He was working, to the sea of Galilee, where it would not be so easy for His enemies to carry out their secret plan as they had in the arrest of John the Baptist a few months before.

The fame of Jesus had spread far and wide over the land. and when He withdrew from the grasp of His enemies to the sea, a great multitude followed Him from Galilee, Judea, Jerusalem, Idumea in the far South, from the regions beyond Jordan, and from Phoenicia or the regions of Tyre and Sidon. So great was the throng of people about Him now at the sea side, that He spoke to His disciples to keep a little boat ready all the time near the place on the shore where He was working, so that if the multitude of those who were diseased and pressed forward to touch Him and be healed by Him should throng Him, He might step into the boat and pushing off a little preach to them from this novel pulpit. There were so many who were afflicted with plagues, as strokes of paralysis and other incurable diseases, who were so eager to be healed that they "fell upon Him"—as Mark graphically notes—and their eagerness became even a peril for Him. Another phenomenon of frequent occurrence was the appearance of those possessed of unclean spirits, who kept on falling down before Jesus and proclaiming Him to be the Son of God. Jesus did not wish the testimony of these demon-possessed men and kept on charging them repeatedly that they should not make Him known.

Matthew found, in this incident of Jesus' enjoining silence upon the demon-possessed, a fulfillment of Isaiah's prophecy about the Messiah. In popular conception the Messiah would be political, making use of military means, being exclusively Jewish, and becoming the imperial successor of David and Solomon in a kingdom which would surpass in glory any that had preceded it.

But Jesus manifested the fact now, at the very initiation of His organization of the kingdom, that the Messiah was to be such as Isaiah pictured (Isa. 42:1-4). The quotation of this prophecy is a free reproduction of the Hebrew, possibly from an Aramaic collection of *Testemonia*. Matthew seems to have been familiar also with the Septuagint translation. The prophecy applied proximately to Israel but also remotely and principally to Jesus the Messiah. It is this fulfillment of prophecy in Jesus that Matthew points out.

The words of the prophecy call attention to the suffering servant, who is the central figure in Isaiah's message from the fortieth chapter to the end. He was the chosen one. The Jews understood that Isaiah was talking about Israel, the people chosen of God. The expression, "my beloved in whom my soul is well-pleased," reminds us of the words of the Father, spoken at the baptism of Jesus (Matt. 3:17). This rendering of Matthew particularizes and applies the prophecy to Jesus. The Spirit of God would be upon this beloved servant in a special degree and manner. He would announce the whole body of God's justice and righteousness for the nations. His mission was not exclusively for the Jews or to the Jews. He would not "wrangle" and dispute like the Scribes, or as the false prophets or leaders of revolt, such as Judas of Galilee. Nor would He "cry aloud" just to attract attention. Jesus preached in the streets not to attract attention or praise to Himself but always for the good of others. The ministry of this servant would be one of gentleness and kindness. He would not break off the tender bruised reed of a crushed spirit but console and uplift the broken-hearted. He would not quench the spirits bowed-down and disheartened just like the smoking wick, with a little oil left and bordering on extinction; but hearten them again. Such would be His tender ministries, unlike the harsh monarch or ruthless conqueror. Such would be His character until He should victoriously and mightily set forth and fully manifest and establish righteous judgment. "On His name the nations (Gentiles) shall hope." His mission would ultimately compass the conversion of the Gentiles.

It was opportune that this character of His mission and the kingdom He was just about to organize should be understood. The busy ministry of preaching, teaching, and healing impressed Matthew and others of the followers of Jesus as one of tenderness, sympathy, helpfulness; and not of harshness, violence, and ruthless suppression of His fellowmen as that of a worldly conqueror.[1] He was not that kind of Messiah and all His activities so declared.

2. After a night of prayer Jesus selects from His disciples twelve apostles (Mar. 3:13-19; Luke 6:12-16).

The *occasion*, demanding the choice of the twelve and organization of the kingdom work in a more compact way, arose from various circumstances. The enemies of Jesus had been organizing the forces opposing His ministry for some time already. This called for definite organization of His followers to resist the shocks of this ever-growing antagonism. More fundamental still, the increasing work in the growing kingdom demanded a more complete organization of its working forces, looking to thoroughness and a complete work. Growing out of this, was the need of thorough training for His workers. They were to be with Him at all times and in all places, companions in His travels, witnesses of all His work, students of His doctrines, fellow-laborers in His practical school of experience, and finally to become in reality as now in name, commissioned apostles of His world-wide campaign for the establishment of the kingdom. For the time, they were learning by daily companionship with the Master what they should be, do, believe, and teach, as His witnesses and ambassadors. From this time on their training would occupy a large part of the time and attention of their Teacher.

The *time* when the election was made is not absolutely determined; but we may safely place it "in these days" after the first Galilean tour and soon after the "unnamed feast" in Jerusalem, when the opposition took more definite shape around the Sabbath question. The movement of Jesus' ministry had assumed large proportions and was rapidly extending itself over the whole land. There are no means of deciding the exact locality of the choice, though circumstances seem to favor greatly the traditional double-peaked hill *Horns of Hattin* four miles west of the Sea of Galilee and about eight miles southwest of the site of Capernaum (Tell Hum). "The[2] mountain" into which Jesus retired from

1 Broadus Commentary on Matthew, pp. 264-5.
2 Greek article making definite.

the midst of the throng for a season of prayer and meditation before choosing the twelve, seems to have been well known and a favorite haunt of Jesus.

The selection of the apostles was a "new departure" and advanced step in the ministry of Jesus. He needed a band of followers bound to Him by hooks of steel. He is to select now twelve teachers and teach them through a period, preparing them to build later upon the foundations laid by Himself. All depended on the right choice of these men. It was a real crisis in the kingdom work, and He went up into the mountain and was continuing in prayer to God[1] the Father all night long in preparation for the choice.

Before going up into the mountain, He called out from the vast throng those whom He wished and they came to Him. Then after retiring from them and passing the night in prayer in the mountain, He descended to this select group when it was day and chose from them twelve, whom He appointed "that they might be with Him and He might send them forth to preach and have authority and power to cast out devils." He named these twelve, *apostles,* because they were to be *sent* out by Him. Their twofold mission was preaching and healing. They were to constitute an inner circle of friends and companions to whom He would confide His thoughts more fully than to others. They were to be witnesses to His unabated enthusiasm and devotion. Through the experience they would gain in His companionship and the tests to which they would be submitted, they would become qualified for the work which He later would send them forth to do.

The *reason for choosing just twelve* is not here disclosed, though there are various hints later on in the ministry, pointing to the half-hidden and symbolic significance of this number.[2] It was the purpose of God that the Gospel be preached to Israel first. The twelve were to represent the twelve tribes. Jesus was the divine Messianic King who had come to set up the kingdom whose advent was foretold in prophecy. It is probable that the apostles understood the mystic significance of the number to refer to the idea of the Messianic Kingdom. Certainly in the mind of Jesus, there was some good reason for choosing this definite number, and His later methods as well as disclosures seem to point to this as another veiled manner of declaring His Messiahship. He had already used the title Son of Man for the same purpose.

Jesus chose these apostles from among the disciples who had been longest with Him and whom He had proved. They be-

1 Periphrastic imperfect active, continued action.
2 Matthew 19:28; Barn. Eph. 8

longed to the simple, unlearned, plastic class of people whose minds were relatively untrammeled by the traditions of Rabbinism which had its chief center in Jerusalem. In the choice, there was no regard to former social position, political party, or religious sect. Several of them, if not the majority—according to Arruenian tradition—were married. Some were fishermen, one a publican, and one a zealot. Most of them were Galileans and seven or eight from in or around Capernaum. Judas, who bears always the sad epithet "the one who betrayed Him," was the only one from Judea. John and James belonged to a family of means. Their father Zebedee had hired servants, and their mother Salome had means to support Jesus in His ministry (Mar. 15:41). Matthew was a man of some education and business ability. In the group there was a fine variety of natural gifts, temperament, and education. A few of them were men of extraordinary ability, who rose above the others in intellectual power and attainments.

There are four lists of the apostles given in the New Testament (Mar. 3; Matt. 10; Luke 6; Acts 1:13). Each list is divided into three groups of four each. The names are identical in the groups and headed by the same name in each case. The name of Peter appears first in all the lists and that of Judas last. There are at least three pairs of brothers, two of which constitute the first group of four. Seven of the twelve are better known than the other five about whom we know very little. Six of the seven who are better known became disciples in the very beginning of the ministry of Jesus; Matthew the publican, six months later; and the other five we meet here for the first time. Nathanael is identified with Bartholomew and Thadeus with Judas the brother of James. These men had much to unlearn and much to learn; but they were privileged to sit at the feet of the greatest teacher of all time.

The *personality* of each of these men stands out distinctly. Simon, son of Jonas, to whom Jesus gave the name Peter (Rock) as a prophecy of what he would become, was bold, impetuous, versatile, alert, sensitive. He was the "mouth of the Apostles." Prone to err, he was quick to repent, and he loved Jesus. He denied his Lord in a critical hour and repented bitterly but became a pillar of the church, and according to tradition sealed his testimony with a martyr's death after forty years of faithful and able service. His force of character was extraordinary and his activity intense. From the vacillating Simon, Jesus made the firm and stable Peter, a veritable Rock. Tradition says he was crucified with his head downward, not deeming himself worthy to be crucified like Christ.

Of Andrew we do not know much. He did a notable service,

the first day of his discipleship, in bringing his brother Simon to Jesus, and thus giving initiation to the great missionary movement of Christianity. Andrew was a man of personal work, counsel and decision. When the five thousand had to be fed he seems to have sensed the object of Jesus and counseled bringing in the little lad with the loaves and fishes. Murillo's painting of the Martyrdom of St. Andrew has a little lad standing with his face turned to one side, as if he could not stand the terrible sight, and with tears streaming down his cheeks. Tradition says that the artist had in mind the lad of the five loaves and two fishes. Andrew showed decision in introducing the group of Greeks to Jesus. He saw in the coming of these Gentiles the promise of a world-wide movement, and through his prompt work as usher they were brought to Jesus, who confirmed Andrew's interpretation of the event. There is a firm tradition that Andrew was crucified at Petrae in Achaia, and that as he hung upon the cross for two days he taught the people all the while.[1]

James was practical, energetic, vehement, and a man to be trusted. He was one of the inner circle of three, with Peter and John, his younger brother. These two brothers, because of their ardent spirit, were called Boanerges (sons of thunder) by Jesus. They would have called down fire from heaven on the Samaritan village when its people did not offer their hospitality to the Master.

John was zealous, affectionate, sympathetic. He would have silenced an unknown worker who spoke in Jesus' name, because he did not belong to the apostolic group. Of all the apostles, John drank deepest of the Master's spirit and doctrines. It is no wonder he was the "disciple whom Jesus loved." Meditative, tender, full of earnest zeal, he alone braved all and stood at the foot of the cross at last. Of Zebedee the father of these two brothers we know little beyond the fact that he was a man of some means. Their mother Salome seems to have been the sister of Mary, the mother of Jesus. She was ambitious for her sons but a devoted follower and liberal supporter of Jesus in His ministry. She was of the brave women who surrounded the cross, and visited the sepulcher early on the morning of the resurrection. Of these two brothers James was the first of the apostolic group to become a martyr, being beheaded by Herod Agrippa (Acts 12). Tradition says that he was accused by Josias, a scribe, who when James was being dragged through the street by a halter sentenced to die, repentant fell at his feet and cried out: "Pardon me, thou man of God, for I have repented of the things which I have spoken

1 Abdiae History Apost. III. 41

against thee." James kissed him and said "Peace to thee, child, peace to thee and pardon for thy transgression." Josias confessed himself a Christian there and was beheaded with the apostle. John came to old age, having a fruitful ministry for many years in Asia Minor. He was profound in his understanding of theology but highly practical in his teaching. His love was ardent and at times vehement. It is said that when he heard that the great heretic Cerinthus was in the same building with him in Ephesus, he hastened out lest the roof should fall on all. There are many things said of the last years of his ministry but none more interesting than his favorite and almost only text in his old age was: "Little children, love one another." The ardor of his young manhood had been tempered down by the experiences of his long life into a character full of sweetness, patience, and fraternal love. He had been a great defender of the faith as well as a preeminent constructive theologian. Tradition says that John was put into a cauldron of boiling oil but escaped death and was banished to Patmos. It was given to him to serve the Lord for long years and to be the only apostle to die a natural death.

The name of Philip comes first in the second group. He was practical, prudent, thoughtful, inquiring, but somewhat slow of heart and dull in spiritual understanding. He was a matter-of-fact man who insisted on getting the facts. He had the mind of a bookkeeper. When Jesus wished to feed the five thousand, he would make a calculation of the probable cost. He was largely lacking in imaginative faith. It is probable, judging from his Greek name, that he was a Hellenistic Jew. His prudence in dealing with the Greeks who came to inquire about Jesus led him to move very cautiously. He wanted an occular demonstration of the Father when Jesus spoke about going away to the Father (Jno. 14). Philip did not have vision; but he did have a practical mind which moved with the precision of a machine. Of such a type of mind Christ has use in the varied work of His kingdom. Tradition says he was hanged against a pillar in Phrygia.

Nathanael (Bartholomew) was a man free from guile. He was a bit skeptical but a student of the Scriptures. His name is associated with that of Philip who led him to Jesus. His home was in Cana. Little is known of Nathanael. Tradition says he wrote a gospel and preached to the Indians. He was with six other disciples fishing on the lake when Jesus appeared to them (Jno. 21:1-14). Tradition also adds that he sealed his testimony as a martyr, being flayed alive.

The names of Thomas and Matthew come next in the list. Thomas received the name of "Doubting Thomas" from the expression of his doubt when the apostles told him of the appearance of Jesus. He had a melancholic temperatment. When Jesus spoke about *the way*, Thomas could not understand how they were to know the road when they could not see the goal. But he was heroic. He had his hours of high courage and was ready to go into Judea and die with Jesus when He went to the rescue of the home of Lazarus. He wanted occular evidence on which to base his faith. It is a comfort to us today that there was a doubting Thomas among the apostles, who demanded to see the prints of the nails in His hands and put his finger into them, though that was not necessary. If doubting Thomas was convinced of the resurrection the evidences were surely unimpeachable! Tradition ascribes to Thomas the authorship of a gospel.[1]   It is interesting that his name was associated with that of Matthew who wrote the *Logia* or sayings of Jesus. There is a tradition also that he carried the gospel to India where he suffered martyrdom at Coromandel, his body being transfixed. Matthew Levi reveals in his gospel the fact that he was a publican, though Mark and Luke do not mention it. He would reveal his identity, probably, that he might show how Christ broke down the social barriers which separated the publicans from respectable society in Palestine. He would have men of all classes who were boycotted by the *respectables* to know that with Jesus they could find acceptance. Matthew was a methodical man of business habits. Moreover he was an educated man who had natural gifts as well as mechanical skill for writing. While he had been a *Mokhes* or tax-gatherer in the custom-house located on the Via Maris by the sea in Capernaum, his leisure hours had been utilized in some measure in the cultivation of these gifts. Otherwise he could not have written the gospel which bears his name. His outline of the Sermon on the Mount is more adequate than that of Luke. His genius for orderly grouping gave us the finest group of Christ's parables. He was a man of affairs and a valuable asset in the constitution of the aposolate. He finally suffered martyrdom by the sword in Ethiopia.

Of James the Less and his brother Judas (Thaddeus) we know very little. Simon Zelotes belonged to the party of desperate patriots who had pledged themselves to hostility to the Roman government. It took courage to receive a member of this party into the apostolic group. Judas Iscariot, the only apostle who was not a Galilean, was from the little town of Kerioth in the south of Judea. He was lacking in spiritual discernment. It seems he had a capacity for finance and Jesus certainly gave him a fine opportunity but he threw it away. Yielding to the baser impulses of his nature he sold his Master for thirty pieces of silver. The choice

1 The apocryphal Ev. Thomas.

of Judas for the apostolate remains a mystery, seeing that Jesus knew from the beginning the diabolical character of the man. Greed was his weakness, mixed with ambition. He had probably nurtured the ambition of a splendid worldly kingdom, and when Jesus manifested clearly that "his kingdom was not of this world" Judas was disappointed. He resolved to avenge himself, and get what he could out of what he considered at the last a lost cause, by selling his Lord. After the base betrayal he went out and hanged himself.

3. Jesus sets forth in the Sermon on the Mount a declaration of His kingdom ideals and principles (Matt. 5-7; Luke 6:17-49).

Jesus delivered this greatest of all sermons recorded in human history just after the choosing of the twelve—according to Luke's account which is generally chronological. It was urgent now that Jesus define the ideals and objectives of His kingdom. The twelve just chosen to be apostles of the kingdom would need a declaration of the principles and ideals of Jesus to serve as a basis for their teaching and guide for their conduct. The ministry of Jesus had grown so rapidly in its influence, that vast throngs now pressed upon Him from all parts, coming from Jerusalem and Judea and even from the regions as far as Tyre and Sidon. They pressed upon Him to be healed of their diseases, and so eager were they that many sought just to touch Him because power kept coming forth from Him and healing them.

Jesus, after the night of prayer, had come down to the group of disciples already called apart the day before, and chosen from their midst twelve. This occurred in the level place on the Horns of Hattin, likely, which today is pointed out as the most probable site of the delivery of the sermon. Jesus stationed Himself on a slight elevation on the upper edge of this "plain" place, and lifting up His eyes with an earnest steadfast searching look into their expectant faces, He opened His mouth so that everyone could hear His words and began to teach them.[1] It was a momentous occasion long to be remembered. The azure blue of beautiful Galilee was spread out as a picture map before Him as He raised His eyes. His newly chosen apostles sat in an attentive group before Him and back of them a vast throng of disciples and a multitude of others who had come from near and far, many of them bringing their sick ones to be healed.

Jesus was fully conscious of the importance of the occasion. He had not until now given much attention, apparently, to the organization of His work, though He had been abundant in His activities of healing and preaching. He had called into definite

1 Ingressive aorist.

discipleship a small group "to be with him," and they had accompanied His ministry assiduously for some time; but now the
need was pressing for more definite organization. The first step,
He had taken in the choice of the Twelve; the second, was to set
forth in a succinct declaration some of the fundamental ideals
and principles of His kingdom.

The Sermon on the Mount was a kind of inaugural address
on the theme: The Ideals of the Kingdom of Heaven. It was a real
connected discourse at a definite time and place. It had special
application to the twelve just chosen, serving as a kind of ordination sermon. But it was also applicable to the great number
of believers present and the multitude of others who had not yet
definitely accepted His teaching. Many of the splendid things
said on this occasion were repeated at different times later in His
ministry. We have only a brief outline recorded by Luke and a
somewhat fuller one by Matthew; and by no means all of the
things said by Jesus in this sermon are recorded in these outlines.
Many of His teachings pronounced on other occasions did not
constitute a part of this discourse at all. But He did lay down
here, at this critical juncture of His ministry, a platform of important principles for the enlightenment and guidance of His
kingdom forces. This sermon is not a mere ethical code but its
sublime moral principles far surpass all human moral standards.
Christ's idea of Righteousness as here set forth, became the kingdom's ideal of Righteousness which has never yet been approximately realized by humanity. In His universal eternal principles
in this sermon, Jesus laid the basis for the kingdom work for all
time. In one discourse, He superseded all previous standards and
set up the new and final religious goal for the human race. He
here uttered the final word about character and privilege, conduct
and duty, religious ideals, the divine and human relations of men,
and the supreme objective and goal in life and how to attain it.

It is not strange that an analysis of this sermon is difficult.
It is so comprehensive in its scope and many sided in its teachings
and applications, that there is a great divergence in the manner
of its analysis by different interpreters. In the Beatitudes Jesus
described the ideal character and glorious privileges of the kingdom subjects (Matt. 5:3-12). Following this He delineated in
two beautiful similes their function and responsibility. He then
answered forever the objection which had been raised to His attitude toward the Mosaic regime. He had not come, as they accused, to abrogate, but to fill up to the full and complete the
law (Matt. 5:17-48). The ideal moral standards of the kingdom
were far superior to the laws of Moses, especially as interpreted
by the Scribes and Pharisees. In practical religion these teachers

had exalted the ritual, formal, and ceremonial, to the point that all spiritual life was crushed out. Jesus on the other hand emphasized the spirituality of the duties in practical religion. All religious acts must be performed honestly in view of the approval of God and not of men. He urged in man's relation to God single-hearted devotion and whole-hearted trust. He gave the Golden Rule to govern in man's relations to His fellowmen. His appeal in the conclusion of His discourse to His auditors was to enter into the straight way and pursue it to the narrow gate leading into life. They must avoid false teachers and build on the rock of the doctrines of Christ.

(I) The character and privileges of the ideal subjects of the kingdom. These are set forth in the so-called Beatitudes (Matt. 5:3-12; Luke 6:20-26). Jesus tells His disciples the qualities and characteristics which will make them truly happy and rightly to be congratulated. Men are to reach happiness by the method of inwardness. The virtues praised are not the active ones only but also the passive; not merely those of doing but those of bearing. The first four in Matthew's narrative corresponding to the four in Luke, describe the characteristics of the inward self; the others deal with the attitude of the soul to one's fellowmen. Luke's narrative presents the first group, in the simpler more universal form: the poor, the hungry, the sorrowful and the downtrodden. Jesus had a word of comfort for the millions in the world who are found in these classes. But one is not happy just by being poor, hungry, sad, or oppressed. There were as many poor in those days as now. Jesus was a friend of the poor and oppressed and would extend a hand of loving sympathy to them. He wished to tell the great class of these miserable ones in their wretchedness that there was a kingdom of happiness very near and accessible to them. Their material conditions were no bar or hindrance to their entrance into that land of happiness. He would say to them, that human life is more than mere material plenty or creature comforts. The true riches are in the heart. Man may enjoy the riches and happiness of the kingdom in spite of poverty, hunger, sadness, and oppression. Nay, the very poverty which seemed to constitute a barrier might become a help instead of a hindrance to their entering the kingdom. Indeed, Jesus taught that it was hard for a rich man to enter the kingdom. Poverty is no virtue, and wealth is no sin; but poverty and oppression may serve to drive one to seek refuge and relief in the realm of the kingdom because of their very grimness and hard realities.

In the form in which the *beatitudes* appear in Matthew, they probably more clearly express the thought of Jesus as to the characteristics of the kingdom subjects. The *poor in spirit* are happy with that high and holy happiness which grows out of the pure character. The poor in spirit is one who recognizes his poverty in spiritual things and seeks the blessing of God in his own spiritual enrichment. The Jews thought and taught that outward material prosperity was a sign of God's favor and blessing; Jesus declares here that man cannot pertain to the kingdom of God, apart from humility of spirit which recognizes one's own spiritual poverty and is thus prepared to receive the riches of the kingdom. Another paradox Jesus presents in saying that the *sad* are blessed. The world thinks quite the contrary. But the man who *mourns* because of his own evil deeds, in true repentance, reaches consolation in an alleviated conscience. The *meek* who are strong but gentle, courageous and energetic but patient under affront, who govern their spirits in the midst of severe trials, suffering silently, are pronounced by Jesus happy because they shall inherit the earth. It is not mere physical *hunger* that Jesus pronounces blessed, though He sympathized with the hungry and He would have hunger drive people to Him with a real *hunger and thirst after righteousness.* Such will experience a growing satisfaction of their dearest desires for spiritual things. Another characteristic of inwardness pronounced blessed by Jesus was *purity of heart.* The one who is pure internally in thought and imagination is to be congratulated, because he will have the privilege of entering into the very presence of God, as the favourites to oriental monarchs, whose doors were shut to all others. They will see God and enjoy His intimate friendship. The pure in heart seek with singleness of purpose the rule of God in the world. Their reward is to see God in His intimate fellowship. In the clear mirror of a pure heart one will see the purity of God reflected. Like discerns like. Sin clouds and befogs the heart so that one cannot see God; but the very glory of God is reflected in the clear depths of a pure soul.

The remaining beatitudes refer to the attitude of the kingdom subject to his fellowmen. The *merciful* are those who have pity on the guilty or anyone who suffers a real need. The blessing on the merciful is that he receives mercy, according to the eternal law that like produces like in the spiritual realm. The world had always honored great conquering warriors. But Jesus said "happy are the peacemakers." The work of the peacemaker is one of great difficulty. It is hard enough to keep peace; it is harder to bring it about where it does not exist. In the Messianic kingdom, the one "settling up difficulties," shall be recognized as one whose character partakes of the divine (Eph. 2:14f). Jesus was the Prince of peace. He who would be like Him must be a peace-

maker. The God of Christians is called the God of peace. The
name of pacifist shall have a different atmosphere as the kingdom
gains ground in the world. The peacemaker is often held in dis-
esteem now and persecuted but he will be honored with the name
of a "child of God" in the kingdom. It was natural for Jesus to
speak next of the *"pursued"* or persecuted ones. It is a favorite
stunt to pose as persecuted; but the one who really is *pursued* and
harried because of righteousness (goodness) is to be congratulated. Jesus frankly foretells that His diciples will have to suffer tribulations both of the character of persecution and obloquy.
Christ appeals to the heroic in men. They would be slandered
and maltreated because of loyalty to Christ. But these persecuted
ones are blessed because the kingdom is theirs and they wield its
power. They may well rejoice when they are calumniated, reproached, and persecuted, because they are placed thus in the
line and fellowship of the prophets and become God's prophets to
their own times. There is no prize for the one who deserves all
the bad things said about him; but there is great reward in
heaven for the truly persecuted, for just as the prophets suffered
for God and exulted so the disciples may endure persecutions
for Christ and rejoice. Christ here claims in another way equality
with the Father.

In these Beatitudes (beatus) Jesus shows that true felicity
depends not on outward position but on inward disposition; not
primarily on how others treat us but on how we behave toward
others. What are you doing for others? How are you reacting
to your environment? Not the rich, the full, those who laugh
now, those who are now well-spoken of as the false prophets,
nor the proud warriors, or the favourites of kings, are to be
congratulated. On the other hand, the humble, the repentant, the
meek, patient sufferers of injustices, the sincere, true pacifists, the
persecuted, are the sons of the glorious promises of the kingdom.

(II) The function and responsible mission of kingdom subjects
(Matt. 5:13-16). In carrying out their prophetic mission to the
world the apostles of the Kingdom are to be the "salt" of human
society. There is sin in the world and consequent decay and corruption. Salt saves from corruption only by contact. The kingdom subject must be a cleansing, purifying, preserving element in
contact with the human social environment. The believer may
lose his influence becoming *foolish* (moron). When the salt in
Palestine lost its taste and became insipid it was piled out on
the *street*. On the *ground*, (soil) it might become prejudicial,
robbing it of its fertility. The salt arrests the processes of decay
and corruption and stimulates the forces of life, but sacrifices its
own force in so doing. The disciple can only save the world by

sacrificing himself. Again, the mission of the disciples was compared to the light (lamp). They were to be the light of the *whole
world.* They must not as the Essenes put their light under the
bushel. Those professedly holy ascetics lived in secluded places,
out of living contact with human society. Thus, they contributed
nothing toward the leavening and enlightening of humanity. The
light of the Christian should not be hidden, as a lamp in a
Palestinian cottage which was put under the earthenware grain-
measure to hide or extinguish it at night. The proper place for
such a lamp was on the lamp-stand or projecting stone in the wall
on which the lamp was accustomed to be placed.[1] There was only
one lamp for a whole room. The kingdom man must seek not only
a pure light of intensity and clarity, but an advantageous position,
like the cities on the hills around the Sea of Galilee, whose white
stone houses could be seen from long distances in the light of
the sun. The influence of the good works of the disciples must
illumine the world, rebuking the sins of men and saving them
from self-destruction. Such a mission fulfilled would shed brilliance and intense light, revealing the Father in heaven, whose character of this same kind of light would thus be demonstrated before men, who would be eager to recognize His glorious character.

(III)   The ideal moral standards of the Kingdom in relation to
the Pharisaic interpretation of the Mosaic laws (Matt. 5:17-48;
Luke 6:27-30, 32-36).

One of the most fundamental of all things needed to be
understood by the disciples of Jesus was the exact relationship
which His new kingdom organization was to sustain to the old
regime of the Mosaic Law. The Pharisees were already accusing
Jesus of being disloyal to the Law. He had set aside deliberately
their traditional Sabbath laws and had taught His disciples to do
the same. Yet He continued to frequent their synagogues and
teach the people with unabated popularity. Doubtless these Pharisees were putting forward all their effort to undermine His popularity by declaring His frank, daring abrogation of their laws.

(1)   Jesus declares the moral and ethical standards of His
kingdom to be the fulfillment of the Law of Moses (Matt. 5:17-20).
The foundation of the great work and example of Jesus as a
teacher was the Old Testament Scriptures, summed up in the
expression — "the law and the prophets." He accepted these as of
divine authority but quietly brushed aside the immense accretion
of traditional interpretations of the Scribes and Pharisees. He discussed at greater length the relation of His teaching to the law and
prophets than any other topic of His general theme of kingdom
ideals and righteousness. In the Beatitudes, He had assumed in

1 The Land and the Book by Thompson.

the kingdom man a new heart of regeneration. Now, He proceeds to declare that far from coming to break up or "loosen down" the Law, He came to fill up to the full the moral law and the ceremonial law which pointed to Him through types for its fulfillment. He would reveal the depths of the meaning of the law and the prophets. He asserted, in the face of their accusation of His being a law-breaker, that the law and the prophets were dearer to Him than the whole physical universe both "the heaven and the earth." Not one iota or one smallest letter or particle, "not one jot or tittle" would pass away from the law until all should be fulfilled. Jesus here assumes the championship of the law and carries its demands to the utmost limit of Rabbinical expression. The tittle was a tiny little horn to distinguish one Hebrew letter from another. In the teaching of the Rabbis, "the guilt of altering one of these is pronounced so great, that if it were done the world would be destroyed." Jesus goes to this Rabbinical limit. "The heaven and earth may pass away but not one of the least commands of the law shall pass away unfulfilled." The Scribes and Pharisees did not recognize of course that many of the types of the ceremonial law were being fulfilled and completed in Jesus. To them, whose eyes were fixed on the letter, He seemed a destroyer, but to the one who sees through the letter to the deep underlying principles, Jesus was the fulfiller of the law and prophets. He distinguished between the eternal and temporal, the universal and national, the spirit and letter. This was the reason Jesus was different from the Scribes and Pharisees in His teaching. He spoke with authority born of conviction wrought out in experience. He was seeking to meet the real needs of humanity. He understood those needs and sympathized with them. He brushed aside verbosity and all formality and dealt with those needs in a clear, definite, and concrete way. Jesus asserts next, that the teacher must apply the doctrine to himself first before he is qualified to teach others. The test of the greatness of the teacher in the kingdom, He declares to be in his *doing* and *teaching* the law faithfully. This was a total denial and refutation of the charge made against Himself. Having thus clearly set forth His attitude toward the law, He proceeds next to throw a bomb into the camp of His enemies. The Scribes and Pharisees had not met the real spiritual needs of the people in their synagogue sermons. Their endless ceremonial and exacting regulations were a burden to the soul too heavy to be borne. The helpfulness of the preaching of Christ was a complete contrast. Jesus adds significantly now the startling statement, that if the righteousness of His hearers should not exceed that of the Scribes and Pharisees they would in no wise enter into the Kingdom of the heavens. He was not making "righteousness" secondary in

His kingdom regime. In the teaching of the law they must excel the professed Scribal teachers and in living the law they must surpass the Pharisaic separatists — the orthodox pietists.

(2) Jesus illustrates variously the superiority of the righteousness of the Kingdom over that of the Scribes and Pharisees and their interpretation of the Law (Matt. 5:21-48). They taught the Old Testament plus their oral law or interpretation of it. The latter covered up the former. They were not content with the prescriptions of Moses and added a tedious system of meritorious works such as fasts, washings, alms, and prayers. The Essenes and John the Baptist discarded most but held on to some of these in a partial reform. Jesus pierced to the heart of the truth repudiating all merely human traditions, and proclaimed the eternal spiritual principles of the Law. He carries the teaching from the letter to the spirit and illustrates it concretely in six examples.

The first example was that of *murder*, which was the prohibition of the sixth comandment (Matt. 5:21-25). For the Scribes murder meant the actual slaying of a man. They added to the simple words of the law (Ex. 20:13) that the criminal was "in danger of the judgment of God" in some cases and "of the Sanhedrin" in others. There was a small Sanhedrin in certain cities and the homicide was subject to the sentence of the tribunal of his nearest city. Jesus located murder in the seed thought of anger and hatred. He thus assumed superiority over the Mosaic regulations, and interpreted the law of Moses to condemn anger itself and its expressions of contempt as in the Aramaic word *Raca*, which meant *stupid or empty head*, and the Greek word *More*, *thou fool*, which expressed contempt for the heart and character, as our expression, *you scoundrel*. The latter was a graver expression and put its author into the danger of the Gehenna of fire. Abusive language even was thus prohibited by the new principle of Jesus. The disciple therefore who should come in the solemn act of worship, bearing his gift to the altar, and there remember that his brother had something against him, must go and get himself reconciled[1] taking the initiative himself. There should be mutual concession in the reconciliation[2] which involved two persons. Anger retained in the heart breeds insults and leads to homicide. Worship is not acceptable to God when there is hate in the heart. He who does not make up with his enemy opportunely, may be delivered into the hand of the judge and thence to the underling servant officer and be cast into prison whence he will not emerge without first paying the last tiny two-mite farthing.

The second example was that of *adultery*, prohibited in the seventh commandment (Ex. 20:14). Jesus found the germ of

1 Ingressive second aorist passive imperfect.   2 Preposition dia, between two.

adultery in the lascivious look (Matt. 5:27-30). The Scribal interpretation of the Law restricted it to the overt act itself. The new
kingdom doctrine condemned the unclean glance as virtually a
commission of the crime. Jesus arraigned the secret lusts of the
breast and called upon His disciples — using hyperbolical language — to exercise the strictest guard and greatest self-restraint. It
would be better to pluck out the best (right) eye or cut off the
right hand than to yield to the temptation to satisfy these lusts
and go into hell. Adultery is in the eye and heart before the outward act. The heart is not merely the seat of affections but includes the intellect, affections, and the will. Jesus was near to
quoting the Rabbis in this expression. They said that "the eye
and the heart are two brokers of sin" (*Wunsche*). The eye is like
the stick in a trap that springs and lets the trap close on the animal
that touches it. Here is a great plea for self-mastery. Jesus does
not want man to mutilate the body but control it against sin.
If your right hand is causing you to stumble and be slandered,
cut it off. It is better to cut out a bad appendix then to die of
gangrene. It is better to suffer the loss of one member than all.

The third example was that of divorce. The Pharisaic doctrine
of divorce was wholly inadequate. It sanctioned divorce at the
mere whim of the husband. If a man should see a woman pret-
tier than his wife, he might dismiss his wife and marry the other.
The school of Hillel allowed the husband to put his wife away
for poor cooking or for any greivous bodily affliction. In the time
before Moses, the Israelites were very loose about divorce and a
man could divorce his wife "for any cause." Moses placed restrictions by obliging the one desiring a divorce to give a "divorce
certificate." This was a protection of the wife against the mere
whim of an angry husband. During the time necessary to arrange
this written document, reflection might lead to reconciliation.
Jesus taught that neither husband nor wife has the moral right to
dissolve the marriage relationship, except for the single cause of
unchastity or unfaithfulness.

The fourth illustration of the superiority of the new kingdom
law was that of the *oath* (Matt. 5:33-37). The law of Moses condemned the false oath (Ex. 20:7; Lev. 19:12). The oath was a
debt to God. There was abuse then in the use of the name of
God, as now, in profanity. Jesus prohibits all forms of profanity.
The kingdom man's word must be as good as his oath. The Rabbis
had laid down minute rules as to many different kinds of oaths
which might be used. Men might swear by heaven, earth, the sun,
the prophets, the Temple, Jerusalem, the altar, the sacrifices,
vessels, and by their own heads.[1] Jesus expressly refers to some of
these as illustrations, and then cuts the whole practice of profanity

1 Hor. Heb. Vol. II, pp. 127, 128.

up by the roots. The Rabbis' casuistry had added to the words of
the law — "Thou shalt not swear falsely" — their own words: "but
shalt perform unto the Lord thine oaths." Hence they concluded
that any oath that did not have a vow of sacrifice as a part of it
was not binding. This opened the door for perjury without blame.
Jesus cut the whole practice out for the kingdom man.

The fifth example was the law of *retaliation*, "an eye for an
eye and a tooth for a tooth" (Ex. 21:24; Lev. 24:20). This was a
restriction on unrestrained vengeance by fixing an exact compensation for injury (McNeile). Jesus removes personal revenge
wholly from the hands of man, including lynching and offensive
or aggressive war (Matt. 5:38-42). He said it was better to suffer
injury by personal violence (v. 38), by litigation (v. 40), by public requirements (v. 41), or by insistent requests for loans (v. 42)
rather than cultivate the spirit of vengeance. He warned His
disciples that they would be maltreated, giving these examples of
the kind of treatment they might expect. Smiting on the cheek
was a common form of insult in the East.[1] A fine of two hundred
denarii was imposed for the first blow and for the second the
fine was doubled. It was not the injury but the indignity and even
a slave preferred scourging to a buffet.[2] Both Christ and Paul
had to suffer this shameful experience. The disciple must "turn
the other cheek" not literally, but show a dignified reserve of
patience and remonstrance instead of striking back. "When he
was reviled he reviled not again." The creditor might take the
coat of a debtor but must return his cloak, which served as his
blanket at night. The disciple must forego even this right to
claim his cloak. He was not to resent the forced service which in
customs prevailed in the Roman Empire. Jesus meekly remonstrated but did not resist insults and impositions. The disciples
should give what they could honorably and justly give to everyone
that should ask. Meek endurance puts the oppressor to shame.
The law of equivalent revenge was to be superseded by the law
of complete self-denial. His disciples must overcome evil with the
good. They must suffer wrong patiently that the wrong-doer
might be won to repentance by the non-resisting meekness of the
wronged.

The last illustration Jesus used was *love of one's enemies*
(Matt. 5:43-48). The Rabbis taught love for one's neighbor and
hate for one's enemies. Jesus repudiated this Rabbinical inference
from Lev. 19:18. He Himself prayed for His enemies on the cross.
Shammai and others made use of the Mosaic law to justify
national and religious hatred. Jesus rose with His disciples to the
highest pitch of heroism when He commanded them to love their

1 I Kings 22:24; Matt. 26:27; Acts 23:2.   2 Seneca.

enemies.[1] The Old Testament commanded kindness and mercy but sanctioned revenge and triumph over one's enemies. Jesus taught that all men who need us are our neighbors. Our love must be universal, without distinction of race, merit, color, or rank. A new standard is set up. No human standard would suffice. The one standard and ideal for all humanity was *the Father*. He had love in His heart for all, the good and the bad alike, sending His sun for both and His rain upon the just and unjust. His motive in bearing patiently the sins of His creatures against Him is to bring them to repentance. With the Rabbi, religion was a transaction with God. The literal fulfillment of the legal requirements put God under obligation to him. They said: "love them who love you; do good to him who does good to you"; but the new kingdom ideal called for greater heroism and the imitation of the Father in heaven. To be able to rise to the height of working for the salvation of their enemies, they would need to look up to the divine ideal frequently. Be full grown, complete, compassionate as your heavenly Father. This was the highest ideal possible — that of perfection.

(IV) The ideal of kingdom righteousness in practical religion (Matt. 6:1-7:12). The spirituality of the duties in all the acts of religion as well as in all the relationships of life, Jesus illustrates, in contrast with the formalism, hypocrisy, and self-righteousness of the Scribes and Pharisees.

(1) The kingdom ideal in all religious acts of worship was that of *honesty* and *sincerity* (Matt. 6:1-18). The practical righteousness of the Pharisees was in no wise superior to the unsound teaching of the traditionalists. The practice of real righteousness is cited in three characteristic religious acts: almsgiving, prayer and fasting.

Jesus warns His disciples against the kind of hypocritical ostentatious righteousness, with the motive of getting praise from men, which was common in the practice of the Pharisees. They were commanded to put their minds on this in strict attention.[2] Their motive in all eleemosynary as well as other *giving* must be with a view to God's approval and not man's praise. There were thirteen trumpet-shaped chests in the Temple to receive the contributions. The Pharisaic hypocrites passing by would cast their coins into these metallic chests and make such a noise as to attract the attention and commendatory remarks of men. "They have their receipt in full," said Jesus. The praise of men is what they sought and that is what they "are receiving." The kingdom man must not let his right hand know what his left hand is doing, that none may know how much he is giving. His Father seeing in

1 Ps. 7:6; 14:7.   2 The verb prosechete with the noun nous.

secret will reward him. Jesus does not promise public but sure reward.[1] Almgiving had been made by the Rabbis a meritorious work before God. "For one farthing given to the poor, a man will receive heaven," said the Rabbis. Alms were given to earn a reward from God.

Greater emphasis is put on the illustration of *prayer*, which is the "holy of holies" of worship (Matt. 6:5-16). The same motive of God's approval and not man's praise, must actuate the prayers of the kingdom subject. The Pharisaical hypocrites loved to pray in the synagogues and also standing on the corners of the street where they could be seen from all sides. Real prayer lays open wholly the inner man to the light of God. It is a self-dedication to God (vs. 22-24). But the prayer of the Pharisees had as its motive the praise of men. They were getting public notoriety when they prayed and that was their pay. Following the warning against the spirit of ostentation which is so commonly seen in prayer, Jesus gives some indications as to how the kingdom man should pray. He should go into his *secret place*, whether a private chamber, office, or other place, where he can shut the world out. Prayer in the congregation is not forbidden but prayer must be sincere and not a hypocritical show. As to the manner, they must not use vain and lengthy repetitions as the heathen (Gentiles), who think there is virtue in verbosity. To them prayer is a mere babble of many words, an empty repetition like the prayer of the Mohammedan or the paternosters and aves of the Romanist. Prayer was to be intensely personal. Jesus dropped the plural and used the second singular, "thou."

He gave a model prayer to suggest the scope of prayer and the attitude of the praying soul toward God and men. It is also always easier to follow a pattern than to obey a mere precept. Jesus gave the model prayer in order to make it easier for His disciples to pray. This prayer, brief, simple, universal, and spiritual, contains an invocation and six petitions, three looking Godward and three manward, only one of the latter referring to material sustenance and that in a most spiritual manner. The doxology was a later insertion in the text. "The Lord's Prayer," as it is called, was not meant for liturgical use by others. Jesus wanted to teach His disciples how to pray, as was the custom of Rabbis, but in a different way. The invocation was *social*, using the plural pronoun "our." It was universal, revealing the God of all humanity. In all the petitions the *aorist* imperative is used, expressing urgency. One supreme objective is stated in the first three petitions: God's glory, kingdom, and will, the worshipper's needs being made secondary. The things of God, His name, His kingdom, His realized

* *future indicative.*

will come first, and the needs of the body in one and soul in two petitions follow. The highest ideal of perfection and felicity for the race is offered in the will of the Eternal Father's being done on earth as it is in heaven. Childlike trust and dependence are expressed here toward the Father's daily bounty. The spirit full of love and forgiveness toward others stretches out its hands for the Father's pardon. In no place in literature do we find a more complete expression of thought and feeling in so small a compass. Bread for the body is asked, but just for a day in simple faith in the Father. The request for pardon must be based on the spirit of pardon extended to one's fellowmen. "Our *moral debts* to God will be forgiven" in proportion to "our forgiving spirit." The petition not to be submitted[1] to severe trial or "sifting" has its complement in the plea to be delivered from evil or the evil one. The reference to trespasses[2] is not a part of the model prayer (vs. 14, 15) but points to the fact that forgiveness is dependent on forgiving.

The final illustration Jesus chose of the practical righteousness of the Pharisees was that of fasting (Matt. 6:16-18). There was only one fast in the Mosaic system, that of the Day of Atonement; but the Pharisees had added many others, especially Mondays and Thursdays. On these fast days they strewed ashes on their heads, put on their worst clothing, did not trim their beard or wash or anoint themselves.[3] The Romans satirized this sad and mournful custom in their theatres, by leading a camel on the stage covered with mourning cloth. "Why is the camel mourning?" asked a player. "Because the Jews are keeping the Sabbath year and growing nothing, but living on thistles," was the reply. The Rabbis were forbidden to wash and anoint themselves on the fast days. They put on a sullen, gloomy, sad countenance, and even disfigured their faces in a hypocritical show of their great piety. Kingdom men were not to follow this vain and hollow show, but on the contrary anoint their heads and wash their faces that they might not appear unto men to fast. To seek effect, applause, or gain, by a show of godliness must be avoided.

(2) The ideal attitude of the kingdom subject toward God (Matt. 6:19-34).

The kingdom man must maintain the attitude of single-hearted devotion and whole-hearted trust toward God, and make the kingdom of Heaven the controlling objective of his life.

The necessity of single-hearted devotion to God and His kingdom, is illustrated first by the "laying up of treasures" (vs. 19-

1 Permissive imperative.
2 A falling to one side, a lapse or deviation from the truth
3 Lightfoot, Vol. II, p. 155.

27). "Do not have the habit of treasuring up treasures for yourselves upon the earth," said Jesus. Personal selfish interest in
treasure-getting and hoarding is one of the greatest and most prevalent weaknesses of the human race. Thieves are always digging
through and stealing, now, as they did then through the walls
made of mud or sun-dried bricks. Even steel safes are unsafe
now. There are other natural destructive forces, as the moth
which attacks clothing and rust which consumes most metals.
"Have the habit of laying up treasures in the heavenly sphere,"
He added, "for there none of these destructive forces will affect
them." The reason for so doing is, that when the treasure is laid
up on earth the heart will be thoughtless and careless about heaven.
Divided loyalties dissipate the energies and neutralize the effort
for the kingdom. The kingdom man must seek to have a united
heart, in which there is no warring between opposite desires and
affections.

Another illustration of single-hearted devotion Jesus adds,
that of the eye (vs. 22, 23). One cannot have spiritual sight and
insight when he has one eye fixed on the world and the other on
heaven. Then, too, if the moral vision is diseased or *bad* it will
confuse the spiritual perception. Seeing double is double-minded-
ness. Just as lack of focus of the eye gives a double retinal picture and produces confusion in the vision, so the lack of a united
heart and concentration on one supreme spiritual objective leaves
the soul in darkness. The eye is not only the organ of vision but
the seat of expression, revealing the inward disposition. If the
inner light be darkness how terrible is that darkness. Finally, the
illustration of the slave is added. Many try to be slaves of God
and Mammon, the money-god, at the same time. The slave of
Mammon may pretend to serve God but will surely, "line up with
Mammon and depise God."

The kingdom man must maintain an attitude of whole-hearted
trust in God (Matt. 6:25-32). A second enemy, to a heart united
on the grand kingdom objective, is anxious worry about food and
clothing. Stop being anxious and having the habit of petulant
worry about making a living. Your life is more than food and
your body than clothing. The confidence of the kingdom man in
God's providential care must be absolute and whole-hearted. God
gave the life, how much more will He give the food and clothing
to sustain it. This is an argument from the greater to the less.
Jesus adds an argument from the less to the greater, in the birds
of the heaven, which are accustomed neither to sow nor reap nor
gather into barns, but the heavenly Father goes on nourishing
them. If He takes care of them how much more will he take care

of our lives which are of more value. Thus, He shows why we should not be anxious about food. After all, our anxious thought will do no good. It will not help in our growth physically nor will it prolong our life one day. In the illustration taken from the botanical world and in particular from the lilies and other wild flowers like the anemones, poppies, gladioli, and irises (McNeile), Jesus urges us not to be anxious about clothing. "Put your mind on the lilies of the field how they are growing, not sowing nor reaping." Yet not even Solomon in all his glory "was putting around himself" such clothing as one of these. Now, descending to the common grass of the field Jesus heightens the comparison and force of His illustration. "This common grass which exists a day and then withers up and is used for making a fire in the cooking ovens, God clothes; how much more you, O little-faith men. Do not grow anxious.[1] It is *heathenish* to be thus anxious about these things," said Jesus.

He concludes the exhortation to single-hearted devotion and whole-hearted faith, by pointing out the supreme objective of the life of the kingdom man — the kingdom of God and His righteousness. He who puts the kingdom first may be assured he will never have lack of food, clothing, and other necessities. The reason is that God knows we have need of these things and provides. Do not let the ghost of tomorrow come stalking forth with its hobgoblins of doubt and distrust. This is what the anxious soul is tempted to do when all other doubts are allayed. Do not borrow trouble from tomorrow; each day has enough of its own.

(3) The ideal social law of the kingdom (Matt. 7:1-12; Luke 6:37-42). Jesus next gave the social law of the kingdom, warning against censoriousness; stimulating proper discrimination, counseling prayer as the only means of maintaining the proper relations with others, and summing up all in a Golden Rule which should serve as our guide. There is no habit more prevalent or more vicious in human nature than that of captious criticism and censoriousness. "Do not go on being a critic and prejudging people," said Jesus. We may have our opinions about others but they should be based on real facts. If we condemn men here, we will be condemned by God hereafter. Jesus would have us be charitable respecting the errors and shortcomings of others, that we may not have our own sins brought up against us in the judgment day. Judgment belongs to God. We may not condemn our brother. We must have a desire to release or acquit rather than to condemn him. The opposite of censure and condemnation is commanded, with the promise that bountiful measure in return, pressed down well, shaken together firmly, heaped up to the point of being over-full, and actually

1 Ingressive aorist (V. 31)

falling off around the sides, will be given into our laps by God. This will be in accord with the law of requital — love in return for love. Luke adds two metaphors referring to the over-critical Scribal teachers who were full of this fault of captious criticism. If a teacher is thus full of the censorious, he is like the blind leading the blind and both fall into a terrible pit, such as one of the un-curbed wells or unfenced quarries in Palestine. Self-explanation is enjoined especially upon the one who teaches, since it is a long process to get the pupil "patched and mended" up to the plane of his teacher; and what if the teacher who does the patching needs patching himself?

Jesus adds another metaphor which illustrates the vicious practice of censorious criticism. "Why are you looking at the small piece of trash or splinter in your brother's eye and not con-sidering the log sticking out of your own eye?" This was an Arabic proverb which Jesus used with certain alterations. The point of the illustration is, that self-examination is forgotten and kind offices are offered benevolent and condescendingly, to help correct the little fault of the brother, while the great big fault in one's self is ignored. People who do not try to correct their own faults should not criticize the mistakes of others and especially of the brother. According to the pronouncement of Jesus such people are self-blinded hypocrites.

On the other hand, man's God-like powers of discrimination are to be employed for their high ends. The meat to be offered in sacrifice which had been "set apart" or holy, should not be given to the yelping savage dogs in the Palestinian street. The disciples would meet with ungodly and hardened men who would dishonor the truth when they received it; or like the wild boars of the Jordan valley would trample the precious pearls underfoot in lack of appreciation and by rejection. The prostitution of our high powers of discrimination and judgment into use for cen-sorious criticism and captious cavilings, to say nothing of cynical sneers, is to be guarded against. But we are to use discrimination in dealing with men. There is such a thing as a mistaken zeal in trying to make converts though we are most apt to err through the lack of zeal. To cast the pearls of beautiful evangelical ideas which are precious before unappreciative minds, and sacred things of the gospel message down before those who have devouring appetites for low things, without discrimination, is a vain practice.

The means of attaining this kingdom ideal in judgment and discriminating conduct, is through prayer (Matt. 7:7-11). It is very hard to avoid censorious criticism and use wise discrimina-tion. We are to seek divine direction in this diffcult task through prayer. We are commanded by Jesus to so resolve this problem.

"Begin to ask and keep on asking habitually and you shall receive; begin to seek and keep on seeking and you shall find; begin to knock and keep on knocking and it shall be opened unto you. For the one who continues asking is actually receiving, and the one who continues seeking is already finding, and to the one who continues knocking it shall be opened." The illustration of the earthly father, who is ready to give in a discriminating way the proper and useful thing in response to the request of the son is adduced to stimulate our faith in the heavenly Father's readiness and ability to give us the good things when we ask Him.

The Golden Rule (Matt. 7:12) sums up the substance of the warning and counsels about the proper attitude toward our fellowmen. It is found in different, incomplete, and negative forms in Socrates, Menander, Confucius, and the apocryphal book of Tobit. Someone asked Rabbi Hillel to teach him the whole law while he stood on one foot. He replied: "What you would not like done to yourself, do not to your neighbor; this is the whole law: all the rest is commentary on it." But this declaration was misleading, leaving God out of account, and giving as a result a mere moral code without a religious basis. Jesus made this rule the *second* great commandment, following that which made God supreme in man's affection and loyalty (Mar. 12:28-34). All of our duties toward our fellowmen are summed up in this rule or social law. Jesus made use of the precepts of others to build His teaching on, but He so transformed and glorified them as to make them ideal, and in this case a perfect spiritual law for all humanity.

(V) The conclusion of the sermon was highly practical, pointing out how the kingdom men might attain the high ideals set forth in the body of the discourse (Matt. 7:13-27; Luke 6:43-49).

In this solemn appeal there are four exhortations and warnings given to the disciples.

1. They are commanded and warned to enter into life by the narrow gate and the narrow or compressed way, which leads like the difficult mountain defile between high rocks (vs. 13, 14). Jesus made use of the metaphor of the two ways familiar in Jewish writings (Ps. 1; Deut. 30:19; Jer. 21:8), to impress upon His hearers the difficulty and strenuosity of the way of the kingdom, in contrast with the facility of the worldly life. The contrast is sharply drawn in the reason assigned for choosing the one and avoiding the other. The gate is wide and the way is broad which leads to destruction and many go by that way. On the contrary the gate is narrow and the way compressed which leads into life and few are they that find it. One must not walk with the multitude in the broad and easy way but will have to go against cus-

toms, fashions, and conventions. The way of life is not easy, but calls for strenuous effort, passing through narrow places and afflictions (Rom. 8:35).

2. They are warned in the second place to beware of false teachers. (Matt. 7:15-19; Luke 6:43-45). There were many such then and in all times since. In appearance, they are innocent and harmless as sheep; but inwardly they are full of ulterior motives of greed for power and gain. They can be "known fully" and should be tested out and "recognized" by their fruits, as you know a good or a bad tree. Works correspond to doctrines and conduct reveals character. A good tree does not progressively bring forth bad fruit nor a corrupt tree good fruit. "Make the tree good and the fruit will be good." This is the pragmatic test. A regenerated character is the primary consideration in the teacher or disciple. Men do not gather grapes from thorn trees nor figs from bramble bushes. The mouth will speak out sooner or later what is in the heart. The disciples must not follow teachers recognized to be false by the fruits of their lives. Such teachers will be cut down by God and cast into the fire.

3. Jesus warns against false personal religion (Matt. 7:21-23; Luke 6:46). All disciples as well as teachers must face the test of the Lord's perfect insight. Mere profession before the world will not suffice. The disciple must be a doer of the will of the heavenly Father. Nor would a religion of mere works, though "mighty" and done "in the name of Jesus," meet their needs in the final day of judgment when they should appear before Him as their judge. Unless they take care to have a real religion of obedience and loyalty, He will in that day have to "confess" no favorable knowledge of them and send them away from Him as workers of "lawlessness."

4. Finally, Jesus says that all successful outcome in life depends on building upon the doctrines set forth in the sermon (Matt. 7:24-29; Luke 6:47-49). The one who responds to this appeal favorably, He likens to the wise man, who dug down deep until he struck solid rock and there laid his foundation sure and strong. The winter came with its rain, torrential rivers arose in a flood, and the winds and stream beat and broke upon the house, but it did not fall because it had been well built upon the rock. On the other hand, the one hearing these teachings of Jesus and not putting them into practice He compares to the foolish man (moron) who built his house upon the surface, sandy soil. The winter rain came down, the river rose in a flood, and the winds and stream beat and broke upon that house, and it collapsed, and the fall and ruin was great. It is impossible to ignore or neglect the

teaching of Jesus. One who does so will have his life-house tumbling in upon him, and being all he has how great will be the ruin! But he whose character is built upon the eternal foundations of Christ's words will withstand all the forces of adversity forever. But the whole wall must be built on the solid foundation lest there be a breach somewhere and great damage.

It is no wonder that when Jesus had finished speaking, the crowds expressed their wonder in a buzz of astonishment. They were literally swept from their feet. It was different from the sermons of the Scribes which they were accustomed to hearing. Specimens of these discourses in the Mishna and Gemara show that they were dull collections of disjointed comments on many subjects. Their teachings were narrow, dogmatic, second-hand, having no freshness, force, or power to move the heart to emotion or the will to action. They dealt with the minutiae of mint, anise, cummin, the length of fringes and breadth of phylacteries, thus neglecting the weightier matters and vital subjects. The sermon of Jesus, quite to the contrary, with a swift intuitive insight pierced to the depths of the human heart, stirring the conscience and moving the will to action. He knew the life of man, rejoiced with him in his joys and wept with him in his sorrows. Such words of grace fell from His lips, spoken in such a gracious manner, that the world said: "Never man spoke as this man." There is no wonder that when He came down from the mountain great multitudes followed Him.

CHAPTER XIV
SECOND MISSIONARY CAMPAIGN IN GALILEE
(Harm. §§ 55-60)

Following the Sermon on the Mount, Jesus returns from the Horns of Hattin with His newly organized body of apostles, to Capernaum, the town exalted to heaven in these days of His ministry in Galilee.

1. He cures the Centurion's slave-boy at Capernaum (Matt. 8:5-13; Luke 7:1-10). It is at this time that we must date one of our most interesting incidents — the cure of the grievously tormented paralytic slave boy of the Centurion. This slave, who was highly esteemed, nay very dear to his Gentile master, was getting on so badly that he had been for some time just at the point of death.[1]

It is not strange that this "Captain of a hundred" should have turned to Jesus for help. Though he was a Gentile and not a proselyte to the Jewish faith,[2] yet he must have witnessed the cure of the paralytic in Capernaum a few months before, and known of the healing of the Gentile nobleman's little boy, whom Jesus had cured while in Cana. In these miracles, which had passed under the sober observation of this soldier, Jesus had not discriminated against the Gentiles; furthermore, He had certainly demonstrated His power to cure paralysis and heal *in absencia*.

There are certain discrepancies between the narratives of this cure by Matthew and Luke, but they are only apparent and are due to the fact mainly that Matthew did not give unessential details while Luke searches more into the facts as they occurred. This Gentile centurion came to Jesus, not personally, but through the representation of the synagogue elders of Capernaum, asking Him that He should come and save the servant lad. These Jewish friends added insistence to the request and "were beseeching him" to come with haste.[3]

They gave their testimony to the character of the centurion. "He is worthy that thou shouldest do this for him," they said, "because he loves our nation and himself built for us a synagogue." It is a significant fact that of all the ruins of Capernaum (Tell Hum), the cornices and capitals of this, what seems to have been the sole synagogue of the town, are best preserved. The fact that the centurion did not come personally to Jesus with his request would indicate that he was not a proselyte to the Jewish faith[4] and so did not feel the liberty to approach a Jewish rabbi. More-

---

1 Luke 7:2; imperfect of verb, emellen.   2 Edersheim Book III, p. 546.
3 Luke 7:4.   4 Schurer, H. J. P. II:2.

over, the facts of the narrative show him to have been kind-hearted
as well as public spirited. He held this Jewish slave boy to be dear
and not only had him cared for in his own home but went forth
to seek means for his cure, in humility appealing to Jesus, who
was a Jew. Such treatment of a slave was in those times rare,
though it was occasional, as in the case of Seneca, the Roman
philosopher, who "sat down at the same table with some of his
slaves because they *were* worthy and with others that they might
become so." This centurion in the service of Herod Antipas was
a good man, in spite of the fact that he was a centurion.

Chrysostom charged the Jewish elders who came with syco-
phancy. They might have used adulation with ulterior motives, or
they might have been moved with jealousy that the Centurion
should have called in the aid of Jesus who was the rival of the
Rabbis. It is more probable however that they were well disposed
and really sought to serve their friend the Centurion, who had
been so liberal in his patronage of their cause. Then, too, opposition to Jesus had not developed yet to the point that He did
not find a welcome with the elders of this synagogue in which He
was invited various times later to speak. The fact that Jesus immediately responded to the request, saying: "I will come and cure
him," and was going along with them,[1] would it seems, sustain this
supposition.

Either the elders exceed their commission in their zeal, inviting Jesus to come to the Centurion's home; or the Centurion by
later reflection resolved on a different plan; for he sent a group
of his friends who met Jesus when He was not a great distance
from the house, and bade Him in the Centurion's name not to take
the trouble to come further. He humbly assigns, as a reason for
sending these friends with this request, his own unworthiness,
which had led him not to come personally to Jesus but send the
elders, and which was now the motive in sending the messengers
to say that his home was unworthy or unfit, by being a Gentile
home, to receive Jesus. In one who had built the fine synagogue,
we would expect a different spirit from that of extreme humility.
This home was probably not far out from the synagogue on the
road to Tiberias, the seat of government of Herod Antipas. The
Jews considered the Gentile home unclean. This Roman soldier
had to swallow a good deal of pride to say: "My house is unfit
to receive you."

Coupled with this humility, we find a faith in the unlimited
power of Jesus which elicited the highest praise of our Lord. Using

1 Imperfect indicative passive.

his own position of a subordinate officer in a great military organization, in which he exercised over his own unit in the organization absolute power to command and send, he illustrated the
position Jesus occupied in the realm of the spiritual hierarchy in
which He was supreme. His conception of Jesus was that He
could speak a word of authoritative command, and the "demons of
malady" which by popular superstition were thought to cause diseases would have to go forth in obedience. It was only necessary
that He should speak with a word[1] where He was and the slave
boy would be healed. The Centurion placed the Saviour on the
throne of the universe; and he was not the only Centurion of the
time who pierced through to the thought of the deity of Jesus.
Three times the gospel states that Jesus marveled: once at the
unbelief of the people in Nazareth, once at the faith of the Canaanitish woman, and here at the faith of the Centurion. "I say unto
you, I have not found so great faith, no, not in Israel." Here was
an absolute trust which deemed all things possible with Jesus,
and that, too, in a man who made no claim to outward or inward
fitness to receive the blessing.

Faith, so clear, undoubting, humble, expressed by the lips of
a heathen man, a Gentile despised by the Jews, caused Jesus to
reflect on the high destiny of His Kingdom. Here, were appearing
first-fruits of a vast harvest, world-wide in its extension. "And
I say unto you that many shall come from the east and the west
and shall recline at the table of the feast with Abraham, Isaac
and Jacob in the kingdom of heaven (Ps. 107:3; Isa. 49:12); but
the sons of the kingdom shall be cast forth into outer darkness;
there shall be weeping and gnashing of teeth." The Jews thought
the kingdom their special heritage and that Israel would be
gathered to a great feast together with the patriarchs and the
heroes of the Jewish faith. Their outward and hereditary connection with the Jewish race was the basis of this hope. Gentiles
would have no part in that feast.

But we have here the teaching of Jesus about the future of
the kingdom in marked contrast with the traditions of the Jews.
John had also taught that outward or hereditary connection was
not sufficient, but an inward change was necessary. In the day of
the kingdom feast, the honored guests who would recline around
the table of social fellowship with Abraham, Isaac and Jacob,
would not be the hereditary "sons of the kingdom." On the contrary, these would be cast into outer darkness, "where there would
be weeping and gnashing of teeth." The spiritual privileges of the
kingdom would be taken away from those who rejected Christ and
their place of privilege would be given to other nations. In one
of their Rabbinical lessons the Jews made God say: "I shall spread

for you Jews a great table, which the Gentiles will see and be ashamed." They prided themselves on being the "sons of the heavenly kingdom," and despised all others as doomed to sit in the darkness outside the banquet hall of the Messiah. In the usage of the Jews, *Gehenna* was a place of darkness to which in the day of the Lord the Gentiles would be consigned.[1] The merit of the circumcision would deliver the Jewish sinner from Gehenna. But in the language of Jesus Gehenna is a place of hopeless and endless night where there shall be deep sorrow (weeping) and intense anger (gnashing of teeth).

We may well believe that Jesus did not stop until He came very near the house of the Centurion. To him personally Jesus doubtless spoke the words of great cheer and comfort: "Go thy way, as thou hast believed so be it done unto thee." And with what joy it must have been that those who had been sent, both the elders and friends, returned and found that the slave boy had been healed in that same hour.

2.   He raises the widow's son at Nain (Luke 7:11-17).

It came to pass providentially soon afterwards, some think on the next day[2] after the healing of the slave boy in Capernaum, that Jesus went to the walled town called Nain twenty-five miles southwest from Capernaum. He was now entering upon His second missionary campaign in Galilee. He probably took a boat at Capernaum to the southern extremity of the Sea of Galilee, and from there pursued His way on foot, accompanied by His twelve recently chosen apostles, a larger band of other disciples, and a considerable[3] crowd of others.

Nain was located according to Robinson about two miles west of Endor on the north slope of Little Hermon (Tabor). The site has been identified with that of the modern Nein, a miserable Moslem village of a few houses of mud and stones with flat earth roofs and doors three feet high, sprinkled here and there without order or system among the debris of former and better days.[4] The ruins are extensive and indicate a walled town in the days of Jesus, its gate opening out to the north on the plain of Esdraelon, so intimately connected with many events in the history of ancient Israel. Shunem was only a short distance, just on the other side of mount Tabor, where Elisha had restored to life and given back to his mother an only son. Elijah, his predecessor, had performed a similar miracle at Zarephath, also not far distant, nine hundred years before. Nain must have been a "fair" city, as its name

1 Yalkut II, p. 42.   2 Many ancient authorities read, on the next day.
3 Hikanos.   4 Land of Israel by H. B. Tristam, p. 125.

means and one of considerable size as the extensive ruins indicate. There are traces of its walls and so it would have a "gate"
as in the Gospel record.

To the east of the town, about a mile in the direction of
Endor, is an ancient unfenced burying-place still used by Moslems,
marked by a few graves and rock-hewn sepulchers and identified
by Tristam and others as the most probable site of the cemetery
to which the mournful procession, bearing the body of the only
son of the widow, was slowly wending its way. Leading the procession[1] came first the widowed and bereft mother, the only real
mourner, but followed by the women making loud lamentations
according to the Palestinian custom. Next came the bier borne by
men, a mere board with narrow sides attached, and on it the open
wicker-basket coffin on which the body wrapped in linen cloth
lay with the face exposed. Luke, the physician, states that the
young man was really dead.[2] The well-known blast of the horn
had announced that once more the Angel of Death had visited
the town. All the last sad offices to the dead had been rendered.
There is a great concentration of sorrow here. The mother was a
widow who had doubtless struggled hard to rear this *only* son and
was depending on him as her main support in age. It was a double
sorrow and the heartless lamentation of the mourners about her
did not relieve the anguish of her grief-stricken heart. There was
no consolation for her lonely life as she contemplated the sad days
out ahead. He was her only son, so young and full of promise.
His death left a vacancy in the home and in her bleeding heart.

Following Jesus was another great crowd but one full of rejoicing and eager hopefulness. He was the Prince of life and inspired joy and expectation as He led His disciple band forth to
the abundant activities of His glorious ministry of teaching, preaching, and healing. Here was the triumphal procession of life with
singing and rejoicing, going to meet the sad procession of death
and the sound of mourning and the funeral dirge. It was no mere
coincidence that the Lord of life here met in the way near the
gate of Nain at the evening hour the sad procession of sorrow
and death. It was a plan of providence. If He had come a little
later the funeral would have been over.

Jesus recognized the grief-stricken mother as she went before the bier,[3] and going forward a few steps in front of His disciples advanced near her. "Seeing her, His heart was filled with
sympathy and deeply moved with compassion for her."

"Do not go on weeping,"[4] He said tenderly.

Then going forward a little He touched the open wicker-coffin.

1 Wetstein on Luke 7:13.   2 Perfect tense indicating permanent state.
3 Leading back to death whom she had brought into life.
4 Present imperative of progressive action.

The pall-bearers stopped immediately. It was ceremonial pollution of the worst type to touch the dead, and by Rabbinism frought with the most terrible consequences. Jesus dreaded not the imagined defilement and brushed away all such useless traditions. A superstitious awe fell upon the great crowd of people. The mourning ceased in breathless expectation of what this strange Rabbi should mean by thus stopping the inviolate funeral procession in the way. Suddenly His clear command rang out on the vibrant air and was heard by all:

"Young man, I say unto you, Arise!" And immediately "he who was dead sat up and began to speak,"[1] and Jesus gave him, whom He had brought back to life and might well claim as His own, to his astonished mother. The curtain drops there so far as the rejoicing mother was concerned and we are not permitted to witness her gratitude and joy. The young man began to speak but we are left in surmise as to what he said. The act of Jesus was unsolocited. His sympathy had not been merely passive but active. He had told her not to weep but He proceeded to remove the cause of her weeping. He was so full of spiritual life that He could not be polluted by contact with sin, sorrow, and death. He was the Lord of life and could speak the word of command which sounded through the silent corridors of death, electrifying the dead into life again. Elijah and Elisha had been used of God to bring life again to the bodies of two boys, with the greatest agony of effort; but Jesus with the ease of a simple word called back the soul of the young man and restored his physical strength in the instant so that he sat up and talked.

A reverent fear seized upon all present, and they began and went on glorifying God by repeated expressions.[2] The conclusion which they reached unanimously and the cause they assigned for their glorying, was that a great prophet had risen in their midst. They remembered the incidents in the ministries of Elijah and Elisha nine hundred years before, and jumped to the conclusion that "God had visited his people" once again with a prophet. This kind of report went out into all of Judea and all the surrounding country concerning Him. We have no subsequent record in the Scriptures of the young man or his mother but the news about the miracle, like and yet so unlike those of the ancient prophets, spread like wildfire out over the country and penetrated even into the dungeons of Machaerus far down east of the Dead Sea where John was imprisoned, leading him to send a deputation to ask Jesus the question: "Art thou he that should come or do we look for another?"

1 Inceptive imperfect.   2 Inceptive imperfect.

3. The message from John the Baptist and the eulogy of Jesus (Matt. 11:2-19; Luke 7:18-35).

It was just a few days later that two disciples of John come to Jesus, bearing an agitated message from their Master who had languished in the prison of Machaerus for seven months in hourly expectation of a violent death. Herod Antipas had imprisoned John under the pretext of the peril of a popular uprising but motivated really by his infatuation for Herodias, his brother Philip's wife, whom he had illegally married. John had denounced in unsparing terms this sinful union. Antipas kept John under arrest, rather than execute him, because he feared the consequences if he should kill this idol of the people. For the same reason he shielded John from the wrath of Herodias for a time, allowing him to receive visits from his disciples. He had occasional interviews with his distinguished prisoner which deeply stirred his conscience and perplexed his soul.

But John had been taken from intense activity to this inactive life of solitude and the closeness and darkness of the dungeon. From the height of being a popular idol, he was snatched away to isolation and the prospect of a martyr death. It was a dreary life, utterly different from the wild freedom of the wilderness. He kept himself informed through his disciples of the doings of Jesus; but the dark days of prison life had bred within him doubts. Similar moments of heart-breaking despondency had been experienced by his great predecessors Moses and Elijah. Many times in the world's history dauntless spirits have been crushed by hopeless captivity. We do not condemn Savanarola, Jerome of Prague, and Luther because of wavering or being agitated in the dark hours. The case of John was worse. It was one of seeming to be neglected by God above and by the Messiah whose harbinger he had been.

John's question did not indicate a loss of faith in the coming Messiah. It was rather an expression of faith that the Messiah would come.

"Art thou the one coming or shall we look for another?" was his question, expressed by the two commissioned disciples. He had been clear in his testimony to Jesus as the Messiah at the time of the baptism and later also even after his own ministry had paled like a star before the rising sun of Jesus' popularity. But now he seemed confused in his mind. He had waited patiently for months in prison as reports came in by his disciple-messengers of the extraordinary cures wrought by Jesus and the ever-growing multitudes that attended on His ministry. As he looked out from behind prison bars upon the black lava-crags and deep gorges, yawning in the seemingly bottomless depths beneath his prison window, and around him at the dimly lighted dungeon walls from which he had no reasonable hope of ever emerging alive, held as he was in the relentless grasp of the pettiest, meanest, weakest, most contemptible of princelings, dominated by the most designing and profligate of women, there is little wonder that he should have raised the question in his own mind of why Jesus did not come to his help. "Could he have been mistaken in thinking Jesus to be the Messiah?"

An examination of John's ideal as to the Messiah as expressed on other occasions reveals the fact that his messianic ideal differed radically from the current conception of a mere temporal ruler, who would subject the surrounding enemies and exalt Israel in power through violence though it might be. John had foretold a Messiah-Reformer, with His "fan in his hand" to purge and separate the good from the bad. "He would hew down every tree that should not bring forth good fruit." The activities of Jesus as reported to him did not seem to correspond to this ideal. His ministries, unlike those of His forerunner, were in gentleness and patience. John had caught the vision of the suffering servant and pointed his own disciples to the "Lamb of God that taketh away the sin of the world." In His great popularity, Jesus did not seem to John to reproduce this ideal of the prophecy of Isaiah. There were more than sixty pretenders to the Messiahship first and last. Could he have been mistaken about Jesus? Should he look for another? He resolved to refer the matter to Jesus for decision. One so truthful and faithful would not refuse to give him a final and frank answer.

When the messengers of John came, Jesus was busy in the midst of His ministries of curing and preaching to the popular throng made up of all classes.[1] He did not pause, but continued for a time His work in the presence of the disciple-messengers of John, healing many "in that hour" of diseases, plagues, evil spirits, and all kinds of bodily ills. To those in particular who were blind He gave as a free gift their sight.[2]

Jesus was characteristically wise in His answer to John's inquiry. "When you go back announce to John what you have heard and are hearing, what you have seen and are seeing. The blind are receiving their sight, the lame are walking, the lepers are being cleansed, the deaf are hearing, the dead are being raised, and the poor are being evangelized."[3] These were the things the Coming One would do according to a true interpretation of Isaiah (Isa. 2:18-19; 35:5, 6; 61:1). Jesus doubtless raised others from the dead beyond the three mentioned in the Gospel record. Here

1 The poor were there.   2 Luke 7:21 verb echarisato.
3 Present tenses of progressive action.

was the answer of *works* which showed the character of Jesus. He intimated to John the peril of sinful doubt which might entrap him and the blessedness of not "being tripped up" by the popular Messianic ideal. John had misread his prophecy of Isaiah. Let him make a new examination of Messianic prophecy and possess himself with patience. The Messiah would suffer later and His forerunner must suffer now. If Jesus were the Messiah of current Jewish expectation He would have long ago intervened on behalf of His forerunner. The reply was dramatic, leaving John to draw his own conclusions. But it was a clear assumption on the part of Jesus to the fulfillment of the Messianic prophecies in Himself. His closing words sent to John were a gentle rebuke for his doubts and encouraging stimulus for a firm faith in the Messiah whom John had already splendidly introduced. Jesus had deep sympathy for His forerunner but John was not a man to be pitied or coddled even in a dungeon of suffering. The wisdom of His answer was in giving direction to the independent thought and resolute character of this hardy son of the desert.

When the disciple-envoys of John had just left, Jesus poured forth the high eulogy on John's character, which was reserved for good reasons while they were present. Praise in their presence would be misinterpreted as flattery and would add nothing to the consolation of the prisoner in the dungeon of Machaerus. Wishing to prevent His hearers from cherishing deprecatory thoughts about John, He paid him the most wonderful tribute ever passed on a mortal man, couching it in language of rhythmic beauty:

"What did you go out in the wilderness to gaze on?
A reed shaken by the wind?
But what did you go out to see?
A man clothed in soft raiment?
Behold those who are luxuriously dressed are in king's
    palaces.
But why did you go out? to see a prophet?
Yes, I tell you, and far more than a prophet."

It was no weak and wavering man bending like a reed shaken by the wind, that his auditors had gone forth to gaze on in wonder, when John was preaching in the desert of Judea. They were not to think now, that his sending messengers with the inquiry indicated any weakness of character or bending before the winds of adversity in the prison of Machaerus. The reeds of the Jordan valley bent before the winds but John's nature was as rugged as the mountain oak. Nor had they gone out to see a man clothed in luxurious, soft raiment, such as the courtiers around Herod Antipas wore. He did not need to remind them of the simple coarse

camel's-hair clothing of the poor used by John, nor of the fact
that he lived the hardy life of an ascetic, subsisting on the locusts
and wild honey of the desert. This hardy son of the soil was
not, by sending these messengers, turning from his former loyalties, or by recanting or adulation of Antipas seeking his own
personal freedom.

Just why they had gone out was to see a prophet. John was
popularly held to be a prophet. In this the people were right.
Jesus seals their opinion with the testimony of His own judgment.
John was "much more than a prophet." He cites Malachi's prophecy
in substantiating this declaration.

So it stands written:

"Behold I send my messenger before thy face
Who shall prepare thy way before thee." (Mal. 3:1).

"Solemnly, I say to you: There has not been raised up on
from among those born of women, greater than John the Baptist."
So the eulogy of Jesus, pronounced almost as a funeral oration
over His forerunner, was tender, lofty, and fervent. He was the
greatest of the prophets surely in privilege if not in character,
because he was the Forerunner of the Messiah. After all, this was
the underlying thought. John had wanted to know if Jesus was
the Messiah. The reply of Jesus was that John was the fulfillment
of the prophecy of Malachi — the forerunner of the Messiah. This
was an explicit declaration of His own Messiahship; and John
as forerunner was the last of the prophets of the old dispensation
and the Elijah-like prophet who should usher in the new order.

Then reflecting on the doubts of John and the privileges of
His hearers and especially His disciples, now, Jesus added:

"Yet he that is but little in the kingdom of the heavens[1] — the
Messianic Kingdom — was greater than John in spiritual privileges.
"The least of that which is greatest is greater than the greatest
of that which is least,"[2] is a legal maxim. The least disciple of
Jesus has more fellowship with the Father, more hope, more revealed knowledge in the new Covenant, than the greatest of the
prophets of the old regime. This was John's serious limitation.
He did not clearly perceive the character of the kingdom because he had not experienced the things in the sphere of the new
Kingdom life. His disciple-auditors should therefore use great
charity in judging of John's conduct in sending the committee of
inquiry. At the same time they should recognize their own heavy
responsibility flowing out of their high privileges in the Kingdom.

But the Kingdom men should not lightly esteem the great
work done by John. From the day that John began to preach in

1 Locative case of sphere within which.   2 Maldonatus.

the wilderness there sprang up a great religious movement. He broke with the old order and set the imagination of the people on fire. Many were desiring to take the movement into their own hands and establish a temporal kingdom, by violent and revolutionary methods, like an army storming a city. Jesus had to meet and overcome this. But the kingdom also like a rushing mighty wind was forcing its own way.[1] The strong force started by John was now bringing the throngs around Jesus. His disciples must not forget this great work of John but give him full credit.

Until the time of John the prophets and prophecies in the law spoke of the Messiah who was to come and about His forerunner. Jesus now endorses John as the forerunner promised in Malachi as the Elijah who was to appear. This amounted to a veiled declaration of His own Messiahship because John had pointed forward to Jesus. For emphasis He added:

"Who has ears to hear let him hear."

John wanted to know if He was the Messiah. Let these disciples about Him now open their ears. He had sent John a reply adequate to the needs of that wise but dejected prisoner. But did these hearers of His understand that He was the Messiah? He had just declared to them directly that He was.

But what had been the result of the wonderful ministry of John? For a time when John's message of repentance sounded out, "the people, and even the corrupt tax-gatherers had felt that God was just and righteous in making the demands He did make of them through John, and submitted to the rite of baptism in the river Jordan, confessing their sins." But the Pharisees and the lawyers rejected for themselves[2] the baptism of John, refusing to admit the need of confession of sin on their part.

What reception was Jesus having and going to have from these Pharisees and lawyers? They were already rejecting Him as they had rejected John. They were not pleased by the methods of the one or the other. This fact Jesus illustrated by children playing charades in the market place. In the game representing the marriage, one group would pipe while the other group danced; or in playing funeral they would sing the dirge while the other group beat their breasts in token of their sorrow. But through peevishness the game was spoiled. John came and sang the dirge of an ascetic life of self-abnegation and severity but that did not suit the Pharisees and lawyers. They said of him: "He has a *daemon.*" Then the Son of Man came mixing freely with society, identifying Himself with them in every way, eating and drinking with them as their friend in their homes, participating in their marriage feasts helpfully, and they say: "Behold a glutton, a drinker of wine, and a friend of tax-gatherers and *sinners*" — in

---

1 Verb biadzetai either middle or passive.   2 Middle voice of the verb.

the low sense of that word. So they could not be pleased by either the method of John or that of Jesus; but both of these methods were wise and were justified by their results. Wise men recognized this.

4. Jesus upbraids the unrepentant cities of opportunity and assumes the moral burden of the world (Matt. 11:20-30).

Most of the mighty works (dunameis) of Jesus were done in Galilee, and principally around the Sea of Tiberias in the populous districts of Chorazin, Bethsaida, and Capernaum, the last named, preeminent among the three, being His adopted city. Much of this mighty work was in His preaching but some lay also in miracles. But the people of these cities had not shown any general and genuine penitence; and Jesus felt that so far as they were concerned His ministry had been a comparative failure. He had already referred to the fact that the Pharisees and lawyers did not accept John or Himself.

Now he began to upbraid these three neighboring cities which had been the scene of His greatest activities because they did not repent. He pronounced woes on the first two for their impenitence, comparing them to the wicked heathen cities of Tyre and Sidon. Those characteristic heathen cities, had they witnessed the dynamic works wrought by Jesus, would have shown their repentance as did ancient Nineveh, using sackcloth and ashes to do so. He assumes further the authority to pronounce that in the final judgment day it would be more tolerable for Tyre and Sidon than for these privileged cities. He thus calls attention sharply to the fact that privilege entails responsibility and also to His authority in the judgment. Capernaum, He separates from the other two cities in His denunciation, because it was His own adopted home-city and so exalted to the very heavens in honor and privilege. But high opportunity rejected brings down judgment all the more severe. Capernaum would go down to Hades. Sodom was the worst city He could choose with which to compare it. If the dynamic manifestations of power seen by the people of Capernaum had been witnessed by the people dwelling in Sodom, that city would have remained until today and not have been totally effaced as it was. Then He adds: "Solemnly, I say unto you, it shall be more tolerable for Sodom in the day of judgment than for you." Almost all these people were seeking a temporal kingdom. Even John did not have a perfectly clear conception of the spiirtual character of Jesus' work. Much more were others desiring to violently precipitate a religious movement looking forward toward the establishment of a *bread* king. They needed repentance but they were persistently unrepentant. They did not understand His appeal.

There was one encouragement in the midst of what seemed to be a failing ministry. While the Pharisees and lawyers rejected His message and led many others to do so by their influence, there were some of the plain simple-hearted folk that heard the message gladly and accepted the offered gospel. Reflecting on these at this discouraging juncture of His ministry — an opportune time for such reassuring thoughts — Jesus gave expression to His feeling of thanksgiving, praise and prayer. He praises (Exomologoumai) the Father, Ruler of the heavens and the earth, because He had hidden these things of the Gospel message from those who were wise in their own conceits and proud of their own judgment, and had revealed them by deliberately uncovering their meaning, to the "babes" of humble mind who were conscious of their own spiritual ignorance and religious need. This was to be the plan of the gospel of God. The great physician would go to those who recognized that they were sick. The teacher would minister instruction to those who confessed that they were ignorant. This was the Father's plan and was "well pleasing in his presence." The humbler more ignorant class of people would be the first always to hear and accept the kingdom message.

Jesus reveals further that He accepts the moral burden of the salvation of the race and will walk the lonely way, suffering the rejection of the leaders of His people and their antagonism.

All these things of the gospel had been given unto Him by the Father at a definite time[1] in the past. His messianic consciousness takes Him back to that transaction in the preexistent state. This was a moment of high fellowship with the Father. He undertook to come into the world and reveal the Father. "No one is knowing thoroughly[2] the Son but the Father." His loneliness in the world was complete. Nor did any know the Father thoroughly save the Son. He was the only one who could reveal the Father. He "will reveal him to whom he desires." He is the absolute steward of the knowledge of God but He wishes to reveal Him. He would have all men come to the knowledge of the Father.

How He is to bring men to this knowledge we see in the wonderful invitation that follows (Matt. 11:28-30). He is the teacher, final and absolute, of the Father. He sounds forth a world-call to men to come to Him as their teacher and "take his yoke upon them." He commends Himself as a teacher who is meek and lowly, not like their Rabbis, hard and haughty. Their yoke of endless ceremonial exactions and formal duties was heavy and galling but His is kindly (chrestos) and helpful. The toiling ones are bidden to come, who through active effort to perform all the multiplicity

1 Aorist tense.   2 Epiginoskei, to know accurately.

of difficult and painful duties of Rabbinic regulations and exactions, found the "yoke of the Law" galling. The ceremonies of the law and the traditions of the elders were a yoke which Peter said: "neither our fathers nor we were able to bear" (Acts 15:10). The invitation also was to those who in passive endurance were bowed beneath the heavy "burdens grievous to be borne" which the Scribes and Pharisees "laid upon their shoulders and themselves would not move their finger" (Matt. 23). The actively toiling and passively enduring include all men in an invitation which is universal. The suffering servant stands forth in the midst of suffering humanity the greatest sufferer of all, and with His own heart breaking with His failure to make men see the Father, extends His hands in gracious invitation to every man to come to Him for rest, which would bring refreshment and rejuvenation. This would replace the vain toiling[1] and state of weariness.[2] There is no other religion that offers to toiling and burdened humanity the rest of pardon, peace, security, fellowship, eternal life. Jesus was the "great rest-bringer." He is the final and authoritative Teacher of humanity in all things pertaining to man's life and destiny. He claimed absolute knowledge of God the Father and presents Himself as the lonely, meek and humble Teacher, ready to reveal God to every man. The condition of learning at His feet is that of "coming" simply to Him in response to His gracious invitation. He who yokes Himself up with Jesus will have the rest of fellowship increasingly through the years as experience grows ripe in His school.

5.   The anointing of the feet of Jesus by a sinful woman in the house of Simon, a Pharisee (Luke 7:46-50).

Somewhere in Galilee on His second missionary campaign, the first with the twelve apostles, Jesus was invited by Simon, a certain Pharisee, to eat with him. This Simon is not to be confused with the cured leper in Bethany who entertained Jesus a few days before His crucifixion. The exact place of this incident is not revealed. It might have been in Capernaum, more probably in Magdala, the circumstances not being so favorable to Nain. Though the antagonism of the Pharisees toward Jesus had not developed greatly at this time, Simon seems to have been characteristically proud, a truly exclusive Pharisee, and his invitation not to have been sincere and from a motive of true loyalty and friendship. This is borne out by the fact that Simon coldly omitted all the ordinary attentions shown usually to invited guests. Jesus was received with hauteur; no one brought water to wash His sandalled feet; no kiss of welcome was given Him by His host; no cool

1 Active participle.   2 Perfect passive participle meaning "state of weariness."

fragrant perfume was poured upon His head.[1] Simon felt that he was conferring a great honor on the visiting Rabbi. He had doubtless heard of the works of Jesus in neighboring places and wanted to study Him at closer range. Jesus was being proclaimed, since raising the widow's son at Nain, as a great prophet. Simon would, with the help of a few of his intimate friends, submit Jesus to close examination, and find out if He were really a prophet.

Jesus neither sought nor refused such an invitation. It offered one more occasion to touch the life of the Pharisaic class and for this reason He accepted it. He had said about His own ministry, that "he came eating and drinking" with men in their homes and on their festive occasions. He neglected no class of society or condition of individual as is patent in the occasion under review.

When they were at the table they "reclined," according to the custom long ago brought over from Persia in the days of captivity and now universally prevalent among the Jews, resting with the left elbow on the table and the feet extended out perpendicularly behind. In the banquet hall were arranged ordinarily seats along the walls for those who might wish to avail themselves of the freedom of Oriental custom to be present even though uninvited.

On this occasion came a woman, known by reputation and appearance to be a sinner, wearing her hair unbound, a sign of her sinful profession. Doubtless she had heard of the wonderful prophet who was reputed to be the friend of tax-gatherers and sinners. She may well have heard Him preach in the streets the sweet message whose burden was: "Come unto me all ye that are toiling and heavy laden." Was she not in a terrible struggle in her own conscience and was not the burden of her sinful past crushing her life out? She resolved to brave ridicule and come to Jesus. Knowing that He was reclining at the banquet-table in the house of the Pharisee, and bringing an alabaster cruse of ointment — a very costly perfume — she slipped in through the curtained entrance and coming stood behind Jesus, near His feet, weeping. It was not customary for any woman to appear under any circumstances on such an occasion, much less unveiled as she. Her actions betokened a woman of generous, affectionate, and impulsive disposition, who was the victim of others' depravity.

She stood weeping because of her wicked life, brought home to her the more by hearing the gracious words of Jesus. She also met with the icy scowl of Simon. "What was she doing there?" Ashamed, repentant and grieved, she bent over to hide her confusion, and as she did a shower of tears fell upon Jesus' feet. As if in apology and having no cloth, she began to wipe the tears from

1 Wetstein on Matt. 27:7.

His feet with the long tresses of her hair. Among the Jews it was a shameful thing for a woman to let down her hair in public, but she made this sacrifice[1] as did Mary of Bethany on the eve of His death (Jno. 12:3). Next taking the flask of fragrant perfume she anointed His feet and kept on showering kisses[2] upon them in deep repentance and reverence.

> "She sat and wept beside his feet: the weight
> Of sin oppressed her heart; for all the shame,
> And the poor malice of the worldly blame,
> To her were past, extinct and out of date;
> Only the sin remained the leprous state.
> She sat and wept and with her untressed hair,
> Still wiped the feet she was so blessed to touch;
> And He wiped off the soiling of despair
> From her sweet soul, because she loved so much."

Simon had wanted to find out what kind of man Jesus was and he now jumped to the conclusion: "This fellow[3] if He were a prophet would have known who and what manner of woman this is that is touching Him that she is a sinner." So he reasoned within his heart. He was more than horrified. The very touch of such a woman to his way of thinking was pollution. A prophet would have discerned the woman's character and spurned her from him. Simon was filled with disgust and looked it. But he held his tongue in perfect politeness while his thoughts of Jesus were full of evil and uncharitable judgment.

But Jesus soon gave Simon reason to think otherwise. By a searching parable He revealed Simon's inmost thoughts about Himself and about the woman. In this brief but inimitable parable or illustration, Jesus assumed the place of the one who forgives sin and to whom both the sinful woman and Simon alike were accountable. He puts Simon at once on the same plane with the woman whom he despised.

"Simon, I have something to say to you," said Jesus.

"Teacher, speak," was the coldly supercilious reply.

"There was a certain lender," said Jesus, "who had two debtors: the one owed five hundred pence and the other fifty; and when they had nothing to pay he freely forgave them both. Tell me then which of them will love him most?"

"I imagine," said Simon, with a touch of patronage and assumed unconsciousness of any application to himself, "that he to whom he forgave most."

"You have judged rightly," said Jesus.

---

1 Plummer on Luke, Com. in loco.   2 The Greek verb is progressive in action.
3 An expression of contempt.

Then follows in rhythmical language of antithetical Hebrew parallelism the application of the parable to Simon. Turning now for the first time to the woman, who sat at His feet covering her face with her hands and dishevelled hair, He said:

"Simon, do you see this woman?
I entered your house (as your guest)
You gave me no water for my feet.
She washed my feet with her tears,
And wiped them with the hairs of her head.
No kiss thou gavest me;
She, since I came in, has not ceased kissing my feet.
With ointment, thou didst not anoint my head;
She, with nard, anointed my feet.
Wherefore I say to you:
Her sins which are many stand forgiven,
Because she loved much.
But he to whom little is forgiven,
Loves little."

Then He said to the woman: "Thy sins have already been forgiven!"

The guests around the table understood the assumption, and began to whisper around "Who is this that is even forgiving sins?" Jesus then addressed the sobbing woman tenderly: "Thy faith hath saved thee, go into[1] peace."

Thus, with irony, Jesus applied the parable. Accepting Simon's evaluation of his own person — because he thought he had little sin and so owed little and needed little forgiveness — Jesus laid down the principle, that in proportion to one's recognition of his own sin and his desire to forgive and be forgiven would he obtain forgiveness. Simon was thus in a desperate situation because he was blind to his sins and showed a most unforgiving spirit toward the woman. He would have scouted the idea of himself being forgiven by Jesus. But Jesus assumed the power once again to forgive sins and sent the poor woman on her way into a redeemed and peaceful life.

The evangelic record with delicacy withholds the name of the woman who was thus rescued by Jesus from a life of shame. Tradition in the Latin branch of historic Christianity[2] identified her, whether rightly so or not, with Mary Magdalene out of whom Christ cast seven devils. The other tradition, that Mary of Bethany is the same, is not compatible. The Rabbis ascribed drunkenness and lust to the immediate agency of demons.[3] Magdala was a wealthy city of shameful reputation, destroyed for harlotry.[4] Without tearing away the veil of delicacy spread by the Gospel over the

1 The preposition eis.   2 Ambrose, Jerome, Augustine, and Gregory.
3 Smith's Dict. of Bible, Art., Mary Magdalene.   4 Lightfoot on John 12:8.

name of the woman, may we not recognize that it would be the very spirit of Jesus to take the depised but repentant woman who had fallen to a life so low, and raise her to the heights sublime of a life of purity and holy devotion to Him? It would be a signal triumph of the Gospel to cast out the demons of passion from one who had prostituted her beauty and wealth of natural talents to a life of disgrace and shame, and plant within her the enthusiasm and devotion for a holy life of service and sacrifice, such as that which we see in Mary Magdalene who brought sweet spices to the sepulcher.

The woman went out to endure cruel slights and heartless criticisms of men. But she went with peace in her heart and assurance from Jesus of His loving care. He Himself had endured the affront of Simon when He entered his home and knew how to sympathize with her who sustained the scowl of the Pharisees at the table. She was quick to recognize His willingness to break over all tradition and receive her sin-stained soul into His eternal and heavenly friendship. Jesus demonstrated, over against the haughty self-righteous attitude of Simon who was fearful lest his own reputation might be tarnished by the contact, how His disciples should reclaim the erring.

> "Deal kindly with the erring,
> Oh, do not thou forget,
> However darkly stained by sin
> He is thy brother yet.
> Forget not, thou hast often sinned,
> And sinful yet must be;
> Deal kindly with the erring one,
> As God hath dealt with thee."

6. Jesus extends more widely His campaign in Galilee, accompanied by the twelve (Luke 8:1-3).

The campaign of Jesus now gathered force and assumed more definite organization. The twelve apostles had been able to dispose of all preliminary arrangements, so that they could enter upon a protracted campaign throughout the province. Jesus had taken them with Him down to Nain and possibly to Magdala. His work had now taken deeper hold in the hearts of the people. The miracle at Nain had attracted wide attention. His preaching had a great appeal and was reaching some of the worst sinners and drawing them back from lives of depravity. The work of healing went on with unabated vigor and was the cause and occasion of ever-growing throngs about the great Healer.

Now comes the systematic organization of the tour through the province, city by city, village by village. The twelve were with

Him, but thus far He did the heralding and evangelizing. His theme was the good tidings of the kingdom of God.

The financial support for the tour was arranged by the first woman's missionary society in the history of Christianity. Some of these women had been healed of evil spirits and sicknesses. Luke records the name of three who must have been specially active. Mary, from Magdala, a town down the coast of the sea a short distance from Tiberias, is the first mentioned. The site of the ancient town is marked today by a few miserable peasant huts of the Arab village El Mejdel. The ancient watch-tower which gave the place its name is still there. If she was the Mary with whose name tradition has bound up the opprobrious name of *Magdalen,* she quit at that time the scene of her shameful life and went with the Saviour as a witness to His redeeming grace. Joanna, the wife of Chuza, Herod's steward, a woman of prominence and means, is mentioned next. She remembered with profound gratitude that Jesus had healed her little boy in the very beginning of His work in Galilee.[1] Susanna is the third mentioned, unknown elsewhere in the gospel record but doubtless well-known in the primitive church. There were other names not mentioned, recorded in heaven, who had a part in the support and activities of this first general tour of Jesus with the twelve. These women continued their ministrations[2] to Him and the twelve apostles throughout this missionary journey. Their kindly offices enabled Jesus and His apostles to give themselves wholly to the work of the gospel. Here we see a completely organized band of workers going forth to the populous districts of Galilee. Such organized effort would naturally attract wide attention from the people and increased vigilance and antagonism on the part of the enemies of Jesus.

1 John 4:46-54.
2 Imperfect of the verb diakonein indicating repeated and continued action.

CHAPTER XV

A BUSY DAY IN THE LIFE OF JESUS

(Harm. §§ 61-68)

When Jesus returned to Capernaum after His tour of the cities of Galilee He entered into the house of Simon. Mark's narrative, full of action, does not tell of all Jesus did after the choice of the twelve, but jumps over to this crucial time and gives us graphically a picture of one of the busy days in the life of the Master in Capernaum. The multitude comes[1] together again in such numbers, anxious to see and hear and many to be healed, that Jesus and His apostles could not find time or place to rest and have their meals. So great was the tension on His nervous system that some of His friends got over-anxious about Him. Their anxiety was reenforced by the fact that the enemies of Jesus were present now from Jerusalem, and were spreading a slander about Him "that he was crazy." He was so intense in His activities, that some of His friends could not interpret it otherwise than as the Pharisees, "that he was becoming over-balanced mentally." They went out to lay hold of Him and by gentle violence remove Him from the intensity of this movement.

1. Jesus, accused by the Pharisees of being in league with Beelzebub, responds to the accusation (Mark 3:19-30; Matt. 12:22-37).

At this juncture they brought to Him a blind and dumb man who was possessed of a devil. The exorcists said that the dumb was hopeless, unless there was some combination with diabolic power to remove the demon. Jesus performed these three miracles in one in such an easy and simple way, that when the people saw the man with restored sight and speaking they were almost "beside themselves"[2] with excitement. They were excitedly repeating over and over: "Is not this the son of David, the Messiah?" Respect for Jesus was growing in spite of all that the Rabbis were doing covertly against Him.[3] This was the first time the people had openly expressed this new messianic opinion, and it enraged the watching enemies of Jesus. Something radical must be done immediately.

The Pharisaic emissaries had come from Jerusalem for the express purpose of checking the progress of this popular movement and undermining the influence of Jesus. They came forward now with the explanation of this undeniable miracle, asserting that He was in league with Beelzebub, the prince of demons. The Scribes from Jerusalem went repeating it around. "This fellow does not cast out demons except by the power of Beelzebub, the prince of demons. He has Beelzebub, and in the power of the ruler of the demons, He is casting out demons."[1]

1 Historic present.   2 Imperfect of the verb, existanto (were standing out of themselves).
3 Keim, Vol. II, p. 289.

213

Here was a contemptuous accusation of voluntarily possessing[2] Beelzebub and using his power to effect these miracles of demon expulsion.

Jesus, seeing the seductive influence of these religious leaders, called them into His presence and addressed His words directly to them. They had been whispering their slanders about Him among the people and He revealed to them the fact that He knew their very thoughts and called them now to face the responsibility of their vile calumnious accusation. He employed three concise arguments in His reply to their charge. "How can Satan cast out Satan?" He said. "If a kingdom be divided against itself, that kingdom cannot stand. Every kingdom divided against itself is brought to desolation.[3] And if a house be divided against itself that house will not be able to stand; every city or house divided against itself shall fall. And if Satan is risen up against himself and is divided, he cannot stand but hath an end. If Satan cast out Satan, he is divided against himself; how then shall his kingdom stand?" Jesus thus by simple reiterated illustrations, irresistable logic, and pungent sarcasm, lays bare the absurdity of their accusation and their hollow insincerity. Satan does not cast out Satan. They believed that the malady of dumbness was due to demon-possession. If Jesus had cast out the demon by power of the prince of demons then the kingdom of Satan was divided against itself. Even the simplest-minded of the people could understand that.

The second argument was directed against them personally. The exorcists were of the Pharisaic party because they believed like the Pharisees about spirits. Jesus casts their slur—"that he was using the black art"—back in their teeth, by calling the exorcists their "sons." These Pharisees were seeking to separate His followers and the people from Him. He now drove a wedge of dissension into their own ranks with consummate skill. These exorcists claimed to be able to expel demons. Rabbinical exorcists made use of the oath Akal and the "number of Kesbeel" to expel demons. The oath and number were revealed, according to their teaching, by the wicked angels who had allied themselves with women and brought on the flood (Gen. 6:2). Would the Pharisees their "fathers" declare that these "sons" of theirs were expelling demons by the power of Beelzebub?[4] These same exorcists should be their critics and He would leave them to fight out that question among themselves. They had tried to divide His forces and now found their own party divided

1 Matt. 12:24; Mar. 3:22 (See tenses and locative case).
2 Present active indicative echei, "he is having or holding."
3 Third-class condition.   4 Beelzebub the "filth god," was the name given through Jewish wit and contempt to Beelzebub the "lord of the royal habitation," a god of the Phoenicians.

by their own misstep. Jesus did not mean to admit that the exorcists could really expel demons. It was an *argumentum ad hominem.*

With these two arguments He had battered down the wall of their accusation; and now with a third He carries the war into their territory. His whole life was before the people. His character as well as His works were well known. His aim manifestly was to fight against evil and do good. The idea that He would tie himself up with the prince of darkness, for any purpose, was contradictory to these facts. Manifestly He was doing these works by the Spirit of God, and that being so, He was sent from God, the Messiah, to do these works, using God's power to do them. The fact that He had been able to cure this difficult case under observation undeniably showed that He had a power superior to that of Satan. How could He enter into the house of the strongman Satan and spoil the goods in the demon-possessed man, unless He had power to bind the strong man Satan first? The conclusion is, that He is allied to a power superior to that of Satan, and there is only one such power, that of God. "The kingdom of God has thus come upon them," He declares. Indirectly He asserts what the people had just been declaring—"that He is the Messiah."

"The Pharisees should be careful what attitude they took toward Him. The power of God was being manifested in their midst in these wonderful cures." He adds: "He that is not with me is against me; and he that gathereth not with me scattereth." Their attitude toward Him determined whether they were on God's side or Satan's. They had begun by accusing *Him* of being in league with Beelzebub, the prince of demons, and now wind up by finding *themselves* lined up against Jesus and therefore classed with the prince of demons. They dropped into the snare they had set for Him and were silenced before the people whom they had sought to pervert.

Jesus then brought sharply against them a terrific countercharge of blasphemy against the Spirit. He warned them that there was a limit to the antagonism of man to the Spirit of God. Calumny against Jesus whom the people did not yet know would be forgiven on repentance. But these men were convinced in their minds that Jesus was the representative of the kingdom of God, and yet in the very face of this fact attributed His works, done through the power of the Spirit of God, to Satanic power. Such a blasphemy would never be pardoned, neither in this age nor in that which is to come. These men said that Jesus had an unclean spirit and this work of expelling the demon was done through the power of Satan. Jesus pronounced this act of their judgment, the "eternal unpardonable sin." These Pharisees had determined to reject Jesus, whatever proofs He might offer of His divine mission. Their prejudices and self-interest had blinded them; they deliberately refused to be convinced; their consciences had been deadened and their hearts were now incapable of repentance. They willfully and deliberately showed enmity and antagonism toward Him, blaspheming God. Eternal sin is antagonism to the manifest work of the Spirit of God, attributing it to Satan (Heb. 6:4-10).

The very words of His accusers condemned them. Their words of accusation revealed their evil hearts. The heart "spurts out habitually"[1] good or evil according to the supply within it. Words like deeds form a basis for the interpretation of character. Useless words are pernicious and reveal corrupt fruit. Their words were like the venom of snakes injected into others and showed that they were the offspring of a viper-race. This was a severe punishment of these hypocritical and astute slanderers in the presence of the people! "The good man" adds Jesus, "out of his own good treasure in the heart brings forth good things, and the evil man in like manner evil things." They would have to give account of every useless pernicious word in the judgment. He will then be their judge.

2. Certain of the Scribes and Pharisees demand a sign. (Matt. 12:28-45).

Jesus had clearly defeated and routed His enemies in argument and, demolishing their accusation of His being in Satanic alliance, had silenced them. But these astute slanderers were not to be disposed of so easily. The visiting emissaries from Jerusalem probably put some of the local Pharisees to the front now, to ask Jesus to substantiate His implied claim to be the representative of the kingdom of God, the Messiah, by showing them some sign. With bland hypocrisy they feigned perplexity, and expressed their wish to see Him perform a miracle which might resolve their doubts about His Messiahship. This was in strange contradiction and inconsistency with their charge of just a little while before, "That He was in league with Beelzebub," the Ekron Insect-God and ruler of the nether world.

The people expected that the Messiah when He came would repeat the great deeds and miracles of Moses and Joshua. Theudas drew out the Jews, to see his people walk through the Jordan dry-shod again. Other false prophets and claimants to Messiahship did similar things. Jesus had to resist the temptation to establish a world-kingdom when He met Satan in the wilderness; and the repetition of the same temptation later when He fed the five thousand with five loaves and two fishes. This was the popular messianic conception and the Pharisees were "playing to the

1 Present active indicative. ekballei. indicating progressive and habitual action.

grandstand" when they astutely presented this demand, couched in the hypocritical language of a "wish."[1] The pressure of the request was in the fact that the people thought Jesus should be willing to do this if He were the Messiah.

The answer of Jesus was characterized by His unusual wisdom and prudence. To their previous charge He had given a remarkable demonstration of irresitible logic and a sarcasm that pierced to the core of their Pharisaic hypocrisy; He now gives another wonderful proof of His wisdom and mental alertness in presenting immediately without the slightest hesitation the sign which they demanded but not the kind they asked. He upbraids them as "an evil and adulterous generation" unfaithful to Israel's God, because they were asking for a sign, when He had just been giving demonstrations in great number and variety of the true power of God at work in their midst through Him. Had they not seen even that day the difficult case of the blind and dumb demoniac cured? Had they not known of the widow's son at Nain raised from the dead?

"There shall no sign be given this generation but the sign of Jonah, the prophet, for as Jonah was three days and three nights in the belly of the whale so shall the Son of Man be three days and three nights in the heart of the earth."

His life, preaching, and works, were before them as a living miracle. They wanted to see some great miracle of supply of their material wants and gratification of their fleshly desires and appetites. He gave them a spiritual sign of His sacrificial life, terminating in His atoning death and three days in the tomb. This was what they needed but not what they "wished." It involved His perplexing resurrection.

Jesus next assumes to declare future judgment and condemnation on them by contrasting them with the Ninevites and the Queen of Sheba. At the sign of the preaching of Jonah the men of Nineveh believed and repented; but now at the preaching of Jesus who was greater than Jonah these Jews repented not. The Queen of Sheba came from the south a long way to hear the wisdom of Solomon. She put forth effort to avail herself of that privilege; but these hard-hearted Pharisees were not willing to accept even the wisdom of Jesus, who was far wiser than Solomon. Here were high claims for them to ponder over and a sign-enigma for them to puzzle their brains with while He should go on with His work. "What did He mean by the Son of Man being three days and three nights in the heart of the earth, anyway?" They had asked for a sign and they got one! Jonah three days in the whale's belly and then recovered was a type of the three days' en-

1 Matt. 12:38. verb Thelomen.

tombment of Jesus followed by His resurrection. But none of this they could figure out!

Jesus concludes His denunciation of their faithlessness and unfaithfulness with the parable of the unclean spirit. He had just cast out an unclean spirit from the blind and dumb man and His illustration was peculiarly apt and opportune. It was adapted to show the futility of the religious reformation instituted by John the Baptist and carried on further by Himself to effect any permanent change in the Jewish people. His words, which were a prophecy of His own final failure to change the Jews, were based on the attitude of these official representatives of Jerusalem Rabbinism toward His ministry. His claim to Messiahship therefore did not refer to temporal rulership, but a Messiahship of a spiritual nature calling for a life of loving sacrificial service and a death of vicarious and atoning character. They would continue to disbelieve in spite of all He could do; and at last they would put the Messiah Son of Man to death. But after three days in the grave He would arise again, a sign for their confusion.

The Jews believed that certain maladies were due to demon-possession. They thought that when the demon was expelled it went to the wilderness, but wandered about discontented, watching its opportunity to reenter the man and work out its unholy purposes with increased ferocity. Jesus made use of this popular belief by way of illustration. These Pharisees who had accused Him of "having a demon" were really themselves possessed of demons of unbelief and impiety. For a time John had expelled the demon and Jesus Himself was continuing that work, but in a little while the demon of unbelief would come back and take complete possession,[1] with seven other demons more evil than itself, and the last condition would be "worse than the first." So it proved to be with this generation after they crucified Jesus.

3. Christ's mother and brethren seek to take Him home (Mark 3:31-35; Matt. 12:46-50; Luke 8:19-21).

Jesus was in the midst of the intense activities of this busy day when another interruption took place. Hardly had He finished His calm but keenly logical reply to the bitter accusation of the Pharisees, and His stinging and terrific denunciation of them as a venomous generation of vipers, when it was announced to Him that His mother and brothers were standing on the outside of the house desiring to see Him privately.

Jesus was probably in Simon's house in Capernaum. News quickly spread in the town that the Pharisees and Scribes had come up from Jerusalem and intervened in the work of Jesus,

1 The number seven is sympolic of completeness in Jewish thought

accusing Him of being in league with Beelzebub. The rumor of the debate that followed had brought additional numbers to the already great throng of people, and among these Mary, the mother of Jesus, and His half-brothers. The family had already been living in a suburb of Capernaum for some time. Joseph, the husband and father, was dead.

These brothers were friendly toward Jesus earlier in His ministry (John 2:12); but after He was rejected in Nazareth (Luke 4:16-31) there seems to have developed in them a disbelief as to His claims; and later on they ridiculed Him, calling Him the "Secret Messiah" (John 7:5). At the present juncture they were unbelieving and indifferent, not to say hostile, or at least ready to interfere with His work in favor of a kind of quiet and respectable life for the family. They had been forced to move from Nazareth on His account and now the Rabbis from Jerusalem were present in Capernaum and might institute judicial action against Him.[1] They had better interfere now, else the fanatical zeal of this brother of theirs might oblige them and their mother to the inconvenience and difficulties of another change of residence. They had doubtless heard the slander that was being spread by the Scribes, "that Jesus was acting very queer and was probably mentally unbalanced." They had been witnesses to the intensity of His activities and perhaps reasoned among themselves that His intense effort amounted to excessive zeal, not to say fanaticism. He was not taking time to eat and rest. The nervous tension was telling on His mind. This they argued, and persuaded Mary to come along with them to bring her oldest son home and let the excitement die down while He should get needed rest. We can only hope that the brothers did not sympathize with the accusation of the Pharisees, that Jesus was employing the "black art" to expel demons.

So the family came in a group. Surely He would be persuaded by this show of interest and solicitude on the part of all of them. But when they arrived, the crowd had grown so great that it was wholly impossible for them to enter the house. They "could not come at him for the crowd" which was sitting around Jesus in a circle, the disciples naturally forming the inner ring and others behind them and partly mingled with them filling the house. Then a certain one at the request of the family wedged his way in and interrupting Jesus said: "Behold thy mother and thy brothers are standing outside seeking to speak with thee." There was a stir in the room and then the quiet of expectation fell on the crowd. What did they want? The situation was tense. Jesus had just scored a victory over His enemies. Now His friends, whether moved by fear or affection, came with an interruption of His work.

1 Lightfoot, Vol. II p. 205.

What would He do about it? They were calling Him to them now.

We must not forget, in interpreting the failure of Jesus to respond to this summons, the deep reverence among the Jews for their parents.[1] He did not stop His work, but made use of the occasion to lay down a far reaching principle with reference to His own work and all the works of His kingdom workers for all time.

"Who is my mother and who are my brethren?" He exclaimed. Then extending His hand dramatically and looking around on the disciples sitting about Him in a circle, He said tenderly:

"Behold my mother and my brethren.[2] For whosoever shall do the will of my Father which is in heaven, he is my brother and sister, and mother; those hearing the word of God and doing it." Jesus loved His mother and His brothers but they must not interfere with His messianic work. He did not condemn His mother but put His Father in heaven first (Benzel).[3]

"Family ties are at best temporal; spiritual ties are eternal."[4]

One has to sympathize with Mary here. She gave no credence to the slander "that he had a demon." She may have been partially persuaded that the intensity of the work and now the added antagonism of the Jerusalem authorities were depressing Him physically and mentally. "He was not in full possession of Himself perhaps." She was persuaded by the sons to come and if possible bring Him home for a while.

It was from no lack of tenderness that Jesus replied to this summons as He did. Mary would dissuade Him from over-exertion. But in so doing she interfered with His work. He had rebuked her gently twice before for the same mistake.[5] She was again presuming too much on her near blood relationship, being influenced perhaps by the sons. Jesus points out clearly again, that all human relationships must be subordinated to the higher spiritual relationships of the kingdom. He had entered the earthly family that He might be able to found the spiritual family. Mary was yet under some misapprehension as to the true nature of His mission and of the kingdom. He clearly teaches here the spiritual nature of His kingdom. It is to be a great spiritual family. They who do the will of the heavenly Father are His true kindred. His own earthly relatives, His brothers, possibly His sisters and even His mother on this occasion failed to understand Him. But there were those around Him in the circle of disciples who understood the reason for the intensity of His work and His untiring zeal. They knew the joy He got out of it all and the power that sustained

1 Edersheim p. 577.   2 Cf. Jno. 15:14.   3 Non spernit matrem, sed ante-
        ponit patrem.   4 Plummer, in loco.   5 Luke 2:41 and Jno. 2:8.

Him in it. It is good to reflect that the family of Jesus did understand Him more perfectly later on. Even these brothers finally came to understand and accept Him, though it was only after His resurrection. Mary had partly lost her way in confusion now, but she would find her way out again and follow Him with her prayers, her solicitude, and her admiring reverence to the cross at the last.

4. Jesus delivers His first great group of parables in Capernaum (Mark 4:1-34; Matt. 13:1-53; Luke 8:4-18).

Jesus had occasionally made use of brief parables in the earlier part of His ministry; now He adopts this style of teaching, making frequent use of it. On this busy day, when He had met His enemies in determined opposition in the house of Simon and afterwards went out in the afternoon by the seaside to teach, He sat on the beach at first where the waves broke at His feet and taught until the great crowd grew greater and thronged Him; then He entered into a little boat and sat while the multitude had taken their stand and so stood on the beach, and He began and continued teaching[1] them many things in parables.

Jesus did not invent the parables. The Rabbis were fond of this method of instruction. But He transformed the parable marvelously by His use. There is nothing distinctly approaching its depth and power, its felicitous brevity and manifold applications, either in the Old Testament or in the entire literature of humanity, either before or since His life on earth.[2]

A parable is an utterance which involves a comparison.[3] It is an objective parallel to moral and spiritual truth. It is not a mere simile but a connected narrative of events in human life or of a process in nature by which some great spiritual truth is illustrated or enforced.[4] "In the hands of Jesus the parable became a vehicle of instruction and warning, of comfort and condemnation." His parables usually, as here, grew out of the immediate circumstances and needs.

We do not know just how many He spoke on this day out in the beauty and freshness by the seaside as the afternoon hours passed. The eight preserved fall into four pairs: the Sower and the Seed, the Tares and the Wheat, the Leaven and the Mustard Seed, the Hidden Treasure and the Pearl of Great Price. Each illustrates some phase of the Kingdom of Heaven.

The aim of Jesus in using parables, He makes plain to us. He made use of the parable-story first of all to gain and hold the attention of the people and instil vital truths in a concrete form

1 Imperfect indicative of repeated action   2 Farrar, Life of Christ, pp. 227-8
3 Parable means a thing cast alongside.   4 Taylor, The parables of our Saviour,
    p 1.2.

which would be easily retained by the memory. He was a master teacher. He chose scenes, incidents, and objects with which the people were familiar, thus heightening the effect. The great aim of Christ beyond all question in all His teachings was to illuminate human minds and soften human hearts. All prophets desire to illumine, soften, and save; not darken, harden, or destroy. Another reason for using the parable was that His disciples might understand His disappointment and the failure of His ministry to reach and convert great multitudes. It seemed that such a messenger and such a message ought to win every man who came within its range, but such had not been the case. Growing out of this was another reason for using the parable. The disciples would soon be in the midst of the activities of the work He had instituted, and as His apostles to the world would have to suffer the same disappointments He now suffered and meet with the same failures. They must learn now that the failure was not due to them or their message but to the conditions in the hearers. This brings us to one of the main reasons Jesus cited for using parabolic teaching. It was the moral and spiritual condition of the people whom He was teaching. He had started out with Beatitudes and plain teachings and they did not accept them. He followed up with similitudes but with no better success. The ears of the people were dull; their eyes were covered over with scales; their hearts were surrounded with fat. So here Jesus adopts the parabolic form of teaching to *sift* His hearers. His fan was in His hand. Those who were disposed to understand and willing to accept the truth would be stimulated the more by this method to make investigation; while those who were willfully rejecting would be incensed the more against Him and go on hardening their hearts. The preaching of the Gospel in any way has that effect; but the parabolic form of teaching did not sell the precious gospel cheaply but made it a thing to be gotten only by those who sought after it, while at the same time making it more attractive to those who really desired it. As the cloud which led the people of Israel out of the desert separated between them and their enemies at the crossing of the sea, with the bright side to them and the dark side to the enemy, so the parable illuminates the initiated and brings confusion to those who willfully reject the truth.

Then the parable avoided the offensiveness but not effectiveness of direct rebuke. He exposed the conduct and character of His antagonists in this way, without driving the people away from Him. The parable was a test of character and intended by Jesus to awaken the divine consciousness within, and lead the people gradually to understand that which in parabolic form served in the beginning only as a stimulus.

(1) The first parable by the sea was that of the Sower (Mark 4:3-25; Matt. 13:3-23; Luke 8:5-18). This parable explains the causes of the success and failure of the gospel and finds them to be in the kinds of soil or disposition in the hearers. Jesus looked on the crowd assembled and perceived the various dispositions in them and the motives which led them to be present now. Some came through mere curiosity; some through hatred; some to really hear. All needed to know that the capacities they brought would determine what they would get out of the sermon. Most of them would be ready to criticize and lay the fault of the failure on the preacher and His message. But there was no fault either in this preacher or His message; yet many rejected both it and Him.

There was the *wayside* hearer in Jesus' audience. Like the hard beaten path through the grain field in Palestine his heart was impervious to the seeds of the word of God which fell upon it. He did not "understand" or "take it in;" but on account of stupidity, indifference, preoccupation or lack of attention, the seed of the word lay there until some subsequent conversation, some thought of other things, some distraction on the way home used by Satan, snatched it away like the bird snatches away the grains of wheat on the hard worn path.

There was a second class of hearers who were *shallow* and superficially *emotional*. Like the thin crust of soil on top of the ledge of rock, such a heart receives immediately the message of the word when it is presented, with joyful demonstration of emotion but not with reflection and deliberate thought. He is swept away by the emotional wave of excitement in the religious movement and makes a profession before he experiences a real change of heart. He does not understand what it all means or count the cost. The consequence is that he is a temporary professor of Christianity merely. There is no depth to his nature and the word cannot become well rooted. When the sun of tribulation or persecution comes up, his shallow enthusiasm vanishes away like a fog before the morning sun, and the impressions of the word like the plant in a dry soil on a burning rock wither away. He stumbles and falls in temptation. There are many such 'converts' in great revivals who do not prove to be stable Christians.[1]

The third class of hearers is represented by the *dirty soil* that has not yet cleared up thoroughly. Such a hearer has a preoccupied heart. He is neither stupid like the first nor shallow and superficially emotional like the second class of hearers; but his mind is occupied with many other interests of a hurtful worldly character. The thorn seed are already in the soil.[2] There are many

---

[1] Proskairos, for a time.   [2] The preposition epi. Matt. 13:7

other views, projects, cares and desires there. The soil is good, has depth, and receives the seed of the gospel in understanding. But the nut-grass roots are down beneath the surface and spring up first. The seeds of the kingdom come up; but in the struggle for the mastery the thorns win out and the real crop of the word succumbs. Here then is a picture of a divided heart. Such a man never develops a ripe Christian character.

One kind of plant that "chokes out" the word is the "care of the world!" The carking care and anxiety about food, clothing, and other things, suffocates the plants of the kingdom. Another type of weed is the "deceitfulness of riches," the vanity and pride of wealth. Business crowds out religion. Ambition for position, whether social, political, or other, is another pestiferous briar that smothers out the seed of the word, making it turn pale like the wheat in a briar-infested patch or the corn in a grassy field. Yet another type of thorn that prevents the fruit of the kingdom from coming to maturity is that of inordinate affections and "desires for many things." Some form of selfish or sensual indulgence or of worldly pleasures makes the word become unfruitful. "It brings no fruit to perfection."[2] Against domestic cares and trivialities, the encroachments of business, or the ordinary vocational and common activities of life; against the ambitions for preeminence in literature, science, politics, or religion or the life of fashion and frivolity, the parable warns all men. These things will certainly choke the word and prevent it from coming to fruitage.

The fourth class of hearers is represented by the *good ground*. They not only "receive" the word into the heart; but "understand" it, "retain" it, and "bring forth fruit." "The honest and good heart" is soft, deep, clean soil. This hearer does not receive the message with his "decision already made up beforehand," but with a heart sincerely desirous of knowing the truth, and with the intention to abide by it. He does not allow other things to come in and remove the word as the birds pick up the seed; but holds it fast.[2] He takes measures to retain it by meditating upon it. He first hears with active attentive mind; then meditates on that which he heard; and finally puts in practice the word in obedience. Meditation is one of the greatest means of fixing the message in the memory and the learning art is complete when one gives himself to active obedience.

Such then are the four classes of hearers: the spiritually stupid, indifferent, and hard hearted, who does not receive the word into his heart or understand it; the shallow, impulsive, superficially emotional in whom the seed springs up quickly but

1 Luke 8:14   2 Luke 8:15

soon withers away; the preoccupied, divided mind in which the word germinates and springs up but is choked back, pales into sickliness, and never matures or ripens into fruitfulness. The last class of the good soil receives with attention, cultivates through meditation, and bears in obedience, the yield varying according to individual talents, environmental circumstances, and relative application.

Jesus concluded this parable designed especially to prepare the disciple against future disappointments in the work by an appeal to them to be careful how they received it. He had cited the people of the times of Isaiah "who seeing saw not and hearing heard not; whose heart was so fat as to be insensible to any impression." The teaching by parables was "such," that the one who had been initiated into the "mysteries" of the kingdom and had already some knowledge of the truth, would be stimulated to further investigation, like research-students seeking out the facts and realities. Others who had no desire for seeking the truth, but were obstinate and determined not to receive it from Jesus and especially since it did not agree with their traditional beliefs, would have their resentment stirred all the more against the teacher and His message. The lamp of the truth must not be covered up by the earthenware bushel measure, and thus smothered out, or put under the bed where it would be concealed, but on the rock lamp-stand jutting out from the wall, that all entering the room might be illumined by it. The hidden and the secret things are to be revealed. It was not the purpose of Jesus to hide the light from anyone. Let them take this as a principle to act upon. The light must be placed where it would shine forth to all. Let the disciples take heed how they heard.

(2) The parable of seed growing by itself: first the blade, then the ear, and finally the full corn. (Mark 4:26-29).

This parable, which teaches the gradual and slow growth of the word of the kingdom, is supplementary to that of the Sower. The labourers in the kingdom are prone to exaggerate their own importance as instruments and to interfere with the process of development according to the spiritual laws of the kingdom. Wanting to see immediate results they become impatient and even despondent. Jesus would cultivate in His disciples the virtues of dependence, faith, and patience. The blade, the ear, and the full corn suggest progress according to natural law through successive stages. This is the kernel of the parable.

The agent of the sowing is immaterial. The husbandman who "cast the seed upon the earth," recognized that he had done his part and the rest depended on the seed and the soil. Hence he

was patient and unconcerned about the outcome, not fretting but
waiting. Christ did not fret, when the seed He scattered so widely
did not spring up in a day. He patiently trained a few disciples
that He might win the world.

The labourer in the kingdom must remind himself that in
the seed itself and in the soil are the natural elements and efficient causes of a harvest. He must be willing to scatter the seed
diligently and then wait patiently the issue. The element of time
is necessary in order that the process according to spiritual law
may be complete.

The full ripe ear is what He desired; but there are preliminary stages which lead up to it. First the blade comes, then the
green ear, and finally the ripe ear. Enlightened and sanctified
character is not produced in a day. The blade and the blossom
represent the conscious beginning of the divine life in the soul.
The green ear corresponds to an undeveloped stage. It is a time
of unfulfilled desire, unrealized ideals. It is sometimes a period of
doubt and misgivings. But in the good soil the green ear will
finally ripen. At length appears the ripe fruit of nature, Christian
character filled with love, joy, peace, long-suffering, gentleness,
goodness, faith, meekness, temperance. Until the ripe ear appears,
the labourer must wait patiently and work earnestly.

(3) The parable of the tares (Matt. 13:24-30; 36-43).

Jesus added another parable[1] to that of the Sower, to illustrate the chequered fortunes of the kingdom in the world. Like
the parable of the Sower this parable was interpreted for His disciples by Him. In it He warned them not to expect to see society
completely transformed in their time. His Kingdom was not to be
a temporal kingdom. The good and bad must continue to exist
together in the world. There would be a final separation in the
end of time.

Jesus the Messiah sowed, and continues through His servants
to sow down the world-field with the good seed of the kingdom.
At the same time Satan is secretly sowing down on top[2] of the
wheat tares of darnel, which in the early stages of its growth
is so like the wheat that it is impossible to discriminate between
them, that becoming possible only when the grain is developed.

There has been much discussion as to the meaning of this
parable since the time of the Donatists early in the history of
Christianity. The cause for such divergence of opinion as to the
import of the parable is the persistent tendency to apply modern
theories of the church and church discipline to the interpretation,
reading into the simple language of the parable our own thoughts

1 Paratheken   2 Epiespeiren, to sow upon.

and theories. The language of the parable is not so difficult. The seed of the kingdom are the sons of the kingdom. They are different in character from the darnel or tares which are the sons of the evil one or devil. Good and bad men must continue to coexist in God's world-field until the end of time, much as God's servants may wonder that He should so permit. The kingdom will not make conquest of all the evil until the end of the age. The disciples must understand that and not lose faith and courage. Jesus is talking here about His kingdom and not about the visible church.

The parable teaches an important lesson as to the attitude of the servant of the kingdom toward the soil-men of the world. He will encounter in them villainy, fraud, lust, cruelty, malice, in-sincerity, intolerance, superstititon and many other things of im-piety and unrighteousness. He will suffer their antagonism, treachery and persecution in the form of calumnies and violence. But he is to suffer all these things with patience. Jesus did not destroy the Samaritan village which refused Him allegiance, not dealing with them according to their deserts. He suffers the righteous and the wicked to live together in the world intertwined in their relations until the end. The mission of the servant of God is not one of destruction but of salvation. In the same world with saints — the meek, pure, reverent, and pious — exist the infidels, reprobates, criminals, "the lawless," and God's servant must have patience and suffer much while he perseveres in the work of the kingdom. It is hard for him to tell always the good from the bad. There is no way of extirpating the things of scandal and the lawless men by force. He must expect that their kind will con-tinue to the end of time in spite of all that may be done by king-dom men to the contrary.

But there is to be a final separation. The kingdom is to be established universally. The things of scandal will be removed then along with "those doing lawlessness," by the angels who are to be the harvesters. Sent by the Son of Man they will gather the wicked as bundles of tares and bind them for the burning. The righteous on the other hand will be gathered into His garner. The destiny of the wicked will be the furnace of fire, not literal perhaps but worse. There shall be the wailing of sorrow and hopelessness and the gnashing of teeth of anger and bitter hatred of rebellion. The righteous shall shine as the stars forever and ever. But we can-not believe in a heaven without believing in a hell also. While this parable has no direct reference to the visible church as an exclusive field, still the principle holds true and it is a fact that there are good and bad men in the church which is included in the world-field. Many counterfeit professors of Christianity are to be found in the church who are so much like the true Christians in appearance that it is almost impossible to discriminate between them. This is one of the devil's greatest devices to thwart the purposes of Christianity. He makes use of hypocritical professors to contaminate the whole church. The Donatists thought this parable warned against violent extirpation of heretics in the church. While it does not teach the existence of the evil men within the kingdom, it is true that wicked men can be and are members of the visible church. The world-field, by anticipation, was to be the kingdom in the end, and so in that sense the "lawless men" are to be gathered up "out of the kingdom" in the final consummation of the times, and the field be cleared up. Even in the particular matter of church discipline the same principle of patience and forbearance, of rigid self-examination and lenient judgment of others, should prevail. Even in our private and social intercourse we must be tolerant toward others and severe toward ourselves. In this Christ gives us the example.

(4)   The parable of the drag-net (Matt. 13:47-50).

The kingdom is next compared to the seine-net cast into the sea. It enclosed fish of all kinds, and when full they drew it up on the beach at the place of the breaking of the waves and sitting down deliberately gathered the good into vessels but cast the bad out.

So it shall be at the end of the age. Angels shall come and separate the wicked from the midst of the righteous and shall cast them into the furnace of fire. There shall be weeping and gnashing of teeth. The wicked and righteous shall thus be separated at the time of final assizes and the wicked suffer terrible destruction. This seems to be the main point of the parable. The parable of the Tares called attention to the need of patience and endurance on the part of disciples, in relation to the evil in the world and in the visble church too. To try to uproot the tares by violent process is dangerous. The one truth emphasized in the parable of the drag-net is that in its own suitable time the separation will be effected and will be according to the character and the worth of each to God.

(5)   The parable of the mustard seed (Mark 4:30-32; Matt. 13: 31-32).

The parable of the mustard seed presents another aspect of the kingdom. The preceding parables emphasized the difficulties which the kingdom meets with in its progress and the necessity of perseverance and patience on the part of the kingdom labourer. In this parable Jesus chose another illustration from the agricultural life of Palestine. The mustard plant native to that coun-

try springs from the least of seed, so small as to be scarcely
visible, black, very pungent, and of great vitality. The plant which
springs from it, however, is not so small, growing to the height
of ten to twelve feet, so that the branches sprangle out and furnish to the birds a hospitable protection from the strong rays of
the Syrian sun by day and a place of secure repose at night.

The point of the illustration is that the kingdom had a small
beginning. It did not begin as the Jews had hoped, on a great
scale of temporal grandeur. In the interpretation of a parable like
this, we do not make application of all its details. The fact that
the birds came and made their nests in it has no spiritual significance, but is merely one of the ways incidentally of explaining the
final greatness of the plant. The kingdom began with a small
group of disciples; it will terminate in becoming a universal rule
at the second coming of its king (Dan. 4:12, 21). The small beginning, the gradual development and growth, and the final greatness are the points of illustration. The disciples must not be discouraged with the small beginning, for great results will come with
time. The seed is small, but like the acorn from which comes the
oak, the small congregation will some day grow into a great
church if the seed is cast in the earth. This seed of the kingdom is
a vital seed.

(6) The parable of the leaven and many other such parables
(Mark 4:33-34; Matt. 13:33-35).

Yet another aspect of the growth of the kingdom is set forth
in the parable of the leaven which the woman hid in three measures of meal. The parable of the mustard seed was taken from
agricultural life; this of the leaven from domestic activities; that
illustrated the small beginning and great growth; this the imper-
ceptible introduction of the kingdom leaven into the mass of
humanity which it was destined to transform. It was natural that
Jesus should speak of "a certain woman" in this parable because
it was not the custom for the man to make the bread for the
family. The number of measures of meal which He chose was the
usual number for a week's baking for a medium-sized family,
being a peck and a half to the measure or a little more altogether
than a bushel. There is no spirtiual significance in the number
three. It might have been five for a much larger family. Some of
the ancient writers who were fond of the allegorical method of
interpretation, said that the three measures referred to the Jews,
Greeks, and Romans; others found in the number *three* reference
to the doctrine of the Trinity or three persons in the godhead,
a purely fanciful and absurd idea.

The leaven operates according to the spiritual law of influence through contact. It is necessary that the kingdom men should be in contact with the unbelieving world in order to leaven it. The influence of the kingdom elements must be real, vital, and active, producing spiritual change and transformation in the contiguous elements of society. It operates silently and unobstrusively; but is penetrating, pervasive, and will be complete in the end. Wherever the leaven of the kingdom is placed a mighty change will be wrought.

Both Mark and Matthew testify that Jesus made use of many such parables in His teaching, as the people were able to hear it. We do not know how many He used on this occasion. There are ten recorded in the narratives of the two gospels. Matthew found in Jesus' use of parables the fulfillment of prophecy in a Messianic Psalm (Ps. 78:2).

(7)   The parables of the Hidden Treasure and the Pearl of Great Price (Matt. 13:44-46).

These two parables illustrate the intrinsic worth and preciousness of the kingdom of the heavens and the willingness of the man who once perceives its incomparable worth to do everything in his power and sacrifice all else in order to come into possession of it. In Palestine, where the armies of Assyrians and Egyptians passed through the country frequently, always devastating, stealing and destroying — because the Jewish nation passed frequently from one allegiance to another — the inhabitants would hide their treasures by burying them in the ground. It not infrequently happened that the owners, being killed or carried away in captivity, the treasures would be left, and occasionally would be found accidentally by others. Such a happening was one of great joy to the fortunate finder. The illustration therefore was apt and well-understood by the hearers.

The man of the parable came upon the hidden treasure accidentally. It had been hidden well out in a field. The man doubtless recognized it as ancient and pertaining to none so much as the finder. Such might well be the case in the changes of ownership through a long period and especially after the great alterations of the long years of exile. At any rate there is no incorrect moral conduct recommended, since the point of illustration is not how he went about to come in possession of the treasure, but rather the incomparable worth of the kingdom and the reasonableness of selling all one has and buying it with great eagerness and joy. That it was a great treasure is an implication of all the circumstances. There are many who come upon the kingdom treasure while they are engaged in the honest and industrious pursuit of life's common tasks. Happy is the man who recognizes the value of the treasure when he sees it and joyfully sacrifices all else that he may possess it.

The merchant who was seeking beautiful and costly pearls points to the same matchless worth and beauty of the kingdom. The pearl was as precious to the ancients as the diamond is to us today. The merchant in his quest came upon a pearl of great price. He went immediately and sold unconditionally all that he was possessing[1] and bought it. Many come upon the kingdom treasure apparently as an accident, while others find it through earnest seeking; but it is equally precious to both when found. The difference between the accidental finders and the earnest seekers is not so much one of disposition as of position. The merchant was in pursuit of his common trade in pearls; the tenant-farmer was in the industrious activities of cultivating the soil. Both alike welcomed the new-found wealth and sacrificed all to make it theirs.

The intrinsic worth of the kingdom revealed in these twin parables should be a stimulus to all men who have it not, to seek it and sacrifice all to possess it. The worker in the kingdom should learn that though it may be difficult to get men to recognize the value of this treasure and jewel, once they have perceived it they will give everything in exchange for it.

When Jesus finished this afternoon of parabolic teaching by the seaside and His private interpretations to the disciples in the house, He closed His discourse with a question and an illustration (Matt. 13:51-53). "Have you understood all these things?" He asked. They responded in the affirmative and He added:

"As Christian teachers, who have been instructed in the sphere of the kingdom, you are like the house-holder who brings forth out of his treasure things new and old." They could draw from the things of ancient prophecy and the accumulated treasures of the knowledge of the past, but also from the new truth revealed now in His teachings parabolic and other. The true teacher must be a wise conservator of the old facts and realities while receiving with open mind the new truth. This is a splendid guiding principle for all Christian teachers.

5. In crossing the lake Jesus stills the tempest. Mark 4:35-41; Matt. 8:18, 23-27; Luke 8:22-25).

When evening had almost passed, filled with earnest teaching, first of the multitudes on the beach and from the boat and then of the disciples in Simon's house, Jesus was very tired. The great multitudes continued to press around Him and it was impossible to get any rest. It had been a very busy day. The struggle with

---

1 Imperfect tense of verb denoting continued action.

234

232 THE CHRIST OF THE GOSPELS

the Pharisees, the misunderstanding and interruption of His work by His own family, the healing of the blind, dumb, lunatic and other miracles of cure, the intense work of parabolic teaching, together, had left Him quite exhausted. So He took the initiative in suggesting a trip across the lake, a distance of some seven miles. The disciples were ready when He said, "Let us go over to the other side of the lake." They recognized that He sadly needed the repose and so they take Him[1] without any preparation "just as He was" into the boat. They did not stop to get food or make any provision for the trip. They must get Him away from the crowd as quickly as possible. In spite of their resolution and haste they did not rid themselves of the people at once, for other boats followed them as they set sail.

They started out from Capernaum, probably expecting to land somewhere in the vicinity of Bethsaida-Julias on the north-east side of the lake. There they could seek out some quiet nook in the hills near enough to the town to get food, and spend some hours in complete repose.

On board the boat, weary, He sank down on the leather boss of the steerman's seat placed near the stern of the boat and fell asleep.[2] This is the only time the gospel record speaks about the sleep of Jesus. Faintness, weariness, exhaustion, dominated the physique of the human Jesus, and He lay immersed in profound slumber, fanned by the breeze of the lake and soothed by the gentle rhythmic motion of the boat. Here is a picture unspeakably sublime of the human Saviour in repose, in the boat on the bosom of the beautiful Sea of Galilee. Near Him, His disciples converse in subdued tones about the happenings of the day, while others quietly manage the sails and guide the gliding craft over the placid waters. The last glimmerings of the day fade from the western horizon and the night spreads its mantle over this peaceful scene. The myriads of glittering stars dot the Syrian sky, and furnish all the needed light for the sailing craft now midway the placid sea.

But this quiet idyllic scene was destined soon to be changed. Suddenly the northeasterly breeze stiffens and along the horizon of the lake to the north and east the clouds thicken. The heavens rapidly grow darker and darker and in just a few moments a wild wind swoops down[3] the gorge of the Jordan from the heights of Hermon on the north and the cyclonic storm[4] (lailaps) is upon them. All they could do was rapidly to adjust their sails and seek to weather the gale. With every moment the storm grows

1 Historic present active.   2 Ingressive aorist.   3 Came down, Kateba.
    second aorist.   4 Such cyclonic gusts are frequent on this lake even today.
    The lake is 682 ft. below sea-level and is surrounded by mountains so that the
    heated rising and the cool air rushing down from the mountains give rise to
    sudden squalls which at times are severe—Thomson, Land and Book, Ch. XXV.

worse until it becomes a great tempest (seismos) heaving the sea like an earthquake. Now the waves were lashing furiously and breaking over the sides of the boat so that it was already filling. Again and again the boat was buried amid the foam of the breakers which burst over the lower parts completely. They were in great danger and the Master lay on the seat of the stern steeped in the profound slumber of exhaustion.

They had not wanted to awaken Him, such was their love, reverence, and care for Him. But their situation was critical and growing more so every moment. All their efforts to bail out the water were unavailing and the sails were beyond their management.[1] Another wave might send their boat to the bottom and hurl them all into the hopeless struggle for life in the midst of the fury of the elements. They forgot they had the Lord of Life on board, forgot everything in their panic of fear in the face of death.[2] They rush to Him and awake Him with a cry of anguish and fear.[3]

"Master. Master,[4] we perish! Save us quick, Lord, we are perishing!" He hesitated a moment with a look of pity and rebuke. "Teacher,[5] carest thou not that we perish?" they add. For a moment more He paused to calm their fears.

"Why are ye fearful, O ye men of little faith?"[6] Jesus was still Master even if He were asleep. But they had not yet come to understand that He was the Lord of nature. He stood forth now in the midst of the howling storm, calm and unruffled in His majesty. Not one tremor of alarm or one token of confusion. "Silence," He said, addressing the winds as human beings. "Be muzzled," He commanded the turbulent dashing waves as if they were animals. Instantly the winds hushed into peace and the waves subsided placidly. It was a miracle! Always after the storm the swell remains for a time after the wind has died down; but the lake in this case became calm at once.

> "The winds were howling o'er the deep
> Each wave a watery hill;
> The Saviour waken'd from his sleep;
> He spoke, and all was still." — Heber.

Again turning to the disciples with chiding voice, He said: "Why are ye fearful? Have ye not yet come to have faith?" They had witnessed many miracles of His. They should have recognized before this His power over all nature. "Where is your faith?" He said in gentle rebuke.

These bronzed, experienced sailors were profoundly impressed.

1 Land and Book, Ch. XXV   2 Historic present, of vivid description, Mark 4:38.
3 Epistata.   4 Kurios.   5 Didaskalos.   6 Little faith men (oligopistoi)

They feared exceedingly and no wonder. Here was one who in the same day had cured a blind-dumb lunatic, met the learned Scribes and Pharisees in debate and defeated them, taught many wonderful things in beautiful but half-enigmatic parables, and now with a word makes the cyclonic winds cease and calms the raging sea. They were filled with amazement.

"Who then is this?" they said. "What kind of man is this, who commands even the winds and the water and they obey Him?" They were growing in their apprehension and comprehension of Jesus, but they had much to learn yet and needed to grow in the knowledge of the *Lord* Jesus Christ. At least they had caught one more glimpse of His majesty and were filled with dread and wonder. He was not just the human Jesus then; He was also the divine Christ.

6. Beyond the lake near Gerasa Jesus heals two demoniacs (Mark 5:1-20; Matt. 8:28-34; Luke 8:26-39).

The stormy night ending in the miraculous calm had almost passed, when their boat, driven by the tempest to a point south of their intended landing, touched the eastern shore near the little town of Gerasa marked today by the village of Kersa.[1] Scarcely had they landed when the blood-curdling cries of raging lunacy and human distress sounded from the rock-hewn tombs of the near-by precipice. In the dim light of the moon they descried two "exceedingly fierce" madmen issuing from the sepulchers of the Wady Semak and coming toward them, one well in advance of the other. They had just passed from the experience of the raging sea, to one now of human fury and degradation even more terrible, cast as it was on the background of the weird desolate night-scene of the Gadarene tombs.

The description which the Gospels give of these fierce, naked, homicidal demoniacs is vivid. Matthew was deeply impressed by the fiercer[2] of the two who was originally from the town of Gerasa, but had for a long time put on no clothes nor did he abide in any house but in the tombs night and day, filling the stillness of the night with his horrible cries which struck terror into the hearts of all who heard him. So fierce was he that "no man dared[3] pass that way."

There were no asylums in those days in spite of the boasted civilization of the Greeks and Romans. Unfortunates of this class who were too dangerous to be harbored within the town, were driven forth to live in the rock-hewn tombs in the midst of ghastliness and pollution which served only to aggravate the nature of

1 Tristam's Land of Israel, p. 465.   2 Matthew mentions two demoniacs, Mark and Luke describe one, who was probably the leading and worst one.
3 Had courage or strength—ischuein.

their malady. No measures were taken to alleviate their misery but only to protect others against their violence. This man had been bound often with fetters and chains but ineffectually for he had broken the fetters in two[1] and the chains in many pieces. The people from the town and surrounding country places testified this when they came out now to see what had happened. He had been given up as a hopeless case, for no man had the strength or courage to tame him. He kept up a continuous bedlam of hideous shrieks through the day and night and his violence was a menace to all passers-by as well as a peril to himself, for he was constantly cutting himself on the sharp stones as he ran hither and thither, to say nothing of his frequent suicidal attempts.

The explanation which the Jews had for the condition of this man was that "he was possessed by an unclean spirit." According to Jewish demonology, evil spirits of the wicked dead dwelt especially in lonely desolate places and among the tombs.[2] It was chiefly at night they thought that evil spirits were wont to haunt burying-places. But this incident recorded in three of the Gospels is no mere accommodation of the teachings of Jesus to the traditional notions of the Jews as some would have us think. We have here a real case of demon-possession and perhaps the worst recorded in the Scriptures.

What then is the explanation of this extraordinary phenomenon? The subject of demon-possession is one of great difficulty. But the plain teachings of the three distinct evangelical narratives present the matter as a reality. We may not believe with some that it was a mere case of insanity or epilepsy. Demon-possession in the Gospel narratives was often accompanied by physical diseases, as dumbness and blindness, but many times was not. It was set apart in Jesus' classification of the ills of humanity in a distinct category by itself (Matt. 4:23-24). He dealt with the demonized in a different way. Moral depravity might precede and accompany the possession, but while the demonized was an active agent in the condition, at the same time his spirit was dominated by the unclean spirit who is represented as the active agent ruling the spirit of the man. In the case of this poor man there was apparently a double personality. The unclean spirit was ruling in his soul, driving him hither and thither, making him a terror and menace to the neighborhood and to himself. He was himself conscious of this domination of his spirit by the demons and said they were Legion.

Many have ridiculed the idea of demon-possession; but experience and observation, aside from revelation, go to prove that

1 Diaespasthai.   2 Edersheim's Life and Times of Jesus. p. 607.

Satan works in the hearts of men and completely dominates their spirits, bringing many to utter degradation of their physical, intellectual, and moral powers. We would naturally expect the greatest manifestation of Satan's power in the sphere of human life just at the time when Jesus was active in His ministry of salvation in the days of His incarnation. We would not expect such signal manifestations in later history as this case, after Satan had been vanquished by Jesus on the cross in decisive victory. But there are many instances in modern times, especially in pagan lands, of demon-possession, the characteristic manifestations of which parallel those in the evangelical narratives. Any fair and honest interpretation of the narrative in this case recognizes the reality of demon possession. Jesus dealt with the demon as a reality beyond question and this is final.

As the two demoniacs came nearer in the light of the breaking dawn, they recognized Jesus and cried out: "What have we to do with thee, thou Son of God? Art thou come hither to torment us before the time?" With irresistible power they were drawn on to Jesus, and as they came nearer the one who was the fiercer, instead of falling on the timorous disciples in violence, came rushing forward and fell down on his knees before Jesus in the attitude of worship.

Jesus, meanwhile, was ordering the unclean spirit repeatedly:[1] "Come forth thou unclean spirit out of the man." The demon, dominating and using the man's powers of speech, remonstrated: "What have I to do with thee or thou with me, thou Son of the Most High God? Art thou come hither to torment us before the time? I beseech thee, I adjure thee by God, do not begin to torment[2] us yet." Luke the physician adds parenthetically, that "for a long time the spirit had seized the man with such extraordinary manifestations of violence that he had to be kept constantly under guard, bound with chains and fetters." Even these proved unavailing, and breaking the bands asunder he was various times driven by the devil into the desert places. The recognition of Jesus by the demons (daimonia) and their confession of His supremacy and divinity is in perfect accord with the presence of Satan and his agents in the universe. It was consciousness of subjection and fear in the presence of Jesus that caused the unclean spirits to cry out. The usual effect when the demonized came into His presence was a fresh paroxysm of physical violence. But here we see an act of quiet homage on the part of the unclean spirit. The demon, speaking for the Legion, begged that they should be for a season at least exempt from torment, recognizing that there was an ap-

---

1 Imperfect of repeated action, Luke 8:29.   2 Ingressive aorist.

pointed time reserved for their endless punishment in the abyss. The poor man was obsessed with the idea that many demons had entered into him.

"What is your name?" said Jesus, addressing the man, perhaps with a view to aiding his regaining possession of himself. But the demon retained his power over the man's spirit and he replied:

"My name is Legion for we are many." The man could not even remember his own name or recognize his identity, so completely was he under the tyranny of the demons.[1] The Roman legion, in the popular conception, was six thousand armed strong warriors. The presence of Roman legions in Palestine and everywhere at that time is sufficient to explain the use of this Roman term by the man. The demons dominating his power entreated through his lips that they should not be sent into the abyss. In the popular conception there were three doors to Gehenna: the desert (Num. 16:33), the sea (Jonah 2:2), and Jerusalem (Isa. 31:9).[2] Under the impression of this current idea the demonized besought Him "that he would not send them away out of the country." Was the man thinking about the desert wilds to the east? The demons entreated by the man that they should not be sent into the abyss or bottomless pit, the deep sea (Gen. 1:2; 7:11), the eternal abode of demons (Rev. 9:1-11).

At this point the narrative presents one of the greatest difficulties for the interpreter. There, on the mountain side not far away, was visible a herd of swine feeding. The devils through the dual personality of the man besought Jesus that He would send them into the swine,[3] or at least give them leave[4] so that they might go into the swine. He simply did not hinder it.[5] Here we are not dealing with any mere human phychological device of Jesus, making use of the destruction of the herd of swine in the sea, which was popularly considered one of the gates to the abyss, to convince the demoniac that his legion of demons had gone into the swine and had been precipitated into the very abyss which they entreated to escape.[6] Some may ridicule the idea of the devils entering the swine; but they should not forget how Satan made use of the serpent in the Garden of Eden (Gen. 3). The narrative says that the demons came out of the man and entered into the swine. It further adds graphically that the great herd of two thousand swine race impetuously down the precipice[7]

1 Luke's narrative confirms the view of the man that many demons had entered him. Seven demons were expelled from Mary of Magdala.
2 Lightfoot on Matt. 5:22; See Matt. 12:42 also.   3 Mark 5:12.   4 Luke 8:32.
5 Luke 8:32.   6 David Smith, In the Days of His Flesh, pp. 192-3.   7 Kata.

into the lake, and perish, one by one,[1] choking in the waters. The evangelists, recording this extraordinary occurrence confirmed wonderfully by the topography of the place, clearly connected the release of the man from the thrall of the demons with the violent destruction of the herd of swine in the sea. Even the wild cries of the demon-possessed, if he had been above the herd and if he had cried out earlier, would not have been sufficient to produce a panic in the swine sufficient to precipitate the entire herd into the sea. Such a supposition is far-fetched. How the demons could enter into the swine need not occupy our speculative attention while we understand so little about the subject of demon-possession as a whole. Here is a picture of vivid, terrible realism, which no human brain could ever have conceived apart from the actual occurrence. The wild panic, the mad rush down the precipitous place, the splashing waters, the seething mass of choking animals, was so violent an occurrence that it is no wonder the swineherd turned, "fled," and spread the startling news in the town and all the countryside. They told all the details of what had happened[2] but especially what had befallen the two demoniacs. They had doubtless watched with fearful interest, at the early dawn, the two frantic madmen as they ran to meet Jesus. Then quickly followed the unaccountable panic of the herd of swine. With wild terror these men fled to bear the news.

There was a great stir in the town. Wild with excitement, curiosity, and concern for their property, the whole town poured out to the place not far away, to find the erstwhile terrible madman on account of whom no one could pass by the road, sitting at the feet of Jesus calm as a child. Someone had charitably thrown a cloak about his naked form.[3] They were stricken with sudden[4] and protracted fear.[5]

We would suppose that the sight of the transformation of the demoniacs would have filled the people wtih joy and gratitude to Jesus. But quite the contrary, when they had heard how the men were cured and how the herd of swine was lost they began to beseech Jesus unanimously that He would "depart out of their coasts." They were probably seized with a superstitious dread, the crowd being composed largely of pagan Gentiles. They feared lest further disaster should befall their possessions. They loved their sins, their demons, and their swine better than all else. Jesus turned sadly but at once to take the boat and return to the other side. His return to Capernaum was the only course left open to Him.

1 Imperfect graphically describes the process, Mar. 5:13.   2 Matt. 8:38.
3 Farrar, Life of Christ, p. 242.   4 Ingressive aorist passive, "begin to be afraid."
5 Imperfect passive of sunecho with instrumental of photos.

Then occurred one of the most beautiful of incidents! The worst of the two men from whom Jesus had expelled the demons came forward and begged and kept on begging[1] that he might accompany Him. He wanted "just to be with Jesus." But Jesus did not grant this touching request. He had a work for the new convert to do, a place both difficult and dangerous for him in the Kingdom service. "Go to thy house, unto thy friends, and tell them how great things the Lord hath done for thee and how he had mercy on thee." Jesus would not leave even these ungrateful grovelling multitudes without an evangelist. And the man fulfilled his mission in a manner worthy, filling all the region of Decapolis with his message of how great things God had done for him. His personal testimony was powerfully confirmed in his own transformed person and life. The demons had gone out to stay.[2] What a glad messenger and what a wonderful message he had for his fellow-townsmen and for the world!

7. Returning to Capernaum Jesus performs various miracles of faith (Mark 5:21-43; Matt. 9:18-26; Luke 8:40-56; Matt. 9:27-34).

The stilling of the tempest and expulsion of demons had demonstrated His power over nature and the world of evil spirits; those now to be considered His power in the realm of disease and death.

These miracles were performed in Capernaum. After expelling the demons from the two men on the eastern shore, the Lord returned by boat to the other side, where He was welcomed on the plain of Gennesaret by a large and expectant crowd. The news of His return soon spread through the town of Capernaum and a great multitude gathered about Him at the landing place.

One of those who came while Jesus was addressing the crowd was Jairus, the chief ruler of the synagogue (Mark 5:21-43; Matt. 9:18-26; Luke 8:40-56). He was probably one of the elders who had formerly sought Jesus in Cana on behalf of the Centurion's little boy, who was very sick. Now he hastens to Jesus greatly agitated because his own and only child, a little girl of twelve, was extremely ill at the very point of death.[3] Even now, as she lay dying,[4] she passed through the death-struggle and sinking into a state of coma died.[5] In his anguish, the ruler had dismissed all pride, and first falling on his knees before Jesus in worshipful recognition of His superiority, he next prostrated himself with repeated and urgent requests[6] that the Lord come and lay His hands on the little daughter that she might be made whole and

1 Iterative imperfect.   2 Perfect tense denoting permanence.   3 Eschatos echei, Mar. 5:23.
4 Imperfect tense, Luke 8:42.   5 Aorist tense, indicating the death as actual.
6 Imperfect tense denoting repeated action.

live. In tenderness Jesus knelt beside the prostrate father, speaking words of comfort to his troubled soul. In a moment He arose and with the disciples — for they were about to witness one of the greatest miracles of all time — followed Jairus as he led them in the direction of his home. The way led through the narrow streets of Capernaum, and as Jesus followed the ruler a great crowd accompanied and crowded around so as to almost suffocate Him.[1]

The anxious father felt that there was not a moment to lose. Though the child was dead the breath had but now left her body. He had hopes that if Jesus should arrive without delay and lay His hands upon her she might recover.[2] He was almost frantic with the slow progress of the thronging crowd as they impeded Jesus in the narrow streets. Great was his consternation when the Teacher stopped still and turned around in the crowd. "Who touched my garments?" He demanded. Suddenly a death-like stillness settled down upon the hitherto chattering Oriental crowd.

In the midst of the throng there was a poor woman who had suffered for twelve years from a chronic hemorrhage. Mark explains that "she had suffered many things at the hands of many physicians and had thus spent all she had; nor was she the better for it but had grown worse." There were various remedies for the dread malady proposed by the quackery of the medical profession of those times. Geikie cites a number of prescriptions then in vogue.[3] One recorded in the Talmud and resorted to in extreme cases was to "set her in a place where two ways meet, and let her hold a cup of wine in her right hand and let someone come behind and frighten her and say: 'Arise from thy flux.'" Over ten such cures are recorded, always terminating with the same command: "Arise from thy flux." Pliny's Natural History reveals the generally low condition of medical science in the world at that time. Physicians were accustomed to prescribe doses of curious concoctions made from ashes of burnt wolf's skull, stags' horns, heads of mice, the eyes of crabs, owl's brains, the livers of frogs and other like elements. For dysentery powdered horses' teeth were administered, and a cold in the head was cured by kissing a mule's nose. It is no wonder that this poor woman grew worse under twelve years' treatment by such physicians.

Her faith in Jesus might have been tinged with superstition but it was a real faith. She said within herself, "If I may touch His tunic I shall be saved." She was positive in her faith that if she might succeed in touching so much as the hem of His garment she would be saved from her physical malady and consequently

1 Thronged him (Mark)   2 The subjunctive mood, indicating a weak faith, (Mark 5:23).
3 Geikie's Life of Christ, pp. 157-8.

from her life of social isolation. Trembling, she made her way
with difficulty through the throng and creeping up behind Jesus
touched the blue fringed border of His cloak.

Jesus was careful of His dress. The Rabbis thought a man's
appearance might reflect on his theological profession. They were
willing to eat simple food in order to be able to dress well. Jesus
did not wear phylacteries and extend His fringes but various references to His dress indicate that the seamless robe and the cape
or cloak were of fine material and that to the four corners of His
cloak were attached the fringes (Numbers 15:38-41) indicative
of His vocation of Teacher. Weak, nervous, and shrinking, the
poor woman, realizing that her touch meant ceremonial defilement,
yet dared touch the fringed border of His cloak. Immediately
she felt different in her body and knew she was healed of her
malady. She shrank back into the crowd, hoping to escape detection,
but at the same time rejoicing in her cure.

Perhaps she had hoped to steal away unobserved but it was
not to be so. Jesus knew in Himself that power had gone out from
Him. He turned about. At His question as to who had touched
Him His disciples wondered, and Peter called attention to the
throng that pressed upon Him. But He continued to look[1] around
searchingly to see the one who had done this. "Who touched my
garments?" He said, "For I was conscious of the touch and perceived clearly[2] that power went out from me."

Now, the woman, afraid and trembling, conscious of what
had happened to her, knowing that she was not hidden, came and
fell down before Him and told Him in the presence of all the whole
truth, both as to the motive that led her to touch Him, the pitiable
tale of years of chronic misery, and her present joyful experience
of immediate cure. Instantly Jesus responded to this frank confession.

"Daughter, be of good cheer," He said, "your faith has saved
you. Go in peace. Continue to be whole from your malady of
body and soul." She had found healing for her body and with it
sympathy, and pardon for her sins. The latter she would not have
obtained had she been allowed to steal away and disappear in the
crowd without confession. A tradition says she was a Gentile
woman, which seems reasonable enough since a Jewess would
scarcely have ventured forth into the midst of the crowd, contaminating all whom she touched with her ceremonial pollution.

While Jesus was yet speaking they come from the ruler's
home with a message of the little daughter's death.

"Why do you go on troubling the Teacher?" they ask. But
Jesus turned a deaf ear and did not heed this word spoken. On

---

1 Imperfect tense of continued and interested action.
2 Mark 5:30, epignous denoting accurate and clear knowledge.

the other hand He addresses words of reassurance to the ruler of the synagogue.

"Do not fear," He said, "only believe and she shall be saved and made whole."

At this juncture they come to the house. Leaving all but three of His disciples, Peter, James, and John the brother of James, He entered and found the flute-players and hired mourners making a very bedlam with their much wailing and ostentatious grief. "Give place," He said, "Why are you making a tumult and weeping, the child did not die but is sleeping." But His words were met with a scornful laugh and derision for they knew that she was dead. To Jesus physical death is but a sleep.

Then Jesus asserted His authority and expelled them all from the house. Taking the three disciples and the parents of the little girl, He entered the death chamber. And now a marvelous thing took place. Jesus took the child by the hand and said: "Maiden, arise!" Instantly her spirit returned into her and she rose up and walked around. There was no convalescence. Her recovery was immediate and complete. The parents were beside themselves with amazement. Jesus recalled them to their senses by ordering them to give her something to eat. They could hardly believe their eyes. Jesus enjoined upon them repeatedly that no one should know this. She was alive and well. Could they keep the fame of such a miracle from spreading? Once before Jesus had called back the spirit of the dead (Luke 7:11-17). Would the people believe Him now?

As Jesus hastened away from the home of Jairus, realizing that a great commotion would follow as soon as the restoration of the little girl should be known, two blind men came after Him crying and saying: "Have mercy on us, Son of David." (Matt. 9:27-34). This was the first time Jesus had been called by this title. He did not heed their request at first, desiring to escape from the crowd. He could not deny the title and it was dangerous. But they came on and when He entered into the house, probably Peter's home where He often lodged, they pressed in to Him. Then He addressed them, testing their faith. "Do you believe I am able to do this?" He asked. They reply: "Yes, Lord." Then He touched their eyes to confirm their expectant faith and said: "According to and in the measure of your faith be it done unto you," and their eyes were opened. Then with a shake of the head and a stern look He commanded them:[1] "See to it, let none know it." He would avoid the growing attention to His miracles. The popular demand for such would impede His work of teaching. The sick folk would throng Him and prevent His work of preaching. But the blind men going out scattered the fame of Jesus in all the

1 Enebrimatha, commanded sternly.

land. They were glad of receiving their sight, but little did they know how much they were hindering the work of Jesus by disobeying His command to keep quiet. Jesus added another miracle shortly. A dumb man possessed with a devil was brought to Him. When the devil was cast out, the dumb man spoke. The effect on the crowds was to produce in them amazement.

"Never at any time was such a thing seen in Israel," they exclaimed. But the Pharisees had their explanation ready.

"By the prince of demons he is casting out demons," they declared. It was not the first time they had resorted to this explanation for His mighty works of healing and it would not be the last. As the days went by their antagonism grew ever more bitter.

CHAPTER XVI

THIRD PREACHING TOUR IN GALILEE

(Harm. §§ 69-71)

Jesus now leaves Capernaum with His disciples to pay a last visit to His native town of Nazareth before launching His third and final missionary campaign in Galilee. He was, on the occasion of His first visit, rejected, and a violent attempt made on His life (Luke 4:16-31). He now comes back after many months to offer His fellow-townsmen a second chance.

1. The last visit to Nazareth (Mark 6:16; Matt. 13:54-58).

There is no reason to confuse the first and last appeals in Nazareth. It was most natural that Jesus should desire to give His townsmen the first chance when He began His work in Galilee. The same motive would lead Him to give them another chance as He was initiating His last preaching tour of the province.

From Nazareth as a starting point, He would launch His campaign in the province, sending the Twelve two by two into all its towns and villages. In the interval of His absence some changes would have come in the feeling and attitude of the people toward Him in "his own country." The fame of many wonderful things done by Him in other places would have reached them and caused them to reflect. After all He was a citizen of their town. He had been "the builder" of the town, taking the place of the deceased Joseph. He had won a special place there as a constructor (techton). It would be far from Christ's attitude to fail to give His fellow townsmen a last opportunity for repentance and acceptance of His ministry.

On the Sabbath day, He repaired to the synagogue for worship, as was His custom everywhere and always. His religion functioned normally and His reputation throughout Galilee made for Him a second opportunity in the synagogue of Nazareth. When He was beginning to teach, many of His hearers were filled with amazement saying: "Where does this fellow get these things and this wisdom?"

They questioned not only His "wisdom" but the "powers" which were being wrought by His hands. They were amazed, incredulous, and insolent. He would use every means this time. On the first visit He did not perform miracles; now He does, laying His hands on the sick and healing them that the people may see and believe. But the Nazarenes refused to believe.

"Is not this the son of the widow Mary and brother of James, Joses, Judas, and Simon, the family that left Nazareth and moved

244

to Capernaum? And are not His sisters living here with us in Nazareth?" They were more scandalized the more they thought of it.[1] He was a stumbling-block to them. They were literally trapped like game[2] in a snare because they allowed the circumstances of His life to blind their eyes to His real nature. How could one reared in their midst and who had never studied in the schools of the Rabbis know such things and work such miracles? They thought they knew all about Him; but they did not know the manner of His birth. He was born in Bethlehem, a place far away in those times of simple life.

In His reply Jesus claimed to be a prophet. His answer also indicated that those even of His own house did not believe in Him. His countrymen, neighbors, and even His own family did not understand His actions. No prophet could find lasting honor in His own country among His neighbors and His own kith and kin. He had formerly made claims to be the Messiah and the Son of God (Jno. 4:26; 5:22). If He was a prophet, as He now claims, and a true prophet as His life indicated, then His former claims were true also. Jesus had divine knowledge and marvelous understanding of the human heart; and He marveled at the lack of faith in the people of Nazareth. His human limitations were real and their extent is not clear to us. In this skeptical atmosphere He could do no mighty work. He passes out of the life of Nazareth now once for all. He must have been sad indeed as He went down the valley toward the plain of Esdraelon and looked back for the last time on His native town. He needed their friendship and moral support as He faced His work in Galilee and His destiny in Jerusalem; but they needed Him worse. They had sadly lost their last opportunity to have Him.

2. The third missionary tour (Mark 6:6-13; Matt. 9:35-11:1; Luke 9:1-6).

From Nazareth, Jesus descended to the populous plain of Esdraelon, and began His missionary campaign with the disciples, who had up to this time been serving their apprenticeship in missionary work. He was leading them around[3] about all the villages and cities teaching in the synagogues. A second phase of His program was that of preaching or heralding the gospel of the kingdom. The third type of His work was that of healing every disease and every complaint.

As they went on with the campaign, Jesus, seeing the crowds, was moved with compassion concerning them. The reason for His pity was that the people were in a terrible plight, for they were in

---

1 Imperfect of continued action.
2 Eskandalizonto, the skandalon was a snare used to catch game.
3 Imperfect, periagen, a progressive campaign from place to place.

a constant state of concern, vexation, and bewilderment, religious-ly,[1] due to those who should be teaching them the right way but were only laying ceremonial burdens upon them instead. They were cast down beneath the feet of the Pharisees. Their mental dejection had become chronic.[2]

Jesus used two beautiful illustrations, familiar in the life of the people, to characterize their state of religious abandon. They were "as sheep not having a shepherd," He said. This people was as an abandoned flock: scattered, harassed, and fleeing from the invading wild beasts. Some of them were cast down, prostrated, harried, and torn. They had no shepherd to lead them into the safety of the fold in the hours of peril by night or out for feeding into the green pastures of true instruction by day.

Another figure illustrating their religious condition was that of the "abundant over-ripe harvest" just ready for the reaping. The greatness of the harvest stood out in striking contrast with the fewness of the laborers. The population of Galilee was con-gested—over two hundred cities and villages—and His disciple band was just a handful of workers as yet.

"The way to meet this need," He said "was to appeal to the Lord of the harvest," recognizing His sovereignty in all things that He might "thrust out[3] workers into his harvest." After all the harvest and the workers were His and they were to make their prayer to Him. Jesus well knew that one who sincerely prays the Lord to supply workers will be more ready to respond if the Lord calls Him personally to the task.

The Master had now come to a new departure in His method in the work. Hitherto He had gone out with the disciples and they had been permitted to observe His work. Now they are to go out without Him to learn independence and use their own initia-tive. This was necessary in order to complete their training and equipment as workers, and especially in view of the now distant future when He would no longer be with them. Another reason was the vast needs of the thronging multitudes. The number of preachers must be increased and their efficiency and ability to carry on alone must be secured. He therefore called together[4] to Him the twelve disciples, who had been learners mainly in His "walking seminary" up to the present time, and sent them forth as missionaries. They were to be His "apostles" henceforth—those sent out by Him on a special mission. He sent them by twos for mutual consultation and assistance—a wise provision for the in-experienced and timid disciples.

---

1 Skullo, distressed, harrassed, bewildered.
2 Perfect, periphrastic tense, Erimmenoi esan.
3 Ekballa—to hurl or thrust out.   4 Sunkalesamenos, Luke.

They were given their commission with power[1] over unclean spirits, to be able to cast them out, and to heal every kind of disease and every malady. Every kind of demon[2] was to be subject to their authority and power. He sent them out to herald (karuchein) the kingdom rule of God and to heal. Matthew seems to give emphasis to the power given them continuously[3] for their healing ministry, and to the restriction on their work of preaching to the simple, heralding the kingdom of heaven. This restriction would naturally arise from their limited experience in preaching and from their meager equipment in doctrinal understanding. They were told explicitly to preach a kingdom "not of this world" in contrast to the popular conception of the Messianic Kingdom. This was a safe and wise limitation. Their message then was the Messianic Kingdom—a message which electrified their hearers—but with definite limitations as to the heavenly character of this kingdom.

Matthew gives an interesting list of the twelve apostles. They were not chosen now (Luke 6:12-16) but on the occasion of His preaching the "sermon on the mount" (Luke 6:17). There are four places in the New Testament where lists of the twelve are given. Peter's name always comes first and that of Judas Iscariot last. There are three groups of four each with varying order within the groups. Bartholomew is the name for Nathanael and Thaddeus is Judas, the brother of James. Matthew names them here in pairs and probably as they were sent out on this missionary tour.

Before sending them forth Jesus defined the sphere and character of their work and gave them minute instructions as to their equipment, conduct, method, and approach in their task.

The field of their labor was limited practically to the province of Galilee for the present campaign. Their power for healing was unlimited, because vanity could be corrected in the worker later,[4] as was actually done when Jesus told them "not to rejoice because the evil spirits were subject to them but rather in the fact that their names were written in the book of life." But their field of labor was wisely limited, because the time was not yet ripe for the institution of the world-wide campaign, mainly because the workers were not yet sufficiently trained and instructed in the universalism of the gospel. They were not to go "in the way leading to the Gentiles." There were various Greek and other Gentile cities in Galilee largely composed of foreign populations. While Jesus ministered to the Gentiles who came to His ministry, there is no record of His having entered into any one of these

1 Exousian, power rather than authority (Moffat, Robertson) but Luke had both.
2 Luke 9:1.   3 Edidon. Mark 6:7.   4 The Training of the Twelve, Bruce.

cities. This prohibition against spreading out to the Gentiles and the hybrid Samaritans was for practical ends in the present tour. Later on, Jesus would send them out on the campaign of world-wide evangelization (Matt. 28:19, 20). Concentration on the harried and scattered "lost sheep of Israel" was to be the first step in world-wide expansion of the kingdom.

As they went on to their mission, they were to preach that the kingdom had already drawn near and was permanently present.[1] They were itinerant preachers, who were to go on heralding the kingdom at the gates of all the walled towns and in the presence of the smaller groups of the villages.[2] These apostles would be able to tell a good deal about the king of the kingdom (Bruce). Their message was to be backed by their work of healing the sick, raising the dead, cleansing the lepers, and casting out demons (Moffat). Before this time the apostles had not been given such power nor did they exercise it widely later on. It was out of the ordinary that their exercise of such power now was unlimited. Never had it been seen in Jewish history that a prophet should give such power to his disciples, not even Moses.[3] This would naturally lead the people to think of Jesus as the possible Messiah and such was the purpose of these missionaries. Their message was wisely restricted to heralding the kingdom and calling the people to preparation for the Messiah through repentance. Their gospel was not a full gospel including the complete revelation of the nature of the kingdom and the doctrines of the cross. They were to make it plain that the kingdom they heralded was a heavenly kingdom and not a temporal kingdom. This would be necessary not more because it was true than to avoid any political excitement.[4] In their administration of their message and their works of beneficence alike they were to be unstinted. "You have received without cost, give without pay."[5]

The minute instructions given by Jesus to the apostles as to their equipment, support, and simplicity of life are divided into two parts: first those relating more to the immediate work, given by all the synoptic gospels; and second, those relating more to the distant future, given by Matthew alone (Matt. 10:16-42). Matthew, following the topical method in his gospel, brings together, as if given in one discourse, various instructions delivered probably on several different occasions or at least repeated in part at various times. All of the instructions were applicable in part to the present and more largely to the future. The horizon of the Kingdom work was to gradually enlarge and the instructions were of

1 Present tense.   2 Present imperative of progressive action.
3 Andrew's Life of Our Lord.   4 The Training of the Twelve Bruce.
5 Moffat and Twentieth Century Translation for rendering of dorean.

the nature of prophecy[1]—preaching for the present and prediction for the future.

Their equipment and entertainment or support, as well as their reception, were duly cared for by the Master. "Do not acquire or procure for yourselves[2] gold nor silver nor coppers for your girdles (Moffat), nor a wallet, nor a traveling bag for the journey-road, neither two undergarments (Robertson) or change of clothing, nor extra travelling sandals,[3] nor a staff; for the workman is worthy of his food." Their errand was urgent and they must not stay to equip themselves completely or go encumbered with baggage. If they already had sandals they were to use them but not take an extra pair along as was the custom ordinarily. If one had a staff useful for the rocky roads he could take it.[4] "Make no preparations for the journey but go just as you are,"[5] was the tenor of Jesus' instructions. They were not to be troubled about food or raiment but to trust completely in God for these. Jesus here laid down the permanent principle for His workers for all time. The laborer must not be anxious about his material support. God takes the responsibility of providing for His worthy workmen.

Jesus adds immediately an explanation of how God provides the material support for His kingdom workers. It was to be through the instrumentality of His people in every place where His apostles should go. He gives further instruction that these apostles *seek out*[6] these people in every city, wherever they might go. They were not to be changing lodging places daily for the sake of self-indulgence, thus displeasing their hosts, nor to consume their time in being elaborately entertained socially. Their coming unto any house should mean a blessing to that household. It was their responsibility to make this true by their conduct and expressions of peace.[7] They were the bearers of a priceless message and solid comfort and their gracious bearing as guests must convey untold blessings to the home that should receive them. If the home proved worthy, their visit should have this result; but if the home were unworthy, their peace would return upon their own heads in the feeling of satisfaction at having done their duty. Furthermore, the house or city that should be inhospitable toward them, refusing to entertain them or hear their message, would thus incur the divine displeasure and suffer a punishment more severe than that of Sodom and Gomorrah in the day of judgment. In solemn protest against such inhospitality the apostles were to

1 Edersheim in loco. 2 Indirect middle aorist subjunctive
3 Lightfoot and Wetstein. 4 Mark 6:9. 5 Clark on Mark 6:8
6 Third general condition followed by aorist imperative, a general rule of procedure.
7 According to the custom of oriental hospitality. Hastings D. B. Salutations.

shake off the dust from their feet[1] as a testimony against them.[2] According to the Jewish belief Sodom and Gomorrah were to have no part in the world to come.[3] This last and other expressions of these instructions reveal the background of Jewish thought in this discourse of Jesus.[4]

In the second part of His instructions Jesus warns the apostles of persecutions they would encounter and gives directions as to how they should meet them (Matt. 10:16-23). Some of these warnings point forward undoubtedly to the religious bigotry and bitter persecutions suffered at the hands of heathen governors and kings by His workers after the Ascension. But already the opposition to Jesus was becoming more intense in all parts of Palestine and even in this campaign in Galilee it was to be met by these workers. Jesus was sending them forth as weak and defenseless sheep into the midst of the perils of wolves which He knew to exist and which awaited them (v. 16). In the midst of these dangers they would need to become[5] prudent and keen in the recognition of danger and shrewd in the choice of means of escaping from it, even as the serpent is quick and easy to slip away and escape with his life. At the same time they were not to be deceptive as the serpent (Gen. 3:1) but harmless and innocent as doves (Hos. 7:11). Their guilelessness was to be evident to all. They must resort to no trickery or improper means of escaping from danger but with simplicity and courage meet their persecutions fearlessly, and openly confess their Lord at every hazard.[6] They were to be serpents in cautiousness and doves in simplicity, guilelessness, and purity of aim and heart.[7]

They are warned definitely against those devouring types of men which Jesus called "wolves."[8] Such men would hand them over to the Sanhedrins or local courts of justice which were in every Jewish town; and scourge them in their synagogues as if performing a duty of religious discipline.[9] They would also be haled before all kinds of heathen governors or rulers and before Gentile kings, the civil authorities of the land who held exclusively the right to punish with death. This did not happen in the Galilean campaign and so must refer to post-Ascension persecutions.

Such a drastic warning would be calculated to fill the apostles

1 A heathen land was unclean for the Jew who always wiped off dust from his feet on passing into the Holy Land.
2 Dative of disadvantage, Mark 6:11.   3 Sahn 10:3   4 Edersheim in loco.
5 Ginesthe, Acquire these virtues. They were yet inexperienced.
6 David Smith, In the Days of His Flesh.
7 For this proverbial maxim see Wetstein. Matt. 10:10.
8 Definite article points back to lukon.
9 These Jewish scourgings were common in the synagogues. Broadus Matt. 10:17f.

with fear and anxious forebodings. Jesus would have them become completely disillusioned as to the character of the wicked world and to count the cost of discipleship, nor underestimate the difficulty of the task to which He was sending them. But He hastens next to arm them against fear and anxiety.

"Do not become anxious[1] in the face of the terrible ordeal of self-defense before Jewish authorities and heathen kings on my account," said He. "You shall appear there for a constructive witness to *them and to the Gentiles*."[2] Speeches of self-defense and testimony to the Christ would be put into their mouths by the Spirit of God, in the hour when they were *brought up for trial* (Moffat). They must not become anxious as to what they would say on such occasions. Such a guarantee from their Master was reassuring in the extreme. He could add, after that, the further revelation that not only the rulers would be disposed to persecute them, but men in general when filled with religious bigotry and fanatical hatred would resort to the most absurd extremes of persecution. Even in the intimate circle of the family the unbelieving brother would deliver up the disciple-brother to death through the civil rulers, and the father the child; and children would rise up against their parents and put them to death because of discipleship. On account of the name and character of Jesus and their identification with Him they would be hated by *all men*, so sweeping and universal would be the opposition of the forces of darkness in the world. This campaign of hatred and opposition would go on through the ages.[3] But the one who would endure with prudence and simplicity the severity of this ordeal would be delivered out of the perils safely, and suffering with patience every trial, much more would be saved in the attainment of eternal life. Further instruction is detailed as to how they should act when persecuted. They were not, through foolhardiness and pride, to stand their ground in any city when persecuted for fear of being thought cowardly. They were positively commanded to flee into another city and the reason assigned for such conduct was their earnest purpose to reach all the towns of Galilee and prepare the people for the coming of Jesus who was following up their work in this campaign (Moffat). But this counsel (Matt. 10:23) cannot be limited simply to the campaign in Galilee. Jesus evidently refers to the greater coming of the Messianic Kingdom[4] at the destruction of Jerusalem, when the Jewish institutions were over-thrown. It doubtless extends also to the work of His followers of all ages until His second coming. Some recent writers think that this

1 Ingressive aorist subjunctive of prohibition. Robertson, Word Pictures.
2 Broadus on Matt. 10:18.
3 Esesthe misoumenoi, periphrastic future perfect of linear action.
4 See 'Son of Man' (Matt. 16:28), Broadus Com. on Matt.

verse clearly reflects a situation which did not come into existence till the missionary journeys of Paul.[1] But we know that
the early disciples associated the destruction of Jerusalem with
the second coming.

Jesus adds further encouragement for the persecuted by citing His own example. He had already been accused of being in
opprobrious partnership with Beelzebub, the "lord of idolatrous
sacrifices" (Matt. 9:24).[2] The disciples should not expect a better
lot for themselves than that of their Teacher nor the slave than
that of his lord. Defamation had already reached their Teacher
and Lord and martyrdom was yet to follow. They must expect
similar treatment at the hands of their enemies. They are commanded positively not to fear them[3] nor their misrepresentations,
for in due time the Lord would reveal both His and their own
true character, teachings, and work. They were to keep nothing
of His private teachings back through fear but boldly proclaim
them in the most public manner—on the flat-topped roofs—setting aside all regard for personal safety in the fulfillment of their
duty of preaching the gospel. The rather they should have a
reverent fear of God, who had the power to punish eternally the
immortal spirit and destroy the body also in Gehenna. Fear should
not be the main motive in religion but it is a motive still and
should not be disregarded. A wholesome and reverent fear of
God casts out the fear of man. It is the fear of offending God that
frees from the fear of the persecutor.

The apostles should not only dread God's displeasure but
trust in His all-comprehending providence extended to His meanest creatures, even to little sparrows, two of which could be bought
for a farthing, the value of an English penny. For twopence five
could be bought and yet not one of them falls to the ground without the permission of the heavenly Father. Every minutest detail of the individual life of the disciple is ordered by the same
providence, even to the falling of one hair from his head. They
were of more value than many sparrows or "of more value than
sparrows" (Moffat).

In view of this minute providence, extreme loyalty is enjoined.
There is no excuse for shrinking from duty through fear. The
reward for confessing and punishment for not making confession
of Him before the world of men are set forth as a double motive
for loyalty. His followers are to speak out and act as His disciples should under all circumstances and at every risk. The reward of identification with Christ and His kind of life[4] is the

1 Streeter p. 255 M. I.; The Synoptic Gospels, Montifiore.
2 See Bruce in loco.   3 Imperative middle, not subjunctive.
4 Locative case of sphere within which the confession takes place.

gracious act of mutual confession on the part of Jesus in the presence of His Father; but the punishment for saying "no" to Christ will be His positive denial before the Father in the Judgment.

Jesus states that the fundamental cause of persecution is found in the very nature of His principles, which when proclaimed cause divisions and conflicts among men, even in the bosom of families.[1] His kingdom of light was uncompromising in its antagonism to the power of Satanic darkness. His coming was not to bring peace. Let them not for once imagine such to be the case. But He came like the sudden[2] hurling of the terrible short sword,[3] used so much in hand to hand mortal combat in war. Family ties and social ties were rent in twain.[4] Jesus was calling them to a work which would over-ride all mere sentimentalism. Decision for Christ would bring separation from those nearest and dearest, many times. In such a case supreme love and loyalty must be given to Christ. When apparent duty to those of one's own household is found in conflict with duty to Christ, supreme allegiance must be given to Him. The one who keeps on loving father or mother or son or daughter better than Christ is not worthy of Him. He must be before the family, in the affections and loyal obedience of the disciple. Jesus went further and said, "they must be ready to endure bitter suffering, typified in the cross, and uttermost ignominy." The sight of the wretched criminal taking up and bearing his cross out of the city to the place of his dreaded crucifixion must have been familiar to the apostles. Jesus may have had in mind His own approaching crucifixion, now only a year away, when He spoke these words. If the apostles would be worthy of Christ they must be willing to follow after Him in the way of the cross. Jesus lays down as a supreme law of discipleship the paradox which He seven times used: "He who is finding at any time his natural material life, placing it uppermost, shall lose both it and also with it his spiritual or eternal life; but the one who loses at any time his natural life for Christ's sake, shall find and save both it and his eternal life."[5]

The Master concluded His instructions to the apostles by putting a premium on kindness shown to any one of them. Those who did not persecute but receive and aid them would be rewarded richly. One who receives a prophet "because he is a prophet" (Moffat) and from no ulterior motive, so identifies himself with the prophet and the cause he represents as to merit a reward in the coming age equal to his prophet-guest (McNeile). In like

1 Broadus, Com. on Matt. 10:34f.
2 Aorist infinitive signifying a sudden hurling of the sword.
3 Machaira was the short sword of Greek warfare.   4 Dichosai—divide in two.
5 Conditional sentence of the third class, paraphrase.

manner he who receives any righteous worker-layman or minister as such and from sincere motives, shall receive a righteous man's reward. Jesus pursues the same thought yet further to embrace His providential care of the humblest disciple or learner among His followers. "Whoever should give even a cup of cold water to one of these little ones, who was thirsty or in need, because he was a disciple, truly would not lose his reward."

Mark and Luke give a brief summary account of the work done in this campaign in Galilee. Luke says (9:6): "Coming out, they were making a thorough business of going into each village separately[1] and continuing their work[2] of evangelizing and healing everywhere."[3] Mark says (6:12, 13): "Coming out they preached[4] in order that men might repent; and they were casting out many demons and annointing[5] many sick people with oil and healing[5] them." The use of oil was partly medicinal as with the ancients, and might have been partly symbolic or to induce faith in the sick. The campaign lasted probably some weeks, judging from the work done in all the cities and villages. It embraced, it would seem, most of March and some of April preceding the feast in Jerusalem. These apostles responded to the appeal of Jesus with the best that was in them, like Francis of Assisi when he heard this commission read in the chapel of Portinucula. Thrilled, he "laid aside his staff, wallet, purse, and shoes and devoted himself from that hour to his high mission."[6]

Having made an end of detailed instructions to each of the disciples in particular[7] Jesus resumed His own labors (Matt. 11:1). He departed from the place where He had given them instructions and went into their cities to preach. He probably followed after them in many cities, and after the campaign was over the apostles came back to meet Him in Capernaum (Mark 6:30) to tell Him about their work and experiences.

3. The guilty fears of Herod Antipas (who beheaded John) on hearing of the campaign of Jesus. (Mark 6:14-29; Matt. 14:1-12; Luke 9:7-9).

The fame of the name of Jesus now spread over Galilee as never before and penetrated even into the golden Palace of Herod Antipas in Tiberias. To that wicked, crafty, and voluptuous son of Herod the Great, who was himself the greatest monster of cruelty and of crime, had fallen the tetrarchy of Galilee and Perea at the death of his father thirty-two years before. He had been married soon afterwards to the daughter of Aretas, Emir of Arabia; but

---

1 Kata distributive.   2 Imperfect middle of continuous action.
3 Present participle. linear.   4 Constative aorist of summary description.
5 Imperfect indicative tenses of continuous and repeated action
6 Quoted from David Smith, In the Days of His Flesh.   7 Dia—distributive.

while a guest in the home of his half-brother Herod Philip in Rome he became entangled in the snares of Herodias, the kinsman's wife, who not content with mere wealth was ambitious to wear a crown. The upshot of this criminal infatuation was that the daughter of Aretas gained permission to make a visit in Machaerus and fled to her father; while Antipas was united in incestuous and adulterous marriage with Herodias, daughter of Aristobulus and his own niece.

This criminal union proved to be the beginning of the undoing leading to the final ruin of Antipas, in the loss of his tetrarchy and lastly in his tragic death in exile.

It would seem strange that he should not have heard of Jesus before this time. A palace is late in hearing spiritual news (Bengel). The fact that he had not heard or at least given serious attention to the work of Jesus until now may be explained by his absence for a time in Rome, by his hostilities with Aretas, his father-in-law, king of Arabia, in which he suffered defeat, by his preoccupation with his numerous building activities, and as Josephus intimates by his personal love of ease and pleasure leading to a life of voluptuousness and unconcern for religious matters among the Jews or little else of public affairs.

Luke says that three reports reached Herod about Jesus. Some were saying[1] that John had risen from the dead; by others it was said "that Elias had appeared;" by yet others that some one of the ancient prophets had risen again. Herod was in a continual state of perplexity[2] as these reports kept coming to his ears. His conscience was deeply stirred as his memory brought back the gruesome picture of the head of John the Baptist on the trencher borne in before him in an ill-fated hour of drunken revelry and feast-making at Machaerus. He confessed to the guilt of his responsibility in John's death: "John I beheaded." But in half-superstitious dread he asked: "Who is this of whom I hear such things?" To his intimates[3] in the official circle, he went further in his confession: "This is John the Baptist," "John, whom I beheaded, the same rose," he repeated.[4] "He has risen from the dead once for all."[5] John did not work miracles in his life-time such as Jesus and His apostles were now performing everywhere. But according to Herod's philosophy and theology the personality of John had been enhanced by his resurrection, enabling him to do mighty works now which he had been unable to do before his death. At first Herod had questioned the report that John had risen from the dead, but later he adopted that report rather than one of the other two. Perhaps a stricken conscience and guilty

1 Imperfect of repeated and continuous action. 2 Imperfect indicative of aporeo.
3 Pais—those in immediate attendance on him. 4 Imperfect indicative, elegon.
5 Perfect indicative active with the force of permanence and a continuing state.

fear had much to do with the confirmation of this conclusion. The people had been greatly indignant when he beheaded John. Perhaps they would be reconciled now, if their prophet were restored. Herod was stirred by curiosity and kept on[1] seeking an opportunity to see Jesus. He seems not to have desired to interrupt His work or do harm to His person. He would likely be prevented by superstitious fear from any attempt on the life of Him whom he supposed to be John risen from the dead. Later on in the trial of Jesus he had a curiosity to see Him perform some miracle. "On account of his resurrection," thought Herod, "the powers are working in him energizing and reenforcing his natural faculties or gifts" (Mark 6:14). It is interesting to note that the popular reports of the campaign of Jesus placed Him and His work high above the living and among the greatest prophets of the past. He was greater than all of them because He manifested in Himself the greatness of all combined.

The belated account of the death of John is next introduced as a suitable parenthesis[2] in the narratives of Mark (6:17-29) and Matthew (14:3-12). It is likely that the beheading took place during, perhaps near the close of the Galilean campaign. Swete thinks that the tidings of the murder of John seem to have brought the circuit to an end. But the aorist tense of Matthew would indicate that it took place at least a short while before. The disciples of John went and told Jesus and when He heard it He withdrew from thence in a boat (Matt. 14:12f). The beheading took place probably at Machaerus[3] where Herod had imprisoned John in the fortress at the extremity of Perea on the borders of Arabia,[4] on account of John's denunciation of his adulterous marriage to Herodias. He had sent and arrested John, probably at Enon in the midst of his evangelistic activities, and brought him in chains secretly down the east side of the Jordan to his highly fortified summer palace, built at Machaerus on impregnable heights east of and overlooking the Dead Sea. This had probably occurred a year before John's death. John was detained in prison with fair promises of liberation likely, for Herod had frequent interviews with him and for a long time was greatly influenced apparently by John. But the prisoner was kept close in a dungeon "on account of Herodias." John was a fearless prophet and denounced sin in the high and low alike. Some think that Herod invited John to his palace through craftiness and then detained him in prison. This was in perfect accord with the "foxy" charcter of Antipas

1 Imperfect indicative active, continued action, Exata.
2 For this same Herod, gar.
3 According to Josephus John was executed at Machaerus not at Julias or Tiberias as some think. Tristam also agrees with this conclusion.
4 Andrew, The Life of Our Lord.

but if he did, it amounted to an arrest just the same and the motive power behind it all was John's denunciation of the incestuous marriage. It seems that John was summoned previously by Herod for private interviews to see if his attitude might be altered, but various times the austere prophet repeated: "It is not lawful for you to have her" (Lev. 18:16). Such a courageous denunciation of adulterous divorces is sadly needed in our own times. Mark graphically adds that "Herodias set herself against him."[1] She literally "had it in for him" according to the Greek idiom.[2] She was desiring[3] to kill him but (kai adversative) she could not for the time. The power was wanting and not the will (Swete) and she kept her eye on him, abiding her time.

The only reason she could not carry out her malicious design was that Herod was afraid of John.[4] He was alarmed lest the Mosaic curse should come upon him. He knew that John was a just and holy man and innocent of any wrong. He "kept him safe"[5] from the plots and schemes of Herodias. He heard him gladly and was doing many things counseled by John.

But the opportune day[6] for the plotting Jezebel finally came, on the anniversary of Herod's reign or more probably his birthday,[7] when he made a great Belshazzar-feast for his lords, captains of thousands or military authority, and chief men of Galilee of the high social and financial class, in the palace of Machaerus. The daughter of Herodias, Salome herself,[8] was prostituted by her mother to the low level of a scenic dancer and when the guests had finished gormandizing and were flushed with wine, this seventeen-year-old damsel came in with all her enticing beauty and "executed a *pas seul* in the midst of those dissolute and half-intoxicated revelers."[9] The dance was mimetic and licentious (Gould) and pleased Herod and the maudlin group of guests lounging on the divans.[10] She leaped into the middle (Wycliff) and gave a shameful exhibition of lewd dancing as pre-arranged by Herodias.

Antipas, half-drunk, was caught in the snare of the wily Herodias. What she had failed to get by entreaty she secured by craftiness. Herod promised with an oath to give the damsel whatever she might ask for herself, to the half of his kingdom.[12] The girl did what her mother expected, ran to know what she should ask. "The head of John the Baptizer," was the reply. Doubtless the young girl drew back from such a hideous request, for we are told by Matthew that the mother, pushing her forward, in-

---

1 Dative of disadvantage.   2 Eneichen auto.
3 A continued purpose and activity expressed by the imperfect tense.
4 Efobeito, a continuous superstitious fear.   5 Imperfect tense again.
6 Hameras eukairou.   7 For discussion of birthday see Broadus on Matthew 4:6
8 It was not customary for a person of royal family to dance thus as a heteira.
9 Farrar's Life of Christ, Salome.   10 Sunanakeimenois.
11 Aorist subjunctive middle.   12 Same oath made to Esther by Ahasuerus.

stantly prompted her with the words: "Give me here on a trencher immediately the head of John the Baptizer." She came in with haste and made the bloody request with a horrifying levity and indecent haste.

The drunken tetrarch saw that he had been tricked and was grieved. He must have shrunk with disgust from so horrible a murder. He might well have repudiated so foolish an oath which would have been honored in the breaking. But his pride and his fear of the criticism of his drunken guests prevailed over any prompting of conscience or sense of justice, and sending the executioner immediately to the dungeon, he had John beheaded.[1] The gory head of the prophet was brought on one of the golden trenchers which had graced the festive board, and presented to the damsel who gave it to her mother. At last Herodias had triumphed, and now in fiendish delight receives the head of the prophet, whose words had made many hearts quail because of their sins. This woman, a veritable demon, left a name that rivals that of Jezebel in the history of degraded womanhood, and this last picture stands out as one of the most gruesome ones in the annals of crime. Tradition says that Herodias ordered the headless trunk to be flung over the battlements of the castle-dungeon to be devoured by dogs and vultures in the ravines below. But the disciples of John among them perhaps Manaen, the foster-brother of Antipas, who had become a Christian, took up the corpse and after giving it a decent burial came and brought the sad and ominous report to Jesus.

John had sent a committee of these same disciples to Jesus months before to ask if He were really the Messiah. The practical answer Jesus had sent back to him was conclusive. John had penetrated to the conception of vicarious suffering. What did it matter, whether it were by life or by death, just so he should fulfill his mission of forerunner. He was ready for the last ordeal and received the martyr's crown, sealing his life of faithful and courageous testimony with a martyr death. What could be more fitting as the closing chapter of the life of the greatest of the prophets!

The swift hand of retribution soon fell on Antipas and his adulterous paramour Herodias. Even now the furies of conscience pursued him relentlessly and he was sure that Jesus must be John returned from the dead. It was not long before the wicked ambition of Herodias led him to Rome to seek the title of king, given to Agrippa, the brother of Herodias. But in this quest he not only failed to obtain the title he sought but lost his dominions and

---

1 Causitive active tense of apokephalizo.

was banished to Lugdumin in Gaul not far from the Spanish frontier, where he and the wicked Herodias later died in obscurity and dishonor.[1] Salome was married to her uncle Philip, tetrarch of Trachonitis and Batanea, but after a brief time was left a widow and disappeared from history. Tradition says that she met with an early and hideous death.

After Jesus received the news of the death of John and His disciples had returned to Him in Capernaum, He embarked with them in a boat and passed over the sea to the other side for rest, meditation on the death of the prophet, and to hear the reports of the disciples.

1 Edersheim's Life and Times of Jesus and Farrar's Life of Christ.

PART IV

FOUR WITHDRAWALS FROM GALILEE AND SPECIAL TRAINING OF THE TWELVE

(Harm. §§ 72-95)

This period covered six months, from spring to autumn A. D. 29. It was now just a year before the Crucifixion. The main purpose of Jesus during the next six months was to give His apostles special instruction and training. Four separate withdrawals away from Herod's domains and to the mountain retreats are recorded (§§ 72, 78, 79, 81). The causes for the withdrawals were: the hostility of the Jewish leaders, rest and recreation for the tired workers in the mountains away from the tropical heat of the lowlands, to have reports from their work, to give special instruction and training' to the Twelve, to escape the fanatical popularity which would make Him a temporal king, and the possible jealousy and trickery of Herod Antipas. In the withdrawals Jesus and the apostle-band went across the Sea to proximities of Bethsaida-Julias, to the borders of Tyre and Sidon, to the neighborhood of Decapolis south-east of the Sea, and to the region of Cesarea-Philippi. The greater part of the circuit lay within the domains of the tetrarchy of Philip, the least harmful of the Herods.

CHAPTER XVII

THE GALILEAN CRISIS

(Harm. §§ 72-77)

The Galilean crisis embraces the first retirement and its related events, the feeding of the five thousand (Jno. 6:1-25), the walking on the stormy sea (Jno. 6:16-21), the Sermon on the Bread of Life in Capernaum (Jno. 6:22-59) and the crisis results of this discourse (Jno. 6:60-71).

1. The feeding of the five thousand and its results (Mark 6:30-46; Matt. 14:13-23; Luke 9:10-17; Jno. 6:1-15).

The disciples of Jesus on returning[1] to Him at Capernaum gave[2] glowing reports of their campaign experiences (Luke 9:10). Jesus listened to it all greatly concerned (Luke 9:10). He was shocked by the news of the tragedy of John's death. The people were stirred deeply and would like for someone to arise to avenge the death of their prophet. Who could lead a popular movement now better than Jesus? Perhaps this hope was coursing their inmost thoughts. Herod was seeking to see Jesus. He had spirited John away suddenly, while in the midst of his greatest activities. Anyway, the Master and His disciples were tired and needed rest. But already the multitudes were gathering again with their sick to be healed in Capernaum. They had no leisure so much as to eat now. The only way to get a little rest and a chance to quietly talk over the campaign, pointing out the practical lessons of those experiences to the workers, was to get away from the crowds.

"Come ye yourselves apart unto a desert place and rest a little while"[3] He said. The disciples were glad of the invitation and so He took them with Him in a boat and withdrew across the Sea of Galilee—sometimes called the Sea of Tiberias because of the city of that name, capital of the tetrarchy—to the neighborhood of Bethsaida (Julias).[4] There was a fertile but sparsely populated plain to the south of this town which narrowed down at its southern end where there were grassy slopes. This is the desert[5] place where Thompson located the traditional site of the miracle of feeding the five thousand.

When they departed in the boat the crowd saw them and recognized them. They would not allow Jesus to escape unperceived and a multitude followed them on foot by the land route to the north of the lake. This route crossed a ford some two miles above where the river enters the lake. Some of the people actually outwent the little boat which bore Jesus with the disciples, so

---

1 Mark 6:30, historic present, vivid. 2 Constantive aorist, giving a summary.
3 Oligon. 4 Bethsaida of Luke 9:10 was evidently Bethsaida Julias so-called by
Philip the Tetrarch in honor of Empress Julia. 5 Sparsely populated.

261

anxious were they to see His miracle-signs which He was doing[1]
on those who were sick and without strength (asthenounton).
There were others who heard of His departure, and the crowds
from various cities and towns came, some by boat from as far as
Tiberias and others on foot, until there was a vast multitude of
over five thousand men, women and children. Among them were
also many pilgrims on their way to Jerusalem for the feast. Some
also brought their sick to be healed.

Before the large crowd had arrived, Jesus had withdrawn to
the mountain retreat near the southern extremity of the little
plain for a brief period of quiet and meditation. But this period
was soon cut short, and when He came forth from the mountain
retreat, lifting up His eyes and seeing a great multitude coming
unto Him[2] He was deeply moved with compassion for them, because they were as sheep not having a shepherd. They had plenty
of so-called religious leaders, none of whom really fed the people
spiritually, and now John was gone and the responsibility fell all
the heavier on Him and His apostles to supply this need.

Jesus gave the people a warm welcome,[3] began to teach them
and kept it up.[4] He also kept on healing their sick and all those
who needed healing. Some were disappointed, perhaps, that He
did not stir them with a vibrant discourse on the death of John
the Baptist, but He spoke to them on the great central theme of
the kingdom of God and taught them many things.

John throws in a parenthetical note just here, that the Passover feast of the Jews was at hand. Jesus did not go up to this
feast because of the rabid antagonism to His ministry in Judea.
The reference to this feast points the way to the true interpretation of the miracle of feeding the five thousand and to its purpose
as conceived in the mind of Jesus. The people were following
Him to see the signs and were increasingly seeking to see in Him
the promised Messiah. How could He better meet this wave of
enthusiasm for a material, temporal Messiah than to perform a
miracle which would exhibit His power to meet their material
needs and then by sharp contrast call their attention to the spiritual
and sacrificial character of the true kingdom?[5]

Jesus had led up to this idea when He first saw the great
multitude and before there was any suggestion from the apostles
as to sending the multitudes away. He spoke first to the matter-
of-fact, cold, calculating Philip. His object was to attack the
problem of cold materialism in the most bookkeeper-like of the
apostles. "Whence shall we buy bread[6] that[7] these may eat?"
said Jesus with a gesture of the hand toward the gathering mul-

1 Imperfect indicative of customary action.   2 Vivid historic present middle indicative.
3 Apodexamenos antous (Luke 9:11).   4 Imperfect indicative.
5 Bruce, The Training of the Twelve, Cf. Luthardt on Jno. 6:4.
6 Deliberative subjunctive Jno. 6:5   7 Purpose of clause with hina and the aorist
   subjunctive of esthio.

titude. It was yet early in the day. The individualistic method was adapted to the training of each of these apostles personally and that was the main purpose of Jesus during these months. He was putting Philip to the test now. He was not mistaken in His estimate of the character of Philip, for that disciple after rapid mental calculation replied: "Two hundred penny-worth[1] of bread[2] is not sufficient for them, in order that each may take a little morsel." Philip was lacking in faith, and with his eyes fixed on the visible and tangible, lost sight of the invisible things of faith — like so many.[3] Jesus left them to reflect on this matter and went on with the work of preaching, teaching, and healing.[4]

At length the day began to wear away and the apostles became anxious about the situation. The proper hour for lunch had passed and the sun was inclining toward the west. They called attention to the fact that this place was sparsely settled but that there were country places and villages where the people might get victuals[5] and arrange lodging for themselves. To this proposal Jesus replied: "They have no need to go away; give ye them to eat."

They say to Him in protest: "Shall we go and buy two hundred penny-worth of bread and feed them?" To this He answers: "How many loaves have you? Go and see." The Master well knew they had no such enormous quantity of bread with them. He was trying out their ingenuity and preparing the way for a larger faith in His ability to meet every need of the multitudes.

Then Andrew,[6] known principally as Simon Peter's brother, but withal a man of practical turn and quick decision, came forward with a suggestion which proved fruitful. Perhaps Andrew, though half-skeptical, had some glint of faith when he spoke of the little lad who brought in his lunch basket five little barley cakes like crackers and two little sardine-like fish. Jesus accepted the suggestion and acted on it at once. He knew all the time "what he was about to do" even before He had spoken to Philip earlier and now to Andrew and the others. The other apostles had added disparagingly: "We have no more than five loaves and two fishes; unless (Robertson) we should go and buy food for all this people."[7] Luke adds significantly, "For they were about five thousand."

"Make them sit down in companies of about fifty," said Jesus, and then reenforced their efforts by commanding the multitudes to sit down[8] in orderly manner on the green grass.[9] This order was

---

1 The value of about seven pounds or approximately thirty-five dollars.
2 Artoi. loaves.   3 These Twelve, Charles Brown.   4 Imperfects of Luke 9:11.
5 Ingressive aorist active.   6 Charles Brown, These Twelve, Andrew, The Man of decision.
7 A condition of the third class with aorist subjunctive implying nothing as to the reality.
     They had no intention of carrying out such a plan short of a direct order from Jesus.
8 Anapesein "to fall up" literally. We say fall down. The place was likely on a slight incline.
9 A Markan, vivid descriptive touch.

soon executed and the people were arranged[1] in ranks by hundreds and by fifties. John adds that there was much grass there (Jno. 6:10). Thus arranged, the multitude, dressed in Oriental costumes of various colors, looked like garden-beds in bright colored flowers against the green background of abundant grass. Already it was evening[2] and the sun was descending toward the western horizon.

We may well imagine the beauty of the scene as Jesus stood on the grassy slope in plain view of all in the well arranged crowd. Blue Galilee lay below them. The mountains about were bathed in the light of the descending sun. All nature joined in pouring its beauty down upon this wonderful scene, as the Prophet Miracle-Worker was about to perform one of the most wonderful of all His miracles before the eyes of the expectant multitude.

When all were hushed into a reverent silence, He solemnly took the five little barley loaves and the two little fishes of the lad's lunch, and according to the Jewish custom of giving thanks at meal-time, He looked up to heaven, gave thanks, blessed the loaves, and gave them to the disciples, both the loaves and fishes, to distribute to the multitude. There is more prominence given to the loaves in the narrative because the miracle set forth in symbolic form what Jesus was to be for the multitudes of the earth — the bread of life. Thus the miracle was the preparation for the sermon to follow in Capernaum on the morrow.

The people all[3] ate and were filled[4] full. They had all they wished[5] and were completely satiated. Five thousand men besides the women and children had an abundant meal of substantial but not luxurious food that day.

After all were served and had eaten, Jesus commanded His apostles to gather up[6] the broken pieces[7] — not the scraps, but the pieces which had not been served — and there were twelve wicker baskets full left over. He would teach them a lesson in economy in God's work.[8] There had been no lack that day and each one of the apostles had left to him his coffin-shaped traveler's-basket[9] full, enough to last him for some time and serve as a reminder of the great miracle-wonder their eyes had beheld that day. So the record of this miracle is one of the best attested of all, being narrated in harmonious details by all four of the evangelists. Three eye-witnesses report: Matthew in his Logia, Peter through Mark, and John, the Beloved Disciple (Gould).[10]

---

1 They were half-way reclined. Mark 6:30.   2 The first evening lasted until 3 p. m.
3 Pantes, all without exception, men, women, and children.   4 Effective aorist of Chortadzo, to fill completely.   5 Imperfect indicative, ethelon, as much as they were wishing.
6 Second aorist active imperative, a command about which Jesus was careful.   7 Klasniata, broken pieces.   8 Hina with the second aorist middle subjunctive in a purpose clause.   9 Kofinos, (wicliff, coffin), a stout wicker basket different from the sphurides used in a later miracle of the feeding of the four thousand. That was larger, a kind of hamper used for provisions.   10 Robertson, Word Pictures.

The result of so stupendous a miracle was immediate. The men seeing the great sign which He did began to whisper:[1] "This is certainly the looked-for prophet who is come into the world,[2] the prophet like Moses." Were not some already saying that Jesus was Elias or one of the prophets, or John the Baptist risen from the dead?"

Jesus was quick to perceive the mind of the crowd. He knew they were looking for a national king-messiah and that their hearts had been stirred to the white heat of revolt by the recent death of their loved prophet John. He knew[3] that they were about to come and seize Him and make Him their national king. This would bring on wide-spread rebellion against the Roman government, resulting in disaster to all His work and in death and destruction to the Jews as well. He hastened to prevent the revolutionary purpose of the multitude. Recognizing that His disciples sympathized with this ideal of the people, He "compelled"[4] them to enter into a boat and go before Him to the other side of the sea to Bethsaida,[5] while He Himself should send the multitude away.[6] Mark gives a graphic touch with the historic present tense (apoluei) of Jesus in the process of persuading the multitudes to go away. He had already gotten the disciples out of the political atmosphere of revolutionary excitement. It was easier now to dispatch the crowd than it would have been with them present. It was a sad fact that the apostles had not yet come to a clearer conception of the true character of the Messiah and His kingdom. Finally as the dusk fell — we are to believe — He succeeded in persuading the crowd to go away and suddenly He, Himself, slipped off from the lingering ones — lonely in His soul because no man understood — and repaired alone to a solitary spot in the mountain to pray. There He would find strength in communion with the Father to stem the tide of temptation, and quench the flame of revolutionary popularity which had flared up, when He should be again in the midst of the people tomorrow. The crisis had come at last and the rest of His road must be thorny indeed, as He should suffer the necessary alienation of the popular crowds and hear those erstwhile acclaimers of His praises turn in disappointment and bitterness against Him.

Night fell upon the scene of the solitary figure on the mountain height alone in prayer. It was a stormy night on the sea below Him, on which somewhere His beloved disciples were struggling at the oars and sails with raging waves. The tempest of the elements without was not fiercer than that which raged within

1 Inchoative imperfect, elegon.   2 The Messianic hope was strong in Israel then.
3 Second aorist active participle of ginosko.   4 Compelled, enagkasen.   5 This was the Western Bethsaida, probably a port of Capernaum.   6 Heor hou with the aorist subjunctive expressing purpose.

His soul, as He thought of the death of John and His own approaching day of final bitter struggle issuing in His death on Calvary.

2. The miracle of rescue in the storm at sea (Mark 6:47-56; Matt. 14:24-36; Jno. 6:16-21).

The sixth chapter of John with parallel passages in the synoptics, records a series of marvelous experiences in the first period of the withdrawals. Among them the most salient are: the great miracle of feeding five thousand, a great storm on the sea at night in which Jesus rescues the apostles, coming to them walking on the water, a great sermon in Capernaum putting His disciples to a severe test, and a great falling away of the superficial disciples and severe test of the true ones. We are now to consider the second of these incidents, the storm at sea and the marvelous rescue. It was about dark, the beginning of the "second evening," when the apostles embarked for the other side at the urgent bidding of their Master. They had lingered, hoping He would change His mind and join them on the beach before embarking;[1] but it had already become dark[2] and He had not come to them (Jno. 6:17). So they must go at His order without Him.

The curtain of the night suddenly dropped upon the scene and with the night came on one of those sudden storms characteristic of this deep sea-basin surrounded as it was by mountains. The sea was rising up more and[3] more. The apostles had experienced one such storm, not long before, on the sea by night, but that time Jesus was with them and had saved them when the boisterous waves threatened to engulf their boat. Now they were in the midst of the sea, distressed in rowing, making little headway with all their strenuous effort, because the wind was against them (Mark 6:48) and He was not there. Nine hours of that fearful struggle brought them but little over three miles to about the middle of the sea. They dared not approach the shore lest their boat be cast upon the rocks and they precipitated into the waves.

Meantime we are told that Jesus was alone on the land (Mark 6:47). He had spent hours in prayer on the mountain. Another night He had spent alone in prayer in the mountains, months before when He chose the twelve (Luke 6:12, 13). Now He is facing an even greater crisis in His ministry. He could see them from there in the torture[4] of the strenuous pull of the oars as they sought to drive their boat on[5] in face of the adverse wind. The darkness of the darkest stormy night did not hinder His vision

1 Andrew's Life of Our Lord.   2 Past perfect tense, skotia ede agagonei.   3 Graphic imperfect passive. The great wind was the agent in causing the sea to rise.
4 Basanizomenous.   5 Elannein used of driving a chariot (Robertson).

when His beloved disciples were in the peril of the sea. While they were in the toils of the waves He was in the struggle of prayer. This storm was as violent as the first they had experienced and lasted longer. Their strength had been put to a severe test and they were worn out now with the strenuous work at the oars and terrorized at the fierceness of the wind (Jno. 6:18). Perhaps this storm was a preparation for a greater one to follow on the morrow when the fickle crowd would turn away from their Master and they themselves would have to weather the gale of a tornado of apostasy.[1] The trial of their faith, in an absent Lord in the storm at sea, surely would strengthen them to meet that tempest of temptation. Jesus left them for a while in the midst of that affliction to prepare them for the victory of their faith on the morrow and for the years of service ahead.[2]

It is in the fourth watch[3] when they see[4] Jesus coming toward them, walking on the sea. Closer and closer the figure came but they did not recognize it to be Jesus and became sore afraid.[5] He had made as though He would pass by them at first, that He might not frighten them. Perhaps that would give them a better chance to recognize Him (Mark 6:48). They, thinking it was a ghost, were terrified[6] and cried out with fear[7] (Matt. 14:26). But immediately Jesus spoke to them words of peace and reassurance. "Be of good cheer," He said, "It is I, be not afraid." He had come to them in the hour of dire need and relieved their distress. They would remember this in many a subsequent storm and be strengthened. His temporary absence now was a preparation for His perpetual absence later. His miraculous intervention in the hour of greatest need would impress them that though absent from them He would supply their need. Every experience now seemed specially adapted to prepare them for the impending crisis. "Be of good cheer." The storm could not harm them when Jesus was near. They were no longer afraid and were willing[8] to receive Him into the boat (Jno. 1:21).

Matthew alone recorded the episode of Peter walking on the water. Perhaps Peter was not very proud of his experience on that occasion and so we do not find it mentioned in Mark's account (Robertson). With characteristic impulsiveness, that disciple, desiring to be the first to reach the Lord or perhaps moved with a sudden desire to see if he too could walk on the water, called out to Jesus: "Lord, if it is really you, order me to come

---

1 Bruce, The Training of the Twelve.   2 W. M. Taylor, The Miracles of Our Saviour.
3 From 3 to 6 a. m.   4 Historic present of vivid description.   5 Ingressive aorist passive indicative.   6 Etoracthesan.   7 When a Jew met a friend at night he would not greet him lest it should be a demon in his friend's shape. Wetstein on Matthew 14:26.   8 Inchoative imperfect, Ethelon "they began to be willing" (Robertson).

to you upon the waters" (Moffat). It was a rash request. Excitement had borne Peter beyond all reflection. From utter despair the pendulum had swung over to the other extreme of reckless joy. Christ did not negative his prayer but humored the impulse, that He might teach this self-confident disciple a lesson which might serve as a rebuke and a warning. He would need this lesson a little later. "Come," He said.

Jesus was dealing with a man who was presumptuous, overenthusiastic, and self-confident. To deny his request would smother out his independence and initiative. To permit him to try it out would teach him his weakness and dependence on the Master. After all, Jesus was seeking the development and growth of His apostles individually.

Peter did not hesitate. No sooner said than done. He stepped down from the boat,[1] and wonderful to behold, walked off on the waters and came to Jesus. As long as he kept his eyes on the Lord all was well, but when he turned his eyes to the fury of the wind-tossed billows and the dark cavernous depths of the sea below, immediately he began to sink.[2] He was a "fisherman and a good swimmer" (Bengel) but fear seized on him and he shouted out to Jesus: "Lord, save me."[3]

Jesus did not fail him but extended His hand and taking hold of him[4] pulled him up.[5] At the same time He rebuked him, saying: "O little-faith man, why did you doubt?"

When they had embarked in the boat the wind dropped suddenly like a tired child[6] and the waves subsided into a peaceful calm. Peter learned a great lesson and so did the others. Those on board, both apostles and others, fell down in worship before Jesus,[7] saying: "Truly you are God's son" (Moffat). They would soon confess what they were beginning to comprehend now, but in clearer terms, that He was "the very Son of God." They were literally "beside themselves"[8] with astonishment at the sudden calm after so horrible a storm. Mark gives as a reason for their amazement, their failure to grasp the character of the miracle of the loaves the day before, which was itself a great miracle. Here was another of the same kind. But their hearts were in a hardened state[9] and they could not receive it. John notes that when Jesus and Peter had come on board "immediately the boat was at land whither they were going."

There were wonderful lessons in this night's incidents. From

1 Aorist tense.   2 Katapontizesthai—to plunge down.   3 The aorist imperative soson means "and do it quickly."   4 Genitive with epilabeto, take hold of.
5 Epilabeto, imperfect middle denoting that Jesus pulled him up as they went walking on the water (Robertson).   6 Ekopasen, ceased, grew weary or tired.
7 Prosekunesan auto, worshipped him.   8 Existanto, placed out of their normal mind.
9 Was hardened, enpepromene, perfect tense denoting permanent condition.

Peter's experience they had learned not only the weakness of
his faith and theirs but also the possibilities of a strong faith in
Jesus. If like Peter they should fix their eyes on Jesus, they too
might walk triumphant over the swollen waves and so may we.

"He bids me come; His voice I know,
And boldly on the waters go
And brave the tempest's shock.
O'er rude temptations now I bound,
The billows yield a solid ground,
The wave is firm as rock."

Owing to the storm, they landed on the shore of the plain of
Gennesaret several miles south of Bethsaida, their destination.
They moored[1] to the shore. The people of this populous district
recognized[2] Jesus immediately and ran about[3] excitedly to spread
the news of His arrival in all that countryside. And they began
to bring those who were sick,[4] on pallets, to where they were
told[5] He was. And wherever He was going in villages, cities, or
country places they placed the infirm ones in the market places
and kept on begging[6] Him that they might touch the hem of His
garment.[7] And as many as touched Him were healed.

Jesus had a purpose in every miracle He ever performed.
There was no necessity that He should have walked on the water
in the storm by night. What could have been His purpose? Since
the days of Lucean in the latter half of the second century[8] this
miracle has been ridiculed. It has been considered by unbelievers,
from the time of Strauss particularly, to be a myth. Strauss found
it peculiarly difficult to believe, in that the body of Jesus is represented as exempt from the ordinary law of gravitation.[9]
Eighteenth century naturalism sought to explain it away by saying
that the boat of the apostles kept close to the shore and that Jesus
was not walking on the water but on the land.

We will find a clue to the proper understanding of the miracle in the main purpose of Jesus during these months of retirement with His apostles. He was seeking to prepare them for His
approaching death and resurrection. The miracle is a prophecy of
the resurrection. The same body which had walked on the storm-
tossed surface of the lake would then pass through a door closed
and locked without opening it.

3. The collapse of the Galilean campaign brought on by the
sermon of Jesus in Capernaum (John 6:22-71).

On the morrow the crowd which had remained in the neigh-

1. Lashed their boat to a post on the shore.   2 Epignontes, recognize or know well
3. Constantive aroist.   4 Kakos echontas, those having it badly.   5 Imperfect
indicative of continued inquiry and report.   6 Imperfect indicative.
7 Purpose clause.   8 Cf. Wetstein.   9 David Smith, In the Days of His Flesh.

borhood of Bethsaida Julia in the farm houses or villages or perhaps sleeping in the open air on this warm spring night, and
which the previous day had seen that there was only one boat
for Jesus and the disciples and that He had not embarked[1] with
them on the return, got in the little boats driven over from near
Tiberias by the storm during the night, and came across seeking
Jesus. They had thought to find Him somewhere in the locality
where He fed the multitude but had been disappointed. They did
not find Him immediately but later when He was on His way to
the synagogue worship.[2]

The feeding of the five thousand, coupled with the recent extensive campaign of Jesus and the apostles in all the towns and
cities of Galilee, had raised the Messianic expectation to the highest pitch. That miracle was used consciously by Jesus, we must
believe, to bring to a crux the question of the true character of
the Messianic Kingdom and sift out the superficial disciples who
threatened to precipitate a movement for a national Messiah which
would prove fatal to all His work. The Passover feast was just
ahead of them when more than a million Jews would be assembled
in Jerusalem. This, added to the excitement over the recent death
of John the Baptist, made the situation tenfold more tense. The
opportune moment seemed to have come for throwing off the
hated yoke of the Romans, if only the long-expected political
Messiah should appear, clothed with the miraculous power which
prophecy had foretold He would have.

Jesus was obliged to meet this situation promptly by making
clear to them two things: first, that the Messianic Kingdom was
not one of meat and drink or material wealth and power and that
He was not a political Messiah; and second, that the Messianic
Kingdom was spiritual and He was the true manna come down
from heaven.

The first part of the sermon (Jno. 6:22-40) was introduced
by a question put to Jesus. In a blandly flattering way they address Him as He comes to the synagogue: "Rabbi, when did you
get here?" They doubtless added, how they had sought Him anxiously on the other side. How could He leave them when they
were so eager to do Him honor?

Jesus probed to the very core of their inmost thoughts and
uncovered their veiled hypocrisy, reproaching them for their un-
spirituality. To their question He replied nothing. It was not for
them to know how or when He came over.

"Truly, truly I tell you; it is not because you saw signs that
you are in quest of me, but because you ate of the loaves and were

---

1 Second aorist, translated as past perfect in English.   2 It was probably the worship
   of Monday or Thursday. Geikie. Life of Christ.

filled.[1] This was a sharp rebuke for their gross animalism and coarse appetites, which smothered out all true idealism.

"Do not go on working[2] for the meat which perishes," He said, "but labor for the meat which remains unto eternal life, which the Son of Man will give unto you," and He added: "For *this one* God the Father certified" (Moffatt). The miracle of feeding the five thousand was in the mind of Jesus. He knew what the current conception of the coming Messiah was. Their idea of the character of the Messianic Kingdom was that of a Mahomet's Paradise, one of meat and drink, continual satisfaction of their desires, houses of precious stones, beds of silk, rivers flowing with wine and spicy oil.[3]

The Rabbis taught a religion of ritual and ceremonial observances. There were special "works of God" appointed for every hour of the day.

"What may we do,"[4] said they, "in order that we may *work the works of God*."[5] They thought they had been keeping all the current Rabbinical precepts to secure an inheritance in the Messianic Kingdom. What more would He have them do? They professed to want to please God and Him whom the Father had accredited. Yet how far they were from the character of true spiritual religion by basing it all on their *doing!* Jesus next overturned this false conception. He points them to belief in Him as the only "work of God."

"This is the work of God, that ye believe on that one whom He hath sent."[6] Citizenship in the new kingdom depended on nothing they could *do* but on belief on Him whom the Father had sent. The works of God would spring from that faith-relationship.[7]

But they were not satisfied. Perhaps some of the Pharisees in the group were responsible for the next question. They had in mind all the while the wonderful "signs" of Moses, particularly the giving of the manna in the desert during the forty years.

Among the ruins of the synagogue at Capernaum (Tell Hum) has been discovered by archeologists a lintel, bearing the device of a pot of manna, ornamented with a flowing pattern of vine leaves and clusters of grapes.[8] The miracle of the day before had reminded the people of what Moses had done and what the Messiah would

---

1 Literally to have the stomach filled as the stomach of the beast was filled with grass
2 Present middle imperative of linear action.   3 Geikie's Life of Christ.   4 Present active deliberative subjunctive, joiomen, "What are we to do as a habit?"
5 Hina with the present middle subjunctive in a final clause: "that we may go on working the works of God."   6 Present active subjunctive, "that ye keep on believing" as a progressive condition of life.   7 Geikie, Life of Christ.
8 Edersheim, Life and Times of Jesus.

do on a grander scale; and now as they crowd the synagogue to hear the new prophet, the device of the pot of manna—"Angel's food distilled from the upper light, suited to every taste and age or condition, bitterness to Gentiles' palates"—brought home again in symbol what had been done by Moses, an earnest of what the Messiah would do. Such was the atmosphere of tradition in which Jesus proffered His remarkable sermon on the "bread which comes down out of heaven."

To the claim of Jesus to be that accredited One, sent by God with the seal of His truth, on whom they were asked to believe they replied: "What sign therefore are you doing that we may come to see and believe thee?"[1] What are you working? They cited the fact that their fathers had eaten manna in the desert, and reminded Jesus that it was predicted[2] that the Messiah would do even greater things than Moses, who had given them bread for years. The miracle of yesterday was not comparable to that even if the manna did cease with Moses' death.[3] Jesus must show a sign on a far grander scale if He wanted them to believe Him greater than Moses.[4] The Master replied, correcting their false conception of religion: "It was not Moses who gave you the bread from heaven (a blunt denial), but it is *my* Father[5] (mine in a peculiar sense) who is giving[6] you the *true* bread out of heaven." The obvious reason He adds: "For the (genuine) bread of God is that coming down out of heaven and giving life to the entire world." The manna gave nourishment to the Jews; the genuine bread gives life to all. The very ones who ate the manna sinned and perished in the desert. True life must come from more than material bread and faith must be founded on deeper foundations than mere signs and miracles.[7] Would they grasp this profound and for them difficult teaching of Jesus? It seems that for a moment they caught some glimmerings of the truth and exclaimed:

"Lord, evermore give us this bread."[8]

Jesus had now come to the crux of His sermon when He must reveal Himself more clearly.

"I am the bread of life," said He. "The one coming to me shall never become[9] hungry and the one believing[10] on me shall never

---

1 Purpose clause with hina and the second aorist (ingressive) active of houras and first aorist (ingressive) active of pisteuo.
2 They cited Ps. 72:16; Ex. 16:15; Ps. 78:24; Deut. 8:3.
3 Torg. Psuedo-Jon. on Deut. 34:8.
4 Bruce, The Training of the Twelve.
5 Same claim as that He made in Jerualem (Jno. 5:17f) months before, which so angered the Jews.
6 Present indicative active of linear progressive action.
7 Farrar's Life of Christ.　　　　8 Cf. the woman at Jacob's well.
9 First aorist (ingressive) active subjunctive with strong double negative. Ou me peinasa.
10 Ho Pisteuon eis eme, present participle of continuous relation of belief or trust.

thirst."[11] Even their Rabbis had explained that the receiving of
the manna was the sequence of having received the Law and Commandments—the real bread. The manna after all was but symbolic
of the true bread. Wisdom said, "Eat of my meat and drink of my
wine." But their mood to ask for the bread of true instruction was
transient and their minds were wholly engrossed with the idea
of material benefits of the expected Messiah. Vainly had Jesus
sought to free them from the shackles of their gross materialism.
He was the bread of life in two senses: there was life in Him and
He imparted life to others (Robertson). But He adds sadly:

"You have seen me and yet are not believing."[1] They had been
witnesses of His wonderful signs, but had not believed on Him—
identified themselves with Him—or truly accepted His teaching.
He could only add a promise to the one who should come to Him.
Everyone whom the Father was giving Him would come and the
one coming to Him He would not cast out, because He had come
down[2] from heaven to do the Father's will, who sent Him, not His
own.[3] It was the will of the Father that everyone who would come
to the Son should keep on having[4] eternal life. In the last day
Jesus would raise up such an one.[5] The test of the true bread
was whether it would give life. He repeatedly comes over the
promise, "I will raise him up," because that was the fundamental
necessity for a continued life.

At this point there was a change in the situation. Jesus seems
to have addressed the words recorded in verses 37-40 mainly to
His immediate circle of disciples. Now the angry murmurs of
the leading Jews,[6] His old enemies, burst out with a buzzing[7]
chorus which spread through the synagogue. It was because of
what Jesus had said about His being the bread which had come
down from heaven. They were saying to one another over and
over[8] in a complaining, disturbing murmur:

"Is not this Jesus, the son of Joseph, whose father and mother
we know? How now is he saying, I have come down from heaven?"

Jesus met the rising tide of protest and interruption of His
discourse by a firm call to order, followed by a clearer declaration
of the truth which He had presented. "Stop murmuring[9] among

11 Future indicative active with even stronger form of negation—popote.
1 Present indicative active, second person plural, linear action.
2 Perfect active indicative of permanent transaction in the incarnation.
3 Present active subjunctive of poieo, "not that I keep on doing my will but that I keep
      on doing the will of the Father."
4 Present active subjunctive with hina.   5 Volative future of promise.
6 Jno. 41, 52.   7 Imperfect indicative of the onomatopoetic verb gogguzo.
8 Imperfect tense of repeated action.   9 Present imperative of prohibition with ma.

yourselves," He said. "No one is able to come unto me, except the Father who sent me may draw him, and I will raise him up at the last day." To His claim of being the bread of life and having life in Himself, He adds that He will definitely impart that life not only here and now in the creation of new life, but also hereafter in the raising up of the redeemed body in the last day. The experience of this new life was dependent on coming to Him, and that in turn on the initiative of God in moral attraction playing on the life of the individual. Jesus cited Isaiah's declaration: "And they shall all be taught of God," adding that it was not sufficient merely to hear but there must be a human initiative in learning[1] and receiving the attractive teachings of God. The one who does this will inevitably come to Christ.

It is not necessary that any one see God with his physical eyes in order to hear and learn. That privilege was given to the only one who was with God. Jesus had just told them that He came down from heaven. He implies now that He has seen[2] the Father and continues to see Him. He was the medium of revelation between the Father and the world. The one believing in Him already has and continues to have progressively[3] eternal life.

Again Jesus repeats His remarkable statement about His own person: "I am the living bread."[4] In explanation He calls attention to the fact that the manna which their fathers ate in the desert did not prevent spiritual death. Anyone eating His bread would live always. He identifies His own life to be offered up in sacrificial death as the means of life for the world. The central fact of the atoning death for the spiritual life of mankind is here set forth; but they did not understand it.

In the first part of His discourse (Jno. 6:22-40) Jesus had led His hearers up to His declaration of the fact that He was the bread of life come down from heaven. He asserted that He had life in Himself and would impart life to the one believing on Him. He also set forth plainly the fact of His incarnation.

In the second division of the sermon (Jno. 6:41-51) He discusses His own personality as the true bread giving life to the

1 Second aorist active participle of Manthano. permanent state.   2 Perfect indicative, permanent.
3 Present indicative active, linear action.   4 Ho artos ho zon, the bread, the living.

world, and leads His hearers on to the further declaration of His sacrificial and atoning death, as the bread to be broken in a fleshly body.

This declaration brought about a contention in the ranks of the leading Jews, His enemies. There was a battle of words[1] among them over this last expression of Jesus, about the bread which He would give for the life of the world being His flesh. The discussion degenerated into a bitter wrangle over these words. "How is this fellow able to give us His flesh to eat?" they said. Jesus now presses the disillusionment still further. His purpose is evidently to thrust away from Him all superficial mere bread-seekers, who could never come to the truth until their eyes were open and who could do His ministry much harm indeed, as a few hours ago was all too apparent.

"Truly, truly, I say unto you, if you do not eat the flesh of the Son of Man and drink his blood you have not life in yourselves. The one who goes on eating my flesh and drinking my blood has eternal life in him as a progressive reality; and I will raise up his body too at the last day. For my flesh is the true bread and my blood is the true drink. The one eating my flesh and drinking my blood remains in me and I in him. As the *living Father* sent me and I am living on account of the Father, even as the one *eating me* shall live on account of me. This is the bread which came down out of heaven. Not as the fathers ate and also died, the one eating this bread shall live forever." With these expressions He brought His sermon to a close.

Jesus thus dealt with the subject of how the individual is to appropriate the incarnate Son and His atoning sacrifice. How is Christ to be assimilated as the bread of life?

The idea of eating, as a metaphor for receiving spiritual food and the benefits flowing therefrom, was familiar to the Jews. "In the Rabbinical literature, sacred instruction was called bread and those who eagerly absorb it were said to eat it."[2] "Thy words were found and I did eat them (Jer. 15:16)." In the Talmud Hillel says: "The Messiah is not likely to come to Israel, for they have already eaten Him in the days of Hezekiah." The Rabbis spoke of their instruction as "the whole stay of bread." It was a common saying among the Jews: "In the time of the Messiah the Israelites will be fed by Him."[3]

1 Emachonto, make war or battle.
2 David Smith, In the Days of His Flesh.   3 Geikie, Life of Christ.

Augustine's interpretation of the discourse of Christ in Capernaum was summarized in the expression: "Believe and thou hast eaten." To Calvin the "eating was not faith but rather followed from faith." Of course the eating and drinking of this discourse had no reference to the Lord's supper. Bruce gives as his conclusion: "that through faith alone may we attain all the blessings of salvation."[1] "By eating the flesh and drinking the blood of the Son of Man, we are to understand the personal application of His Death and Passion to the deepest need and hunger of our souls."[2] "Faith in Christ and not mere works, whether ceremonial or practical, is the touchstone of Christianity."[3] They asked for manna as a sign of His being the true Messiah; He used it as a symbol of His personality as the true Messiah, even the bread which, as the manna sustained physical life, must be appropriated to create and sustain spiritual life.

The discourse of Jesus was not understood by His hearers, It was intended to serve as a means to sift out the superficial believers and test the faith of those who were sincere, clarifying their understanding as to the true character of the Messianic Kingdom. Jesus said these things in the synagogue while teaching in Capernaum. We cannot but believe that this was one connected discourse and not several as some think.

The result of the sermon was a real sifting, like a winnowing breeze blowing away the chaff and leaving a small residuum of wheat behind. Doubtless the enemies of Jesus who had started the murmuring at first also began the criticism this time. But many others of the superficial type of disciple also joined in the adverse remarks:

"This saying is a harsh one," they declared, "who can hear it?"[4] To some of His hearers the doctrine was incomprehensible; for others the difficulty was in the will to accept it. Jesus meant to put an end to mere selfish hopes. To some, even of the disciples, the saying was harsh and repulsive. Augustine thought that "the saying was only hard to the hard and incredible to the incredulous." Jewish literature was perfectly familiar with the symbolism of "eating" as an entire acceptance of and incorporation with

1 Bruce, The Training of the Twelve.   2 Edersheim, Life and Times of Jesus.
3 B. H. DeMent, Bible Reader's Life of Christ.   4 Auton.

the truth.[1] It ought not to have been hard for most of His hearers to comprehend His discourse in the main. We must admit, however, that it would be difficult for them to understand the connection between Christ's flesh and eternal life and how eating the flesh would confer any benefit or what eating it might mean anyway.[2]

Jesus, knowing that some of His disciples were murmuring concerning this expression, said to them: "Is this causing you to stumble?" These words He directed to the disciples exclusively perhaps and apart. "If therefore you may see the Son of man ascending where he was before?"[3] He prophesied that His ascension would soon show them that He had come down from heaven where He had existed before. What would they say and think then? He tried to make it as easy for them as possible. To do so He added a further statement as to how they ought to interpret His metaphor about eating His flesh.

"The spirit is life-giving; the flesh profits nothing," He said. They were not to take His words literally. It was not His flesh they were to eat but His atoning sacrifice they were to appropriate by faith and His life and teachings they must assimilate.[4]

The disciples were destined to undergo a severer trial yet, when He should be offered up and ascend to heaven, leaving them to struggle alone. How would it be with them then, if they became offended now by a mere clear intimation of His vicarious sufferings and atoning death? The realization of that sacrifice would bring a severer trial. He points them again away from bald literalism to the spiritual character of His religion. He had explained in His sermon just before, how His teachings were the bread and how His whole life and atoning death must be appropriated or "eaten" by them. The Jews spoke about "eating the Messiah," meaning by that "receiving him joyfully and devouring his instruction." So Jesus adds now a clearer statement: "The words (of definite teachings) which I have (just) spoken to you (in the sermon) are spirit and life." They belonged essentially to the region of eternal being and conveyed what in reality existed.[5] The breath and life of God were in the words of Jesus (Robertson). "But there are some of you who are not believing," and unbelief kills the life in the words. Hearing must be mixed

1 Farrar's Life of Christ.   2 Bruce, The Training of the Twelve.
3 Third general condition.   4 Geikie, Life of Christ.   5 Wescott, Com. on John.

with faith in hearers. Jesus was progressively conscious[1] of the unbelief in some of those who professed openly to be His disciples. He could distinguish between mere lip service and sincere worship. He had long ago detected insincerity in Judas and John had come to understand this fact and comments on it. Jesus was not surprised on this occasion to descry signs of wavering in the one who was destined to "hand him over"[2] to His enemies at last and was even now doing so in His heart. It was for this reason that He had made the statement in His sermon, that no one was able to come to Him unless[3] he were attracted by the Father first. The initiative in man's salvation is with God.

At this point the final break came with them as it does with many, when disillusioned as to the real sacrificial character of the Christ-life. From that moment and after that expression many of the so-called or professed disciples turned away from Jesus. They drift "to the rear." The battle of discipleship was too hot for them at the front. These half-hearted seekers after loaves were not caught "walking around with Jesus"[4] after that. He was not their kind and they had found Him out at last. They wanted a worldly political kingdom and a national Messiah. He had denounced their program and refused to be such a Messiah. They walked out of the synagogue and left Him coldly.

Then came the acid test for the twelve apostles. Everybody was leaving their Teacher who had been for months the idol of the people. What were they to do about it? Would they desert with the "camp-followers" or would they stand for Jesus? With sadness He addressed them:

"You do not wish to go away too do you?" Jesus used the form of the question which indicated that He expected or hoped for a negative answer.[5] His question was appealing and He was anxious that they should stand firm, but He would not unduly constrain them. Their choice must be wholly voluntary.

They were placed in a position which severely tested their faith, and tempted them to turn back. Hundreds were going off in disappointment and bitterness. Had Jesus made a mistake? His sermon had deeply offended His hearers. It was so different from all the discourses which had attracted the multitudes for months before. They were tossed in a storm of doubts. But they did come through the storm safely. It was Simon, as usual, who spoke first and expressed the firm decision of the apostle-group. "Lord, to whom shall we go? You have the words of eternal life. And we

1 Imperfect tense denoting progressive understanding.
2 Paradoson, present participle.   3 Third class condition.
4 The imperfect of peripateo.   5 The particle ma expects a negative answer.

have come to believe (firmly)[1] and to know permanently, that
you are the Holy One of God." They had made their choice. They
could not go to John who had been beheaded by Herod; nor
would they think of going to the Pharisees whose hypocrisy and
vain ostentation Jesus had exposed. The only alternative was to
abide with Christ though they were perceiving already what that
would involve of sacrifice. They had learned through their contacts of two years with Him that He was the Holy One of God.
They could not doubt His character. He was from God and His life
was pure and holy.[2] They might not understand all that was implied in His deep and remarkable sermon which had driven the
people away from Him, but they had unshaken confidence in Him
as a person. The confession was inadequate, but a step in the right
direction of the more complete expression of faith in His divinity a
little later.[3]

Jesus was glad for their confession but sad to feel that, even
among the twelve, there was one who was a deceiver who would
betray Him.

"Did not I choose you the twelve, and among you one is a
devil,"[4] He said. Such a strong expression—not so unusual in the
ears of the Jews perhaps—would at any rate shock them and warn
them against the real and imminent danger of defection and apostasy. This is the first time Jesus clearly speaks of His betrayer,
and significantly so in connection with the first definite prophecy
of His atoning death. Judas must have manifested on this occasion, to the intuitive glance of Jesus, some attitude of faltering.
John adds significantly, that Jesus spoke of Judas who was about
to betray Him, and that He was of the twelve—a sad commentary.

4. Jesus once again meets with Pharisaic opposition and denounces their tradition about ceremonial defilement (Mark 7:1-23;
Matt. 15:1-20; Jno. 7:1).

Pharisaic opposition did not lose its good opportunity now to
press the fight. Jesus had voluntarily, to all intents and purposes,
alienated the vast multitude of His disciples which had been ready
but yesterday to make Him king. For some months He had not
been able to do the work of itinerant evangelist in Judea, because
the Jews had been seeking[5] to kill Him ever since He had broken
with their Sabbath traditions.

The opposition had been deepening for months. Its earliest
manifestation in Galilee was when He spoke forgiveness to the

1 Perfect tense of a complete faith of conviction and understanding born of a clear
      perception on their part through progressive experience.
2 Bruce, The Training of the Twelve.
3 "Thou art the Christ, the Son of the living God," at Cesarea Phillippi.
4 Imperfect active indicative of peripatein describing his method of work (Jno. 7:1)
5 Imperfect active ezetoun, signifying their habitual and progressive attitude.

paralytic in Capernaum. He had silenced the murmurs of His enemies at that time by the miracle of physical healing (Luke 7: 48-50). The Pharisees had accused Him later "of being a glutton and habitual wine-drinker," and He retorted by showing that they were "like peevish children playing wedding and funeral in the market place," who were pleased neither by John's austere semi-ascetic ministry nor by the social program He himself had followed. Again, they had criticized the disciples of Jesus for not fasting, thus seeking to drive a wedge between Jesus and John and their mutually friendly groups; but again they had come out worsted in the encounter. When Jesus had broken over the social lines of caste and chosen Matthew to be one of His disciples, they had accused Him of identifying Himself with the publicans and pariahs of society. He had replied: "They that are whole need not a physician but they that are sick."

Once again now they launch their attack, under what seemed for them, to all outward appearances, more favorable circumstances. The Jerusalem Pharisees had kept their detective committee on the job in Galilee for months. This committee, aided by the local Pharisees and Scribes who sympathized with their views, gathered now around Jesus to enforce their criticisms, while He was suffering from the result of the wholesale defection following His sermon in Capernaum on the bread of life. They had observed that the disciples of Jesus disregarded the observance of the traditions of the elders about ceremonial defilement of the hands.

Mark refers to the traditional custom of the Pharisees, which had become general among the people, not to eat without diligently washing their hands. Indeed these ablutions had grown to be exceedingly numerous and very binding. Before and after every meal and whenever they came from the market-place or town-square, they had to wash or take a bath according to certain ceremonial restrictions. All cups, pots, and brazen vessels as well as tables and perhaps dining couches must be thoroughly cleansed. The Pharisees carried their ablutions to such an extent, as to completely overshadow with their ritual the fundamental moral principles of the Scriptures. The Sadducees remarked in derision when a Pharisee washed the golden candle-stick of the Temple, that "soon they would think it necessary to wash the sun."

The Pharisees claimed that these oral traditions had been handed down in part from Moses, consisted partly of decisions made by the judges from time to time and partly of explanations and opinions of eminent teachers. The body of these traditions continued to accumulate until after the time of Christ, when they were codified in the Mishna and its commentaries. Traditional rites and restrictions stood higher in the esteem of the Jews than their

Scriptures.[1] Where Scripture and tradition seemed opposed the latter was treated as the higher authority. The Pharisees said that the Covenant was made on account of the oral law. The Talmud adds: "My son, give more heed to the words of the Rabbis than to the words of the Law."[2] This attitude of Judaism toward their oral law has been a deciding factor in the high esteem in which the Church of Rome holds oral tradition as "of equal weight with the Scriptures."[3]

The legal washing of the hands was considered of great importance by the Rabbis. To slight hand-washing was a crime worthy of death. "Better go four miles to water, than incur guilt by neglecting hand-washing." One who neglected hand-washing after eating was "as bad as a murderer." Hillel and Shammai, two great rival teachers and heroes of Jewish traditionalism just before the time of Christ, united on eighteen decrees which might not under any circumstances be modified.[4] These decrees were designed to separate the Jews from all contact with the Gentiles. To touch a Gentile involved defilement; hence the necessity of a complete bath (immersion) after returning from the market-place. The opposing schools of Hillel and Shammai though antagonistic in many points were agreed on the ordinance of hand-washing. "It had come down from Solomon," they said, "and must be honored with the highest reward. Anyone living in the land of Israel eating his daily food in purification, speaking the Hebrew of the day, and morning and evening praying duly with the phylacteries is certain that he will eat bread in the kingdom of God."[5]

It nettled the Pharisees, and especially the Scribes, that the disciples of Jesus were indifferent to the Pharisaic traditions, evidenced in the fact that they did not wash their hands according to the prescribed rules before and after meals. Doubtless these self-constituted critics had observed that the disciples did not wash when the five thousand were fed and perhaps at other times. The principle of inwardness which Jesus had inculcated constantly[6] was changing their conception of religion. These heresy-hunters came to Jesus and called His attention to this very serious offense of His disciples.

"Why is it that your disciples are not walking according to the tradition of the Elders (Hillel and Shammai) but are (habitually) eating with common (unwashed) hands?" they asked. They could not understand how a teacher like Jesus could permit His disciples to neglect this custom imposed by their wise fore-

1 Geikie, Life of Christ, p. 194.   2 Eisenmenger, Vol. I, pp. 329-30.
3 Decrees of the Council of Trent.   4 Edersheim, Life and Times of Jesus, Vol. II,
   P. 13, 14.
5 Shabbath, f 3, 4 (Geikie).   6 See Sermon on the Mount. Cf. also lesson on fasting.

fathers. The disciples were transgressing habitually[1] the oral law and that was "worthy of a death penalty."

Jesus at once accepts the challenge. That His disciples had neglected the traditions of the Elders, He admits. He offered no excuse for their conduct in so doing. But these traditions were only man-made. Though the Pharisees claimed a basis for them in Scripture the whole spirit of the ordinances was contrary to prophecy. With biting sarcasm Jesus denounced them:

"Well did Isaiah prophesy about you *maskers*, you play-actors!

'These people honor me with their lips
But their heart is far from me.
But in vain do they worship me
Teaching as their doctrines the precepts of men.' "

He then answered their question by a question, as He often was wont to do:

"Why do *you* transgress the commandment of God on account of your tradition? You accuse my disciples of transgressing a ceremonial restriction invented by men; why do you transgress the law made by God himself? For he said: 'Honor thy father and thy mother (Exodus 20:12), and let the one speaking evil of his father or mother go on to premature death', but you dodge the responsibility of this highly important and much esteemed fifth commandment of the Decalogue by saying: 'Whoever may say to his father or mother (in order to evade his duty of support or help in their old age),[2] Corban (Gift), that whereby thou mightest have been profited by me is given (to God), shall not be under obligation to honor his father or his mother.' You thus have made void the word of God through your tradition."

This was a heavy charge and Jesus made it good by citing particular cases of such violation. The Ten Words were the Holy of Holies of the Law and the particular law to honor the parents carried with it a promise and was the most rigidly observed of all the ten, perhaps, among the Jews. It was a monstrous piece of inhumanity, not to speak of the impiety of making use of the votive *Corban* in order to escape the responsibility of the child to the aged parents. A concrete case is related in the Mishna, in which a father was thus shut out by a son from anything by which he might be profited by him.[3] After all, this was a kind of back-door for graft. The one thus exempted by Pharisaic authority from financial onus would satisfy the itching palms of Pharisaic greed. This would be a more frequent occurrence in the case of debtors

---

1 Present active indicative, parabainousi.   2 Dict. of Antiquities, Table (Geikie).
3 Edersheim, Life and Times of Jesus, Vol. II, p. 21.

who wished to avoid the payment of honest debts, resorting to the votive Corban, as a casuistical loophole. They were not merely setting aside[1] the commandment of God in their own conduct but were invalidating His (revealed) Word in the eyes of the people by their hair-splitting and immoral handling of it. They not only were transgressing[2] the commandment of God themselves but were not permitting others to obey it. Many such things they were doing.[3]

Having finished His stinging denunciation of these hypocritical critics and their ceremonial system, Jesus calling the multitude to Himself[4] addressed them: "Hear me all of you and understand," He cried. He was to lay down now the profound principle about "clean and unclean." The Rabbis gave an enormous amount of time to this whole subject of clean and unclean persons and things. Jesus sets forth the principle that there is no such thing as religious impurity attaching to things and material objects. "Not that which entereth into the mouth defileth the man, but that which proceedeth out of the mouth." Religious impurity concerns only the spirit and soul of man, not food or things. This declaration goes beyond the traditions of the Elders and virtually abrogates the Levitical distinctions between clean and unclean (Bruce). Moral uncleanliness alone defiles a man. Jesus had just charged the Pharisees with their immoral handling of the Scriptures. This was too much for them. These pettifogging pretenders fairly shriveled up with such withering words. But they walk out in a high dudgeon and depart in angry and menacing mien, impressing the timorous disciples of Jesus with their threats. These, moved by fear of the consequences, come to Jesus:

"Knowest thou that the Pharisees were offended[5] after they heard this saying" (Moffat). The disciples were uneasy. Had Jesus gone too far in discrimination between the clean and unclean? The Master quieted their fears: "Every plant (of mere human tradition) which my heavenly Father planted not," He said, "shall be rooted up. Let them alone: they are blind guides. And if the blind guide the blind both shall fall into the pit." Jesus seized on a common proverb[6] to stigmatize the proud ecclesiastics and warn all the people of the consequences to any who should follow them.

At length when Jesus had left the multitude which lingered and had withdrawn within the house, probably that of Peter, the disciples sought further instruction on the strange new principle

1 Atheteite (Mark 7:9) cf. Wescott and Hort.
2 Parabainate, to transgress or pass over the mark.   3 Mark 7:12, 13.
4 Aorist middle particle. The Rabbis had taken initiative in seeking to undo His disciples
     before the multitude; Jesus now exposes their hypocrisy to the people.
5 "were shocked" (Goodspeed), "have turned against you" (Weymouth)?
6 See Wetstein on Matt. 15:14.

enunciated by Jesus about the clean and unclean. It was hard for those who had always attached so much attention to the externals of religion to understand this new teaching.

"Explain to us the parable," said Peter, voicing the desire of the others.

"Are ye also even yet without understanding," replied Jesus. It was a discouraging thing that His chosen disciples should yet be so much under the spell of Pharisaic theology. They had been trained in Judaism, in which the distinction between clean and unclean is ingrained, and could not understand the statement abrogating this (Gould). Were they so dull intellectually and stupid spiritually? There must have been a tone of sadness in the voice of Jesus as He reproached them for their slow understanding. But with the patience and forbearance of the master-teacher He detailed the explanation in the baldest and most concrete terms, making them understand that all material things, particularly meats, were clean. Religion was from within outward not from without inward. Defilement is of the spirit of man, not of the meats which he eats to sustain the physical life. It proceeds from the things that come out of the heart. He then adds a significant list of the principal things He had in mind as the sources of defilement: "evil thoughts out of the heart (inner man), fornications (usually of the unmarried), adulteries (of the married), thefts (stealing), covetings (craze for more), murders (often growing out of the other crimes already enumerated), wickedness, deceit (lure with bait), lasciviousness (unrestrained sex instinct), evil eye (the eye that works evil), railing (hurtful speech), pride (holding oneself above others, stuck-upness, snobbishness), foolishness (lack of sense)." These things are in the beginning in the inward character, but soon find expression in the outward conduct in words and deeds. The captious quibblings of the Pharisee, for instance, had come out of evil hearts (Robertson).

CHAPTER XVIII

IN THE COASTS OF THE HEATHEN

(Harm. §§ 78-80)

The encounter with the Pharisees had revealed sharply the spiritual dullness of the disciples, and confirmed Jesus in His resolution to spend a large part of His time for some months, now, in their special instruction, until they should come to a clearer understanding of His character and mission. There were other reasons for His present withdrawal to the borders and parts[1] of Tyre and Sidon. The hostility of the Pharisees, following the defection of the great mass of the "camp-follower" type of His disciples, when He preached the doctrine too stony-hard to be received in His Capernaum sermon, had reached its culmination in Galilee. His enemies had closed the doors of the synagogues to His preaching in Judea (Jno. 7:1) and now redoubled their efforts to do the same in Galilee. He had defended His disciples against the subtle attack of these enemies, with such keen satire and extraordinary ability, as to leave them defeated and humiliated before the people and so thus embittered. They would doubtless resort next to violent means to do away with Him, and in this would find a willing and astute instrument in Herod Antipas who had just beheaded John. The wiser policy was to temporarily withdraw from the vicinity of Tiberias, the seat of Herod's government, and seek repose and privacy with His apostles in some place not too distant from the scene of action. Such a place He had sought across the lake to no avail. He must needs get out of the tetrarchy of Herod, and the nearest place was the borders and regions of Phoenicia some thirty-five miles to the northwest. Thither He repaired with His apostles and found a lodging near the border.

1. The second withdrawal and the healing of the Syro-Phoenician woman's little daughter[2] (Mark 7:24-30; Matt. 15:21-28).

No place could have offered safer retirement; but Jesus was too well known to be hid, much as He might desire it. He did not go to Phoenicia for the purpose of initiating a public ministry there. To do so would be to put a veto on His work among the Jews—the main purpose of His personal earthly mission—due to the fanatical attitude of His people toward the Gentiles. But it was "impossible to be hid" and soon a Syro-Phoenician woman, descendant by race from the Canaanitish people, who had inhabited all this region and all Palestine before the Israelites came in possession of it, found out about His presence. It is possible she

1 Within Phoenicia near the border.
2 Thugatarion, diminutive, little daughter.

might have been one of those "who came out of Phoenicia" to attend the ministry of Jesus in Palestine months before. She was a pagan Greek in her traditional belief, possibly, though she might, like the widow of Zarephath or Cornelius, have been a seeker after the light. Coming[1] "from those borders" somewhere in the neighborhood of where Jesus and the apostles were lodging, she cried out to Him in a distressed wail: "Have mercy upon me, O Lord, Son of David! My little daughter is badly demonized." Mark explains in detail that this affliction with an "unclean spirit" was a continued malady.[2] Whether she had been an attendant on the ministry of Jesus in Galilee or not, she had come to know something of the current Jewish messianic hope and the idea that some nurtured that Jesus might be the expected Jewish Messiah. She had doubtless witnessed personally or at least heard of His wonderful miracles of cures wrought on the multitudes; and stimulated by hope of securing some relief from the long affliction in her home, came, making her little daughter's case her own. "Have mercy on *me!*" she pleaded. "It was a piteous sight to see a woman crying with so much feeling, and that woman a mother, and praying for a daughter and that daughter so ill bested" (Chrysostom). But, strangely, Jesus did not answer her one word. It was so different from His usual way. What could be His reason?

Then the disciples took a hand. They disliked this kind of sensational public attention, of a strange foreign woman crying after them. They were insistent[3] when they came and asked Jesus to send her away. It would be inconsistent with their known Jewish prejudices that they should ask Jesus to grant her request, still His words to them in reply would indicate they did make such a suggestion, perhaps the rather to get rid of her. Their main interest in the matter was that she be sent away: "for she is wailing[4] (Moffat) after us," they said.

Meanwhile the anxious mother kept on begging[5] Jesus that He would cast the demon out of her daughter (Mark 7:26). But He, disregarding the woman, answered the apostles and said:

"I was not sent except to the lost sheep of the house of Israel." In Galilee He had freely ministered to the Gentiles who attended His preaching; but now the case is different. He had come to this Gentile country. If He should engage in extended ministries here He would forever close the door to all further effort on behalf of the *"lost sheep of the house of Israel."* This would be to defeat His

---

1 Aorist participle.
2 Eichen, imperfect of echo, denoting a progressive or continued state.
3 Imperfect tense indicating their repitition of the request.
4 Present indicative of linear action.
5 Imperfect indicative of continued action from erotao, to ask. She kept on asking begging. It was not a mere question she was asking, cf examples in papyri (Robertson).

wider ministry to the world later through the Jews, who were to
be His emissaries when enlightened. For the same reason no other
incident is recorded of any work done in Phoenicia except this one
significant cure. With this observation, made mainly to the disciples, but perhaps in the hearing of the woman, Jesus passed with
the apostles into the house of their lodging. Unabashed, the persistent mother followed them within, and making use of the liberty
of Oriental hospitality, continued to press her plea, falling at the
feet of Jesus in worshipful[1] reverence and humility, as he took
His place with the apostles at the table.[2] "Lord, help[3] me!" she
implored again, identifying herself with the afflicted daughter in
her entreaty.

Jesus repeated — *to her now* — and more explicitly, what He
had said to the disciples: "Let the children first be filled." He said,
"It is not well to take the children's bread and cast it to the little
dogs." He was evidently making a test of her faith and humility.
He knew she had an initial faith, for she had addressed Him as
"the Son of David," which in current terminology meant a profession of her belief that He was the Jewish Messiah. He would
strengthen that faith by testing it. She must be brought to recognize, too, that it was no little thing she was professing and asking.
She was reminded of the wide breach between the Jews and the
Gentiles. The Jews thought of themselves as God's children and of
the Gentiles as "dogs." The Gentiles resented and heartily returned
this ill-will. Edersheim thinks that the main purpose of Jesus,
in what seems to us the harsh attitude He assumed toward the
distressed mother, was to teach her that, while He was the Jewish
Messiah she addressed in the high sense, and she must recognize
that "salvation was from the Jews," at the same time He was
mainly the "Lord" of all, both Jews and Gentiles. This view, while
too exclusive, expressed doubtless one of the motives for Jesus'
manner, since in her second address she used the title "Lord,"
saying only: "Lord, succor me!" All racial prejudice must disappear. Such was His lesson to her and to the apostles as well.

It seems to us a very harsh expression in the mouth of Jesus
and a very severe test of the poor, afflicted, suppliant mother. A
closer view of the words, however, softens greatly their harshness,
and doubtless the kindly mien of the tenderest of all manly men
contributed to the same end. Making use of the fact that they were
sitting at the table, and that by custom the little pet dogs were
allowed to run about the room and under the table, He suggested
with a kindly play on the situation and the words, which render
these so different from Rabbinic exclusion:

1 Prosekunei, imperfect of continued action of bowing the knee as in the act of
    worship.
2 David Smith, In the Days of His Flesh.   3 Succor me, Boethei moi.

"It is not well to take the own children's bread[1] (from the table) and cast it to the little dogs"[2] (on the floor under the table). We must not fail to remember that the chief interest of Jesus during these months was to prepare His apostles for a world-wide mission of evangelization. Two things He would demonstrate to them in this incident: their own wrong exclusiveness, the heartless sinful attitude of the Jews toward the Gentiles, and the relative worthiness of many Gentiles. They must come to these conceptions before they would be ready to enter upon the world-wide missionary campaign. Their race prejudice must be corrected and their sympathy broadened.

The quick wit of this versatile Grecian woman took the very words of rebuff from the lips of Jesus and turned them with playful raillery to her own advantage: "Yes, Lord," she said, "and the little dogs under the table eat of the 'little morsels' falling from the table of the 'little children their masters.'" Here are three diminutives[3] which make a delightful and pleasing picture,[4] which, added to her desperate and tragic plea and her heroic faith in a loving Saviour, won for her one of the greatest of victories. On account of her faith and humility, but also "on account of this word" of quick wit and keen intelligence, taking the adverse wind in the teeth and soaring like the eagle in the storm to the cloudless empyrean, this poor heathen woman rose in a few brief moments from lowly obscurity to the highest pinnacle of famed heroism. Her faith was truly omnipotent, moving the heart and changing the purpose of God.

"O woman," said Jesus, "great is your faith! Be it done unto you even as you wish." Great faith and a keen rejoinder won her case (Robertson). "The demon has gone[5] out of your daughter," Jesus added. Joyfully, she must have gone back to her home; and she found it just as Jesus had said. The hitherto frantic lunatic child was lying calmly on the couch and the demon had gone out. She had been cured "from the very hour" Jesus had spoken.

The poor mother had brought her trouble to Jesus and through humility, persistent prayer, devoted love, a great faith, and keen intelligence, secured the physical cure of her little daughter, and what was a far greater blessing — her own salvation and one of the highest places among the heroines of faith in all times.[6] Jesus is revealed to us in this incident as the master interpreter of the human heart, the skilled teacher of His apostles, and the wise builder of His kingdom.

---

1 Teknon not huion.   6 W. M. Taylor, The Miracles of Our Saviour.
2 The diminutive for dog kunarion is used signifying a little house dog in contrast with other kinds of pariah dogs living in the streets on the garbage.
3 Little dogs, little morsels or crumbs, and little children.
4 Robertson's Word Pictures.
5 Perfect tense, signifying permanent and complete cure.

2. The third withdrawal and the feeding of the four thousand in the region of Decapolis (Mark 7:31-38; Matt. 15:29-38).

How long Jesus and His apostles remained in the borders of Tyre is unknown. Possibly the fame of the miracle forced Him to leave sooner than He had proposed.[1] He did not return south to Capernaum, but took His way in a north-easterly direction, up through the region of Sidon.[2] He likely followed the caravan road from the region of Sidon on the south side of the river Bostrenus, crossing a lofty spur of the Lebanon range amidst peaks six thousand feet high, and passed over the natural rock-bridge spanning the Leontes. This road led down into the valley of the upper Jordan. He would thus avoid entering the tetrarchy of Herod Antipas, as He pursued His course to His old haunts further south and east of the Sea of Galilee. How long He took for this journey we are not told. He may have spent some time in the villages of the Lebanon range, a most suitable locality for snatching a few days of repose in the exhilarating climate and beautiful surroundings, so conducive to recreation of the exhausted energies both of Himself and His apostles, and to quiet meditation and communion while He carried forward as rapidly as possible the particular instruction of the Twelve.

His destination was further to the south, in the borders of Decapolis, the territory of the ten allied Greek free cities. This region lay to the east of the Jordan and extended possibly from Damascus on the north to the river Jabbok, which was the border of Perea on the south. The ten cities[3] were occupied by heathen people, the Jews never having recovered them after the Babylonian captivity. The reception accorded to Jesus on arrival in this semi-pagan district seems to have been favorable.

Where the healing of the man, who was deaf and partly dumb — graphically recorded[4] by Mark — took place, is not stated[5] exactly. The people bring unto Jesus somewhere in this region, a man who was deaf, and thick of speech or a stammerer,[6] and are beseeching Him[7] to lay His hands on him. Jesus took him to one side away from the multitude, to avoid excitement and the better to get the attention of the "deaf and dumb demoniac" (Robertson). For some reason, best known to Jesus, it was desirable to make the cure gradual and visible.[8] The man could not hear what Jesus said, so Jesus put His fingers into the man's ears and then touched his tongue with a finger moistened with saliva. Then He looked up into Heaven and sighed. And He says[9] to him,

1 Geikie, Life of Christ.   6 Clark's Com. on Mark, 7:32.
2 He would hardly pass through the city, which would be contrary to His general purpose.
3 Decapolis, from deka and polis, means ten cities.   7 Historic present in graphic description.
4 Dramatic present tense.   8 Farrar's Life of Christ.
5 Philip Vollmer, The Life of Christ.   9 Historic dramatic present.

Ephatha, which is Aramaic trans-literated into Greek and means: "Be thou unbarred."[1] The process Jesus carried the man through was doubtless to awaken faith in him. Saliva had no virtue to effect any such cure as this, but would serve to stimulate faith, since it was believed by the ancients to possess remedial properties. Jesus "looked up" into heaven, probably in token of the fact that the source of the cure was with God. Why He sighed is a matter of conjecture; perhaps it was because of His pity for the man, or His reflection on the maladies of mankind, caused by sin and vividly represented in this poor specimen of humanity, or maybe it was an unarticulated prayer for the man's recovery. At any rate we know that there was a perfect and instantaneous, and so miraculous, cure.[2] His ears were opened and immediately the bond of his tongue was loosed and he "began to speak correctly."[3] Jesus began to charge them and kept on insisting[4] that they should tell no man about the miracle. He did not want to attract a great crowd about Him now in this period of retirement. He had other more pressing and vital work to do, in the instruction of the Twelve. But the more He charged them "the more they were heralding" the matter everywhere. These Gentile crowds were "beyond measure astonished." Jesus had not been in their borders very much. True, they had besought Him to leave their neighborhood once — the only time He had ever visited them — when He cured the two demonized men, who were wildly living in the sepulchers near the Lake. They had sustained a grave loss of a drove of two thousand hogs on that occasion, which was too much for them. But they had come to recognize in the meantime that Jesus did a great work on those men, whose presence in their midst since had been convincing. This had prepared them now to receive the wonder-working Rabbi in a more kindly way. They are ready when they see this added cure to declare their settled conviction about Him.[5] "He hath done all things well," they say, "He is making both the deaf to hear and the speechless to speak."

It is no wonder that when the news of this wonderful miracle was spread abroad, the crowds began to gather about Jesus, bringing their lame, blind, dumb, maimed, and many others. All hope for seclusion was now at an end. Jesus had gone up into the mountain to escape the crowd and was sitting there, possibly teaching the twelve, but the crowds soon swamped Him, and in their eagerness and hurry pressed in with their sick and "cast them down at his feet" to be cured. The Master did not deny them but healed every

1 Robertson's Word Pictures, Mark 7:32-37.   2 Euthus, immediately.
3 Elalei orthos, inchoative imperfect indicative, began to speak, straightly or correctly. He had
    some impediment in his speech, perhaps he was tongue-tied or a stammerer.
4 Imperfect of continued action.   5 Present perfect tense denoting firmness of their
    conviction about the permanent and abiding character of the work of Jesus.

one. It must have been a beautiful sight up on the side of the mountain, east of and in plain view of the Sea of Galilee, to witness the Master in this ministration of mercy. These were the "other sheep" He had of the Galilee flock and "not of this fold" — even more needy than the Jews because they were blinded by heathen superstitions. Jesus pours out His love in healing on them, semi-pagan though they were, until they were filled with amazement at seeing the dumb speaking, the crippled made whole, the lame walking and the blind seeing, and "glorified the God of Israel."

In those days again,[1] there was a great crowd around Jesus. We do not know how long He continued His work of healing and teaching in this region. Only one of the many cures is given in detail, that vividly recorded by Mark (7:32-37).

The crowds grew larger and larger until there was a vast multitude, a kind of "camp meeting"[2] where many had come bringing their lunch-baskets, and some groups even bringing the larger hamper baskets[3] of provisions, that they might remain longer. For three days the people held on, sleeping on the ground at night and eagerly pressing around the great wonder-worker by day, that they might witness every miracle and catch every word.

Jesus was touched[4] deeply by the sight of this multitude, composed largely of Gentile peoples. To Him it was symbolic of the wider conquests of His kingdom in the future. During the three days, naturally, they had exhausted their supply of food, and yet they hung on and would not leave. These Gentiles had never witnessed things like these and were charmed beyond words.

Jesus called His disciples to Him and said to them:

"I am sorry for the crowd; they are three days with me now and they have nothing to eat. I am not willing[5] to send them away, for if I send them away fasting to their own houses they will faint in the way, for some of them are from a long distance."[6] The disciples held in their memory distinctly as one of the numerous miracles, the feeding of the five thousand. But those people were mostly Jews. Would He feed this multitude of Gentiles also? Then too, He had been in many crowds before and had fed only one. Such prodigality as was witnessed in that miracle was not to be expected frequently.[7] At any rate, they would feel a delicacy in making any suggestion to Him about what He should do. The disciples were also slow of heart to believe. They had seen so many

1 In contrast perhaps to the occasion of the feeding of the five thousand in a locality to the north of this. 2 As Bishop W. M. Taylor would say.
3 The "hamper" baskets (sphurides) like the one used in letting Paul down from the Wall of Damascus were there for they took up seven such baskets full of fragments later.
4 Splagchnizomai, to have compassion. 5 Ou thelo, I am not wishing or willing. Present indicative, linear action. 6 Apo makrothen, from a long whence.
7 Farrar's Life of Christ.

wonders and signs that there was no novelty in it now for them. Later on Jesus reminded them of how easily they forgot about both of these miracles. They say to Him in reply to His expressed concern about the hungry crowd:

"Where are *we* to get[1] loaves enough in a desert like this to fill so great a crowd?" Some modern critics[2] have taken this expression to imply that the two miracles of feeding the five thousand and the four thousand could have been but one. On the contrary, the former was recorded by all four evangelists and the latter by Matthew and Mark alone. Furthermore, Jesus Himself afterwards referred to both miracles, as teaching the same thing[3] (Mark 8:19, 20). Then too, the miracles differ in many details: as locality, the former being near Bethsaida in Galilee, the latter in the territory of Decapolis to the south; the number of loaves and fishes and quantity of fragments taken up; the kind of baskets used in gathering up the fragments, the number of people fed, the time the multitude stayed, difference in the grassy or barren character of the places, indicating different times of the year, and the events which preceded and followed the two miracles.[4] Anyway, there is no reason why Jesus should not have repeated a nature miracle, just as He repeated certain of His teachings, and for the same purpose.

Jesus took all the initiative in providing for the four thousand, just as He had done in the case of the five thousand.

"How many loaves have *ye*?" He asked. Surely they could not have thought that He would expect *them* to arrange food enough in this "sparsely settled or desert place" to feed so great a multitude. They must have caught the hint of His purpose now, for they respond immediately:

"Seven, and a few little fishes."

Jesus then commanded the multitude to recline on the ground, and taking the loaves and fishes He gave thanks, broke the bread, and gave[5] the bread with the fish to the disciples to set before the multitude.[6] They already knew what to do and all the details of arranging the people and serving them, so that Jesus did not have to give detailed instructions. Of their own initiative, they gathered up this time seven large "hamper baskets"[7] full of the broken pieces that were left over.[8] Mark says there were about four thou sand but Matthew gives his report more like an eyewitness, saying: "there were four thousand men besides women and children."

1 Dative of possession.   2 Montfiore, The Synoptic Gospels, Vol. I (Mark 8:1-9).
3 Broadus' Com. on Matthew, Chap. 15.   4 Philip Vollmer, Life of Christ.
5 Imperfect active indicative edidou, "kept on giving out," the bread and fish.
6 Hina with present subjunctive, a continuous process as Jesus purposed.
7 Sphurides in contrast with kofinoi of the miracle of the five thousand.
   This was the kind of basket used in letting Paul down from the Damascus wall.
8 Periseumata, overplus, remains of broken pieces.

3. The brief visit to Magadan (Dalmanutha) in Galilee and the combined attack by the Pharisees and Sadducees (Mark 8:10-12; Matt. 15:39-16:4).

Once more Jesus gets away from the multitude as soon after the miracle of feeding the thousands as He could. It would be hard to hold their attention to the message of His preaching after the miracle. They would hardly be less material in their thought than the five thousand Jews who sought Him afterwards for the loaves and fishes. He took the boat[2] with His disciples immediately after He had sent the multitude away, and crossed over to the "borders of Magadan" (Matthew) also probably in the region or neighborhood of Dalmanutha (Mark). Both places are unknown but probably to be identified with Magdala,[1] at the lower end of the plain of Gennesaret and not far from Bethsaida and Capernaum, the headquarters of the hostile Pharisees. Much as He would like to return to His adopted home, He realized that to do so would precipitate the conflict again immediately. He had left His enemies there a few weeks before, defeated, humiliated and embittered. While He was away they had been busy organizing the forces of the opposition. Though the Pharisees were traditionally opposed to the Sadducees, they had meantime succeeded in securing their cooperation against Jesus. This is the first time the two parties appear together against Him. Ordinarily the Sadducees did not take much interest in religious matters, being a skeptical, half-religious, mostly-political sect, to which the high priests and members of the reigning family belonged.[3] Even before this the Pharisees had lined up the Herodians with them against Jesus in the Sabbath controversy (Mark 3:6). The latter was a political party, favoring the influence of the Romans and the reign of their tetrarchs, the Herods. The Scribes had been in the last encounter with Jesus. They were the repositories of Jewish orthodoxy. All parties were united now in their hate and in a conspiracy to hinder the work of Jesus. The hostility of the leaders had not decreased but the rather increased in His absence.

As soon as the boat,[4] which had been arranged to bring Jesus and the apostles over, touched the shore on the western side of the lake, the Pharisees sallied out from their lair in Capernaum to meet them, accompanied by the Sadducees, and beginning[5] at once to dispute with Him,[6] kept it up.[7] Their motive in asking Him captious questions and disputing with Him was to tempt Him

---

1 Most manuscripts give Magdala.
2 A special boat possibly arranged by Peter and his colleagues, the fisherman-brothers, Greek definite article.　　　　3 Geikie, Life of Christ.
4 Both records give the boat, not a boat, cf. David Smith, In the Days of His Flesh, Introduction II.　　　5 Inceptive aorist.　6 Dative of accompaniment indicating a controversy.
7 Present infinitive of progressive action.

to do or say something He would afterwards regret. They expected from Him some "sign."

Many of the people were believing that Jesus was a great prophet and secretly hoping that He might turn out to be the Messiah. The best way the enemies of Jesus knew to discredit His claims, intimated at least in the title Son of Man — which He customarily used when speaking of Himself — was to ask for "a sign from heaven." There had been signs enough in the miracles of Jesus to convince an open mind, but these they had attributed to the prince of demons, Beelzebub. A sign from heaven would be different. If He would make a rainbow span the world; or like Joshua make the sun stand still; call down thunder or hail like Samuel, or fire and rain like Elijah; or if He would make the sun turn back like Isaiah, they would believe that the King-Messiah had come.[1]

Twice before, they had come asking for a sign.[2] The first time was in Jerusalem during the Passover, at the beginning of His ministry. He gave them there the sign of His resurrection in enigmatical language, which they misinterpreted in His last trial. Even His disciples had puzzled their brains over the allegory of the destruction of the temple and its raising up in three days. The second demand (Matt. 12:38f) He "met with indignant contempt,"[3] but gave them another enigma to puzzle over — the double sign of His preaching as a warning to them, under the allegory of Jonah's warning message to Nineveh, and of His own death and resurrection under the parable of Jonah's experience in the whale's belly for three days and nights. He said their condemnation would be deeper than that of the Ninevites, because of their attitude toward Him, a greater than Jonah.

Jesus had warned them, along with the multitude, not to be seeking for "bread-from-heaven" signs. The people had turned away from Him at that time because He would not repeat the sign of the miraculous feeding and keep it up, like they said Moses had done, for years. His enemies thus brought Jesus before the tribunal of the people to force Him to repeat such a *sign*, as they well knew He would not at their demand. They thus put Him into a trying situation to vex His soul and exasperate Him. If He refused the sign — as they knew He would — the people would be alienated all the more.

The way He met their third demand for a sign was by absolute refusal. The revised version of Matthew's account retains the reference to the signs of the times, probably taken from a parallel

1 Geikie, Life of Christ, pp. 213, 214.   2 Jno. 2:18f; Matt. 12:38.
3 David Smith, In the Days of His Flesh.

incident which occurred later (Luke 12:54-57), though the passage (Matt. 16:2, 3) is "quite certainly not the original text."[1] Jesus might well have used the illustration twice, as He repeated various other teachings at different times and places. The reason for His refusal to accede to the demand for a sign was that it would have been wrong for Him to work a miracle just to please His enemies; and even if He had done so they would again have attributed it to demoniacal agencies. Later on Jesus said to the people who had been contaminated with this desire to see a sign:

"When you see a cloud rise in the west, you say: There is a shower coming; and so it is. And when you see the south wind blow you say: There will be heat; and so it is" (Moffatt).

Whether Jesus actually said on this occasion the words given in Matthew 16:2, 3 or not, we do not know. These words are in entire accord with what He would say and essentially what He did say a little later. Some think that He did use here the beautiful figure of the weather signs, pointing as He did so to the western sky, now tinged crimson with the deepening hues of sunset.

"When it is evening ye say: Fair weather! for the sky is fiery red; and in the morning: Storm today! for the sky is red and frowning. Ye know how to discern the face of the sky; can ye not learn the signs of the times?" These same Pharisees pretended to be able to tell by the way the smoke blew on the last evening of the Feast of the Tabernacles what kind of weather there would be through the year. If it turned northward there would be much rain, and the poor would rejoice; if it turned south, they said the rich would rejoice and the poor mourn for there would be little rain.[2]

Many unmistakable signs had been given: in the fulfillment of the Scriptures, in the events of the day, in the preaching of John, in the preaching, miracles, and life of Jesus pointing to His Messiahship. The Pharisees were successful in discerning the tokens of the weather; why did they not look around them and read the signs of their own times? If they had so done, they would have seen that soon Jerusalem was to be destroyed and the Jewish state overturned (Robertson).

Jesus "sighed from the depths[3] of His soul," when He saw the obduracy of their determined opposition under the hypocrisy of religious zeal. He had been well received and sought after by thousands among the Gentiles of Phoenicia and Decapolis during the past weeks, and now when He returns for a brief visit to the neighborhood of His adopted home-town, He is met by these astute enemies, who hound His every step with their persistent antagon-

1 Broadus, Com. on Matthew (16:1).   2 Geikie, Life of Christ.
3 The perfective use of the preposition ana reenforcing and intensifying the meaning of the verb.

ism. The Lord's human spirit was stirred to its depths (Swete). He was deeply pained, grieved, and filled with sorrow and resentment by the settled and determined prejudice of these mutually antagonistic parties, now banded together against Him. It was the most ominous token of the beginning of the end which He had yet met with in His ministry.

"Why does an evil and adulterous generation seek after a sign?" said He. "Truly, I say unto you, there shall no sign be given unto this generation but the sign of Jonah." He had given them the sign of Jonah on a previous occasion (Matt. 12:39-41) but the mention of it now is a mere reference — "a refusal to give any sign such as they demanded"[1] (Bruce). That they did not understand the enigma was abundantly proven when He rose from the dead (Acts 3-5).

It was unsafe for Him to remain longer in the proximity of Capernaum and Tiberias. His enemies would move heaven and earth to compass His destruction. He was outlawed now in His own town and almost in all Galilee. He could not force His mercies on those who rejected Him. With a heavy heart He reembarked in the boat with His disciples and directed them to steer their course northeast in the direction of Bethsaida Julias.[2] Soon they were gliding over the mirrored surface of the sea, in plain view of Bethsaida, where Peter, Andrew, James and John had been reared. In the distance stood out, in the slanting rays of the westering sun, the synagogue of Capernaum, where He had preached to many an eager throng in the earlier part of His ministry. The home of Peter, too, was visible where He had made His headquarters and preached and healed. What of Mary and the younger brothers, now that He was practically barred from further residence there? He was fully conscious that His ministry was closed in Galilee. Whither should He turn now to escape the plotting of His desperate enemies? The pagan territory to the north, as far from Jerusalem as possible, seemed the only place where He could find a few weeks in which to complete His final instruction to His apostles, leading up to their firm confession of their belief in His divinity; and then break to them in plain and unmistakable terms the tragedy of His approaching death on the cross. This was the only retreat left open for their temporary refuge.

1 Robertson's Word Pictures. Mark 9:12.   2 Farrar's Life of Christ.

CHAPTER XIX

THE GREAT CONFESSION

(Harm. §§ 81-84)

As the western shore receded with the loved scenes of the greatest days of His past ministry, Jesus sat in the boat in meditative mood. He was sure that the disciples did not realize the danger which He and they were facing in the conspiracy which had just been formed by the Pharisees, Sadducees, and Herodians. Already there had been a great defection, brought about in large measure by the false doctrines, standards, and leadership of these men. The Pharisees hated Him with an inveterate hatred and would leave no stone unturned to defeat His ministry and do away with Him.

One of the things these enemies had tried repeatedly, was to alienate from Him His disciples. They had succeeded with many already. The greatest danger for the twelve apostles on whom so much depended for the future was that they might become contaminated with false teaching of these combined enemies. Those astute Pharisees had just placed Jesus in a trying position, where He might easily be misunderstood, by their asking for a sign from heaven. His disciples might wonder why He did not give a sign. Had it not been foretold that the Messiah would do so? The twelve must be warned against the seductive influence of these hypocritical enemies, who, under the appearance of religious zeal, were seeking the destruction of the Lord.

1. On the way across Jesus sharply rebukes the dullness of the disciples and in Bethsaida Julias heals the blind man (Mark 8:13-26; Matt. 16:5-12).

"Take heed and beware of the leaven of the Pharisees and the Sadducees," Jesus commanded.[1] Over and over he charged[2] them "Look out and beware of the leaven," not only of the Pharisees and Sadducees, "but also of Herod."

But the disciples were slow to understand. They had disposed of the seven large hampers of bread left over from the feeding of the four thousand, perhaps in Magadan among the poor, and on re-embarking, in their preoccupation with the hard discussion which had just before taken place between Jesus and His old enemies the Pharisees — this time reenforced with their new allies — they forgot to provide themselves with food. There was only one loaf left in the baskets they carried, not enough for thirteen hungry men. They were evidently upset about the matter as they continued to discuss it among themselves. They kept up[3] the discussion

---

1 Present active imperatives, a progressive command calling them to habitual alertness.
2 Diestelleto, imperfect of repeated action.
3 Imperfect indicative active, kept on coming back to the subject.

297

for a time. This gave rise to the expression of Jesus about the leaven. He saw how slow of belief the apostles were. They were far from exercising such faith in Him as was necessary to their success as kingdom workers. They had wholly misinterpreted His language about the leaven and applied it to their loaf[1]-less condition. This revealed to Jesus yet more clearly their blinded faithlessness. The Master was deeply grieved with this unbelief and disproportionate concern about *loaves*. He, on the contrary, had been engrossed as He sat looking out over the waters at the fading picture of His beloved Capernaum, wondering what the result of the day's conflict would mean, in the weeks just ahead, for His kingdom. He knew His own fate personally was sealed, but what of His kingdom? Would His apostles stand the test? If they were to do so they must get their eyes opened to the insidious plans and subversive teachings of the enemies. Their stupidity saddened and vexed Him. Their mistake in this present instance in supposing Him to be speaking of loaves to eat was absurd, and revealed the gross materialism of their thought and concern, when they should be thinking of the spiritual things.

He turned to them with a sharp rebuke. There was something of indignation in the six questions (Mark) which He fired at them in rapid succession.

"O ye little faith-men," said He, "why do you keep on preoccupying[2] your minds and discussing among yourselves[3] about not having loaves? Do you not yet perceive, neither understand? Have you your hearts (permanently and irremediably) hardened?[4] Having eyes do you not see and having ears do you not hear? And do you not remember when I broke the five loaves among the five thousand, how many lunch-baskets[5] full of the fragments you took up?" They say to Him, "Twelve." "And when the seven among the four thousand how many large hamper-baskets[6] full of the unconsumed broken pieces you took up?" And they say, "Seven." "Do you not understand now?"[7] These pungent questions reveal the disappointment of Jesus about the intellectual dullness of His pupils. They refer to the intellect (perception, *noeite*, and reflection, *suniete*), the heart in a hardened, callous state, the eyes, ears, and memory (both the perceiving powers and the retentive powers).[8] In these questions Jesus pointed out their absurd mistake but offered no correction.[9] He calls attention to the fact that He was not talking to them about loaves and repeats His warning about the leaven (Matt. 16:11).

1 It is "loaf" not bread.   2 Reasoning in yourselves.   3 Matt. 16:8.
4 Perfect passive participle, indicating a continued and permanent state.
5 Kofinous, the baskets ordinarily used for luncheon.
6 Sphurides, a large, hamper-like basket.   7 Present indicative active, linear.
8 Robertson, Word Pictures.   9 Farrar's, Life of Christ.

At last it dawned upon them. Their dullness had seriously taxed the patience of the Teacher. They had been wayside hearers and the seed could not get into their hardened hearts. They were yet unsuspecting and hard of understanding, but He had been patient in His instruction and finally they had gotten the idea. "He was talking to them of the teaching of the Pharisees and Sadducees and not about loaves."[1] How sorely they needed instruction! He was warning them against the seductive heresies, the leavening influence of the false teaching of these astute, hypocritical enemies. They did take the lesson home to their hearts in part at last, as their conduct shows afterwards. They fought shy of the Pharisees and Sadducees and learned that the teaching of Christ was antagonistic to the fundamental tenets of those religious sects. It would take them a good while to discriminate clearly between the religion of Jesus and that of these Pharisaic teachers, but the fundamental line of cleavage had been pointed out. They would look out and beware of it from now on, and this was worth the Master's patience. Food and raiment would not occupy so large a part in their thinking from this time forth, nor would they be so blind[2] and deaf to spiritual things. They would seek to perceive and by reflection to understand the true doctrines in discrimination from the false, and to have a greater faith in the providence of Jesus over the lives of His workers, by treasuring up in their memories the things they had experienced with Him in the past.

Arriving in Bethsaida—Julias late in the afternoon, probably, they must have spent the night there. His entrance into the town was not unnoticed. Early the next morning the people come[3] bringing a blind man and beseeching Him that He would touch him.[4] Jesus took the man by the hand and led him outside of the village[5] that He might not attract the multitude about Him. He was on the way to the region of Caesarea-Philippi and had no plan to make an extended visit in Bethsaida now. He therefore used the utmost secrecy in performing the miracle. Proceeding in this cure after the same manner as that performed on the deaf and dumb man in Decapolis, He used a gradual process to awaken the faith in the man and his semi-pagan fellow-countrymen. He put spittle into the man's eyes and placing His hands upon him asked: "Are you seeing anything?" The man looking up said: "I see the men, because as trees I see them and they are walking around." Here is a vivid description of the dawning sight. Evidently the man had lost his sight at some time or else it was a

1 Farrar's Life of Christ.   2 Bruce, Training of the Twelve.
3 Present indicative active, dramatic present, a Markan touch.
4 Hina with present active subjunctive, denoting purpose.
5 It had been a village, but Philip had made it a town and named it Julias in honor of Julia, the daughter of the Emperor Augustus.

double miracle, as in the case of the man born blind, for he did not have to go through the process of educating his vision. The cure was incomplete but the man knew the objects he saw were men because they were walking around.[1]

Again Jesus put His hands on the man's eyes and he saw thoroughly[2], and was completely and permanently restored, be cause he kept on seeing[3] clearly[4] all things. Immediately Jesus sent him to his home in the country bidding him not to enter into the village.

2. Near Caesarea-Philippi Jesus tests the faith of the twelve in His Messiahship (Mark 8:27-30; Matt. 16:13-20; Luke 9:18-21).

From Bethsaida-Julias, Jesus went forth with His disciples into the "regions" of Caesarea-Philippi, where He visited the villages round about the town. This was a beautiful district, and most favorable of all the retreats they had sought for privacy, rest, and instructive fellowship. "Everywhere there is a wild medley of cascades, mulberry trees, fig-trees, dashing torrents, festoons of vines, bubbling fountains, reeds and ruins, and the mingled music of birds and waters" (Tristam). The fields, between and around the three sources of the Jordan here at the base of Mount Hermon, are fertile, producing breadstuffs and rice; and "in summer the whole district is a sea of flowers, whence the bees gather a rich harvest" (Keim).[5] Caesarea-Philippi was an important town, built by Philip the tetrarch, through the enlargement of Paneas (modern Banais), and re-named Caesarea in honor of Tiberias the emperor, and Philippi, to distinguish it from the other Caesarea on the Mediterranean coast. The inhabitants of the town and surrounding "parts or borders" were heathen, and for this reason it was the easier for Jesus to be secluded here, where He doubtless remained for some weeks instructing the twelve.

Luke records the significant fact that Jesus was engaged in protracted, secret prayer at this time.[6] He ever met thus the great crises of His ministry—and this was the greatest by far to this time. Even in this heathen territory, far removed from the haunts of His greater activities, the people were attracted to Him. But most of His time was given to confidential talks with the twelve. He evidently took the apostles into His confidence, not only in conversations but also in some of His hours of communion with the Father.

In one of these hours, "when they were with Him and away from the crowd" (Luke 9:18), after their prayer-hour was past and they were walking along the way, He asked His disciples what the people were saying about Him currently. This was no mere

1 Peripatountas, walking around.   2 Dieblepsen, see thoroughly, effective aorist.
3 Imperfect of continued action.   4 Distinctly from a distance, tele, far, and auge, far-
     shining.   5 Broadus, Com. on Matthew.
6 Periphrastic articular present infinitive.

vain desire to receive the praise of men. Jesus had a more serious purpose. He began[1] to question them:

"Whom do men say that the Son of Man is[2]?" This question was designed to prepare the way for another more important one to follow. Jesus knew that the people did not think He was the Messiah. They were expecting a different kind of Messiah, one who would free them from the bondage of Roman dependence and make them a free nation.

The disciples, in mingling among the people, had heard many opinions expressed about Him. He did not have to wait for their answer. They tell Him frankly what the people are saying:

"Some say that you are John the Baptist." This had been the immediate conclusion of Herod Antipas when he heard about the wonderful works of Jesus. His opinion was reflected in others also. Yet others, impressed by His fiery denunciation of sin and call of the people to repentance, thought that He was "Elias", who had gone to heaven in a chariot of fire, and in the popular tradition, would return as the forerunner of the Messiah. Others still, detected in His preaching the plaintive notes and tenderness of Jeremiah. A larger group could not identify Him with any one prophet and were content to speak about Him as "one of the old prophets[3] risen from the dead." They could not find a contemporary great enough with whom to compare Him except John who had been recently beheaded. But in their blindness they had not been able to think of Him as the Messiah, especially since He flatly turned down their Messianic program in His last sermon at Capernaum. The examination through which Jesus was putting the disciples[4] had registered one sad conclusion: the people might accord Him a high place among the prophets but they had not arrived at the understanding of His real character — they had not recognized Him as their Messiah.

The more important question is next put to them:

"But you,[5] whom do you say that I am?" Upon their answer much depended. Jesus had been teaching them many things by precept and by example, in order to bring them to an intimate understanding of His real nature and mission. Had they come to understand and catch the vision of the Messianic Kingdom and its king? They had, with the people, recognized His surpassing greatness as a man, His superiority to any one of the prophets, and His likeness to and comprehension of all of them in one personality.

1 Arota, conative imperfect tense, began to question (Matt. 16:13).
2 Infinitive with accusative in indirect assertion. Jesus was conscious of the identity of himself with the Son of Man. This expression, Son of Man, in the mouth of Jesus meant Messiah. Jno. 8:20; 12:23; Matt. 12:8.
3 Perhaps Ezekiel or Daniel. who used many parables also.
4 The imperfect tense of the verb indicating that he kept up his questioning, erota.
5 The pronoun occupies the place of greatest emphasis.

But He was not content to be classed merely as a prophet or even with Elijah and Jeremiah, who in popular opinion were the greatest of the prophets.

It was the "warm-hearted" impulsive Peter, who was so many times the speaker of the group, or as Chrysostom called him, the *coryphaeus* of the apostolic choir, who instantly responded: "Thou art the Christ, the Son of the living God." He was very definite in his statement[1]. For Jesus this noble confession, bubbling up out of the warm heart of His devoted disciples, was exceedingly reassuring after the great defection which had swept away most of His Galilean following. He had never claimed definitely to be the Messiah in the presence of the twelve apostles. Their conception of the character of the expected Messiah was largely that of popular tradition, and to claim to be the Messiah would seriously endanger all His work even with them. He had patiently waited for them to find out for themselves, through contact with His life work, what the real character of the Messiah and His Messianic Kingdom was to be. He had openly refused to be the kind of Messiah the Jews wanted. At the same time He had accepted Messianic homage and used Messianic authority in cleansing the temple. He had confessed Himself the Messiah to the woman at the well (John 4:26).

There had been a growing comprehension of His Messiahship on the part of the twelve, from their first contacts with Him, revealed in various partial confessions.[2] Andrew had said to Peter: "We have found the Messiah" and had brought Peter to Jesus (John 1:41). Nathanael had called Him the Son of God and King of Israel (John 1:49). When He walked on the stormy sea they had said: "Of a truth thou art the Son of God" (Matt. 14:33). After the great defection, a little while ago, Peter speaking there for the others as here, had affirmed: "We have believed and are sure that Thou art the Holy One of God" (John 6:69). But in spite of these and other expressed confessions, their Messianic hope was yet deeply tinged by popular notions concerning the Messiah. But this clearest of all expressions from them until now, revealed the fact that though they did not understand fully all about Him and His mission, they were going to follow Him on to the end. They had come to a settled conviction that He was the Messiah, even though His conduct might not accord perfectly with their traditional idea of what that of the Messiah would be. Peter had gone beyond the most favorable opinions expressed by the people and asserted what was lacking by classing Jesus above all the prophets as the Messiah. But He was more than merely the

1 There are four definite articles used here, the Messiah, the Son of the God, the living one.
2 Andrews, Life of Our Lord.

Messiah: He was the Son of the living God, partaking of the super-human divine nature of the real and living God[1] of whom Peter and the others were presently conscious as an abiding reality in their experiences. For Peter and his colleagues now, Jesus was *the* expected Messiah of Jewish prophecy and *the*[2] real and only begotten Son: not just *a* son as formerly said in a partial committal (Matt. 14:33); but *the* son of *the* only true God, *the*[2] living and real one, not like the lifeless heathen gods.

Jesus had expressed neither satisfaction nor His sorrow, when popular opinion was reported to Him, at the failure of the blinded people led by the blind Pharisees in not seeing the true character of His Messianic mission. He now received with solemn joy the clear confession of Peter to His Messiahship and His divinity.

"Happy art thou, Simon Bar-Jona, because flesh and blood did not reveal it to you, but my Father, who is in the heavenly places." Jesus congratulates Peter joyfully with a special beatitude, that he was so privileged in receiving and had been so happy in ex-pressing what had been revealed to him by the Father in the heavenly places of prayer, service, and fellowship. Jesus appre-ciated the devoted love and admired the daring and courage of Peter. He might make blunders in the future but Jesus would know him to be His friend and would be the first to befriend Peter after his failure. The terms in which Jesus speaks of Peter are characteristic, warm, generous, and unstinted. The style is not that of an ecclesiastical editor laying the foundation for church power and prelatic pretensions, but of a noble-minded Master eulogizing in impassioned terms a loyal disciple (Bruce). Peter had not learned these great facts from human teachers or con-tacts, but in the school of prayerful experience with God. It was the own Father of Jesus, His Father in a peculiar and intimate sense, who had revealed this to Peter.[3] His own Father-God had helped Peter get this spiritual insight into the Master's person and work (Robertson). Peter could not have attained to this new revelation by the unaided effort of his own mind. Jesus asserts that this was a new light from heaven. He accepts the confession as true to the facts, thus putting His stamp of approval on the words of Peter and asserting His claim to be the Messiah and the divine Son of God.

"Now I tell you, that your name is Peter (petros) and upon this rock (petra) I[4] will build my church, and the powers of Hades shall not succeed against it" (Moffatt). One of the characteristics of

---

1 Present active participle of continuous existence.
2 The definite article in Greek helps to make definite the confession here.
3 The use of the personal pronoun mou emphasizes the intimacy of the relationship.
4 Kago, kai-ego, is given the place of emphasis. Jesus assumes the place of the authoritative master-builder.

this rock-nature was a devoted love for Jesus and another less conspicuous, but there nevertheless, was the humility which would not permit Mark to write down in his gospel later the eulogy pronounced on him by Jesus, while at the same time inserting the sharp rebuke administered to him the next day.[1]

Jesus himself[1] now adds important statements that assign to the truth confessed a fundamental place in His kingdom-building (Matt. 16:18-19). Jesus did not fail to give Peter, personally, His warm commendation. He had become the *rock* which Jesus prophesied he would become the first time they met face to face (John 1:42). By the experiences through which he had passed, Peter had been transformed from the mere Simon son of John, into Cephas (Aramaic) or Peter, a foundation stone for the kingdom. This transformation had gone on to the extent that Peter thus spiritualized and divinely aided could pierce through the mist of things human and catch a glimpse of the divne nature and truly Messianic character of the Master. The same transformation now enabled Peter not only to see this great fact but to express it with conviction and definiteness.

On the rock of the messianic character and the divine nature of Christ, personally incarnated in a living faith in Peter and others, and publicly confessed to the world, Jesus would build His house of the spiritual Israel (Deut. 18:26; 23:2; I Peter 1:1). He doubtless here plays on the name of Peter[2] which denoted a smaller detachment—a stone broken out of the quarry for building purposes. The rock on which Christ would build was the massive ledge of the eternal truth of His divinity, incarnated in the personality of all believers, transforming them, as it had transformed Peter, into the rock-nature, suitable for the purposes of kingdom-building. To Peter was given the honor of being *primus enter pares*, the first to have expressed the *great confession*. Jesus did not assert the supremacy and primacy of Peter, as Romanists contend. He expressed first to Peter, His purpose to found His church, because Peter had been the first to confess Him confidently as the Messiah and Son of God. Peter is to be one of the foundation stones[3] along with the other apostles, and he has the honor of being the first mentioned. He is worthy of this first mention because he was the first to make the *bold* confession, just following the great defection, and in the face of the united hostilities of a far-reaching conspiracy.[4] Peter was the kind of man Jesus could use in building His great spiritual temple of the universal church— a living stone.

1 Matt. 16:17; 16:23.
2 The play on the masculine and feminine forms of the Greek words petros and petra cannot be pressed too far here because the Aramaic Kepha is the same in both cases.
3 Eph. 2:20.   4 Matt. 16:5-12.

So here the fugitive Jesus, banished from His own province, is declared king of the universal spiritual Israel by a small band of Galilean fishermen. It is He who will build His church on such secure foundations, that death[1] shall not be strong enough to prevail or gain the victory over it. The church's hope would not be swallowed up when Jesus should die on the cross. He would break the bonds of death and come forth from the grave. Hades would not be able to prevail by keeping Him imprisoned. He would presently reveal them this truth more clearly.[2] As the risen Lord, He would have in His possession the keys of death and Hades.[3] His people need not fear Hades because He holds the keys. There would never be a time when death would swallow up His church. It was to be perpetual in human history.

Jesus adds another momentous declaration, addressed to Peter as the representative and spokesman of the twelve, which has been the occasion of endless controversy.

"I will give you the keys of the Realm of Heaven; whatsoever you prohibit[4] on earth will be prohibited[5] in heaven, whatsoever you permit on earth will be permitted in heaven" (Moffatt). Advocates of papal supremacy insist on the primacy of Peter here and the power of Peter to pass on this supposed sovereignty to others. But this is all quite beside the mark (Robertson).[6] The power of the keys given to Peter belongs to every disciple of Jesus. All are stewards (oikonomoi) of the teachings of Jesus and gospel of the kingdom. What a gigantic system of spiritual despotism and blasphemous assumption has been built on these two sentences about the rock and the keys! But neither the "arrogancies of sacerdotalism, nor the disgraceful abuses of the confessional, nor the imaginary power absolving from oaths, nor the ambitious assumption of a right to crush and control civil power, nor the extravagant usurpation of infallibility in wielding the dangerous weapons of anathema and excommunication, nor the colossal tyrannies of Popedom and the detestable cruelties of the Inquisition," and all in the name of the church, have been able to prevail against the true spiritual "assembly" founded by Christ.[7] In the use of the keys, Peter is only *primus enter pares*, and not the sole or principal agent. Neither Peter nor the other apostles understood that he was receiving the supreme authority.[8] Peter was to follow the teachings of Jesus as his standard. All of the disciples would have the same prerogative of binding or loosing here given to Peter.[9] The keys

1 Death is called the gates of Hades (Greek) or Sheol (Hebrew).
2 Matt. 16:21.   3 Rev. 1:18; 3:7.   4 To "bind" in Rabbinical language is to "forbid" to "loose" is to "permit."
5 Future perfect indicative, periphrastic form, a state of completion.
6 Word Pictures.   7 Cf Farrar's Life of Christ.   8 Matt. 18:1; 20:21.
9 Matthew 18:18.

of the kingdom are the conditions of entrance into the kingdom, revealed in the teachings of Jesus. The disciples all alike have the privilege and prerogative of proclaiming these conditions. There was no such power given to Peter here as the Romish priest claims for himself in the power of absolution. Jesus did declare here that Peter had the prerogative of laying down the conditions of salvation in accord with His teachings and that the approval and sanction of heaven would be upon what he did thus bind or loose. The terms "bind" and "loose" in Rabbinical writings signify to interpret and apply the law and traditions on any subject with strictness or laxity, and hence in general to "forbid" or "allow."[1] Rabbis of the school of Hillel "loosed" many things that the school of Shammai "bound". Paul loosed the Gentile Christians who were being bound by the Judaizers.[2] He did so by applying the principles of Jesus to the local situation. Such is the proper function of every disciple of Christ, especially of the preacher or worker in the public teaching of the word. The sanction of heaven rests upon all work done under the direction of the Holy Spirit and in accord with the teachings of Jesus, whether in the proclamation of the conditions of salvation, in indoctrination, or in the discipline of the church.

Jesus sharply charged[3] the disciples that they should tell no man that He was the Messiah. The declaration of such a fact would be taken by the people in a political sense. They were to follow the same plan He had followed with them, and let the impact of His life and teachings, and their own, reenforced by the events of His sufferings, sacrificial death, and resurrection out just ahead, convince the world. About these things He would presently give them more explicit revelations. He was grateful and happy with their confession. They had the keys of the knowledge of the profound mysteries of His divine nature, to use in unlocking the doors of entrance to the kingdom for all men. But for the present they were to remain silent.

3. Jesus clearly predicts His death and resurrection (Mark 8: 31-37; Matt. 16: 21-26; Luke 9: 22-25).

Jesus enters "from this time" upon a new epoch of His ministry. He is now definitely accepted as Messiah by a small group of thoroughly convinced disciples and Himself clearly acknowledges to them that He is the Messiah. Such a confession on His part might lead them to carry out erroneous notions about the Messiahship and precipitate a popular movement which would defeat His kingdom plans. He charged them strongly that His confession of

---

1 Broadus, Com. on Matt.   2 Acts 15.   3 Epetimasen, to admonish or charge sharply.

Messiahship should not be made known. For a time this fact must remain in the inner circle, concealed from the general public.

The time was ripe now for the revelation to the twelve, of the tragedy of His death, only a little more than six months ahead. There had been half-veiled intimations from the beginning of His ministry of this sad necessity. He had told Nicodemus that "the Son of man must be lifted up[1] like Moses lifted up the brazen serpent in the wilderness." He had spoken about "giving His flesh for the life of the world."[2] He foretold how the "children of the bride-chamber would fast when the bridegroom should be seized away.[3]" He had given as a sign of His authority, in enigmatic language, "the raising up in three days of the temple of His body when the Jews would have destroyed it.[4]" When the combined enemies had exacted a sign recently, He had referred to the previously given sign of Jonah, symbolizing not only His ministry of warning but His death and days in the grave.[5] None of these symbolic references had been fully understood by the disciples, who were yet filled with the current Jewish conceptions about the Messiah. But they had avowed their belief on Him and loyalty to Him, and were now prepared, if ever they would be, for the rude shock of the revelation of His impending death. They would need to learn with Him the fuller revelation of the character of that death and its meaning, as He would go on instructing them through the months ahead.[6]

"From this time" He begins[7] to reveal to them clearly and openly, in plain matter-of-fact statements, and no more in mere intimations, the fact of His approaching sufferings, death and resurrection. He had never referred to His death that He did not connect it up with His resurrection. It was necessary and safe for them now that He should speak in unmistakable terms on this dark subject. In the midst of the black cloud of His tragic death He placed the rainbow of His resurrection. But the disciples only saw the blackness of the clouds and not their silver lining.

Jesus revealed four things about the sad necessity that faced Him. There was a must[8] in His life which had to be met. First, He must leave in a little while for Jerusalem. It was impossible that a prophet should perish outside of that city, the murderess of the prophets. His ministry in Galilee was practically finished already. The ecclesiastics had succeeded in closing the doors of opportunity there. It remained to face them in their greatest stronghold, in the most public place, and in a heroically dramatic manner, surrender His life. Second, He must "suffer many things at the hands of the

1 Jno. 3:14. 2 John 6. 3 Matt. 9:15. 4 Jno. 2:19. 5 Matt.16:4.
6 Matt. 17:9, 22; 20:18; 26:2, 12, 31f. 7 Inceptive aorist.
8 Dei, it is necessary, a necessity.

elders, and chief priests, and scribes". It was entirely foreign to any conception of the Jews that their Messiah should suffer. He was to be a conquering king. Even the Hebrew Christians of a generation later stumbled over the sufferings of the Messiah.[1] Jesus only refers here to the "many things" He must suffer; later on He will draw the veil aside and show them clearly some of the many things:[2] how He would be mocked, scourged, and spat upon. It was sufficient for them to know now that He would be rejected after trial[3] and killed by the Jerusalem ecclesiastics, who had long since forced Him to withdraw from Judea and had dogged His steps in Galilee, until they paralyzed His work there also. "Gray-browed elders sitting in council would solemnly decide that He was worthy of death; high priests would utter oracles, that one man must die, that the whole nation perish not; scribes, learned in the law, would use their legal knowledge to invent plausible grounds for an accusation involving capital punishment."[4] The third thing was the plain, rude, shocking fact of His death. He must be killed. To them He spared for the time the revelation of the dread specter of the cross, which already cast its sinister shadow athwart His path. The fact of His death must be revealed first; its manner and the reason for it would be made known to them later, when they had in some measure recovered from the first terrible shock. Finally, it was fitting that the dark message of death should be relieved by the bright hope of the resurrection. It is a sad thing that the disciples did not catch that bright vision, though He stated definitely the time He would be in the tomb. He would be raised up on the third day.[5] These four things Jesus had to go over and over again[6] with the disciples, to try to get them to understand. Even then they but poorly comprehended.

The twelve were gravely disappointed. They could not understand how the Messiah might be subject to such treatment. Surely He had taken too gloomy a view of the situation and was too much depressed by the united opposition of the Pharisees and Sadducees. They found a ready spokesman of their thoughts and feelings in Peter, who had but now received such a warm expression of approval from Jesus for His whole-hearted confession and such an important responsibility in the leadership of the twelve. Peter plucking Jesus by the sleeve, took Him to one side to himself[7] apart and *began* to rebuke Him:

---

1 The letter to the Hebrews written to correct this error.   2 Mark 10:34.
3 Luke 9:22, Apodokimazo, to reject after trial.   4 Bruce, The Training of the Twelve.
5 ta trita hemerai, locative of point of time, on the third day, Matt. 16:21 same as "after three days" (Mark 8:31). It could not thus be on the fourth day.
6 Imperfect tense elalei shows that Jesus did it over and over.
7 Proslabomenos, aorist middle participle, taking him to himself.

"God have mercy on thee, Lord,"[1] he said, "this shall never be unto thee." Peter spoke as if he knew far better than Jesus what was best and would not let this happen. He would have had Jesus save Himself at any cost. This was exactly what Satan had suggested in the wilderness temptation, when he told Jesus to change the stones unto bread to satisfy His own hunger. Jesus was now called by Peter with the air of one who would give superior counsel. He is rebuked by Peter apart. But the lesson to Peter, for such a mistaken conception, was for all, and must be administered in the presence of the group.[2] It was a withering rebuke to all for their mistaken Messianic views.

Quick as a flash Jesus turned[3] upon him with a stinging rebuke. Peter had been presumptuous. Great as was his devotion to Jesus he had made a great blunder.

"Get behind me, Satan! Thou art a stone of stumbling unto me: because thou art not thinking the things that be of God but those that be of man." It grieved Jesus that the one who had made such a noble confession of faith should so soon reveal such absolute blindness as to the necessity of His following in the way of self-sacrifice. Peter had been honored by being called a foundation stone in the great spiritual temple of the church; Jesus now calls him a stone of stumbling for his Master.[4] He was taking the place of Satan, tempting Jesus as Satan had, to deviate from the right course. For his forwardness, presumption, and irreverent attitude he gained for himself the opprobrious epithet of Satan. He had sinned against the purposes of God, and in seeking to dissuade Jesus from the way of the cross, unconsciously or through ignorant presumption delivered himself into the hands of Satan to be used by him. He would not forget this experience in the years ahead, when he should come to understand what a temptation he had brought to his Master, whom he loved and whom he had just confessed to be the Messiah and Son of God. This rebuke was deserved. He had placed himself on the side of the great *Adversary*, thinking things after the manner of the current thought of men and not the things of God. In Peter the banished tempter had once more returned (Plummer) because his outlook was not God's but man's (Moffatt). Jesus reduced him, who had presumed to dictate the course of the Messiah, to his right level and left him squelched and silent. He had before given Peter the place of leadership and honor; now he orders him to the rear, humiliated in dishonor. Peter's newly won honors had made him too proud and his pride

---

1 Probably a colloquialism. cf. Wetstein.
2 Mark 8:33, a characteristically Marcan descriptive touch and noted especially by Peter in contrast to his silence on the subject of Jesus' previous commendation.
3 Second aorist passive participle, quick ingressive action (Robertson)
4 Objective genitive, a stumbling stone for Jesus.

and self-confidence brought him to disgrace.

Having rebuked the unspiritual affection and ignorant loyalty of Peter, Jesus called to Himself[1] the multitude with the disciples. Mark notes the unexpected presence of the multitude in this isolated district. Jesus had separated Himself from the disciples and the crowd for meditation and prayer doubtless for a season, and now calls them to Himself, that He might teach them the principle that cross-bearing was the fundamental law of discipleship. The essence of all highest duty, the meaning of all truest life, is found in the law of self-sacrifice.[2] Jesus states this law in words which have sunk into the consciences of mankind:

"If any man would come after me, let him deny himself and take up his cross daily, and follow me." The disciples had received the revelation of a fact hard to understand and accept; that Jesus, whom they had confessed to be the Messiah and the Son of God, must suffer and die. This brought great confusion to their thought and difficulty to their understanding. Why should Jesus, whose character was beyond reproach, and who admitted that He was the Messiah and Son of God, suffer and die? Such an idea was incompatible and impossible to reconcile with all their previous conceptions. But now they are to learn another lesson which would be equally difficult for them and all mankind to accept. The disciple must also bear his cross day by day. Readiness to bear his cross was to be the condition of discipleship. In the law of discipleship the Master enumerated three essential things: first the disciple must deny himself. To say no to himself[3] is a difficult thing for anyone to do. Then he must pick up his cross at once.[4] The disciples understood what the cross meant. Hundreds of Jews had been crucified by foreign rulers in their times. The cross was for them a symbol of suffering and shame. The other condition was that the disciple must begin and keep on following[5] Jesus in character and conduct. Jesus assigns next three fundamental reasons for this philosophy of the life of the disciple. Each reason is introduced by "For". First, "for whosoever may wish to save his life shall lose it and whosoever may (at any time) lose his life for my sake and the gospel's the same shall find and save it." In this paradox the word "life" or "soul" is used in two senses as also the words "save" and "lose". The one who wishes to save his natural life and worldly well-being at the cost of spiritual things, shall lose his eternal life. On the contrary, one who gives up a life of worldliness, the lower life of animal happiness, for the sake

1 Present middle particle. He had a purpose of peculiar interest to Himself in calling them.
2 Farrar, Life of Christ.
3 Ingressive first aorist middle imperative, reenforced by the reflexive.   4 Aorist tense
5 Present middle imperative, linear action.

of Christ and his gospel, will himself find and save the higher
spiritual life. Righteousness, godliness, faith, love, patience, meekness, are the price many pay for worldly enjoyment.[1] The second
reason assigned was: "For what shall a man be profited if he gain[2]
the whole world and lose his own life, self, or soul? Or what should
a man give in exchange[3] for his self, life, or soul?" The whole world
would have no value to a lost soul. But there are many who, like
Judas, sell their souls for thirty pieces of silver or less. A man
must give or surrender his life, and nothing less, to God; no
antallagma is possible (McNeile). The wisdom of Sirach says:
"There is no *exchange* for a faithful friend (6:15). There is no
exchange for a well-instructed soul.[4]" The devil said: "Skin for
skin all that a man hath will he give for his life" (Job); but he
was mistaken. A man's eternal life is truly worth more than all
else to him. It is interesting to note how the three evangelists here
use the words life, soul, self, or himself interchangeably. All of a
man's life, whether physical, intellectual, or more properly spiritual,
is wrapped up in his self or soul.

4. The coming of the Son of Man in that generation (Mark 8:39-
9:1; Matt. 16: 27, 28; Luke 9: 26,27).

Jesus assigns as a third and final reason for His philosophy of
the life of discipleship,—that the Son of Man is to have the final
victory.[5] There is reality in the kingdom, for which the disciple is
called on to suffer. The Son of Man was to endure the shame of
the cross for the disciples soon. They in turn are called upon to
bear their crosses and not be ashamed of Him and His gospel. Paul,
even before the proud Romans, was not ashamed of the good news
of the crucified Messiah of the Jews nor did he refuse to stand in
Mars Hill and be laughed to scorn on His account. The individual
disciple has, laid out before him as one of the motives for
his conduct, the reward of faithfulness and loyalty to Him in the
present life. Virtue is virtue's own reward but the reward of honor
for loyalty is yet a real motive in human conduct. Every disciple's
reward will be according to his deeds. A fundamental principle in
the life of the disciples, as well as in future judgment, is that the
attitude of Christ in the present and final evaluation of the disciple's life must be based on the present conduct and attitude of
the disciple toward his Lord. If he is ashamed to endure for Him
the suffering and opprobrium of the cross now,[6] Christ will be
ashamed[7] of him when He comes in the glory of the Father with
His holy angels in the second advent. But some of those who were

1 Third general conditional laying down the general rule.
2 Aorist subjunctive, punctiliar action.
3 Antallagma exchange, the soul has no market price.
4 Quoted from Robertson's Word Pictures. 5 Robertson's Word Pictures (Matt. 16:28).
5 First aorist passive subjunctive in condition of third class.
7 First future passive indicative of verb.

standing there would not taste death until they should see the Son
of Man coming in His kingdom with power, and that kingdom
was coming to stay.[1] The disciples would see in just a few days
the glory of the kingdom power in the transfiguration. With the
crucifixion came an enlargement of the power and glory of the
kingdom of Christ. The majesty of His sacrifice made a great
light which flared up from Calvary and sent out its beams through
the darkness of the world afar and down through the centuries to
follow. The resurrection also would demonstrate the power of the
kingdom over the grave. Pentecost would illustrate the power of
the kingdom over the hearts and consciences of men, and among
them some of those who had slain the Lord of glory. Within another generation the hand of retributive judgment would fall upon
the city of Jerusalem and the Jewish nation, when Titus with the
Roman army should come.[2] This providentially lifted the Messianic
reign to a new stage.[3] Jesus had been coming in judgment and
glory down through the centuries and will have the final victory
when He appears upon the clouds in His second advent for the final
judgment. This was probably the first distinct intimation of His
second coming. It was fitting that this great fact should be revealed at this time.

1 Perfect active participle, completed action, already come. (Mark 9:1).
2 This was in 70 A. D., less than forty years later.   3 Broadus, Com. on Matt. 16:28.

CHAPTER XX
THE TRANSFIGURATION
(Harm. §§ 85-86)

The announcement of Jesus that He was to be rejected by the religious and civil authorities and die in Jerusalem soon, to rise after three days, was incomprehensible to the apostles. They were perplexed and confused in their thinking, unable to fathom the mystery of this confessed Messiah. He had opened a door to the understanding of the secret of His atoning death in declaring another hard fact, that the disciple also must live a life of self-sacrifice, taking up his cross daily and following in a life of self-abnegation, such as the Master had demonstrated. That was more easily understood than the infinite condescension of the Messiah and Son of God to a lowly life and ignominious and violent death.

The transfiguration fitted exactly into the progressive plan of instruction for the disciples, just at this time. They were discouraged. He had announced that if they should lay down their lives for Him, they would find and save them unto life eternal; but what did He mean by this paradox? He foretold His resurrection on the third day; but this did not accord with their Jewish theology.[1] Some of the Rabbis said Israel alone would rise; others that the resurrection would include the heathen also, who had kept the seven commandments given to the sons of Noah; others still that all the heathen outside of the Holy Land would be raised, but only to shame and everlasting contempt before Israel; and yet others said that neither the Samaritans nor the great mass of their own nation who did not observe the precepts of the Rabbis, would have a part in the resurrection.[2] Furthermore they had been trained to believe, that at the coming of the Messiah all Israel would be raised immediately. It was hard for them to discard all the traditional theology and penetrate at once into the thought of Jesus, new and strange to them, that "the Messiah was to be raised from the dead on the third day." Another promise He had added: that He would return to them briefly with victory. How could this be? So the Transfiguration must bring to them the testimony of the redeemed host of heaven—of just men made perfect—represented both by the great founder Moses and the outstanding prophetic defender of the old Jewish economy, Elijah, as to the *exodus* of the Messiah-Leader through sufferings and death. It was to be to them also a presage of the resurrection of Jesus, and

---

1 Geikie's Life of Christ, p. 240.   2 Eisenmenger, Vol. II, pp. 904-907, (Matt. 11:4)

by implication, of their own life beyond the tomb. It was to open
up their understanding as to the glorious victory of the kingdom
through the atoning death, resurrection and final advent of the
Messiah.

But it was to mean much to Jesus also, as He faced the closing
months of intense struggle against the antagonisms of His enemies,
which would, He fully knew, bring Him to the inevitable cross.
After the experience on the holy mount, He could calmly face the
final issue.

1. The transfiguration of Jesus on a mountain, probably Hermon,
near Cesarea-Philippi (Mark 9:2-8; Matt. 17:1-8; Luke 9:28-36).

During the six or eight days which followed the first lesson on
the principle of the cross,[1] Jesus went over and over that lesson
with the disciples, seeking to get them to understand it. They were
ill-prepared to receive it and unwilling to accept it. Wisely, now,
Jesus took the three most spiritual of the twelve, Peter, James,
and John, who had been with Him in the upper chamber of the
home of Jairus, when He called back the life of the little maid,[2]
and would be with Him in Gethsemane[3] later, and brings them[4] up
into a lofty mountain apart by themselves. Evidently there was
some purpose in withdrawing with this smaller group of the most
favored and beloved disciples, aside from the object of prayer.
That was the initial and preparatory purpose,[5] but Jesus evidently
had some further special object in view and was expectant.

The traditional site of the transfiguration according to the Greek
church was Tabor, where they celebrate annually, on the sixth
of August, the Feast of the Transfiguration, the *Thaborium*. But
this is an impossible fancy, since Tabor is almost fifty miles from
Caesarea-Philippi and Jesus was at this time avoiding Galilee. The
summit of this mount was also occupied by a fort and was no fit
place for such a scene. Furthermore, Mark states that Jesus did not
"pass through Galilee"—in which Mount Tabor is situated—until
later.[6] The most probable site of this wonderful event was one of
the lower spurs of snow-clad Hermon, visible from all parts of
the land as far south as the Dead Sea. There could be no more
suitable place in all Palestine than the accessible slopes of this
famous mountain, cool and fresh with the evening breezes from the
snow-clad heights above, where solitude reigned, and one of the
grandest scenes of all nature and history lay out visibly before
them.

1 Mark 8:31-37; Matt. 16:21-26; Luke 9:22-25.   2 Mark 5:37.   3 Matt. 26:37
4 Historic present of vivid description.
5 Aorist middle infinitive, prosenxastai, expressing purpose.   6 Mark 9:30.

It was evening when they ascended.[1] At this hour the whole
land to the south, bathed in the slanting rays of the westering sun,
presents a picture of incomparable beauty. Stopping to rest at
intervals, the little group, wrapped in thoughts too deep for utterance, would look down upon the province of Galilee, dotted with
its many towns and villages, and recall the experiences of the
busy weeks of the campaign and the sad hour of withdrawal,
when persecuted and driven by their enemies; or look away to
the greater distance to Jerusalem, where as He said He must soon
suffer and die. As the sun sank into the great sea[2] and dusk stole
silently about them, they turned their thoughts more immediately
upon the great object of their visit here and entered into a period
of prayer. Jesus ever prayed at the seasons of greater crisis in
His ministry.

The season of prayer was a long one. The burden of the
world's sin was heavy on the Master's heart. Doubtless He prayed
for nerve to drink the bitter cup of suffering and death just before Him. He must have prayed for faith and patience and such
manifestation of the Father's approval as would give Him assurance.
He was also solicitous for the better understanding on the part of
His apostles of the mystery of His death and resurrection. He Himself was already entering the penumbra of Calvary's eclipse and
needed the strengthening power of heavenly communion; but the
apostles were His chief concern. They were weary with the day's
work and the ascent of the mountain and were weighed down[3]
with sleep. Wrapping their *abbas* (outer garments) about them,
they sank upon the carpet of grass; and fanned by the gentle
breeze brushing the heights, fell into a profound slumber.

At midnight He prayed in Gethsemane alone; at midnight,
now, on Hermon's heights He prays; and as He prays His soul rises
above all earth's sorrows and misery into the sphere of heavenly
radiance. While He was praying[4] "the appearance of his face became different." Matthew says: "He was transfigured[5] before them,
his face did shine as the sun, and his garments became white as the
light." Mark says: "His garments became exceeding white, whiter
than any wool-carder on earth is able to whiten them." Luke adds:
"And his garment was white radiant."[6] There was a kind of efful-
gence—a celestial radiance—shining out over all. The Divinity
within broke through the veil of the flesh and shone out, until
His very raiment kindled to the dazzling brightness of the light.

1 Luke 9:32, 37; cf. 6:12.   2 The Mediterranean.
3 Periphrastic past perfect of Bareo, late form of baruno, indicating state in which
    they were and continued to be (cf. Gethsemane).
4 Articular infinitive, en toi proseuchesthai, in the locative case indicating the point of
    time when the transfiguration took place.
5 Metemorphothe, aorist passive, a change of form, used by Paul (Rom. 12:2) of an
    inner change.
6 Exastrapton, present active participle from astrapto, flash out, and ex,out.

Roused by the splendour the disciples were filled with awe, and when they were wide awake[1] they saw His glory, and there appeared two men, Moses and Elijah, who stood talking together with Him. The subject of their continued[2] conversation in this aureole of glory, was His decease or departure[3] which He was about to accomplish at Jerusalem. Here were two representatives of the old economy: Moses its founder, representing the Law, who led the people out in the *exodus* from the bondage of Egypt; and Elijah its best known prophet, who was taken up to heaven in a chariot of fire, and would return—according to popular tradition—as the forerunner of the new dispensation. Jesus was to lead His people out in a new exodus from the bondage of sin, and be the prophet of the new dispensation, calling the people to repentance and new life for God. He was to accomplish this through His atoning death. Heaven sent these dignitaries of the Old Economy to testify to the New and its Founder and strengthen Him for the task.

The disciples were bewildered and over-awed. As the vision began to fade and the majestic visitants were separating themselves[4] from Him to depart, Peter, anxious to detain them, amazed, filled with exceeding great fear as were the others,[5] and not understanding really what he was saying,[6] exclaimed:

"Master, it is best[7] for us to be here. Let us make three tabernacles, one for Thee, one for Moses, and one for Elias." He volunteered his services to make these little booths or tabernacles, such as the Jews would construct now in a few days at the Feast of Tabernacles in Jerusalem. Perhaps Peter had mistaken the import of the conversation about the *exodus*. Could they not commemorate the exodus here on Mount Hermon, with the excellent presence of these two heavenly visitors? It would be far better than to go to perilous Jerusalem. Truly Peter did not know what to say and in child-like simplicity offers this suggestion, hoping to lengthen out the delight of this hour. But he received no answer to this wild suggestion of dreamy words,[8] however generous his purpose. Peter's implication was still in line with his rebuke of Jesus a few days before. Why descend to the plain and resume the conflict? Why go to Jerusalem and die? Would it not be better to remain on the mount in this heavenly fellowship?

Even as he was speaking a white cloud began[9] to over-shadow them[10] and kept on until it completely covered them up.

1 Diagregoresantes, aorist active participle.
2 Imperfect active indicative, elegon, signifying a continued action.
3 Exodou, exodus or departure from earth to heaven.
4 En with the articular infinitive in a temporal clause.   5 Mark 9:6.
6 Luke 9:33.   7 Superlative sense of kalon, good, beautiful.
8 Farrar, Life of Christ.   9 Ingressive aorist tense.   10 Nestle's reading, autous.

The disciples began to be afraid[1] as they entered into the cloud. God had come down on Sinai in a thick cloud of darkness. Doubtless they remembered that and were expectant and filled with awe. Suddenly a voice came out of the midst of the cloud: "This is my chosen and beloved Son in whom I am well pleased: hear ye him."

That awful voice had been heard before at the baptism, when practically the same words were addressed to Jesus; they would be heard in yet different form by the people later in Jerusalem just before His death. When the disciples heard the voice they fell on their faces in awe and were exceedingly afraid. So, they were to "hear" His words of awful prediction about His death just ahead, and His message about the resurrection of the Messiah and future return in glorious victory. Still they could not understand what these words might mean. Peter remembered vividly this voice years afterwards, when he wrote his second Epistle.[2] He had come to understand fully the import of the voice then. "We were eyewitnesses" says he, "of his Majesty. For he received from God the Father honour and glory, when there came *such a voice* to him from the excellent glory, 'This is my beloved Son in whom I am well pleased; hear ye him.' And this voice which came from heaven, we heard, when we were with him in the holy mount." The brightness of this vision had remained with Peter.[3] Three things stand out in the vision: the personal glorification of Jesus, the appearance of the two heavenly ministrants, and the theophony and divine voice.[4]

For Jesus the transfiguration brought new strength to faith and added patience, through a foretaste of the glory He should experience after His passion. It was a great solace also to His already broken heart, to be honored while yet in the flesh with the visit of the greatest leaders of ancient Israel who expressed to Him the admiring approval of the heavenly host of the redeemed, upon the manner and purpose of His *exodus* through vicarious sufferings and death soon to be accomplished. But to Jesus the greatest help of all in the event, came in the true approving voice of the Father, who expressed His good pleasure in the Son and confirmed the faith of the disciples and all mankind in His divinity and His plan to redeem the race.

The disciples were taught by the transfiguration that vicarious sufferings and death were not incompatible with the Old Testament conception of the spiritual Messiah. The current Jewish conception was wrong and the new interpretation of the prophecy by Jesus was right. They were confirmed by the voice from heaven in their

---

1 Ingressive first aorist passive, began to be afraid.   2 II Peter 1:17, 18.
3 Geikie, Life of Christ.   4 Godet quoted in Broadus, Com., Matthew 17:2-5.

confession of Jesus as the Messiah and Son of God.[1] This belief in His divinity would give tremendous conviction and impulse to their ministry. They were prepared by the admonition of the voice to hear His further explanations on the necessity and manner of His sufferings and death. They would thus gradually come to know the purpose and plan of Jesus in the redemption of mankind. The vision of His temporary glory also brought to them new light on His resurrection and return in glory about which He had spoken. Jesus had given them His instruction as to His divine nature and the necessity of His vicarious death; heaven's testimony is now added in confirmation of His teaching. According to Moses and Elijah His exodus was to be a splendid triumph, and then the Father's approval was on it.

They were lying prostrate on their faces filled with exceeding great fear, when Jesus came and touched them and said, "Arise and do not be afraid." When they lifted up their eyes they found themselves alone with Jesus. How wonderful it all was.

2. The discussion about the resurrection and question about Elijah in the descent from the mount (Mark 9:9-13; Matt. 17:9-13; Luke 9:36).

Day dawned and the first rays of the morning sun kissed the snow-capped peak of Hermon into a dazzling brightness. It was a day of new hope for Jesus and for the disciples. As they descended the hill to rejoin their companions, their first eager impulse would be to break to them the wonderful news of the night's vision; but Jesus charged them over and over[2] to tell no man about the vision until[3] He should rise from the dead. He hoped that this night's experiences would greatly strengthen them for the things out ahead and especially clarify their understanding of the resurrection. They obeyed His wishes even from that hour[4] and kept silent. They went on discussing on the way among themselves about what the rising from the dead should mean.[5] The previous allusion[6] of Jesus to that subject seems to have made little impression on them.

Another serious question arose in their minds about Elijah. They saw Elijah and Moses with Jesus. But the Scribes had taught that Elijah was to come first and restore all things before the Messiah should appear. But Jesus the Messiah had come first. They could not reconcile these wonderful facts of their experience with the traditional theology of the Jews. Such is the hold of traditional beliefs on mankind, whether true or false. Had not the Scribes,

1 II Pet. 1:17, 18.   2 Imperfect indicative signifying a repetition of the action.
3 Conjunction with the subjunctive for future event.   4 Ingressive aorist, Luke 9:36.
5 Mark 9:10.   6 Mark 8:31.

the Jewish theological authorities, the prophecy of Malachi in their favor?[1]

The Rabbis said Elias was to come three days before the Messiah.[2] Jesus was familiar with this tradition which said, that Elias would come and stand on the hills of Israel and weep and lament over the desolated land till his voice should be heard through the world and then cry: "Peace and blessing come into the world! Salvation cometh!" After this, he would gather all the scattered sons of Jacob and *restore all things in Israel* as in ancient times.[3] Elias was to turn the hearts of all Israel to the Messiah, the disciples thought. How could they reconcile the present situation of Jesus, rejected by the leaders of Israel already and deserted largely by the people, with this traditional belief?

They bring the question to Jesus and eagerly[4] explain to Him:

"The Scribes say that Elijah must first come. Why then did the Scribes say this, seeing that Israel is turned away and Elias came after the Messiah?"

Jesus replied: "You are right in thinking that Elias must first come before me. It is also true that according to Malachi he is to restore all things. But let me ask you how it stands written,[5] that the Son of Man, the Messiah, should suffer many things and be set at naught?" Doubtless He referred them to the fifty-third chapter of Isaiah, in confirmation of the treatment He was receiving at the hands of the Pharisees and Sadducees. He now clearly states the facts about the coming Elias:

"But I say unto you that Elias has already come, and they did not recognize[6] him but they did unto him as their hearts wished." Jesus had alluded to the fact, when the committee came from John,[7] that John was "the Elias that should come." The disciples had not understood the passing reference in the eulogy pronounced on the great prophet that day. "Elias had to suffer," He said, "even as the Son of Man at their hands." They saw it clearly at last. He was talking of John the Baptist, who was beheaded. Again the principle of vicarious suffering is driven home on them in the example of John, making it more possible for them to believe His prediction about His own death. Was not John a holy prophet? — and did he not die?

1 Mal. 4:5, 6.   2 Eisenminger, Vol. II, p. 696, 697.   3 Geikie, Life of Christ.
4 Imperfect indicative, descriptive of their eager repeated action.
5 Perfect indicative middle, it stands written.
6 Epegnosan, second aorist active indicative, recognize.   7 Matt. 11:14.

CHAPTER XXI
THE RETURN TO CAPERNAUM
(Harm. §§ 87-95)

The period of comparative isolation was now drawing to a close. Jesus had led His apostles, through the experiences of nearly six months, to a more intimate understanding of His own nature and the true character of His kingdom. He had brought them to a confession of their faith in His Messiahship and divinity and then revealed to them the impending tragedy of His death, explaining its necessity on the principle of vicarious suffering, through which He was to redeem the race. They had been led to understand that the same principle was basic in the life of the disciple. Finally, He had taken the three best equipped and most spiritual of the twelve up on the mountain with Him, that they might receive the testimony of heaven as to the right character of His plan for leading out the race in the exodus from sin through His sacrificial death. They must serve as witnesses of these things after His death and resurrection. He now returns through Galilee privately for a brief stay in Capernaum before He should go to Judea for His last ministry and final struggle in Jerusalem.

1. Jesus heals the demoniac boy whom the disciples could not heal (Mark 9:14-29; Matt. 17:14-20; Luke 9:37-43).

Before Jesus and the three favored apostles who had been with Him during the night on the mount had reached the other nine, who had probably spent the night in a village not far from the foot of Hermon, news had gotten abroad that the Teacher was in the neighborhood.

A distressed father had brought his only son to Jesus, that He might "look upon him" and cure him. The nine apostles, who had been commissioned to perform similar miracles in the Galilean campaign, undertook in the absence of the Master to cast out the demon from the boy, and had failed.

When Jesus and the three came to where the nine were, they "saw a great multitude about them and the Scribes arguing[1] with the disciples." It was impossible for the enemies of Jesus, who had closed the doors to His ministry in Judea and Galilee, to leave Him alone. They dogged His steps everywhere and a few of their emissaries were present now, stirring up the local rabbis and Jews against Him. They had taken advantage of the absence of Jesus in the early morning and made use of the occasion of the failure of the nine to cast out the demon to ridicule them and malign the

1 Sunzatountas pros autous, exchanging questions and discussions.

character of both the Teacher and His disciples. They were taunt-
ing the nine with questions and discussions when Jesus suddenly
appeared in their midst. He came so opportunely, just in the nick
of time, that they were all thunderstruck.[1] The disciples were
glad of His sudden appearance, and with others who were curious
to see what Jesus would do, running to Him, began to welcome
Him.[2]

Jesus saw the embarrassment of the nine and took their defense: "Why are you disputing with them?" He sternly asked the
Scribes. There was something so terrible in His look as He faced
these enemies, that they were abashed and did not reply. Nor did
the nine disciples — conscious of their failure — give an explanation.

But at this juncture, the disappointed father of the afflicted
boy came out of the crowd, and kneeling in humility before the
Teacher, cried out his grief and disappointment. "Master, I beseech thee to look upon my son,[3] have mercy upon him,[4] for I
brought him unto thee;[5] he is epileptic[6] and suffereth grievously.[7]
He has a dumb spirit. I asked thy disciples that they should cast
it out and they were not able."

He then detailed the symptoms dramatically, saying: "Wherever it seizes him (in a fit), it dashes him down in rending con-
vulsions, and when it tears him he foams at the mouth[8] and grinds
his teeth,[9] and —,Teacher, he is wasting away! His body is withering up with this malady. It hardly ever leaves him,[10] and he is
all bruised up from falling. Worst of all, ofttimes he falls into the
fire and into the water. I begged your disciples to cast it out, but -
though they were willing — they could not do it."[11]

Such a dramatic recital of distressing symptoms in the tones of
disappointment at the failure of the disciples, who had formerly
cured so many, and despair lest there should be no further hope,
deeply touched the Lord. He had been a long time with the disciples, patiently teaching them the secrets of power and success
in such cases. His mighty acts had been witnessed by the people
far and wide in the land during more than two years. Both the
disciples and the people should have learned to trust in Him before
this.

"O faithless and perverse generation," He exclaimed, "how
long shall I be with you, how long bear with you?" Jesus was indignant with the crooked brood of malicious and captious Scribes;

---

1 Exethambetheson, ingressive aorist, they suddenly began to feel amazed, that He should
     not be seen and suddenly appear thus.
2 Imperfect middle indicative, they were personally glad to welcome Him.
3 Luke 9:38.   4 Matt. 17:15.   5 Mark 9:17.   6 Seteniazetai, moonstruck, lunatic,
     a disease which was thought to be aggravated by the changes of the moon.
7 Has it badly, literally.   8 Luke 9:39.   9 Mark 9:18.   10 Luke 9:39.   11 Luke 9:40.

but His soul was also weary with a generation of faithless or half-believing disciples and unbelieving multitudes of people. "Bring him to me," He added. They brought the boy at once.[1] The moment he saw Jesus, as he was coming, "the spirit tore him grievously and he fell down on the ground and wallowed, foaming at the mouth."[2] A sad spectacle it was! Jesus now takes the case in hand. The father's faith must be strengthened as well as that of the disciples. The people also must have time to draw near and see. "How long has he been in this condition?" Jesus inquired, addressing the father. The man's attention was thus attracted and his hope inspired by these calm words of one who approached the case as any human physician would do.

"Ever since he was a mere child," the father replied, catching a new glimpse of hope. "If thou canst do anything, have compassion on us." Thus, like the Syrophoencian woman, he identified himself with the son in his desperate situation. The disciples' failure had shaken his faith and almost left him in despair. But maybe the Teacher would be able to do something. The leper had said, "If thou wilt." He did not doubt the ability of Jesus but rather His willingness.[3] This man doubts whether He will be *stronger* than His disciples. Here again Jesus makes a play on the words.

As for the "If thou canst?"[4] answered Jesus, "All things are possible (canst) to the one who believes." The poor father had made the cure hinge on the ability of Jesus to cure; but Jesus returns the responsibility to him, making it depend on his faith. The unhappy father, recognizing that his faith was utterly weak, cried out desperately in words which have since been used to express the plea of many a struggling soul:

"Lord, I believe, help thou quickly[5] mine unbelief."

Jesus saw that the crowd was hurriedly gathering more and more. The people were anxious to see what the famous Healer would do. The Lord rebuked the unclean spirit, addressing him as a separate being from the boy, as He had done in other similar cases.

"Thou dumb and deaf Spirit, I command thee, come out of him and enter no more into him." There was a screech or wild cry and a fierce convulsion, and the child lay motionless and to all appearances, dead. Most of the bystanders thought that he was dead. But Jesus took him by the hand and raised him up and the boy stood up. All the people were greatly astonished at the easy victory of Jesus, when the nine had failed, and at the greatness

1 First aorist active.   2 Mark 9:20, 21.   3 Mark 1:40.
4 Durtata Cf. verb dunei which precedes, both from same root. Historic present, indicative linear action.   5 Aorist imperative.

of God. Jesus tenderly delivered the boy, soundly cured, into the arms of the glad father.

When He and His disciples came into the house, where the disciples had lodged the night before, they asked[1] Him:

"Why were we not able to cast him out?" They had cast out many demons in their campaign in Galilee, and wondered, seeking an explanation of the reason[2] for their failure. Jesus explained to them frankly the reason:

"Because of your little faith," He said. "If you have faith as a grain of mustard seed you shall say unto this mountain: 'Remove hence to yonder place' and it shall remove; and nothing shall be impossible unto you." Their failure was because of their unbelief. They dreaded lest they had lost the power He had given them when He sent them out on the campaign in Galilee.[3] They did not have the power to expel the demon. Why they "were not strong enough" was the question that perplexed them. The secret of the lack of power Jesus revealed a final lesson to them. "This kind can come out by nothing save by prayer," He explained. Some scribe wrote into the copies of the manuscripts the words "and by fasting." Though these words were not those of Jesus, the prayer that prevails is so intense at times as to remove all desire for food. Such intense prayer increases vital faith in Jesus, which is the secret of such power as removes mountains of difficulty.

Raphael's great painting of the Transfiguration may not be wholly true to the facts in representing as simultaneous the conflict of the nine at the foot of the hill and the glorious experience of the three with Jesus on the mountain-top; but it does immortalize the great truth of the contrast between peace, glory, and heavenly communion on the mountain heights with God, and the unbelief, confusion, agony, and suffering in the low plains of human life. In this case, on the mountain top was the harmony, gladness, fellowship, understanding, vision and inspiration of heaven; in the valley there was the discord, unbelief, defeat, shame, desolation, and despair of the earth. These disciples learned that they could not dwell always upon the mountain tops; but gaining understanding and inspiration there, must descend to the plain for the sacrificial service of humanity. Such was the lesson that Jesus taught by His immortal example.[4]

2. Returning privately through Galilee He again foretells His death and resurrection (Mark 9:30-32; Matt. 17:22-23; Luke 9:43-45).

It was no longer possible for Jesus to be alone with the twelve

---

1 Imperfect, questioned Him repeatedly.   2 Hoti, really means why here. Cf. Robertson Grammar, p. 730.
3 Chrysostom.   4 Farrar's Life of Christ and W. M. Taylor's, Miracles of Jesus.

in the region of Cesarea Philippi. The enemies had found out His retreat and were on hand to dog His steps at every turn. The multitudes learning of the cure of the deaf and dumb lunatic boy would soon make it impossible for Him to have privacy for the further instruction of the twelve. So He turns His steps once again toward the south, passing through the hills and valleys of Galilee, probably to the west of the Jordan.[1] He did not wish[2] that anyone should know them as they went but rather that the group should escape recognition, thus giving opportunity for Him to administer such further instruction as the disciples needed. On this brief return journey, He did reiterate[3] His teaching about His death and resurrection, adding a clearer statement than the previous allusion to His betrayal.[4] He declared that the betrayal was already going on now.[5] But the disciples continued[6] as dense as ever, not grasping the meaning of His declaration. They added to this a persistent timidity in being afraid to ask Him any question about it.[7] While all were wondering at the things He was doing[8] He commanded the disciples:

"Put[9] these teachings, about the death and resurrection, into your ears." He would impress these things deeply on their memories. But they ignored the word and it "continued to be hidden from them[10] in order that they might not perceive it." This was a self-inflicted judgment[11] on them, because of their dullness and unwillingness to accept the truth.[12] But they seem to have understood that He was going to die, and He said He was going to rise again. They did not understand how it could be; but they could not doubt that some dread tragedy was ahead of them. On this account they were exceedingly sorrowful.

3. Jesus the Messiah and Son of God pays the Temple-tax (Matt. 17:24-27).

It was Matthew, who had previously been a tax-collector, who records for us this interesting incident, giving us a glimpse into the private life of Jesus during the days of His last brief visit in Capernaum. It was doubtless in the home of Peter, where Jesus was accustomed to lodge, that the incident took place.

Jesus could not resist the temptation to return to the old haunts of the busiest days of His intense ministry, when

1 Matt. 17:22 Sustrefomenon.   2 Imperfect tense, he was acting on this impulse.
3 Edidasken gar—Imperfect of repeated teaching and with "for" giving the reason for the secrecy.   4 Jno. 6:70.   5 Present passive indicative of progressive action.
6 Imperfect tense of connected state of mind, agnooun to rhema.
7 Imperfect tense, ephobounto.   8 Imperfect of poieo.
9 Thesthe, second aorist imperative.
10 Periphrastic past perfect, expressing a continued state.
11 Negative of purpose with second aorist middle subjunctive, Luke 9:45.
12 Robertson, Word Pictures, Mark 9:32.

the multitudes crowded about Him to see many wonderful things and hang upon His gracious words. He had come to tacitly bid farewell — He knew — to these loved scenes, and to intimate friends who lived in these parts, before He should "set His face to go to Jerusalem."

His entrance to the town was not undetected by His enemies, who were alert to His every move. The local tax collectors, prompted doubtless by these enemies, with seeming but hypocritical politeness, approached Peter and not Jesus, and said:

"Does your teacher not pay the Temple-tax?" Something in their manner, coupled with the previous warning that Jesus was soon to suffer at the hands of the elders in Jerusalem, led Peter to suspect instantly some trap that might be laid for the Master. So he immediately replied in the affirmative without waiting to ask Jesus about it.

The Temple-tax was a small kind of "religious poll-tax" provided first by Moses for the erection of the Tabernacle. It was payable at first only at the census but after the Babylonian captivity was required annually of every Israelite over twenty years of age.[1] From the time of the Maccabees it was paid in half-shekels and after these coins became scarce, with the Roman didrachma — about thirty cents in our money but probably with a purchasing power six times as great. Peter knew on general principles that whatever was right in such a matter his Master would do; and so responded instantly and confidently. He would take full responsibility for the conduct of Jesus and so not allow any question to be raised. This small tax was due on the fifteenth of the month of Adar (March), now nearly six months overdue for Jesus and Peter, owing to their protracted absence from Capernaum. It was not a compulsory tax, however, like that collected by the publicans for the government. "The tax was like a voluntary church-rate; no one could be compelled to pay" (Plummer).[2] Originally the Mishna laid it down that the goods of those who had not paid might be detained after the twenty-fifth of Adar; but it is scarcely credible that this obtained at the time of Christ, especially in Galilee. It had to be deposited in the (three) chests of an inner chamber of the temple in Jewish shekels, and must be changed by the money-changers in the Temple from Roman and other foreign coins into Jewish shekels, as it was, with an annual graft of over two hundred thousand dollars. The tax itself constituted a vast treasure in the Temple, a strong temptation to lawless greed and enticement to foreign rulers, and one of the chief causes of the great war that finally destroyed the city and Temple.[3] The yearly receipts of this tax were destined to pay for the animals for the

1 Ex. 30:11-16. 2 Geikie, Life of Christ. 3 Josephus, Bell. Jud. 2:3, 14, 15.

general sacrifices, pay the Rabbis, inspectors of sacrifices, copyists, bakers, women who washed the Temple linen, water and other supplies, and for repairs of the Temple.

It is possible and quite probable that the prompt appearance of the tax-collectors was due to a plan of the alert enemies, to involve Jesus and Peter in a breach of a recognized obligation, or to reveal if He were really following the idea of the Zealot, Judas of Galilee, who would not pay the Temple-tax so long as the Holy City was polluted by the Romans. The form of question they used did not call for an affirmative answer,[1] such as they received from Peter, but rather implied doubt.

When Peter came into the house to speak to Jesus, he seems to have hesitated, embarrassed. He did not like to speak to the Master about so trivial a matter. Jesus anticipated the whole problem.

"What thinkest thou, Simon," He said, using the name that reverted to Peter's beginning days of immaturity. Peter was forgetting again that Jesus was the Son of God.

"The kings of the earth," continued Jesus, "from whom do they receive toll or tribute — direct and indirect taxes — from their own sons or from those of others?" Obviously a king does not receive taxes for the maintenance of his palace from his own children.

"From those of others," promptly replied Peter.

"Therefore," said Jesus, "the sons are exempt." By this simple parable, declaring the sons of the earthly king "free"[2] from the payment of taxes for the support of the king's palace, Jesus claims for himself the exemption from the Temple-tax, which was for the up-keep of "his Father's house" in Jerusalem. The implication of His claim was His sonship of God, which Peter had days before near Cesarea Philippi emphatically confessed, representing the thought of the twelve. After His clear acceptance from Peter and the others of the title Son of God, for Jesus to pay Temple-tax without explanation would be contradictory and cause misapprehension;[3] to pay it in the ordinary way would be to acknowledge that He was a mere subject of the kingdom.[4]

On the contrary, if He should refuse to pay it, people would think He was objecting to what all the Jews considered a religious obligation, to be met cheerfully.

"But lest we cause them to stumble," He said, "go thou to the Sea and cast a hook, and take up the fish that first cometh up;

1 The negative me indicates an affirmative answer. Their question looked to assent, since Jesus had not paid and the tax was overdue.
2 Eleutheroi, free or exempt.   3 Edersheim, Life and Times of Jesus.
4 This tax was redemption money for the ransom of each man's soul. How could the Redeemer of all men pay ransom money?

and when thou hast opened its mouth, thou shalt find a shekel: that take and give unto them for me and thee." Jesus asserted that He had the right to be exempt from the Temple-tax; but in order that He and the disciples might not be misjudged and cause some to stumble by giving the wrong impression, He preferred to waive His rights.

He did not resort to a miracle to pay this tax because of the depleted treasury of the apostolic group, as some have assumed.[1] Nor did He make use of His supernatural power for mere personal ends, contrary to His action in the first temptation in the Judean desert. This miracle which seemed not to be a necessity, was so designed as to once again impress His disciples that He was the Son of God and should be so treated by men. By the miracle, Jesus demonstrated His universal foreknowledge and supremacy over all nature. No lesson could have been better suited to Peter and the other disciples at this time.

Paulus and other critics have tried to laugh this miracle out of court by calling it "a miracle for half-a-crown." Even others, who defend it, admit that it does not fall under the same category as the other miracles.[2] But it was in every sense a genuine miracle, and not a mere resort by Peter, at the suggestion of Jesus, to use "his long disused craft," to get by an hour's work enough fish which sold in the market would pay their tax. The narrative of this miracle is entirely different in nature from the Rabbinical story of Joseph the Jew, famed for his strict observance of the Sabbath, whose wealthy neighbor — warned by fortune-tellers that Joseph was after his property — sold all and purchased one great pearl. Taking a ship, to escape by sea, the pearl was lost overboard, and swallowed by a fish, which afterwards being caught and sold in the market, Joseph bought.[3] This miracle of foreknowledge is not unlike the one when the seven "toiled all night and caught nothing, but casting on the right side at the bidding of Jesus, enclosed a multitude of fishes."[4] The effort of Rationalism to get rid of the miraculous by putting the non-miraculous meaning into the words of the narrative is vain.[5] The purpose of the miracle was to teach the deity of Christ. That is why it was so displeasing to Strauss and other critics. The narrative, however brief, furnishes a fine example of the consummate wisdom of Jesus in dealing with the most commonplace problems of life, turning them to account for the work of His kingdom. It is better to waive our rights and submit to the wrong than to prejudice the cause in any way whatever.

1 David Smith, In the Days of His Flesh.   2 Farrar's Life of Christ.
3 David Smith, In the Days of His Flesh, cf. Wetstein on Luke 4:1.
4 Jno. 21.   5 Weiss (Robertson's Word Pictures).

4. Jesus teaches the ambitious disciples that the kingdom subjects must be childlike (Mark 9:33-37; Matt. 18:1-5; Luke 9:46-48).

On the return trip from the regions of Cesarea Philippi, the
disciples were discussing the experience of the previous days,
when some observation was made on the special privileges, once
again[1] accorded to Peter and the sons of Zebedee, in being chosen
by Jesus to go up into the mountain with Him. This led on to a
dispute[2] as to who was greatest anyway, and who would be
honored with the highest places in the kingdom, when Jesus should
establish it. They could not, in spite of all the recent teaching of
Jesus about His sufferings and death, get rid of their traditional beliefs about a messianic kingdom of materialistic character. The
expectation of some great development in a kind of messianic
kingdom stimulated in them ambitions which easily degenerated
into jealousies as to who should be greatest and occupy the highest places. The fact that Peter was to the front again in the
incident of the payment of the Temple-tax probably gave a new
impulse to this discussion. Jesus allowed the discussion to pass
without comment on the way though He was fully conscious of
what was going on in their minds.

After their arrival in Capernaum and the Temple-tax had been
provided for, as they were entering the house, probably of Peter,
the disciples brought up the subject which had occupied their attention on the way, but now in an impersonal form.

"Who, then, is greatest[3] in the kingdom of heaven?" they
asked. They had covered up from Jesus the fact that they were
discussing the subject jealously on the way. But He probes to the
heart of the question, grasping the situation, as ever, and administers a far-reaching lesson on humility as a requirement for
membership in the kingdom. Jesus was fully cognizant of the fact,
that the work of disciplining their temper, disposition, and will
was the most difficult phase of His work in training them.[4] First,
He asked them the direct question on entering the house:

"What were you arguing about on the way?" They recognized
that He had understood and so they maintained[5] a confused and
embarrassed silence. It was a sad fact, that they were concerned
chiefly about their own offices, in the political kingdom they were
expecting. They knew that their discussion on the road had centered around who among them was[6] greatest in the kingdom and
that Jesus was cognizant of the thoughts of their hearts.[7]

1 They were admitted with Jesus and the parents into the death chamber when Jesus raised
   the little daughter of Jairus from the dead.
2 Dialogismos, a reasoning or dispute, Luke 9:46.
3 Meizon, comparative degree of megas, used as superlative in the koine.
4 Bruce's Training of the Twelve.   5 Imperfect indicative of continued action.
6 Historic present, Mark 9:35.   7 Indirect, middle voice aorist participle.

Their Teacher now sat down as was the custom of a Rabbi in formal discourse, and calling the twelve about Him, began His sermon with a direct thrust at their selfish ambitions and jealousies:

"If anyone wishes to be first, he shall be the last of all and the servant of all."

Then wishing to enforce the teaching in a concrete and impressive way He called to Himself[1] a little child—probably Peter's as it was likely the incident took place in his home — and taking the child in His arms said:

"Verily I say unto you, except ye may turn[2] and become as one of these little children, you may not enter[3] into the kingdom of heaven." Jesus thus denounces their selfish ambitions with great severity such as He only used in denouncing Pharisaism.[4] They were headed in the wrong direction and must turn around.[5] There is nothing more difficult in the training of the disciples than to get them to recognize the claims of the law of love and expel ambition, jealousy, and envy from the heart, in their relationships with the brethren and all men. Many, who attain great excellence in prayer, in knowledge of the Word, in many accomplishments and attainments of service and other virtues of the disciples' life and character, fail just here, where the twelve showed one of their greatest weariness. When the disciple-worker is full of ambition for place, preferment, and honor, the cause is compromised in his hands and brought into contempt. This is why Jesus put the case so strongly and made admission to the kingdom[6] itself dependent on childlike humility and unpretentiousness. The little child knows no pride of rank or distinction. So the disciple must consciously put aside pride and selfish ambition for the highest place and give himself unreservedly to the work, leaving his promotion in service in the hands of the Lord. In His kingdom, the honors are given to the meek and lowly, who are self-forgetful and only seek a higher place that they may serve in a greater way. The very genius of the Christ-like life is to be unpretentious and self-forgetful. There is a holy ambition for great accomplishment and service in the kingdom but it is not of the kind that is hurtful to others, and does not partake of the spirit of vainglorious egotism. Jesus did not declare that these disciples were not disciples indeed, but lays down the principle by which they must govern their conduct, if they would be true followers of His.

---

1 Mark 9:36.   2 Second aorist passive subjunctive in a third-class condition undetermined but with prospect of determination.
3 Second aorist middle subjunctive with double negative, meaning they would not get into the kingdom at all unless they were lined out with the conditions.
4 Bruce, Cf. Matt. 23.   5 This would involve conversion in their thinking, Matt. 18:3.
6 Matthew 18:3.

"Do you want to know who is greatest," He added, placing His hand on the little child's head. "Whosoever shall humble himself as this little child, the same is the greatest in the kingdom of heaven."[1]

We may well imagine with what tenderness He placed the little child by His side[2] as He went on with His discourse. He had something more to say to them before He should leave so important a subject. He would draw for them another lesson from the character of a little child.

"Whosoever may receive one such little child[3] in my name[4] receiveth me, and whosoever receiveth me, receiveth him that sent me. For he that is the least among you all the same is great."[5]

Jesus throws His arms around every humble and unpretentious believer in these gracious words, even as He did typically around the little child. There is a blessing for every man who receives, with tenderness and favor, the believer, in whatever time or place. The humble Christ-like disciple, however insignificant and unknown, is to be honored and received as we would receive the Lord himself and in so receiving him we receive a blessing from the Lord ourselves.[6] Jesus loved little children and has raised their estate in all the world. He loves the childlike believer and sets him by His side[7] in the midst.[8] He knew that worldly ambition made a difficult time in the world for little children. The ambitions of military rulers in the World War brought suffering and death to many innocent children. Jesus would crush in the bud, if possible, the spirit of a self-seeking ambition, especially in His disciples. Hazael of Syria could hardly believe Elisha when he foretold how that ambitious ruler would "set the strongholds of Israel on fire, slay their young men with the sword, dash their children to earth, and rip up their women with child." But the prophet knew to what lengths of cruelty ambition will lead any man. Jesus knew, that even in His disciples, ambition, jealousy, and envy would be a canker to corrode the heart and spoil the gospel work in the life. To the long-suffering disciple He said: "The least among you, the one who makes himself least, is great indeed."[9]

5. The mistaken zeal of John rebuked by Jesus (Mark 9:38-50; Matt. 18:6-14; Luke 9:49-50).

The discourse of Jesus struck home. John remembered an experience which he and James had in the Galilean campaign, which was suggested by the expression "in my name," used by Jesus

---

1 This saying is repeated a number of times, (Cf. Matt. 23:12).   2 Luke 9:47.
3 Luke 9:48, any humble believer.   4 On the basis or ground of my name.
5 Great positive degree and very strong (Robertson).
6 This same blessing was offered those who should receive well the twelve in the evangelistic campaign in Galilee.   7 Luke 9:47.   8 Mark 9:36.
9 Luke 9:48, positive degree and very strong (Robertson).

just now in His discourse. They had seen a man who was casting out demons in Jesus' name and had tried to hinder him.[1] John frankly gave as their reason for doing so, that the man was not following them.[2] John wanted to follow out the teaching of Jesus about those who were in any sense disciples. Had they done right in hindering the man? He had some compunction when he remembered the incident. Their main reason for hindering him, he confessed, had been that the man did not "run with the group of the Twelve." The subject of their selfish ambitions had been dealt with so frankly by Jesus, that John had spoken up in the meeting.[3] Perhaps a change in the subject would relieve the smart of the salt in the wound. It did not divert the speaker from His main theme, however. This man was doing the Master's work in the Master's name and with the Master's power.[4]

"Stop hindering[5] him," said Jesus, "for no one who shall perform a miracle in my name will be able easily to speak evil of me. For whosoever is not against us is for us."[6] This is a lesson of tolerance toward all who work for Jesus in any way, and enjoy His manifest approval on their efforts in the bestowment of His power, and in the actual accomplishment of the work the Master laid down for His disciples for all time.[7] The principle on which Jesus based this rule of tolerance was that the "one who is not against us is for us" in the work of the kingdom. This profound saying of Jesus in proverbial form throws a flood of light in all directions.[8] The complement of this expression He used later: "He that is not with me is against me."[9] He who refuses to take a stand with Christ is against Him. But the one who takes a stand with Christ and is doing His work, however imperfectly, is not against Him. We are to use all tolerance toward such, whether he "be of our party" or not. In using tolerance, however, we may not excuse error or approve wrong doctrine or practice.

To alleviate the sting of the rebuke which had cut deeply, Jesus adds:

"For whosoever shall give you a cup of water to drink because ye are Christ's, verily I say unto you, he shall in no wise lose his reward." He here addresses them as the recipients of His divine providence. They are safeguarded by these gracious promises, if they assume the role of humble disciple workers, who seek the good of the kingdom and not the ends of selfish ambition.

With this brief digression, He reverts once again to the general theme. Using greater force even than before and tactfully em-

1 Vivid conative imperfect indicative. They repeatedly tried to hinder him.
2 Associative instrumental, hamin, with us.
3 Luke 9:49.   4 Robertson's Word Pictures.   5 Me with the present imperative.
6 Cf. Moffatt's translation.   7 Present imperative of continued action, applicable in all times, general prohibition.
8 Robertson's Word Pictures.   9 Matt. 12:30.

ploying the indirect approach to the subject, He impresses upon them the greatness of the unpretentious disciple in his humility. This He does by showing the tragedy of leading any one of "these little ones" into sin.

"Whosoever shall cause one of these little believers to stumble, it is better for him if a heavy mill stone — of the kind turned by the ass in grinding — were tied around his neck, and he were sunk once for all[1] into the depths far out in the open sea."[2]

To make the matter more solemn still Jesus pronounces one of His infrequent woes[3] because of the stumbling-blocks.

"Woe unto the world (of humanity) because of the occasions of stumbling, for these are inevitable (in the present status of things); but woe to the man through whom the occasion of stumbling comes."

Assuming then the second person of pointed address, He administers a direct and pungent warning as to cases in which they might become stumbling-blocks to themselves and to others: "Better cut off the right hand and enter into heaven maimed, better hew off the right foot and enter into heaven halt, better tear out the right eye and enter into heaven one-eyed, than suffer hand or foot or eye to be the minister of sins, which should feed the undying worm or kindle the quenchless flame."[4] Jesus had spoken in the sermon on the mount about plucking out the right (best) eye if it should by the look of evil desire corrupt the soul, and cast it away.[5] So no member of the body should be allowed to become an instrument of stumbling to them or to "his little ones," lest the offender suffer the unquenchable (abestos) fire of the ages. Jesus taught that there is eternal (ageless) hell (Gehenna) just as truly as there is eternal (aionion) life.[6] The valley of Hinnom, desecrated by the sacrifice of children to Moloch in Canaanitish days, was an accursed place used for the garbage of Jerusalem, where worms gnawed and the fires burned perpetually. It was a vivid picture of hell (Gehenna) and eternal punishment.[7]

The Master winds up His sermon by giving another admonition about the little ones, and about their own conduct in disputing over who should be greatest. They were to be the salt of the earth; but if the salt should lose its saltiness, through wranglings and disputes over the chief places, wherewith would it be seasoned. They should let the fire of His disciplinary sermon salt them and live at peace with one another.[8] The Jews offered salt with their

1 Perfect active indicative of completed action and permanent continuing state.
2 Matt. 18:6 (McNeile).   3 Matt. 18:7.   4 Cf. Farrar's Life of Christ.
5 Matt. 5:29.   6 Matt. 19:16, 29; 25:46.   7 Cf. Robertson's Word Pictures.
8 Mark 9:49, 50.

sacrifices,[1] a symbol of the incorruptible.[2] Jesus meant by the
reference, that they were rendered unfit for the sacrificial fire
while they should harbor selfish ambitions within their hearts.
Their souls would be purged by the fires of self-sacrifice in the
future. Let them purge themselves now with the fire of searching
self-judgment and put away disputes.

Let them remember that the humble believer, unpretentious
and unselfish, is the favorite of heaven. They must not "look down
upon"[3] these little ones. The Father takes special care of His little
ones, through ministering angels who wait to do His bidding in
heaven. The Jews believed each nation had a guardian angel.[4] According to their theology the chiefest angels were before the face
of God within the veil, while others were ranged on the outside
and awaited His behest. Those within enjoyed the most intimate
knowledge of His counsels and commands. The classification was
one of knowledge. Jesus teaches that those representatives—it may
be guardian angels—nearest to God, are not those of greatest
knowledge and merit or worth; but those less conscious of self,
more humble, less pretentious. Reasoning from heaven to earth,
the greatest in the kingdom is the humblest, least pretentious
disciple.

If God cares for the "lost one" who has gone astray[5] as the
sheep from the fold, how much more will He care for "each one
of his little ones." Humanly speaking, the one who has voluntarily
cast himself away in sin is accounted of little worth; but the Father
places a high value on those who are thus considered by men of no
account.

6. How to deal with a brother who has wronged you and the
duty of patiently forgiving a brother (Matt. 18:15-35).

From the initial subject of the mistreatment of one another
through unholy ambitions and the warning as to how they should
treat the "little ones" of God's brotherhood, illustrated further in
the example of one such "who followed not with them", Jesus
passes on to deal with a related subject, the proper treatment of a
brother who does you any wrong, through his unholy ambition.
This is the obverse view of the former subject. With mankind,
wrong too often depends on "whose ox is gored." Jesus deals now
with the question of sinful ambitions, jealousies, and envies, and
their hurtful consequences from the side of the one who has suffered the wrong. How shall he proceed with reference to the brother
who has wronged him?

1 Lev. 2:13.   2 Edersheim, Life and Times of Jesus.
3 Kataphronete, think down upon, with the assumption of superiority (Robertson).
4 Daniel 10:13, 20f; 12:1.   5 Luke 15:3-7.

"The Rabbis enjoin that the offender shall go to him whom he has injured and own his fault, and that if he cannot thus procure forgiveness, he shall take others with him and seek to obtain it; but require that he who is wronged forgive the offender, that he may show his humility and his patient love for a guilty brother. But the stubborn offender who refuses private amends is at last publicly reproved in the synagogues and in the schools."[1]

The same principle of humble love which Jesus urged as a remedy for self-seeking ambition, resulting in jealous wranglings and envious disputes, should lead the offended brother to seek the good of the offender. The method of Jesus, as well as His principle, is superior to that of Rabbinism, which was derived with some modifications from Moses.[2] The Rabbis placed the responsibility of the initiative in any move for the reconciliation or amends on the offender; Jesus, on the offended. It is obviously easier for the offended to make the first approach than the offender. The delicate tact and kindness of showing the brother his fault in private so as not to put him to shame, is the same in the method of Jesus as that practiced by the Rabbis. The superior spirit of the *act*, in the teaching of Jesus, is that of a yearning brotherly heart, seeking to win back his brother who has wronged him.

"If (at any time) your brother may sin[3] (against you) go and reprove him[4] (show him his fault) as between you and him alone. If he may hear you (listen to you), you gained[5] your brother. If he may not hear you (will not listen to you), take along with you yet one or two (brothers) in order that out of the mouth of two or three witnesses every word may be established." On the evidence of two or three witnesses every case may be decided (Moffat). If he may refuse to listen to them let them tell it to the church (assembly). Then if he refuses to listen to the church treat him as a pagan or a tax-gatherer (Moffat). In these few words Jesus deals with the very difficult subject of church discipline, as well as personal relationships and private offenses between brethren under all conditions, laying down far-reaching principles. The whole procedure is based on fraternal consideration and Christian tact and charity. First, strictly private dealing on the part of the offended with the offending is required; then when that is patiently tried out and has failed, two sympathetic and impartial brothers are brought in as assistants and witnesses, that if possible the offender may be convinced and led to acknowledge his fault. He will thus be not able to deny or repudiate

---

1 Geikie, Life of Christ, p. 258.   2 Deut. 19:15 in Sept.
3 Ingressive aorist subjunctive, harmatano, in a third class condition laying down a general
    principle.
4 Elegxon, convict or convince him of his fault, without delay.
5 Aorist, indicative, punctiliar action.

afterwards the confession he makes. Finally, as a last resort, if
he refuses to listen and admit his fault, the matter must be brought
before the assembly or local church, which will deal with the
brother, first through their representatives, seeking to bring him
to the right attitude of mind, and finally, on stubborn refusal, by
public elimination. This method of dealing with offenses bridles
the scandalmonger, prevents resentment and rapid estrangement
in the offender, and eliminates busybody, pharisaical trouble-
hunters. Stubbornness and obduracy in the offender are punished
by the severity of the severance of religious fellowship and the
application of a limited social boycott. He is to be to the church
"as a heathen" religiously, and as a "publican" socially. The
heathen was excluded from the Temple, having no part in religious
rites; and the publicans were treated by the Jews as social pariahs.
Jesus has in mind, by the "church", either an actual body of believers already in existence or is speaking prophetically of the
local churches which would be formally organized later (Acts).[1]
Some think that the twelve Apostles already constituted the "nucleus" of a kind of moving church (Bruce). They are not to des-
pise or persecute the eliminated brother or "refuse him the common offices of humanity, but still love and seek to win him back
even to the last."[2]

Jesus now adds that the sanction of heaven is upon whatever
act of discipline is enacted thus in accord with the spirit of His
teachings and His method of procedure.

"Truly I say to you, whatsoever you may (at any time) bind
or prohibit on earth shall remain in a state of being forbidden[3] in
heaven, and whatsoever you (as a church) permit on earth shall
be permitted in heaven." The disciplinary measures adopted in
accord with Christ's mandate are ratified and approved in heaven.
This is a great responsibility, which was at first placed on Peter
and the other apostles,[4] and here extended to the local churches
of all subsequent time, to forbid or allow what is necessary for
the proper discipline of its members.

Here is not a hotel theory[5] of church discipline such as prevails
too often in modern times or an ark theory such as Cyprian an-
ciently taught and Catholicism has always practiced. In a hotel,
people of all types of character meet and sit down for a brief time
at the table together and then part, knowing and caring little about
one another. In the ark of Noah, there were all kinds of animals,
the ferocious lion with the innocent lamb, and all were saved alike
by being in the ark. Such is the Catholic theory of salvation inside

1 Robertson's Word Pictures.   2 Geikies' Life of Christ.
3 Future passive periphrastic perfect indicative, a continued state in completion.
4 Matt. 16:19.   5 Bruce, The Training of the Twelve.

the church. But in a true church every member is vitally responsible for the character of the group as a whole and must insist on the right character in each individual composing it. Considerate love must always be balanced over against holy severity. The body must be heavenly in character, and in its measures to make itself so may count on the cooperation of heaven. Scandalous sin may not be tolerated in any individual member of a society, without contaminating and demoralizing the whole. In discipline, the stubborn offender is "turned over to Satan" by elimination[1] that he may have a foretaste of the hell of religious disfellowship and social ostracism, which may help to purge away his sin and lead him to repentance. There is great danger in such severe disciplinary measures, lest the church should be dominated by a self-righteous pharisaical group, who "thank God that they are not as other men." The greatest evil in discipline, however, is in that laxity which "allows the sheep and the goats to be huddled together in one fold." Such a condition too often grows out of a desire to multiply members. Many a local church has no back door.

Jesus adds another related thought, in the form of a promise. Contrary to the divided state of a church, filled with dissensions and jealousies, and thus impotent with God and man, the united church however small shall easily reach the ear of God in prevailing prayer. "If (even) two of you shall agree on earth as touching anythng that you shall ask, it shall be done for you of my Father which is in heaven." This promise will hold true, not only in dealing with questions and measures of discipline, but also in small gatherings of believers assembled for worship and service of the kingdom. "For where two or three are gathered together in my name there am I in the midst of them." Two in concord are spiritually stronger than a thousand who are in dissension.

The other phase of the question, of how to deal with the brother who has wronged us, is set forth in the parable of the unmerciful servant.[2] There must be readiness to forgive great and often repeated offenses.[3] The parable was given in answer to a question of the irrepressible Peter, as to how many times one should forgive his brother who wrongs him.

"Lord, how oft shall my brother sin against me and I forgive him? Until seven times?" It struck Peter that seven times would be an unusually liberal number since the Rabbis said three times was the limit.[4] Such a question demonstrated more childishness than

1 I Corinthians 5, 6.
2 Matt. 18:21-35. 3 Broadus, Com. on Matthew. 4 Amos 1:6.

childlikeness. The man who asks such a question does not know what forgiveness really means (Plummer).[1] The answer of Jesus reveals Peter's lack of comprehension of the true character of forgiveness by showing what real forgiveness is in the kingdom, illustrated in the Father's forgiveness of us and what our forgiveness of our offending brother must be, to measure up to the kingdom standard.

"I say not unto thee, until seven times; but until seventy times seven." Forgiveness is not a matter of mathematics but of love and character. The character of Lamed was so vindictive that he wished to be avenged seventy times seven;[2] the character of the disciples must be so forgiving as to patiently and graciously receive the offending brother seventy times seven—an unlimited number of times, always and everywhere, with complete forgiveness. The unlimited revenge of primitive man has given place to the unlimited forgiveness of Christians.[3] A loving mother does not keep a memorandum of the offenses of her child, though she may not allow them to pass without due notice and correction.[4] A vindictive temper grows out of selfish ambition such as had afflicted the twelve. An ambitious man is quick to detect offenses and slow to forgive injuries.

The parable of the unmerciful servant[5] is designed to set forth the character of forgiveness in the kingdom.[6] The "certain king" who was wishing to "cast up accounts" in a general reckoning with his servants or satraps, and who liberated the debtor who owed the enormous sum of ten thousand talents—equivalent to ten or twelve million dollars—and freely cancelled his debt, sets forth the example of the Father-God who forgives the incalculable moral debt of our sins, graciously, patiently, and freely. The example of the forgiven servant who went out and seized his fellow-servant, holding him by the throat,[7] who owed him the paltry sum of a hundred pence—the value of about twenty dollars —and cast him into prison until he should pay, illustrates the unforgiving spirit in many who pass for disciples of Jesus. God is slow to anger and of great kindness in dealing with our offenses. We should not be mean, little, and inhuman, in our treatment of the offending brother, who truly repentant for the injury he has done seeks our forgiveness. The "kingly" man quickly forgave and received his creditor back into his good graces and friendship; on the contrary, the forgiven but unforgiving servant persistently refused[8] forgiveness to his fellow-servant.

1 Robertson's Word Pictures.   2 Gen. 4:24.   3 McNeile (Robertson Word Pictures).
4 B. H. DeMent, Bible Reader's Life of Christ.   5 Matt. 18:23-35.   6 Matt. 18:23.
7 Imperfect indicative probably conative, began to choke him.
8 Imperfect indicative, persistent and arbitrary refusal, ethelen.

The application of the parable was obvious and simple. There must be real forgiveness, not a mere lip pardon; a receiving back of the offender into full fellowship and not a mere liberating of a criminal from prison into the continued ostracism of cold alienation. It must be a genuine transaction "from the heart" such as the Father's forgiveness is in our experience. We were all God's debtors; we had naught with which to pay; He forgave us freely and expects us to forgive our brothers and all men, who repentant seek our forgiveness. The injured brother must take the initiative in opening the door to reconciliation, and then meet acknowledged fault with free and full forgiveness. Peter learned that forgiveness is qualitative, not quantitative.[1] It is not a matter of arithmetic but of a loving character. Unless we have that forgiving spirit which is demonstrated in God, it is a sure indication that we are not akin to Him and cannot truly call Jesus' Father[2] our Father. Even those who are true disciples in the kingdom cannot enjoy the perfect fellowship of God without a forgiving spirit which can say: "Forgive us our debts as we forgive our debtors."[3]

7. Three aspirants to discipleship are warned to count the cost (Matt. 8: 11-22; Luke 9: 57-62).

Jesus was probably yet in Galilee when these incidents occurred. His Galilean public ministry was ended and the days of His being received up were being fulfilled. "He set his face steadfastly to go to Jerusalem." His purpose was to travel slowly through Samaria and cross over into Perea. His ministry in Galilee, judged from a worldly standard, had ended in failure. The door was closed for Him in Judea. He would give Himself during these last months to an effort to evangelize Perea.

On one of these days while He was lingering yet in the midst of the loved haunts of His earlier ministry in the neighborhood of Capernaum, He was approached by a Scribe who impulsively volunteered to follow Him.

"Master, I will follow thee anywhere"[4] he declared. Evidently he did not know that Jesus was just on the eve of His departure for the tragic days in Jerusalem.

"The foxes have their lurking dens and wild birds of the air their roosting places," replied Jesus, "but the Son of Man hath not where to lay his head." He thus warns the unsuspecting Scribe that privations are ahead. His life was more unsettled now than ever. Rejected in Judea and Galilee He was about to cross over into Perea for a temporary ministry before being offered up in Jerusalem. The Scribe had probably thought that Jesus was

1 Edersheim, Life and Times of Jesus.   2 Matt. 18:35. My heavenly Father.
3 Cf. Lord's Prayer, Matt. 6.   4 Present middle subjunctive with indefinite relative
        adverb ean.

the Messiah and would soon establish a temporal kingdom. Those among the disciples who were as distinguished in rank and learning as he, would then come in for a large share in the high honors and offices. He did not understand what Jesus meant by "Son of Man," His veiled title for Messiah. Jesus knew the measure of the Scribe's enthusiasm.[1] His own was a wandering life, which His would-be disciple, knowing, probably would not accept.

There were two other volunteers who subordinated His spiritual claims to their temporal plans, purposes, and comforts. They were among the "casual disciples" of whom there are always many. They put other objects first and not their loyal duty to Christ. One of the problems of life is the relation of duties—which comes first.[2] Jesus called upon this second Scribe to follow Him but he offered an excuse:

"Suffer me first to go and bury my father," he demurred. He wished to wait until his family obligations were fulfilled first and then he would follow Jesus. He could not go as long as his father was alive. The Oriental held it as a sacred duty to bury one's father when he died.[3] Speaking about his future prospects one was heard to say even in the presence of his father: "But I must first bury my father."[4] There are many who put duty to their relatives before duty to Christ. A third, Jesus warned against delay or indecision and the fatality of looking back.

8. The unbelieving half-brothers of Jesus counsel Him to exhibit Himself in Jerusalem and He rejects the advice (John 7:1-9).

The Feast of Tabernacles, which came on 15-22 of Tisri or October, was at hand. That was the holiest and greatest of the feasts of the Jews,[5] intended to commemorate the wanderings of the Israelites through the desert. During those days, the vast throng of Jews, numbering ordinarily about two million, lived in booths made of the thickly-foliaged boughs of olive, palm, pine, and myrtle, and carried in their hands small branches of palm, willow, peach or citron.[6] All the courses of priests were employed in turn. The feast followed on the heels of the great day of Atonement, when sacrifices were made for all the sins of the people. It was celebrated with great joy, the Law being read daily,[7] and seventy bullocks being sacrificed for the seventy nations of the world, in token of Messianic ingathering of the nations.[8]

The visit of Jesus in Galilee after His return from Cesarea Philippi had been brief and of a very private character. All Galilee was now astir in preparation for the annual caravan which would

1 Plummer, Com. on Luke.   2 Robertson's Word Pictures.   3 Tobit 4:3; Gen. 26:9
4 Plummer, Com. Luke.   5 Jos. Ant. 8:4.   6 Jos. Ant. 3:10.
7 Neh. 8:18; Jno. 7:19.   8 Edersheim's Life and Times of Jesus, Vol. II. p. 130.

start in a few days to the feast. Jesus had not been in Judea for eighteen months. His work of itinerant evangelist in Judea had been cut short at that time because the Jews were seeking[1] to kill Him.

The half-brothers of Jesus, who held the current conception about the messianic kingdom as one of temporal power and grandeur, came to Jesus and urged Him to go up to the feast and manifest His messianic powers. Apparently, now, and in contrast with His former popular methods, He was avoiding the crowds. He was fast losing His hold on the people. According to their judgment He had made a great mistake when He vetoed the desire of the multitude to make Him king when He fed the five thousand. If He was ever to regain His popularity and if indeed there was anything in His pretense to being the Messiah, He should manifest His power before the people. To force Him to some decisive step and induce Him to come out of His hiding of these last six months, they taunt and ridicule Him with being a "secret Messiah."

"Remove hence,"[2] they say, "and begone to Judea that thy disciples may gaze at the works which thou art doing. For nobody who aims at public recognition ever keeps his actions secret. Since you can do these deeds display[3] yourself to the world." They were hostile toward the messianic assumptions of Jesus. This insult of His half-brothers who had been the object of His fraternal care in their younger years and after the death of their father, Joseph, is a painful illustration of the lonliness of Christ in His work at this time. He was hated in Jerusalem, disliked by many in Galilee, haunted by His enemies, and ridiculed and insulted now by these half-brothers who had lost faith in Him[4] and would "force him out of his hiding."

Surely, the Feast of the Ingathering, prophetic of the messianic ingathering of the nations, was an appropriate time for such a manifestation. They thought they knew better than Jesus himself what He should do. He replies to their taunt of "secret Messiah" with a naked revelation of a sad truth about themselves:

"My time is not yet come; but your time is always ready. The world is not able to hate you but it is hating me because I testify concerning it, that its works are evil." He returns sarcasm for sarcasm. The "opportune predestined time" for Him to reveal Himself in His capacity of Messiah had not yet[5] come. Their time was always ready because they had nothing out of the ordinary to

1 Imperfect indicative (Jo. 7:1), signifying a continued attempt.
2 Aorist imperative active, an impertinent and urgent command.
3 First aorist active imperative in a condition of the first class implying nothing as to the fulfillment.
4 Imperfect indicative active oude, episteuon eis auton, persistent refusal to believe in His messianic assumptions.   5 Oupo, Nestles' text.

reveal. The world could not hate them because of the "law of moral correspondence."[1] They were like the world and the world liked them. Jesus exposed[2] the unbelieving world and consequently the world hated Him.[3]

"You[4] go up to the festival yourselves," He commanded, "I go not up yet[5] to this feast because my (predestined) season has not been filled to the full."[6] He did just the opposite of the impudent advice of His brothers and afterwards went *privately* to the feast, passing through Samaria instead of going with the caravan down the east side of Jordan. Nor did He follow their counsel any better when He did arrive later in Jerusalem; He was not their kind of Messiah, seeking notoriety. He refused to fall in with their idea of a grand messianic procession with the caravan on the way to the feast, and their desire for a great display of messianic miracles when He should arrive in Jerusalem. So He stayed on[7] in Galilee for some days after they were gone and then went with His disciples through Samaria. This was a very wise provision to keep down excitement on the part of the multitudes in Jerusalem until He should arrive.

9. Jesus goes privately with His disciples to Jerusalem through Samaria (Luke 9:51-56; John 7:10).

At last the days had been fulfilled[8] for the Ascension. He was fully conscious of the near approach of His death, resurrection, and ascension on high.[9] He himself "set his face with fixedness of purpose" in spite of all difficulty and danger, "to go to Jerusalem." As He went, there was such a look on His face, that the disciples, following, were amazed, and afraid.[10] In view of the fact that He was to pass through Samaria, He sent special messengers ahead to make arrangements for their lodging place at night. What was the dismay but[11] surprise of the disciples, already deeply impressed with the shadow of the impending tragedy, to receive the news that the Samaritan village had refused obstinately and persistently[12] to receive their Master, and for the mere obscure reason that He was going toward Jerusalem. Such was the bitterness of the hostility between the Samaritans and the Jews that the fact that a Jew was traveling[13] across their country, passing by the altar of Gerizim and going to Jerusalem to a feast, was resented.

James and John, the sons of thunder (Boanerges), were deeply incensed and grieved by this inhospitality of the Samaritan town.

1 Wescott Com. on John.   2 Jno. 5:42, 45.   3 Jno. 3:19; 18:37.
4 Humeis, you, place of emphasis in contrast to their command to him, he commands them. Second aorist imperative positive and urgent command.
5 Onpo. Nestles' Text.   6 Perfect indicative.   7 Aorist indicative active emeinen.
8 Articular infinitive with the accusative of specification.   9 Luke 9:22,27,31; Acts 1:2, 11, 22, analambanein.
10 Mark 10:32.   11 Adversative use of kai, but.
12 Imperfect indicative of repeated and persistent action.
13 an poronomenon, periphrastic imperfect middle, a continuous journey, Luke 9:58.

Surely it was enough for Jesus to be rejected by His own fellow-countrymen, and much too much to be slighted by these "Samaritan dogs."

"Lord, if you are willing," they insisted, "shall we call down[1] fire from heaven to destroy them?" They had recently been with Jesus on the mount of transfiguration and had seen Elijah, the prophet who once called down fire from heaven on Carmel. They themselves had been endowed by Jesus with wonderful powers in the recent Galilean campaign. It did not require a great leap of the imagination for them to conceive of the idea of calling down fire now to wipe this inhospitable town of detestable Samaritans, who dared to cast a slight upon their Master, immediately and completely[2] off the map.

Jesus turned quickly[3] and rebuked them. Some ancient mss. add here: "Ye know not what manner of spirit ye are of"; and a smaller number also: "For the Son of Man came not to destroy men's lives but to save them." While these words are not a part of Luke's gospel they express undoubtedly the spirit of the Master and might well have been a part of His rebuke of the two disciples in the bitterness of their mistaken zeal. For the night's lodging they went to another village, probably across the Jordan in Perea. The usual route of the Galilean Jews in going to Jerusalem was on the eastern side of the Jordan. This road would be free of pilgrims by this time and would relieve further embarrassment with the Samaritans.

---

1 Deliberative subjunctive, eipomen, after theleis.   2 Analusai, effective aorist infinitive.   3 Strapheis, second aorist passive participle. A dramatic act (Robertson)

PART V

LATER JUDEAN MINISTRY

(Harm. §§ 96-111)

This ministry in Jerusalem and the surrounding provinces of Judea occupied the brief period of about three months, from the Feast of Tabernacles to the Feast of Dedication. John gives the account of the work in Jerusalem and Luke that in the surrounding province of Judea. Jesus had been forced to withdraw from Judea early in His ministry, on account of the intrigues of His enemies, who sought to bring His ministry in conflict with that of John the Baptist. The last opportunity had now arrived for Him to make a thorough job of evangelizing Judea before He should face His enemies in the final issue in Jerusalem. Once again He initiates His campaign in Jerusalem during the Feast of the Tabernacles, and when the antagonism of His enemies grows too bitter and their hostility too open to pursue His work safely in the city, He withdraws into the surrounding country, visiting the various towns and country places whither He had sent the seventy disciples two by two in order to prepare the way before Him. When this rapid campaign came to a close at the Feast of Dedication we find Jesus again in Jerusalem. During this Feast the Jerusalem enemies tried to stone Him and He withdrew to Bethany beyond the Jordan and gave Himself to teaching in Perea until He was called to the home of Mary and Martha, when He raised Lazarus. This miracle inflamed the minds of His enemies yet more, who were now openly bent on His destruction. It was necessary that He withdraw to Ephraim, probably, in the edge of Samaria, whence He departed by way of Samaria and Galilee later to join the caravan of pilgrims coming down the east side of the Jordan to the Feast of the Passover.

CHAPTER XXII

THE MINISTRY IN JERUSALEM

(Harm. §§ 96-101)

When Jesus did not appear in Jerusalem during the first three days of the feast, the hostile Jewish leaders were seeking[1] Him, anxious to attack Him as soon as He should arrive. They went everywhere about the city inquiring for Him. "Where is that fellow?"[2] they asked with disdain. There was much murmuring[3] concerning Him in animated whispers among the crowds.

1. The coming of Jesus to the Feast creates intense excitement concerning the Messiahship (John 7: 11-52). The multitudes from various parts were divided in their opinion about Jesus.[4] Some were saying and repeating here and there:[5] "He is a good man, of pure motives." But others led by the enemies of Jesus were affirming: "Nay, but he is leading the multitudes of the common people astray." No one yet dared to be speaking about this subject openly, because of the fear of the national leaders,[6] who, though they were evidently against Jesus, had not yet pronounced their judgment.

(1) First discussions "in the midst of the Feast" (John 7:14-36). Suddenly when all were agog with curiosity, and excitement about Him was at its highest pitch, Jesus went up[7] to the Temple, probably to Solomon's porch on the side to the east, and there began His teaching.[8] There were three different groups of men that Jesus encountered in the midst of His discussion on this first day: the Jewish leaders, the inhabitants of Jerusalem, and the officers sent by the chief priests.

The Jewish enemies of Jesus were wondering and repeating around sarcastically: "How does this fellow know literature?[9] He never studied in either of the rabbinical schools of Hillel and Shammai!" It was His knowledge of their sacred writings—which had to be learned—that disconcerted the Jewish leaders. Jesus showed Himself familiar with the literary methods of the times, which were supposed to be confined to the scholars and popular teachers. They were not aware or were unwilling to admit that a talented man, though unschooled, outstrips many times a man with lesser gifts with school training, which is no argument against true education. In the eyes of these Jewish leaders Christ was a mere self-taught enthusiast!

---

1 Imperfect indicative active of Zeteo.   2 This is the emphatic and contemptuous
   force of ekeinos.   3 Onomatopoetic word goggusmos.
4 Cf. Jno. 6:66.   5 Imperfect, elegon.   6 Objective genitive.
7 Effective aorist, anebe.   8 Inchoative imperfect, edidasken.
9 The people were surprised after all the bluster of the enemies but the rulers
   were amazed at His effrontery.

344

Jesus met the defaming ridicule of these Jews with a significant declaration: "My teaching is not mine but his that sent me." He had not originated His teaching and He was not a mere self-taught enthusiast. With the Jews a teaching derived its authority from being in accord with tradition, traced back through teachers to Moses and God. On this ground He claimed for His teaching the highest authority, being from God, whose messenger also He claimed to be. He thus asserts the superiority of His teaching over that of the Rabbis. They had erudition, He learning; they knowledge of books, He practical wisdom. They traced their teaching back through rabbis to Moses; but His came direct from God. He tells them the only way they can test out the truth of His teaching: "If anyone desired to do the will of God he should know[1] for himself experimentally whether his doctrine was from God or whether he spoke of himself." There must be harmony with the will of God, sympathy, an open mind, an obedient heart, before there can be understanding. He adds His own absolute devotion to God, the fact that He was not seeking His own glory but that of God who sent Him, as evidence of His own faithfulness and the truth of His teaching.[2] He was not the kind of teacher that pushes His own claims for position and glory—"blows his own horn"—but the kind that seeks the glory of God. Such a teacher is true and no unrighteousness is in Him. He thus gives them an inward criterion— their spiritual perception if they had any—and an outward criterion —His own character and conduct—by which they might judge of the truth of His teaching. He next points out the cause of their failure to understand His teaching: because they were "not wishing" to be faithful to the truth they had received already. "Did not Moses give you the law?" He injected, "and no one of you is keeping the law." A point of evidence He adds immediately: "Why are you seeking to kill me?" He was conscious and so were they that such was their secret intent. This was a violation of the law of Moses.[3]

The scene changes now, and another group, people from Galilee, take up the debate![4] This crowd of pilgrims who did not understand the purpose of these enemies of Jesus broke in on the discourse coarsely: "You have a demon! Who is seeking to kill you?" They took Him to be a monomaniac laboring under the hallucination that people wanted to kill Him. Jesus went right on with His reasoning in spite of the interruption: "One work I did and all of you, both rulers and people, are wondering why I did it." He cited the work of curing the man at the pool of Bethsaida

1 Future middle indicative of "ginosko."   2 Wescott, Com. on John.
3 Matt. 5:17-48.   4 Jno. 7:20-24.

eighteen months before, because it was on account of that cure
that the national leaders had desired to kill Him.[2] They had been
unable to understand His conduct in that cure. He now calls
attention to their own frequent violation of the Sabbath law,
in order to[3] carry out the command of circumcision, when the eighth
day happened to fall on the Sabbath. They had received through
Moses the law of circumcision which came down from Abraham.
The circumcision was only a sign of looking toward deliverance,
whereas He made a whole man every whit sound, not just mended
one member of his body. They kept the law of circumcision by
violating the Sabbath law. Why should they get all yellow-green
with anger at Him.[4] If the circumcision, an act of partial healing,
took precedence over the ceremonial observance of the Sabbath,
how much more the complete healing of a whole man. Let them not
be superficial in their criticism, but come to some principle of
righteous judgment, such as the unwritten law of human need.

A group of the resident citizens now take a hand in the discussion. Some of these Jerusalemites kept on saying, and now
with surprise and an injection of sarcasm directed at the leaders:
"Is not this the one whom they are seeking to kill?" Evidently
they were in on the secret plans of the Pharisees, as the group
of pilgrims had not been.[5] With sarcasm now they tantalize the
rulers: "He is going on with his preaching openly in the Temple
and they are saying nothing to him to prevent it. They did not
come to find out that he is the Christ, did they?" These Jerusalemites were hostile toward Jesus and impatient with the temerity of
their rulers. They boldly assert now their own opinion, following
their popular theology. "We know positively where this fellow
came from; but no one shall know whence the Messiah is when he
comes." He should emerge suddenly from concealment, with
the anointing of Elijah, or drop from the skies in the Temple, as
suddenly as a Godsend or a scorpion, (Sanhed 97a), they thought.[6]

In reply to their interpretation of popular Jewish theology,
Jesus claims a knowledge of God which they do not possess. He
passes over their popular theology to point out their ignorance of
God, who sent Him. He admits that they know His own birthplace
(7:42) but asserts that they are ignorant of His real origin, which
was God. These facts Jesus announced in a loud voice in the
Temple so that all might hear. In contrast with their ignorance
He asserts His knowledge of God and His consciousness of His
mission for Him. His unique claim through all His controversies

1 Marcus Dodds, Com. on John.   2 Jno. 5:18   3 Purpose clause with negative me.
4 Jno. 7:23.   5 Perhaps referring to the examination of Jesus by the rulers, Jno. 5:10
6 Apoc. of Baruch 19:3, II Esdras 7:28; 13:32; Justin Martyr Myth 110.

with the Jews was, that He himself was the interpreter of God to men.

These Jerusalemites now angered by His bold claims began to seek ways for taking Him prisoner, not waiting for the timourous leaders. But none laid hands on Him because His predestined hour had not yet come (Bernard). The outcome of the discussion was that many out of the crowd came to believe[1] on Him. He made new converts to His cause.[2] Some, by this discussion, were openly and repeatedly saying: "When the Messiah comes will he do greater signs than those done by this one during these many months?"[3] The multitude was divided now, some accusing and some defending Jesus.

Once again the scene changes. (Vs. 32-36). The Pharisees had from the beginning taken the initiative in the antagonism to Jesus. They heard the multitude—now divided in opinion—murmuring concerning Him, their disputes rising like the hum of bees. They introduced at this juncture the Sadducees, who had already been enlisted in Galilee in cooperation against Jesus. The political group known as the chief priests, including all those who had ever held the office of high-priest, together with members of the hierarchical families, had their sessions in a stone hall of meeting, within the precincts of the Temple. They were within ear-shot of Jesus and kept themselves informed by emissaries of all that He said and did. When they knew of the divided opinion of the multitude and the espousal of the cause of Jesus by some they were stimulated to send officer-assistants[3] to arrest Him.[4] Jesus went on calmly with His work. When the officers appeared in His audience, He simply stated that after a little while He proposed personally to withdraw from their midst and return to the one who had sent Him.

"You shall seek me and shall not find me," He added, "and where I am you shall not be able to come." He would be in eternal fellowship with the Father (Vincent). Into such a fellowship they could never come—an environment wholly different from their character. His enemies were puzzled over this unintelligible saying. They sneeringly venture an explanation among themselves.

"Where will this fellow go that we shall not find him," they inquired. "Is he not about to proceed to the Jews of the Dispersion and to teach the Hellenists?" All over the world there were groups of Jews settled in heathen lands. When the Jews were taken in captivity to various countries many became after a time

1 Ingressive aorist active indicative.
2 Constative aorist, summing up all the miracles of Jesus.
3 Servant-officers.   4 Hina with subj. in final clause.

planted in those distant parts. They clung to their ancestral faith for the most part but embibed the customs and languages of the people to whom they were subject. Because of this taking over of things foreign they were called Hellenists, and for the same reason were hated by the strict Jews of Judea. The enemies of Jesus now concluded that since He had been driven to the wall in Judea and Galilee, He meant to go next to the Jews scattered abroad. But they could not understand His saying:

"You shall seek me and shall not find me and where I am you shall not be able to come." This was a puzzle to them.

(2) The last day of the feast was called the Great Day or Hosanna Rabba and celebrated as a Sabbath, probably in memory of the entrance of Israel into Canaan. During the seven days preceding, seventy bullocks were sacrificed for the seventy nations of the world; but on this eighth day one was offered for Israel herself. Each morning of the seven, at an early hour, came the joyous ceremony of pouring the golden ewer of water, brought by a priest from the pool of Siloam near Mount Sion outside the Water-gate of the Temple, into the silver basin on the western side of the altar. The Hallel was sung by the gaily-clad worshippers and as the water was poured they shook their palm-branches in triumph.[1] A multitude of pilgrims also marched around the city with music and shouts in commemoration of the taking of Jericho. Others passed the brook of Siloam to drink, while chanting the words of Isaiah: "Ho everyone that thirsteth, etc. With joy shall ye draw water from the wells of salvation" (Isa. 12:3).

It was near this procession doubtless that Jesus was standing, moved by the enthusiasm of the people, but saddened by the de-lusion which mistook mere ceremony for religion—the symbol for the reality. Water was a magic word in that sultry dry climate. Raising His voice suddenly until it sounded out in soft clearness over the throng He cried:

"If anyone thirst let him come to me and let him drink!" He had the water of life for everyone who would come. The water from Siloam was only a type; He offered them the reality. "He who believes in me" He added, as the Scriptures echoed, "rivers of living water shall flow in a constant stream from his heart." Once the spiritual thirst is satisfied with faith, then follow the refreshing energies of faith. The riches of divine grace and truth drunk in, become in the believer's heart a living spring flowing forth from his lips and life in holy words and deeds, quickening the thirsty around him. The evangelist John found the greater fulfillment of this quickened missionary zeal and power in the in-

1 Farrar's Life of Christ.

spired activity of the apostles after Pentecost. Then, after the receiving up of Jesus into the glory He had before the world was, would come in permanent and manifest revival, the Holy Spirit, and streams of holy influence like rivers of living water would go forth from His Apostles, through the Spirit's overflowing fulness in their souls. "The structure of Christianity was to stand upon four great pillars: the norm-life of Jesus, showing us the true standard of life; the cross meeting sin, suffering, and death in decisive victory; the resurrection, sealing the victory of the cross by bringing life and immortality to light; and Pentecost, making available that life in present human experience."[1] While Christ was in the flesh, His historical presence excluded the realization of His abiding presence, which followed the resurrection and Pentecost.

Again there was division of sentiment in the multitude of those hearing these words. Some were saying: "This is truly the prophet." Others went further and affirmed more specifically: "This one is the Messiah." But others diverged in their opinion and reasoned: "The Christ does not come from Galilee does he?"[2] The Rabbinists were there with an explanation as always. They now cited the fact that the Scriptures stated that the Messiah should come of the seed of David and from Bethlehem, the village where David had lived. This division in the crowd worked well for Jesus. His enemies wanted to lay fierce hands on Him as a Sabbath-breaker and blasphemer but they dared not do so because of His strong supporting party.

It was momentarily becoming more difficult to carry out their plan to arrest "this audacious pretender." At this juncture their exasperation was greatly increased by the empty return and irritating report of the Temple police, who had been sent to effect His arrest.

"Why did you not lead Him away?" demanded the chief priests and Pharisees, of these servant-officers. "Never at any time spoke a man as this man was speaking," they confessed frankly. These hard police officers had been carried away by the power and charm of the personality and discourse of Jesus.

"Are you also led astray?" sneered their employers. "No one of the rulers has believed on Him has he, or anyone of the Pharisees? But only this ignorant accursed street rabble who are ignorant of the law" they added with dogmatic finality. What right had these subordinate officers to have minds of their own? (Dods). They were mere employees of the Temple authorities!

The cautious voice of Nicodemus was now heard in suggestive defense of Jesus. He was timid when he came to Jesus by night.

1 Stanley Jones, The Christ of Every Road.
2 Me expects a negative answer to the question.

He is more bold now but yet cautious and prudent. Moreover he was a ruler and Pharisee and member of the Sanhedrin. He would be expected to have an opinion and it was perfectly in order for him to express it about this case in question. He had months before confessed secretly to Jesus his profound impression of Him "as a teacher sent from God." His legal opinion on this present case was now submitted in the form of a searching but prudent question.

"Our law does not judge the[1] man, does it, if it may not first hear him and know what he is doing?" Without assuming to be His defender, Nicodemus had scored a point in the defense of Jesus. These men who were supposed to be exponents of the law were themselves violating the law of criminal procedure. There was no legal answer to this suggestion of Nicodemus and he was a ruler and a Pharisee. His Pharisee colleagues of the Sanhedrin sneeringly reply to his comment:

"You are not from Galilee too are you? Will you class yourself with this ignorant crowd?" These Jerusalem aristocrats had a scornful contempt for the rural Galileans, the Am-ha-'Aretz or country people. They next fall back on their traditional dogmatism:

"Search and see" they demand, "that from Galilee no prophet comes." As a matter of fact Jonah came from Gathhepher, Nahum from Elkash, and Hosea from a northern town, all in Galilee. Also Elijah, Elisha, and Amos, possibly were from that province. Most of God's great servants have come from rural districts. But dogmatic prejudice is blind. It is no excuse for their ignorance to say that reference was to the future. It was wilful ignorance and incurable prejudice![2] Their taunt silenced the timid Nicodemus, and his voice was no more raised in the Sanhedrin on behalf of Jesus and justice. But he stood for Him this time, even if he did bring down on his own head a vial of wrath.

2. The story of an adultress brought to Jesus for judgment (John 7:53-8:11). This narrative is certainly not a genuine part of the gospel of John. The oldest and best manuscripts do not have it. It is probably a true story, for it is like Jesus and in perfect accord with His teachings. The story is possibly a part of the tradition preserved by Papias.

Jesus came very early to the Temple on the morning after the last day of the Feast, arriving probably near daybreak. He may have lodged in the home of Lazarus, Martha, and Mary that night, or at some place on the Mount of Olives. The crowds which had assembled from far and near for the Feast would this day depart, but Jesus would remain a few days, and He came early

---

1 Article points to Jesus definitely. 2 Robertson, Divinity of Christ.
1 Article points to Jesus definitely. 2 Robertson, Divinity of Christ, p.80,

to catch a part of the crowd ere they departed. Taking His place
in the Court of the Women, the most public part of the Temple
where the trumpet-shaped collection boxes of the Treasury were,
He sat down according to the custom of teaching Rabbis and began to teach.[1] According to this traditional story, the Scribes
and Pharisees come,[2] leading a betrothed virgin who had been
caught in the very act of adultery. They had a court for the trial
of such cases, but since it was customary sometimes to ask the
opinion of a Rabbi, the opportunity presented itself to entrap Jesus
and to that they addressed themselves. They remind Him that
stoning was prescribed by their Jewish law for the case of a
betrothed woman guilty of adultery.[3]

"Now what do you say?" they insisted. The writer of the
narrative adds that they were tempting Him in order that they
might have whereof to accuse Him.

Jesus quickly stooped down in apparent embarrassment, and
began to write with His finger on the ground. He might well be
embarrassed over the woman's evident guilt but He was not shamed
so much by the deed as "by the brazen hardness of the prosecu-
tors." Tradition says that He wrote the names and sins of the
accusers on the ground, but for this there is no evidence. These
hard-hearted men continued to prod Him with questions, thinking
that they had at last brought Him into confusion. If He should
condemn her and insist that she be stoned (Deut. 22: 23 ff.), it
would alienate the people from Him, for the law in this particular
had long been obsolete from the very commonness of the offense. If
on the other hand, He should dismiss her, they would at once
charge Him with slighting the Law, for it was still formally binding.[4] As quickly as He had stooped down, so now He suddenly
arises and looking them straight in the face, He demands:

"Let him who is without sin among you cast the first stone at
her." He knew their evil design and dissimulation. He merely
repeated what the chief witness of the law was required to say
in such a case.[5] Once again, He quickly stooped down and wrote
something on the ground. Their consciences made cowards of
them all and they began to go out, beginning at the oldest unto
the youngest, until Jesus was left alone with the woman, standing
there abashed and repentant before Him. Then Jesus arose and
seeing no one except the woman, addressed her:

"Woman, where are those accusers of thine? Has none condemned thee by casting a stone at thee?"

1 Inchoative imperfect.   2 Dramatic present.
3 In a state of guilt, perfect passive indicative. (Robertson).
4 Geikie's Life of Christ, pp. 279, 280.   5 Deut. 13:9, 10, 17:7.

"None, Lord," she humbly answered, not making any excuse for her sin.

"Neither do I judge thee," He said, "go, and henceforth do not go on sinning." He gave her another chance to live a decent life. He felt that even a wicked, outcast woman can be saved.

3. After the feast of the Tabernacles in the Temple, Jesus claims to be the Light of the World (John 8:12-20).

Again Jesus took up His discourses in the Temple, within earshot of His enemies. He still sat in the court of the women, sometimes called the Treasury. This court was a thoroughfare to that of the Israelites on a different level fifteen steps above it. He had the day before applied to Himself one of the miracles of the Exodus, that of the water poured out in libations. To give water to drink was a common phrase for teaching and explaining the Law. Now, He applies to Himself the type of the fiery pillar. The great golden candelabra were close beside Him, fifty cubits high and sumptuously gilded. Every night these lights were lit and shed their soft light all over the city. Here, the people joined in festive dances to the sound of the flutes and other music and the Levites chanted the Songs of Degrees.[1] Such a scene had been acted, doubtless, the night before and was fresh in their memories. "I am the light of the world," Jesus exclaimed "The one following me shall not be walking around in darkness, but shall have the light of life." He had said but yesterday that He was the water of life, satisfying the individual need of every soul coming to Him; now He declares He is the light of the world, shedding forth His benefits for the whole race, like the lights in the Temple — types of the pillar of fire which led Israel through the desert ways by night, or the glorious sun now rising over the Mount of Olives. John the Baptist had called Jesus "the true light." The Psalmist called God, "his light." Isaiah spoke of the Messiah as the everlasting light. The Light was a Jewish title of the Messiah.[2] Jesus here claims to be the light of the whole race, Jew and Gentile, a claim which startled the Pharisees, and raised within them a spirit of fierce antagonism. His claim was that of being the light which springs from the fountain of life and produces life. Whoever should follow Him wouldn't walk in the darkness of ignorance, sin, and spiritual death.

Such a sweeping claim could not go unchallenged by the Pharisees. Enraged by their last failure to entrap Him, they were embittered and enfuriated by this new and bolder claim.

"You are bearing witness concerning yourself," they said, "and your witness is not true." According to their tradition

1 Pss. 120-134.   2 Ech. Rabb. 68:4 Cf. Lightfoot in Loco.

"no man could give witness for himself."[1] Judged by their pedantic rules and external tests, His testimony concerning Himself was not pertinent, and for all practical purposes was worthless. The trouble was with their rules and not with the nature of His testimony. Jesus reminded them that their legal rule was wholly inapplicable to His case.

"Though I do testify to myself my evidence is valid," He said, "because I know where I have come from and where I am going to, whereas you know neither where I came from nor where I am going to." He asserts that His mission justifies His testimony. He was not just praising Himself as they insinuated. He had a mission to fulfill of which He was conscious. It was necessary that He testify concerning Himself, because He, alone, was conscious of His origin and destiny. They were not to judge Him, because they did not know anything about His mission. His very character was light, evidencing His origin and mission. Though His testimony to Himself might not be considered competent, judged by their traditional rules, nevertheless, it was true, because light testifies to itself. None need argue that the sun is the sun or that light is light. The very character of Jesus was sufficient basis for His words. The witness of Christ to Himself was essentially complete, but as He had before acknowledged, Himself, the technical need of supplementary evidence and furnished it in the form of the testimony of John the Baptist, His Father, His words, and the Scriptures so now He refers not only to His conscious knowledge of the fellowship with the Father in the preexistent state, His consciousness of His mission in the world, and His destined return to the Father, but presents the testimony of the Father also. Over against the true character of His testimony, stood the false character of their judgment upon Him, because they judged according to mere appearance, without knowing the mystery of the incarnation. He, Himself, did not assume to judge anyone, either Himself or them. He came to save, not to assume a harsh dogmatic attitude toward anyone. Even if He should pass judgment on anyone at any time, His judgment would be genuine, because it was linked up with the Father's. This kind of testimony satisfied all the requirements of their law just cited, because it called for only two witnesses who should agree. His own testimony in words, coupled with the approving testimony of His Father — evidenced in His sinless life and incomparable miracles — met all the legal requirements. These two testimonies were not only in perfect agreement, fulfilling the legal requirement, but were true in their absolute character. The testimony of a life was the final

1 Mishnah Ketub 11:9.

appeal, as always. Both His character-life and the approval of the Father on Him substantiated His claim to being the light of the world.

The Pharisees retorted, deriding Him: "Where is the second witness, your father?" He had referred to God as His very Father before, but now they effect to misunderstand Him.

"You neither know me nor my Father," He replied. "If you knew me, you would know my Father also." They intimated that an absent witness was worthless. If they had been spiritually minded, having a just conception of Jesus, they would have been able spiritually to perceive His Father also.[1] God is only known spiritually. Their failing to perceive Him reveals their lack of spirituality.

These words Jesus spoke in the Temple's treasury-chamber, near the room where the Sanhedrin was accustomed to meet. They were bold words to be spoken in the very stronghold of His enemies; but when He arose and went out no one laid hands on Him, for His predestined hour had not yet come.

4.   The Pharisees attempt to stone Jesus when He exposes their sinfulness (John 8:21-39).

Later on, possibly the next day, Jesus draws the line of cleavage sharply between Himself and His enemies in destiny and character. He repeats His warning that He is going away. They will seek Him, in that day of calamity, in despair, but will not be able to find Him. In reply to His first warning, they had intimated that He would go to the Dispersion. When He gave them this second warning, they insinuated that He was insane and meditated suicide. He had said their search for Him would be one of despair. They retorted with bitter and subtle mockery with this question:

"He will not kill Himself, will he?" with the insinuated suggestion that He would. They knew that He spoke of going away to the next world and suggested the deepest depths of Gehenna — the suicide's hell — as the destination. That was the only way they could explain His expression: "Where I go you will not be able to come." "Of course they would not follow Him to Gehenna," they jested insultingly.

Jesus points out the contrast between their origin and character and His, as the cause of their inability to understand Him. They belonged to the lower sensual sphere of the fleeting world-order; He to the higher spiritual sphere to which entrance is only by a spiritual birth. Their natures and hearts were in keeping with their sensual origin; He, on the contrary, had the higher wisdom

---

1 Second class condition, contrary to fact.

and divine life of the spiritual Kingdom. He warns them that because of this difference of character they would die in their
sins, unless they should believe that He was the eternal spring of
life and light, which He had claimed to be. Jesus here claims absolute divine being. They wish to pin Him down and charge Him
with blasphemy; so they ask, feigning sincerity:

"Who are you then?" They hoped He would make some
clearer declaration of His Messiahship that they might entrap Him.
But He avoided the title Messiah and with an enigmatical expression stands by His claims. A plainer revelation of Himself
was impossible at present. His life substantiated before their
eyes, anyway, all that He claimed to be. His person was teaching
(Westcott). How could He even speak to them at all. They and
He belonged to different worlds and communion was impossible
between them. They did not want to understand or receive what
He told them. But they could not evade the responsibility of their
antagonistic attitude of unbelief toward Him. He had the responsible mission of speaking the things from the Father. The utterance
of those things would widen the chasm between Him and them,
but it was His duty to communicate them. They were hopelessly
preoccupied with thoughts of an earthly deliverer and could not
recognize Jesus as one sent from God.

But the time would soon come when all would be made clear.
"Whenever you shall lift up the son of man, then shall you perceive
that I am and that from myself I do nothing; but just as the
Father taught me, these things I speak." The being and action
alike of the Son were in absolute union with the Father, who
had not left Him alone in the incarnation. There was perfect coincidence in the will between the Father and Son, as was demonstrated in the positive, active, energetic obedience of the Son,
which was pleasing to the Father. When He was speaking these
things, many came to believe on Him in the truest, fullest sense;
not merely accepting His statements as true, like some other superficial believers to whom He refers next.

Jesus proceeded to submit to the test the faith of those
who believed in Him and did not believe on Him. He was not
willing to commit Himself to the Jerusalem Pharisees, because He
knew that their belief was a superficial belief, mingled with a
thousand erroneous ideas. His test soon revealed the hollowness of
their profession. He wished no false disciples now, but only
those who would hold out and stand by His word. For this reason
He said to them:

"If you may remain in the sphere of my teaching, learning and
obeying it, then you are truly my genuine disciples, and you

shall have a progressive conception of the truth and the truth shall set you free!" He spoke of course of intellectual, moral, and spiritual freedom — emancipation from ignorance, superstition, false doctrines, and especially sin. Patient continuance in the study of His doctrines, and the new faith in Him, would have this elevating and purifying influence on them.

But they misinterpreted His words, and referring them blindly to their political status — their national pride ablaze — they exclaim: "We are the seed of Abraham and were never at any time in bondage to any man. How are you saying that we shall *become* free?" Thinking only of their physical descent from Abraham, and of their being the chosen people of God, they failed to grasp the spiritual meaning of Jesus. In the heat of the controversy, they had uttered an untruth; for they had been in bondage in Egypt, Syria, and Babylon; and even now they were smarting under the gall of Roman rule. Though the prudent Romans did grant their subject nations much autonomy, at the same time their domination was real and exacting. In their pride of race, these Jews resented hotly the insinuation that they should be subject. It was an offense punishable by excommunication for one Jew to call another a slave.

Jesus earnestly calls their attention to His deeper spiritual meaning. He was not talking about political status, and now lays down a broad principle as to their spiritual freedom. "Everyone that habitually practices sin is the slave of sin," He declared. They might be of the chosen people; but morally they were enslaved, and were — just as other peoples — in the bondage of sin. Being thus slaves even within the household or chosen nation of God, they could not hope to remain in that household of privilege forever; because the bond-slave, like Ishmael, does not continue endlessly. The true son remains permanently, as did Isaac. He had suggested that if they would continue in His truth, it would free them spiritually. If He should free them, they would be free spiritually and really. He states frankly that they are the physical descendants of Abraham. But He cites a concrete fact, showing their bondage in sin. They are even now seeking to kill Him; and the reason was that His word had no place in them. Some of these professed believers were even now glowing with murderous vengeance. Far from remaining in the sphere of His word, they had no room for that word among them or in their hearts. He was speaking the things He had seen in the presence and communion with His Father; they, on the other hand, were practicing thus, in seeking to kill Him, the things they had heard from their father, the Devil. Since they clearly understood that He referred to God as His Father, the implication is that the Devil was their father. They saw what He meant and answer: "Our father is Abraham." "If ye were the children of Abraham," He replied, "you would do the works of your father." They were the physical descendants of Abraham, but they were not doing the works characteristic of their great progenitor according to the flesh.

"Even now ye are seeking to kill me," He added. "a man who has spoken the truth to you, which I heard from God. Abraham did no such work as this." They were entirely unlike Abraham, and were doing the works of *their* father. Descendants should manifest similarity in character. If they were spiritual sons of Abraham, they would do the works of Abraham. In seeking to kill Jesus, which they did not deny, they were showing their true origin. They understood His denial of their spiritual descendance from Abraham and affirmation of spiritual affinity with the Devil. Stung with this insinuation, they reply:

"We were not born of fornication — as the son of Joseph. Sarah our mother, was not unfaithful to Abraham." He had intimated that God was not their father; they declare that He is. "We have one father, God." They affirm that they are spiritual descendants of Abraham. That did not make it true.

"But," said Jesus, "If God were your father you would love me,[1] for I came out from God and am here."[2] He declares that His incarnation was not self-initiated or independent of "that one who sent me."[3] He clearly claims to be the Messiah, sent from God, though He avoids using the title.

He further declares that their incapacity and failure to recognize and receive understandingly His manner of speech and His doctrine evidenced their true origin. They were of their father the Devil and wished to go on doing the works of their father. "He was a murderer from the beginning. He was not standing in the sphere of the truth because there was no truth in him. Wherever he speaks the lie, he is speaking of his own, for he is the father of the lie." This was the reason why they did not believe Jesus when He spoke the truth to them. He had spoken frankly and not flatteringly about their sins. He now throws down the challenge to them: "Who of you convicts me of sin? If I speak the truth why do you not believe me?" The conclusion is clear; because they were not hearing, they were not from God. The one who is from God hears the words of God. The challenge of His sinless life was before them. They could find no flaw in His record anywhere. That being so, He had no untruthfulness in Him. If they were the children of God they would believe on Him. The one who is of divine

1 Second class condition with implication that failure to love Jesus was proof they were not children of God.
2 Present active indicative with sense of perfect tense.   3 Jno. 8 :42-47.

origin is ready to hear divine things. With irresistible logic, He
drove them into a corner. They were of the earth and of the
Devil and not of God. This was a terrible indictment. John had
called the Pharisees "a brood of vipers"; Jesus calls them "sons
of the Devil." Filled with rage and fury, they hiss back:

"Do we not say well that you are a Samaritan, and have a
demon?" He was speaking evil of the chosen people, as the Samaritans did. They retort to His accusation of "sons of the Devil," by
accusing Him of being an enemy of His people and a demonized
maniac. These were two of the meanest things a Jew could say
about anyone and a return of both His charges of illegitimacy and
sonship of the Devil.

Jesus does not deign to answer to the coarse abuse of being
called a Samaritan, but calmly replies: "I have not a demon, but
am honoring my Father, while you are dishonoring me. I am not
seeking my honor. There is one who is seeking it and judging you."
The rather, He comes to a more important matter, and claims to be
able to prevent spiritual death! Introducing His solemn declaration
with the usual phrase to mark the importance of His words, He
says:

"Truly, truly I say unto you: if anyone keep my doctrine, he
shall never see death." At this, they laugh Him to scorn, saying:
"Now we have come to complete knowledge that you have a demon.
Abraham died, and the prophets, and yet you are saying that if
anyone keep your doctrine he shall never taste death. You are not
greater than our father Abraham who died, are you? And the
prophets who died? Who do make yourself out anyway?" Infuriated, they exclaim: "You are not yet fifty years old, and have
you seen Abraham? He has been dead two thousand years!" I
mean to say far more than that, replied Jesus: "Verily, verily I
say unto you, before Abraham was born, *I am.*" They understood
this language now. He had used the title Jehovah employed in
announcing Himself to Israel in Egypt. There was no mistaking
it. He was claiming the independent continuous existence, from
the beginning, of the uncreated eternal God. Full of rage and fury,
they rush to take stones from the incomplete building parts of
the Temple, to put an end to Him by stoning — the penalty for
blasphemy. But in the confusion, Jesus passed into the midst of
those who were His friends in the crowd and quietly but boldly
came out from the Temple. He escaped this time the violence of
the mob, but He would not be able much longer to evade the
wicked plots of His enemies, the Pharisees.

5. The healing and conversion of the man born blind. (Jno.
9:1-41.)

It must have been on a Sabbath sometime after the Feast of

the Tabernacles that Jesus performed this important miracle. His enemies had been ready to take His life by mob violence the day after the Feast. With supreme poise and calmness, He had passed out of the Temple, and was hidden in the midst of the crowd. Some days and perhaps weeks had elapsed, and Jesus bravely presents Himself again in the Temple in Jerusalem. It was there that the battles must be fought out to the finish against the ceremonialism of the Rabbinical system.

The narrative of the cure — embracing the conversation of Jesus with His disciples about the poor blind beggar sitting probably at the Hulda gate of the Temple, the mode of the cure, and subsequent discussion of the case by the man's neighbors — is full of vivid details. It was not permitted to the beggar to ask or to receive alms on the Sabbath day; but his presence there on that day would be an advantage to him on other days. Jesus and the disciples were passing and observed this pitiable man, into whose soul no light of heaven had ever penetrated. Such a case never escaped the sympathetic observation of Jesus. The disciples might have passed the poor man casually but Jesus would not. Why He should stop and give attention to this miserable wretch, when they were busy in the Temple with their religious duties, the disciples could not understand. But His attitude caused them to reflect.

"Teacher," they asked, "who sinned, this man or his parents, that he should be born blind?" They probably did not think Jesus contemplated curing the man. He had cured many blind people, to be sure, for blindness was very common in the Orient. But it was the Sabbath, and He had but recently escaped mob violence in the court of the Temple. Furthermore, this case was one of peculiar difficulty due to hereditary sin, a very difficult problem in itself; or else to pre-natal sin on the part of the man — a curious notion of the Jews. In either case, the disciples would consider the case hopeless and treat it as a matter of speculative interest rather than of sympathetic helpfulness. But Jesus did not so consider the poor man's desperate and gloomy estate. His chief concern was not to place the blame for the man's pitiful condition on one of his parents or himself, but to do something to get him out of his miserable lightless state. They must learn to look upon such cases of diseased and afflicted humanity as opportunities for the manifestation of the works of God's redemptive love. He lays upon them the necessity and urgency of giving themselves to this activity, while the hours of their day of opportuntiy are theirs to fill up with golden deeds of uplifting helpfulness. He invites them into His fellowship in this work. He also reminds them that His own day of active service is limited and He must be about His work, while He is present to light the world. This consideration was sufficient, if for no other reason than that He should disregard the Sabbath rules of a fettering ecclesiasticism and break the bonds from the darkened soul of this man. Once before He had chosen time and place, and had dared to assail the traditional Sabbath, which hung like a burdensome yoke around the necks of the Jewish people. Now, He will make another and final attack on this Rabbinic stronghold, though it will incense His enemies and hasten His tragic end.

With these explanations, Jesus proceeds to the work of the cure. In so doing, He accommodated Himself to the current popular belief in the curative effects of saliva and clay, especially in the case of weak eyes, in order doubtless to stimulate initial faith in the man, as well as to technically violate the traditional rules. He spat on the ground, made clay of the spittle, smeared it on the blind man's eyes, and told him to go wash in the pool of Siloam not far from the Temple. The application of spittle to the eyes on the Sabbath was expressly prohibited by Jewish tradition. The kneading of the clay was a further aggravation of the offense. Jesus did not believe in the efficacy of these remedies of current medical traditon to cure this man born blind. He only used this method as an aid to the man's faith in Him.

The man obeyed, went and washed, and returned seeing. His obedience was prompt and the cure instantaneous. The occular education of an infant takes six months; but this man had perfect vision immediately, a complete proof of a very extraordinary miraculous cure.

It is no wonder the cure attracted at once the attention of the neighbors. The great change in the beggar's appearance prevented his full recognition. The neighbors were amazed and wondered. Some went around inquiring and commenting:

'Is not this the one who was accustomed to sit at the gate and beg?" Others were saying: "He is the same man." But others in doubt said: "No, but he is like him." But the man said: "I am he." That was final; he knew. Then they began to question him: "How were your eyes opened?" The beggar answered: "The man called Jesus made spittle-clay, smeared my eyes with it, and said: 'Go wash in the pool of Siloam.' When I went and washed, I received my sight." They asked: "Where is that fellow?" He replied, "I do not know."

The next part of the enacted drama is the trial through which the man passed. The neighbors came bringing the beggar to the Pharisees, the accepted professional teachers, who posed as those who knew everything. They began to question him as to how he was healed. The fact of his being healed or as to his identity they did not deny at first. John records significantly in this connection the fact that it was the Sabbath. That was probably the reason the neighbors thought it prudent to bring the cured man to their religious overlords to be examined. The cure had been effected on the Sabbath. When the Pharisees questioned him about how he was cured, he narrated faithfully the facts. They could not deny the miracle, but they would discredit the character of Christ. He had dared to break the law of the Sabbath both in act and in word. Some of the Pharisees repeat their former accusation that "He was an habitual Sabbath-breaker."[1] "This fellow cannot be from God," they exclaim, "because he is not keeping the Sabbath." But on the contrary, others were saying: 'How is a man who is a sinner able to do such things?'" So there was a division among the Pharisees themselves. Consequently, they come to the blind man again to know what his opinion was.

"What do you say about him? You should know, since He opened your eyes." The man replied: "He could open my eyes, because He is a prophet." The Pharisees were hopelessly divided. Some of them were probably too honest to deny the fact of the miracle, but if they should admit that it was a miracle wrought with God, their Sabbath tradition laws were doomed. The cured man promptly took the position of identifying Jesus as a prophet. "Jesus was not a sinner, but a prophet, in spite of the traditional laws of the Sabbath." This reply did not satisfy the Pharisees. They had hoped that he would give some other explanation of the cure.

These enemies of Jesus saw they must seek some other way out of the difficulty. The cured man could not be moved. They could not intimidate him. So they just refused to believe that he had been born blind. If he had gone blind after birth there might be some natural explanation of the cure. There had never been a cure in the case of those born blind. So they send for the parents of the man who had regained his sight.

"Is this your son," they asked, sternly, "the son whom you declare was born blind? How is it that he can now see?" They hoped perhaps to intimidate the parents and get them to deny their relationship to this man who had never seen them. They had let these humble people know beforehand that if they confessed Jesus to be the Messiah, they would be excommunicated — a severe sentence among the Jews, involving direct consequences socially and religiously. One thus put out of the synagogue was as one dead. The burial ceremony was used, there could be no circumcision or mourning for the dead in his house, and none dared come within four cubits of the excommunicated but the wife

1 Present indicative active, linear action, Cf: Jno. 5:10, 16, 18.

and the children! They had not been able to intimidate the beggar son; they did succeed in making the parents timid and cautious. They answer: "We know that this is our son and that he was born blind." Thus far, they were able to go without involving themselves. They refused to go further and draw any inferences, and so cast the responsibility back on the son. "He is of age, ask him," they suggested. The Pharisees had tried to confuse these simple people by their triple question but had not succeeded. The parents confirm the fact of the son's identity and of the cure, leaving the enemies of Jesus to puzzle over the manner or cause of the cure.

There was nothing for them to do now but to turn again to the cured man himself and try to browbeat him into some expression, suitable to their desires. They had succeeded in intimidating the parents; perhaps now the son would follow their example. They first put the man on strict oath: "Give God the glory for the cure." They assure him that they know Jesus very well and that He is only a sinner. "He was accustomed to violate the Sabbath," they declared. They cannot deny the cure, in face of the testimony of the parents. So they will now dragoon the man into denying that Jesus had healed him. They oblige him to choose between Jesus and Moses. "God gave the Sabbath law through Moses," they say. "Even now, Jesus had violated the Sabbath by mixing clay with spittle and applying it to this man's eyes," they explained. As a matter of fact, the act practiced by Jesus was in entire accord with the spirit of the true Sabbath, as Jesus had shown before. But they made the man think he must choose between Jesus and Moses.

The courageous young beggar did not accept the conclusion. Their false logic would have driven him to admit that Jesus was a sinner. He would not be overawed by their authority. Over against their dogmatic declaration that Jesus was a sinner, he declared that he did not know whether Jesus was a sinner or not, but did know that being blind he now saw. He was too sharp to be caught in their trap and too brave to be browbeaten. Foiled in this attempt, they went back to their first question:

"What did he do to you? How did he open your eyes?" Seeing their critical spirit, the man responds with sarcasm: "I told you already and you did not listen. Why do you wish to hear it again? You do not want to become His disciples, do you?"[1] There was the keenest irony in this jibe.

They reviled him, saying: "You are his disciple; we are the disciples of Moses. We know God spoke to Moses but as for this man we know not whence he is."

1 He expects a negative answer.

The man is keen in his reply: "Why, in this very point is the wonder, that you who profess to know all do not know whence he is; but he opened my eyes." Then he adds a bit of theological reasoning on his own account. "We know that God does not listen to sinners." The conclusion was evident; Jesus could not be a sinner. "If anyone is a worshipper of God and continually does his will, God listens to him."[1] This was a fine argument, good logic, and sound theology. "It is unheard of since the world began that anyone opened the eyes of one born blind. If this man wasn't from God, he would not be able to do anything." His reason was conclusive.

They retorted, storming at him: "In sin thou wast begotten, all of thee, and dost thou presume to teach us?" He was either tainted wholly with herditary or with pre-natal sin, according to their understanding. Would he presume to teach them — the religious authorities? He *had* taught them, and out-argued them. But they were casting him out, excommunicated from the synagogue, an outcast of society, deprived of all religious privileges. They faced the force of logic with the violence of excommunication. This has ever been the policy of persecution.

The report of the incident soon reached Jesus. The moment the door of the synagogue closed on him, the door of the kingdom swung open to receive him. Jesus heard that they cast him out and immediately went in search of him. "Do you believe on the Son of Man?" Jesus asked. He eagerly answered: "And who is he, Sir, that I may believe on him?" "You have seen him, and the one speaking to you is that one." Jesus reveals Himself to the man as the Messiah, but not with the expressed title, as to the Samaritan woman, for the Pharisees were near. The man, who had so courageously given his testimony before the council, at once accepts his Saviour, the very moment He is revealed. "Lord, I believe," he said, and bowed down in reverent worship before Him.

Meanwhile, the crowd had gathered about Jesus and the man, attracted by the extraordinary proceeding. Among those who came crowding around were some of the Pharisees, who were ever alert to watch every action and every word of His whose destruction they sought. Jesus was also awake and made use of every opportunity to impress His message upon the people. So addressing those about Him, He declares:

"For judgment I came into this world, in order that those who are confessedly blind may receive their sight and go on seeing, and those thinking they see may become blind."

The Father had turned over the sifting to the Son when He came into the world. He was engaged in that work even now in

1 Third class condition, laying down a general principle.

the miracle. This man now sees physically and spiritually. The Pharisees were being separated as chaff. They caught the point, and gathering their partisan crowd about them, take up the challenge: "But we are not blind, are we?" They suspected that Jesus was insinuating that they were blind, but thought He would hardly dare face their authority, demonstrated but now in the excommunication of the man. He responds in no uncertain terms: "If you were confessedly blind, you would not have sin; but now that you are saying, 'We see,' your sin continues." They had arrogantly asserted superior knowledge; consequently, their rejection of Jesus sealed their fate. They were blinded by the smoke of their own presumption and pride. Jesus made the application directly to them.

6. In the allegory of the fair (good) shepherd, Jesus contrasts the false leaders and teachers with Himself (Jno. 10:1-21).

Going on from the thought[1] of the blindness of the Pharisees, who professed to be the teachers of the people, Jesus spoke a self-explanatory allegory in their presence about the true and false teachers, contrasting Himself with them. They had just cast out from the synagogue the blind beggar whom Jesus had cured and saved. In relation to the fold of the Kingdom and church, Jesus is the door (Jno. 10:1-6) and in relation to the flock, He is the good shepherd (Jno. 10:7-16). The background of the allegory is found in the shepherd life of Palestine in that historic period.

Jesus starts out with a general statement as to the true and false shepherds. The true one comes through the door of the sheepfold — which was a roofless enclosure in the country where sheep were herded. Any other one, climbing up by some other way over the wall, is both a thief who comes to steal, and a bandit-robber who steals by violence. Several flocks were kept in the same fold at night. To a true shepherd the porter opens the door and the sheep listen to his voice. He calls his own sheep each one by his own name and leads them out. It is common for the Eastern shepherds to give individual names to their sheep (Bernard). The loneliness of pastoral life bound the shepherd and his sheep together in companionship, dangers, and pleasures mutually enjoyed. There were dangers of ravines, torrents, wolves, thirst, the winter storms and mountain mists, and straying, in which the sheep looked to their shepherd for protection. There were occasions of care and tenderness on the part of a true shepherd, leading his flock out in the morning and returning with them to the safety of the fold at nightfall. From the tenderness of this intimate relationship, Jesus drew the lesson of the true shepherd-teacher. The sheep follow the true shepherd who goes before them. He has led them out before

1 Amen never introduces a fresh topic.

and they trust him. The true shepherd does thrust out every reluctant sheep "which wishes to linger too long," and then, staff in hand, goes before them and they follow him. The sheep will not follow a stranger, but will flee from him as from a wolf. This "wayside saying" the Pharisees did not understand. He had to tell the story over and explain it in detail to their dulled understanding, because they were too self-satisfied to comprehend that it was pointed at them. They did not recognize themselves in the picture He drew.

Leaving the general picture now, Jesus interprets His relation to the fold under two aspects: that of the door of the fold, and that of the Fair Shepherd. With this object in view, He again took up the allegory with the solemn declaration: "I am the door of the sheep" — a saying which reminds one of other declarations re-recently made about His nature and mission as the bread of life and the living water. To the assembled crowd, He adds, "All who come before me have been thieves and robbers; but the sheep did not listen to them." Jesus claims here to be the only door of the spiritual fold by which the true shepherds enter. There had been many false Messiahs and self-appointed leaders who had worked havoc with the flock.[1] The Scribes and Pharisees had just given an illustration of this by excommunicating the poor beggar whom Jesus had cured. But they themselves must enter the spiritual fold by Jesus if they wished to be saved. Jesus repeated: "I am the door. If anyone enter through me, he shall be saved, and shall come in and go out in the daily routine of the flock and shall go on finding pasture."[2] In me he shall have salvation, liberty, and support. Again He draws the contrast sharply between Himself and the false teacher. "The thief-teacher does not come except that he may steal, kill and destroy." In contrast, "I came that they may go on having life and a surplus or overflowing of it, with all that goes to sustain it."

Having thus passed from the figure of the door to that of the shepherd, Jesus now depicts His character as the "Fair Shepherd" under two aspects: His perfect self-sacrifice and His perfect and superhuman knowledge. "I am the Fair Shepherd," He declares. The fair shepherd is not only true, but beautiful and attractive in character. He lays down his life in self-sacrifice on behalf of his sheep, unlike the hireling, who is working for wages and is not a true shepherd.[3] Such a hireling does not feel that the sheep are his very own property, nor does he have the real interest in the sheep that the shepherd has. "He sees the wolf coming, leaves the sheep and flees."[4] The wolf seizes them quickly and destroys them

1 Josephus Ant. 18:1, 6.   2 Future indicative active, linear action.
3 Cf. Edersheim in loco.   4 Graphic historic present tenses.

completely, because the hireling does not care for the sheep but only for his own life.

Again Jesus repeats His declaration: "I am the Fair Shepherd." Between Jesus and His sheep there is the same mutual experimental knowledge of character as that which exists between Jesus and the Father. This perfect sympathetic understanding between the shepherd and the sheep which follow, has its origin and fruit in complete love, loyalty, and sacrifice, which led the Fair Shepherd to lay down His life for His sheep. Looking forward to His cross and the universality of His Gospel, Jesus adds: "Other sheep I have which are not of this Jewish fold" (Wescott). Those of the Gentile world, I am morally[1] obliged to bring in, and they will listen to my voice; and all the Christian Jews and Gentiles will become one flock under one shepherd. Christ's horizon took in all races and nations. His world mission was no new idea to Him.

For this reason, that the Son lays down His life voluntarily for the world-flock, the Father's love is drawn out. The purpose of the Passion was not merely to exhibit His unselfish life, but that He might resume His life, now enriched with quickening power as never before.[2] There is spontaneity in the surrender to death and in the taking of life back again.[3] Once again, His discourse was the occasion of division among the Jews. Many of them kept on saying: "He has a demon and is gone mad. Why do you listen to him?" But others firmly contradicted and repeatedly affirmed: "These are not the words of one possessed of a demon. Is a demonized man able to open the eyes of the blind?"

1 Impersonal use of dei.　　2 Bernard in loco.　　3 Dods. Com. on John.

CHAPTER XXIII

FINAL CAMPAIGN IN JUDEA

(Harm. §§ 102-111)

Jesus came back to His work in Judea determined to thoroughly evangelize that province. Starting His campaign from Jerusalem, He reached out to all the towns and populous districts of the surrounding country.

1. The mission of the Seventy; Christ's joy in their work and prayer of exultation (Luke 10:1-24).

It was some days after the incidents of the trip down from Galilee (Luke 9:46-62) that Jesus publicly announced His choice of seventy "other disciples" for a special mission. He had chosen twelve some months before and sent them forth by twos in an evangelistic campaign in Galilee (Luke 9:1-6). He now employs the same method on a more intensive scale in Judea. The extreme antagonism of His enemies called for a more rapid and intense work here. As there was special significance in the previous choice of twelve representing the twelve tribes of Israel to whom they were sent primarily, so now the number seventy was not merely a larger and convenient number for the work in hand, but pointed to certain important things in the Jewish history and tradition, linking this number — as the Tubingen School would indicate — in the interest of his universal gospel; but Christ consciously chose seventy to do what the seventy Sanhedrists had failed to do in preparation of the people for the coming Messiah (Hahn). This number harked back also to the seventy elders appointed to assist Moses.[1] The symbolic meaning of the number seventy continued in the seventy translators of the Hebrew Bible into Greek. A more significant symbolism even is found in Jewish reckoning of the number of the nations of the world to be seventy. Here was an implication of the universalism of the Kingdom work, a representative missionary for each nation.[2] Certainly this idea would be in accord with the universalism of Luke's gospel and the mission of Christianity as revealed more clearly later, whether it was the conscious teaching of Christ at this time or not. They were sent by twos for the advantages of companionship and efficiency, as in the case of the campaign of the Twelve and in the early apostolic missions of Paul and his companions. Their work was temporary, unlike that of the Twelve, and so their names are not recorded in the narratives of the gospels, though tradition of the early centuries of apostolic history points to Barnabas, Mark, and others as being of the number.

1 Edersheim: Life and Times of Jesus, Vol. II, p. 136.   2 Genesis 10.

It was the purpose of Jesus to follow after them into every city and country-place and investigate their work, as well as enter into the open doors of opportunity prepared by them. He submitted to them certain considerations and instructions, as He had done in the case of the Twelve, with a view to helping them to a correct and efficient conduct of the campaign. First He stated as the reason for the campaign that "the harvest was abundant (much) and the laborers were few." The way they were to increase the number of laborers was by earnestly and definitely "begging the Lord of the Harvest to thrust out urgently workers into his harvest." Prayer is the primary way of increasing the number of preachers and Christian workers. They must be God-sent and sent in response to definite prayer. Second, they were warned sharply[1] of the perils they were to encounter among the wolf-like enemies, and the necessity of maintaining a harmless lamb-like innocency and inoffensive conduct in the midst of those perils. Third, they were to depend for their material support on those to whom they ministered spiritually, not taking with them any purse for coins, traveling bag for clothing or food, or even an extra pair of sandals. They must be so intent on their work as to waste no time in palaver by the way. Oriental greetings were tedious and caused delay and sometimes danger. The usual Oriental greeting or salutation should be given, first, on entering any home: "Peace be to this house!" If the head of the household proved to be a man well-disposed and inclined to peace, the blessing of God's peace would rest upon him. But if not, then the peace of God would return back in blessing upon the one who spoke the salutation. Once the worker was received into the hospitality of a home, he was to comport himself in a manner worthy. He must stay on in that house, not changing from house to house with every new invitation, thus wasting much time. "The laborer is worthy of his wages," and Matthew's account adds "of his food" (Matt. 10:10); but he must not be troublesome, the rather genteel, eating and drinking the things the family should furnish. Fifth, the workers should be proper in their conduct toward any town into which they might enter. If the people, Jews or Gentiles, received them with good will, they were to accept with all courtesy their hospitality, eating the things placed before them, putting aside all Jewish scruples. Sixth, their mission was to be one of healing and preaching, and their message —summing up — was: "The Kingdom of God has come nigh to you." Seventh, they were to deal with their opponents fearlessly. If they might, at any time, enter into any city and not be well received; coming out of the inhospitable homes, they should say: "Even every speck of dust of your city that has stuck to our feet we are

1 Idou; look! behold! see!

wiping off as a protest against you."[1] This solemn act must be
followed up by an equally solemn declaration: "But though you
reject us, you must go on learning this, that the Kingdom of God
has drawn nigh." "I tell you, that for the people of Sodom in that
day of reckoning, it will be more tolerable, than for that town that
rejects you." Eighth, Jesus adds a forceful illustration of the consequences to those who should reject Him, taken from His own
personal ministry: "Woe unto you Chorazin! Woe to you Bethsaida!
For if the miracles had been done in Tyre and Sidon which have
been done among you, a long time ago they would have repented,
sitting in sackcloth and ashes.[2] But it will be more tolerable for
Tyre and Sidon in the judgment than for you. And you, Capernaum
will not be exalted to the glory of heaven, will you? No, down to
Hades, the depth of shame and destruction, you shall go." Thus did
He pronounce a solemn farewell to the cities in which He had
preached and done many mighty works in vain. The mention of
Chorazin shows how much of the activity of Jesus was not recorded
in the Gospel narrative. The cities, which should reject the workers He now sends forth, would suffer the same dreadful fate. Finally the Lord points out to them the authority and power of their
mission. The one who should reject one of these workers, rejects
Christ, and the one rejecting Christ rejects God.

The campaign, which was initiated probably after the Feast
of the Tabernacles, had been in progress for some weeks. Many
of the activities of Christ during the campaign are not recorded in
the Gospel narratives. Jesus had been forced to retire to Bethany
beyond the Jordan and it was to this place most likely that the
seventy came back to Him.

They returned with joy over their success which had ex-
ceeded even their fondest hopes and expectations. When they went
forth they were not expressly endowed with the power to cast
out demons, but marvelous to tell "even the demons were subjected and they continued to have power over them." The condition
of exercising this power was identity with Jesus in character and
work as they commanded the demons "in his name." Every Christian worker has to grapple with demons in people and can overcome them only in the sphere of the name and character of Jesus.[3]

The observation of Jesus on this report was, that He was seeing in the defeat of the demons while this work was going on the
quick-as-lightning and complete downfall of Satan, the chief of
demons, from the highest seat of power. He adds: "Behold, I have
given to you as the representative workers, and to those who shall

1 Dative of disadvantage.   2 Sackcloth was worn by penitents and supplicants. Ashes were
        used for self-humiliation and punishment (Robertson).
3 Locative of sphere within which.

follow you, the power and right to tread upon the venomous ad-
ders and scorpions of hell and trample down all the power of the
Devil-enemy and nothing shall in anywise harm you in the least."
Protection from bodily harm and, especially, victory over spiritual
foes is guaranteed to them in their pursuit of this high task of
the kingdom. "But do not go on rejoicing in this power over demons
important as it may be." In this very elation, in their victory over
demons, there might lurk a temptation to pride over their spiritual
powers. Satan fell from heaven in the beginning through pride.
The rather should they "keep on rejoicing" in something better —
"that their names were permanently recorded[1] in heaven as citizens
of the Kingdom of God."

At that very hour, Christ exulted in the Holy Spirit over the
present victory of His disciples, prophecy of the future final victory
of His Kingdom on the earth. The return of the joyful, victorious
band of disciples, was the occasion of holy joy in Jesus, who
through the Holy Spirit, foresaw the glorious future. In this ecstacy
and transport of high exultation, He uttered a prayer of thanksgiving and praise: "I confess to thee, Father, Lord of heaven
and earth, my thanks and praise because thou didst hide these
things of the Kingdom from those who are wise and learned in
their own conceit and hast revealed them unto those who are mere
babes in intellectual things." The twelve were chosen from the
midst of the unlettered fishermen of Galilee. "Yes, thou Father of
all, because thy good pleasure made it so." Then He adds the
whole of the christology of the fourth gospel in a single expression:
"All things were definitely intrusted to me by my Father, not only
the power of revelation, but all power." There is perfect equality
and understanding between the Son and the Father. Here is His
claim to deity in a definite declaration uttered in this prayer, in
supreme fellowship with the Father, as He contemplated the final
victory over Satan. Here is also a declaration of His divine
sovereignty. The Son reveals the Father "to whom He may wish."
This prayer was uttered publicly.

Turning next to His disciples, probably a little later in private,
He uttered a Beatitude: "Blessed are the eyes that are seeing
what you are seeing: for I tell you many prophets and kings wanted
to see the things you are seeing and did not see them and hear
the things you are hearing and did not hear them."

2. A lawyer's question and the parable of the good Samaritan.
(Luke 10:25-37.)

It might have been in some synagogue in Judea, that the incident took place which called forth such a remarkable teaching

---

1 Perfect tense, denoting completed action and continued state.

of Jesus and one of the most beautiful of all His parables, that of
the good Samaritan. A certain lawyer stood up, from among those
seated in the synagogue around the great Teacher, and asked Him
a question. He was testing out the ability of Jesus as a teacher.
He probably felt the pressure of such teaching as placed the
lawyer-scribes in the embarrassing category of the "wise and
prudent," to whom God did not reveal the things of the Kingdom.
His motive might have been to entrap Jesus with some question,
though it is likely he may have had an earnest desire to know
better the way of life. His question, at any rate, revealed an incorrect conception of the eternal life, about which Jesus had much
to say always:
    "By doing what heroic deed shall I inherit the larger and
unending life about which you say so much?" he asked. By the
very form of his question, he had placed emphasis[1] on "doing" as
a means of coming in possession of eternal life. The answer of
Jesus showed fairness toward one who might be among the "wise,"
but who at least showed a desire to learn. It also assumed in the
lawyer a previous knowledge of the law. "In the law, what stands
written?" The lawyer wore a phylactery bearing the Shema,
which the Jews recited twice daily (Deut. 6:3; 11:13). Jesus knew
the lawyer had studied the law at length and was familiar with
the letter of the law at least. He also knew that the cardinal vice
of the times was the divorcing of the letter from the spirit, religion
from moral life and conduct.[2] "How do you read it?" Jesus wanted
to see how the lawyer would interpret the law. This very question
assumed the previous study of the law, involving the process of the
memory, on the part of the learned jurist. The lawyer answered,
reciting the Shema, which called for love to God with all man's four
powers of Heart, Soul, Strength, and Mind, covering his physical,
intellectual, and spiritual capacities. The second part of his answer
shows he knew the law and probably reveals a sincere desire that
this man might have had to connect up religion in a real way
with life.
    Jesus treated this answer as sincere and thorough-going in
His reply: "You have answered in a straight-forward way. Go on
doing this, and you shall live." As far as the lawyer's words
went, he had answered correctly. The trouble with this plan of
obtaining eternal life is that no man ever lived up to the requirement. No man was ever able to live a life blameless before the
law. One slip brings failure. If one could live up to this standard
perfectly, he would inherit eternal life. But no man can do this.
The lawyer felt that he was himself in a trap and was embarrassed
because he had asked such a *simple* question. There was much

1 Place of primary emphasis, in Greek sentence, is the beginning, the first word.

hair-splitting among the Jews over the question, "Who is my neighbor?" The lawyer wanted to excuse himself for asking a question, the answer of which was so evident, and now carried the discussion into this debatable field. The Jews excluded from the category of *neighbors* the Gentiles, especially the Samaritans.[1] Everybody recognized that, but what would Jesus say?

Jesus took up the rejoinder immediately in the form of the following beautiful story, the so-called parable of the good Samaritan:

"A certain man was descending by the precipitous, robber-infested road leading down from Jerusalem to Jericho." Secular history records the dangers of this road from antiquity.[2] These bandits were the meanest type of robbers. "They violently took from him his money and even his clothing, beat him up, and left him half-dead in this dangerous, bloody way." The vivid details in this imaginative story corresponded with frequent tragic occurrances in the mountain defiles of this perilous road. "Now, by chance, a priest was going down that way. He came alongside,[3] took a momentary look, and passed on the other side of the road," to avoid ceremonial contamination. Here is a vivid picture of ceremonial cleanliness at the cost of moral principle and duty. "And likewise, a Levite came down to the place and on seeing him," more heartless even than the priest, "passed on the other side." Another vivid illustration of how the world, even the religionist, treats those in distress. There was no neighborly love in the conduct of either one of these men for the poor, abandoned, and helpless man.

"But a certain Samaritan, being on a journey, came down upon him and, seeing him, took pity on him." The contrast here is sharp between this despised Samaritan "dog" and the robed priest and Levite, the orthodox clergy of the Jews, supposed to minister religiously in matters of human welfare. The Samaritan gave a demonstration of true neighbor-love. Immediately on seeing the man he had compassion — a fellow-feeling or sympathy for him. Nor did he stop with mere looks of pity, but hastily administered first aid — "binding up his wounds, pouring in soothing oil and antiseptic wine," the common household remedies. Then he helped the man to mount his own beast and himself walked beside him, until he came to one of the two solitary inns on this deserted way.[4] On arrival, he personally took special care[5] of him. At dawn the next morning, when he must resume his journey, probably on business to Jericho, with careful but prodigal generosity, he paid

1 Robertson, Word Pictures.   2 Tristam, Eastern Customs.
3 Ingressive aorist.   4 There are ruins of two inns about half-way between Jerusalem and Jericho.   5 Intensive preposition with verb.

the innkeeper for the expense of the night and said: "Take good care of him, and, whatever you may spend in addition, on my return trip I will pay you." Here is the genius of true neighbor-love. It renders help with promptness, thoroughness, self-sacrifice, fearlessness, and unwearying patience.[1] The kindness of the Samaritan wasn't one of the letter but of the Spirit, not circumscribed by national or racial prejudices but universal, not limited by personal convenience but sacrificial.[2]

In the interpretation of this beautiful parable, regard must be had especially to the question put by the lawyer: "Who is my neighbor?" That question revealed the wrong point of view in the jurist who asked it. He was limiting in his thought the conception of neighbor to the one who was near to him, and from whom he received helpful treatment for himself. Evidently, his point of view was wholly selfish. Jesus substituted the conception of an outgoing love: "To whom may I be neighbor?" "Whose claims on my neighborly help do I recognize?" He required the lawyer to answer his own question: "Which of these three men seems to you to have acted as neighbor to the man who fell among the robbers?" The lawyer was moved perhaps by the wonderful pathos of the story. He could not but see the point. He gave the correct answer, but his race-prejudice kept him from using the hateful name, "Samaritan." Jesus had chosen that name advisedly, that he might deal a knockout blow to all kinds of caste and racial barriers. The lawyer's answer was: "The one who took pity on him."

"Go on and keep on doing likewise," said Jesus. The neighbor-love renders help when and where needed, having regard to nothing beyond the fact of need. My neighbor is any "certain man," Jew or Gentile, black or white, rich or poor, learned or ignorant, who needs my help and whom I have power and opportunity to help. A love that makes us do that for every needy soul is the kind of love God had for sinful men when He sent His Son to be their Saviour. It is the kind of loyal love we must have toward God and men if we are to have eternal life.

3. Jesus, the guest of Martha and Mary at Bethany (Luke 10:38-42).

If we are to put much by the chronology of Luke, who made "an accurate examination of all things from the beginning" of the evangelical work, we may think that the incident of this visit to the Bethany home took place some time before the Feast of the Dedication and perhaps after Jesus had received the Seventy

1 A. B. Bruce, The Parabolic Teaching of Christ. 2 Taylor, Parables of Our Lord.

back in Bethany beyond the Jordan, to have their report of the campaign in Judea. The Bethany where Martha, Mary, and their brother Lazarus lived was distant some two and a half miles southeast of Jerusalem. Why Luke did not mention the name of the town in his account of this incident is unexplained. Whether Martha, who received Jesus into her home, was a widow or the wife of Simon the Leper, is a matter of conjecture. It seems that Martha was the owner of the house, or, at least, the dominant figure and older sister. Whether Mary is to be identified with Mary Magdalene, and Jesus was a special guest in this home because he had rescued her as a run-away girl from a life of shame in Magdala, a town in Galilee, is also a matter for conjecture, and improbable, though there may be some arguments seeming to favor such a theory. We cannot believe that this was the first touch of Jesus with that home, contrary to the opinion of some. When He came to the town with His disciples, He received the personal invitation from this beloved family to be their guest. Circumstances indicate that it was a family in easy circumstances, and enjoying a certain position of social esteem and regard in Bethany and Jerusalem.

The character of the two sisters stands out in marked contrast in the circumstances of the visit. The younger sister Mary took her place, seated on the floor in the recognized posture of a disciple, and right in front of the feet of Jesus. Her attitude as depicted in the narrative was one of an eager learner, alert to catch every word of her Lord's teaching. It is significant that Luke uses here the title, Lord. Mary recognized that Jesus was her Lord and she was desirous of knowing what He would have her do. But Martha, on the other hand, was "drawn about in different directions," much distracted[1] with the household service. She was preoccupied with the preparation of an elaborate meal for Jesus. That was a praiseworthy desire, if a partly mistaken one. At least it was born out of a dear regard for her great guest, and excusable in this beautiful and affectionate hostess. She chose a good part, if Mary did choose the better. There are worse faults than being a hard-working, bustling housewife and hostess, though too much nervous distraction over household duties may sometimes stand in the way of more important hours of quiet meditation at the feet of Jesus. We ought the more easily to excuse Martha for this mistaken zeal, because it was all done for Jesus. We, who have worse faults, could never blame or criticise her.

---

1 Periespato, imperfect, denoting a continued state of nervous distraction.

In her "much service" and over-occupation, she grew tired and nervous, and then a bit of jealousy crept into her heart as she bustled to and fro, and, in passing, saw the younger sister sitting calmly at the feet of Jesus, too engrossed with His conversation to pay any attention. All of a sudden, Martha lost hold on herself and suddenly burst in on the conversation and said:

"Lord, don't you care that my sister has been leaving me to do the work alone? Tell her to take hold and help me."[1] This was a little show of jealous temper, which, when given way to, always works evil. Doubtless Mary would have complied with any gentle appeal from the elder sister for help. Martha, instead reproaches Jesus for monopolizing Mary and complains that both He and Mary had forgotten her. She even intimates that Mary might not heed an appeal from her and that Jesus must command her to take hold of her part of the dinner job.[2]

The answer of Jesus was a tender rebuke to His amiable but over-anxious hostess: "Martha, Martha," He repeated with tenderness and evident affection, "you are filled with inward anxiety and outward agitation about many things in the preparation of a too elaborate meal. There is need of only a few things, or 'one dish would be sufficient.'" Here, Jesus must have played on the word. Just one staple dish would have required little time and attention and left her unencumbered for other things more important. There is one thing which is more important than all else, the spiritual "one thing" which Mary had chosen as her "good part, which shall not be taken away from her." Jesus must have been smiling as He administered this loving rebuke. Fret and fussiness He must reprove, even in this lovely matron, as well as the superfluous hospitality which occasions it. At the same time, He exalts fellowship with Him to a very high place of excellence and permanence in the life of the disciples. This is the principal thing needful for life and its reward is permanent and "will not be taken away." It was not Martha's service that Jesus rebuked, but her over-occupation with the material side, her nervous distraction, her anxiety, and her jealous burst of temper. It was Mary who braved all ridicule, scorn, and criticism later when she broke the expensive alabaster box of wonderful perfume and anointed Jesus "against his burial." The reason she attained that height of devoted service in a perilous hour was because she before had chosen, "the good part, of sitting at the feet of Jesus." Her reward has never been taken away.

4. Jesus again teaches His disciples how to pray (Luke 11:1-13).

1 Ingressive aorist.

2 Sunantilabatai, literally to seize hold of her end of the job along with the elder sister.

The whole section of Luke's gospel (9:51-18:14) is largely didactic. One of the main elements in all the work of our Lord, and now especially in this intensive campaign in Judea, was prayer. The example of Jesus in prayer in this campaign inspired His disciples to a desire to know better how to pray. Their request that He teach them "the habit of prayer,"[1] showed their familiarity with the fact, that John the Baptist had emphasized habitual prayer in his ministry, just as he did fasting. Prayer was systematic in the conduct of His campaign in Judea and habitual in the life of Jesus. He now repeats His teaching on the content of prayer and giving them once again His model (1-4), reenforces the perseverance of prayer in a parable (5-8), and exhorts them to perseverance in the practice of prayer (9-13).

(1) Why Luke gives a more abbreviated form of the model prayer than Matthew, is not expressly stated. Jesus, having given the fuller instruction on the subject of the content of prayer to the Twelve at the time of the initiation of the campaign in Galilee, here gives the substance of the prayer in shorter form. He did not intend it for formal, ritualistic use. There are certain changes in words and tenses of verbs which show an accommodation to the intense needs of the present campaign in Judea and to the request to teach them the habit of prayer. Jesus avoids the formality of ritual, which the form of their request seemed to imply characterized the ministry of John. Instead of using the same phrases exactly that He had employed earlier in His ministry, He alters the words and phrases to teach the spontaneous and intensely practical character of true prayer. He took it for granted in His first expression that prayer was going to be systematic and habitual.

"Whenever you pray say:

"Father, hallowed be thy name;

Let thy Kingdom come;

Keep on giving[2] us our bread each day for the incoming day;

Forgive us our sins, for we ourselves forgive everyone owing us;

And bring us not into temptation."[3]

Jesus divests the model prayer of all Jewish restrictions and makes it universal by omitting even the pronoun "Our." The characteristic teaching of Jesus in revelation of God is found in the word "Father." He is the Father-God of every loyal individual believer in His Son.

"Let thy name (or character) be acknowledged as holy." We must pray that God's character become known and reverenced

---

1 Present infinitive, indicating continued, progressive, habitual prayer.
2 Robertson's Word Pictures, present active imperative.
3 From the Greek text, Nestle.

by men and His relationship to us be understood. "Let thy Kingdom (reign or dominion) come" or be extended from heaven to
this world (now ruled by the adversary) so as to extirpate
wickedness. Jesus did not forget the personal needs, which we
put in the first place usually in our prayers, thus reversing the
model prayer's order, which puts the highest good first. He
reminded them of the habitual need of persistent daily prayer, by
limiting the supply to one day's necessities. They were to ask
daily for the daily supply for meeting the current, temporal, and
spiritual needs. Prayer must be recurring, constant, just as God's
supply in answer must be continual. "Keep on giving¹ us daily
our bread for the incoming (current) day." Also: "Go on for-
giving² us our sins as we are habitually and continually forgiving everyone owing us." The flow of the present tenses drives
home the habitual character of prayer at every turn.³ Notice also
the more universal character given to the prayer in Luke's narrative by the use of the word "sins" in contrast to Matthew's use
of the more Jewish "debts." The Jews would understand debts
to include sins, but Luke's Gentile readers would not. At the
same time, he notes carefully that we are not able to forgive sins,
but only debts, in the common sense of mutual human relationships. The effectiveness of our prayer for forgiveness of our sins
is measured just by our forgiving attitude toward our fellowman
who has offended against us.

"And bring us not into temptation." God does not tempt man
to evil (Jas. 1:13). Here, we are bidden to pray for guidance
that we may not come into temptation, or better, into a Geth-
semane-like trial which would be too hard for us.

(2) The parable of the friend at midnight, and of the selfish
neighbor, teaches perseverance in prayer (vv 5-8), which is never
out of season and must be importunate. We ought always to pray
and not grow faint-hearted when the answer is delayed. To teach
this great fact about the character of prayer, Jesus supposed a
case which might happen, couching His teaching in beautiful
parabolic form. At midnight,⁴ one goes to his supposed friend and
neighbor with the simple request for a loan of three loaves of
bread, to meet the emergency of unexpected need arising from the
visit of a friend, who came in upon him at a very late hour, tired
and hungry from the journey. His guest caught him with an
empty pantry and nothing to set before him. Bread was lacking —
as might happen where the bread was baked daily, and in quantity

---

1 Present imperative, didou, indicating a continued, progressive process.
2 Present imperative again.   3 Cf. The use of the aorist tense in Matthew's narrative,
       showing the practical end and adopted form of the prayer, here.
4 Genitive of time.

measured to meet the daily need alone. But the neighbor had
already retired, tightly bolting and barring his doors for the
night, and his little children were in bed with him. "Stop troubling
me,"[1] he said to the persistent and repeated knocking, "I cannot
get up and give you anything." What he meant in effect was that
he did not wish to get up and undo the tedious bolts and bars, rous-
ing up the little children in the same room with him at the dead
hour of midnight. The supplicant, however, was not to be denied,
and continued to knock and beg clamorously. His persistence
became even shameless and impudent.[2] The conclusion Jesus confidently asserts: "I tell you, it is not from true friendship, but
from his own selfish desire to be rid of the troublesome applicant
who persists shamelessly that he will arise and give him as many
as he needs."

There is not in this parable a picture of the God-Father, to
whom Jesus would have the disciples pray habitually, except by
contrast. God is not selfish, indifferent, heartless, as He may sometimes seem to the believer who prays for some time without apparently receiving any answer at all. On the other hand, He is loving,
tender, and fatherly. His ear is ever open to them who wait upon
Him in humility, faith, and patience.

Jesus sets forth in this parable one of the main conditions of
successful prayer. We have to wait and persist in prayer if we
would have the "desires of our hearts" fulfilled. The revent,
believing and importunate prayer of a true child of God will always prevail with an infinitely kind and loving Father. By contrast, if the petition of the persistent supplicant prevailed at last
with his selfish and lazy neighbor, how much more will the earnest,
persistent pleading of the believing child be heard and answered
by the heavenly father. It is necessary that an all-wise Father-God
should wait for a long time to fully answer our prayers, many
times, that the conditions may be first fully worked out in us.

There are many conditions which must be met in successful
prayer. Persistence in the supplicant gives the opportunity for
the fulfilling of those conditions. Successful prayer depends on
the character of the supplicant as well as the nature of the
things petitioned. Without holiness of character, purity of heart,
submission to the will of God, willing obedience and a vital
faith-connection in loyal attachment to Christ, there can be no
successful outcome of prayer. True prayer is not a mere wish
that flits across the soul like a shadow of a cloud that passes
over a field of grain.[3] It is the "soul's sincere desire uttered or

1 Present active imperative with me   2 Anaides, shamelessly.
3 Taylor, Parables of Our Lord.

unexpressed," which goes up in unerring thought-waves to the ear of God. The supplicant must abide in Christ and His words abide in the character and conduct of the one praying. True prayer must be characterized by devotion, which is willing to wait for an answer. The successful prayer is shameless in its persistence and will not take a refusal. Importunate prayer will prevail even in the face of discouragements and difficulties. We have Christ's authority that those who pray to God persistently will be heard and fully answered.

The Father-God tests our faith by delaying the answer. He knows our needs far better than we do, and appears in the hour of sorest trial with the answer, "full measure, shaken down, and running over." So, Jesus teaches us that in the disappointing experiences of the individual disciple, grappling with the problems of growth and development in grace and Kingdom-life, when progress seems so slow, there must be persistence and patience, to keep on praying and await the final and successful outcome. God is working out in us His purposes and our petitions must always be conditioned by His will and purpose in our lives. He deals with each individual as the physician deals with his patient, according to his disease, temperament, and constitution.

(3) Jesus concludes the lesson on prayer "with a threefold exhortation, a threefold promise, and a threefold statement based on experience, with an illustration from human relations." He prefaced the final exhortation, by an emphatic, authoritative expression: "So I[1] say to you." The parable had taught the successful outcome of persevering prayer, but the disciples have here the authority of the Master explicitly declared. The three commands[2] form a climax in earnestness, after the manner of the teaching of the parable. "Go on asking, and it shall be given unto you; Go on seeking and you shall find; go on knocking[3] and it shall be opened to you." We must ask earnestly, seek energetically, and knock intently and loudly. There is no racial limit placed on prayer in the threefold promise: "For everyone who is asking[4] is receiving; and everyone who is seeking[4] is finding; and to the one who is knocking[4] it will be opened."

The threefold illustration taken from the analogy of the human relationship between father and son, brings the lesson on prayer to the final conclusion: "Now what father among you, if his son asks him for a fish, will hand to him a snake? Or if he asks him for an egg, will hand to him a scorpion?" Matthew adds: "If he asks for bread will he give him a stone?" (Matt. 7:7).

1 Ego, in the first, or emphatic position.   2 All in the imperative mode.
3 All, present imperative active, denoting continued and progressive action.
4 The progressive present tense in each case.

In each case there was certain similarity between the thing asked for and the thing that might have been given in deception. The loaf of bread resembles in some cases a stone, the fish a serpent, and the scorpion, with its legs closed about it, an egg. The form of argument of the final conclusion is from the less to the greater. If an earthly father, with all his evil human limitations, knows how to give good gifts to his children, how much more will the Heavenly Father give the highest, and sum of all spiritual gifts, the Holy Spirit, to those who habitually and persistently pray to Him. God gives in response to earnest and persistent prayer neither a useless thing, like the stone, nor a harmful thing, like the serpent or scorpion, but the Holy Spirit, the supreme object of desire for all true disciples.

5. Jesus casts out a demon and is accused of being in league with Beelzebub (Luke 11:14-36).

In the ministry of Jesus, it was easy for similar cures to be performed on different occasions with correspondingly similar results. On such occasions, there might be partial repetition of the same teachings, as well as similar charges by His enemies, answered by substantially the same arguments Jesus had used before, under like circumstances. It would be but natural that the Pharisees, who had hounded the tracks of Jesus everywhere in Galilee with their emissaries, should be acquainted with the methods there used to antagonize His work and make use of them now in Judea, where vast throngs attended His ministry.

Jesus cast out a dumb demon one day, and when the demon had gone out, the man who had been dumb began and went on speaking. The crowds marveled, but certain ones from the crowd, probably the Pharisees, and particularly the Scribes, judging from what had happened in Galilee (Matt. 12:25), malignantly criticized His work, saying: "By Beelzebub, prince of demons, he casts out demons." Others at the same time, putting Him to the test from another angle, were seeking a sign from heaven from Him. He was attacked from two sides at the same time: from one side with brazen scorn and derision which would attribute His high works of mercy in the cure of the miserably demonized to the black art of Satanic powers, and on the other side by those who under the pretext of piety would seek to force Him to a physical demonstration of His assumed Messianic powers. He knew their malicious machinations, and simply replied to the first attack with the unanswerable argument used before in Galilee. "Every Kingdom divided against itself undergoes desolation and house topples against house." Here is a graphic picture of what happens when a kingdom is divided against itself.[1] Satan's kingdom, if divided against itself, as they were assuming, could not stand. Division leads to destruction. Thus He showed how unreasonable and inconsistent was their accusation, and refuted unanswerably their foolish charge. Following this with an *argumentum ad hominem*, He asserted that their own sons in the Pharisaic doctrine, the exorcists, claimed to be able to cast out demons. If[2] Jesus cast out demons by Beelzebub, by whom did these exorcist-sons of theirs cast them out? Of course, the exorcists would vehemently deny such a Satanic source for their power. Jesus does not assert that they did actually cast out demons. The Pharisees would have divided the followers of Jesus, putting some against Him, but they fell into their own trap and found their own disciples, the exorcists, who taught the Pharisaic doctrine of the spirit world, arrayed against themselves by this reply of Jesus. A third argument brought Jesus to His conclusion. In the practice of the military art, he who would go in and spoil the house or court of a strong man must be stronger than the one who protected that house and its goods from within. Jesus with ease, by the finger of God, had cast out demons. The Kingdom of God, therefore, had come upon them. He was the stronger man, who had come into Satan's house and despoiled it. His casting out demons was a demonstration of this process. In this evident conflict between His work and that of Satan, there could be no neutral ground. Every man must be on one side or another. It was evident now whose side His antagonists were on. They thus started out by charging Him with being in league with the prince of demons, and wound up by finding themselves revealed to the people as allies of Satan. Jesus further draws the moral and applies the lesson to the people who were led by these Pharisees. The unclean spirit of idolatry had finally been cast out of Israel's house, which had been swept and garnished with Pharisaic self-righteousness; but the house had been left empty and was being reoccupied by Satan with many unclean spirits, such as pride, self-righteousness, and unbelief.[3] The last state promised to be worse than the first.

At this juncture, a woman in the crowd burst into exclamations about the mother who had borne and nurtured such a Son. She had doubtless been deeply impressed by the "demolishing words of Jesus."[4]

"Happy is the womb that bore you, and the breasts you sucked."[5] In Galilee, He had been interrupted in the midst of His discourse following the encounter with the accusing Pharisees

---

1 Robertson, Word Pictures.   2 Condition of the first class, determined as fulfilled,
    but deals only with the statement, not with the facts.
3 Edersheim, Life and Times of Jesus, in loco.   4 DeMent, Bible Reader's Life of
    Christ.   5 Robertson, Translation of Luke.

and Scribes, by the appearance of His mother and half-brothers who had come to fetch Him home, believing, according to the report of the Pharisees, that He had become mentally unbalanced, such was the intensity of His work. In that case, as in this, the human relationship was exalted above the divine mission, and asserted to the detriment of His work. In both cases, Jesus exalts the divine above the human:

"Yes, rather happy are those who are listening to the Word of God and keep observing it." Thus He points the woman away from His person to His mission. Spiritual knowledge leading to spiritual kinship was the most blessed wish for them all.

This led him to the kindred thought of the need of the light of God's word, as revealed through His own ministry. He plainly told them that their generation was an evil one, and needed the light. That such was the case was evidenced in the fact that these Jews were seeking even there and then a sign, instead of accepting the evident sign of His beneficent ministry in their midst. Jonah, who was delivered from the belly of the fish and sent to Nineveh, became, through his very miraculous presence and glorious ministry, a sign to the Ninevites. The only sign which would be given to this present generation was that of the miracle-working, preaching and teaching ministry of Jesus. He does not here point to the sign of the three days in the tomb typified in Jonah's experience in the fish. The Queen of Sheba would rise up in the judgment to condemn the men of this generation because she came from the ends of the earth, recognizing her need and seeking to derive from Solomon a greater wisdom than she possessed. A greater preacher than Jonah and a wiser sage than Solomon was here, making the greater their condemnation for rejecting Him. "She was a heathen queen and they were Jews, God's chosen; she came from the ends of the earth, while they were here; she applied to Solomon while they rejected Him, a greater than Solomon; therefore, their condemnation was great" (Plummer).

Jesus concludes His discourse by a parabolic application of the principle laid down in the previous discussion, as to the character of the spiritual light of His ministry and how it should be received. He made use of a part of the sermon on the Mount in His illustrations. (Cf. Matt. 5:15; 6:21; Mark 4:21).

"No one, after lighting a lamp, puts it in a cellar or under a bushel, but upon the lamp-stand (jutting from inside of the rock wall of the house), that those who come in might enjoy the light." This figure is taken from the domestic life of Palestine, where one grease-lamp served for the whole family. We should not expect that God would light the spiritual lamp of the Messianic reign and place it in a dark vault of the unbelieving hearts of an unreceptive people and allow such to hide it under the common bushel-measure of their indifference. They should look to the inward conditions of their receptiveness. If the eye is sound, the whole body receives the benefit of the light; but if the eye is diseased and suffers from myopia, it distorts and gives a confused double-image. Those who darken their God-given spiritual light by deliberate indifference or impenitence, are not able to see things straight or to judge them correctly. The faculty of faith, when diseased, becomes the organ of superstition. Those who look to the soundness of the eye of reception will experience no difficulty in the reception of spiritual truth and light.

"Keep on the watch to see whether the light of inward condition has not become darkness through willful opposition." This was the note of warning sounded out by Jesus to an unbelieving generation.

6. While at breakfast with a Pharisee, Jesus severely denounces the Pharisees and lawyers (Luke 11: 37-54).

Now on the occasion of His speaking while in the campaign, probably somewhere in Judea, a Pharisee invites[1] Jesus to take breakfast[2] with him. This meal was served at midday and after returning from morning prayers at the synagogue, Jesus accepted without question the invitation and circumstances would seem to point to sincerity on the part of the Pharisee. At least he did not omit the courtesy of water to wash the hands of his guest. Simon, the Pharisee, who had entertained Jesus formerly in Galilee, did omit the accustomed courtesies. This Pharisee, seeing that Jesus reclined on the lounge at the table, without first dipping[3] His hands in water for the ceremonial purification, was filled with amazement. The Pharisees had many regulations about the meal. First, a basin of water was brought for each to wash one hand. Then a blessing followed and all partook of a glass of wine. After this, they reclined at the table in the order of worthiness, another basin of water was presented, and they washed both hands, preparatory to the meal. It was probably the first basin of water that Jesus refused, with the purpose of showing that religion must not spend its energy on such trivialities.[4]

In a previous encounter with the Pharisees in Galilee, Jesus had denied that the ordinance of the Elders was binding. He now shows that mere externalism militates against the internal and spiritual character of religion. Then He showed how mere

1 Dramatic present Indicative.   2 Note hopos rather than hina.
3 First aorist passive of baptidzo.   4 Edersheim, Life and Times of Jesus.

traditionalism was in conflict with the written law; now He points out how it supersedes the principles which underlay the law. Then He had explained how defilement came not from without inward; now He reveals how higher consecration imparts purity. He takes the initiative this time, seeing the evident surprise of the host at His conduct in omitting the traditional ablution before eating.

"You Pharisees do now what the Pharisees have always done: keeping the external regulations scrupulously, cleaning the outside of the cup and plate, while your hearts within are full of greed and malice. Fools! Did not he who made the outside make the inside also?"[1] The very meat and drink before them now was probably the product of plunder and certainly was the means of excess.[2] This meal was not proving very peaceful. The critical attitude of the Pharisees drew forth from Jesus a strong expression: "Senseless men!" He said, "did not God, who made the material things make men's souls also?" It was foolishness to wash hands, cups, and plates, and leave the souls polluted with rapacious greed and wicked excess. Let them learn to give this same excessive food in the cups and platters, to the poor, and along with it their sympathy and true charity, and they would have a "pure religion and undefiled" before God. True internal benevolence expels external defilement.

Jesus next addressed Himself particularly to the Pharisees of the group (vv 42-45), castigating them with three woes. The first was against their *ritualism*, tithing little things such as mint, rue, and every garden herb, but passing by deliberately the meting out of justice and love, the kind[3] that characterized God. Jesus did not condemn the tithe, but rather approved of it; but their sin was in neglecting the weightier matters of the inward state of heart. The second woe He pronounced was against their *pride*, exemplified in their love of prominence in taking the principal seats on the semi-circular bench facing the congregation in the synagogues. Even at this meal, He doubtless observed how they were arranged in the order of "worthiness" at the table (cf. Matt. 23:6). This was a well-known characteristic of the Pharisees. They also liked to be saluted in the marketplaces, another evidence of their pride and self-assertion. A third woe Jesus hurled at them was against their *hypocrisy*, comparing them to the unmarked tombs which had not been white-washed according to regulation. It was a seven days' ceremonial pollution to come in contact with one of these "indirect graves," full of corruption within; and men stepping on them unaware would

1 Robertson's, Translation of Luke's Gospel.   2 Harpagas kai ponerias. (Plummer)
3 Objective Genetive.

sink down and come into contact with one of the dead bodies. Jesus called them masked men, whose outward appearance belied their inward character.

At this juncture, a conceited lawyer (scribe) spoke up. He was a professional student of the Law, and thought that he was just a little better than the ordinary Pharisee. Jesus had condemned the whole system of their traditionalism. He would cut it up root and branch. The scribe might wink at the denunciation of the Pharisees; but Jesus had gone so far that "even[1] he and his lawyer-colleagues were insulted." So Jesus turns the guns of His woes on them. The first was against binding upon the people, burdens of traditionalism, too heavy to be borne. To the already too heavy burden of ceremonial rules, received as a heritage from the past, they continued to add others, but never raised a finger to put aside one. Moreover, they themselves evaded in practice the very rules they required the people to observe. Their petifogging interpretations of the written Law were later compiled in the Mishna and in the Gemarah.[2] They had no sympathetic touch to relieve the burden they imposed. The second woe was against the persecution they waged against the messengers of God. Their fathers had killed the prophets because they had brought the message of God's changing order in new revelation. These enemies of Jesus now built tombs for the prophets, who had been persecuted to the death by their forefathers. Thus they seemed to be putting their disapproval on the persecution waged against them and their murder. But in reality they were opposing even now the teachings of Jesus and His apostles, and would later persecute Him and some of them to the death. Divine Providence[3] had sent the ancient prophets. This Jesus asserts authoritatively. These enemies "are witnesses and are giving their approval on the works of their Fathers." The reason for the truth of this statement was that both the murder of the prophets of old and the building of their tombs centuries later were motivated by the insane desire for an unreasonable traditional conservatism. Jesus asserts that all the blood of the prophets which had been shed from the foundation of the world, from that of Abel to that of Zachariah, the last recorded in the Old Testament, would emphatically be required of this generation. The third and last woe He thundered against them was for taking away the key to the door of knowledge. This was a charge against their obscurantism.[4] They were teachers of the people, but they refused to go into the house of knowledge themselves and locked the door and held the

1 Kai, even.   2 Edersheim, Life and Times of Jesus.
3 The wisdom of God.   4 Cf. Matt. 23:24.

key, thus hindering those who were attempting to enter.[1] The knowledge of the way of salvation was to be obtained through the Scriptures. The Scribes had cut off access to this knowledge by false interpretations, which were fatal to themselves as well as to the people, whom they despised.

What happened to the breakfast? We are left to infer that it did not go forward. Finishing His denunciation, Jesus "went out from thence." His enemies were enraged and followed Him out. They "had it in for Him" and pressed upon Him with relentless hatred, plying Him with questions about many things. At the same time, they were "laying in wait, as it were in ambush for Him that they might ensnare Him in some word." He was now hunted by them like a wild beast,[2] such was their fury against Him. He would never be forgiven for this offense. They would soon nail Him to the cross, too.

In this lesson, in the school with Jesus, we learn the inwardness of true religion. It is not predominantly ritualistic, though Jesus did not abrogate all ceremonialism. Ritualism has a proper place, when rightly understood and used. It was to be a religion of humanity and not of pride and self-assertion, though Jesus would not condemn self-confidence, and personal initiative and ambition of the right sort. He, Himself, showed His own ability on this same occasion, to push forward and assert Himself, in cutting up by the roots the traditions of the Elders. His religion was also to be one of sincerity and not double-facedness or hypocrisy. This has ever been the most stubborn and ingrained of all human faults in religionists. The Pharisees were separatists and they claimed for themselves great holiness. They were so sure of their own sanctity that they saw nothing good in others, whom they judged severely, measuring them by the Pharisaic yard-stick.

In dealing with the lawyers on this occasion, Jesus further taught about His religion, that it must not over-burden people with rules and regulations, but must be a religion of the spirit and of principle rather than a system of traditional precedents and man-made laws to govern the conduct of man. Another trait of His religion was open-mindedness which is willing to hear the new interpretations of God's messengers to each generation. Progressive thinking, not over-liberal, will not build the tombs in honor of the prophets of a past generation while persecuting to the death the living apostles. Finally, the teachers of His religion must not assume a dogmatic attitude of finality, in

---

1 Imperfect participle, conative action, were continually trying to enter.
2 Thereusai and enedreuontes, they lay in wait in ambush for Him to ensnare Him through some word He should speak.

handling the keys of the door of the saving knowledge contained
in God's word. They must not cover up with man-made interpretations the word, or deny the people access to that word,
with a right to think and interpret for themselves, thus making
themselves Lords over God's heritage. On the other hand, they
must use those keys to unlock the doors of the saving truth of the
Gospel. Jesus, under the most difficult conditions in the home
of this Pharisee, gave a demonstration of His supreme ability as
a fearless and authoritative teacher of His religion.

7. Jesus speaks to His disciples and a vast throng about hypocrisy,
covetousness, worldly anxiety, watchfulness, and His own approaching Passion (Luke 12).

The consequence of the bold attack of Jesus on the whole
system of Pharisaic and Scribal traditionalism was to precipitate
great antagonism on the part of His enemies and draw about
Him a vast throng of people (tens of thousands). Many of them
were curiosity-mongers who desired to witness the debate between the discerning Rabbi and the keen lawyers, whose undying
enmity He had incurred by His deliberate and daring denunciation
of them. In the vast throng, there were many determined and
enraged enemies, a considerable group of disciples, not a few
sympathetic friends who had not yet become professed disciples,
and many others, who were either indifferent or slightly prejudiced
for or against Jesus.

(1) In the midst of these conditions of a varied assembly,
Jesus wisely began[1] His discourse, which would cover many topics
according to the needs, by first addressing His disciple-group
primarily, but in the presence of the vast multitude,[2] so vast that
they trampled on one another to get close enough to hear the
speaker. He warned His disciples against the Pharisaic leaven of
hypocrisy. His third, last, and severest woe, pronounced against
the Pharisees at the lunch, related to their hypocrisy, though He
did not actually use the word. He there called the Pharisees
"senseless ones"; here He shows His disciples how utterly senseless
and foolish is hypocrisy. Jesus had warned the disciples against the
corrupting leaven of the teaching, and influence of the example of
the Pharisees, Sadducees and even Herod, earlier in His ministry.
They were apt to become tinctured with the erroneous teaching
of Pharisaic materialism (Mark 8:15). Such a leaven of erroneous
doctrine had a tendency, when coupled with the predominating
numbers of those who followed the Pharisees, and the fear which
the enemies of Jesus sought to instill in the disciples, to cramp
them into compromise, or at least into non-aggressive silence in

1 First aorist middle, inceptive aorist.   2 This is the largest crowd mentioned in the
ministry of Jesus.

respect to the Gospel message. The warning of Jesus on the present occasion was directed more particularly against such timidity, being a stimulus to courageous testimony to the truth in the face of such strenuous opposition. The Pharisees fooled many of the people and thought they were fooling God. Hypocrisy toward men is bad enough, but to delude oneself into thinking that one can fool God is the height of folly. The corrupting leaven of hypocrisy pervaded all the teaching and character and conduct of the Pharisees. Jesus warned the disciples to beware and separate themselves[1] from contact with this baleful influence. The reason for the utter foolishness of hypocrisy, the leading Pharisaic vice, was that there is nothing, which seems to men to be completely and permanently covered up from all sides, that shall not be uncovered.[2] The hypocrite is always unmasked at last. Even the things spoken in the darkness, though in a whisper, shall be heard in the light. So Hillel said: "Think of nothing that will not easily be heard for in the end it must be heard." Even what was whispered in the ear or in the secret stone-chambers shall be proclaimed from the housetops.

Jesus here reenforces His warning by a solemn declaration: "I tell you my friends, not to become afraid[3] of those who are killing the body and have no power beyond these things of persecution and death to do you any worse harm. But I will show you whom to fear. I command you[4] to fear him, who, after killing has power and authority to cast the soul into hell (Gehenna) the place of eternal burning,[5] for only God has power over the eternal destiny of the soul." They were to have reverent fear and regard for God under the pressure of persecution, and not act faithlessly or hypocritically toward Him. They were to beware of any Pharisaic influence which might intimidate them or make them waver in their sincere allegiance toward God and His own ministry, as they faced the enemies from now until Calvary.

For the consolation of these friends, who were facing a dreadful crisis of persecution, which would soon sweep Him and many of them to a violent death, He adds an illustration of Divine Providence, which He had already used on another occasion. Five sparrows cost only a farthing, one of the smallest of all coins, but even this least significant of all God's creatures never stands forgotten in God's care. "More than that, the hairs of your heads are all numbered.[6] Cease being afraid. You are worth more than

---

1 Put their minds on themselves.   2 Apokalupto, reveal, apocalypse.
3 Ingressive aorist subjunctive.
4 Imperative, different accent from preceding aorist subjunctive.
5 The valley of Hinnom, where babies were sacrificed in the red-hot arms of Moloch, and where the refuse of Jerusalm was "a continual burning," a figure of Hell.
6 Perfect passive tense, they stand numbered.

many sparrows." If God cared for each little sparrow, and was so mindful of each disciple that not even the falling of one hair should escape His notice, how much more He would take care of them in the midst of their persecution.

He further reenforces His exhortation to courageous witness-bearing: "I tell you, everyone who will confess me (as Messiah) before men, the Son of Man also will confess him as a loyal disciple before the angels of God." Equally, on the contrary, He declares the results of denial of Him in the same terms. The law of conduct works both ways, in blessing or for curse. Furthermore, He adds that the one who opposes the Son of Man in His ministry, yet has an opportunity to repent and be forgiven; but for those who show deliberate preference of the darkness to the light, and are constant and stubborn in their opposition to the Holy Spirit to the point of defiant blasphemy, there will be no forgiveness. Such high-handed sinning against the light so deadens the conscience as to render repentance morally impossible. God's grace is sufficient for every repentant sinner; but repentance becomes impossible to those who set themselves in defiant opposition to the Holy Spirit.

Jesus concludes His exhortation, more especially directed to the disciple group than to His hearers, with a further word of consolation. "When you are brought before the local synagogue courts for scourging or excommunication, or before the heathen magistrates or legal authorities, do not grow anxious about how you are to defend yourselves or what to say; for the Holy Spirit will teach you in that very same hour what to say." What could be more consoling than this final word as to their conduct in the face of opposition, given at this time in the midst of the already fierce but ever growing enmity of the enemies? Here was comforting reassurance not only for the preachers, but for the humble disciple-followers of the Cause. They must be bold in their witnessing and not fear the consequences.

(2) Jesus rebukes an avaricious brother and teaches in the parable of the rich fool the peril of covetousness (vv 13-21). The Lord attracted and deeply moved the multitudes. The character of the hearer is always revealed by his reaction to the sermon. Jesus spoke to the disciples about when they should be called before the Jewish courts or the Gentile magistrates and authorities, that they should not be anxious about their defense. This was sufficient to stimulate the thought of one of His hearers who was in legal altercation with his brother about the division of the paternal inheritance. The Jewish law fixed the division at two thirds for the elder and one third for the younger brother. This avaricious brother did not ask Jesus to arbitrate the question,

but to take his side and use His influence, as the Rabbis sometimes did in such cases, to impose on the brother his will. Jesus
refused flatly, repudiating either the position of judge, to decide
the right or equity of the case, or of arbiter to carry out the judgment. The man had attracted the attention of the multitude by
his question. He had betrayed his greedy character. Jesus makes
use of the opportunity to teach a profound lesson about covetousness. "Look sharply and guard yourself," He said, "against
every form of covetousness; because it is not in the superabound-
ing to anyone of the things he possesses, that his life consisteth."
Man's life is sustained only by what he actually needs. Why
then be covetous and desire more than we actually need? The
love for wealth laid-up, will engross the mind and heart and drive
out the higher thoughts and aims. A man's life does not consist
in what he has, but in what he is or character. The acquisition of
wealth to be used in the service of God and humanity calls for
frugality, develops the mind and body, teaches self-denial and
free thought, and wealth thus gained is a great blessing. But the
desire for wealth just to hoard it, making all else subservient in
life, and coming to be dominated by it, is a great curse to man. It
is far more important to learn how to use money than how to make
it.

The parable of the rich fool or foolish rich man teaches the
folly of laying up superfluous wealth or hoarding money, and
the sin of possessing it for ourselves, regardless of God's claims on
us, and crying needs of humanity which we should meet. The
rich man's farm produced bountifully, and he began to reason with
himself;[1] "What shall I do, because I have nowhere to store my
crops." He was proud, selfish, and self-indulgent. He forgot God,
and spoke of his possessions as his very own. "I will pull down
my storehouses and I will build bigger ones, and I will store in
them all my grain and my goods. Then I will say to my soul: 'Soul,
you have many good things laid up for many years; go on taking
your ease, eat, drink, and be merry'." Alas, for the man, he had
left out of account God, death, judgment, and eternity. All shrewdness, industry, drudgery, and cleverness came to naught, because he did not take God into account. The Bible plainly calls
such a man a "fool" for want of sense.[2] To such an Epicurean,
God always says as in the parable: "Fool, this very night, they
are requiring thy soul from thee!"[3] What a pathetic spectacle!
Whose would be the hard-earned possessions now? All his hard
work, anxieties, material success, looking forward to a time of
ease and enjoyment, had been in vain. His heirs might quarrel over

1 Middle voice, imperfect tense, continued action.
2 Aphron, fool for the lack of sense, a privative and phren sense (Robertson).
3 Dramatic present tense.

the inheritance he could not take with him, that was all. This was a lesson to the brother who had solicited the intervention of Jesus on his behalf in the quarrel with his brother. And the loss of his soul was irreparable. He had cut religion out in favor of business and now he was facing eternity without God. That has been the sorry end of many a soul.[1] Jesus draws the moral of the parable: "So is the man who lays up treasure for himself and is not rich toward God." Amassing wealth without reference to the God who bestows it is covetousness, and is a fool's bargain.[2] Material things are not the proper food for the soul which feeds on God. It is far better to be rich in faith, good works, peace, holiness and heaven.

(3) After speaking the parable of the rich fool or the foolish rich man, Jesus turns again more particulary to His disciples, and resumes the thread of His discourse to them about not being anxious when they should be brought before the courts. They should not be anxious at all about anything. Anxiety about material things would lead them to covetousness, against which He had warned them, and with them all the multitude hearing the parable. The following topic (vv 22-34) therefore is logically and probably chronologically connected with the preceding. They were not to be anxious about material or spiritual things. When He addressed Himself to the disciples, He no longer spoke in parables. Many of the sayings of this topic of His discourse were a repetition of teachings of the Sermon on the Mount, just like any popular preacher or teacher will repeat his favorite expressions on different occasions and in different places.

"Stop being anxious," He exhorted His disciples, "for your life, what you may eat and for your body what you may put on; for life is something more than food and the body than raiment. He who gave the one shall supply the other. Think (put your attention or your mind on) on the ravens, the mere scavenger birds, which neither sow nor reap, nor have storerooms or grainaries, yet God feeds them." In the first place, to be anxious is unreasonable, for, if God feeds the ravens and had even made the ravens feed His servant Elijah, how much more He would feed these disciples. Worry is the most common malady of the human soul, but it is both unreasonable and useless. "Which of you by being anxious can add half a yard to his stature?" If then you cannot do a little thing (which God can do, and does very easily) why are you anxious about the rest? Consider the lilies how they neither toil nor spin. "And yet I myself[3] solemnly declare to you: not even Solomon in all his glory was adorned as one of these. Now if God clothes the grass which today is in the field and

1 David Smith, In the Days of His Flesh.   2 Plummer on Luke.
3 Position of emphasis.

tomorrow is consumed in the oven, how much more will he clothe you, O men of little faith!" So Jesus throws these disciples who had followed Him from place to place, who "had not where to lay his head," back upon the providence of a wise and tender Father. Everything great and small, has a place' in His beneficent care. Worry about the future but embitters the present and does not remove the trouble which most times is but imaginary.

"So then stop seeking[1] what to eat and what to drink and cease living in suspense!" This Jesus commands. If they were worrying about those things, they must cease and not go on worrying. They must not be anxious because it was unreasonable and useless but more important still it was heathenish and contradictory to the very character of their religion. In manifesting this doubtful mind, they were like the passengers on the storm-tossed vessel, now up on the swell of anxious hopes, now down in the valley of depression and despair. The life of a Christian should not be so. "The heathen nations of the world, the non-Christian peoples, go on seeking after these things in their own strength and with the attendant anxieties, but your Father knows you need these things."

The remedy for all worldly anxieties is to believe utterly in the Heavenly Father's love and wisdom and make His Kingdom and righteousness the supreme concerns, trusting to Him to provide for all lesser interests. "But begin and go on seeking his Kingdom and these things will be added to you." Here is the secret of a tranquil heart, a repose of strength and resourcefulness.

The little band of disciples, beset now by enemies on every hand, were not to be anxious even about the future of the Kingdom. Its future now seemed dark enough as the angry mob of enemies surrounded them in this vast throng of people. "Stop fearing, little flock," He said, "because your Father takes pleasure in giving you the Kingdom. Sell your belongings, if you have fear of losing them in the threatened persecution, and give alms. If you are afraid of someone stealing or seizing the little money you have, make for yourselves purses that do not grow old, a treasure unfailing in the heavens, where a thief does not enter, nor moth destroy." Heaven cannot be bought by alms-giving, but money invested in true charity is safe and becomes a help instead of a cause for anxious care, or an occasion for temptation to covetousness. Wealth stored up in this world has many enemies, but that which is invested in heavenly work of the Kingdom is safe, and serves to draw the one who invests it heavenward (Plummer). "Where the treasure is, there will the heart be also."

1 Me with present imperative active.

(4) Jesus exhorts the disciples to loyal vigilance (vv 35-48). "Let your loins be girded[1] for speedy action, and your lamps be continually burning[2] like men watching for their lord when he is to return for the wedding feast, that they may open the door for him when he comes and knocks." In the first watch of the night, the feast was going on. The fourth watch would be too late for his return. They must be ready the second or third watches, the hardest time to keep awake. "Happy are those slaves whom the lord will find watching. I solemnly declare to you, he will gird himself, and make them recline at the table, and serve them himself."[3] At this juncture, Jesus inserts the parable of the Master of the House—a warning as to the sudden coming of the Son of Man. It was in the second or third watch of the night that the thieves usually broke into houses, because at that time, the servants would most likely be asleep and the thief would easily dig through the mud wall of the house. If the Master of the house had known[4] at what hour the thief was coming, he would have watched and prevented his entrance. "But you keep on becoming ready, because in the hour in which you least think the Son of Man is coming."

Then Peter broke into the sermon with a question. He did not understand whether Jesus intended this parable and admonition just for the Twelve — to whom He did not usually speak in parables when alone with them — or whether He was speaking to the whole crowd. The parable of the stewards replied to the question not categorically and explicitly, but parabolically. Peter must understand, that, though Jesus had favored the disciples with interpretations of the parables on the side, at the same time He ought to be able to speak to them in parables, with the assurance that they could use their understanding of the principles. He had taught them how to make their own interpretations. All that He had ever taught in parables was surely applicable to the disciples. In this parable, all the disciples and especially the Twelve were stewards and slaves who knew the will of the lord. If they did not make good use of this knowledge, they would merit many stripes. The general disciple-group was composed of some who were well instructed and some who were ignorant of their duty, in a large measure. Those who did not know so well, doing things worthy of stripes, would be beaten with few stripes. Others who were not professed disciples, were yet responsible for their life and conduct, and also must give account at the coming of the Lord.

1 Perfect periphrastic passive imperative.   2 Periphrastic present middle imperative.
3 Future active.   4 Second class condition determined as unfulfilled. ean with the second aorist subjunctive in protasis. an with aorist indicative in the attodasis.

The parable gets its background from the customs of the country. The steward was the house-manager who was left in charge of all the supplies. His duty was to organize and superintend the activities of the working force, measure out the rations, and attend to the interests of the Lord of the household in his absence rendering an account of the service on his return. Happy the reliable and thoughtful steward whom the lord should find at his post of duty when he returned; his reward would be immediate promotion to a larger and more responsible work. On the contrary, the steward who secretly in his heart should say: "My lord takes his time in coming," and should begin to harshly and cruelly maltreat and beat the slaves, depriving them of their proper food, while himself indulging in excessive eating and drinking to the point of getting drunk, that steward-servant would meet with sudden and just judgment, being "cut in two" and given a part with those who were unreliable and guilty of gross abuse. The conclusion from the parable was, that every man is responsible for his stewardship in life. The degree of light one has, determines the measure of responsibility and the relative reward or punishment. "Much will be required of him to whom much is given, and people will demand much more of him to whom they have entrusted much." God also acts on this principle, commonly known and accepted by men as just.

(5) Jesus further clarifies the nature of His Messianic mission and warns His disciples what to expect (vv 49-53). He explains to them that His teaching inevitably provokes opposition and that divisions will come. He lays emphasis on the fact that He came to cast fire[1] upon the earth, the fire of a burning, purifying, life-giving message, the fire of an unquenchable zeal in the hearts of His disciples, the fire of the Holy Spirit. "What do I care if it was already kindled?" It had been started by His ministry, though it was not yet a general conflagration. The friends of Jesus were on fire with enthusiasm and zeal and His enemies with a burning anger of antagonism. Jesus quickly passes from the metaphor of the fire to that of the water, to explain the effect and results of His mission on himself. He would be submerged in a baptism of blood. He emphasizes the baptism as He had the fire.[1] The urge of the cross was upon Him, and He was already drinking the cup of Gethsemane in anticipation. There was in Him a tremendous urge of passion driving Him on to Calvary (Robertson). He further states with reference to His mission that He did not come to introduce a reign of peace and prosperity, according to the popular Jewish conception of the Messianic realm. His mission was not

1 First word in sentence places emphasis on the fire and on the baptism of blood.

one of "peace at any price," but would bring dissension and division of the most intimate character, separating between the inner circle of friends, and many times breaking up the bonds even of the family. In this world the disciples were to expect tribulation. Wherever His gospel should go, it would be accepted by some and rejected by others, thus causing a division in loyalties and introducing inevitable antagonism. They must recognize this divisive character of His teaching and accept philosophically the consequences. Loyalty to Christ must be put above every other loyalty or early tie. The tie binding the family of believers together, entered by the second, spiritual birth, must be stronger than those of the human family. There was before the disciples a period of work, waiting, and trial. He would prepare them for it.

(6) In concluding His discourse, Jesus points the multitude to the necessity of spiritual vision. (vv 54-59). The things He had spoken to the disciples had a wider application in Israel's relationship to their Messiah. The Pharisees and their numerous followers among the multitudes professed to be able to understand the weather signs well enough. Whenever they saw a cloud rising out of the Mediterranean to the West, they were accustomed immediately to say: "A thunder shower is coming," and they rarely missed in their prediction. Also when they saw by the leaves and branches that a hot East wind was starting up, they said: "There will be a scorcher,"[1] and it so happens. But the same ones who professed such intelligence and discernment in judging of the signs of the earth and sky, showed utter dullness or hypocritically assumed not to interpret any of the too evident tokens of the critical time through which they were passing. They ought to be able to interpret the signs as the birth, preaching, and death of John the Baptist, and the preaching and miracles of Jesus. But their worldly interests were tied up with their weather-wisdom. They were obviously dull when it came to matters of spiritual discernment. They ought "from themselves" without any help from others like Jesus and John, to be able to judge what was right, and foresee the gathering tempest of judgment that was coming on their nation, like a scorching sirocco from the desert, He closes with an illustration from common experience in legal relationships, to explain His exhortations to spiritual vision and discernment. When anyone was led away to the magistrate by an adversary, he put forth strenuous endeavor to come to agreement with him and thus be rid of him, before he was dragged before the judge for judicial action and turned over to the collector or court officer, whose business was to collect the debts after the judge had decreed the penalty. This court officer or executor of

1 Sirocco.

the fines had the power to thrust anyone into prison until he should pay his debt. Jesus thus warned His hearers of the timeliness of repentance before the judgment should come. They should make terms with God while they had the opportunity. There is a great deal of hypocritical blindness and dullness in interpreting the signs of the spiritual judgment, which should be easily understood by those whose eyes are open to the events of human life and current history. Willful sinners against the evident offers of God's mercies will pay the "last pittance" in the judgment.

8. Jesus urges repentance in the light of two tragic incidents and by the parable of the barren fig tree (Luke 13: 1-9).

It must have been in close connection with His discourse about the impending judgment, the signs of which He upbraided the Jews for not being able to interpret, that certain ones who were present on the occasion and heard the discourse announced, by way of reminding Him, the incident about the Galileans, who probably on account of rebellion had been slaughtered by the order of Pilate while in the Temple. According to the account of the event preserved by Luke, the blood of those turbulent Galileans was mingled with that of the animals they were slaughtering in the Temple for the sacrifices. It was an opportune hour,[1] probably, for His enemies to get Jesus to make a rash statement about this recent incident, which seems so in accord with the general character of Pilate and some of his drastic and ruthless acts. We cannot but interpret their motive to have been to entrap Jesus. At least in His answer, He gave no ground for an accusation before Pilate of starting up rebellion against the Roman government, like Judas the Galilean, who had previously led a revolt and perished.

The Jews also popularly connected the idea of suffering and calamity with the idea of punishment for sin. One who was prospering materially they considered the favored of heaven; whereas suffering was an indication of the displeasure of God and His punishment visited on the sufferer for some secret sin.[2] The case presented for the pronouncement of Jesus put Him in a dilemma. If He should speak some word that they might interpret as against Pilate, they would imperil at once His life; on the other hand, if they could get Him to contradict the popular belief of the Jews about suffering as punishment for sin, they would possibly alienate the sympathy of the crowd from Him.

In His reply, Jesus condemns neither the Galileans nor Pilate. He does condemn the whole nation, and warns the Jews against the coming judgment. "Unless you repent, you shall all likewise

1 En auto kairo, in the same opportune time.   2 Cf. the case of Job.

perish." This was literally fulfilled in the fall of Jerusalem when the city was violently destroyed by Titus, and thousands perished, slaughtered in the streets.

Jesus cited another incident Himself to reenforce His exhortation to change their ways of thinking.[1] There were eighteen men who were crushed by the falling of the tower of Siloam, probably when Pilate was constructing the aqueduct, which he paid for by appropriating the Temple treasure (Jos. Ant. 2:9, 4). The Jews thought these fellow townsmen did wrong in working for Pilate on this construction, and that they perished because they ought to have paid back their wages into the treasury.[2] Jesus denied that those men were any worse than the rest of the Jerusalemites. Again, He warns them against the future and in language most prophetic of what would happen. In the destruction of Jerusalem, many perished beneath the falling walls of the city and their Temple.

In concluding His exhortation, Jesus sets forth the longsuffering and severity of God, in the parable of the barren fig tree, (vv. 6-9). "A certain man had a fig tree planted in a most favorable place, in his vineyard. He came, seeking fruit, and did not find any, He said to the vinedresser: 'See here, it is three years I continue to come[3] seeking fruit on this fig tree, and I do not find any. Cut it down! Why does it cumber the ground!'" There were two reasons[4] for not letting the fig tree continue longer. It had not produced fruit, and was taking up the place which should be occupied by a tree which would produce.

But the vinedresser replied: "Let it alone yet this year till I dig around it and throw in manure. Then, if it bear fruit—; but if not, you may cut it down." The story was such an apt illustration of the longsuffering patience of God with the Jews, His favored people, who occupied the place of His chosen people, but did not bring forth the fruits He sought in the national life, that it must have sunk deeply into the conscience of the multitude. The whole nation was guilty of fruitlessness. It took three years for a fig tree to attain maturity. The nation had been the object of God's special providence for centuries, when it should have reached maturity, and of other centuries of longsuffering and patience from Him, when it should have been producing fruit. Still Christ, the vinedresser, even now was asking for another period when the nation might repent and bring forth fruit. Israel was on probation. Would the Jews repent? When God puts a nation into a most favored position, He expects exceptional results. To

1 Metanoette, present subjunctive active, change of mind, one side of repentance.
2 Opheletai, offenders, debtors.   3 Present indicative active, progressive tense.
4 Kai; also calls attention to the second reason.

occupy such a place entails extraordinary responsibility and, in case of failure, the greatest consequences and severest punishment. This was a clarion note calling Israel to repentance in an opportune time. The Jews heeded not the warning, with the direst results, in a judgment spread over centuries of national dispersion and punishment. Nations and individuals alike should heed this warning.

9. Jesus heals a crippled woman in the synagogue on the Sabbath and defends the act. He repeats the parables of the mustard seed and the leaven. (Luke 13: 10-21).

The picture of the cure of the aged woman in the synagogue is very vivid, leaving no doubt in the mind of the reader of this narrative, recorded by Luke alone, of its true historicity. This is the last recorded incident of the work of Jesus in the synagogue. It was His custom to repair to the synagogue for worship and teaching on the Sabbath days wherever He happened to be, until, in the course of the development of Pharisaic opposition, the synagogues were closed to His teaching activities.

The circumstances of this incident would point to a rustic situation, a synagogue in a country place. The drama begins: "And, look, there was a woman present, who for eighteen years had suffered weakness caused by an evil spirit;[1] indeed she was bent double," moving around in this state[2] with much difficulty, "and was not able to straighten herself up at all," not even to raise her hand properly. What a picture of affliction!

"When Jesus saw her, He called her attention and said to her: 'Woman, you are released from your infirmity'." She had not even asked to be healed. He took all the initiative in the cure. It was one more opportunity to cut up by the very roots the traditional rules which had covered up the real meaning and true use of the Sabbath. "Then he placed his hands on her," as a kind physician would, "and at once she was straightened up and began to glorify[3] God."

The rustic ruler of the synagogue, being indignant and greatly pained[4] because Jesus healed on the Sabbath, gruffly spoke to the crowd: "There are six days on which work must be done, therefore coming on these days get healed, and not on the Sabbath day." The ruler was furious with Jesus and indirectly censures His act by addressing angrily the people.

This ruler of the synagogue is a picture of narrow-minded bigotry. In the picture, so well painted by Luke, we can see him coming forward "confused, irresolute, perplexed and very angry," with a scowl on his face for Jesus, and a scold for the people.

---

1 Objective genitive. indicative.   2 Periphrastic imperfect.   3 Inchoative imperfect active
4 Agan, Achomai, to feel pain.

This man was more angry than wise. He admitted Christ's healing power, but does not dare attack Him directly.[1] He did not even undertake to silence the woman, who was now praising God. He recognized that the majority of the people were in full sympathy with the work Jesus had wrought on this poor, long-time-afflicted and aged woman. He appealed to the law of the Sabbath,[2] but misinterpreted the meaning.

In His reply, the Lord tore off the mask of his hypocrisy, addressing him and a small group of his sympathizers. "Hypocrites," He said, "does not each one of you on the Sabbath loose his ox or his donkey from the stall and lead him away to water?" Their own Rabbinic law allowed this, and it was a common practise among them. The people were acquainted with this, and the ruler could not deny it. "Now, ought not this woman, being a daughter of Abraham, whom Satan had bound for eighteen years, to be set free from her bondage on the Sabbath day?" Jesus thus appeals to a reasonable interpretation of the Sabbath law,[3] one which was even in accord with their traditions. It was common sense that the Sabbath should be a blessing and not a burden. He was dealing not with a mere animal but with a human being, a woman, a daughter of Abraham, one very ill for a long time. Moreover, she had been bound by Satan for eighteen years, and the ruler had just admitted that Jesus had the power to cure. Was it not an obligation[4] to release this poor woman at once on the Sabbath? Would it not be a shame to put it off?

As Jesus piled up argument after argument "all those who were opposed to him were confounded and put to shame[5] before the people who were rejoicing at all the glorious things that were taking place at his hands."

While the people were rejoicing over the cure and enjoying also the discomfiture of the ruler of the synagogue, who had not merited his sympathy and held them constantly under his yoke, Jesus makes use of the occasion to point to the future growth and inevitable conquest of His Kingdom, by repeating here in the synagogue the parables of the mustard seed and the leaven. The enthusiasm of the multitude coupled with the praises of the cured woman were prophetic of the greater triumph of the Kingdom in this world. Both the parables illustrated the insignificant beginning and the great, inevitable, and complete growth of the Kingdom. The practical application of these parables was obvious to all. The mustard seed, the tiniest of all seeds, cast into the garden soil, grew and became a tree, large enough to furnish protection

1 Edersheim, Life and Times of Jesus.   2 Dej, it is necessary.   3 Exodus 20.
4 Edei, it was not necessary.   5 Imperfect passive, to put to shame.

in its branches to the birds of the heavens by night and shelter from the burning Syrian sun by day. Such would be the outward historic development of the Kingdom in the world. The success of the work of Jesus was but an earnest of the greater works which would be done through history. The little lump of leaven buried deep in the bushel of flour illustrated the all-pervasive silently-penetrating influence of the Kingdom teachings and life. Internally, the Kingdom would transform all human life and so ciety. By simple contact, the leaven takes up gradually and transforms completely the measure of the flour; even so, the Kingdom inevitably changes all it contacts into its own character.

10. At the Feast of the Dedication, Jesus gives final testimony to Himself before His passion (Jno. 10:22-32).

Nearly three months had elapsed since Jesus left Jerusalem after the Feast of Tabernacles. The busy days of the Judean campaign had sped past rapidly and the time for the Feast of Dedication, which fell on Dec. 20-27, had come.

It was a joyous festival in commemoration of the restoration of the altar and purification of the Temple by Judas Maccabeus, six and a half years after its defilement by Antiochus Epiphanes. During the eight days of the Feast, the Hallel was chanted, both in the Temple in Jerusalem and in the private homes in all parts of the land. In the rededication of the Temple in 164 B. C., only one unpolluted flagon of oil was found, just sufficient for the illumination of one day; but it was miraculously replenished for eight days, according to the Jewish tradition, and, for this reason, the feast lasted eight days. This feast, like that of the Tabernacles, commemorated a Divine victory, when the land was restored to Israel. It was a time which brought anew the aspiration of the Messianic hope.

Being a cold day, Jesus sought a protected place for His teaching, Solomon's porch on the eastern side of the Temple. This was the only part of the Temple which had escaped the devastating fury of the Babylonians in 586 B. C. Jesus was walking around on this porch when His enemies came and circled Him,[1] perhaps in a friendly mien, and asked Him: "How long are you going to hold us in suspense? If you are the Christ (Messiah), tell us plainly." It was no honest question. They desired to elicit from Him some confidential confession which might serve as a basis for accusation before their Jewish Sanhedrin, or the Roman Pilate. They were looking for a Messiah, but not His kind. Still, He might adopt their ideal yet.

1 Aorist active indicative, punctiliar action.

The reply of Jesus was sincere but wise. He understood their motives. He did not go back to His former declarations at first, but merely cited His previous claims (cf. Jno. 5:17). They had not accepted His testimony there and "are not now believing[1] in him." He declares the mute but powerful witness of His works. The Father's approval could be seen in these deeds. He points out the reason why they did not accept the testimony of His claims, confirmed so abundantly by the approval of the Father on His works. Reverting to the allegory of the Fair Shepherd He had given them when He was present in Jerusalem three months before, He declares to them that they did not believe because they do not belong to His flock. His sheep "are following Him." For His own sheep, He had provided fulness of eternal life, through His complete fellowship with the Father. They would never be destroyed. Even now, complete destruction threatened the Jews. But His flock would never, never[2] be destroyed. This flock was precious to Him. No enemies would ever be able to snatch His sheep out of the hand of His power. The reason was that they were given to Him by His Father, who "is greater and stronger" than the fiercest, strongest, and most cunning enemy. He guards them with absolute faithfulness and no one can seize them and snatch them out of His hand. Here, Jesus identifies His work and power in guarding the sheep with that of His Father, placing Himself on equality with God, the very declaration He had made formerly:[3] "I and the Father are one." Thus He claims to be one in essence with the Father, while separate in person.[4] He had answered their question. He was the Messiah, but not their kind of Messiah. Nor would He be tempted to become so, though they might fall down and worship Him or acclaim His praises as those of Judas Maccabeus, their great national hero, who was even now the center of their patriotic thoughts in this Feast. He was the true Messiah and the Son of God. Such was His daring claim, stated clearly and tersely, and to be repeated later (Jno. 17:11, 21) in His great high-priestly prayer on the evening before the Crucifixion.

This statement enraged them. They had heard the same blasphemous expressions from Him once before here in the Temple (Jno. 8:59) and had attempted to stone Him then. Again they run from the Cloister to the builders' litters to fetch stones, that they might pelt[5] Him to death, the penalty for blasphemy (Lev. 24:16; I Kings 21:10, 13). He remained calmly in His place until they had returned. They had expected Him to retire precipitously and were awed to find Him composedly awaiting their return. For

1 Present tense.   2 Double negative.   3 Jno. 5:16-47.
4 Hen, neuter, not masculine.   5 Esmen, plural in number.

a moment, their wicked purpose was checked. His voice sounded out clearly on the hushed scene:

"Many beautiful works I have shown you, proceeding from my Father." They would remember the healing of the man now impotent for thirty-eight years, another man born blind, and many others. "For what sort of work, from among these, are you trying to stone me?" It was not lawful to stone one for good works, but for crimes. They must at least cite the offense in the presence of the people before they carried into effect their wicked purpose.

"We stone you not for a good work, but for blasphemy," they replied, "and because you, being a mere man, are making yourself a God." Jesus had before, by their declaration which He approved by His silence (Jno. 5:18) called God His own Father, making Himself equal with God. Now He claims equal work and equal power with God. They were right in their accusation, but wrong in their conclusion, that it was blasphemy. They could not conceive of His being anything but a mere man.

Jesus now appeals to their Scriptures. "Does it not stand written in your law: (Ps. 82:6) 'I[1] said you are Gods?' If he called them Gods to whom the word of God came,[2] and the Scriptures cannot be destroyed or discredited, then do you say to him, whom the Father consecrated and sent into the world: 'You blaspheme,' because I said, I am the Son of God?" Jesus here makes use of the Rabbinic form of argument, a deft turn of dialectic. In the Scriptures, the judges were called Gods because they were God's representatives, standing for God. These Jews claimed to be the special custodians of the Scriptures of the Old Testament. They could not go back on their own Scriptures. They faced now the dilemma of acquitting Jesus or destroying their idolized law. Jesus had called Himself the Son of God. By using this argument, He stopped the mouths of His enemies, without disclaiming His own deity. The judges had been called Gods because they wielded delegated power; but Jesus had been consecrated to the office of Messiah and sent forth directly from God on a divine mission into the world. Then He appeals to His irrefutable works again in confirmation of this statement. He goes on to reaffirm His deity in a different expression.

"If I do not the works of my Father, stop believing[3] in me. If I am doing them, though you may not believe, believe in the works, in order that you may know and recognize that the Father is in me and that I am in the Father." His works, which were going right on every day, constituted an irrefutable argument in favor of His verbal testimony. Those works manifested the

---

1 Late form of second aorist indicative a instead of on.
2 Condition of first class assumed as true.
3 Present active imperative with me in prohibition.

fact that Jesus was clothed with the weighty power of God and was full of grace and truth. Let them believe in the testimony of those works that they might come[1] to perceive and keep on knowing experimentally[2] that in reality He and the Father were one.

With this skillful argument, of their own Rabbinic kind, He had parried the assault of His enemies and rendered it impossible for them to carry out their plan to stone Him, while He asserted His claim to deity in the most complete claim up to this time in His ministry. Overawed and outwitted, they had let their stones fall from their hands to the ground. But they kept on seeking to seize Him, and drag Him before their tribunals. But His time had not come, and He "went forth out of their hand"—just how, we do not know.

1 Second ingressive aorist active subjunctive.
2 Present active subjunctive, both in purpose clause.

PART VI

THE LATER PEREAN MINISTRY

(Harm. §§ 112-127)

The Perean Ministry occupied probably three and a half months: from the Feast of Dedication, 29 A. D., to the end of the last journey to Jerusalem in the spring of 30 A. D.

CHAPTER XXIV

OPENING THE PEREAN MINISTRY

(Harm. §§ 112-117)

1. The withdrawal from Jerusalem to Bethany beyond Jordan (Jno. 10:40-42).

Jesus now found it necessary to leave Jerusalem and Judea for a time. The campaign in Judea had profoundly stirred the people. But the antagonism of His enemies had also grown more bitter, culminating in a renewed attempt to stone Him in the Feast of the Dedication, when He so adroitly parried their assault, making skillful use of one of their own Rabbinical methods. All doors to His ministry were now closed in Judea. For some time Galilee also had rejected His ministry. There was only one place left to His choice for the work of the remaining brief months before He should face the last issue in Jerusalem—the half-heathen province of Perea across the Jordan. Thither He repaired with His disciples, choosing as the center from which He would work out in His evangelistic activities, Bethany, where John passed the first times[1] of his ministry of some months.[2] There Jesus was remaining[3] in the place where He had been baptized by John in the Jordan—place of hallowed memories—where He had met and won His first disciples in the surrounding parts of this province, largely Gentile. He had success here, away from the prejudiced atmosphere of Jerusalem. Many poured[4] in from the surrounding places to attend His ministry. Jesus ministered to them: preaching, teaching and healing. The report of those who came was the same everywhere. They "were saying" in comparing the ministry of Jesus with that of John, as people will do, that "John did no sign" or miracles, but all the things he had said concerning this new preacher, Jesus, were true. John's testimony had prepared the soil for this last fruitful campaign of Jesus in which "many believed in Him." John had painted the picture of the coming Messiah so faithfully in his preaching that the people recognized Him at once and believed in Him readily.

2. Teaching in Perea on a journey toward Jerusalem, Jesus is warned against Herod Antipas (Luke 13:22-35).

This incident might have occurred on the way to the home of Martha and Mary. It seems that Jesus made another brief visit to Jerusalem after the Feast of the Dedication and before that of the Passover, three and a half months later.[5] Somewhere

1 Proton, the accusative extent of time.   2 Periphrastic imperfect, continued action.
3 Imperfect indicative, continued ministry there.
4 Second aorist.   5 Robertson, Harmony of the Gospels.

in Perea on this journey to Jerusalem, as Jesus was making[1] His way through the cities and villages teaching, someone asked Him "if those being saved were few." This question, of the number of the elect, was a familiar theological problem with the Rabbis. It was one of the hard knots, and a certain one, unknown in person or motive, brought it to Jesus. He directed His reply to the whole group:

"Keep on straining every nerve[2] to enter in through the narrow door (of salvation)," He said, "because many, I tell you, will be seeking to enter but will not be strong enough[3] (to force the door open) when once the Master of the house may arise and may slam the door fast, and you may begin[4] to stand without and knock repeatedly at the door, saying: 'Lord, open to us at once;'[5] but he, answering, will say: 'I do not know whence you are.' " The plea will be cut short by a brief and unreasoning reply. "Then will you begin[6] to say: 'We ate and drank in your presence and you taught in our streets.' " There were many present in His audience now, perhaps, who came in intimate contact with Him as His host or at least were His guest-hearers in the street services. But rejecting His message of salvation, they would hear in the final day the dread sentence:

"I do not know whence you are. Depart[7] from me all ye workers of iniquity." There outside, in your place of punishment, will be the weeping of deep anguish of spirit and gnashing of teeth of rebellion and defiance, when you shall see Abraham, Isaac, Jacob and all the prophets in the Kingdom of God, but you are being continually cast out. So they will come from the east and west and north and south, and shall recline at the table of the feast of salvation in the Kingdom of God. "And lo, there are last who will be first, and there are first who will be last" (Cf. Math. 19:30; Mk. 10:31; Math. 20:16). Some of these who seem to be first will appear as last and some who apparently are last will be first in the final reckoning. The thing of supreme importance is to secure a place at once among those who are in the process of being saved. Strain every nerve to enter into the way of personal salvation. This is the supreme concern. The implication is that many shall fail and relatively few shall succeed.

In that very hour[8] and on the same occasion of the above discourse, certain Pharisees came to Him saying:

"Get out and move on from here, for Herod (Antipas) wants to kill you." Jesus was not far from the very place where this

---

1 Imperfect middle, oporeueto. 2 Agonisthe, agonizing like the wrestler in the struggle. 3 Ouk ischousousi will not be strong (enough).
4 First aorist middle subjunctive. 5 First aorist active imperative.
6 Ingressive aorist middle subjunctive. 7 Second aorist active imperative.
8 Locative case expresses the point of time.

same crafty king had arrested John the Baptist and dragged him in chains to the dungeon of Machaerus, where later he had him beheaded. It might have been an astute plan of the wily Pharisees to frighten Jesus into going on into Judea, where they could get Him more easily into the clutches of their Sanhedrin. At least it was a peculiar role for the Pharisees, that of warning Jesus against the craftiness of Herod Antipas. But it was not all false alarm, if we take Jesus' reply as a cue to the interpretation of the real situation.

"Go tell that fox," He said, "Look, I cast out demons and perform cures today and tomorrow and on the third day I finish my task." Herod had been wily, deceptive, crafty, and cruel in dealing with John, disposing of him secretly and defending his act on false grounds. He would like to dispose of Jesus in the same way. But Jesus is not afraid of him and replies, stating His plan clearly to Herod and the Pharisees:

"I go on my way (for a brief but definite period[1]) today, tomorrow and the next day, because it is not permissible for a prophet to perish outside of Jerusalem." The course of the Messiah is determined and will not be abbreviated or changed, because of the threats of Herod or the pressure of the Pharisees. His task in Perea would be finished in a few days. This reply was wise and would probably satisfy Herod, who had already suffered the odium of the people for having slain John. He would like to be rid of Jesus, but not repeat his crime, which had deeply pained his conscience, seared as it might be. At the same time Jesus reveals to the Pharisees that His face is set to go to Jerusalem. When His brief ministry is complete in Perea, He will go up to Jerusalem to die. In severe irony, He reminds the Pharisees that past history revealed that rarely a prophet of Israel had died outside of Israel's land. "That could not be allowed," He said. Then He broke into the lament repeated later on the vesper of His crucifixion: "O Jerusalem! Jerusalem! You who are accustomed to slay the prophets and stone those sent to you! How oft have I wished to gather together to me your children, as a hen her own brood under her wings, but you refused to come. Look! Your house is abandoned to you. But, I tell you, you will not see me till you say: 'Blessed is he who comes in the name of the Lord.' " The abiding character of Jerusalem was that of a murderess. Christ did much work there. He yearned over her people. But now with His death the beloved city of the Jews was abandoned by God. The prophecy of doom was soon fulfilled in her complete destruction.

1 Plummer on Luke.

3. Breakfasting with a chief Pharisee, Jesus again heals on the Sabbath and defends Himself (Cf. Harm. 49, 51, 110). Three parables suggested by the occasion (Luke 14: 1-24; Harm. 114). Jesus was still journeying toward Jerusalem, somewhere in Perea, when He was invited to dine with one of the Pharisees on a Sabbath day. In spite of their scrupulous observance of many Sabbath rules, the Pharisees had many social gatherings on the Sabbath, with sumptuous servings prepared the day before. On this occasion a Pharisee had invited a number of his colleagues and a lawyer friend and added Jesus to the list of his guests, either out of curiosity, or, more probably, through evil intent. Jesus accepted the invitation, though He knew well enough the general attitude of the Pharisees toward His ministry. This was one of the leading Pharisees, and Jesus treats his invitation with all candor and good will. He would give all men a fair chance to know Him and accept Him. On this occasion the Lord, after healing the dropsical man and defending His miracle performed on the Sabbath (vv 1-6), administered in His familiar discourse in the form of tabletalk, a lesson on *humility* or taking the lowest seats (vv 7-11) directed to all and especially the guests; another on *hospitality*, of inviting lowly guests, intended more especially for the host but also for all; and then adds the Parable of the Great Supper or Gospel Feast, meant for all.

(a) The cure of a dropsical man (vv 1-6) is the only record of such a case in the ministry of Jesus, and is not the same as the miracle of the withered hand.[1] "Now it came to pass that on His going into the house of one of the leading Pharisees on the Sabbath to take a meal, that the Pharisees and lawyers kept watching[2] Him insidiously. And look! a certain dropsical man" making use of Oriental liberty "came into the house and placed himself immediately in front of Jesus." It seems to have been a surprise[3] to the guests, though the Pharisees might have arranged it beforehand as a trap for Jesus. At least the lawyers and Pharisees had some malevolent thoughts and intentions, which Jesus answered.[4] The mute appeal of the diseased man, who was afraid even to speak before these scrupulous guardians of the Sabbath, touched the heart of Jesus. Answering the inmost reasonings of the Pharisees, which He read in their outward mien and whisperings, He asked:

"Is it allowed to heal on the Sabbath or not?" They had brought Him into a pocket of embarrassment and now they found *themselves* in a dilemma. The Rabbinical law allowed the applica-

---

1 As against Strauss and Keim.   2 Periphrastic imperfect middle, continued watching
   with malevolent intent.   3 Idou.   4 Apokritheis.

tion of remedies on the Sabbath in case of peril. Was this man in peril? They were afraid to say that it was allowable to cure on the Sabbath but they did not dare to deny the man the cure for fear of alienating the people. They were not able to answer and became silent.[1] So Jesus "laid hold of the man, healed him, and then dismissed him" from the company, to get him away from these critics. Jesus had read the mute look of appeal of the diseased man and understood the hostility of the Pharisees. Seeing the displeased looks of the lawyers, who should have known how to respond, and also of the Pharisees, He said:

"Which of you, if your son or your ox fall into a well, will not at once draw him up on a Sabbath day?" This was a powerful question which put the Pharisees and lawyers on the defensive. "How do you act when your own personal interests are concerned?" There were many uncurbed cisterns, wells, and pits in Palestine. The natural instinct was too strong to allow one's own son (or donkey) or ox to remain in the well and perish. Unhesitatingly, without any thought about the Sabbath rules, they "would at once draw them up, even though it were on the Sabbath day." "They had no power[2] to reply to this," but were helpless before this argument based on their known practice.

(b) The lesson on humility or counsel to take the lowest seats (vv 7-11). Jesus doubtless observed now as the guests began to take their places on the couches around the table, that there was a maneuvering for the places of honor and distinction. He made use of the occasion and the puerile conduct of the guests—which would have been amusing if it had not been disgusting—of scuffling for the chief seats, to teach a lesson on humility. This was done in tactful, parabolical language.

"When you are invited by anyone to a wedding-feast," He said, "do not recline in the place of honor, lest one more honored than you be invited, and the man who invited both of you come and say to you, 'Make room for this man'; and then you will begin with shame to take and keep the last place." On a couch holding three, the middle place was for the worthiest, the one to the left next, and the right third. On occasions of formality, such as the marriage-feast, there was more desire for the places of distinction. It was the place of the host to arrange the guests, if their positions did not suit him. Sometimes he would rearrange them and one who had sought for himself the place of honor was asked to take the lowest seat permanently.[3] "Take the humblest seat when you are invited," counseled Jesus, "that when the host

---

1 Ingressive aorist active indicative.   2 Ouk ischusan, were not strong (enough).
3 Present progressive tense.

comes he may say: 'Friend, come up much higher.' Then you will have honor in the presence of your fellow-guests." Christ was not giving a mere lesson in table etiquette. He applies the general principles of humility to all human conduct:

"For everyone who lifts himself up shall be humbled, and he who humbles himself shall be exalted." The moral of the parable is a great law of the Kingdom for all human conduct.

(c) The lesson on hospitality was intended more especially for the host (vv 12-14). Doubtless Jesus observed that the Pharisee had invited only his friends, relatives, and rich neighbors. "When you make a breakfast or a dinner," He said good-humoredly, "do not always invite[1] just your friends, or your brothers, your kinfolk or your rich neighbors, with the hope that they will invite you in turn, and so you will get a requital. But when you have a reception,[2] have the habit of inviting[3] the poor, the crippled, the lame, the blind." The motive in entertaining friends, relatives, and rich neighbors would be selfish, as it could not be in having a reception for those who had no money, physical ability, or fitness to repay the favor. Jesus painted here, with a master-stroke, the ways of fashionable society in their rounds of mutual entertainment, at great cost and little profit. The same money spent on the poor, the crippled, the lame, and the blind would be rewarded in this and especially in the world to come, in the resurrection of the righteous.

(d) A certain one of the guests reclining at the table, hearing this said: "Happy is he, who eats bread in the Kingdom of God." This was a mere superficial, pious remark uttered by one who fully expected to participate in the feast at the beginning of the Messianic Kingdom. The ground of his hope was doubtless in being a Pharisee. He had certainly misinterpreted the teaching of Jesus he had just heard, on hospitality. The final remark of that discourse, about "the resurrection of the righteous," led him to a commonplace observation which was either mere ignorant pious talk, or made with a hypocritical evil intent. In reply Jesus spoke the parable of the great supper, which is not to be identified with that of the Marriage of the King's Son (Math. 22:1-14) because of many vital differences of detail. It is a parable of warning, predictive of the reception of the Jews, and calling of the Gentiles, and though spoken in answer to the remark of one guest, showed to the whole company the nature of the privileges they were then enjoying, as well as the responsibility they were facing

1 Present imperative active, habitual or progressive action.
2 Like Matthew's reception for Jesus.   3 Present.

and the danger and peril in which they were standing, if they rejected the Gospel.

"A man was (in the process of) giving[1] a great dinner and he had invited many. So he sent his bond-servant at the hour of the supper to say to those who had been called: 'Come[2] because it is now ready.' But they all from the same motive began to beg off." It was the custom then, as it is now among the wealthy Arabs, to send a second summons at the hour, and a refusal at that hour amounted to an insult, or, among the tribes, to a declaration of war.[3] The motive which led them to beg off or ask to be excused was that of preoccupation with other things they considered more important. They were moved by the same impulse and demonstrated the same disposition. Their excuses were all mere pretexts. They did not go because they really did not care to go. None of the excuses they offered could have kept them away if they had thought it worth while.

The first said to him: "I have just bought some land and am obliged to go and look at it. I beg you consider me excused." He had most likely seen the land before he bought it and any further inspection now might be deferred easily for another day. Another said: "I have just bought five yoke of oxen and am on my way to prove them. I beg you consider me excused." The oxen could be tested out or broken in to the yoke later. And another said: "I married a wife and for that reason I am not able to come." No bride would have objected to the brief absence of her husband to attend an important function such as this reception. The host would not under such circumstances object to his bringing the bride along with him. These three excuses were doubtless samples of many others.[4] Some said they would not come now; others that they would not come at all.

When the slave returned and reported these answers to his Lord, the master of the house became angry[5] and said: "Go out into the (broad) streets and (narrow) lanes of the city and bring in here the poor and crippled and blind and lame." He had prepared a great feast and expected many guests. He invited the "high-ups" of the city first. The Pharisees would not find it difficult to understand Jesus' allusion to them by this class. Those Jews who respected the Law had a prior claim in the presentation of the Gospel. But when they rejected the Gospel, its messengers were sent out into the broad streets and even into the back alleys, or the habitat of the publicans and sinners. They were to bring

1 Imperfect indicative.
2 Present imperative, begin to come (Robertson).   3 Tristam, Eastern Cust. p. 82.
4 Pantes would include more than the three.   5 Ingressive aorist passive participle.

in the poor who had no other invitations and would offer no excuses, the blind who could not go to see farms, the lame who
would not go to prove oxen, and the maimed who would not
likely marry.[1] The bond-servant[2] executed the order and reported
back: "Sir, what you ordered has been done and yet there is
room." Then said the lord to his servant:

"Go out into the highways (public roads outside the city)
and hedge-rows (where vagrants slept) and compel them to come
in, that my house may be filled. For I tell you that not one of
those men who have been invited shall taste of my dinner." The
invitation was broadened now to include not only the poor, the
diseased, the publican and sinner class of the Jews but the *heathen*
outside of the *city* of the Jewish privileges. The servants who
bore the invitation should compel them by persuasion to come
in. The host was resolved that his preparation should not be
wasted. He opened the way for the outcast class of humanity to
come and occupy the places of high privileges in His Kingdom.
These Pharisees must feel that they were in the place of privilege
but of peril as well, and by rejecting the Gospel message they
would be counted less worthy than the poorest, most ignorant,
most degraded of men, since that class by acceptance was entering
into the Gospel feast.

The Gospel is a great feast of pardon, forgiveness, peace,
access, joy, and a thousand other blessings. The invitation is frank
and the entrance to the feast free. The great majority of men,
however, make flimsy excuses, putting things of the world first;
and religion must occupy a secondary place, if any, in their lives.
In this they are self-deluded. The result is, those who reject Christ
are themselves rejected. But there shall be no lack of guests at
the Great Supper of the Master of the House.

4. Great crowds follow Him and He warns them to count the
cost of discipleship to Him (Luke 14:26-35; Harm. 115; Cf. Harm.
70, 83).

Great crowds were following[3] Jesus now as He went on His
way toward Jerusalem. He realized, as they did not, that soon
His enemies would nail Him to the Cross of Calvary. There were
many who were coming close to Him now with the purpose of
being His permanent disciples. It was necessary that they should
know the real conditions of discipleship. Earlier in His ministry
He had discussed this subject in Galilee (Matt. 10:37-39). At
that time He pointed out the conditions of being worthy disciples;
now He reveals the conditions of *effective discipleship*. He presents
the conditions of discipleship under five aspects: (a) a choice of

1 Bengel.   2 Doulos as above.   3 Suneporeuonto, were going along with him.
(Imperfect tense).

loyalties to be made (26); (b) a cross to be borne (27); (c) the cost to be counted, illustrated by the rash builder and the rash king (28-32); (d) all possessions to be renounced (33); and (e) the spirit of sacrifice and service to be maintained (34, 35).[1] Under these topics He elaborated His sermon on the conditions of discipleship, warning those who were thinking of embracing His teaching, as well as His disciples previously won, against precipitancy in beginning and the futility of half-heartedness in following the life of discipleship. He knew that the enthusiasm of many of them would evaporate and their eager applause cease if they knew they were facing in Jerusalem a cross instead of a throne.

(a) In dramatic gesture Jesus whirled around suddenly to the crowds following and said:

"If anyone is coming to me now (for permanent discipleship), who does not hate his own father and mother and wife and children and brothers and sisters, and still more, his own life, also, he cannot be a disciple of mine." The strong Oriental term *hate* really expresses, but strongly, the preference we are to give Christ when called on to choose between supreme loyalty to Him or loyalty to any member of the family, or even to one's own apparent best temporal interests. Christ must have the first place in the loyal devotion of the disciple's heart. Not even the dearest earthly tie of family may stand in the way of loyal devotion to the Cause of the Master.

(b) The second condition is that of carrying the cross of discipleship (27). Hundreds of Jews had been crucified in Galilee in the rebellion under Judas (6 A. D.). The idea of cross-bearing was a familiar one to the people. They understood that Jesus meant to point out to them with the utmost candor the extreme difficulty of being effective disciples. It was no easy task they were embracing when they became His disciples. "Whosoever does not bear his cross and keep on bearing it every day[2] cannot be a disciple of mine."

(c) With great skill the Master Teacher drove home the lesson of the difficulty of discipleship and the necessity of careful reflection in choosing it, with the two brief parables of the rash builder and the rash king, taken probably from current events, or at least familiar to the experience and thought of the people. "For which of you, wanting to build a tower, does not first sit down and calculate the cost,[3] to see if he has enough to complete it? Lest perchance, when he has laid a foundation and is not able to finish it, all who behold it begin to poke fun at him saying:

1 Plummer on Luke.   2 Present indicative active, progressive action.
3 Psephizie, cast a pebble used in voting and so counting.

'This fellow began to build but was not able to finish.' " It was not an uncommon experience then as now for one to overestimate his resources, or underestimate the cost of building. The watchtower in the vineyard was common in Palestine but here the allusion is to a tower-like house built strongly for ornament or special protection, and so a costly structure. The point of illustration was "counting the cost".[1]

"Or what King, going to clash with another King in war, will not first sit down and deliberate whether he is able with ten thousand men to meet the one who is coming against him with twenty thousand? And if not, while the other is still at a distance, he sends an embassy and asks for peace." In that age of "ostentatious building and reckless warfare" there were not a few exampples of not counting the cost. Many a leader of an army had come to grief in rashly attacking a superior force without first counting the cost. By this additional illustration taken from military life, the Teacher impresses the necessity of rational foresight and reflected insight into the conditions of discipleship.

(d) Jesus next sums up all He had said before on the subject by a sweeping assertion of "renunciation of all," whether family or property, in order to put Christ first and His Kingdom service in the first place. "So then no one of you who does not renounce all of his belongings can be a disciple of mine."

(e) He concludes His discourse with a repetition of one of His beautiful metaphors of the Sermon on the Mount (Matt. 5:13) and a saying to reenforce the necessity of a careful hearing and attentive concentration on what He was saying.

"Salt indeed (as I have said) is good; but if even the salt becomes tasteless, with what will it be seasoned? It is fit for neither soil nor manure. People throw it out." Jesus had said that genuine disciples are the salt to a corrupt world, but spurious disciples are as salt that has lost its savour (Matt. 5:13f). Disciples without the spirit of self-denial are like tasteless salt which has lost its strength. It cannot even be used as many other things, for manure to fertilize the land.

It takes a conscious effort for one to understand and accept the strenuous program of discipleship, therefore: "He that has ears (the capacity for hearing) let him hear (make use of that ability)."

5. Jesus, criticized by the Pharisees and Scribes for receiving sinners, defends Himself in three parables (Luke 15:1-32; Harm. 116).

The discourse of Jesus revealing the exactions of discipleship doubtless alienated some of the people who were following Him in such crowds. The multitudes dwindled "but the tax-collectors and

---

1 Dapanen, devour, consume, expense which eats up one's resources.

sinners at the same time were drawing near[1] to listen to Him "[2]
Jesus had long since bridged the chasm between Himself and the
publicans by calling Matthew Levi to be one of the Twelve. He
had taken the initiative in this and entered wholeheartedly into
the reception given Him by that disciple when he invited many of
his colleagues from the custom-house to be present. It was a
constant thing in His ministry for Jesus to approach the "down-
and-outs" with His gospel-invitation, extending them friendship's
hand of sincere helpfulness and not approaching them condescendingly. This feature of Jesus' ministry was ever growing more conspicuous. The outspoken sinners had come to recognize in Him a
friend though He manifestly did not approve of their sins.

The Pharisees took the lead on this present occasion, accompanied by the Scribes who are usually mentioned first, in
criticizing Jesus for breaking down all social and moral barriers.
They were alert always to make use of every favorable opportunity to undermine the work of Jesus. Their murmuring, which
started among themselves, spread out (imperfect tense) and grew
in proportion as the sinner-class crowded around the Teacher.
eager to hear.

"This fellow," they said with contempt, "welcomes[3] sinners
and eats with them."[4] They implied that Jesus preferred these outcasts (untouchables) to the respectable classes, "because he was
like them in character and tastes, even with the harlots" (Robertson). Such an evil insinuation was made with a view to injuring
the reputation of Jesus and bringing His ministry to naught.

To this meanest and basest insinuating attack, Jesus replies
with three parables of encouragement to the penitent sinner, setting
forth the love of God for man in his lost estate in three of the
most beautiful stories of all His ministry: the lost sheep (3-7),
the lost coin (8-10), and the lost son (11-32). In these parables
He presents three pictures of the sinner: how he becomes lost and
how he is to be saved; and three pictures of God showing His
attitude toward the sinner before and after repentance. He points
out to the Pharisees and Scribes, in the presence of the people,
what His own attitude toward sinners is, what theirs should be
and justifies this attitude by revealing what God's attitude is toward the lost. He winds up this most beautiful parabolic discourse
with a vivid picture of what the attitude of the Pharisees and
Scribes actually was—in the disgruntled elder son—rebuking severely their self-righteousness and exclusiveness in relationship to
the lost. Jesus here lays low the conventional laws and social

1 Periphrastic imperfect, customary action. 2 Present infinitive active of purpose.
3 Present indicative active, progressive and habitual action, cf. Pantes, all sinners everywhere.
4 Imperfect of customary action.

caste of contemporary Jewish society and shows God's love for the
outcast. The very accumulation of three parables enabled Him to
set forth this great love under various aspects: that of the great
shepherd-heart taking all the initiative in going after the helplessly lost sheep, that of the careful and diligent housewife who
estimated highly the smallest coin, that of the yearning father
anxiously hoping for the return of the lost son. The Pharisees
and Scribes did not evaluate highly the souls of the publicans
and sinners but considered them "infinitely insignificant" (Bruce).
So the interpretation of these parables should be from the apolo
getic or defensive point of view, but Jesus also attacked the attitude of His enemies strongly and denounced their sinful exclusiveness unsparingly. In it all, Jesus was still a reconciler of
alienated classes and a healer of social breaches.

The character of the three parables is such as to depict all
aspects of the relationship between a loving God and a lost man.
The first emphasizes "God's possession and attachment, the second God's ownership and man's intrinsic worth and the third
God's kinship and supreme affection."[1] The first sets forth God the
Son, the great Shepherd, the second, God the Holy Spirit seeking
diligently for the lost, and the third, God the Father anxiously
yearning for the return of the Prodigal. The first parable emphasizes the loss, the second the search, and the third the restoration.[2]
The three parables form a climax:[3] the pasture, the house, the
home; the herdsman, the housewife, the father; the sheep, the
treasure, the beloved son. They teach other correlated truths:
God's feeling of His loss and His joy in recovering the lost. The
first two have their start in the heart of God and the last in the
heart of the sinner. The full truth concerning the conversion of any
sinner is attained by combining all three.

(1) The parable of the lost sheep (3-7).

"What man of you," said Jesus, "having a hundred sheep, having lost[4] one of them, does not leave behind the ninety and nine in
the desert and go on after the lost sheep till he find it? Then after
finding it he puts it upon his shoulders full of joy, and on reaching
home he calls his friends and his neighbors saying:

" 'Rejoice with me because I have found my sheep that was
lost!' "

The figure of the Good Shepherd had been used by Jesus
before (Jno. 10:1-10) to characterize His own work and mission.
"No simile has taken more hold upon the mind of Christendom"
(Plummer). He is the Shepherd but also the owner[5] of the sheep.

1 DeMent, Bible Reader's Life of Christ.   2 Edersheim, Life and Times of Jesus.
3 Taylor, Parables of Jesus.   4 Aorist active participle.
5 Echon, having or possessing.

He has particular love for each individual sheep. He does not leave the ninety and nine exposed while he goes forth to seek the lost. If they are true sheep they are left in the care of an assistant, to be guarded in the fold by night and led forth in the pasture by day. The shepherd goes forth and keeps going until he finds the lost sheep.[1] There is no cessation of seeking until the lost is found. When the shepherd finds the lost sheep he does not drive or even lead it back, but himself carries it, placing it back on his neck on both shoulders in a comfortable position, safely held by both hands. There is no upbraiding of the wandering sheep, nor murmuring at the trouble (Plummer). But rejoicing on the way, he calls forth his friends and neighbors immediately on arriving at home, to rejoice with him because he has found the lost sheep.

The other picture in the parable is that of the lost man who like the sheep that strayed away, leaves the Shepherd and wanders away through ignorance and folly. The lost sheep was in the midst of many deadly perils, of wild beasts, ravines and rugged precipices, hunger and thirst; the man lost in sin is in the midst of the perils of temptations, spiritual adversaries, fatal disease, and sudden death with eternal loss. Christ misses even one who wanders away, and with a yearning shepherd heart, goes after him until he finds him. In solemn declaration Jesus draws the moral of the parable:

"I tell you that just so there will be more joy in heaven over one repenting sinner than over ninety-nine righteous persons who have no need of repentance." The joy in heaven over the recovery of just one of these publicans or sinners would be universal. Heaven's approval was on His ministry of seeking the lost. With fine irony Jesus takes the Pharisees at their own estimate. They professed to be righteous. If they were "righteous" they did not need to repent. Let heaven rejoice then at the repentance of the lost ones. The grumbling Pharisee had to shut his mouth and let the work of Jesus go on. But Jesus did not mean to say that the Pharisees were righteous. He could not change their stubborn wills, but He could brush aside and receive with open arms the publicans and sinners.

(2) The parable of the lost coin (8-10).

"Or what woman having ten coins, if she may lose one coin, does not light a lamp and sweep the house clean and keep on seeking[2] carefully 'til she find it? Then after she finds it she calls together her women friends and neighbors saying:

" 'Rejoice with me because I have found the coin I lost!' "

1 Poreuetai, present middle indicative, continued or progressive action in which the subject is interested and active.
2 Present progressive active indicative, linear action.

This parable, like the one which precedes it, sets before us the loss, search, and recovery of the lost soul with the resultant joy. The poor peasant woman of the Syrian village, living scantily in a rude adobe hut, with a reed-covered dirt floor and no windows, lost one of the small silver coins, worth about eighteen cents, which constituted a tenth of the cherished dowry handed down to her from her forbears. Disturbed because of the loss, she lights the lamp and thoroughly sweeps[1] the floors of the ill-lighted house, and keeps on looking under beds and boxes and among the reeds, until she discovers the shining coin. Then she rushes over to the homes of her neighbors and breaks the glad news of the recovery of her lost coin, inviting them to rejoice with her.

All of the ten coins of her dowry put together would not excell in value five dollars, which, though a considerable amount for a poverty-stricken woman, was yet insignificant—a true picture of the low evaluation put upon the human soul by the Pharisees of all times. The coin, though lost to use, yet bore the image of the emperor on it and was intrinsically valuable. Jesus would have us understand that the soul of the lost man bears the image of God, however much it may be covered up with the rust or filth of sin. It is recoverable, though while in the sinful unrepentant state it is lost to its proper use and the service for which God intended it. The interest of this parable centers in the *search*. The Holy Spirit, fitly symbolized in the woman of the parable, makes diligent, thorough, and unceasing search for souls in all the house of God's humanity and in every crack and cranny of the heart of the lost man. But Jesus would have us understand that, like Himself, every disciple of His should join in the recovery of souls to the uses and service of the Kingdom. The sinner is so precious in God's sight that no effort is too great to reclaim him. The details of the search are graphic in the parable. There was earnestness, thoroughness, and persistence until the result was obtained. The house was turned upside down until the coin was found.

Again Jesus draws the moral of the parable in a solemn declaration:

"So, I tell you, joy comes in the presence of the angels of God over one repenting sinner." The value of a single sinner is the outstanding thought in these two parables. God rejoices when the sinner repents. The Pharisees taught that there was joy in the presence of God when those who provoke Him perish (Plummer). But the angel-neighbors of God rejoice and joy is in the heart of God over one repenting[2] sinner.

1 Present tense.   2 Present participle, the process of repentance is progressive, continued, habitual.

(3) The parable of the lost son (11-32).

In this most famous of all the parables of Jesus we have a picture of the willful sinner departing from God, wasting his life, and finally returning repentant to God; and a picture of the Father-God yearning over the lost man in his prodigal life of sin and receiving him back repentant into the loving arms of parental care and eternal abundance. We also have a picture of elder-brother Pharisaic religion which is selfish and exclusive in its nature, presenting to the repentant sinner a barrier of moral severity, filled with a feeling of resentment that repulses the returning prodigal, and unlike God, would boycott him and leave him in a social isolation with only a frown of disapprobation for his past life, and no encouraging sympathy for a new and better one.

(a) The prodigal (11-19).

"A certain man had[1] two sons: Now the younger of them said to his father: 'Father, give me the share of the property that is going to fall to me.' So he divided the estate (living) between them. Then, not many days afterwards, the younger son, gathering together all, went away into a far country and there threw his property away in spendthrift living. Now when he had spent it all there came a great famine throughout that country and he himself began to be in want. Then he went and glued himself to one of the citizens of that country, who sent him into his fields to feed hogs. He was even longing to fill his stomach with the horn-shaped carob pods which the hogs were eating and no man was giving him (anything). Then coming to himself he said:

"How many of my father's hired men have more food than they can eat, while I am perishing here with hunger. I will arise and go to my father and I will say to him: 'Father, I have sinned against heaven and before your face. I am no longer worthy to be called a son of yours. Make me as one of your hired men.' Then he rose up and came to his own[2] father.''

The parable of the lost son completes the trilogy of three parables showing the grace of God toward the sinner. The first two give the divine side, the seeking love of God; the third, the human side, the rise and growth of repentance in the one-time prodigal heart.[3]

The prodigal in the parable (11-24), the inexperienced younger brother, a self-willed, unfilial, sensual youth brings himself want and misery by his folly. This winds up finally in desperation, repentance, and resolution to return to the paternal home, where he is accorded a gracious and royal welcome followed by a joyful celebration in view of his long-deferred but final actual return.

1 Imperfect active indicative, the status of ownership.
2 Heauton, of himself, reflexive pronoun.   3 Plummer on Luke.

The self-will of the prodigal had manifested itself in asking for a premature disposition of the *will* of the father, so that he might receive the one-third share of the estate, which would naturally fall as his part later. In such an early surrender of the property to the sons, the law called for the maintenance of the father by the sons until death. Eager to be free from paternal restraint, this unthinking youth makes a hasty departure, gathering up everything he could, not providing anything for the maintenance of the father, burning all bridges behind him by going to a far away country. Base ingratitude, mixed with heartless rebellion, led him to seek in the distance, freedom from all conventional shackles. His motive is soon revealed in the breaking out of passionate impulses and hungry sensual appetite in a life of dissolute and riotous living. While his money lasted, he had hilarious companions to help in his spendthrift[1] abandon. He had freedom to sow his wild oats and he drank to the depths the cup of sinful pleasures.

His folly of sensual indulgence soon brought the enslavement to passion and the absence of self-control. His physical powers were soon seriously diminished, his health undermined, his intellectual capabilities dulled, and his moral nature vitiated. All the finer feelings of the soul, all the beautiful aspirations of youth were dissipated. The once firm will became flabby and unresisting before the recurring storms of temptation to sensual appetite.

In the midst of this crisis came the retributive hand of a providential drouth to aggravate his now recognized defeat, and deepen the misery of his humiliating poverty. He had fallen behind with his accounts, became debtor to those who would lend to him, until no man would longer give him credit. In desperation then he went and glued himself[2] like a leech to a Gentile citizen of the country, who had nothing to offer in the way of employment except that of a swineherd, living in rags in the field and feeding on the food used for the hogs. Such an experience is apt to cause the worst sinner to reflect. To "tend hogs" was an abomination to a Jew, but it was deeper humiliation that he should be forced to subsist on the horn-shaped carob pods, the common hog-food. He had been out of his right mind and now he was "coming to himself" and seeing things as they really were. Reason was getting the upper hand of sensual appetites and he remembered now in the midst of his hunger the abundance of food served out even to the hired men back at home, while he himself was suffering here from actual hunger.[3]

In desperation he resolves to arise and return to the protection of the parental roof. He even formulates in his mind the words

1 Zōn asotos, living without saving, in a prodigal fashion, a spendthrift.
2 Ekollethe, first aorist passive, to glue together.
3 Present middle, linear action in which the subject was supremely concerned.

of his confession, which might possibly conciliate the father. He recognizes that he has been an offender against his father but primarily against God, his father being testimony to this. Hunger and stern necessity had driven him to this repentance, which was probably partial, until he met the unexpectedly gracious reception on his return. But he had come home, it matters not what might be the character of the motive. There must be self-recovery to give ethical value to the event.[1] He recognized that he sinned (failed) and failed to hit the proper mark of life. When he made his high demand as he was leaving home, he missed the mark, and he had been missing it ever since. He no longer felt worthy now to be in the home as a son and would ask to be considered merely as one of the hired men. Such was his resolution as he wended with difficulty his way home, clothed in filthy rags, emaciated with the life of sensual vice and filled with a sense of shame.

(b) The father and his reception of the prodigal (20-24).

"But while he was yet a long way off his father saw him, and took pity on him and ran and fell on his neck and kissed him again and again." The son said to him:

"Father, I have sinned against heaven and before your face. I am no longer worthy to be called a son of yours." But his father spoke to his slaves:

"Quickly fetch a robe, the finest one, and put it on him; and give him a ring for his hand and sandals for his feet; and bring the calf, the fatted one, slay it and let us eat and make merry; because this my son was dead and he has come back to life, he was lost and has been found."

So they began to be merry.

The picture of the father of this penitent prodigal is perhaps the most vivid one we have of God in the Bible. There are four graphic touches[2] of the artist's pencil in the picture: (1) recognition at a distance, implying a vision sharpened by love and a habit of looking expectantly down the way for the son's return; (2) instant pity awakened by the distressing and miserable conditions of the son when he arrived close enough to be identified completely; (3) running and excitement of the aged father demonstrating his eagerness to receive the son in whatever condition; and (4) falling on his neck in affectionate embrace and kissing him again and again.[3] Here was love that kept on waiting and watching ready to do anything for the recovery of the lost. The son repeats his premeditated confession, perhaps half mechanically. Meanwhile the slaves had heard of the coming of the son and had rushed out down the way after the father, coming near to witness

---

1 The Expositor's Greek Testament.   2 Ibid.   3 Katefilesen, perfective use of Kata.

422   THE CHRIST OF THE GOSPELS

the touching scene of the meeting of father and son. The confession of the son was but partly uttered when interrupted by the father's orders to the slaves: (a) "Be quick! and bring forth the best (first), the kingly robe and put it on him." This robe was a mark of distinction. (b) "And give him a golden ring for his finger and sandals for his feet," both marks of a freeman, as slaves were bare-footed.[1] The son was not merely to be fitted out anew but was being honored and accorded a real welcome. (c) "Bring also the fatted calf which has been fattening for a high festive day, kill it and let us make merry." (d) The reason for all is that this "my son was as good as dead and has come back to life again, he was in a state of one lost and after a long time he is found."

(c) The elder son (25-32).

The main point of the three parables is the Pharisees' atti-tude toward the mission of Jesus on behalf of the publicans and sinners as illustrated in the elder brother. He was exemplary in his moral life, correct in conduct, respectable in society, indus-trious, prosaic, methodical, but had the spirit of a hireling. When he came from the field where he had been working, and drew near to the home, he heard the harmony of the band of music and danc-ing. Then he called one of the lads to him and began to enquire repeatedly and eagerly[2] what these things might be. The boy, in-nocently and sincerely, told him:

"Your brother has come and your father killed the wheat-fattened calf because he has gotten him back safe and sound." Then the son began to be angry and soon his long pent-up jealousy ex-ploded in a rage. Sullen, he was not willing to enter into the house. Then his father came out and began to urge him repeatedly;[3] but he answered and said: "See how many years I have slaved to you and never yet overstepped a single command of yours, but you have never given me even a little kid that I might make merry with my friends. But when this son of yours, who has eaten up your estate with harlots, came, you killed for him the wheat-fattened calf." He refers to the brother as "this son of yours" in contempt and bitter sarcasm.

Then the father meekly replied in tender, conciliating tone:

"My child, you have always been with me and all mine is yours. To make merry and to rejoice was our duty,[4] because this your brother was dead and has come to life, and though lost he has been found again."

The spirit of the elder son was mercenary. He was jealous toward his younger brother and resentful when the father made

1 Robertson's Word Pictures.   2 Imperfect middle.   3 Imperfect active indicative.
4 Edei, it was necessary, imperfect tense.

a feast on his return. Haughty and self-complacent, he dwelt on his own model behaviour and saw only the sin without the repentance in his younger brother. Jesus loved sinners deeply, while the Pharisees were filled with the cold pride of virtue. There is much irony in the story. The Pharisees were greater sinners than the publicans. The picture Luke gives of the father's love for the lost son and his tender and patient dealing even with the elder brother, explains the reason for the coming of Christ to the world to save the lost.

6. Three parables on stewardship: the unjust steward, to the disciples; the rich man and Lazarus, to the Pharisees; the unprofitable servants, to the disciples (Luke 16:1—17:10; Harm. 117).

Among the disciples of Jesus not a few were converted publicans and sinners. Jesus had been defending His conduct in receiving them graciously and had manifested His sincere love for them. But these men had followed for years the course of making ill-gotten wealth the main aim in life. They, and all the other disciples of Jesus as well, needed to learn the right use of wealth, and Jesus teaches this important lesson in two parables: the Unjust Steward (1-13), and the Rich man and Lazarus (14-31), which later was directed also, and mainly, to the Pharisees. Both parables teach that riches do not necessarily involve sin but bring responsibility and are accompanied by peril.

(1) The parable of the Unrighteous Steward (1-13). The parable, covering eight verses, is followed by the moral and its application (8b-13).

There was a certain rich man who had a steward (manager) who was accused[1] of squandering his goods. So he called him in and said to him:

"What is this I hear about you? Render the account of your stewardship, for you cannot be steward any longer." The Master had weighed the evidence and decided that the accusation was true. He now asks the manager to wind up the accounts, with the understanding that he was to prove his innocence or be dismissed. The steward thought the matter over and said to himself: "What shall I do now that my lord is taking away[2] the work of steward from me? I have not strength to dig (for a living) and I am ashamed to begin to beg.[3] Now I know[4] what I will do so that when I am discharged from my position, they (friends) may receive me into their own homes."

1 Aorist passive indicative, a slanderous report by gossip. full of malice, though in this case, true.
2 Present middle indicative, linear and middle, taking away from himself.
3 Present infinitive, not participle, which would mean, ashamed while begging.
4 Egnon, second aorist active indicative, I am resolved.

So he called to him separately, one by one, his lord's debtors, and spoke privately to the first:

"How much do you owe my lord?"

The man answered: "A hundred baths (nine hundred gallons) of oil."

Then he said to him: "Take your papers (bond) and sit down quickly and write fifty."

Then he spoke to another: "And how much do you owe?"

And this one said: "A hundred cors (a thousand bushels) of wheat."

He said to him: "Take your papers and write eighty."

Then the lord praised the dishonest steward (factor) because he had acted shrewdly.

The steward on the point of being deprived of his stewardship is a fit emblem of a man who faces death and must make provision for the future life. He recognizes that he faces an impossible task since he is "not strong enough to dig and too proud to begin to beg." Man is *unable* to work out his salvation and often too *proud* to depend on another for it. But he was intelligent and reasoned within himself, coming soon to a shrewd plan. Once conceived, the plan was acted upon with promptness and consummate tact and sagacity. He quietly called in for private conference all the debtors of his lord, leaving no opportunity for division of sentiment among them. He would make them understand that he was their friend doing them a good turn, freeing them from the injustice of his lord. He asked each separately, in private, how much he owed his master and in each case used his assumed authority as steward to reduce the debt of each one, not all on an equal percentage basis but varying tactfully in accord with the individual needs and character. This would avoid a too apparent fraud, would impress upon each the power of the manager and the necessity of respecting it, and at the same time give each a friendly feeling toward him for dealing out justice to them.

When the lord of the steward found out what the rogue had done and saw with what sagacity he had dealt, he caught the humorous side, ludicrous though criminal, of the whole affair, and good-naturedly said: "What an amazingly shrewd fellow!" He himself had been robbed, probably, though it is possible the steward-manager had been the perpetrator of former injustices to the debtors, the work being farmed out to him, as was the tax-collecting to the publicans by the Roman government. At any rate, it was the lord of the steward and not Jesus who commended his shrewdness in rascality. Some have wondered why Jesus chose this bad man for an illustration. The reply is that there are some commendable traits in the worst of men and such characteristics may be singled out for our instruction. We are not taught to imitate the vices but the prudence and shrewdness of the man.

The moral and application of the story are set forth (8-13) in the words of Jesus:

"Now men of the world (this age) are shrewder toward their own generation than the sons of light (the spiritually enlightened)." Here is the moral of the whole parable. Men of the world in their dealings with men like themselves are more prudent (shrewd) than the children of light are in their intercourse with one another. Worldly people are far-sighted and sagacious in their transactions for temporal ends. The spiritually enlightened ought to be equally ready in making one another promote heavenly objects. There is a great lack of intelligence, not to say stupidity, in the cooperative work of the Kingdom.[1]

Jesus goes on then to make application of the parable in solemn words:

"So I say to you, make friends for yourselves by the use of the mammon (money) that tends to unrighteousness, so that when it fails, they may welcome you to the eternal tabernacles." Jesus knew the evil power in money. So He warns His publican-disciples and all others against the evil and shows how to use money in such a way, for helping others and promoting the ends of the Kingdom, that when death or misfortune should come, and their money should be swept away or be of no further service, they might find a welcome in heaven on the part of many who had been benefitted by them. One cannot buy his way into heaven with money but by the right use of it for the service of God on earth he may lay up treasure in heaven.

He further explains in application of the parable: "He who is faithful in very little is faithful also in much, and he who is dishonest in very little is dishonest also in much." This is an infallible principle in the business world. The man who can be trusted in small things can be promoted to large responsibilities; and he who embezzles with small sums will wind up in large thefts. "If, therefore, you did not prove faithful in the use of tainted mammon, who will entrust to you the genuine riches? And if you did not prove faithful in what is another's who will give you what is yours."[2] Our earthly wealth is given us as a trust. We may possess it permanently only if we use it properly in the service of God. Unless we do so use it, at any moment it may be withdrawn.

The whole conclusion with reference to the *wise*, intelligent, shrewd use of money is finally set forth in another illustration:

1 Robertson and Plummer.   2 Variation of texts, but yours is the reading in accord with the meaning of the context (Robertson).

"No house-servant can be a slave to two lords; for either he will hate the one and love the other or he will stand by one and scorn the other. You cannot serve God and Mammon." Here Jesus repeats one of the sayings of the Sermon on the Mount. Our service of God with money must be wholehearted. God must be our Master, and not Money.

(2) The parable of the rich man and Lazarus (14-31).

(a) Introduction to the parable (14-18).

Jesus had been addressing His disciples on the subject of how to use material wealth in order to make for themselves eternal friends and lay up treasure in heaven. The Pharisees who were "lovers of money" were standing hard by listening[1] to all these things. They received the words of Jesus about the wise use of money for laying up treasure in heaven with contemptuous ridicule, and began to turn up their noses[2] with disdain at Jesus, "this crazed enthusiast!" Their eyes, noses, faces were expressive of their utter scorn. So Jesus said to them: "You are the type of men who justify yourselves before the face of men, but God knows your hearts. Now, what stands high among men is abomination in the sight of God." These Pharisees considered their wealth a sign of special blessing of God upon them because of their scrupulous observance of the Law. The teaching of Jesus, that wealth involves peril and tends to promote unrighteousness, struck at the root of their avarice and covetousness. They curled up their lips at this penniless Rabbi. "They thought they knew perfectly well why he spoke against wealth." Their pretended holiness and scrupulous outward observance of the law was an abomination to God. They were hypocritical, and explained away the law when it suited them. They insinuated that Jesus did not observe the law. He explains:

"The law and the prophets held until John. Since then the Gospel of the Kingdom of God has been spreading and everyone is pressing into it. But it is easier for heaven and earth to pass away than for one iota of the law to fail. Everyone who divorces his wife and marries another woman committeth adultery, and the one who marries the divorced woman committeth adultery." The Pharisees had disregarded the greatest and most fundamental teaching of the law and prophets, which related to the coming of the Messianic Kingdom. John had ushered in the Messianic Kingdom. They were rejecting that Kingdom while multitudes were pressing into it, with tremendous moral enthusiasm and spiritual

1 Ekuon, imperfect active indicative.   2 Examukterizon, imperfect indicative active, to turn up the nose, to sneer, to scorn.

passion.[1] Jesus further cites the example of their loose divorces which Moses could not remedy because of the hardness of their hearts. With these introductory remarks as to their avaricious character, known to God, though it might be justified in the eyes of men and their wrong use of the law, Jesus comes back to the subject of the right use of money and adds another parable to show the evil consequences of using one's wealth for selfish and wrong ends, neglecting at the same time opportunities for its right use.

(b) The parable of the rich man and Lazarus (19-31). There are two scenes depicted in strong contrast: one of the earthly life (19-22) and the other of the future state in Hades (23-31). It hinges on to the preceding parable of the Unjust Steward and draws the lesson that "to possess great wealth and use it selfishly for oneself, is fatal."[1] "Now there was a certain rich man who was accustomed to clothe himself[2] with purple and fine linen, making merry every day with magnificent display. And a certain beggar by the name of Lazarus had been cast down[3] at his gate, full of ulcers, and longing to satisfy his hunger with the scraps falling (from time to time) from the rich man's table. Nay, even the dogs were accustomed[4] to lick his ulcers."

There could be no greater contrast in the material conditions of two men than in this first scene of this parabolic-drama. The rich man was accustomed to wear the finest and most costly clothing, the upper garment being made of the costliest Egyptian cotton dyed purple, a garment worn only by princes, and the under garment of fine linen made from Egyptian flax. Daily he entertained friends with merry feast-making at a table both sumptuous and glittering with the richest vessels. The poor diseased beggar of the parable, to whom Christ gave the name Lazarus, a type of the wretched humanity always evident in Palestine and other places as well, had been brought, helpless as he was, and cast down[5] at the gate of the rich man's palatial home. His only companions in misery were the half-fed street scavenger dogs, with which he contended in the scramble to get the scraps left over, which were dumped out in the street after the man's family, guests and household servants had been served. Half-starved, he longed[6] to fill himself from these left-overs thrown out from time to time. His gnawing hunger was never satisfied and even the dogs tormented him by licking his unbound sores, exposed the more by the scantiness of his clothing. If there was ever given to anyone an

1 Plummer on Luke.   2 Imperfect middle.   3 Perfect passive tense.
4 Imperfect.   5 Perfect passive, he could not move when set down in the place.
6 Present participle.

opportunity to alleviate human misery, it was to Dives, the rich man, who passed in and out and beheld daily this sad sight of wretchedness at his very gate. But he was criminally indifferent and neglectful, and hardened his heart as he daily beheld the disgusting beggar. This went on for times and the beggar died. Dives' last opportunity to befriend his need was lost.

Then the scene changes.

"Now it came to pass that the beggar died and was borne away by the angels to Abraham's bosom. Then the rich man also died[1] and was buried." Heaven ministered to Lazarus in his death because he had been a patient, suffering servant of God. Never a word of complaint from him!

The scene in Hades unfolds:

"Now in Hades he lifts up his eyes, being in torment, and sees Abraham from a great distance and Lazarus in his bosom. So, he called and said: 'Father Abraham, take pity on me and send (quickly) Lazarus that he may dip the tip of his finger in water and cool off my tongue because I am in anguish[2] in this flame.' "

But Abraham said: "My child, remember that you got your good things in your life and Lazarus likewise the evil things; but now here he is comforted while you are tormented. And through all these regions a great chasm remains fixed between you and me, that those who wish to cross from this side to you may not be able nor may they pass from your side to us."

Then he said: "In that case I beg of you, father, to send him to my father's house, for I have five brothers, that he may bear witness to them, that they at least may not come to this place of torment."

But Abraham says to him: "They have Moses and the prophets. Let them give heed to them."

But he pled: "No, Father Abraham, but if one from the dead go to them, they will repent."

Then he answered: "If they do not listen to Moses and the prophets, not even if one rise from the dead will they be persuaded."

According to the popular tradition of the Jews, Paradise or "the bosom of Abraham" was in sight of Gehenna, the place of torment, both being in Sheol or Hades, the place of departed spirits. Jesus couched this parable in the language and symbolism of that belief, that He might in understandable terms teach a profound truth about the unseen world. We are not to believe this detail and some others given in anthropomorphic terms, in relation to the realities of the unseen world, except in a symbolic way. There

---

1 Aorist, the simple fact, nothing of the rich funeral, which in nothing would help the lost man.
2 Present middle, his torment arose from himself, his internal condition.

are great truths behind the symbols and the reality is in character true to the symbol. For instance, the pious servant of God, true in character and faithful in service, will surely pass from this life into the Paradise of God, while those who reveal by their wrong conduct, illustrated in the selfish use of their wealth and characters incompatible with that of Heaven, will pass into a place of eternal separation from God and true sons of Abraham. The place of torment,[1] symbolized by the stocks, where prisoners were tormented in ancient times, is pictured here as a place of fire, and the terms descriptive of the scene are those of the body in flames. The reality of eternal punishment is thus symbolized by the worst type of suffering known to mankind, the reality being always an exaggeration of the type.

In the conversation with Abraham, the rich man excuses himself, begs for pity, and for a slight service now at the hands of the poor beggar whom he had not befriended on earth. He had not made eternal friends through the beneficient use of his money. Lange thinks this is the finest master-stroke of the parable, that Dives asks for the slightest services for the alleviation of his misery now at the hands of the poor beggar whose misery he had done nothing to relieve on earth.

But Abraham points out that the time of preparation and probation has passed. There is no remedy now for his loss. He had his opportunity to use his wealth for the service of God and man and spent it in luxurious living with criminal neglect of suffering ones about him. He had his good things on earth and Lazarus his evil things; now the situation is reversed and Lazarus was being comforted and Dives tormented. The memory of the past must convince him of the eternally unalterable conditions of his status in the place of torment. On reflection, the man who had vainly spent his life on earth recognized the irremediable separation between Paradise and Hell and begged that Lazarus be sent back to earth to warn his five brothers not to follow him to this place of torment.

Jesus puts in the mouth of Abraham the words of warning: "They have Moses' law-writings and the book of the prophecies. Let them give heed to them."

Still he pled with Abraham, that a miraculous appearance of a messenger from the dead would lead his brothers to repentance. But the final reply of Abraham draws the moral and closes the question:

"If they would not listen to Moses and the prophets, not even if one rose from the dead would they be persuaded." These brothers needed a profound moral change which could not be effected

1. Enbasanois a rack for torturing people.

by a mere apparition. There must be repentance leading to a godly life. They had been living lives of luxurious ease; they must live lives of thoughtful service to humanity and reverent regard for God. The rich man was not condemned for being rich but for neglect in not using his wealth for the right ends. We are trustees for God in the use of material wealth for the benefit of our fellowmen. The rich man was merely a picture of the Pharisees; he was not a monstrous specimen of humanity. Nothing is said of ill-gotten wealth, nor of his being a miser. He liked to have his friends enjoy themselves and spent on them his money lavishly. He even allowed the poor diseased beggar to be placed at his gate. But he formed the habit of selfish, thoughtless living, oblivious of the misery around him. Such a character can never be at home with God.

> *"The wounds I might have healed,*
> *The human sorrow and smart,—*
> *And yet it never was in my soul*
> *To play so ill a part.*
> *But evil is wrought by want of thought,*
> *As well as want of heart."*—Thomas Hood.

(3) The parable of the unprofitable servants (Luke 17: 1-10). This parable (7-10) is prefaced by three sayings of Jesus leading up to the parable. These sayings about the sins of causing others to sin (1, 2), the duty of forgiveness (3, 4), and the power of faith (5, 6) followed by the parable (7-10) constitute a fit conclusion of the discourse on stewardship. There is a vital connection between the several sayings which form the introduction to the parable. The opening verses deal with the matter of giving offense, or causing others to stumble. This might well have been directed against the Pharisees who were seeking to alienate His disciples from Him. They would succeed with some of the weaker disciples and this would be a cause for discouragement to others. There would be disputes and divisions among the disciples owing to the intrigues of these licensed enemies. So Jesus warns the disciples, as well as His enemies:

"It is not possible for offenses[1] not to come, but woe to the man by whom they come. It is advantageous[2] for him if a millstone is hung around his neck and if he has been hurled into the sea rather than that he lead into sin one of these little ones." This woe was pronounced mainly against the designing Pharisees, but also against any disciple who should be deluded and led by them into divisional or partisan strife. "Take heed that you neither mislead or are misled."[3]

1 Ta skandala, snares, accusative of general reference.   2 Dative of advantage
3 Dr. Geikie, Life of Christ.

The subject of the duty of forgiveness naturally grows out of that of offenses. Forgiving love would be the only remedy for them when the leaven of divisional strife should be introduced by the Pharisees. Jesus had taught the Twelve earlier in His ministry the lesson of unlimited forgiveness for a repentant brother (Matt. 18: 21, 22). He now repeats this teaching to the whole group of disciples in a slightly different form.

"Look out for yourselves," He said. They must stick together and look out for one another. "If your brother wrongs you,[1] take it up with him and gently rebuke him, and if he may repent, forgive him. Even if he may sin[2] against you seven times a day and seven times may turn to you saying: 'I repent,' you shall forgive him." Seven times a day would be a hard test for their forgiving love.

The disciples felt the strain of such a precept, almost discouraged with its high moral standard. They realized the need of a stronger faith to be able to meet such an exacting principle of life. Humbly they petition the Master: "Give us more faith," they plead. "If[3] you have faith as a grain of mustard seed," He replied, repeating a former teaching, "you would say[4] to this mulberry tree;[5] 'Be rooted up and be planted in the sea,' and it would have obeyed you." Things impossible humanly speaking can be accomplished with God's help through a minimum of faith. Jesus seems to have made use of a Rabbinic saying here; for His teaching He drew from all sources.

Then He concludes His discourse with the brief parable of the unprofitable servants (7-10). "Now which of you having a slave ploughing or tending sheep will say to him when he has come out of the field, 'Come at once and recline at the table.' But will he not rather say, 'Get ready what I am to have for dinner, and after getting dressed keep on waiting on me 'till I eat and drink and after that you shall eat and drink?' Does he thank[6] the slave because he did what he was ordered to do? So you also, when you do all the things ordered you, say: 'We are unprofitable slaves; we have only done what we were under obligation to do?' "

The disciples were not to be of a mercenary spirit or think of their own merit. If they would preserve this humble attitude of dependence on Him and readiness to serve Him as dutiful slaves, they would be able to give good account of their stewardship. The Pharisees served God for reward; the disciples were to seek to avoid that leaven of false doctrine.

1 Third class condition, with second aorist ingressive subjunctive.
2 Condition of third class.   3 Condition of the first class, assumed to be true.
   He meant to assume that they did have such faith.
4 Second class conditions assumed as unfulfilled.   5 The black mulberry-sycamore.
6 Me expects negative answer. He does not thank the slave, does he? The answer
   expected is 'No.'

CHAPTER XXV

RAISING OF LAZARUS AND FLIGHT TO EPHRAIM

(Harm. §§ 118, 119)

According to the testimony of John in the arrangement of his gospel, the raising of Lazarus constitutes the climax of the miraculous manifestation of the divine-human personality of Jesus, the Messiah, unto the outside world. It is the last of a series of several signs chosen by John to illustrate the work of the Master in the revelation of the incarnate truth. It falls naturally into its place in this purposive arrangement of the author John, in the manifestation of His glory and the production and nurture of faith in men.

There is no real ground for questioning the literal exactness of the evangelical record. The objection raised, that this miracle is not mentioned by the synoptic gospels, is offset by the fact that neither did John mention the raising of Jairus' daughter (Matt. 9:22-26) nor that of the widow's son at Nain (Luke 7:11-17). The fact is, John gives special emphasis in his gospel to the ministry in Jerusalem and Judea, while the synoptics emphasize more the Galilean ministry. Furthermore, the dramatic vividness of details, the remarkable delineation of personalities, and the numerous minute touches in the historic record, leave no room for doubt, that an eye witness wrote it. He made use of it to show forth the divine personality of the Saviour. This sign is tied up indissolubly with the whole argument of the fourth gospel. He who questions it will also doubt the divinity of Jesus and His resurrection from the dead.

For convenience in the treatment of this narrative we consider it under two heads: (1) the raising of Lazarus from the dead (Jno. 11:1-44), and (2) the effect of the miracle and flight to Ephraim (Jno. 11:45-54). The narrative falls naturally under four topics: (a) the preliminary circumstances (vv 1-16), (b) the arrival at Bethany (vv 17-32), (c) the raising of Lazarus (vv 33-44) and (d) the effects of the miracle (vv 45-54).

The prelude (vv 1-16) to this highly dramatic incident of the ministry of Jesus opens in Perea, probably at Bethany, near where John baptized. It was one or two days' journey[1] from the other Bethany—the home-town of Mary and Martha, whose brother Lazarus was now critically ill, having been sick for some time[2] (cf. Jno. 10:40). It is significant that Mary is given the first place and special mention here, whereas Martha comes first, as elder sister and hostess elsewhere (Luke 10:38; Jno. 11:19). The home

---

1 The two Bethanys were about twenty miles apart.
2 Imperfect active indicative, continued state.

of the infirm Lazarus and his sisters was situated some two miles from Jerusalem, a little south of east, on a slope of the Mount of Olives, and its sight is marked today by the little village of El Azariyeh. Mary is identified by John as the one who anointed[1] Jesus later with ointment, in the home of Simon, who had been cured of leprosy by Jesus. This anointing took place some weeks after the raising of Lazarus and on the vesper of the crucifixion. The identification of Mary with Mary Magdalene is a mere conjecture supported by no direct evidence and opposed to the general tenor of the gospels.[2] The act of devotion of Mary stood out in the memory of John and gave her first place in this allusion. Her eager devotion in learning at His feet had also been commended by Jesus on one of His frequent visits to this hospitable home (Luke 10:38). Later, in the narrative of this incident, Martha bears away the palm by her sane calmness and high confession of faith, when sorrow reigned in the home (Jno. 11:19). The individualities of these two sisters shine out in bright contrast of emulation in their devotion to the Master, as two distinct types among the highest examples of Christian womanhood in all history.

Their message to Jesus about the illness of their brother was sent, doubtless, with anxious hearts, but reveals a complete confidence in His friendship, a tactful restraint on any suggestion which might inconvenience His work, and a restful assurance that He would do what was best. "Lord, behold your loved friend is critical from prolonged illness."[3] When the messenger delivered this message Jesus sent back the reply: "This illness is not to end in death, but is for the honor of God, that the Son of God may be glorified through it."[4] This was a most comforting message to the sisters. They were sure of their wonderful Friend. The mere suggestion in their message was sufficient without an urgent request. He gave them, in His reply, the right view of the experience of illness in the believer's home—it should always be useful, in the providence of God. This illness of Lazarus would be "for the glory of God." The ultimate purpose of it all in God's scheme, was the revelation of the Glory of His Divine Son. Jesus sent the messenger back to the sisters with this understanding: "They would trust him to do what was best, as they had revealed by their message they had been doing." More than this, He confessed to them intimately and before His disciples that He was the Son of God, the Divine Son. This was the clearest statement He had made up to this time of His divine Sonship, and accounts for the calmness and wonderful confession of Martha, after He arrived

1 Aleipsasa timeless aorist participle, proleptic illusion to Jno. 12:1-8 (Robertson).
2 Westcott on John in loco.   3 Imperfect indicative active.
4 Hina with the subjunctive in a purpose clause, the purpose of the illness of Lazarus was to reveal the divine Son of God.

later in Bethany (vv 11-27). John thought it worth-while to inject
into this narrative here a significant parenthesis: "Now Jesus
loved Martha and her sister Mary and Lazarus,"[1] with an abiding
love. But it was a high spiritual love, far deeper and more abiding
than the love of mere human frienship could ever be.[2] They
had based their message merely on human friendship and attachment; He responded in terms of an unfailing spiritual affection,
which would not spare effort or sacrifice on their behalf. They
were to rest assured of this. But the Lord does not always act,
as we would like, in His care of us. When He heard that "Lazarus
was critical from protracted illness, he remained in the same
place where he was for two days."[3] He probably continued with
His program of work, recuperation, meditation, and prayer during
this delay. He was conscious that the disciples might misinterpret
His hesitation to return to the proximity of Jerusalem, to be the
dread of facing His enemies there. He also knew it would be a
severe strain on the faith of the sisters in Bethany, and the cause
of disappointment and suspicion of neglect. Lazarus died probably
hours before He received the message of the sisters.[4] Jesus announced His decision to return to Judea two days after the message
came. It was a test of the faith and confidence of the sisters, to
await, for three long days after the death of their only brother,
the coming of Jesus. He had said the sickness would not end in
death; surely He could not be mistaken. There was hope, according to popular tradition among the Jews, during the first three
days after death. The soul yet hovered about the body and life
might return. During two days the disciples watched their Master,
wrapt much in deep meditation and often going apart for prolonged prayer. Finally they saw on His face a look of decision and
determination. "Let us go back to Judea[5]" He announced. "Master,
the Jews have just been trying[6] to stone you," they replied amazed,
"and are you going back there again?" Jesus calmed their fears.
Until His work was finished He bore a charmed life. His hour had
not come and He was sure of divine protection. They would share
with Him that protection and need not fear. "Are there not twelve
hours in the day?[7] If anyone walks around[8] in the day he does
not go stumbling and cutting himself or bumping into things,
because he can see the light of this world; but if he travels around
in the night he goes stumbling along because the light is not in
him." There was no danger or peril for Jesus, who was walking

---

1 Imperfect active indicative, an abiding love.
2 ēgapa, not efilei, the love of mere human friendship.   3 Accusative of duration of
    time.   4 Lazarus had been dead four days when Jesus arrived in Bethany. It
    took the messenger a day to come. Jesus delayed two days before starting, it
    took him a day to make the journey.
5 Hortative subjunctive.   6 Conative imperfect active indicative.
7 Genitive of kind of time, daytime.   8 Condition of third class.

in the full glare of noonday brightness of God's truth and had the
moral light of the truth in Him. Man's work for God must be done
in the appointed and opportune time allotted, and must move in
the sphere of God's truth; but the truth must dwell within the
heart and conscience at the same time. After thus preparing their
minds, He announces Lazarus' death in enigmatical terms: "Our
friend Lazarus is fallen asleep; but I am going there to awaken
him."[1] But the disciples had not been wholly persuaded of their
safety and His and sought to dissuade Him from his purpose:
"Lord, if he is fallen asleep[2] he will recover,[3]" they tactfully suggested. Now Jesus had referred to Lazarus' death but they thought
He was speaking[4] of taking a rest in sleep. So Jesus then tells
them plainly: "Lazarus died, and I am glad, on your account, that I
was not there, so that you may come to believe.[5] But let us go to
him!" If Jesus had been in Bethany and healed Lazarus, even
though very ill, such a miracle would not have had as tremendous
effect on the disciples and others, as that of raising one four days
deceased. The determination of Jesus to return to Judea, into
the very jaws of danger, served to reveal the fears of the disciples. They considered such a return only a journey to His
death. This conviction was expressed by Thomas the Twin, sometimes called Didimus among his Greek friends. He said to his
fellow-disciples, when he saw the look of determined decision on
Jesus' face: "Let us go also to die[6] with Him." They were sure that
this would be the result of His returning to Judea; but, in spite of
his skeptical attitude, this disciple revealed here a courageous
devotion to Jesus rarely encountered.

The second scene of the drama is laid at Bethany, suburb-town
of Jerusalem (vv 17-32). The circumstances of the arrival (17-
19) bring us to His encounter with Martha, who came out to meet
Him (20-27), followed by that with Mary, to whom Martha reported His coming (28-32).

On His arrival Jesus found that Lazarus had been already
four days in the tomb. This fact was reported to Him as He lingered on the outskirts of the village, resting awhile from His day's
journey before He should enter the grief-stricken home. John
inserts a parenthesis here as to the exact locality of the town
which was situated about two miles southeast from Jerusalem.
According to the custom among the Jews, a number of friends had

---

1 Goodspeed's translation.   2 Condition of first-class, condition assumed as fulfilled.
3 Future passive, will be saved.   4 Present active indicative in indirect discourse.
5 Hina with ingressive aorist active subjunctive, that you may come to believe.
6 Hina with the subjunctive expressing result.

come out to see Mary and Martha and console them about their brother. Some of these friends, of a family which moved in the best circles of society, would be sympathetic with Jesus, while others were doubtless hostile; all the more reason why He should linger for a brief while outside the village, before entering the home of the sisters. Lazarus was buried, according to Jewish custom, on the day of his death, and the family would also naturally observe the customary seven days of solemn mourning. The fact that there were "many friends" reveals the high social position of this noble family. We do not meet here with the extravagant demonstrations of grief by hired mourners, customary in funerals among the Jews of high society. The fact that these sisters had become disciples of Jesus would cause them to dispense in part, at least, with such superfluous and for the most part hypocritical demonstrations. Lazarus was probably buried not in the public cemetery, outside and a mile distant from the town, but in a private family tomb in a near-by garden.[1] In the customary cave or rock-hewn tombs, the bodies were laid in niches, after elaborate anointing with spices, aloes, myrtle, hyssop, rose-oil, and rose-water. Though a close friend of Jesus, Lazarus was not regarded as an apostate from the synagogue. He and the two sisters probably attended all the feasts in Jerusalem and regular services in the neighboring synagogues—if there were such—subscribing to all the routine ceremonies, as good Jews would expect to do. The early disciples continued regularly to do this for some time after His death, until the breach between Judaism and Christianity widened.[2]

The four days had been sad and trying ones for the bereaved sisters. They had fasted the day of burial and had eaten nothing since but an occasional egg or some lentils. The funeral procession had been very depressing with its dirge flutes and the wailing friend-mourners, who "wept as those who had no hope." These were followed in the procession by the two sisters, neighbors, and relatives. At the tomb the men had chanted the ninetieth Psalm and circled the bier seven times, while friends spoke words of comfort to them in formal mien. How they wished for their great Friend, Jesus, in those weary dragging hours, and cast many an anxious look down the Jericho road. In their desolate home they sat on the floor heavily veiled, with unsandalled feet, surrounded by the mourning friends, with their rent clothes and dust-covered heads.

The arrival of Jesus in the neighborhood could not take long to become known in the village. He would have been descried

---

1 Edersheim, Life and Times of Jesus.   2 Cf the case of Peter and John, Acts 4.

by someone, afar off, climbing[1] the Jericho highway—the Ascent of Blood; and the news would be brought first to Martha the elder and more active of the sisters, and always the hostess in the household. Quietly wrapping her mourning dress and veil about her and slipping away from the mourning friends quietly, to avoid being followed, she hastened to go out[2] in the way to meet the long-wished-for Teacher (vs. 20-27), leaving Mary sitting quietly in the house. "Lord, if[3] you had been here my brother would not have died," she exclaimed on meeting Him, but added immediately, when she recalled in an instant the message of Jesus: "Even now I know that whatsoever you may ask[4] of God he will give you." Martha doubtless knew about the little daughter of Jairus and the young man, son of the widow at Nain. But, even this very morning, she had looked with dismay at the blackened corpse of her brother in the tomb, and with a sinking heart, realizing that decomposition had set in already and all traditional hope of resuscitation was cut off. If Jesus had said now: "He shall live," she might have some hope, but when He said: "He shall rise again," her mind flew immediately to the general resurrection and with sad words of resignation she replied: "I know that he will rise at the resurrection on the last day." She had faith in the future life, but her heart craved now something more. The quick reply of Jesus startled and caused her soul to leap up with a great joy: "I even myself am the Resurrection and the[5] Life. The one believing now in me, though he may die (physically) shall go on living and everyone living[6] and believing in me shall never die.[7] Do you believe this?" Now, He is not speaking of far-off future events but present realities. The resurrection is one manifestation of the Life; it is involved in the Life.[8] The believer is not dead when he dies physically but goes on living. Jesus submitted Martha's faith to the test. She might not understand perfectly all the turns of thought in the remarkable declaration of Jesus—as few do—but she responded to His appeal to her faith:

"Yes, Master," she affirmed, "I do believe that you are the Christ (Messias) the Son of God, who was to come into the world." She believed in the future resurrection, but she went further and asserted her firm conviction[9] in the present eternal life for the believer, and in the power of Jesus to raise even from the dead here and now. Her confession reminds one of Peter's at Cesarea Philippi, but outranks his, because she believed under trying cir-

1 Present middle indicative, he was putting effort and energy into the climb with a good
      will.   2 First aorist (ingressive) indicative.
3 Second class condition, contrary to fact.   4 First aorist middle subjunctive.
5 Note the use of the article.   6 Future middle of zoo, spiritual life.
7 Not die forever, spiritual death.   8 Westcott on the gospel of John, in loco.
9 Perfect active indicative, an unshaken firm conviction.

cumstances in the power of Jesus to raise her brother even then (cf. Matt. 16:16).

Desiring that Mary her sister should share with her this joyful hope, she interrupted the conversation, and hastened back to call her sister secretly, saying: "The Teacher is here and is asking for you."

When Mary heard it, she rose up quickly and started out to go to Him[1], for Jesus had not yet come into the village, but was in the place where Martha met Him. Now, the Jews who were with her in the house and were condoling with her, when they saw that Mary rose up quickly and went out, followed her thinking, "she is going to the tomb to weep[2] there." Now, Mary on coming to the place where Jesus was, and seeing Him, fell down at His feet, saying to Him:

"Lord, if you had been here my brother would not have died." Now, when Jesus saw her weeping thus at His feet and the Jews who had come out with her wailing in their half-hypocritical fashion, He restrained a groan[3] in His angered spirit but was manifestly agitated. Here was sincere grief pouring out its heart at His feet; and here also was a sham of insincere lamentation enacted in the name of friendship. It was enough to stir the heart of God to anger. But Jesus restrained Himself with an effort from any expression of rebuke to the "wailing friends." He would now proceed to His work of raising Lazarus (vs. 33-44).

"Where have you laid him?" He asked. They say to Him, "Sir, come and see." The group then moved on toward the tomb, and as they did, Jesus silently began to shed tears[4] of sympathy for the grieved sisters.

Some of the more sympathetic "friends" of the family remarked on seeing this:

"See how much he loved him." Even they were moved at the tears of this strong man, and recognized His true friendship[5] for Lazarus. But there were among these "friends" some who were hostile towards Jesus. These muttered words of criticism, insinuating malicious words:

"Was not this fellow, who opened the eyes of that blind man, able to keep this one from dying?" These words muttered in sly insinuation reached the ears of Jesus and raised again His indignation, just as He comes[6] to the tomb. Again He restrains Himself, as He stands before the rock-hewn tomb where He was to demonstrate His power over death. The door of the cave-tomb was closed,

---

1 Imperfect (ingressive) middle indicative, started toward him.
2 Hina with the aorist subjunctive in a purpose clause.
3 First aorist middle indicative.   4 First aorist indicative active (ingressive).
5 Imperfect active indicative of filein.   6 Present middle, active indicative.

with a large stone laid against it. Jesus issued the order:
"Take away the stone."

Martha, the sister of the one who had died, quietly reminds
Him:

"Lord, already the corpse is in decomposition[1] for he has been
dead four days!"[2] She shrank[3] with horror from seeing the now
blackened corpse exposed to the public gaze. But Jesus reminds
her of the word He had spoken to her a few moments before: "Did
I not say to you that if you may believe you will see the glory of
God?" He had also sent the message to them that the sickness of
Lazarus "was not to end in death but was for the glory of God."

So they lifted away the stone.

Then Jesus looked upward and said: "Father, I thank thee
that thou heardest me. I know[4] that thou hearest me always.[5]
But because of the multitude which is standing around I said it,
in order that they might begin to believe[6] that thou didst send me."
This was the purpose of the great miracle, declared even before it
was performed—the production of faith in the people. After saying
these things He cried with a loud voice that all might hear:

"Lazarus, come here, outside!"

The one who had died came out immediately, bound both as to
his feet and hands[7] with grave-wrappings and his face bound
around with a napkin. Jesus says to them:

"Loose him and let him go his way." It was a majestic moment!
At last it was clear, Jesus was the Master of death. He, who seemed
troubled and perplexed a few moments earlier, and was derided by
some as being helpless and weak even to the shedding of tears,
now stood forth calm and self-possessed, in majestic silence,
before the amazed disciples, the shuddering and panic-stricken
multitude, and the horrified enemies. Then the curtain drops on
the remarkable drama.

(2) The effects of the miracle on the people, the Sanhedrin, and
on the movements of Jesus (Jno. 11:45-54).

The evangelist, who recorded as an eyewitness the vivid details of the incident, does not describe the joy of the devoted sisters in receiving Lazarus back to life and their amazement and
adoration as they received their great Guest into their hospitable
home that day. John remembered that many of the friendly Jews
who had come to comfort the sisters in their bereavement, seeing
this great thing which Jesus did, put their trust in Him. But there

---

1 Ede ozei, gives off an odor already.   2 He is a fourth day man (corpse).
3 Aorist participle, punctiliar action.   4 Past perfect indicative.
5 Present active indicative, linear action.
6 Hina with ingressive aorist active subjunctive in purpose clause,
7 Accusative of specification, specifying the part affected.

were others in this same group who went back to Jerusalem and reported to the Pharisee enemies of Jesus the things which He did.

There is one more scene in this memorable drama, and this time the scene is laid in Jerusalem. The chief priests got busy, and began to call together[1] the Sanhedrin, in special call session. In their excitement and haste they were saying over and over to one another:

"What are we doing[2]? because this fellow is doing many signs."

"If we allow him to go on his way, everybody will believe on him, and the Romans will come and take away from us both our place and our nation."

It would not do for them to allow Jesus to go on raising the dead right at their doors, here in the very suburbs of Jerusalem. The people would be insisting again, presently, on making Jesus their political Messiah. There was a great hubbub in the meeting of the council. The chief priests were much concerned about their place. The Pharisees would have welcomed a successful political Messiah but they well knew that Jesus had refused to be even thought of as such. Still they foresaw that such a miracle as this, transcending all previous human experience and reason, must bring to Jesus a vast increase of popularity. Should the multitude take Him and acclaim Him their Messiah, it would bring immediately the bloody legions of Rome upon them, and there would ensue just such a massacre as that experienced in the time of Judas the Galilean. They shuddered at the very thought of it. There was much discussion, hesitation, and confusion in the council as to what should be done. But something must be done, else the gravest consequences would follow, and all their efforts to diminish His popularity would prove unavailing.

At this juncture all turned to the High Priest Caiaphas. Surely he ought to give some solution to the difficult problem. For some twelve years already he had been their leader. He was the successor of Annas in the High Priesthood since 18 A. D., having been appointed at that time by the Roman procurator Valerius Gratus. He was identified so thoroughly with the Romans that the Sadducean leaders in the Sanhedrin would accept with confidence his decision in this important affair. Then, too, he was the religious head of the nation.

The discussion suddenly ceases as the long-robed president of the Council rises sedately from his priestly throne to announce his decision. All are breathless with attention to hear what the sentence will be. Here was another august moment in its conse-

---

1 Second aorist active (ingressive) indicative.   2 Present indicative active, linear action.

quences on future generations. "You know nothing at all," he declared solemnly. Your discussion and indecision will not solve
the problem. You are not reasoning or thinking clearly about
your interests. "It is fitting and to your best interest[1] and advantage that one man should die on behalf of the people, in order that[2]
the whole nation may not perish." His decision expressed the
inmost thoughts of most of the members of the council. They had
been hesitant and timid in giving expression and vote to so drastic and final a measure, which involved death for the Nazarene.
Their consciences had made cowards of them all. "But Caiaphas
was right. The time demanded action and a drastic though bloody
measure. Jesus must die or else the nation would be swept away."
So the Sanhedrists thought.

Caiaphas had unconsciously uttered a prophecy, and a deeper
truth than he knew. He meant to be selfish and mean and he expressed the bloodthirsty decision of the Sanhedrin council. He
fairly represented the Jewish people in his decision. He never
realized at all that he was prophesying the downfall of the Priesthood (their "place") and the destruction of the people whom he
professed to be saving by his decision against Jesus. He did not
"reason" that an unjust decision on the part of a judge against
an innocent victim will always revert in curses on the head of the
one who pronounces it. This was the last prophecy of the High
Priesthood in Israel, pronouncing sentence against itself. Jesus
would indeed die "on behalf of the people" in a sense far deeper
than Caiaphas would ever understand. Caiaphas, in virtue of his
office as High Priest, unconsciously announced the eternal plan of
God—that His Son should die instead of the nation and on behalf
of not only the Jewish people but all the children of God who
should be gathered from among the nations, scattered over the
whole face of the earth. By His atoning death Jesus would gather
these children of God from among all the tribes and nations of the
earth. The die was cast; Jesus had committed the final and unpardonable act in raising Lazarus from the dead. So, from that
day, they began to plan[3] to kill Him.

In some way, perhaps through His friend Nicodemus, Jesus
came to know of this dark decision (in private session) of the
Sanhedrin. In consequence of this, He did not continue to go
around openly among the Jewish enemies, but withdrew to a
place near the desert, to a town-place called Ephraim, the identity
of which is not known. It was probably northeast of Jerusalem,
near the margin of Perea and Judea. There He remained[4] for a

1 Humin, data of advantage.   2 Hina with me and subjunctive in sub-final clause.
3 First aorist (ingressive) middle.   4 Imperfect, continued action.

time with His disciples in meditation and prayerful preparation for
the last attack on the stronghold of Jerusalem. He would soon face
the final issue at the Passover. He and the disciples, especially,
needed a brief session of rest and communion in anticipation of
that struggle. But the words spoken in front of the tomb of Lazarus in Bethany, "I am the resurrection and the life," continue to
ring down the corridors of time, are read beside every death-bed,
and repeated in every Christian burial service, with the same
wonderful results of stripping death of its sting and the grave of
its victory.

CHAPTER XXVI

LAST JOURNEY TO JERUSALEM

(Harm. §§ 120-127)

A few days of needed rest and meditation; perhaps a visit to the desolate region near, where He was tempted of the devil in the beginning of His ministry, to fortify His spirit for the conflict out just ahead; a brief lull in the tempest which now raged about Him was all the time that the intense spirit of Jesus would permit before He should enter on the last journey to Jerusalem which was to terminate with His death. The Passover Feast was some days ahead yet, and since Ephraim must have been somewhere near the northeast corner of Judea, Jesus took His way up the boundary line[1] between Samaria and the narrow strip of Galilee west of the Jordan, until He should strike the road on the northern border of Samaria leading across the Jordan near Bethshean into Perea. There He would find a caravan of pilgrims from Galilee crossing over to the road east of the Jordan to go on their way down through Perea to the ford near Jericho and thence up to Jerusalem to the Passover Feast. He had many friends in Galilee, and it was particularly fitting that He should take this route, accompanied by old friends.

1. Jesus heals ten lepers and explains the nature of the kingdom of God to the Pharisees and His disciples (Luke 17:11-37). (1) It is Luke the beloved physician, who records the healing of the ten lepers (vs. 11-19). It was an incident which lent itself to the presentation of the universality of the gospel, one of the major interests of that evangelist. Even the despised Samaritans found a welcome place in the program of Jesus, according to Luke.

(1) Now, it came to pass that as He was going on to Jerusalem, He was passing through[3] the midst of Samaria and Galilee.[4] As He was entering into a certain village,[5] there met Him ten leper-men, who rose up, stood at a distance, and lifted up their voices[6] in a chorus, saying: "Jesus, Master (Superintendent) take pity on us!" And when He saw them, He said to them: "Go and show yourselves to the priests." Now it came to pass that, as they were going,[7] they were cleansed. But one of them, perceiving that he had been healed, turned back, glorifying God with a great voice, and fell on his face at the feet of Jesus, thanking Him. Now, *he* was a Samaritan. Then Jesus said to him: "Were not the ten cleansed?

---

1 Luke 17:11, 12.   2 En with the articular infinitive, a favorite Lukan idiom (17:11)
3 Dia with accusative use.   4 Perfective use of dia with erchomai.
5 Some unknown village near the border.   6 First aorist active of aireo.
7 Articular infinitive with en.

But the nine, where[1] are they? Were none found[2] to return and give glory to God except this foreigner?" Then in a moment He added: "Get up and go on your way. Your faith has saved you."

Luke had given the account of the healing of a leper in the very beginning of the ministry of Jesus in Galilee (Luke 5: 12-16) and now adds this very extraordinary case of the ten, who met Jesus outside of a village near the border of Samaria. Nine of them were probably Jews and the village was likely a Jewish village. Fellow-sympathy in misery had broken down the barriers of race and the one Samaritan stood up with the others, who were probably Jews, and joined with them in a heart-rending plea for pity. According to the ceremonial law of the Jews (Lev. 13:45f) they might not come near anyone but must stand afar off and cry: "Unclean! Unclean!" Miserably afflicted with this malady which was itself a living death, they spent their days in hopelessness, waiting for the end. But, where Jesus goes, humanity cannot be hopeless. These men stricken with leprosy had doubtless heard of the remarkable cure wrought months ago on one of the worst lepers in Galilee, not far from here. They knew the name of the Nazarene prophet, and recognized in their desperate plea that He was the Master-superintendent and had power to overcome their disease. Jesus had told the leper whom He had cured months before, that His cure depended not on the willingness of the miracle-worker, but on the will or desire of the leper himself to exercise a vital faith in Him. These beg for His pity and leave the case with Him. At first Jesus did not see them, for they stood afar off, but when He did, and heard their cry, He did not hesitate, but ordered them to go at once[3] and show themselves to their priests, according to the instructions of their ceremonial law. Each would go to the priest nearest his own home,[4] and the Samaritan to the temple on Gerizim. Jesus came to fill up to the full the law, not to destroy it. He would build on the old regime a new, larger, and better order.

Now it happened that in going they were cleansed. Their confidence in obeying the order of Jesus proved the occasion of their immediate cure. The dry scales fell from them, the white spots disappeared, a healthy color returned to their flesh, their disfigured members were restored, a thrill of new life coursed their veins, and with exceeding joy they perceived they were made whole. Surely they were all thrilled and should be deeply grateful to the Master. But not so; nine hastened on to put an end to their social isolation, thinking only of themselves, in anticipation of a

1 Emphatic position.   2 First aorist passive.   3 Aorist imperative active, denoting prompt action.   1 Edersheim Life and Times of Jesus.

glad reunion with their families and friends. Only one remembered with gratitude Him who had wrought the cure, and hastily
turned back, praising God with a loud voice, and fell down beside
the feet of Jesus, thanking Him. Luke inserts the significant explanation that this man who came back was a Samaritan. Ten
had received the blessing; only one returned to give thanks—a
percentage too true to history.

Jesus was disappointed. This was characteristic Jewish ingratitude. He did not find gratitude where it should have been
expected. But it was gratifying to find it where it would not be
expected. Pharisees would reject Him; but publicans and harlots
would press into the Kingdom. "Where are the other nine?" is a
question which has passed into a proverb for expressing the frequency of ingratitude. Nine received benefits through Christ; one
received Christ through His benefits. The nine Jews received
physical cure; the one Samaritan received cure of the body and
salvation for the soul. Jesus concluded the incident: "Rise and go
your way," he said. "Your faith has saved you once for all and
eternally."[1]

(2) Jesus explains to the Pharisees and His disciples about the
nature of the Kingdom and the coming of the Son of Man (Luke
17:20-37).

The Pharisees in the Jewish village, near where Jesus cleansed
the ten lepers, were chagrined by Jesus' commendation of the
grateful Samaritan and His indirect but effective thrust at the ingratitude of the highly privileged Jews. With a contemptuous
sneer,[2] they approached Him with a question, as to when the proposed King—of His discourses—would come (vs. 20, 21). They
themselves looked for a visable Messianic Kingdom of great outward display of pomp and splendor. When would this Jesus the
wanderer, even now a fugitive from His own people, set up His
Kingdom? His reply to their insinuating question and derisive
sneer was keen and cutting, revealing their utter misconception
of the nature of the Kingdom of God: "The Kingdom of God is
not coming[3] with outward display," nor will men say: "Look, here
it is!" or, "There it is!" for "See, the Kingdom of God is within
you." To be sure, it was not within the Pharisees but it was
among them (entos). It was in the hearts of the disciples, and that
is what Jesus meant. This was a knock-out blow to the externalism
of the Pharisees. Once more they came out worsted in their insinuating and sneering attack on His Messianic claims.

1 Perfect active indicative, denoting permanence.   2 David Smith, In the Days of
   His Flesh.   3 Present indicative (deponent), indicating actual present coming
   then in process.

Jesus then turned to the disciples, and addressed them mainly, though perhaps in the presence of the Pharisees, revealing to them and others present the true character of the second coming of the Son of Man (Messiah). This subject grew immediately out of the discussion with the Pharisees. He had told them that the Kingdom would not come with outward display. It would not be possible to predict the *when* of its appearance, like the astronomers do stellar events, by close "observation" of the heavenly bodies. Days would come when these disciples would long and yearn for a day of the future glory of the coming Messianic King. They must not be disappointed because they would not see it in their day. There would be many false signs and false prophets of the second Advent. Those prophets would say: "Look, there He is!" "Look, here He is!" The disciples must not allow themselves to be deluded, and, leaving their daily occupations, run away after false prophets, pursuing them here and there. The second coming of the Son of Man (Messiah) would be sudden and universally visible. There would be no need that one should be told when or where. It would come with the shock and suddenness of a flash of lightning, rending the sky from east to west, from horizon to horizon. But the disciples need not be speculating about any early realization of the august event. The cross must be faced first. There was no advantage in idle speculation about when the Kingdom would come; He would teach them how it must come, and that through the suffering of the cross and rejection by the present generation.

Jesus had told them that the Kingdom was not to come soon, in great outward display of power. He now reveals that the second coming of the Son of Man (Messiah) will be with such outward demonstration as to be recognized universally and instantly. But the realization of the Kingdom of God now in their hearts called for suffering and much disappointment on His part and theirs. He passes now to reveal the fact that the second coming, being sudden, would find the world unprepared. He cites the times of Noah and Lot as illustrations of the vain worldliness and careless enjoyment which would prevail at that time in the world. His expression falls into the most beautiful, almost rhythmic, movement of the Greek tenses. The imperfect tenses: "They were eating, they were drinking, they were marrying, they were giving in marriage," set forth in vivid manner the unceasing stream of worldly pleasures and occupations which engrossed the attention of the people in the times of Noah. Then the aorist tenses follow: "Noah entered (the ark), the flood came, and destroyed them all," like repeated strokes of judgment and destruction. The same use of the tenses is repeated in the other incident cited in illustration, but this time lengthened out: "They were eating, they were drinking, they were buying, they were selling, they were planting, they were building." These words sound out with the rhythmic swing of continued midnight revelry; but they are followed quickly by the fatal beat and cadence of the aorists of sudden, final, and awful judgment: "Lot went out from Sodom, God rained fire and brimstone from heaven, and destroyed them all." He definitely applies the illustration to the theme in hand: "It will be the same way in the day when the Son of Man is revealed."

Jesus instructs the disciples how they are to conduct themselves at that time (vs. 31-33). "He who happens to be[1] on the flat-topped roof and his goods in the house, let him not go down[2] to take them; and likewise let not the man in the field turn back. Remember Lot's wife." She looked back, "desiring to recover her worldly possessions and enjoyments and so proved herself unworthy of the salvation that was offered her" (Plummer). Jesus summed up the spiritual lessons of His instructions in words similar to those used before:

"Whosoever seeks to use his own life for himself shall lose it, but whoever shall lose it shall preserve it."

The Teacher closed His address to the disciples, pointing to the final separation (vs. 34-37). "I tell you solemnly, on that[3] night there will be two on one bed, one shall be taken away and the other left. Two women shall be grinding together; one shall be taken and the other left." Those most intimately associated will have the most widely separated destinies.

Then they reply to Him: "Where Lord?" And He said to them: "Where the body is, there will the vultures be gathered together." The vultures of judgment will find the corpse of carnal nature, which clings to earthly things, wherever it may be; like the carrion-vultures, the animal corpse.

2. Two parables on prayer: that of the importunate widow and that of the Pharisee and Publican (Luke 18:1-14).

The delayed coming of the Son of Man would be a test to the faith of the maltreated disciples. So Jesus adds a lesson on the necessity of persistence and humility in prayer for deliverance. The need of importunity in prayer, He illustrated with the case of the unjust judge, who might have been any one of a number of irreverent and disregardful Gentile magistrates, noted for their selfishness and oppression.

a. The parable of the unjust judge carries in its preface the purpose of the illustration. It was spoken to show the necessity of

---

1 Present passive indicative, prophetic and futuristic.   2 Second aorist active imperative
        with me.   3 Robertson, Translation of Luke.

praying always and not giving up[1] under difficult and discouraging circumstances. The Jews taught that men ought to pray three times a day at the most and not to weary God with incessant prayer.[2] But Christ here teaches that we should pray always and about everything[3]; not to lose heart, turn coward, or give in to evil,[4] but persist and not faint. There is danger of "giving up" and abandoning prayer, if the answer does not come soon. The parable warns against this.

The personages of the parable (vs. 2-5) are well chosen. On the one hand, there is the irreligious or irreverent judge, who has no regard for God or conscience, who is unprincipled, lazy, selfish, who cares naught for executing justice or for public opinion. He is hopelessly unscrupulous and defies divine and human authority. On the other hand, we have the widow, a very symbol of defenselessness. "She had no protector to coerce nor money to bribe." Widows have ever been subject to the oppression of bad men and unprincipled officers of the law. Even the religious leaders of the Jews were denounced by Jesus, because "they devoured widows' houses," while professing, at the same time, great piety by their "long prayers."

The case of the widow was desperate. The judge was professedly neither pious nor humane. He had regard only for his own pleasure and comfort. The widow had no bribe for his itching palm. She certainly could not intimidate this insolent fellow. She resorted to the only method left, that of "pestering" him with her persistent complaint, until he should grant her redress from her oppression. So we are told in the parable: she kept on coming[5] to him day after day, with her request for protection and redress. "Give me justice against my adversary," she said. For some time, she kept on coming, and he kept on refusing.[6] At last, however, her persistence, like a continual dropping, wore him out, and he decided to grant her request in order to be rid of her. She had become an unbearable bore to him, and he was afraid that the tempest of her sharp words, motivated by her deep feeling of wrong and injustice, would bother him beyond measure,[7] "pestering him to the end."[8] It might also possibly result in violence— a scene in the court.

Jesus, after a brief pause, draws the moral of the parable (vs. 6-8). "Will not God give justice to His elect, who call to Him day and night?" This was what the parable of the unrighteous judge[9] said to the disciples. An affirmative answer to the question

1 Robertson, Translation of Luke.   2 Plummer on Luke.   3 Pantote.
4 Me enkakein, not to give in to evil.   5 Imperfect tense, denoting repetition.
6 Double negative ou and me.   7 Imperfect, continued action.
8 Hupopiazei means iterally to beat under the eyes, the insolent judge humorously excused his conduct by saying "he was afraid she would give him a black eye."
9 Genitive of kind or quality of judge.

is implied. The unjust judge is no complete picture of God, nor is the widow a true symbol of the disciple who prays. The illustration is an argument *a fortiori*. If the unjust judge would yield to the importunity of the defenseless widow, who came daily to speak to him, how much more will God, who is just, hear the unceasing cry for succor from His own elect people.

But God's method is not well understood always. "He is patient (forbearing) over them." He will reward their patient believing prayers in due time, though His answer may seem to be delayed. "Is He slow to help them?" The point is that the disciple must not try to browbeat God into answering this prayer, nor must he trust in his own importunity; he must have faith in the faithfulness of God to answer always, though the answer may be delayed. The parable teaches that God does delay and we are to be faithful, persistent, and faith-filled in our praying. We must pray always, in all circumstances, and not get discouraged and give way to evil. Will Jesus find, when he returns, such persistent[1] faith and faithfulness as this on the earth? That is a challenge.

b. Luke connects the parable of the Pharisee and the Publican (vs. 9-14) with that of the Unjust Judge, because Jesus wanted to teach both His disciples and the Pharisees a very important lesson as to the character of true prayer. The Pharisees had just raised a question about His Messianic Kingdom, deriding Him, and instilling into the minds of His disciples a doubt as to the Kingdom. So Jesus drew a picture of the Pharisees, who have confidence in themselves that they are righteous and who scorn everybody else, in contrast with the Publicans, whom they utterly despised. His purpose was to show to the Pharisees and to the disciples the real character of self-complacent Pharisaism and so humble the pride of the Pharisees, bringing them if possible to repentance before God. This exposure of the vain and hollow hypocrisy practiced in the very act of prayer, which called for sincerity and humility before God in the one praying, would also be wholesome in its effect on the disciples, whom the Pharisees sought to separate from Him by every means possible. Thus He spoke:

"Two men went up into the temple to pray, the one a Pharisee and the other a tax-collector. The Pharisee took his stand and began to pray thus to himself: 'O God, I thank thee that I am not like the rest of men, robbers, rogues, adulterers, or even as this tax-collector. I fast twice a week; I pay the tithe on all I acquire.'" Such is the picture of the Pharisees which Jesus with consum-

1 Goodspeed's translation. Cf. Weymouth, "will he be tolerant to their opponents?"

mate skill dashes on the canvas with a few strokes of His artistic brush. He was a true representative of many Phariees, "who set all others at naught," and in their self-complacency depreciate the rest of the world, treating others as nothing.[1] The Pharisee utterly despised all other men, whom he considered inferior to himself. When he went up to the temple on Mount Moriah, he planted himself in a place where he could be seen by the crowd, and struck an ostentatious posture, Jesus was dealing with realities in this parable, for standing was the common posture at prayer among the Jews, and the Pharisees had made it so for purposes of ostentation. Jesus calls attention to their desire for preeminence in other places and condems this very spirit in His Sermon on the Mount. The words the Pharisees repeated were not a prayer, but rather a soliloquy of self-congratulation. He was standing before the people, boasting[2] of his own character. He asked God for nothing. He congratulated himself on not being like the rest of humanity, whom he confessed by his words to consider as mere "plunderers or dishonest rogues, workers of injustice, and adulterers." He addressed God on the subject of his own virtues and congratulates Him on having such a servant as he is, not a Gentile but a Jew, not a man of the common rabble but a Pharisee of the *elite* class. The most detested of all, whom he cited by contrast in his self-praise, was "that fellow," the despicable tax-collector, who had dared to come up to the temple for prayer at this same hour. Such a fellow should not be allowed within the Temple. He confessedly condemned all other men of gross and flagrant crimes; but was he innocent of those things?

He further cited ways in which he was superior to others. He was accustomed to fast twice a week, Mondays and Thursdays, the year around. The Mosaic law enjoined only one fast in the year, the Day of Atonement. There were many other fasts added by the Rabbis, but the Pharisee boasted that he went beyond all the requirements of written or oral tradition. In like manner, he went beyond all requirements of the law of the tithe, which embraced only the produce of the lands and herds. The Pharisees as a class did go to fanatical and ludicrous extremes in tithing even the kitchen herbs: the anise, mint, and cummin; while they neglected the weightier matters of the law. A recitation of his own praises, in the spirit of self-righteousness, was the core of the whole soliloquy. Along with this spirit of complacent self-satisfaction went a spirit of cruel contempt for others. He was better than all his fellow-mortals.

1 Exouthenountas tous loipous, treating as nothing the rest.
2 Imperfect, repeated words of self-praise.

Over against this vivid portrait of the Pharisee, stands in sharp contrast that of the Publican or tax-collector. He did not take a chief place in the temple, but stood afar off. He did not raise his eyes to heaven in ostentatious pose, but in contrition bowed his head. His prayer was a sob of repentance and a cry for forgiveness. His whole attitude was eloquent of his deep conviction and his grief for his sin. He stood beating[1] upon his breast in demonstration of that grief. His words were few but expressed a real prayer to God. "God, have mercy on me *the* sinner" he pled. He recognized that he was *the* sinner. To him, his sin was definitely conscious.[2] He did not think of comparing himself favorably with any man.

In solemn declaration, Jesus again draws the moral: "I tell you, this man went back home accepted with God rather than that one (the Pharisee); because everyone who lifts himself up will be humbled, while he who humbles himself will be lifted up."

Here Jesus claims to know the secrets of men's hearts and of God's judgments (Plummer). God approved of the Publican because of his self-satisfaction, his humility, his self-abasement, and his sincerity in prayer. He disapproved of the Pharisee because of his self-complacency, self-praise, snobbishness toward others, ostentation and hypocritical insincerity in prayer; lack of repentance and recognition of sin in his own life and unjust judgment of all others, whom he considered different from and inferior to himself. Effective prayer depends on the character of the one praying, the nature of the thing asked for, and the spirit in which prayer is offered.

3. Going from Galilee through Perea, on the way to Judea, Jesus teaches concerning divorce (Mark 10:12; Matt. 19:1-12).

It was in Perea on His last journey to Jerusalem that Jesus was again beset, in the midst of His work of teaching and healing, by the Pharisees, who tempted Him with another difficult and captious question. Their motive was evidently sinister. There were great crowds following Him constantly, while He continued[3] to teach them, as was His custom. This popularity of Jesus was more than His enemies could bear. If they could only bring up some decisive question that would make Him unpopular with the people! They sought for such a question and soon found it. The divorce question was a burning one then, as it is now. The two great theological schools of Hillel and Shammai debated this question hotly, Hillel taking the liberal side and Shammai the

---

1 Imperfect tense denoting repeated act.   2 Use of the Greek article makes definite.
3 Imperfect tenses of continued action.

conservative. The Pharisees would force Jesus to line up with one side or the other of the theological factions and so alienate a part of the crowd. Or perhaps, knowing already what Jesus thought about such questions, they wished to bring Him again into direct conflict with Herod Antipas. That wicked ruler was living with Herodias in open adultery. John had denounced their sin and lost his own head. If they could get Jesus to denounce openly this Herod and the wicked Herodias, they might succeed in doing away with Him soon. They had worked that plan successfully in John's case, and that right at the height of his ministerial success. This would be even better than to push Jesus into a controversy with one of the Rabbinical schools. They therefore raise the question of divorce in its current form, as reported by Matthew: "Is it lawful for a man to put away his wife for every cause?"

The school of Hillel said it was lawful "for every cause," even for the most trivial offenses. The Jewish woman could not divorce her husband, as could the Roman and Greek women; but the man could put his wife away for almost any senseless excuse. They took the words: "matter of shame" in Deuteronomy, in the widest possible sense: if "she found no favour in his eyes," or "he found another woman more attractive" — which sounds modern enough — he could put her away. Many specific[1] offenses were enumerated, such as going in public with uncovered head, entering into conversation with other men, speaking disrespectfully of the husband's parents in his presence, burning the bread, being quarrelsome or troublesome, getting a bad reputation or being childless (for ten years).[2] The school of Hillel had prevailed, and there was great general moral laxity now. The Mosaic law really permitted divorce only for the cause of unfaithfulness, but the popular conception among the Jews at the time of Jesus was that of the Rabbinical interpreters of the school of Hillel. Woman had become a mere chattel of man, subject to his inhuman and cruel treatment. The Pharisees understood well that if Jesus took the side of Shammai or the stricter view of divorce, He would alienate a greater part of the multitude.

But Jesus avoided the cavils and disputes of theological parties by piercing at once to the great fundamental law of marriage, recorded in Genesis. "Did you never read that the creator from the beginning made them male and female?" God made, at the beginning of the race, one woman for one man, suited to each other; and there was only one for one. For the same reason, it was declared that all other human relations, even the most intimate ones, as that existing between children and their par-

1 Deut. 24:1-4.   2 Edersheim, Life and Times of Jesus.

ents, must be secondary to that between husband and wife. The strong cohesive force of sex was purposed by God to be the basis of an inseparable unity. The union, in a true marriage, is one of body, mind, and spirit. In the Hebrew conception, body stood for all three. Therefore this yoke of God, by which He bound[1] two souls together, "let not man try to separate."[2] Thus Jesus soars far above the fog of controversial opinions and bears the question to the open skies of God's establishment of the law of marriage in the beginning. They had gone back to the Mosaic legislation; but He, farther back to the beginning. They could not answer this argument. Jesus was deeply moved by the wrongs suffered by womanhood among the Jews and all over the world, and here lays down the eternal law of God for marriage, which has never been changed since the beginning of the race. He clearly placed His seal of approval on the institution of marriage in its original form, and He speaks the last word of authority on this subject. Such a marriage did not contemplate the subjection of woman to man's caprice, but their union on equal terms of mutual helpfulness. Their complementary natures fitted them for each other and their union constituted the basis for the propagation of the race, the building of civilization, and the development of the Kingdom of God on earth.

But the Pharisees were not to be put off thus. They had failed to precipitate Jesus into a controversy with the theological school of Hillel or bring Him into acute conflict with Herod. But they acutely insinuate now that by His statement He has contradicted Moses, who sanctioned divorce. They assume — with injured air, we may well imagine — the defense of Moses. They say to Jesus: "Then why did Moses command us to draw up a written bill of divorcement (for the divorced woman)?" They emphasize the fact that Moses had commanded[3] this practice. Thus they would have placed the blame of prevailing moral laxity on Moses and so excused themselves. Jesus hastens to correct this impression and defend Moses:

"It was on account of your hardness[4] of heart that Moses permitted you to put away your wives: but from the beginning it has not been[5] so." The original ordinance had never been abrogated or superseded, but continued in force (Vincent). Moses' bill of divorcement was a convenient arrangement to mitigate the moral evil and was a great advance for the time. It was a *permission* because he could not bring them to a higher standard. Such

1 Sunedzeuken, timeless aorist.   2 Present conative imperative with me of prohibition.
3 Deut. 24:1.   4 Skleros, tough, dried up, stony.
5 Ouk gegonen, perfect tense, permanent state.

a bill of divorcement served as a protection for the woman being divorced, and also caused delay, which might give time for reflection and readjustment of relationships. Jesus placed the blame not upon Moses, but upon the people of uncircumcised hearts, who were not willing to be governed by the restraints of so high and holy a law. Moses desired a better state but had to permit the people to have divorce because they demanded it. The Master-Teacher was doing some real preaching at that hour, when He was surrounded by disciples of Hillel with their prevailing laxity so popular with the people. He proceeds to lay down next more specific details as to how this law of marriage must be respected. In solemn words, He says: "I tell you, that whosoever divorces his wife except for fornication[1] and marries another, himself commits adultery." Shammai was not the worse for agreeing with Jesus about this, but the Master-teacher had already lifted the subject out of the plane of controversial fog, before He touched on this technical point. Jesus, by implication, allows the innocent party of a union thus disrupted the privilege of remarriage, but not the guilty one (Robertson). A crying need of our times, as of theirs, is a faithful application of this principle by religious and civil leaders.

In a subsequent conversation with the disciples, He carried His instruction further at their solicitation. They were impressed with the difficulty of carrying into practice so high a standard.

"If that is the sole basis for a man's relation to his wife, it is better not to marry," they said. To limit the causes[2] of separation to adultery, solely, seemed to them impossible. They were so accustomed to the lordly position of man that they could not think of him as tied down to one woman for life. What would he do about the burnt bread and other disagreeable experiences?[2] Obviously their point of view was largely selfish. Jesus with great charity overlooks their low view of the wife as a household drudge to be dismissed at pleasure, and points them to the difficulty of their suggested alternative of a celibate life. The disciples suggested that the unmarried state would be preferable; but Jesus shows them that few have the moral capacity to live a continent life in celibacy. If we take a more charitable view of their question and admit that they were thinking mainly of their service to the Kingdom, we have the clear answer of Jesus, that if one desires to dedicate himself, unmarried, wholly to the Kingdom work, he has the approval of Jesus, with the distinct understanding that few have the moral capacity to carry through such a program. "There are some who are incapable of marriage

---

1 Pornia, fornication, general term inclusive of adultery.   2 Aitian, cause.

from their birth, and some are made eunuchs by men, and there are some who made themselves eunuchs for the sake of the Kingdom of God." Some men and women have remained unmarried that they might dedicate themselves solely to some great cause. This is permissible; and if one wishes to dedicate himself wholely to the service of the Kingdom, like Paul, his life of unimpeded dedication and strenuosity meets with the blessing of Jesus. Thus Jesus, in a few brief sentences, clarifies the whole question of the matrimonial union, which is one of the most vexing problems of all human history. A simple and faithful application of His teaching by religious leaders universally would be one of the greatest of measures for salvaging the wrecked homes of the world.

4. Jesus receives and blesses the little children and illustrates for His disciples the true nature of the Kingdom (Mark 10:13-16; Matt. 19:13-15; Luke 18:15-17).

It was peculiarly fitting that the incident of the parents, who kept bringing[1] their little children to Jesus, should follow immediately His pronouncement on the supremacy of the marriage vow over every other tie, particularly that between children and parents. The Master shows here, in this most tender and touching scene so graphically portrayed for us by the three synoptic evangelists, His love for children, which has made a new world for the children ever since. The incident probably occurred in Southern Perea, just a short while before the triumphal entry. These mothers and fathers, who had great confidence in the goodness of Jesus, were attempting to press in with their children into the house where He had repaired with his apostles for a few moments of rest after the strenuous hours with the Pharisees and His difficult discussion of the divorce question. The disciples, preoccupied with the vexatious question Jesus had discussed and disturbed over the outcome of the discussion, were denying[2] entrance to these anxious parents. They wanted to protect their Master, perhaps, from the crowd, and especially from being annoyed with these children, They thought the time of Jesus was too precious to be spent humoring the caprices of these over-fond mothers, who wanted their little children to see the great Rabbi, and have Him, according to popular tradition, lay His hands on their heads in a prayer of benediction.

When Jesus found out what was taking place, He became indignant.[3] It was painful to Him that His disciples should have so little understanding of Him and His attitude toward children. They might think they were doing Jesus a favor, just as some

---

1 Imperfect tenses denoting repeated process.   2 Imperfect tense denoting repeated action.
3 Ingressive aorist.

people today when they keep the children away from the church. How little they understood the children and Jesus! The pastor who does not like children in his church services has something more to learn about Jesus. The Master not only felt indignant but He did something about it. The disciples must learn a severe lesson: "Leave the little children alone," He said, "Suffer them to come to me!" "Stop hindering[1] them," He added sternly to the uncomprehending apostles, who thought they knew better what was good for their Master, and kept on scolding the parents for bringing them. Jesus wants parents to bring their children to Him for dedication[2] of their young lives.

Just a few months before this, Jesus had taught His over-ambitious disciples a lesson, taking a little child and setting it — in His lap probably—in the midst. They must receive the Kingdom as an innocent, confiding, obedient child, devoid of earthly ambitions and envies. He here repeats this teaching in another form. The Kingdom of heaven belongs to persons who are childlike in disposition. The little child learns to obey confidingly and simply. Jesus does not say here that children are in the Kingdom of God because they are children. He makes the child the model for those who seek entrance into the kingdom of God, not the adult the model of the child.[3] There is no argument here for infant baptism. Children who die in infancy are provided for by the Atonement of Christ. The childlike qualifications for one to enter the Kingdom are humility, receptiveness, meekness, a simple application to and trust in Christ.[4]

There are beautiful graphic touches in this narrative of the evangelists which constitute one of the most wonderful pictures which artists have sought to put on the canvas. We see first the tired Teacher, weary from His hours of strenuous teaching. About Him in the house, where they have sought refuge from the thronging crowd, are clustered the Twelve, anxious to hear more in detail about the great question of divorce. Then comes the group of anxious parents, bearing in their arms their children, some of them too small to walk. Some of the apostles, who remained at the door to prevent the intrusion of anyone, are rebuking these parents and sending them away. But, immediately, when Jesus perceives it, He takes His stand in the door, beckoning to the parents to enter with the children, while He gently chides the apostles and rebukes them for their thoughtless act of hindering the little ones from coming to Him. Then seating Himself, He takes the children each in turn into His arms and on His lap, placing

1 Present imperative with me (Matthew).　2 Prosferon, they were 'offering them" to him, as it were.　3 Robertson, Word Pictures.
4 Edersheim, Life and Times of Jesus.

His hand tenderly on the head of each and pronouncing a brief
prayer and benediction on the child. It is no wonder that artists
have vied with each other in trying to get this picture on canvas.
But they can never exhaust the tenderness and deep meaning of
this remarkable incident, which presents Jesus as the greatest friend
of every child.

5. Jesus teaches the rich young ruler the way of life, and the
disciples the greatness and sovereignty of their reward. Parable
of the Laborers in the Vineyard. (Mark 10:17-31; Matt. 19:16 to
20:16; Luke 18:18-30).

It was as Jesus went forth from the house, where He blessed
the babes, that a certain rich young ruler, probably of a local synagogue in Southern Perea, came running and kneeling to Him,
and questioned[1] Him saying: "Good Teacher, by doing what good
thing shall I inherit eternal[2] life?" He probably thought that by
doing some one great thing he could obtain everlasting life, and he
was ready to make a great effort and large expenditure for it. Here
was a youth of open mind and a good heart, who yearned for something higher than the ordinary experiences of a self-satisfied
religionist (Matt. 19:16-22). He was not flattering Jesus by addressing Him in this extraordinary way,[3] as no Rabbi was accustomed to be addressed. While we may understand that the young
man was sincere in his quest for the *summum bonum*, at the same
time his words reveal that he had a fundamentally wrong conception of the way to reach it. He understood that he might obtain
or acquire eternal life by some great act of devotion to religion,
something that he might do. That he had been zealous for the
law, we get from his confession. He belonged to the same class of
Pharisees[4] that young Saul of Tarsus did. He had zealously kept
all the commandments and traditions of his fathers and with a sincere longing to measure up to the highest standard. But he felt
that there was something lacking yet, and thought that Jesus,
whose great insight into the deep questions of life was so evident,
might give him some help. The answer of Jesus was of such a
character as to reveal to His earnest pupil the real nature of the
"good thing" he felt the need of so acutely. He was an eager but
immature young man, who trusted "too much in himself and too
little in God."[5] Jesus would reveal to him what God's goodness
really was and what a high goal Jesus places before man. Perhaps
the young ruler had heard Jesus preach on other occasions and

1 Imperfect tense, eperota, was asking him, Mark 10:17
2 Matthew, "may get," ingressive aorist subjunctive.
3 No Jewish Rabbi was called "good" in direct address (Plummer).
4 The "let me know what is my duty and I will do it" class. (Robertson).
5 Plummer on Luke.

had been inspired to seek to know what "the good" **really** was, since he had tried out what was ordinarily considered "good" and found it insufficient and unable to give inward satisfaction.

"Why do you call me good," said Jesus, "or ask me about the good? None is good save one, even God."

One of the titles given God in Jewish writing was: "The Good One of the world."[1] Had the young man caught a glimpse of the divine goodness of Jesus? At least Jesus would lead His pupil on to define his attitude toward Him. There were great possibilities in this bright and aspiring youth, if he might be led to the confession of His divine Messiahship.[2] "You have given me a title," He explained, "which belongs only to God. Do you understand and mean it?"[3]

A second element in the reply of Jesus referred to the young ruler's question about "the good" which he might practice or cultivate in his own character, that would enable him to "acquire" or "become an heir of" eternal life. The Talmud said: "There is nothing else good but the law." Jesus first submits the young ruler to the test of his own Jewish standard. "You ask me about the good thing, practice, or character which would make you an heir of eternal life."

"You know the commandments. If you would[4] enter into life keep the commandments." Jesus had taught His pupil the necessity of a thoughtful use of moral epithets. If he really understood what he meant by calling Jesus *good*, he had taken a great step toward defining his personal relationship to Him. Does the young man comprehend the real meaning of the Law? There was such a body of laws and traditions that the requirement laid down by Jesus was very vague.

"Which of these multitudinous commands do you mean?" asked the young ruler. In reply Jesus cites the sixth, seventh, eighth, ninth, and fifth of the commandments of the Decalogue:

Do not kill,
Do not commit adultery,
Do not steal,
Do not bear false witness,
Keep on honoring your father and mother.

As a summary of the second table of the Decalogue, He adds:

"Thou shalt love thy neighbor as thyself."

Can the young ruler measure up to the ethical standard of

---

1 Edersheim, Life and Times of Jesus.   2 Cf. Matt. 16:16f.
3 David Smith, In the Days of His Flesh.   4 Conditions of the first class determined as fulfilled.

man's duty to man? This was the test to which Jesus submitted him. The youth replied thoughtfully and sincerely:

"Teacher, all these things I have observed in their entirety, from youth." He was a young man of high moral character, who put conduct above ritual in religion. He was not an ordinary person but had heroic elements in him. He was honest in his efforts to fulfill to the best of his knowledge all the laws of the Decalogue, as well as the traditional rules of the Rabbis. But there was an inward dissatisfaction which he could not fathom. "What lack I yet?" he added, frankly confessing that dissatisfaction.

He had expected that Jesus would tell him some wonderful thing he must do; but was simply reminded of things he had been doing all his life. Jesus was seeking to define for him the boundary, the true Law, and free him from the shackles of the traditions, while at the same time leading him to think deeply and discover his own inability to live up to the standard of the Law itself. Mark, who reflects the intimacy of Simon Peter with Jesus, graphically adds at this point:

Now, Jesus, looking upon him, began to love[1] him and said to him "One thing thou lackest yet. If thou wouldest be perfect[2] go and sell all thou hast and distribute[3] it to the poor and thou shalt have treasure in heaven; and come and begin to follow me." At last the young man was to learn that goodness was qualitative, as in the character of God, and not merely quantitative, as in a series of religious acts. Jesus agreed with the young ruler that he did lack something. The Teacher had led him to a confession of his lack; He was now prepared to lead him on to discipleship if possible. Jesus recognized in the youth noble character and wholesome aspiration, and let him know that He approved his desires and sympathized with his ideal.[4] Perfection[5] was a high ideal and the means of attaining it would not be easy. The difficulty in the way of the young ruler's complete dedication to God was his property. Jesus sets before him two measures necessary in order to inherit eternal life: (1) to go and sell all his property and give it away to the many poor people and then (2) to come and begin to follow Him. The first was an appeal to the heroic in a life of great self-sacrifice and privations, and the second to sponsor a cause which to all appearances would involve persecution and possibly death. The young ruler had not bargained for so much. He was seeking some counsel at the hands of the learned Teacher, but not so radical a change in his whole life and social status as these measures demanded.[6]

1 Ingressive aorist participle.   2 Condition of first class determined as fulfilled. Jesus assumes that the young man so desires.
3 Second aorist active imperative of diadidomi, gives to various ones.
4 Matt. 19:21.   5 Teleios, full-grown.   6 Present imperative active. (Luke).

So it is not surprising that he, "on hearing this, became very sad," and the reason for his sadness, as revealed by the whole circumstances, was "that he was exceedingly rich." His countenance depicted his disappointment. The sad conclusion of the whole story was that "he went away sorrowful, because he had great possessions."

Jesus points the moral of the story (Matt. 19:23-27). He had to correct the ideas of the disciples about money. They shared the popular belief that money proved that the one who had it was the favorite of heaven. Seeing the young man go away in "the great refusal," deeply impressed the Teacher, and looking around at His disciples to see the effect on them He said: "How difficult it is for those who have property to enter into the Kingdom of God." The disciples were filled with consternation by such words. So that they might be more deeply impressed and might understand what He meant, He added, tenderly addressing them as His very own:

"Children, how hard it is for them that trust in riches to enter the Kingdom of God!" Changing a current proverb cited in the Talmund, about the impossibility of an elephant passing through the eye of a needle, He added by way of illustration: "It is easier for a camel to go through the eye of a surgeon's needle[1] than for a rich man to enter into the Kingdom of God."

This was for the disciples literally a knock-out blow. They were exceedingly astonished and said:

"Who then can be saved?"

Jesus, looking upon them and seeing their amazement, replied: "With men it is impossible, but not with God, for all things are possible with God." It is possible for God to break even the spell which wealth exercises over the wealthy (Plummer). Jesus had exploded one of the current theories! Material prosperity then was not a sign of God's approval? What about their hopes which were bound up with the expected Messianic Kingdom? These thoughts were coursing their minds as Jesus looked upon them.

Reflecting still on the refusal of the young ruler to leave all and follow Jesus, Peter, speaking for the group, began[2] to say (Matt. 27:30): "Behold, we have left all and followed thee." He remembered the bright morning when Jesus called the four by the seaside, and they had left their fishing nets and gone off after the Teacher. They had been following Him for almost three years now and had passed through some pretty hard places with Him. Now the question which came to his mind, as to others of the

1 Luke the physician used the term which means surgeon's needle. Matthew and Mark, the common needle.   2 First aorist middle, ingressive (Mark).

group, was: "What then shall we get?" Jesus responds literally in a solemn declaration:

"Verily, I say unto you, that ye which have followed me in the regeneration when the Son of Man shall sit on the throne of his glory, ye also shall sit upon twelve thrones, judging the twelve tribes of Israel. And every one that hath left houses, or brethren or sisters or father or mother or children or lands, for my name's sake and for the gospel's sake, shall receive a hundredfold, now in this time, houses and brethren, and sisters, and mothers, and children, and lands, with persecutions; and in the world to come eternal life." Job stands out, in the Bible, as an example of one who passed through the fire and flood of suffering with the loss of all, and through faithfulness received again double of all he had lost. Jesus winds up the moral lesson drawn for the disciples with a paradoxical enigma:

"But many that are first shall be last; and the last, first!" He is gently rebuking the disciples for their mercenary spirit. There shall be many reversals of positions both ways. Those who are first now, shall be last then; first in this world's position, last in the Kingdom of God; first in privilege, last in Christian faith; first in zeal, last in quality of service through low motives. They should try to be first in the love of God and loyal service for His Kingdom, and in God's esteem and loving care, and not be looking merely at "the main chance" or what they should get for themselves out of the service. The choice workers are those who love the Lord most and serve the Kingdom from the motive of love for it. Jesus now adds the parable of the laborers in the vineyard to enforce the character, spirit, and true motive of the choice workers (Matt. 20:1-6).

The rich young ruler, when directed by Jesus to go and sell his goods, distribute the money to the poor, and then come and be His follower, went away with a discouraged look of distress on his countenance. Peter was quick to apply to himself and his fellow-disciples — and to their advantage — the lesson of the exactions of the Kingdom. They were looking forward to the coming Kingdom with eager expectations, that when it should come they themselves would greatly profit in a material way. The question of Peter revealing the mercenary spirit of the apostles in their service, was the immediate occasion of Jesus' speaking the parable of the laborers in the vineyard.

He likened the Kingdom of heaven to a man who was a householder, or kind of farmer-employer, who had vineyards in great need of workers. Farmer-like, he went out at the very break of day,[1] and began to employ workers from among the unemployed in the market-place, for his urgent work in the vineyard (vs. 1-7). He hired some laborers at the usual wage of a denarius a day (about seventeen cents in value) to begin at six in the morning and work the entire usual time, finishing at six in the evening. He agreed with these workers on a stipulated price and sent them into his vineyard. About nine o'clock, after three hours of the work-day were gone, he saw that he would not be able to finish the urgent tasks with these workers alone, and went again into the market-place, where he saw others standing idle because no one had employed them, and benevolently sent them also into his vineyard. He only promised to pay them what was just; but they went without a word of barter, trusting in the justice of the em-ployer. Coming out again about the sixth hour or twelve o'clock, and again at the ninth hour or three o'clock in the afternoon, he did likewise, sending other workers in to help. About the eleventh hour, coming out, he found others standing and said to them:

"Why have ye stood here the whole day idle?" They reply: "Because no man hired us." The employer says: "Go ye also into the vineyard." There was no stipulation of price in this case, or even a promise to pay anything. The workers must trust absolute-ly in the fairness and just character of the employer, to pay them something at least for the one hour of service.

At the close of the day, there was a settlement (vs. 8-12). The farmer-lord of the vineyard told his manager to call the workmen and pay them, strangely beginning at those last employed at five o'clock in the afternoon, and paying them each in turn[2] a denarius, or a full day's wage, without exception. Seeing that the eleventh-hour men had received a denarius, the workmen who had been the first employed and had worked the whole day thought they would receive more. Now these also each received a denarius. But when they received it, they began grumbling against the house-holder, saying: "These last-hour fellows worked only one hour, and do you make them equal with us who bore the burden of the day and the scorching sirocco wind?"[3] One of the workers cast down his denarius on the table and would not even accept it.

The householder replied to the disgruntled workman (vs. 13-15). He was wise in replying to the one instead of to the group. "Comrade," he said, "I did you no harm. Did you not bargain with me for a denarius? Take up that which belongs to you and be off.[4] I wish to give to this last as much as to you. Is it not possible for me to do what I wish with my own? Is your eye evil because I am generous?"

1 Hama proi, at the same time with early dawn (Matt. 20:1).
2 Distributive use of ana.   3 The hot, dry, dust-laden wind of the desert which scorched the grain of Pharaoh's dream.   4 Present imperative.

So runs this extraordinary story, designed to set forth the character and motive of true workmen and the point of view of God in His work, caring more for the character and spirit of the workmen than for the work done. Jesus ends the story with the declaration already made before He began it, but in a modified form: "So the last shall be first and the first last."

The parable rebukes gently the hireling spirit revealed by Peter in the apostles. "What shall we have therefore?" That question did not express the right spirit for a loyal worker in the vineyard. Jesus had not rebuked the mercenary spirit immediately, when Peter had asked it. He had graciously answered, enumerating the honors and rewards of the self-sacrificing disciples. They were to sit on twelve thrones and to receive abundant compensation and at last everlasting life. But now He shows in parabolic language that they must beware of the bargaining spirit, which is selfish and vitiates all service. The work done in a spirit of trust and love is wholly different from that of the hireling. God has more regard for the motive which prompts the worker, than for the amount of work done, or time spent in doing it. He has more regard for the worker than for the work. The householder of the parable had a benevolent motive in calling the workers into the vineyard. He was displeased with those who were self-complacent and calculating, but pleased with those who were humble, self-forgetful, truthful, and grateful. Some of the apostles who were first called into the service, and who had just expressed through Peter their mercenary spirit, must have seen in the first-hired laborers their own picture. Jesus points out the fact that there will be a reversal of human judgment in the end. Many who are prominent in the church, highly esteemed and lauded by men will be last in the estimation of God. What kind of workers are we in God's vineyard? Are we dominated by the motive of love and loyalty, which actuated Thomas Aquinas? He, according to legend was addressed by Jesus while in his devotions one day:

"Thomas, thou hast written much and well concerning me. What shall I give thee for thy work?"

He answered: "Nihil nisi te, Domine"—"Nothing but thyself, O Lord!"

"They that work for reward do not get as much as they want; they that work for love get more than they expect."

6. Jesus again foretells the manner of His death and resurrection, and rebukes the selfish ambition of James and John (Mark 10:32-45; Matt. 20:17-28; Luke 18:31-34; Harm. 125; cf. Harm. 83, 85,

86, 88).

Jesus walked in advance of the disciples as they went on the road leading up toward Jerusalem. His followers were terrified[1] and in a fearful state of mind,[2] such was the solemnity and determination of His attitude. Once again He took the Twelve apart in the way and began to explain[3] to them, and this time more in detail than ever before, the things He must suffer in Jerusalem. He had forewarned them twice before: the first time, that He would suffer many things at the hands of the rulers, and be killed; the second, adding His betrayal. Now He unfolded the whole drama of His passion in detail, adding His condemnation in trial, His mocking by the heathen (Romans), His flogging with the cruel Roman scourge, and His crucifixion.[4] Over against this dark picture He mentions the resurrection on the third day.

"See!" He said, "We are going up to Jerusalem, and the Son of Man will be handed over to the high priests and scribes, and they will condemn him to death and hand him over to the heathen and they will ridicule him and spit on him and flog him and kill him; and three days after, he will rise again."[5] Luke adds significantly: "But they understood none of these things." They were so dazed now that they simply received His announcement in bewilderment.

The thoughts of the apostles were on the Kingdom "out just ahead." Jesus had raised Lazarus, four days dead. Such miracles as these were bound to precipitate a final struggle between Him and His enemies, and the apostles were assured of the triumph of Jesus in this conflict. Had He not promised that they should sit on twelve thrones, judging the twelve tribes of Israel? It would not be long now until His Kingdom would be established, and the apostles, especially the more ambitious ones like James and John, were speculating in their own minds as to who would occupy the more prominent place in the Kingdom.

It was at this juncture that Salome, the mother of James and John, came on the scene. She might have joined at this time the caravan going to the Feast, or earlier. She knew, doubtless, about the raising of Lazarus, and shared with her two ambitious boys the current hope of the Messianic Kingdom. Being the sister, possibly, of Mary the mother of Jesus, she was deeply interested in the promotion of her sons, and resorted to the intimacy of his relationship in helping them, also prompting them in seeking the chief places. She even took the initiative and came with her two sons, kneeling before Jesus, as Esther before the Oriental Monarch Ahasuerus, to ask a favor of Him (Matt. 20:20).

1 Imperfect periphrastic indicative active (Mark).   2 Imperfect indicative, continued state of mind (Mark).   3 Ingressive aorist middle (Mark).   4 Mark 10:32-34.
5 Goodspeed's translation of Mark.

Being asked: "What wilt thou?" she replied: "Give orders that these my two sons may sit one on thy right hand and the other on thy left hand in thy glorious Kingdom."

Peter had revealed his mercenary spirit just a little while ago by his question: "What shall we get?" James and John here reveal not only their worldly ambition and mercenary spirit, but that they were plotting—even while Jesus was predicting His tragic death —for their own promotion to the chief places in a worldly Kingdom. They were not sure in their consciences, and drew back from presenting their request, putting their mother forward, like spoiled children, to lay their plan before Jesus. Plainly, their request was ignorant, foolish, and offered in anything but a courageous way. They were presumptious and irreverent to ask Jesus, as if He were some worldly tyrant, to grant them places of political preferment, just on the basis of mere intimacy and friendship. Family influence and court politics are not the pathway to position in the Kingdom of God. Mark records the fact that the sons, after the mother had presented their request, added their plea in that indirect way, seeking to get Jesus to commit Himself before they revealed fully what they desired. "Master, we wish that you may do for us what we ask." It is probable that Salome approached Jesus alone first, though the sons were waiting near and came forward to make their request in almost the same words their mother had used in her plea. Jesus did not rebuke them but replied kindly and sadly:

"You do not know what you are asking?[1] Are you able to drink the cup which I am drinking[2] or be baptized with the baptism with which I am being baptized?" They were brought back momentarily to face the fact that Jesus was suffering and even now had prophesied a crisis out just ahead. They were not able to understand that the Messiah should come to die. He must surely be, in some way, under a wrong impression about this. There would be a struggle. This they were able to see, but thought He would surely come out victorious in the conflict with His enemies, as He always had. The apostles understood that He meant the "cup" of suffering and the "baptism" of extreme suffering, but Jesus was referring to His death. They were ready to suffer for a while, that the victory of the Messianic Kingdom should come, so they responded almost eagerly and surely with conviction: "We are able."

Jesus then as firmly granted their request, to drink with Him the cup of suffering and be baptized with Him in the baptism of blood as they had eagerly asked it. And so it was; James became

1 Aiteisthe, indirect middle voice (Mark).   2 Present indicative, progressive action.

later the first martyr-apostle, beheaded by Herod Agrippa; and John was banished to Patmos (the lost), to seal his testimony with his life. They were to learn that the way to place of pre-eminence in the glorious Kingdom was not by political preferment, but by sacrificial service and suffering unto the uttermost for Jesus,

So they were to suffer disappointment in their request now for the chief places on His right and left. It was not possible for Jesus arbitrarily to confer such favors, regardless of the inward fitness of those upon whom they were conferred. The conditions necessary to be pre-filled in order to occupy such places were just those of heroic character and complete dedication to God and His Kingdom, which would lead men to meet unflinchingly a martyr's death. Little did they understand the character of the Kingdom as yet. They must learn that it was a spiritual Kingdom, which called for spiritual characters, void of worldly ambitions, envies, and the mercenary spirit which they had just revealed. The high places in the Kingdom are destined for those who are prepared in soul for them. Such preparation depends on the ability to drink the cup of vicarious suffering with Jesus.

The ten apostles began[1] to get indignant, when they knew that James and John had tried to over-reach them. They had their ambitious hopes too; but these brothers, who stood nearest to the family of Jesus, had resorted to unfair means to obtain for themselves the first places. Jesus called all of them to Himself, and recognizing that all were in fault—if James and John were most outspoken—sought to illustrate clearly to them what the true character of the Kingdom was:

"You know that they which are accounted to rule over the heathen nations (Gentiles) lord it over them; and their great ones exercise authority over them. It is not so among you. But whoso-ever may wish to become first among you shall be the slave of all." He thus draws a picture by contrast between the worldly heathen kingdoms and the spiritual Kingdom of God. The mode of acquiring preeminence in these two kingdoms is wholly different, as also the manner of using the power when obtained. Hereditary rulers grind down the populace in subjection; but those high in place in the spiritual Kingdom treat others with love and gentle-ness, and serve with loyalty the interests of all, as would those who come up from lowliness to position by service and suffering.

Jesus had taught the apostles before, that the path to pre-eminence is through the cultivation of the humble, trustful, child-like character, and that whosoever wished to be great among them

1 Ingressive aorist.

must be the minister (servant) of all. He now points to His own example, as the way. Out just ahead was the cross of suffering. They must follow in His footsteps the way of the cross if they would win the crown of the power to serve.

"Even as the Son of Man did not come to be ministered unto but to minister and give His life a ransom instead[1] of many." This is a clear reference to His atoning death which was just a few days ahead. Jesus gave His life as the price of freedom for slaves under the bondage of sin. By His atoning death He broke the bonds of sin-slavery and enabled every soul that so chooses, to go free. His death was substitutionary for all men. "We are not our own; we are bought with a price." Jesus died for the sin of the world and by His death provided eternal life for all believers. This is the very heart of the Gospel, the apostolic doctrine of the atonement in germ.

7. Jesus heals blind Bartimaeus and his companion near Jericho (Mark 10:46-52; Matt. 20:29-34; Luke 18:35-43; Harm. 126).

When the caravan crossed the Jordan, on the way to the Feast in Jerusalem, the first place reached was the site of old Jericho, City of the Palms, some four miles from the Jordan ford. Passing by this place of ruins, famous in sacred history, they approached, about a mile to the south the new (Roman) Jericho. This city was situated on an oasis in the Judean desert, watered by streams from the mountains above and springs in the valley. It had a flourishing trade and many fine buildings, including Herod's palace, a theatre, amphitheatre, and hippodrome.

As Jesus went before with His disciples, a considerable multitude followed. Suddenly, as the crowd moved forward slowly, the cries of two beggars were heard. Mark notes the name of the more prominent one, Bartimaeus, son of Timaeus. They were both blind and sat by the wayside begging, not far from the entrance to the town. When they heard the hubbub of the crowd as it approached, they began to inquire[2] of some of those who went in front what the noise might be.[3] They were told: "Jesus of Nazareth is passing by."[4] Immediately Bartimaeus began[5] to cry out with a loud voice and say: "Jesus, thou son of David, take pity on me." Whereupon those of the vanguard of the crowd began to rebuke[6] him and kept telling him to be quiet.[7] But, joined now by the other beggar, he kept on screaming:[8] "Son of David, take pity on me." Then Jesus suddenly halted and gave order for them to be brought to Him. "Call him," He said, referring to Bartimaeus especially. Those who

1 Anti, over against, instead of, the idea of substitution,   2 Imperfect tense,
   ingressive.   3 Optative mood (Luke).   4 Present middle indicative,
   retained in indirect discourse.   5 Ingressive aorist (Mark).
6 Imperfect active indicative.   7 Ingressive aorist subjunctive.
8 Imperfect indicative active, ekrazen.

were chiding the beggars for crying out now addressed Bartimaeus: "Courage," they said, "Get up—He is calling thee." Mark
graphically explains that Bartimaeus cast aside his cape,[1] sprang
up, and came quickly to Jesus. Naturally the other beggar followed, led perhaps by someone as he threaded his way with difficulty through the crowd. When Bartimaeus had come near,
Jesus spoke to him kindly. "What do you want me to do for you?"
He said. The blind man replied in pleading, reverent[2] terms:
"Master,[2] that I may see again."[3] It was a pitiful sight, these two
men lost in a world of darkness, a sight too frequent in Palestine.
Thompson said that in Ramleh he found nearly half the population
with defective eyes.[4] The frequency of blindness was due to dust,
the glare of the sun, and the unsanitary habits of the people. Jesus
was "moved with compassion," as frequently He is reported to
have been in His ministry. He put His finger on their eyes and
said gently: "Receive thy sight; go thy way: thy faith hath made[5]
thee whole." And immediately they received their sight and began
to follow Him in the way, glorifying God; and all the people
seeing it gave praise to God.

These two blind men had doubtless heard of the wonderful
miracles of Jesus, especially that of the raising of Lazarus in
Bethany, only a day's journey from Jericho. They, like the rest of
the people, shared in the expectation of the Messianic Kingdom.
It was due to that fact that Bartimaeus addressed Jesus as the
"son of David," the common designation for the hoped-for Messiah.
There were many among the people who had come to the conviction that Jesus would probably turn out to be the Messiah for
whom they had long waited. This initial faith of Bartimaeus and
his companion was strong. Their prayer was one of faith and humility, since they remained seated in their place by the wayside
until they were bidden by Jesus to approach Him. The people at
first were an impediment to their coming rather than a help.
But once the beggars knew that they were invited to come to the
great Master (Rabboni), they sprang up and came boldly and
promptly.

How graciously the compassionate Saviour received them,
accepting gladly their faith and granting immediately their request.
He touched their eyes, putting His fingers as a gentle physician on
the sightless retinas, to strengthen their initial faith. To the blessing of physical cure, He added the spiritual blessing of faith and
salvation, and the two men, filled with gratitude, became at once
earnest disciples, following Him in the way toward the cross in

---

1 Himation, a kind of cape.   2 Rabboni, more intimate and reverent.
3 Anablepo, to see again, have the sight restored.   4 Land and Book.
5 Perfect active indicative.

Jerusalem, and giving their testimony of praise before the people. And that testimony was effective, too, for Luke says:

"And all the people, when they saw it, gave praise unto God."

8. Jesus visits Zaccheus and saves him and his household. The parable of the pounds (Luke 19:1-28; Harm. 127).

Jesus did not arrive in Jericho unheralded. News had run before, from His crossing at the Jordan ford, and the inhabitants of Jericho, already deeply impressed with the wonderful miracle of the raising of Lazarus in Bethany and the resolve of the Sanhedrin to put Him to death, gathered in the streets, some through curiosity and others through a genuine desire to hear and see the Nazarene Prophet. It was customary for the inhabitants of towns to welcome the pilgrim bands on the way to Jerusalem Feasts; and on this afternoon the extraordinary circumstances would bring the people of Jericho out in mass, a solid wall of onlookers, by each side of the street along which Jesus was to pass.

So, "when he entered the town and was passing through," Zaccheus, the rich tax-commissioner, was among the spectators, seeking[1] to get a good position, where he would be able to see Jesus. This man had no good reputation in the city. He was at the head of a large staff of tax-collectors, farming out the taxes as the representative of the Roman government, in this prosperous center of the balsam trade. His name Zaccheus (meaning "just") was a misnomer. He had lived up to the bad reputation of the unscrupulous "publicans" in his exorbitant demands and unjust extortion from his people. Withal, Zaccheus had a heart for better things. He was wealthy with ill-gotten gains, but used his "tainted" money in charities for the poor. But his conscience disturbed him, and this, coupled with the fact that he had heard of Jesus as the "friend of publicans and sinners," and that Jesus had called Matthew—a tax-commissioner in Capernaum—to be one of his apostles, made Zaccheus doubly eager to at least see, and, possibly —if a good chance should present itself—to meet personally this extraordinary prophet.

When he came forth from his fine residence to seek a place of advantage where he might view the caravan, he met with difficulty. The streets were thronged, and being a man of "little stature," he could not so much as gain a good view of Jesus, being unable to look over the heads of others or to come near for the press. We may well understand that he would also be unwelcome in the crowd. To his fellow-townsmen, he was but a renegade Jew; one who had robbed and oppressed his own people—a despicable

1 Imperfect indicative active.

outcast. There would not be wanting bad looks and even gross insults, expressing the hatred of the people.

But Zaccheus was resolved to see Jesus and not to be outwitted. Being a man of resources, he was quick to find an ingenious way to effect his wishes. He hastened to the front, in the way by which Jesus was to pass with the caravan, and climbed up into a wide-spreading fig-mulberry tree, located somewhere not distant from his own residence. In this way, he would at least get a good view of the Prophet and the crowd, as they approached. At the same time, concealed in the abundant foliage of the tree, he would escape detection and consequently avoid the insults and jostling of the crowd. In his social isolation, hated by his own people, longing for something better, afraid to face the crowd, and bitterly resentful, this wretched soul waited, longing to see Jesus. Now was his opportunity.

One of the most marvelous things in connection with this incident, and one which often escapes detection, is that Jesus knew of all that Zaccheus was thinking, feeling, and desiring. He knew of the good impulses, as well as the bad practices, of this publican's life. He also knew that Zaccheus, the sinner, was seeking the Saviour through curiosity, but also because of an evil conscience and inward impulse for better things, prompted by the spirit of God working in the heart of this lost son of Abraham.

The other side of this pathetic picture of the sinner seeking the Saviour is that of a loving Saviour seeking the sinner. "Now when Jesus came to the spot, he looked up" with that face of infinite tenderness, never to be forgotten, and those eyes which beamed a welcome recognition; and with uttered words which electrified with extraordinary surprise the half-hidden man in the branches above, said: "Zaccheus, come down quickly! for I must stay at your house today." Luke says, almost in the words that Jesus had used, that Zaccheus "came down quickly" and at once received[1] Him rejoicing. But all those present, seeing it, began to murmur[2] saying: "With a sinner-man[3], he has gone in to lodge."

Two remarkable things were apparent in this brief transaction: Jesus had taken all the initiative in inviting Himself to the home and hospitality of Zaccheus; and He who claimed to be the Messiah was going to the home of the outstanding publican and most notorious sinner of the town to be entertained. The latter was the refrain of the buzz of criticism, as the group moved forward toward the stately mansion of Zaccheus, a short distance away. People had been interested before, perhaps to know where Jesus

1 Ingressive aorist middle. 2 Imperfect active of the onematopoetic word diagogguzo.
3 Position of empsasis on sinner-man.

would stop for the night. It was nearing the close of the afternoon and at sundown the Sabbath would begin. Would He be invited by some prominent priest of Jericho to lodge with him? They were aghast with surprise when the honor unsought by others was freely bestowed on Zaccheus, the chief publican. More surprised than all himself, but rejoicing, Zaccheus led the way on to his home. These moments of glad surprise had worked a marvelous change in this hardened man of the world. The rigidly unsympathetic pharisaism of his Jewish fellow-townsmen, far from winning him away from the life of a sycophant and tool of the extortions of the Roman government, had produced in him a resentment as deep as life, and he had resolved in his spirit never to humble his pride in any admission of his wrong-doing to them. Now, by one small act of friendship of one who extended to him as he had to Matthew, the hand of real friendship across the barrier of social isolation, the flood-gates of emotion in his soul had been opened and his heart stirred to repentance; and he made a full and bold confession of his sin to the great Teacher, who had graciously invited Himself to be a guest in this socially boycotted home. The buzz of the criticism had not been unheeded by Zaccheus, as the crowd moved forward. It had served to stimulate him to an open confession of his past sin, an avowal of his loyal acceptance of the Saviour, and his purpose to start out on a new life, regardless of the cost to himself or the incredulity of others toward him. When they came to the front of his residence, he suddenly stopped,[1] and addressing Jesus so as to be heard by those around, he said: "Listen, Sir! The half of my property I hereby give[2] to the poor, and if[3] I have robbed anyone of anything, as I freely admit I have done, I am ready to restore to him, now, four times as much." Here was a full and public confession of his past extortions and a declaration of his purpose to substantiate that confession by full restitution. He even went beyond the requirement of the Mosaic code, which claimed one-fifth for the poor, and in cases of fraud an amount equal to that robbed, plus one-fifth more. This whole-souled confession of Zaccheus, revealing a deeply repentant heart and living faith by which the whole current of his life had been turned, could only meet with a free and full acceptance by the Lord, in unqualified forgiveness and manifest joy. So Jesus said to him in a voice that all might hear: "Today salvation has come to this household, seeing that he himself is also a son of Abraham." By these firm and tactful words Jesus brushed aside forever the paltry barrier of social boycott, by declaring that Zaccheus was a son of Abraham in spite of the social ban, and that every re-

---

1 First aorist passive principle. punctiliar action.   2 Present indicative active.
  linear action.   3 First class condition assumed to be true.

pentant sinner is acceptable to God. His faith in Jesus had saved Zaccheus. Such faith in Jesus makes every true believer a son of spiritual Israel.

Jesus summed up the whole matter for them and for us in the wonderful conclusion: "For the Son of Man came to seek and to save the lost." He uses for himself the title "Son of Man," which in His own thought stood for divine Messiahship and human solidarity. As divine Messiah, He was able to be a Saviour, because He had the ability to save; and as son of mankind, He could be a sympathetic Saviour who Himself was tempted in all points like as we, but without sin. He "came" with a mission to this world, oh glorious fact! That mission was to search for the lost until He found him; and to save him when he was found. What a beautiful picture is here! the sinner seeking the Saviour and the Saviour seeking the sinner!

It was a significant statement Jesus had made about Himself, as the Son of Man (Messiah). His disciples knew this title to carry a half-hidden allusion to His Messianic character and mission, and were eagerly looking forward to the early manifestation of that Kingdom, the character of which they little comprehended. While they were listening to these things and the impression of the incident of the previous afternoon was fresh in their experience, Jesus made use of this special opportunity in Jericho to correct some wrong impressions relative to the Kingdom, particularly the time of its coming. This was all the more necessary since He was near Jerusalem, and the people were thinking that He would establish a temporal Kingdom when He arrived there at the time of the feast. Because of the presence of many enemies, as well as some half-hearted fickle disciples, the Master-Teacher made use of the parabolic form of teaching.

This parable of the pounds (Luke 19:12-27) is different in many details from that of the talents, and serves a different purpose. It is a prophetic sketch, in parabolic form, of the real future before the disciples, the fortunes of the Messianic King, and the various attitudes of men toward Him.[1] It sets forth "unequal diligence in the use of equal endowments and consequent inequality of rewards" (Bruce). It was spoken to a mixed multitude composed of murmuring enemies and enthusiastic, though mistaken, friends. It contained a warning for the enemies of the Kingdom and an important corrective revelation for its devoted friends.

Jesus said: "A certain nobleman went into a distant country to obtain for himself a kingdom and to return. Now, he called ten servants of his and gave them ten pounds, or a pound each

Bruce, The Expositor's Greek Testament.

(about the value of twenty dollars), and said to them: 'Trade
with it till I come.' But the citizens of the country detested him
and sent a deputation after him saying: 'We are not willing for this
man to become King over us.' "

There is probably a hidden allusion in these words of Archelaus, the son of Herod, who went from Jericho to Rome to get a
kingdom in Palestine from the Roman emperor Augustus and come
back to it.[1] This happened, back in the days when Jesus was yet
a boy in Nazareth. Archelaus was followed by an embassy from
Judea, appointed by the citizens who were tired of the adventurous
Herod-dynasty, to ask that their country might be converted into a
Roman province.[2] The palace of Archelaus was in the neighborhood of Jericho, and this fact may explain the allusion to it, by
way of illustration. Not all the details of the parable need fit into
the historical event.

The parable sets forth the picture of the near departure of
Jesus to a "distant country," a journey *requiring a long time*,
which is the occasion of His speaking the parable. The servant-
disciples, like slaves seeking to do the will of their Lord, are to
receive the common-pound privilege of the Gospel—the entrusted
word of the Kingdom—and go forth to make use of it in hard,
obscure, unhonored activity, calling for faithfulness and persevering loyalty, until He should return in His second glorious advent into this world. Thus the curtain falls on the first scene of
the drama.

The second scene opens when the nobleman returns. The
servants, to whom he had entrusted each a silver pound, were
summoned before him, that he might learn what business they had
done. The first came, saying: "Sir, your pound has added ten
more." So he said to him: "Well done, good servant; because
you have proved faithful in a very little, have authority[3] over ten
cities." Then the second came, saying: "Your pound, sir, made
five pounds." So he said to this one also: "And become thou ruler
over five cities." Then another came, saying: "Sir, behold your
pound, which I kept[4] laid away in a napkin. For I kept on fearing
you,[5] because you are a harsh man. You take what you did not
plant and reap what you did not sow." He said to him: "Out of
your own mouth I judge you, good-for-nothing[6] slave. You knew
that I am a harsh man, taking what I did not plant, and reaping
what I did not sow. Then why did you not put my money into the
bank? In that case, on coming back, I should have gotten it with

1 Robertson, Word Pictures.   2 Joseph. Antiq. 17, 11, 1.   3 Periphrastic present
        active imperative, have authority and keep on having it.   4 Imperfect of echo.
5 Imperfect tense of continued action, I was holding.
6 Poneros, evil in sense of good-for-nothing. Second perfect.

interest." Then, to the bystanders he said: "Take from him the pound and give it to the one having ten pounds." And they said to him (in surprise): "Sir, he has ten pounds already!" "I say to you that to everyone acquiring will be given yet more, while even what he has will be taken from the one who does not acquire."[1]

Jesus wished to make plain to all that neither glory, nor material riches, nor power were to be the lot of the servants of the absent Lord, who was to go away in a few days; but rather labour and responsibility. He knew that not all His disciple servants would make the same use of His entrusted work and word of the Kingdom. In the acid test of hard and difficult labour, sacrifice, and persecution, some would be very faithful, trading with their small opportunities and privileges, and gaining larger ones; others would be less ardent, devoted, diligent, and constant; and some would be good-for-nothing, like the slave who hid the money away in a napkin, in that craven, faithless, and slothful spirit. The parable was a prophecy of the departure of Jesus, His return after a long time at His second advent, and the way things would be with the servants in His absence as well as when He should return. To the one who in faith puts the Lord's pound into circulation and use, gaining with it large returns through great diligence and devotion, there will be the highest praise and the greatest reward of multiplied opportunity for service in the future heavenly Kingdom. To those who are content with doing less than their best, while rendering a good service, but not that requiring the greatest sacrifice and labour, there will be praise and opportunities commensurate with their character, but not the greatest. To yet others, who through lack of faith are afraid to invest their lives for their absent Lord, but pass their time in sloth and selfishness, in a spirit of slavish fear and distrust toward Him who generously gave them equal endowments and privileges in the Gospel, there can only await a sentence of condemnation and eternal loss. Even the high Gospel privileges of the Kingdom will be taken away from them forever.

Jesus expresses for us in the end of the parable the law of spiritual capital. To the one who has that attitude and habit of soul of acquiring and holding, more will be given; while from the one who does not have that soul-character will be taken away even the opportunities for acquiring which he once possessed.

The part of the parable which touched deeply on the present circumstances of His life, in relation to the Jewish enemies who would lead their nation to reject and crucify the Messiah in a few days, He reserved for the conclusion. This would naturally anger

1 Robertson's Translation of Luke.

the Pharisaic enemies and might bring the sermon to a violent end. He must have looked around on the long-bearded hypocritical Pharisees present in His audience, when He said: "But these enemies of mine, who do not wish me to become King[1] over them, do you bring here and slay them before me." Here was a prophecy of the destruction of the Jewish nation just ahead!

1 Ingressive aorist active infinitive, to come to rule.

PART VII

LAST PUBLIC MINISTRY IN JERUSALEM

(Harm. §§ 128-184)

Jesus probably spent a part of the day in the home of Zaccheus and a part in public teaching in Jericho.

Services would be held in the synagogue on Thursday, according to the prevalent custom among the Jews of having services on Saturday, Monday, and Thursday. It was perhaps in the synagogue that He spoke the parable of the pounds. On Friday He probably went on to Bethany, a distance of fifteen miles from Jericho, arriving there on the vesper of the Sabbath.

CHAPTER XXVII

THE JEWS' MESSIAH AND THE WORLD'S SAVIOUR

(Harm. §§ 128-131)

Jesus arrived in Bethany the eighth of the month Nisan, six days before the day of the Passover celebration. This Feast lasted a whole week, but the Passover supper was on Thursday, the fourteenth of the month Nisan (A. D. 30).

1. Circumstances of the arrival at Bethany (Jno. 11:55 to 12:1, 9-11).

The vanguard of the caravan from Galilee would begin to arrive in Jerusalem some days before the Passover, an account of the necessary purification in preparation for the Feast. The pilgrims, on arrival, naturally, dispersed to various localities around Jerusalem and prepared hastily their booths. Jesus was received into the home of Martha and her sister Mary, and Lazarus, whom Jesus had, just six weeks before, raised from the dead.

As the people gathered in Jerusalem, the main topic of discussion was Jesus, the Nazarean prophet. Some were seeking[1] for Him, and those standing about the Temple kept on discussing the matter of His coming to the Feast. Would He come? They knew that the high-priests and Pharisees had given order that "if anyone might know where He was, he should reveal it, that they might arrest Him." To have stayed away from the Feast at this time would have meant to surrender to His enemies. The fight was on, now, to the finish. When His bold appearance in Bethany, a suburb of Jerusalem, was known, it enraged His enemies. But His appearance, in the company with a great caravan from Galilee composed largely of those who were friendly to Him to say nothing of many who were His disciples, forestalled the plan of the Sanhedrin to have Him arrested before the Feast. When the pilgrims made known His arrival in Bethany, many of the common people from Galilee and other parts flocked out from Jerusalem to see Him. They wanted to see Lazarus also, who had been four days in the tomb. Such a sight was calculated to draw great crowds. A miracle like this had never been witnessed before in history. This so angered the chief priests that they plotted together how they might do away with Lazarus also. While Lazarus remained alive, they could effect nothing against Jesus. Many of the people, who came and saw Lazarus, went away believing on Jesus. Could a less than the expected Messiah perform such a miracle as this?

This Sabbath must have been spent quietly in Bethany. John places the social feast in the house of Simon the Leper on the eve-

---

1 Imperfect indicative active, repeated action.   2 Subject of Chapter XXVII.
  Carver's Self-Interpretation of Jesus.

477

ning of the Sabbath. Matthew and Mark agree in putting it on the following Tuesday evening. It is possible that John may have simply mentioned this feast in connection with the arrival of Christ at Bethany, since he does not again recur to Bethany in his narrative, and so puts it out of chronological order.[1] At any rate, it would have been a very fitting prelude to the strenuous week before Jesus.

2. His triumphal entry into Jerusalem as the Messiah. (Mark 11:1-11; Matt. 21:1-11, 14-17; Luke 19:29-44.)

Jesus had confessed His Messiahship to the woman at the well in Samaria, had approved the confession of it by Simon Peter, representing the Twelve at Cesarea-Philippi, had recently declared it again to Martha at the time of the raising of Lazarus, but had studiously avoided any open revelation of it to the people in general until now, because of His enemies. His hour, to which He referred frequently throughout His ministry, had now come. He would make an official and open declaration, though in a symbolic manner, of His claims as the Messiah. Jesus deliberately planned this Messianic demonstration. He had in the very beginning of His ministry assumed the Messianic role for a day, the first time He cleansed the Temple. From that day His enemies had their eyes upon Him, and He was a marked man. The people had tried to force Him to accept their idea of Messiahship, and to crown Him as a temporal King.[2] He deliberately refused that offer. Various times His enemies tried to trap Him into an open confession of His Messiahship; now He will gratify their desire in an open but guarded symbolic declaration. Possibly some of the people would understand and believe. Whether they would or not, He is now offering Himself to them as their promised Messianic King.[3] It was not the kind of kingdom they had expected, but it was the kind their prophets had foretold: not a reign of might, a display of grandeur, or a rule of force. He had to be careful in His symbolic pageant to avoid any demonstration of force; so He enters Jerusalem as the Prince of Peace, sitting upon a colt, the foal of an ass, the beast of burden, according to the Messianic prophecy of Isaiah and Zachariah. In the Orient, the ass was livelier, swifter, and very useful; and esteemed as the symbol of Jewish royalty and peace.[4]

Jesus started with His disciples from Bethany for Jerusalem on Sunday morning. It was probably soon after setting out, when they were drawing nigh unto Bethpage, a village not far from Bethany, that He sent two of His disciples forward to get the

1 Robertson, The Divinity of Carist.   2 John 6.   3 Carver, the Self-Interpretation
of Jesus.   4 Stanley, Jewish History, Vol. 1, p. 94.

animal on which He would ride to Jerusalem. He gave them instructions in detail: that they would find an ass and colt immediately on entering the village, both tied at the stake out in the
open street in front of a house. The houses were usually built
around an open court, which was connected with the street by a
tunnel passageway. The ass and colt were tied at this tunnel-
door on the street which crooked around the house.[1] They would
recognize immediately, without difficulty, the place and the animals, designed to reveal a knowledge more than human in Jesus.
They were to bring both the ass and the colt.

The disciples, one of whom must have been Peter—from the
vividness of the Markian description—went and found everything
just as Jesus had said. There was a group of men, among them
the owners of the ass and colt, standing near when the disciples,
in obedience to the instructions given by Jesus were loosing[2]
the animals. "Why loose ye the colt?" they demanded. "The Lord
hath need of him," the disciples replied, "and will send him back
hither."

There were no further objections but immediate compliance
on the part of the owners, who might possibly have been themselves disciples of Jesus. Then, the disciples bring the colt to
Jesus, and throwing their tunics (outer garments) upon him, help
Jesus to mount.

Meantime, the multitude of those Galilean peasants who had
already arrived in Jerusalem, wanting to see Jesus and Lazarus, set
out to come to Bethany. Others, having heard that Jesus would
come to Jerusalem and being convinced that He would now establish His Kingdom, came forth to meet Him and, following the two
disciples who led the colt back from Bethpage at the junction of
the three roads near Jerusalem, cut fronds from the numerous
palms that lined the way and branches from the fig, almond, and
olive trees. These they went spreading in the way as a mark of
special honor. As they approached the place where Jesus had
paused to wait the return of the disciples with the colt, they
broke out in a loud chorus which resounded throughout the hills,
attracting thousands of pilgrims from their booths. "Hosanna!
Blessed is the one coming in the name of the Lord, even the King
of Israel!" Here, the mission and national work of the Messiah
were expressed.

Seated on the colt, preceded by the crowd which had come
from Jerusalem to meet Him and followed by His disciples and a

1 Amphodon, on the road which crooked around the house.

multitude of pilgrims, the Messiah started on His way to the Holy City. Matthew found in this remarkable incident a striking, exact fulfillment of the Messianic prophecies (Isa. 62:11; Zech. 9:9).

"Tell ye the daughter of Zion: Behold, thy King cometh unto thee, meek, and riding upon an ass, and upon a colt, the foal of an ass."

The greater part of the multitude, as He went forward, spread their garments in the way; some had cut branches from the fields as they came from Jerusalem to meet Him and others were cutting branches now from the trees by the road to help pave His royal way. The enthusiasm mounted higher and higher as they went forward until when they were drawing nigh unto the city, the whole multitude of the disciples began to rejoice and burst into an antiphonal[1] chorus of praises for all the mighty works which they had seen:

"Hosanna to the Son of David!

Blessed is the Kingdom of our father David: and He that cometh now in the name of the Lord!

Blessed is He that cometh, the King of Israel, in the name of Jehovah;

Peace in heaven and glory in the highest!"

Such were the rhythmic acclamations of praise, which rever- berated from hill to hill, stirring the multitudes of pilgrims far and wide. They felt that at last their Messiah had come. Had He not fed the thousands by multiplying the loaves and fishes? Moses had not done greater works than these! Even now the tomb gave up the dead![2] This astounding miracle had convinced many of His Messiahship.

The Pharisees, who had been out with the multitude to spy on His every word and gesture, were in despair. They tried to si- lence the acclamations but were unable to prevail.[3] They blamed one another for their failure. They had planned to arrest Him before the Feast; now the vast throng were madly cheering as He moved on toward the city. In their mortification and despair, with blind hypocrisy, they appeal to Jesus: "Master, rebuke thy disciples," they suggest. But Jesus could read their hearts like an open book. "I tell you that if these shall hold their tongues, the very stones will cry out."

Now the city was in full view, as they started their descent toward the eastern gates. Jesus paused and gazed intently on the magnificent view laid out like a picture before Him, seen from this point of vantage on a spur of the mount of the olive-orchards. Overcome with emotion, He broke into a loud wail and sobbing

---

1 Matt. 21:9.   2 The resurrection of Lazarus, of recent date.   3 Jno. 12:19.

lamentation over the city. In contrast to this fair Jerusalem before Him, there arose the prophetic vision of the city of desolation, out just a few decades ahead, when Titus took the city with his Roman legions. In this prophetic forecast of desolation, His very language fell into a natural rhythm:

"If thou hadst known in this day,

Even thou, the things which belong to peace,

But now they are hid from thine eyes!"

The incomplete, broken sentence of the first two lines was the deep emotional expression of a wish: "O that thou hadst known on this very day the things that belong to thy peace!" He, the Prince of Peace, could have brought peace and salvation through their acceptance. But through their rejection of Him, they were blinded and could not see their own good.

He then wails out in sad cadences of rhythmical phrase the desolation that is to befall the lovely city thirty years hence:

"For the days shall come upon thee,

When thine enemies shall cast up a bank about thee,

And compass thee around, And keep thee on every side,

And shall dash thee to the ground, And thy children within thee,

And they shall not leave in thee one stone upon another.

Because thou knewest not the time of their visitation" (See Ps. 139).

Jesus saw in the vision the camp of the enemy, a bank cast up round about with palisades and a rampart hugging the city closer and closer in deadly embrace. The curtain falls for a moment, then rises again on another scene. The city is razed to the ground, not a stone is left upon another, the gory bodies of her children are scattered among the ruins. The silence and desolation of death reign supreme. The fact that this picture was literally fulfilled just three decades later, when the tenth Roman legion encamped just where Jesus was standing when He uttered these memorable words, would be sufficient evidence in itself, apart from any other, to substantiate the Messiahship of the one who uttered the prophecy.

When Jesus broke out into the wailing dirge of a funeral-like lamentation, the voice of the multitude was hushed into silence. The ecstatic vision of the Messianic Kingdom, which had inspired the souls of these pilgrim multitudes as they sang the praises of the Messianic King and had led them to the most extravagant expressions of a fealty, vanished before the dirge-like lamentation of Jesus like a fog before the morning sun. They began now to recognize that their hopes and fond illusions were vain and were not shared by Him whom they boldly acclaimed King. He, from the hill, saw the splendor of the beloved city fade in the twilight and the shadow of irreparable moral disaster darken into deepest night.[1] He had offered Himself as the King of Peace, sitting on the before-unridden colt of an ass, as Zachariah had said the Messiah would come. But neither the populace nor the disciples seem to have understood the significance of the symbolic demonstration (Jno. 12:16).[2] Instead of embracing His theocratic ideal of a spiritual Kingdom of truth, they insisted on a material kingdom which would break the yoke of the Roman bondage and set them free. This ideal of a material kingdom, secretly nurtured in the hearts of an ambitious, arrogant, and worldly priesthood, would soon bring the inevitable collision with the Roman Empire. If the Jewish leaders had followed the teaching of Jesus and confined themselves to leadership in the realm of spiritual ideas, they would have ruled the world by force of truth. But they failed to see the things which would have made for their peace in this day of the visitation of Messianic salvation. At least they are perceiving now, that, just as Jesus had failed to accept their ideals beside the sea of Galilee,[3] so now He turns His back again on an earthly throne and seeks to point the way to the heavenly kingdom.

Once again, the procession moves forward, but now with diminished enthusiasm. Slowly, it wound its way down the western slope of Olivet, past the Garden of Gethsemane, and crossed the valley of Kedron to the Golden Gate which led to the Temple. When it came to the gate, the city was stirred as by an earthquake.[4] From bazaars and homes, the people poured forth to witness the strange pageant, thronging the streets, the city walls, and the roofs of the homes that lined the way.

"Who is this?" cried the Jerusalem Jews in derisive scorn, addressing those in the procession. The brief interval since Jesus had uttered the terrible prophecy about the destruction of their beloved city had brought radical changes. The general enthusiasm had been chilled. Many had already left the procession and sought their booths. Those who had been bold before in acclaiming Jesus as King now responded in tame words: "This is the prophet Jesus, from Nazareth of Galilee." They feared to be accused of sedition. Anyway, He himself had refused to be their King and quenched their patriotic ardour with His tears. Soon, the same multitude that had acclaimed Him King on the way from Bethany would rend the air with their cry of revenge: "Crucify Him! Crucify Him!"

1 Dawson, The Life of Christ.   2 Robertson, The Divinity of Christ.
3 When He fed the five thousand.   4 Eseisthe, shaken as by an earthquake.

Riding on up the valley through the narrow streets, hung with flags and banners for the feast, He came to the Temple. Leaving His beast and entering the Temple, He took possession of it in the name of Jehovah. His enemies, enraged by His boldness, did not dare lay hands upon Him for fear of the populace. This popular demonstration meant to many of them that Jesus had won. The blind and the lame, contrary to all traditional rules of the Temple, came to Him, and He healed them. The children took up the refrain in the procession and sang in the very Temple: "Hosanna to the Son of David." This greatly enraged the Pharisees. "Hearest thou what these are saying?" they asked.

But Jesus did not disavow the Messianic praise they ascribed to Him. He replied: "Yea, did ye never read, Out of the mouth of babes thou hast perfected praise?" For a moment He remained the hero of the hour, the Master of the Temple, looking around steadfastly on all things. The purpose of the Messianic demonstration had been attained. He had declared to the whole world that He was the Messiah. The paschal lamb was selected on this day. He had consecrated Himself to death.

3. The Messianic power demonstrated in the cursing of the fig tree and in the second cleansing of the Temple (Mark 11:12-18; Matt. 21:18, 19, 12, 13; Luke 19:45-48; Harm. 129).

The triumphal entry, in which Jesus offered Himself as the Jewish Messiah and demonstrated His Messianic authority, took place on Sunday. At the close of the day, Jesus with the Twelve passed out quietly with the throng as they retired from the evening prayers and betook Himself once more to the well-loved home in Bethany. Very early Monday morning, before breakfast, He started out again from Bethany, to return to the Temple in Jerusalem. The previous day had been very strenuous, and on the way out from Bethany a short distance, He became hungry.[1] As He proceeded, He saw a fig tree far down the road ahead of them. It stood out conspicuously because of its abundant foliage. The fig season was later,[2] in May or in June, but this tree, with its luxuriant foliage, gave promise of premature fruit. Add to this the fact that on the fig tree in Palestine the fruit appears before the leaves, and also that on the winter-fig tree the old fruit often remains during the winter after the leaves are shed, and we can understand that the leaves gave reasonable hope of finding fruit.

Being hungry, Jesus came to the tree—common property by the wayside—but found nothing on it but leaves. It was a perfect symbol of the "fair profession without a promise," a barren tree cumbering the ground. But a few weeks before this, Jesus had

1 Ingressive aorist.   2 Mark 11:13.

spoken the parable of the barren fig-tree.[1] In this tree so advantageously situated, so abundant in promise yet fruitless, He saw an emblem of Israel. He had already likened Israel to such a tree in His parable, warning her of her boastful and hypocritical insincerity. He now makes use of this barren tree to reenforce the lesson of warning as well as illustrate, in symbolic act, His Messianic power and judgment.

"Let no man eat fruit from thee, and let there be no fruit from thee henceforth forever," He said. These words of Jesus impressed the disciples. They had heard such words as these as He stood on the prow of the boat in stormy Galilee, and with a word calmed the howling wind and muzzled the boisterous waves. To all appearances, this tree remained the same and they moved on down the road toward the city. What did He mean anyway? They wondered but kept silence.

Soon, they passed through the Golden Gate into the city and made their way through the throngs of people up to the Temple. On the way to the House of His Father, Jesus may have explained something of the symbolism of the barren fig tree. They were thus, in some measure, prepared to witness the second cleansing of the Temple, an act the significance of which they could but partially understand. The whole Temple worship was corrupted and doomed to pass away soon, just as the fig tree to wither and die down to the roots before the birth of the next day's sun. In the first cleansing of the Temple, Jesus initiated His ministry as a reformer. The nefarious traffic in the Temple, known as the Bazaar of Annas, He had swept away in a single act of Messianic authority. But during the three years' interval, the trade in all its hatefulness had been restored. Even now, He could hear the bleating of the sheep, the cries of the money changers, and the vociferous bartering of those who bought and sold doves. Jesus felt the same indignation He had experienced three years before, but now intensified. This time He did not come to reform the worship; He came to declare the beginning of the Messianic judgment. The corrupted Temple, its hypocritical scoffing priests, its vain and empty ceremonial were doomed alike to pass away. This cleansing was to be the final judicial sentence of the Messianic king.

"And Jesus entered into the Temple of God and began to cast out all them that sold and bought in the Temple, and overthrew the tables of the money-changers and the seats of them that sold doves, and would not suffer that any man should carry a vessel, through the Temple." He arraigned the officers, saying:

1 Luke 13:6-9.

"Is it not written, 'My house shall be called a house of prayer for all nations?' but you have made it a den of robbers."[1]

The Temple authorities who owned the nefarious traffic were enraged. They brought in some of the principal men of the people with them, and sought how they might destroy Jesus. But the fear of the people was upon them and restrained their violence. With rapt attention, the people hung entranced on His words, astonished and deeply moved by the new and blessed truths which He expounded unto them in His unique, original, and gracious way.

4. Jesus, answering the appeal of the Greek proselytes, reveals Himself as the Saviour of the world. (Jno. 12:20-50; Harm. 130.)

Among the proselytes, going up from various countries with the purpose[2] of worshipping in the feast, were certain Greeks. These men were not merely Hellenistic Jews but real Greeks, bringing the Gentile world in contact with Jesus in the end, as the Magi had done in the beginning of His Ministry. The polite request of these Greeks, tactfully presented first to Philip (horse-lover), who in turn presented it to Andrew (gentleman), both of whose Greek names indicate men of liberal sympathies, might have been connected with the mission of the Gentile prince, Abgarus of Edessa, who is said to have written a letter to Jesus, appealing to Him to come and heal him. In the letter, he confessed his faith in Jesus, based on His repeated power to cure all manner of diseases and raise men from the dead. He also offered to share his own city as a permanent abode, if He would come. As the tradition goes, Jesus promised to send, after His ascension, one of His disciples to heal Abgarus and give life to him and his people. Whether these Greeks were under commission from Abgarus or not, they were earnest and polite in their request to have an interview with Jesus. Addressing Philip, whose Greek name indicates that he was of Hellenic extraction, they began to ask, saying: "Sir, we want to see Jesus and have an interview with him."

Philip, whose mind was of the calculating type, not being able to solve the problem of race prejudice which was thus presented, consulted Andrew, a man of counsel. Together, they wrestle with the problem, which Peter had to face later on the housetop in Joppa, but they reached no satisfactory solution. Together they bring the problem, but not the Greeks, to Jesus (Robertson).

In His answer (vs 23-33), Jesus shows Himself agitated by a storm of emotion. He recognized in these Greeks the forerunners of a vast throng of the Gentile world which would come to Him from all nations, tribes, and kindreds of the earth. It was a presage of the greater things of the Kingdom. Even now the hour of crisis

1 Isaiah 56:7; Jer. 7:11.   2 Hina with the first aorist active subjunctive in a
  purpose clause.

had arrived. The price of the universal conquest of the Kingdom must first be paid. Jesus' answer to the request must have puzzled the two disciples:

"The hour has arrived,"[1] He said, "that[2] the Son of Man might be glorified." The Lord is now vividly conscious of the hour of His glorification by a sacrificial and atoning death, and seeks to lead the disciples into an understanding of self-sacrifice as the supreme law of life (vs 24-26). He would exemplify this law of life in His atoning death soon (vs 32, 33). This supreme principle of life He first solemnly illustrated from the natural sphere:

"Truly, truly I tell you: unless a grain of wheat falls into the ground and dies, it remains a single grain; but if it dies it bears much fruit." Then He proceeds to apply this illustration in affirming the same law of self-sacrifice to be supreme in discipleship: "The one who goes on loving his mere human temporal life, exalting it above spiritual interests, loses progressively[3] even his material life. On the other hand, the one who puts the spiritual above[4] the mere this-world life will guard his spiritual life for eternity." To live is more than to breathe and enjoy physical pleasures and comforts. Eternal living is far different. To experience such real living one must be a true servant of Jesus; must minister to Him, with Him, and for Him; and must keep on following Jesus in place, method, and character. The one who thus keeps on following Jesus in this way of life will find that his own life has taken on the quality and character of the eternal. The servant will also be where Jesus is. The Master led the disciples up thus to the idea of the cross. The one who so does will always be honored by the Father. The cross was out just a few hours ahead. They must learn this lesson quickly.

Jesus was fully conscious of the fact that His death on the cross was the only power under heaven that would remove the racial barrier, and so dedicates Himself to meet it (vs 27-33). But He naturally and instinctively, as a man, shrinks from the cross. A great conflict of emotions now agitates His usually calm soul.

"My soul is in a disturbed state," He said, within Himself, "and what am I to say?"[5] In a moment of human frailty, He prays: "Father, save me from this hour (of trial[6])." But as in Gethsemane, the flickering shadow of frailty passes in one instant, when He reflects on His mission and whole past life: "But on account of this very thing, I came into this hour." The next sentence affirms His purpose to face the issue courageously and meet His end. He

1 Perfect active, indicating completed action.   a purpose clause.   by comparison.   6 Goodspeed and Moffatt.   2 Hina with first aorist indicative in   3 Present tense, linear action.   4 Mison, hating,   5 Goodspeed's translation, momentary indecision.

prays: "Father, glorify quickly[1] thy name." He wants to die such a death as may cast honor upon the name of the Father—which name stands for the Father's character—a death which would be fruitful in eternal life for men.

Such a prayer of resignation and of desire to honor God and serve mankind could not fail to find immediate approval with the Father. All of heaven was watching the struggle in the soul of Jesus, upon the issue of which hung the hope of the world's salvation. Then came for the third and last time in His earthly life the audible "voice from heaven." "I glorified[2] it and will glorify it again." This was the definite answer of the Father to the unreserved prayer of Jesus, to give Him a successful death. This audible voice was variously interpreted. To the unbelieving, it was a clap of thunder out of a clear sky, unmistakable but inexplicable, and perplexing. To more sympathetic disciples the utterance was that of an angel speaking to Him. Jesus interprets the voice for them. It was not principally for His sake, though it did serve to prepare Him to meet the last struggle. It was more for their sake, that they might believe on Him.

The world crisis[3] was on, and the world would be judged and condemned in the hours out just ahead in condemning Him. Satan, the Prince of this world, was to be cast out from his seat of supreme power, and Jesus, by being lifted on the cross, was to draw all men unto Him. The cross would become the central magnet of the universe. The coming of the Greeks at this hour was a foretoken of the future conquest of humanity by the Saviour. Satan, who causes men to hate and kill each other through race prejudice, would be defeated at the cross.

The multitude understood (vs 34-36) that Jesus was talking about Himself, and that He referred to His death. He had often spoken of Himself as the Son of Man. They had understood that this was His half-veiled way of referring to His Messiahship. But now there was a contradiction. They had learned from their Law (Scriptures) that the Messiah was to abide forever and that His reign was to be followed by the resurrection.[4] Again their Rabbinical theology had become their stumbling block. They had misinterpreted their Scriptures.[5] Perplexed, they ask who is this Son of Man, who is to be lifted up. Jesus had claimed to be the Messiah; of this they were sure. But now He speaks of Himself, as "about to be lifted up." Would He tell them plainly what He meant about the Messiah being lifted up? Their difficulty was in the fact that they did not desire such a Son of Man as would die on the cross.

1 First aorist active imperative, note of urgency.
2 First aorist active indicative, punctiliar action, when?
3 Krisis, judgment. 4 Edersheim, Life and Times of Jesus. 5 Ps. 89:36; 110:4.

In His answer Jesus does not discuss the theological question with them, but making use of the metaphor employed before (Jno. 8:12), when He claimed to be the light, urges that they may take advantage of the light during the brief time that they may have it. They are warned not to sin against the light, the value of which they could easily understand from their experiences in their dark and dangerous streets, a terror to travelers. They were to be about their proper religious activities[1] while they had the present moral light of the Messiah. The darkness would soon overtake them, as the sudden nightfall of the Orient, if they did not heed His counsel. The way they were to make use of the Messianic light was by believing in the Messiah. By so doing, they would become sons of light or spiritually enlightened men. With this warning and practical admonition, Jesus withdraws for the private interview with the Greeks. This was the only tactful way to deal with the problem of personal reception of the Greeks at this time. He had already made clear that His atoning death would draw all men to Him.

The evangelist-author, John, reveals the stubborn unbelief of the Jews in spite of the many wonderful miracles such as the healing of the man born blind and the raising of Lazarus. They "kept on not believing."[2] He explains the apparent failure of the work of the Messiah in the light of Isaiah's Messianic prophecy: "Lord, who believed our report, and to whom was the arm of the Lord revealed?" (Isa. 53:1). The complaint of the Messiah, because of the unbelief and indifference of the people to His power in miracles, is here met with the explanation that it was in the divine plan of the ages that the Jews should be spiritually blind to the truth and hardened against the true religious impressions of the Messiah. This was the inscrutable purpose of God—beyond human ken—and its ultimate cause is not discussed. We know that Pharaoh hardened his heart and that God hardened Pharaoh's heart. We know also that when man hardens his heart against the gospel, the preaching of the Gospel hardens man's heart. This is no reason for not teaching the gospel. The reason Isaiah spoke these words was because he saw the glory of Jesus, and spoke a complete and meditated word[3] out of the Messianic theophany.

It is a remarkable thing that many even of the rulers believed on Him, in spite of the previous action of the Sanhedrin. But, on account of the Pharisees, they kept on not making confession of their faith. They feared to be put out of the synagogue—which was a solemn, funereal experience for the Jews—caring more for

---

1 Peripateite, walking around in the daily conduct of life.
2 Imperfect indicative active of continued and persistent action, episteuon.
3 Perfect tense, completed action and abiding status.

their social standing than for Jesus, more for the honor that men might bestow than for God. They were afraid of religious ostracism. There are yet many "cowardly disciples" who are afraid of intellectual ostracism if they should stand by the Christ of the Cross.

In the closing words of John relative to the public ministry of Jesus (vs. 44-50), we have a summary of the teaching of Jesus regarding the nature and consequence of unbelief. John puts the words of this epitome of Jesus' teachings in the mouth of Jesus Himself. He "cried out and said" words which present in outline the whole message of His life and ministry. Faith in Him[1] was faith in the one who sent Him. Seeing Him was seeing God who sent Him. He came as a light to the end and purpose[2] that every man that should believe might not abide in darkness. Those who do not hear[3] and keep His teachings in faith He will not judge now, because the primary purpose of His coming was not to judge but to save the people of the world. But rejection of Jesus and failure to receive His word entails judgment, for in the last day the teaching of Jesus will judge the unbeliever. The reason for this is that He did not speak[4] for Himself, but brought the message commanded by the Father. He had the permanent commission to bring that message. He was absolutely positive about the character of that commanded message. It brings eternal life to the one who receives it, always and without fail. The secret of that fact lies in the source of the message. He had been faithful and unerring in bringing that message.

Thus John ended his gospel record of the public ministry of the Lord. Jesus had, in this last deliverance, laid down sacrifice as the supreme law of life, illustrating it from nature, discipleship, and His own personal atoning death, which He prophesied. He made man's attitude toward Himself the basis for salvation and standing with God. He predicted the universal conquest of the cross, pronounced judgment on the Jews, and prophesied the destruction of Jerusalem and the Temple. He made His ministry and message "the touchstone of destiny" for all who accept or reject His teachings. The content of His message and mission issued in eternal life for men, for whom He yearns.[5]

5. The lesson of the withered fig tree (Mark 11:9-25; Matt. 21: 19-22; Luke 21:37, 38).

It was customary[6] for Jesus and His disciples, after the day's work was done, to go forth to a part of the Mount of Olives known

---

1 Exaggerated contrast.   2 Hina with the subjunctive in purpose clause.
3 Condition of third class.   4 Perfect tense.   5 Carver, Self-Interpretation of Jesus
6 Luke 21:37 cf. Mark, Imperfect tense signifying repeated or customary action.

as Bethany and spend the night. They probably lodged frequently in the open, among the olive trees, beneath the Syrian sky. Having thus spent Monday night in the Mount of Olives, He betook Himself on Tuesday to Jerusalem to resume the intense work of His last days' ministry. On the way, they passed the fruitless fig tree, and the disciples were astonished to find it withered from its very roots. "Rabbi, see!" said Peter, "the fig tree which thou cursedst is withered away."

"Have faith in God," said Jesus. "Verily I tell you that whosoever shall speak to this mountain: Be thou taken up and cast into the sea! and shall not doubt in his heart, but believes that what he saith will come to pass, he shall have it." If they should have faith in God they would be able to accomplish the humanly impossible. The Rabbis made use of the expression later when they referred to the accomplishment of very difficult tasks through a great faith. A simple and undoubting faith honors God and brings the blessing. Jesus employed the terminology known to the disciples in His exhortation. "All things which you pray for and seek, believe that you are receiving[1] them." This is the first condition of successful prayer. They were to face apparently impossible tasks from this time on. They must be prepared to exercise great faith. The second condition for success in these exceedingly difficult undertakings was the right attitude toward frank forgiveness, without anger or revenge, toward anyone who might have committed any offense toward them. The Father in heaven forgives our transgressions, if we forgive those who transgress on the territory of our rights.[2]

1 Present progressive tense.   2 Paraptomata, transgressions are acts of trespass, getting over the boundary.

CHAPTER XXVIII

HIS LAST DAY'S MINISTRY

(Harm. §§ 132-138)

By His assumption of Messianic authority on the two preceding days, Jesus had precipitated a final controversy and conflict with His enemies. Up to the present time, the Sadducees had limited their opposition to merely asking for a sign. They were not concerned vitally with the theological teaching of Jesus, being rationalists, but now that He had assumed control of the Temple it became a matter of political right and authority.

1. Christ's authority challenged and defended (Mark 11:27-12:12; Matt. 21:23-22:14; Luke 20:1-19; Harm. 132).

After administering the lesson of the withered fig tree on the way, Jesus repaired to the Temple early on Tuesday morning and began His teaching in the Temple court. The people soon flocked to see and hear Him. If allowed to continue, He would soon prevail by the very force of the truth of His teachings. Realizing this, His enemies determined to destroy His influence and close the door of His teaching by legal methods, since they were afraid to lay violent hands on His body, because of the people. They would lead Him to make some bold claim as to His Messiahship and oneness with God, such as had brought to a sudden and violent end His last stay in Jerusalem.

(a) Accordingly, a deputation of the Sanhedrin, whether formal or not, composed of chief priests (Sadducees), scribes (Pharisees), and some of the elders (political representatives of the people) came to formally call in question His authority for the teaching work of an accredited Rabbi in the Temple, and especially to demand by what ecclesiastical authority He had interrupted the traffic in the Temple and expelled the money-changers the day before. The Pharisees and Scribes, self-constituted guardians of the orthodoxy of Judaism, reenforced now by the Sadducees, attacked the ecclesiastical and political authority of Jesus. Accredited teaching called for ecclesiastical authorization and Jesus was not a graduate of the theological schools of the Rabbis, nor had He received rabbinical authorization by ordination.[1] It was the unquestioned right of the Sanhedrin to inquire into the authority of any teacher in the proper way. The assumption of Messianic authority on the two previous days was a more serious question still. They interrupted His teachings with a threefold question and demand, with reference to the motive and source of His authority.

1 Edersheim, Life and Times of Jesus, in loco.

"By what kind of authority," they asked, "do you keep on doing these things?" Or, "Who gave you this authority that you may go on doing these things?"[1] Did He claim prophetic authority? Did the Rabbis or the Sanhedrin authorize Him to teach? Was His authority divine, that He should assume to cleanse the Temple?

In His reply, Jesus frankly responded to their question by claiming John the Baptist as the intermediate source of His authority. He was not to be snared, but turned the defense into a counter-attack by retorting with a counter-question. A keen, prompt disputant, He embarrassed His enemies by a question in which was implied His answer to their demand. "I will ask you one word," He said, "If you answer me, I will tell you by what authority I do these things. Was the baptism of John from Heaven or from men? Answer[2] me!" He had thus met their demand with a sharp counter-demand and placed His enemies in great embarrassment. Was the authority of John, in his whole ministry and symbolized by his baptism from Heaven or merely from men? John had baptized Jesus, and thus placed his stamp of approval on His work, pointing to Him as the one whose ministry should increase while his own was destined to decrease.

The reply of Jesus was not a mere dodge, but a thrust. He forced His enemies to face a dilemma, either horn of which would place them in the kind of trap they were laying for Him. They held a secret consultation, reasoning and discussing among themselves as to what should be their answer. It was a hard proposition.

"If we may say 'from Heaven,' He will ask 'Why then did you not believe him?' But if we may say[3] 'of men', we fear the people." The reason was that all the people held John to be a prophet. To denounce John as an impostor was dangerous in the extreme. To accept his ministry as divinely commissioned was to admit the authority of Jesus. What should they do? They sought refuge in a refusal to answer His question. He had answered theirs by implication. He refused openly to declare that He was the Messiah until His hour was come. But He had, by His answer, given the people to understand that He was the authorized teacher and Messiah upon whom John had placed his seal of approval. "Neither will I tell you by what authority I do these things." They ought to have recognized His divine commission long ago as manifested by His works and His sinless life.

(b) Jesus next proceeds to point out, in the parable of the two sons, the character of His opponents by contrast (Matt. 21:28-32). He continued: "A man had two children, and coming to the first, he said: 'Child, go work today in the vineyard.' And he answered:

1 Present tense, progressive action.   2 Aorist tense, calling for prompt reply.
3 Third-class condition, ean with the present subjunctive.

'I will not,' but later regretted it and went. Coming to the second, he said likewise. And he answering said: 'I go, sir' and went not. Which of the two did the will of the father?"

The enemies of Jesus unwittingly said: "The first," thus opening the way for Jesus to make the application of the parable. These religious and political leaders of Israel had assumed at first a receptive attitude toward the ministry of John and were willing for a while to rejoice in his life and light. But when he demanded a baptism of repentance, in recognition of the need of moral cleansing, and that they show worthy fruits first to back up such a profession, they drew back. Openly, they bowed to the popular opinion that John was a prophet, but in their hearts they were utterly out of sympathy with his spirit. Jesus brands the Pharisaic character with the deep, incorrigible vice of insincerity. They were like the latter son who said, " 'I go, sir,' and went not."

They had no reason to reject John, because he had come to them in "their way of righteousness," insisting on the scrupulous fulfilling of the law. He himself fasted, and taught his disciples to fast and observe carefully the ceremonial requirements of the Jewish law. The second son of the parable enabled Jesus to introduce a comparison and contrast between the insincere and unrepentant character of the Pharisees, and the publicans and prostitutes, considered the very scum of Jewish society, but more often repentant. He thus tore the mask of hypocrisy from the faces of the self-satisfied zealots and revealed them to the people as they were.

"Truly I tell you," He said, "that the publicans and prostitutes are going into the Kingdom of God before you. For John came to you in a way of righteousness, and you did not believe him. The publicans and prostitutes, who at first said, like the first son of the parable, that they would not go to work in the vineyard, afterwards, having repented in their hearts, went." But the Pharisaic leaders did not, even after seeing all this, change their feeling[1] about it and believe John's message. This was a stinging insult to the leaders: to be compared, and that unfavorably, with the publicans and harlots. Jesus hated no sin worse than that of hypocrisy. By exposing their insincere and deceptive attitude toward John, Jesus prepared the way for the final blow to their pretended religious leadership of the people.

(c) In the parable of the two sons, Jesus had exposed the insincerity of the Pharisaic leaders in their treatment of John. He now adds the parable of the wicked husbandmen to reveal their rejection of Himself and His ministry by the Jewish people as

1 Metamelein.

a whole, and to warn them of the dire consequences (Mark 12:1-12; Matt. 21:33-46; Luke 20:9-19). He describes the well-equipped vineyard, with its hedge, its hewed-out cistern or wine vat, in which to catch the wine when pressed out. It also had a tower for the guards, and everything belonging to a well appointed vineyard. "The householder let the vineyard to husbandmen (earth-workers), and went into another country for a long time. When the opportune time of the season drew near, he sent a servant to the husbandmen, that he might receive a definite part of the produce, according to agreement. But the husbandmen beat the servant and sent him away empty. Later, he sent another, and they beat him, wounded him in the head, handled him insultingly, and sent him away empty. Still later, the householder sent a third, whom they wounded, cast forth, and killed. The householder, with great persistence, sent other servants—many others—and the husbandmen did unto them in like manner, beating some and killing others."

Finally, in desperation, the Lord of the vineyard said: "What shall I do? I will send my beloved son; it may be that they will reverence him." But when the husbandmen saw him, they said among themselves: "This is the heir. Let us kill him and the inheritance will be ours," so they took him, cast him forth out of the vineyard and killed him.

When Jesus had finished the story, which set forth so graphically, on the background of Isaiah's parable of the vineyard,[1] the theocratic vineyard-privileges of Israel; the special advantages and opportunities that were given to the chosen seed through God's covenant with them; and the horrible treatment they dealt out to God's long line of prophets, from the time of Elijah to that of John the Baptist, to culminate now in three days in the crucifixion of the beloved Son at Calvary, He asked this question: "When the lord of the vineyard shall come, what will he do unto those husbandmen?" The people, who had followed the story with intense interest, unwittingly responded: "He will miserably destroy those miserable men, and let out the vineyard unto other husbandmen, who shall render him the fruits in their season." They did not perceive, in the drift of the parable, that they were pronouncing their own doom. Jesus repeated solemnly the sentence of doom on the people who had rejected the long line of prophets, and were now preparing to kill Him. His words were followed by a deeply resentful and fearful, "May it not be," on the part of some of the rulers and the people, who now began to perceive the import of the parable.

1 Isaiah 5.

Jesus would not let them escape without a complete application of the illustration. With a piercing look at the rulers, He asked: "Did ye never read the Scriptures: 'The stone which the builders rejected, the same was made the head of the corner. This was from the Lord, and it was marvelous in our eyes' " (Ps. 118). The stone rejected by the builders, in a new figure seized upon by Jesus, typified primarily the Jewish nation, rejected by the heathen, but chosen of God as the foundation of His earthly Kingdom. But it also typified in a nearer sense the Messiah. With this citation, Jesus claims once again to be the Messiah. Though they would reject Him and take His life away, He would yet triumph and become the very foundation stone, tying together the whole building of the Kingdom.

Then He adds solemnly the words of doom: "Therefore I say unto you: the Kingdom of God shall be taken away from you, and shall be given to a nation bringing forth the fruits thereof." Woe will be to the builders rejecting Him. The stone though passive is formidable and dangerous. To stumble and fall upon it would prove fatal and injurious: and those upon whom His avenging judgment might fall would be ground to powder!

The rulers were indignant and would have laid hands on Him had He not been surrounded by the enthusiastic multitude among whom He counted many sympathetic friends.

(d) The parable of the marriage feast set forth the contempt of Israel for God's great Kingdom feast. (Matt. 22:1-14). This contempt was shown by the refusal to come, on the part of some, and the utter disregard for the conditions of entrance, on the part of others, illustrated in the case of one who came without the wedding garment. In each case, the judgment on those who despised the gracious feast is set forth strongly. The parable is a drama in three acts. The Kingdom of Heaven is likened to a marriage feast made by the King for his son. It lasted several days.[1] Two invitations were customary: one several days before the feast, to prevent the intended guests from making other engagements; the second a few hours before the initiation of the feast, that the guests might be present promptly on the hour.

In the first act of the parabolic drama, the King sent out his slaves to call those who had sometime before received the first invitation. But they were not minded to come.[2] But the King was anxious that they should come, and again sent out other slaves with a more urgent call, recommending his feast by descriptive touches in detail: "See," he said, "my dinner[3] is complete; my

1 Gamous, a series of festivities.   2 Imperfect tense, ethelon.
3 Ariston, breakfast, but midday meal in this case.

oxen and wheat-fattened calves have been killed, and all is ready. Come hither to the festivities." But the invited—not caring for the feast—made light of it, and went their ways, one to his own farm, another to his business, while the rest laid hold on the slaves, ill-treated them, and then killed them. This made the King angry, and he sent his troops and put those murderers to death and burned their city.

This first bidding to the feast was given to the Jews by the prophets of the Old Testament dispensation. They foretold the Messianic feast of exceeding great and precious promise, peace, and full salvation in the Messiah. But the Jews would not come to the feast. Later, God sent other servants in His chosen apostles and His own Son. They brought a more urgent and explicit invitation. They were more aggressive in their manner and preached a complete gospel. But the result of their preaching was no better than that of their predecessors. Those who were invited became antagonistic to the point of violence, seized upon the servants of the King, maltreated them, and killed them. The apostles were bitterly persecuted, later, even unto death. The parable describes in a most graphic manner the punishment which the pretended but unworthy guests would meet at the hands of an angry God. Jerusalem was to suffer a complete demolition, a century later, at the hands of imperial Rome.

In the second act of the parabolic drama, we hear the King commanding his slaves: "The wedding-banquet is ready, but they that were bidden were not worthy. Go out therefore into the parting of the highways, and, as many as you shall find, bid them to the feast." And those servants went out and gathered all that they found, both good and bad, and the wedding feast was filled with guests.[1]

To the Jewish leaders present, as to some of the people, it must have been apparent that Jesus meant in this second part of the parable that the Gentiles were to be brought into the Kingdom feast. This was a true prophecy of what happened soon. The ministry of the apostles being rejected by the Jews, they turned to the Gentiles, many of whom gladly heard and accepted the invitation to the gospel feast.

The third and last act of the parabolic drama impressed the conditions which must be met by the wedding guests, whether Gentiles or Jews. They must be clothed in the wedding garment of a righteous character and holy life. Rejection of the stipulated wedding garment indicated disregard and disloyalty toward the giver of the feast. The Kingdom of God demands in its subjects,

1 Those who reclined.

not merely profession, but moral character. One who does not have character in harmony with that of the King must inevitably be cast out into outer darkness, where there will be the wailing of anguish and the grinding of teeth in defiance and bitterness toward God.

Jesus here, as in many of His pronouncement-stories, caps the teaching of the parable with a religious precept: "Many are invited, but few are chosen." The gospel message reaches many but few accept it and some do not show the development of corresponding character and life.

2. A political catch-question by the Pharisees and Herodians (Mark 12:13-17; Matt. 22:15-22; Luke 20:20-26).

The rulers had been outwitted in their rabbinical question about the authority of Jesus. He had not only cited His authority, but reasserted, in a veiled declaration, His Messiahship, and exposed their insincerity and disloyalty. They retired for a brief time to take counsel how they might ensnare[1] Him in His teaching. They watched on the side, insidiously, for their opportunity, and sent spies suborned to take Him with crafty words. These spies represented two parties, ordinarily antagonistic but now united in their opposition against Jesus. Part of the group was composed of disciples of the Pharisees, young theologians of the two rabbinical schools in Jerusalem. In the group also were some of the Herodians, though Jews, who sympathized with the Herodian dynasty but not with the Emperor. These young academics "posed as scrupulous persons with a difficulty of conscience." Their purpose was to lay hold of any word that might be spoken by Him against the Roman government, that they might turn Him over to Pilate, the Roman governor, on the charge of sedition. The plot was well laid, since it might easily appear that these young theologians, as inquirers after the truth, had been brought into discussion with the Herodians, who did not profess to favor Jewish independence over the question of paying tribute. With unctuous flattery and piqued reverence, they approach Jesus in the midst of His work in the Temple.

"Teacher," they said, "we know that you are true, that you do not regard with partiality anyone, that you are not guided by personal considerations. You teach straightly the way of God. Tell us, therefore, what you think. Is it lawful to pay tribute to Caesar or not? Shall we give[2] tribute or shall we not give it?"

The ultra-orthodox Pharisees were bitter in their resentment against the restraints of a foreign government and longed for a

---

1 Ingressive aorist subjunctive, expressing their purpose to catch him in a snare, pagideusosin.   2 They used the word "give"; Jesus that signifying "to pay back."

theocratic form of independence. The royalists (Herodians) also were discontented with the present regime. Jesus was known to have at least one member of the apostolic group (Simon), who was chosen from among the party of extreme patriotism, the Zealots. He Himself was also from Galilee, where Judas the Gaulonite had sowed down the doctrine of sedition. All of these circumstances made any opinion of His on this question extremely hazardous. This was a shrewd sly trick to ensnare Jesus. Their question was plain, direct, and frank, demanding a like answer. They could imagine but two replies, either of which would involve Him in very serious or even fatal circumstances. If He should declare the tribute unlawful, He would be haled before the Roman tribunal at once as a revolutionist; if He should say it was lawful, He would alienate the sympathies of a great mass of Jews who were patriotic. They could see no escape for Him.

But in this, they had not reckoned with the formidable genius of Jesus. He sensed at once their craftiness and hypocrisy. They had taken Him for a reckless simpleton. They doubtless expected a stern avowal of the illegality of the tribute. Surely He believed in the theocracy. If they could bring Him to a revelation of His inmost thoughts, they would rid themselves at once of this determined transgressor of the rabbinical law. But He put His mind on the matter[1] in concentration for a moment and replied promptly, with the sincerity, frankness, and directness which their question required.

"Why do you put me to the test, hypocrites? Bring me a coin of the tribute-money." They brought Him a denarius, the kind of coin with which the tribute was paid. He says to them: "Whose is this image and superscription?" "Caesar's" they reply. Then He says to them: "Pay back to Caesar the things that are Caesar's and to God the things that are God's."

It was no wonder they were astonished with His answer, which left nothing to be said on the subject for all subsequent time. Man has a duty to civil government and the tax is the price the individual pays for social order. Tiberius' image on the denarius issued in Rome was the symbol of his government. Paul recognized individual obligations to civil government, and taught that men everywhere should submit themselves to the powers that help to guarantee social justice.

But there is a limit to obligation to the state. Freedom of conscience and loyalty to God in the New Society of the Kingdom take precedence over all other loyalties. Social order is bound up with civil government, which man is obligated to support through

---

1 Katanoesas, putting His mind down on the matter.

the payment of taxes. But man's supreme duty is to God and his theocratic rule. The allegiance to Caesar is limited; that to God is above all.

The catch-question was designated to ensnare Jesus. The tables are turned now. Those bright theologians took the dry grins, opened their eyes in amazement,[1] grew silent, and leaving Him went their way.

3. The Sadducees attempt to deride Jesus with the theological question about the resurrection. (Mark 12:18-27; Matt. 22:23-33; Luke 20:27-40; Harm. 134).

The fact that certain of the Sadducees came "on that same day to him" with another type of question, different from those just brought by the Pharisees and Herodians, gives basis to the statement that all influential Jewish parties had now united forces against Jesus as a dangerous innovator and enemy of the existing Rabbinical "hedge" and social status. The Sadducees were Nationalists and did not believe in angels or any invisible powers, nor in the resurrection. Their main dispute with the Pharisees was as to whether the oral tradition was binding. The Pharisees held it of equal value with the written law; the Sadducees that everything not written might be rejected or was at least open to question. They considered the doctrine of the resurrection a mere matter of pious opinion. They said the doctrine was without authority in the written law, especially since, in their opinion, the prophets were not of equal value with the Pentateuch.

Their question, like those of the Pharisees and the Herodians, was intended to destroy the influence of Jesus with the people. The question, raised by the Pharisees, as to His authority, tended to inspire distrust; that about the tribute, raised by the Herodians and theologians, to raise indignation against Him among the Romans; and this one to cause derision and ridicule by all the people. Not all of the Sadducees publicly refuted the doctrine of the resurrection lest they suffer political prejudices. Here was a group, however, who were accustomed to deny the resurrection and now sought to laugh the doctrine out of court by presenting an old conundrum with which they were wont to flout their usual antagonists, the Pharisees. They would thus not only confound Jesus, but get in a stroke at their old-time enemies at the same time.

They bring forward the imaginary case of the woman who had[2] seven husbands. This case was invented by Rabbinical casuistry, about a woman, who, in accordance with the law, became the wife of seven brothers, each of whom died without children. The law of the levirate, never universal, had fallen into almost universal

1 Ingressive aorist tense.   2 Imperfect tense of successive or continued action or state.

disuse in the time of Jesus. By this law, a brother must, by taking his wife, raise up seed to his deceased brother, in order to perpetuate his name. The current popular idea with reference to the future life was that the resurrection would restore to men their former bodies, appetites, passions, and the usual material conditions and relationships. This low Mohammedan-like sensual conception of the future was the occasion and cause of the Sadducean ridicule and derision:

"In the resurrection-life, of which of the seven will the woman be the wife?" was their question to Jesus. They were sure they would have the laugh on Him.

In His reply, Jesus did not brand the Sadducees as "play-actors," but merely exposed their ignorance of the Scriptures while He corrected the low idea of the future life current among many Pharisees. "Is it not for this reason that you err, because you know not the scriptures and the power of God?" The Sadducees, with all the Jews, and perhaps to a greater extent than the others, esteemed the Pentateuch above the prophets and the Hagiographa. Jesus, in gentle raillery, chides them for their ignorance of the Scriptures of the Pentateuch. They had cited Moses as to the law of the levirate. Jesus, in turn cites the "passage of the bush" where God said to Moses: "I am the God of Abraham, Isaac, and Jacob." He then gave the original interpretation of this passage: "God is not the God of the dead, but of the living." They erred also by not knowing the power of God. "The sons of this age marry and are given in marriage; but they that are accounted worthy to attain that world and resurrection from the dead, neither marry nor are given in marriage; neither can they die any more, for, they are equal unto angels, and are sons of God, being sons of the resurrection."

The Sadducees were not able to bring themselves to believe in the superior spiritual conditions of the resurrection-life. In the life to come, those who attain to the resurrection will not marry or be given in marriage, but will be like the angels. Incidentally, Jesus asserted the existence of spiritual beings in the future life, which doctrine the Sadducees did not accept. He did not mean that there would be no personal recognition in Heaven, or continuance of the spiritual relationships formed in the world. Such relationships will be immeasurably heightened and rendered infinitely more delightful and profitable. In this life, marriage is for the propagation of the race. No such necessity exists in Heaven.

The Sadducees were abashed. They were taken aback. The discomfiture of the Sadducees pleased some of the Pharisaic Scribes who stood by observing, and elicited the eulogy for Jesus: "Master.

thou hast well said." The Sadducees retired, to ask no more questions. Jesus had presented the Scriptural proof of the resurrection in a most convincing manner. He had opened up the very doors of Heaven that all might see the blessed state of the resurrection-life. The people were astonished at His teaching.

4. An experienced lawyer tests Jesus with a hard legal question. (Mark 12:28-34; Matt. 22:34-40; Harm. 135).

The victory of Jesus over the Sadducees so pleased the Pharisees, in spite of their united antagonism toward Jesus, that one of the Scribes openly expressed his approval. It might have been this same Scribe, who had approached the group of Pharisees assembled in the Temple to keep watch on the movements of the Nazarene prophet, who reported to them how Jesus had muzzled[1] the Sadducees into silence. They were really pleased at the discomfiture of the Sadducees, their natural enemies. The Sadducees, in their turn, had dealt a veiled stroke at Pharisaic fundamentals in their theological question propounded to Jesus. When they were routed by Jesus and literally muzzled into a dumb and helpless silence, the Pharisees were filled with glee.

But they would, themselves, make another attempt at the Master. He would not be able to stand before the profound questions of Pharisaic learning, properly propounded by an experienced jurist. Accordingly, they select the most experienced lawyer, likely the same one who had reported to them the discussion between the Sadducees and Jesus, to represent them in their encounter.

The question he was to lay before Jesus was one of the most difficult of current jurisprudence. The Scribes had declared that there were six hundred and thirteen commandments: two hundred forty-eight affirmative precepts—as many as the members of the human body—and three hundred sixty-five negative, as many as the days of the year (Vincent). There was a great discussion between the opposing theological schools of Shammai and Hillel as to which were the "light" and which were the "heavy" commandments. They discussed the distinction between the ritual and the ethical, or the positive and the moral, the prevalent tendency being to attach more importance and greater weight to the positive commandments relating to circumcision, sabbath-keeping, and other ritual requirements (Lightfoot). The result was "the exaltation of the ceremonial element, the curse of later Judaism."[2] The words of the Rabbis were to be prized above the words of the Law. It was commonly agreed that the positive commandments about the minutest details of the ceremonial law were as binding as the

1 To muzzle.   2 David Smith, In the Days of His Flesh.

fundamental moral code. The heavy commandments were the ones to which the death penalty was attached, such as the Sabbath-keeping laws, sacrifices, and purifications. If the Pharisees could get Jesus entangled in the web of current theological, hair-splitting controversy, they would bring the unlettered Nazarene Rabbi into disrepute. They hoped He would take the fatal step of asserting again His divine supremacy. This would precipitate a reaction of violence against Him such as had almost swept Him away on various previous occasions.

"What manner of commandment is the greatest and first of all?"[1] the learned jurist asked.

The reply of Jesus went to the root of the whole matter, by summarizing the Ten Commandments in two, and giving a spiritual interpretation of them. Thus He answered the question: "What is the commandment of primary and supreme import? Hear, O Israel, the Lord thy God is one Lord, and thou shalt love the Lord thy God with all thine heart, and with thy whole mind, and with thy whole soul, and with thy whole strength. And the second is, Thou shalt love thy neighbor as thyself." Then He asserts: "On these two commandments hang the whole law and the prophets." Jesus thus fully answered the question of the Scribes when He declared: "There is no greater commandment than these two." He showed Himself well informed in Rabbinical theology, which thus summarized religion in its Godward and manward aspects. The learned Scribe caught the spiritual import of the reply of Jesus and added: "Of a truth, Teacher, thou hast well said, that 'He is one and there is none other besides him.' " Then, repeating the words of Jesus about loving God supremely and one's neighbor as one's self, he asserted that "so to do was more than all burnt offerings and sacrifices." He seemed to have caught a gleam of the great truth that "love is the fulfilling of all the Law." This Scribe doubtless belonged to the more liberal school of Hillel, some of whose adherents defended the ethical against the ritual in religion. Jesus had once more shown His greatness as a teacher by summing up the whole duty of man in one simple but sublime principle of supreme and whole-souled love to God and self-sacrificing love toward our fellowmen.

When Jesus saw that the distinguished jurist had answered thoughtfully[2], He commended him, saying: "Thou art not far from the Kingdom of God."

This lawyer had approached Jesus with the purpose of putting Him to the test and entangling Him in a Rabbinical maze of controversy. We fail to get the full import of the incident unless

1 Mark 12:28; Matt. 22:36.   2 Goodspeed's translation.

we interpret it in the light of that which followed. The ultimate purpose of the Pharisees in this attempt was to get Jesus to assert more clearly His Messianic claims. They knew well enough His attitude toward the vast mass of traditional rules and His firm support of the ethical element in religion. They wished to drive Him into an open declaration as to the preeminence of the moral and a denunciation of the ceremonial, thus robbing Him in part of His popularity. A more subtle test involved was to place Him in the dilemma of asserting His divine mission as Messiah or denying it.

He had successfully passed through the meshes of their snare by asserting the supremacy of love to the *One God.* He declared His monotheistic belief without reference to His sonship. But He did not let them go until He had fully asserted His Messianic mission and divine Sonship. The half-hearted attempt of the learned jurist, who was selected because of his evident breadth and sincerity, to cover up the malevolent intent of the Pharisees, miscarried, because of the very character of the man himself, who was not far from the Kingdom of God—not far, but on the outside. At any rate, the combined forces and attempts of all the sects or parties of the Jews had failed signally, and "no one any more dared ask him any question."

5. Jesus silences His enemies by a counter-question as to the lineage of the Messiah (Mark 12:35-37; Matt. 22:41-46; Luke 22:41-44; Harm. 136).

All of Jesus' enemies, on this last day of His public ministry, had opened their batteries on Him. When they had exhausted all their resources and had been beaten down by His dexterous defense in defeat, they drew back humiliated, but more determined to make an end to Him. Even while they were in this attitude, He did not ignore them or seek to humiliate them, but rather to instruct them. As He went on teaching in the Temple He turned the defense to an attack on the error of their doctrine by a question to the assembled Pharisees:

"What is your opinion concerning the lineage of the Messiah?" He asked. "Whose son is he?"

They answered glibly, "The Son of David."

"Then," said Jesus, "how does David, speaking by inspiration of the Holy Spirit, call him Lord? 'The Lord said to my Lord, sit thou on my right hand until I may place thine enemies underneath thy feet?' If David calls him 'Lord' how is he his son?"

This was not a mere *reductio ad absurdum* by Jesus, intended to humble the insolent Pharisees. He frankly cited the 110th Psalm as a Messianic prophecy, when the Scribes said that the Messiah was the Son of David, and pointed out to those professed teachers of the Scriptures how far from correct their interpretation of that Messianic oracle had fallen. He took for granted that the Psalm is Messianic, and His Messianic interpretation is in perfect accord with that of all the teaching of the Old Testament in general with reference to the Messiah. The Psalm was undoubtedly held, by the Jewish Rabbis, to be Messianic. David, under the inspiration of the Holy Spirit, in high prophetic vision, was speaking immediately of the Messiah. It was natural that the prophecy should be couched in the Oriental imagery of a 'King in Jerusalem.' The Messiah is necessarily described through images, and in various prophecies is conceived as a King and conqueror.[1] The language of Psalm 110 is of the time of David. Finally, all critical objections fall to the ground when we consider the undoubted Messianic interpretation of the Psalm by the founder of Christianity.

The Scribes had failed in their interpretation of this Messianic characterization by seeking to impose their preconceived ideas as to the Messiah. They insisted on a temporal King, who should be the successor of David in a splendid material rule. They had grasped the fact that He was to be David's son by human descent; they failed to catch the significance of the Lordship of the Messiah. The relationship of the Messiah to David was twofold; He was his son by human descent, but his Lord by reason of His divine Sonship. Jesus did not present to the Pharisees a conundrum to confound them, but sought to lead them once again to understand the true character of their Messiah. His efforts were unavailing, for no one was able to answer Him a word, nor did anyone ever again dare to ask Him anything. But the great crowd of people went on hearing[2] Him gladly.

6. The last public discourse of Jesus, a great indictment of the Scribes and the Pharisees (Mark 12:38-40; Matt. 23:1-39; Luke 20:45-47; Harm. 137).

The enemies of Jesus, though silenced, were impenitent, hypocritical, and more determined than ever to compass His destruction. In His final public discourse in the Temple, it was fitting that He should warn His disciples against the hypocrisy of these corrupt and perverse men. Even while He denounced their spiritual blindness, ritualism, and perversity, He yearned over Jerusalem, and closed His discourse with an apostrophe, deeply pathetic and touching, addressed to the beloved but doomed city which had sinned away its day of opportunity.

This is one of the discourses recorded almost exclusively by Matthew. The introduction presents a vivid portrait of the Scribes

1 Broadus on Matthew.   2 Imperfect indicative, ekouen.

and the Pharisees. There was a group of disciples around Him, and on the outskirts of the group were ranged the enemies. Jesus began with a statement about their official position as teachers in the line of succession to Moses. "They sit¹ in Moses' seat," He observed, in biting sarcasm. "Therefore, all things whatsoever they may speak to you, do and keep; but do not practice after the manner of their deeds. For they say, and don't practice what they preach." Another charge, equally grave, was that they "bound together, like sheaves, heavy burdens of rules for Sabbath observance, and laid them on the shoulders of men, like the heartless camel-driver the heavy burdens on the sore-backed beast of burden; and were not willing to lift a finger to lighten the burden." They did not take the smallest trouble to keep their own rules. With rapid strokes of His brush, He flashes another characterization of them on the canvas and their vanity stands forth in vivid colors. All their works they go on doing² to be seen and praised of men. He cites a pertinent illustration all too well known to the people. "They make broad their phylacteries to proclaim their extraordinary piety and lengthen the tassels on their garments to call attention to themselves." The phylacteries were little boxes, attached to the forehead or left arm, containing small strips of parchment with certain Scripture verses written on them. The larger the box, the greater the piety professed by the wearer, a violent contradiction to all humility. Jesus further exposed their selfish, ambitious, and social vanity. "They love the chief reclining places at the suppers and the first-seats in the front row facing the audience in the Synagogues, being motivated by an insatiable hunger for prominence. Especially were they fond of the salutations before the public in the market-places, being addressed by men with the new title of Rabbi" (Lightfoot). This title means "my great one," "my Master," a title apparently new in the time of Christ. In and aside to His disciples, Jesus adds: "Do you not seek to be called Rabbi. For one is your teacher, and all ye are brethren. Call no man your father on earth, for one is your heavenly Father." This would exclude the application of such a title to priest or pope. "Do not be called teachers, for you have one teacher, the Christ." Jesus here manifests himself intensely anti-prelatic and seeks to inculcate by every means humanity in His disciples. "The greatest of you shall be your servant. Whosoever shall exalt himself shall be humbled, and he who humbles himself shall be exalted."

The seven woes which Christ utters against the Scribes and Pharisees (vv 13-36) are to be interpreted as an effort, not merely

1 Gnomic aorist.　　2 Robertson, Word Pictures, dramatic present indicative active.

to warn others against their vanity, selfishness, and irreligion, but to open their eyes and if possible convert them from the error of their way. There are seven woes, directed against hypocrisy, foolishness, blindness, and avarice of the lowest type; lack of moral perception which made confusion of moral values, exalting ritual above justice, mercy, and faithfulness; hostility to the truth; hatred of the light; and inability to recognize divine messengers and ministries. He denounced the hated antagonism toward the prophets, whose tombs were built in pretense to honor those whom the forefathers had murdered, while inwardly nurturing the same bitter spirit which had slain the prophets, and would, in a few hours, slay the Son of God.

The first woe was uttered against these feigning hypocrites, masked play-actors, because they were engaged in slamming[1] the door of the Kingdom of Heaven in the face of men. They pretended to be on the inside of the palace of the Kingdom, but in the judgment of Jesus they "are not coming in themselves,[2] nor permitting those attempting to come in[3] to enter." Their hypocrisy consisted in the fact that, ostensibly, they were opening the road of the Kingdom, but in reality they were covering up the word, so as to block the way of those who were sincere seekers from entering. The extreme hatefulness of their hypocrisy was seen in their graft-grabbing of the houses of the helpless widows, whom they inveigled into giving their houses to the Temple, only to appropriate the property to their own selfish and private purposes. These same hypocrites would stand in the Temple and publicly make long prayers in pious pretense. Jesus would not let the opportune moment pass to warn them, that "they shall receive the more abundant condemnation."

The second woe was a deadly thrust against their proselytism, which "scoured land and sea, with great partisan zeal, to make a single proselyte" to Pharisaism. The aim was not to bring men into the Kingdom, but into their own coterie of Pharisaism, from among the Jews, principally, and the ultimate end was to enrich their own coffers by the addition of wealthy proselytes, like the centurion of Capernaum. Such a proselyte, they made twofold more partisan than themselves—a veritable son of Gehenna—"the more converted the more perverted, fitted and prepared for hell."

The third woe was a withering charge against their "making confusion in moral distinctions." An illustration of this confusing work of these "blind guides," was to be seen in their spiritual distinctions about the kind of oaths that are binding. They taught that the old general form of oaths was not binding, but only the

---

1 Present progressive tense.   2 Present indicative middle subject participating in the action.   3 Conative present middle participle.

new specific kind. Three instances of this stupidity, lack of spiritual insight, and Jesuitic casuistry are cited: "Swearing by the Temple was no real oath, but swearing by the gold in the Temple was valid." Of course the greater included the less, as any fool or even a blind man should know. "An oath by the altar was nil, while one by the gift on the altar was binding." But they were blind not to understand that the altar was greater than the gift, and he who should swear by the altar swore not only by the altar itself but by all on the altar as well. Likewise, the one swearing by the Temple swore by it and the one dwelling in it; and the one swearing by the Throne of God, swore also by the one sitting on it. The teaching of Jesus was against all use of oaths. A Kingdom man's word must be as good as his oath. These men were blind, deceiving themselves, and blotting out all moral lines and distinctions.

The fourth woe refers to tithe paying, which was scrupulously observed by the Scribes and Pharisees, even to the small garden herbs of the sweet-smelling mint, the aromatic anise, and the cummin (with aromatic seed). The tithe was to be paid on "all increase of thy seed (Deut. 14:22; Lev. 27:30), even on all marketable commodities." They were exceedingly conscientious and showed great zeal in doing the easier things, while shirking the serious and more difficult requirements of duty, such as righteous judgment or justice, compassionate mercy, true-hearted fidelity. Jesus did not condemn tithing, but Pharisaical externalism and ostentation in tithing, while neglecting the weightier matters. He reenforced His severe indictment of those blind guides by the use of a current proverb: "Ye blind guides which strain out (filter) the gnat from the wine, while swallowing the camel" (an unclean animal, chewing the cud but not parting the hoof)! They made small things of great importance and great things of little consequence.

The fifth woe was a vial of wrath, poured out on Pharisaic externalism, rapacity, and incontinence. These masked play-actors habitually cleansed the outside of the cup and platter in which the food and drinks were served, and both cup and platter were full of things gained by plunder and purchased by the wages of unrighteousness. This rapacity was practiced in the name of religion and under the mask of piety. Blind Pharisee, cleanse the moral inside of the cup and plate first, that the ceremonial outside may be clean.

The sixth woe refers to no special vice, but gives a graphic picture of their hypocrisy in general. These play-actors were like the white-washed tombs to be seen everywhere, at that time of the year, in Palestine. The outside looked fair, but, inside, they were full of dead men's bones. It was ceremonial defilement to come in contact with the dead, hence the tombs were white-washed every year, just before the time of the Passover Feast when the pilgrims came up from every part of the land. Many of these tombs were visible around Jerusalem, fit emblems of the Pharisees, who thus from without appeared just to men, but "within were full of hypocrisy and lawlessness."

The seventh and final woe dealt with their inconsistency and the deception of the Jewish people when they professed to be distressed at the murdering of the ancient prophets, saying, they would not have slain the prophets as their fathers did. In their great zeal for the honor of the deceased prophets, they built for them monumental tombs. There are four monuments, called the Tombs of the Prophets, at the base of the Mount of Olives today. Jesus might have had in mind the tomb of Zachariah. He reminds them that they were themselves bearing witness to the murder-taint in their own blood, and adds further that they were sons to their fathers in their very spirit. "Go on and fill to the full the measure of your fathers," He ejected with the keenest irony. "Crown their misdeeds, with killing the Prophet God has sent you! Do at last what has long been in your hearts! The hour has come!" (Bruce).

In His peroration (vs. 34-36), He lashes them with blistering words that remind us of those used by John the Baptist in the wilderness: "Serpents, offspring of vipers," He cried, "you who are yourselves snakes by your own sinful motives, and offspring of your sinful forebears, how shall ye be able to flee and escape from the judgment of the Hell of Torments (Gehenna)?" "See," He exclaimed, "I am going to send you prophets, wise men and scribes. Some you will kill and crucify; some you will flog in your synagogues and persecute from city to city; that on you may come all the accumulated retributive punishment, for all the righteous blood shed upon the earth, from the blood of Abel, the righteous, to that of Zachariah, the son of Barachiah whom they slew between the temple and the altar."[1] By adopting the murderous ways of their forefathers, who killed the prophets, they would become heirs of all the blood of the martyred saints. The blood, it was said, would be avenged (Gen. 4:10). The same was foretold of the blood of Zachariah. A Jewish legend said that the blood of Zachariah bubbled on the Pavement of the Temple Court for two centuries, until avenged by Nebuzar-adan. The legend shows that the murder was held as a notable crime; and Jesus cites these two outstanding murders to point to the fact that men make the guilt of past ages their own, and thus bring upon themselves the penalties for the sins of their forefathers, which they could cut off

[1] From Abel to Zachariah, would include all the murderers. Zachariah was the priest slain by the order of the King (II Chron. 24:20). In Hebrew Bibles Chronicles stands at the end (Broadus).

by repentance. "Solemnly I tell you," Jesus says, "all these things shall come upon this generation." The hailstorm of His denunciation had fallen ever thicker upon these hypocritical leaders of the Jewish nation, and its fury was greatest in this final pronouncement of doom upon national impenitence.

He concludes His fearful indictment with a memorable apostrophe, a dirge of doom, and a lament over the beloved city. For more than half a year, His mind had turned toward Jerusalem, and three times[1] He had broken out in lamentation: "Jerusalem! Jerusalem! which killest the prophets and stonest those who are sent unto her! How often I wished to gather thy children together, even as a hen gathereth her chickens under her wings, and ye would not! Behold, your house is being left[2] unto you desolate. For I say unto you, ye shall not see me henceforth, till ye shall say, Blessed is he that cometh in the name of the Lord." Here is a passionate lament of love. The beautiful city and beloved Temple would soon be places of desolation. The broken-hearted Messiah pours out His soul in prophetic lamentation over His own, to whom He came and who received him not. He would have given them shelter, rest, and divine protection under the wings of His heavenly Shekina; but they would not. He was to leave the courts of their Temple, before the approaching hour of the setting sun, never more to return. Israel would not see Him again until His second coming in Messianic glory, when they would say: "Blessed is the one coming in the name of the Lord."

How fearfully the prophecy of destruction was fulfilled! In a few brief years the Roman legions of the Emperor Titus utterly destroyed the city and its glorious Temple. Over a million Jews perished in the siege in a few days, and a hundred thousand more were borne away in captivity.

At the close of this hour of terrific denunciation, when He poured seven vials of consuming wrath upon the heads of these hypocritical rulers and leaders of the people, Jesus passed into the spacious court of the Women, fifteen feet below, and sat down in the place of the Treasury. His apostles, who had witnessed the tragic scene of the denunciation, and who drew apart in a group, in the midst of the fulminations of His wrath and the scowls and angry mutterings of His enemies, now came around Him with many an anxious look and fearful glances backward toward the upper court, whence the enemies might come at any moment in violence upon them.

1 Luke 13:34; 19:41-44; Matt. 23:37.   2 Present time, progressive action.

In the midst of the certain perils, Jesus was calm, and deliberately sat down to casually watch the passing crowd as they cast their brass coins into the trumpet-shaped metallic collection boxes of the treasury. His was a discriminating observation. Many rich people cast in much, but there came one[1] poor pauper-widow and cast two mites,[2] which together make a farthing. The heart of the Master was deeply moved. He was tired. The nervous strain of the previous hour had been terrific. Even now, the enemies doubtless were plotting His death in the court above, a few paces distant. Even in the midst of these circumstances, Jesus watched the stream of humanity passing by and drew from this slight incident of the widow's contribution a lesson which has become proverbial in all subsequent times.

Calling His disciples around Him, He said to them: "Verily I say unto you, this pauper-widow cast more in than all the rich men put together[3] among the contributors." The basis of His evaluation He adds immediately. "They all cast in out of their superfluity, but she, out of her want, all that she was possessing, even all that she had." The measure of what we really contribute is not how much we give, but how much we keep back for our own personal use. Jesus was pleased with the faithfulness and self-sacrificing spirit of this gift. In His immortal eulogy pronounced on this pauper-widow, He drew the lesson that the very essence of charity is self-denial.

1 Mia.   2 The mite or lepta was the smallest of copper coins. Less than two was not considered an offering.   3 Panton ablative of comparison in the place of oleion.

CHAPTER XXIX

JESUS' PROPHETIC DISCOURSE

(Harm. §§ 139)

Sad and full of forebodings, the apostles went out from the Temple with Jesus to return to Bethany. His scathing denunciation of His Pharisaic and Sadducean enemies, now banded together against Him, would bring inevitable tragedy out just ahead. Their hearts clung with national pride to their Temple and their beloved city, and as they passed out through the Temple gate, they cast a longing and lingering gaze back upon that magnificent structure adorned with goodly stones and offerings.

Herod had built this sanctuary, of hard white limestone, some blocks of which were thirty feet long, eighteen wide and twelve in thickness. The Babylonian Talmud said: "He that never saw the temple of Herod never saw a fine building." Many barbaric spoils offered by King Herod, with votive tablets and other beautiful and costly articles given by the people, adorned the buildings, which including the various courts, covered an area of twenty acres. For strength it was like a fortress and it crowned an eminence, making it visible from afar like a snow-capped hill.

One of the disciples moved by the splendor of the rays of the western sun reflected from the roof and sides of the Temple adorned with gold, exclaimed: "Teacher, see what manner of stones and what manner of buildings!" "You see these greater buildings," replied Jesus, "there shall not be left one stone upon another that shall not be thrown down."

Proceeding calmly on their way by the ascent over the Mount of Olives toward Bethany, they came to the turn of the road and a place from which the city with its Temple was laid out like a map before them, bathed now in the rays of the setting sun. Here Jesus sat down on a knoll for a brief moment of rest. Four of his most loved disciples, Peter, James, John, and Andrew, drew around Him to ask Him privately about the sad words of His prophecy, to them so incomprehensible.

Jesus had predicted six months before, while working in Perea (Luke 13:34), again in the triumphal entry (Luke 19:41-44) and finally in His last address to the people in the Temple, the destruction of that magnificent edifice which for solidity and durability seemed almost indestructible. Well did He understand that the Jews would hold fast to the idea of a temporal Kingdom, until they should call down upon themselves, through repeated acts of rebellion, the vengeance of the Roman legions. Their Pharisaic and

Sadducean leaders were blind guides, discerning the signs of the weather, but unable to read the signs of the times. The disciples of Jesus needed to get away from the current Messianic idea of a temporal kingdom. Jesus would warn them and the people against their dangerous ideal, which was leading them ever nearer the brink of political ruin and spiritual failure. When the Master had given utterance for the first time to the sad lament, as His Pharisaic enemies sought to push Him out of Perea by threats from Herod Antipas (Luke 13:34) and on to Jerusalem where they hoped to compass His ruin, He had referred to two things together: the destruction of Jerusalem and the Temple and the nearness of His second coming and the end of the world. While the disciples still clung to their idea of a Kingdom of temporal power, they were increasingly perplexed and confused in their thought by periodically repeated declarations of their Teacher, which pointed away from this conception to a different kind of Kingdom. Convinced now that something is going to happen shortly, they come to Him with two direct questions: "Master, when shall these things be and what shall be the sign when these things are about to come to pass? What shall be the sign of thy coming and the end of the world?"

In reply to these questions and because He wished to prepare them as far as possible for the tragically shocking experiences out just ahead of them, He there pronounced a most remarkable prophetic sermon on the twofold subject of their inquiry: the destruction of Jerusalem and His second coming and the end of the age.

This extraordinary address of Jesus is the most difficult of all His deliverances to understand. Couched in terms that partake of apocalyptic character, with many expressions of prophetic nature, the sermon deals with two difficult subjects, both of which are fraught with many problems for our understanding. One thing which will help most of all in our interpretation of the discourse is the fact that Jesus here, as in all His sermons, had a very definite and practical end in view. He was a Master in the fine art of teaching and preaching. His aim in this sermon was to divest His disciples of wrong Messianic ideals and inculcate in them correct ideas of the nature of His Kingdom. Another thing which will help toward our clear understanding of His message is to remember that He was speaking to Jews, whose minds were filled with the Messianic ideals which had come down to them as a heritage of Rabbinic teaching of centuries. We must seek to understand in some way, however inadequate, what the Jews currently believed about these subjects dealt with in His discourse, and what His disciples had in their minds about them, in spite of all His teaching and effort during His ministry to correct the wrong and inculcate the right ideas in their thought.

I. We will observe in our study of the sermon that the two subjects are closely connected, We would expect to find that in the master Teacher and Preacher. One subject shades into the other. In fact it is very difficult to draw any distinct line of cleavage between the two in His treatment. The sermon deals with the Messianic Kingdom and gives a prophetic view of that Kingdom as it is to pass through two great crises in the future. One of those crises, the initial one, was just ahead. It would be precipitated in His tragic death by crucifixion in a few hours and would reach its drastic maturity in the destruction of Jerusalem some thirty years later, when the whole city with the Sanctuary would be razed to its foundations.[1] The second and final great crisis would come, when the Messiah should return in power and great glory at the end of time. The subject of the destruction of Jerusalem, which catastrophe would be brought on as a consequence of the Jewish Messianic ideal, the potent cause operating now to bring Him to the cross, is dealt with first; but it is so intimately woven in with the other subjects of the second coming and the end of the world, that it is difficult to say to which of the subjects some expressions primarily refer. In general the narrative of Matthew, which gives the fullest outline of the sermon, may be divided into three sections. The first (24:1-36) deals with both subjects: the crisis of the Kingdom in the destruction of Jerusalem and the end of the world: the second (24:37—25:13) constitutes a transition from the first to the second subject; and the third (25:13-46) deals exclusively with the subject of the second coming and end of the age.[1] There are certain verses, however, in the first section which seem to refer clearly to the subject of the final great crisis (vv 30 and 36). Matthew's outline of the sermon, accompanied by the parallel references of Mark's graphic expressions and Luke's exact narrative, will serve as a guide in our study of this wonderful message, the full import of which the world has never yet fully grasped. Jesus was here acting in His function of interpreter of His own times and prophetic revealer of the times to come, down to the end of the world-age. After all, His subject was one: the future of the Messianic Kingdom, and the coming of that Kingdom which was of the heart and in the power of the Spirit, would find its great advance in the fall of the old Rabbinic regime at the destruction of Jerusalem and its final great victory and consummation at the second advent of the Messiah.

1 Josephus, War 7:1, 1.

1. Jesus first foretells certain things which must transpire before the two great crises should be accomplished (Matt. 24:4-18; Mark 13:1-16; Luke 21:5-21). They had been taught that there would be signs and they asked Jesus "what the signs would be of these things, and especially of his second coming." He warns them first against certain misleading signs (Matt. 24:4-14; Mark 13:5-13; Luke 21:8-19). Among the false signs which would lead many astray were Messiah-pretenders and other false teachers (vv 4,5); wars, famines, and earthquakes affecting the world at large (vv 6-8); persecutions, false prophets, and multiplied transgressions which would directly affect the disciples (vv 9-13). Jesus then adds a corrective of the false signs (Matt. 24:14; Mark 13:10).[1]

The thought of the disciples seemed to run more to the subject of the second advent of the Messiah. So, as He sat in a place on Mount Olivet over against the Temple, looking down upon the devoted city, He began to warn the apostle group now gathered about Him not to be misled by false signs, nor to expect the second advent of the Messiah soon. He could not gratify their desire as to the time of that august event. "Beware," He warned, "lest any man lead you astray." He prophesied that many false Messiahs would arise and lead many disciples and others astray. This prophecy was fulfilled in Barcochba and others, some before the destruction of Jerusalem and others down through the centuries to the present time. They must not be troubled and frightened out of their wits,[2] when they should hear of wars and rumors of wars, or think that they were on the eve of the second coming, as the custom of many has been from the early church in Thessalonica until now. Such social upheavels must of necessity come in the passing away of the old regime and the coming in of the new. These things would be no true signs of the immediate coming of the Messiah, for the deliverance of Israel. The conflicts of the nations were inevitable. Another disturbing factor accompanying social revolution was that of calamities affecting the physical well-being of humanity, such as famines, pestilences, and earthquakes. These again did not fortoken the end, but rather the beginning of the age-long struggle of the Messianic Kingdom just in the birth-throes of its initiation.[3] A harder trial for the Kingdom subjects than all these social calamities and physical distresses—birth-pangs of a new dispensation—were the dreadful persecutions they would have to suffer at the hands of their own countrymen, who would deliver them up to their local Sanhedrins, where they would be

1 Broadus, Commentary on Matthew in loco.
2 Thoreisthe, be excited and terrified by the outcry of false reports.
3 Cf. Book of Jubilees 23:18 Apoc. of Baruch 27-28.

treated with injustice; they would also be flogged in their synagogues, where they ought most of all to expect considerate treatment. That would be a time of great tribulation[1] for the disciples,
leading in many cases to martyrdom. They would have to go on
being hated[2] by the heathen peoples also, to whom they were to
take the Gospel. They would be brought to stand falsely accused
before governors and kings for His sake, that they might give their
testimony to their faith in Him. There would be their opportunity,
as in all the common calamities of life, to give testimony by patient endurance and Christian fortitude.[3] Let them not be concerned or anxious, when thus hailed before the heathen rulers,
as to what they should speak or how to answer. He would Himself give them, through the Holy Spirit in that hour, wisdom
beyond their adversaries. A harder trial, and perhaps the hardest they would meet, was the strife of creeds and disloyalty within the brotherhood of the church and the sacred circle of the
family. Under the heathen pressure many would renounce their
faith and betray or deliver up fellow-Christians. Fathers, because
of creed, would give evidence in the courts against their own
children, brothers against brothers, and children against parents.
Heathen and Jewish fanaticism would deliver up in its fury those
of the dearest earthly ties for trial and execution. This was indeed
a dark and lurid picture that the Master drew of their future prospects. The contrast with current conceptions of the Messianic
reign could not have been greater! The Jews expected a kingdom
of peace and great abundance, and Jesus holds out in immediate
prospect for His Kingdom men this fearful lot. Their current
Messianic conceptions were so far wrong, that this drastic measure
was necessary to prepare them for what they must endure for
His name's sake. Jesus did not leave them, however, to sink in
hopelessness and despair, but gives them assurance. "He that
endureth to the end shall be saved." Their eternal welfare was
guaranteed to them. No real harm would befall them. Though
they should suffer martyrdom, their spiritual safety was assured.
In their Christian patience "they would win their souls." And best
of all, the Gospel of the Kingdom would be preached in the whole
world! That must be done before the end of time and His second
coming, and it would not be done in a day! This sign He gave
them as a corrective for their false conceptions of the second advent of their Messiah. Let them settle down to a long campaign
of world evangelization and not be disturbed by catastrophic signs
which the Rabbis had taught them to expect.

1 Thlipsin, pressure, oppression.   2 Periphrastic future passive.
3 Stanley Jones, Christ and Human Suffering.

Over against this concept was that of the current Messianic ideal, set forth in the teaching of the Rabbis and the Pseudepigraphic writings. The Rabbis said a "happy period would begin with the days of the Messiah" which would end with the "world to come." The duration of this period was undefined. The Messiah was to destroy the hostile powers, especially the Roman power —the fourth and the last empire. Ransomed Israel, including the ten tribes, would be miraculously restored, and circumcised Israel released from Gehenna. The dead would be raised in Palestine, the resurrection being announced by the blowing of the great Trumpet. After the defeat of God's enemies in the great war of Gog and Magog, the sacred city of Jerusalem would be wholly rebuilt. It would be nine miles high and extend from Joppa to Damascus and would be the dwelling place of Israel and resort of all nations. The Temple would be restored with all its ancient services, symbols, and Mosaic and Rabbinic laws. There would be great profusion of wealth and abundance, with the elimination of all diseases, sickness, and outward loss. Jerusalem was to be the residence of the Messiah and capital of the world, and Israel would rule the nations. After a period of Messianic rule, a final rebellion would break out, lasting seven years, after which the final judgment would commence. Abraham would release all the unrighteous Israelites from Gehenna—a kind of purgatory—and the final judgment would be conducted by God in the valley of Jehosaphat, with the aid of the heavenly Sanhedrin composed of the elders of Israel. After the final judgment would come the renewal of heaven and earth. Evil impulse would be destroyed and Paradise restored.[1]

The Pseudepigraphic writings carry in the main the same ideal[2] with few alterations of consequence. On such a background as this, Jesus proferred His prophecy about the signs of the coming Messianic reign. As we shall see more and more, further on, His Kingdom ideal stood out in absolute contrast in its spiritual nature over against the materialism of the Rabbis.

2. Jesus goes on to discuss in the second place, the one great sign in Jerusalem which would be a warning to them of the impending destruction of that city (Matt. 24:15); He also warns them what they should do without delay at the appearance of that sign (vv 16-18). There would be great tribulation in those days (vv 19-22), but they must not think that the second advent of the Son of Man was at hand and be deluded by Messiah-pretenders (vv 23-28).[3]

1 Edersheim, Life and Times of Jesus in loco.
2 IV Esdras, The Sibylline Books, Book of Enoch, and Assumption of Moses.
3 Parallel passages: Mark 13:14-23; Luke 21:20-22.

The Master had foretold the destruction of Jerusalem; He now gives them definite indications which would warn them of its approach and help them escape to safety. When they should see the abomination of desolation stationed in the Sanctuary and the Roman army in the act of encircling[1] the city, let them recognize the fulfillment of the prophecy of Daniel (Dan. 9:27; 11:31; 12:11). The abomination of desolation was the stench[2] of heathen idolatry. Antiochus Epiphanes had sacrificed a hog on the altar of the Temple in other days. The Roman legions of Titus would burn the Temple and offer heathen sacrifices to their ensigns, placed by the eastern gate, when they proclaimed Titus Emperor (70 A. D.).

Two perils would beset the Christians in that time: outward destruction of life and property and further delusions of false Messiahs. Jesus warns His disciples to flee in time. When the Roman armies should begin to encircle the city of Jerusalem, then let those disciples who were in Judea flee to the trans-Jordanic mountains. Those who happened to be on the flat-topped roofs of the houses in Jerusalem should not take time to go down and try to get any baggage out with them, but rather flee from roof to roof until they should come to the city wall and thus escape. Those working in the fields, without the outer garment, should not return to get them.[3] In the fulfillment of this prophecy in 70 A. D., many Christians, heeding the warning Jesus had given, fled at an early stage of the siege of Jerusalem and escaped to Pella, seventeen miles south of the sea of Galilee. It would be a woeful time for those who were with child or tiny babies. They should pray that these things might not happen in the winter or when the streams should be swollen with the season's rains and it would be cold in the mountain hiding-places. Unhappy would it be for those who, clinging to the Jewish Sabbath tradition, would not journey more than two thousand cubits. Greater affliction the world had never seen—would never see—than that reserved for the inhabitants of Jerusalem in that day. Josephus speaks of the horrors of the experiences of the Jews in the siege of Jerusalem in 70 A. D. More than a million perished in a day, and all would have perished if those days had not been abbreviated by the Lord on account of His elect[4] ones—those who were already Christians and those who would later become so.[5] Jesus here speaks as if the dread event had already happened. His prophetic vision was timeless.[6]

1 Present participle, Luke 21:20.   2 Robertson's Word Pictures (Matt. 24:15).
3 The himation, a kind of cape or overcoat without sleeves.
4 The doctrine of the sovereignty of God in election.
5 Titus confessed that God was against the Jews in that siege (Vincent).
6 Timeless aorist.

There would be a greater peril even for the Jews, in the midst of that day of distress upon the land and wrath to that people, when many would fall by the edge of the sword and many be led captive into all nations. That was the peril of false Christs and false phophets who would be skilful in the use of sleight-of-hand signs and wonders, so as to lead astray even the elect if that were possible.[1] Some of these would send out the report that they had found the Messiah in the desert and seek to muster their dupes there in safety. Others would acclaim that He was shut up in secret inner chambers. The disciples were not to give credence to such reports or run after such pretenders. He had given them the warning beforehand; let them give heed. No Maccabee Messiah would rise to deliver them in the coming crisis. "Jerusalem would be trodden down of the heathen until the times of the Gentiles were fulfilled. Long stretches of centuries would roll in those times of the Gentiles" when the nations[2] would have their day of opportunity through divine grace. During those centuries the Jews, dispersed among all nations, would suffer the horrors of persecutions and oppression, until the period of opportunity given to the Gentiles was complete. And that day is not complete yet!

3. The manner and time of the second coming is dealt with next (Matt. 24:29-36; Mark 13:24-32; Luke 21:28-33). There would be visible and unmistakable signs in the heavens (Matt. 24:29-31; Mark 13:24-27; Luke 21:25-28); and these signs would be sufficient to indicate the near approach of the Messiah (Matt. 24:32-36).

The manner of the second coming would be such as to leave no doubt in the minds of the disciples when He should appear. (vv 29-31). The tribulation of the Jews must stretch over a long period of centuries, and following this period, immediately there would be signs in the heavens. "The sun shall have been darkened[3] and the moon will not go on giving her light.[4] The stars shall be falling[5] from the heaven and the powers of the heavens shall have been shaken." Accompanying this extraordinary manifestation in the physical universe there would be great distress[6] of nations in perplexity[7] at the resounding of the sea and surge; men fainting from fear[8] and expectation of things coming upon the world, when the heavenly bodies should be shaken. Then shall appear the sign of the Son of Man in the heavens (Matt. 24:30). When the tribes of the earth shall see this sign—the Son of Man coming[9] in a cloud with power and much glory—they shall mourn,

1 Conditions of second class, contrary to fact, indicating that it would not be possible.
2 Ethnei, nations referring usually to the Gentiles.   3 Future passive indicative.
4 Future active, linear action.   5 Future of pipto.   6 Anguish of soul.
7 In a feeling of one who has lost his way.   8 Ablative of source.
9 The Son of Man Himself was the sign, genetive of apposition. cf. Matt. 16:27.

because of their rejection of Christ. At His appearance the Messiah will send forth His angels with the sound of a great trumpet and they shall gather up the elect from all parts of the earth.

These signs will be sufficient to show the nearness of the coming of the Messiah (vv 32-36). The parable of the fig tree was to illustrate the fact that the before-mentioned signs would be so evident the disciples would be able to judge of the nearness of His coming and of the consummation of His Kingdom. He is evidently speaking now of the second coming and the end of the world. All nations did not mourn when Jerusalem fell. In the end of time when the Son of Man shall appear all the tribes of the earth will mourn because of their sin of rejecting Him. The destruction of Jerusalem as the initial crisis of the Kingdom was in some sense symbolic of the second and greater crisis at the end of the world. The present generation would not pass away before the beginning of the Messianic age had come. This beginning had already been made and would have its first great increase at the fall of Jerusalem. The Messianic age thus initiated would reach its consummation at the second coming and end of the world-age. Before a generation should pass the old regime of ancient priesthood and sacrifices would come to an end and the new age be ushered in at the fall of Jerusalem. They might rely fully on the words of His prophecy. Not one word would fail. We know how fully and literally His prediction of the fall of Jerusalem was fulfilled in history. But the day and hour of His second coming was reserved in the sole keeping of the Father and for a purpose. It was no part of His Messianic Mission to disclose the exact date of His second coming, which in His human self-imposed limitation was excluded from His knowledge and that of all other intelligencies except the Father. To declare that we cannot confide in the revelations of Jesus, as for example in this discourse, because He admitted limitation in knowledge, is beside the mark. Could He have revealed the date of His second coming, He would by doing so have defeated His Messianic Mission. There would then have been no force in His teaching about watchfulness, the duty of faithfulness in work, endurance, purity, and self-denial.

II. The subject of the destruction of Jerusalem gradually drops out of sight in the second main division of the discourse (Matt. 24:37—25:13; Mark 13:3-37; Luke 21:34-36). Jesus having sounded out the warning note to His disciples in the first part, revealing to them the dreadful ordeals through which the Kingdom must pass before its consummation in the end, turns their attention during the rest of the discourse to application of His revelation to their needs. Watchfulness is enjoyed, with endurance and prayer, in four beautiful parabolic illustrations. The necessity for watchfulness was based on our ignorance as to the exact time —a wholesome thing for the Kingdom forces—and on the revelation that it shall be sudden and unexpected.

1. This fact is illustrated first by reference to the times of Noah (Matt. 24:37-44). For the poeple of Noah's time there was plenty of warning, in a hundred and twenty years of that servant's faithful preaching. In those days before the great flood, they went on eating and drinking and giving in marriage[1] until the day that Noah went into the ark, and they did not recognize the peril of their situation until the cataclysm of waters came and swept them all away. "Even thus sudden shall the appearance of the Son of Man be at his second advent. Two (men) shall be in the field; one shall be taken—in the gathering of the elect—and the other left. Two (women) shall be grinding at the hand-mill; one shall be taken and the other left." Many times the mother and daughter were the ones who worked together in the domestic grinding in Palestine. Keep awake,[2] therefore, for ye know not on what day your lord cometh. Persons most intimately associated will be separated by that unexpected coming. Such would be the condition of the world at the second coming.

2. Readiness is next urged by a series of parables.[3] (Mark 13:33-37; Luke 21:34-36; Matt. 24:43—25:13). The refrain of all is: "Watch, therefore, for ye know not the day nor the hour."

a. Mark gives the parable of the Porter,[4] illustrating the assigned duty of watching; "Look out," he says, "watch and pray for ye know not when the time is. It is like a man who, going for a journey in another country, left his house, and giving authority to his servants, assigning work for each, commanded also the Porter to watch. The hour of the householder's return was not marked. It might be at even, at midnight, or near the break of day. "Watch," said Jesus, "lest the householder return and find you sleeping and unprepared to give account of your assigned task!"

"Take heed to yourselves," He warns His disciples again, "lest haply your hearts be made heavy[5] with suffering,[6] drunkenness, and the anxieties of this life, and the day come on you as a snare."[7] Paul speaks of the devil's snares to catch preachers (I Tim. 3:7; II Tim. 2:26). The second coming will catch many people unprepared in all parts of the earth. "Keep awake," Jesus warns His workers and disciples, "at every season, that you may have

1 Periphrastic imperfect denoting a continuous process.   2 Gregoreite, watch. keep awake.   3 Robertson's Harmony of the Gospels.
4 Bruce, Parabolic Teaching of Jesus.   5 Barethosin, weighed down.
6 With nausea following debauch.   7 A net to trap or catch animals.

strength to escape[1] all these things that shall accompany the second coming, and so come to stand before the Messiah as his faithful servants."

b. Jesus further illustrates the necessity of faithfulness and vigilance by two brief parables (Matt. 24:43-51). The parable of the Master of the House illustrates the need for vigilance and readiness (vv 43-45). The houses in Palestine were sometimes constructed of sun-dried brick and the thief could dig through the wall with comparative facility. The vigilant Master of a house could prevent such intrusion of the robber by being awake and ready. The servant of Jesus is warned to be ready "at every watch of the night." A supplementary illustration is found in the parable of the Unfaithful Upper Servant[2]. All of these parables were spoken for the benefit of the workers, both apostles and disciples in general. This might be a surprise to these chosen workers who seemed above the common failing of heedlessness. But the failure of Peter and most of the others, a little later, proved the need of such warning and exhortation. A sudden crisis has a most demoralizing effect on inexperienced disciples; and a long delay produces still worse results in workers, leading to relaxation, carelessness, not to say temporary denials, worldliness, and abandon.

The parable of the Wise versus the Unfaithful Upper Servant, sets forth the fact that the Kingdom was to have a lengthened history before reaching its consummation and the Kingdom workers would have need of great perserverance[3]. The Upper Servant was a brutal overseer and a drunken profligate. Luke warns against the misconduct of such a servant[4]. This servant proved unfaithful in the administration of his absent lord's household. Unlike the wise servant who received the lord's commendation and advancement on his return, he decided that his lord was delaying his return and gave himself up to debauchery, profligacy, drunkenness, and brutal treatment of his fellow-servants. The penalty for such a servant, on the unexpected return of his lord, was to be cut asunder[5]. In this case, of the parable, the penalty is severest in being one of appointment of a portion with the hypocrites, who are grossly offensive to God. The good servant will be exalted to the highest position a servant can have (v 47). Jesus warns His disciples that one who is apparently identified with the working forces of the Kingdom may find himself assigned with the hypocrites in the punishment of hell, where there is weeping of hopeless sorrow, loss, and despair, and gnashing of teeth in bitter hate

1 First aorist subjunctive with hina denoting purpose.
2 Bruce, Parabolic Teachings of Christ, in loco.   3 Idem pp 490f.   4 Luke 21:34-36.
5 Such punishment was practised at times among the Hebrews, II Sam. 12:31; Hebrews 11:37

and rebellion against God. Severe judgment comes upon those, who occupy positions of great privilege in the Kingdom, but through decline into faithlessness and profligacy fall into the snare of the devil. Such has been the fate of many workers, from Judas to the present day! Jesus knew the difficult work of the Kingdom through a long period; His warning against heedlessness was severe, and His commendation for faithfulness was a beatitude. "Blessed is that servant" whom his lord when he cometh shall find in his place of duty, alert to every opportunity, faithful in his task. Such character is high, exceptional, and rare, signifying virtue arduous, heroic, and uncommon; and receives the congratulations[1] of the Lord.

c. The parable of the Ten Virgins (Matt. 25:1-13). This is one of the most beautiful and touching among all the parables of Jesus. It is poetry in prose, an enchanting story, a work of art. For that reason one hesitates before the difficult task of interpretation. The wedding is a happy occasion, the characters brought on the stage are virgin-bridesmaids, full of youth, beauty, and expectation. The setting of the incident is filled with details, which are intensely interesting, based as they are on the customs of a wonderful people and that in the times and country where Jesus lived His glorious life. The parable has been subjected for centuries to wild allegorizing and its didatic element twisted to conform to every particular creed. So potent is the story on human life, when presented in any adequate way, that it is most useful in stirring the heart and moving the will to action in the acceptance of the Bridegroom, whose delayed but sure coming it illustrates.

This parable, like the others which preceded it, points to the second advent and enforces the need of watchfulness and preparedness for that great event.

"Ten virgin-bridesmaids, five wise and five foolish, take their torch-like lamps and go forth to meet the bridegroom." Eastern weddings were celebrated after night-fall, their principal features being the procession and the banquet. The wedding was usually celebrated at the home of the bridegroom's father and the wedding procession accompanied the bridegroom in bringing the bride from her home to the scene of the wedding[2]. Invited guests bore torch-lamps, consisting of a bowl of grease having a rope wick, and being fastened on the end of a staff. Each guest was provided with such a lamp, which served thus collectively to light the procession through the dark Palestinian streets. The bridegroom was de-

1 Makarios, blessed, to be congratulated. 2 I Macc. 9:37-42. Sometimes the wedding was celebrated at the bride's home, the bridegroom providing the feast (Jud. 14:

tained. The hours dragged by and all these bridesmaids, waiting in a house by the way, began to grow drowsy,[1] nodded, and finally fell into a deep sleep.[2]

At the midnight hour the sudden cry was raised: "Behold. the Bridegroom! Come out to meet him!" All awoke with a start and rose up quickly to trim each her own torch-light; for while they slept the oil had burned low. They must needs replenish the oil in the lamps from their flasks. Much to their consternation, the foolish virgins found that they had failed to bring their flasks. In tragic appeal they turned to the prudent ones: "Give us of your oil," they pled. "for our lamps are going out."[3] But the sensible ones answered: "No, there may not be enough for us and for you. Better go to the dealers and buy for yourselves." But while they were gone to buy, the bridegroom came, and those who were ready went in with him to the wedding banquet and the door was shut. Later the rest of the bridesmaids came, saying: "Oh Sir, Oh Sir,[4] open the door for us!" but he replied: "I tell you frankly I do not know you."

Such is the enchantingly beautiful but sad story, and the moral and point of illustration is driven home on the disciples immediately: "Keep awake, therefore, because ye know not the day nor the hour." Jesus realized that by the long delay in His second coming, in many, the hope would flag and zeal burn low.

What is the teaching of this parable? Various interpretations have been given, ranging from the wildest allegorizing, to the most restricted and servile use to sustain some particular ecclesiastical theory. A parable cannot be applied in all its details to teach favorite doctrines or sustain pet theories. The point of illustration is preparedness and readiness for the second coming of the Messiah.

1. The beautiful allegory presents the fact that true preparedness is based on inward condition of character and not on outward appearance and profession. The five foolish maidens to all outward appearances were like the prudent ones. They had the same attachment to the bridegroom, the same equipment outwardly for participation in the wedding procession and banquet, and like the sensible bridesmaids went out to meet the bridegroom. But there were certain fundamental differences. They were improvident, and lacking in good sense and thoughtfulness. They had impulse and emotional attachment but not depth of nature and conviction. Like the seed that fell upon the rocky ground and sprang up immediately because there was no depth of earth, their religion was one of superficial and emotional character, lacking in depth.

1 Ingressive aorist.   2 Imperfect indicative.   3 Present middle indicative, the lamps were just then in the act of going out.   4 Weymouth's Translation. 10).

2. Another distinct teaching of the parable is that crisis reveals preparedness or the lack of it. The sudden appearance of some great emergency, some imminent peril like threatened loss of the steamer on which one is driven before the fury of the blast in a storm at sea, the loss of all one's earthly possessions at one fell swoop of misfortune, constitutes a test of character. In such a storm on life's sea the real character of the disciple is revealed.

3. Another lesson, which is revealed by the necessity of the oil of grace for each individual, is that such a character as prepares for the second advent crisis cannot be transferred from one to another. The prudent virgins could not have given of their oil to their foolish companions, even if they had so desired. Religion is an individual transaction and relationship between God and the soul of each man. There is no such thing as salvation by proxy.

4. Again, true preparedness is not complete without reserve. The prudent virgins took along the reserve supply of oil. Inward grace of salvation wrought into the character constitutes such a reserve. Paul so conceived of the plan of salvation.[1] It was tragic when the foolish virgins discovered their lack of oil. Sputtering, flickering, smoking wicks when the bridegroom had already been announced was a tragic situation. For them then, all was confusion, bustle, and rushing off to the oil-venders, hopelessly, stricken with grief and fear. The tragedy deepened when they returned and found the door shut, to stay shut.[2] There is no chance after the door of death is shut on the lost soul. The opportunity to get ready is given to every man. Many, by neglect, procrastination, heedlessness, allow the door of opportunity to be shut forever in their faces and never enter to participate in the Marriage Feast.

III. In the third main division of this discourse, nothing is in view but the final coming to judgment (Matt. 25:14-46) presented in the parable of the Talents and the Judgment scene.

1. The parable of the Talents (Matt. 25:14-30) enforces the necessity of faithful service of the absent Lord, in order that we may, through making good use of our God-given powers, capacities, and possessions—our talents—receive the commendation and advancement of faithful servants and not the curse of the slothful and wicked.

This parable is not identical with the parable of the pounds. The latter was spoken in Jericho to the disciples and the people, to show that Jesus was not going to establish His Kingdom in a few days; on arrival in Jerusalem the parable of the talents was directed to the disciples to exhort them to be prepared, that they

---

1 Romans: chapters 1-8.   2 Effective aorist indicative passive.

might render a good account to the Lord at His second coming. In the parable of the pounds each servant received one pound, and two used them with different degrees of gain; in that of the talents the capital intrusted was different in each of the three servants. Two made good use of their talents, doubling the amount intrusted. In both parables, one gained nothing at all. In the parable of the pounds we have unequal diligence in the use of equal endowments unequally rewarded; in that of the talents we see equal diligence in the use of unequal endowments equally rewarded.[1] In the former, the words of the Master's commendation were different for each one of those who worked; in the latter, identical for the two who gained in equal ratio.

The story of the parable is true to Oriental life, where it was customary for a wealthy man, on leaving his people,[2] to summon his confidential slaves and entrust to them his belongings. Jesus chose this custom to illustrate the fact that He was going away and was about to leave them as His trusted servants, to develop their own personal talents in the service of the Kingdom and develop the Kingdom interests by the use of those talents. They were to be held responsible at His return for the improvement, both of themselves as Kingdom workers as well as the Kingdom work.

First then, He distributes the talents variously, giving to each according to his particular ability;[3] to one five, to another two, and to a third only one. Each had all he was capable of handling and each was held responsible in the measure of his intrusted endowment; for the Master went on his journey and left them solely on their own initiative.

Next we see the trusted servants at work (vv 16-18). Immediately,[4] without a moment of hesitation or idleness, the one who received five talents (about 1,200 pounds) went and traded[5] with them[6] and doubled them before his Master's return. Likewise the one who received two (about 500 pounds) doubled his. But the one who received the one went away and digged in the earth and hid his lord's money.

Time passed, and the next scene is at the return of the owner of these slaves, when he made a reckoning with them, (vv 19-23). Much time had elapsed, giving opportunity for ample demonstration of their respective initiatives and abilities in the work. The one who had received five talents came to him and brought five additional talents, saying: "Master, you entrusted to me five talents. See! I gained another five talents." The Master replied to him. "Well done, excellent and trusty servant. You were trusty

1 Bruce, Parabolic Teachings of Jesus.   2 Apodemon.   3 Dunamin, power, force
4 Revised version.   5 Ergasato, aorist middle, worked with them himself.
6 Instrumental of means.

over a few things, I will set you over many things. Enter into the joy-feast of your lord." The one of two talents also came and said: "Lord, you handed me two talents. See! I gained other two talents!" In the same terms as to the one who received five the Master replied: "Well done, excellent and trusty servant! You have been trust-worthy over a few things, I will set you over many things. Enter into the joy-feast of your lord."

The final scene in the drama is a sad one, when the man of one talent came up to give account (vv 24-30). In the spirit of self-justification he said to the Master: "I knew thee, lord, that thou art a harsh, stern, hard-hearted man,[1] reaping where thou didst not sow, and gathering where thou didst not scatter; and I was afraid and went and hid thy talent in the earth; lo, thou hast thine own." Then the lord answered him and said: "Thou wicked and slothful servant, thou knowest that I reap where I sowed not, and gather where I did not scatter; thou oughtest therefore to have put my money with the exchange-bankers and at my coming I would have received back mine own with interest.[2] Therefore take from him the talent," said the lord, "and give to the one having ten talents. For unto everyone who hath shall be given, and he shall have abundance; but from him that hath not shall be taken away even what he hath. And cast ye out the unprofitable servant into the outer darkness: there shall be the weeping and gnashing of teeth."

"Do business till I come again," was the urgent message of the Lord to His disciples, as He was now on the eve of His departure. There was a tremendous message, in this parable, for His people of all times. It would be long ere the "times of the Gentiles" were filled up and He would return again. The love of many disciples would wax cold. There would be much of profession but little of true discipleship. There would be much work to be done and few faithful workers. Many workers would never come to mature development and not thus succeed well with the work. Good workers would need the strongest encouragement and stimulus to give their best to the Kingdom tasks. Inactive professed workers would need a drastic warning, that if possible they might be awakened and not lose their lives of service.

In the parable, Jesus frankly recognized (1) that men are not equal in natural talents, capacities, abilities nor in opportunities and hereditary advantages. Some are brilliantly endowed with five talents; more are mediocre, having but two; and still more live in obscurity, possessed of only one.

1 Skleros, stony-hearted, grasping, ungenerous.   2 Not with usury but interest—sun tokoi. The exchange-bankers exchanged money for a fee and paid interest on money deposited (Robertson).

(2)   But all are given opportunity to use and improve their talents and are held responsible for their proper use for the Kingdom. Failure to use the utmost diligence in improvement of whatever talents are intrusted is inexcusable. The servant who received five talents went immediately to his task without losing a moment. He was keen in intellect, persistent in effort, and shrewd in management, and succeeded in doubling the capital intrusted to him. The man of two talents was mediocre in mentality but applied himself faithfully and thus doubled his talents. The servant of one talent kept it[1] and made no effort to put it to use for the absent lord, not recognizing that responsibility corresponds to endowment. He might have won the same commendation, and a reward equal to the other two. Every talent is needed and has its place and use in the great total work of the Kingdom. The wicked and slothful servant depreciated his own gifts and so failed in his part of the general task.

(3)   There is a time of reckoning: a time of commendation and reward for the faithful and diligent servants and of reproof and punishment for the wicked and slothful. There is equality in endowment and opportunity, but there is equality in commendation and advancement for the diligent and faithful servants of the Kingdom. The good and trusty servants, whether possessed of five, of two, or even of one, are delighted when they can increase His Kingdom's possessions. Their service is one of loyalty motivated by love for the Master. They are advanced from the position of mere slaves or bond servants to that of friends, sharing in the eternal joy-feast and lordship of the Master. Their capital is increased from the little to the much in the coming Kingdom. On the contrary, the wicked servant has the wrong view of his Master. He fears him and thinks of him as hard and selfish; he dares not take any risk on behalf of the Kingdom and leaves his intrusted talent hidden in the ground. He passes his time in idleness and sloth and in due time faces his lord, without any show of apology or repentance, but defiantly, and hears the curse pronounced upon his worthlessness and loss of the very talent which had been given him. With him the day of opportunity closes and the words of eternal loss are spoken without recourse. "Take the talent from him and give it to the one who has ten, and cast out the unprofitable servant into outer darkness where there shall be the weeping of eternal loss and gnashing of teeth of hopeless rebellion." Such is the warning Jesus would give to professed disciples and workers who show not fruits for their services.

1 Perfect active participle showing he still had it (Robertson's Word Pictures).

2. The Judgment scene at the coming of Christ (Matt. 25:31-46).

Jesus concluded His wonderful prophetic sermon, presenting the solemn and august scene of the final Judgment. When we remember that these words, which open for us the curtain of time and eternity and reveal to us in a glorious imagery things to come, were spoken just three days before Jesus went away, they become even more sublime. Matthew alone preserved for us this glorious revelation of Jesus—he who had been a publican.

"When the Son of Man," said Jesus, "shall come in all his glory, he shall sit on the throne of his glory." No longer will He be a homeless wanderer, nor even an earthly King, according to current Messianic tradition. The Messiah is to sit upon a throne, surrounded by His holy angels, to judge the nations gathered before Him, making awards for eternity. Such an image of the Judgment was familiar to the Jews in Messianic prophecy. God was to judge the nations in the valley of Jehosaphat.[1] The reference there was to the Gentile nations. But it is hardly conceivable that Jesus should here be referring solely to the Gentiles. The teachings of the New Testament as a whole would oblige us to consider this great Judgment to include all men of all nations, who will then be divided, like the shepherd divides the sheep from the goats— an image familiar in the life of Palestine. Jesus is set forth in the Bible as the Mediatorial King and He so considered Himself in this image under the often used title, Son of Man. This image of the great Shepherd, dividing the good, symbolized by the sheep, from the bad, typified by the goats, is but a homely illustration of a sublime and august spiritual reality of the future, when there shall be a separation between the good to the place of preference (right) and the bad to the place of rejection (left) for eternity.

The King-Judge will first speak to those on His right, calling them blessed of His Father, and inviting them to enter and possess the inheritance of the Kingdom, made ready for them from eternity. The basis of this marvelous judgment is revealed in the spiritual character of the judged, as evidenced in their merciful and benevolent ministries to the King and Judge. With surprise and modest humility, in keeping with their Christ-like character, they asked: "When have we ever ministered unto Thee in any of the beautiful ways mentioned?" Then the King reveals to them that every smallest act of charity in giving sustenance to the hungry and thirsty, every act of hospitality tendered to one of His obscure disciples, every gift of clothing to His poor ones, every sympathetic visit to a sick brother of His, every help rendered His

1 Joel's prophecy about the judgment of the heathen nations.

persecuted followers, was as a ministry done to Him personally.
He thus identifies Himself with the least of His brethren in the
Messianic family.

But His words to those on His left were different (vv 41-45).
"Depart from me, ye cursed, into everlasting fire prepared for the
devil and his angels." These words would seem hard in the mouth
of the benevolent King-Judge were it not for the fact that the
judgment was but inevitable consequence of the character of
the judged. The reason for the terrible sentence of condemnation was exactly the lack of all merciful and benevolent ministries in lives devoid of all unselfish charity toward the world of
men, the Messianic brotherhood, and the King himself. Here was
a tragic surprise, and the greatest part of the tragedy was that the
sentenced did not recognize or confess to their selfish, hard-hearted,
cruel neglect of Jesus and His needy ones.

Hell is a reality. It was prepared, not for men, but for the
devil and his angels (Jude 6; II Peter 2:4; Rev. 12:7). If fire is
but an image in the conception of hell, the reality is far worse.
Men go to hell against God's wishes. He wills not the destruction
of any man. Men do not *inherit* hell with its punishment but are
separated to it by their characters. They gravitate to their own
place through conscious sin committed against God and man. In
this judgment the sins of omission stand out beyond the overt sins
of transgression or commission. "Verily I say unto you: inasmuch
as ye did it not unto one of these least, ye did it not unto me."
There is a present judgment going on all the time. The separation
of the good from the bad is inevitable. Man determines his own
destiny by his conscious choices and acts. Character is eternal. The
wicked character belongs in hell, the place of eternal rebellion
and endless regret, hopelessness, and despair. The son of the Kingdom, clothed with the righteousness of Christ, inherits the estate of
the blessed. He would not be a congenial companion in hell. And
there is a hell as eternal as the heavens.

CHAPTER XXX

THE LAST PASSOVER AND THE FIRST SUPPER

(Harm. §§ 140-149)

It was just two days now until Jesus would celebrate with His apostles the last Passover and institute the Lord's Supper. The paschal meal is not a part of the Christian system. The Supper was to be memorial of the Lord's body to be broken three days hence and His blood to be shed on Calvary.

1. Jesus had been preparing the disciples gradually from the very beginning of His ministry, by various hints, for this hour of tragic suffering and death. He now clearly reveals to them on the return to Bethany, that after two days, He is appointed by the eternal counsels of God to be delivered over to His enemies to be crucified (Matt. 26:1-5).[1] His enemies were alert, watching the thousands of pilgrims pouring into Jerusalem from all parts of the land, bringing with them materials for the construction of their booths. They understood that among the Galileans there would be many friends of Jesus. They had already been taking counsel how they might entrap Him. They now call together the chief priests and the elders in informal session of the Sanhedrin in the palace of Caiaphas, who had given utterance days before to the definite expression, that it was "convenient that one man die rather than that the nation perish." This was to give the official sanction of the high priest to the idea of putting Jesus to death. They now met in informal session, not in the legal place of meeting, the Temple, nor within legal hours, but at night in the palace of Caiaphas to the west of the city. They had met for the purpose of arranging a secret plot to take Jesus by subtlety[2] and kill Him. But they were restrained by their fear of the people and said: "Not during the feast, lest a tumult arise among the people." That, then, was the lobby-decision of the *august* Sanhedrin—a decision worthy of the lowest politics.

2. At the feast in the house of Simon, the leper, Mary of Bethany anoints Jesus for His burial (Mark 14:3-9; Matt. 26:6-13; Jno. 12:2-8).

Arriving in Bethany after this day of intense activity, in meeting the various groups of His enemies in the Temple, who sought to entrap Him with subtle questions, followed by His great denunciation of them, and His prophetic discourse on the Mount of Olives, Jesus found to His great consolation that many sincere friends of His had made for Him a feast in the house of Simon, formerly a

---

1 Mark 14:1, 2; Luke 22:1, 2.　　　2 Dolo, deceipt.

leper. It was natural that Martha, from what we know of her habitual bent, was called upon to take the superintendence in the service of the feast. She had previously assumed that good role in the
domestic program, when Mary sat in devotion at the feet of Jesus
drinking in His teaching.[1] Martha was practical and efficient, and
while she did not rise to the heights of devotion that her sister
Mary attained, she loved her Lord and was glad to serve in the
humbler place. It must have been a remarkable experience to
take one's place on the reclining-couch at the table with Lazarus,
who had been brought back to life from the grave after being dead
four days. All the more thrilling would be the fact that Jesus was
there, the one who had raised Lazarus from the dead—now the
guest of honor at the feast—what a Guest! Others who reclined at
the table were Simon, the host, who had been cured by Jesus of
leprosy—a living death—and many others who had been ministered
to in body and soul by the great Wonder-Worker. These were
sincere friends who now wished to honor Him whom they loved,
taking their very lives in their hands to do so.[2]

Mary, the younger sister of Martha, knowing of the bitter
antagonism of the enemies of Jesus, sensed the consequent peril in
which He now walked and with quick intelligence and intuition
anticipated the tragedy of His death. It was not the custom of the
Jews for women to sit down at the table with the invited guests at
such suppers. Mary came with a flask, made out of the white ala-
baster-stone, holding twelve ounces of very costly[3] genuine spike-
nard[4] perfume. With lavish abandon she broke the narrow neck
of the vase and poured the nard out profusely on Jesus' head as
He reclined on the table-couch; and then turning, anointed with
the same liberality His feet, wiping them with her hair,[5] like the
sinner-woman in the house of Simon, the Pharisee. Ordinarily it
was considered immodest for a woman to wear her hair loose, this
fact giving rise to the supposition by some that Mary of Bethany
was rescued by Jesus from a life of shame early in His ministry.
This act, however, does not brand Mary as a woman of loose
character, nor does it identify her with Mary of Magdala, the
woman from whom Jesus cast out seven devils. In Mary's complete
devotion, she threw all mere custom to the winds, in a love of absolute abandon. The house was filled with the odour of the perfume and the whole world with the aroma of her love. Such gifts
were given to kings.[6] Only such a gift would be a worthy expres-

1 Luke 10:38-42.   2 The Sanhedrin had already given order calling on informers
        in order to arrest Jesus, and were in session even at the hour of the feast
        plotting how they might take him.
3 The price of a day-laborer for a year.
4 Nard is the head or spike of a very fragrant East India plant.
5 Instrumental plural.   6 It was one of five presents sent by Cambyses to the King
        of Ethiopia. (Herodotus 3:20)—quoted from Robertson's Word Pictures.

sion of her deep devotion and profound love for the Master. It was customary to anoint the heads of Rabbis and special guests at marriage feasts;[1] but Mary anointed with the most expensive perfume both the head and the feet of her Lord.

This devoted servant was criticized for her act of sincere love and extreme devotion. Judas led in the criticism and it was easy for others to join in, once the critical word was started. He said it was a dead loss[2] to use all this money for mere sentiment. John reveals the fact that it was Judas who started the criticism. But others weakly fell into the endorsement of what he said. "Why," they asked, "was this ointment not sold for three hundred pence and given to the poor?" This man from Kerioth was the treasurer of the apostolic company, and John adds that he was a petty thief, stealing from the bag. He certainly was not known for his charity to the poor. He did not love Jesus, else he would not have been inconsiderate, trampling under foot rudely the Master's most delicate feelings by his hard words of condemnation of Mary's tender and thoughtful act of devotion. Later John and others saw this dastardly criticism of Judas in the light of his betrayal of Jesus and so interpreted it.[3]

Jesus with tact and revelation of the deep meaning and high value of this act of devotion, defended Mary: "Let her alone!" He said. "Why are you troubling her?" It was a beautiful deed expressing her heart's affection. "She has wrought a good work upon me," He added. Then turning to Judas with emotion He said: "Suffer her to keep it against the day of my burying. For the *poor* you have always with you but *me* you do not have always." Thus Jesus took the words from the mouth of Judas and taught an eternal lesson as to the duty of the disciples to be charitable toward the poor. At the same time, He interpreted the thought of the devoted heart of Mary and confirmed her conviction that in a few brief hours He would offer up His life in sacrifice for all mankind. Mary had with rare intuition grasped the whole desperate situation and brought the perfume of her loving heart to pour it out in tribute on her Lord, in unforgotten affection. This simple act stands out as an eternal monument to the devotion and faith of her who did it. Jesus pronounced upon it the highest eulogy and declared: "She did all she could. She has anointed my body for the burying. Verily, I say to you: Wherever the Gospel[4] is preached in all the world, what she did shall be spoken of as a memorial to her."

1 Geikie's Life of Christ.   2 Apoleia.   3 John 12:4.   4 Good news.

3. Judas, stung by the rebuke, bargains with the rulers to betray Jesus (Mark 14:10, 11; Matt. 26:14-16; Luke 22:3-6).

Jesus' commendation of Mary and rebuke of Judas cut the man of Kerioth to the heart. Satan now began to enter[1] in and take complete possession of that heart with evil feelings, desires, and suggestions; and soon Judas was on his way to seek the chief priests and agree with them[2] about some plan to betray his Lord. Even while the supper was in progress in the home of Simon, the Sanhedrin was gathered in the palace of Caiaphas,[3] planning how they might take Jesus and kill him. Judas slipped out from the supper and arrived at the palace at the opportune moment for his fell purpose. The captains of the temple-guard announced[4] that Judas, one of the twelve apostles of Jesus, had an important proposal to make. He would deliver Jesus in the midst of the feast but without the possibilities of a popular tumult or protest by the people. When those astute politicians understood the offer of Judas to betray Jesus, they were filled[5] with exultation, that one of the twelve should betray Him. Judas had planned to dictate the terms under which he would deliver his Lord into their hands, but he unconsciously delivered himself instead into their power, when he revealed his treachery, and so left them to dictate the price.

"What are ye willing to give me and I will deliver Him unto you?" he demanded sullenly. But his inquiry was received with complacency and hypocritical self-satisfaction by the Sanhedrists. They bartered with him and he quickly consented to their terms— thirty pieces of silver, the price of a slave. Evidently he was disillusioned and disappointed at the price, but what could he do to remedy it? They weighed him out the silver and he planned with them the best time[6] and place for the arrest, to avoid any tumult of the people. He well knew the accustomed haunts of his Lord and it ought to be an easy matter. Little did he anticipate the dire consequences of this treacherous act for himself, just two days hence!

4. Preparation for the paschal meal (Mark 14:12-16; Matt. 26: 17-19; Luke 22:7-13).

On the first day of the feast of unleavened bread,[7] when they were accustomed[8] to sacrifice the Passover with Jesus, the disciples came and asked Him: "Where do you[9] wish that we go and make ready that you may eat the passover?" In response, He detailed two of the apostles, Peter and John, and quietly instructed them, conscious as He was of the treachery of Judas and the

---

1 Ingressive aorist indicative.   2 Second aorist indicative middle of suntithemi, see force of middle, he acted on his own initiative.   3 Illegal in time and place.
4 Dawson, Life of Christ, in loco.   5 Second aorist passive indicative, ingressive aorist
6 Eukairos, a favorable opportunity or opportune time.
7 This was Thursday, the 14 of Nisan, the Day of Preparation.   8 Imp. of customary action.   9 Ex. 12:18; cf. Mark 14:12, second person singular of verb.

necessity of keeping the place of the celebration a secret so as to avoid the intrusion of His enemies in that hour—a wise provision. The Master had evidently had some understanding with John Mark, or more probably his father. Naturalistic explanation will not account however, for another part of the incident. The two were told that they would be met by a man bearing a pitcher. Men did not ordinarily bear pitchers in those times in Jerusalem, and they would easily single out such a man. Peter and John were told to follow this man, whose name Jesus kept a secret for a reason not announced in the group, though it must have been sensed by Judas. He would hardly dare follow the two for fear of being suspected. His conscience was already accusing him. Jesus further instructed them that, when they came into the house of the man with the pitcher, they were to say to the house-ruler:[1] "The Master saith, 'My time is at hand; I keep the passover at thy house with my disciples, *alone*. Where is my guest-chamber, where I shall eat the passover?'" They were told that the Master of the house would at once show them a room already furnished with mats, table, couches, all the necessary furnishings. They went and found everything just as Jesus had said to them and made ready for the Passover meal.

We are not told where or how Jesus spent Wednesday, since the supper in Simon's house was Tuesday evening. The best supposition is that He used this day to get some moments of rest and quiet meditation with His disciples and intimate friends, perhaps in the home of His Bethany friends, Lazarus and his two sisters. On Thursday morning Peter and John, according to the custom, would go to the Temple and provide for the lamb, which they must purchase and take to the priests who had to pass upon it. Early in the afternoon the lamb would be killed in the Temple court, offered at the altar, and, after the blood was poured out at the altar and a certain part of the Lamb was reserved for the sacrifice, the rest would be wrapped in the skin and taken home. Before sunset, the carcass would be roasted in barbecue fashion and made ready for the meal at the blasts of the trumpet just at sunset. The apostles must provide also for the wine, unleavened cakes, bitter herbs, and the charosheth or paste of crushed fruits moistened with vinegar—symbolic of the clay with which the Israelites made brick in Egypt.[2]

At the place already located—probably the home of John Mark's mother and father—the two disciples prepared the meal and then wended their way back to Bethany with sad and foreboding hearts to announce that all was in readiness.

---

1 Oikodespotes, late word for despotes, oikou (Robertson).
2 David Smith, In the Days of His Flesh.

5. Jesus partakes of the paschal meal with the Twelve and rebukes their jealousy (Mark 14:17; Matt. 26:20; Luke 22:14-16; 24-30).

It was permissible to celebrate the Passover at home.[1] The disciples had hoped that Jesus would choose the Bethany home and not return to Jerusalem, thus placing Himself in the hands of His enemies. But, strictly speaking, Jerusalem was the place appointed by the law for the feast. Jesus would personally minister for the first time in His life[2] at this last paschal meal, and institute the new regime symbolized by the Lord's Supper—all in the city of Jerusalem.

Thursday had been a day of dread anticipation for the apostolic group. Judas had slipped back after his barter with the Sanhedrists on Tuesday night. Wednesday and Thursday were bitter days for the traitor, his conscience gnawing within and the understanding eyes of the Master upon him from without. As the sunset hour approached on Thursday, the 14th of Nisan,[3] the Master started for Jerusalem with the Twelve. He had been denounced by the hierarchy. The Temple officers were seeking His arrest. The people who were enthusiastic a few days ago about His Messianic Kingdom were now indifferent, and the apostolic group would pass through the crowded streets unnoticed.

When they arrived at the house of "the goodman," they found the large Upper Room (Aliyah) furnished and ready, with all that was necessary for the feast. The owner of the house was certainly a disciple and might have been John Mark's father or perhaps Joseph of Arimathea. Whoever it was, he had so lavishly prepared the large room that the apostles were impressed with the material abundance, and forgot themselves in their eagerness to occupy the places nearest the Master. Jesus allowed this contentiousness[4] to pass unheeded for the time.

When they were all arranged on the couches around three sides of the table, according to custom, Jesus began solemnly: "I desired very much[5] to eat this passover with you before I suffer; for I tell you I will not any more eat of it until it is fulfilled in the Kingdom of God."

Then with tact and gentleness He reproves their contentious spirit. "The Kings of the Gentiles lord it over them," He suggested in a parabolic way, "and those exercising their authority take the name of Benefactors.[6] But ye shall not be so: but he that is greater among you, let him become as the younger; and he that is chief, as he that doth serve. For which is greater," He

1 Geikie's Life of Christ, p. 434. 2 Edersheim, Life and Times of Jesus.
3 Jesus was crucified on Friday, 15th Nisan, Robertson's Harmony. pp. 274-284; David Smith, In the Days of His Flesh. App. VIII
4 Fondness for contention. 5 Epithumei, instrumental, with desire.
6 Euergetai, well-doers of God.

asked pointedly, "the guest reclining or the servant serving? Is not the guest who is reclining greater?" He asked in irony, "but I[1] am among you as a servant." That He had taken the place of one serving, they were all aware. This had been His example before them always; yet even now they had shown their indisposition to follow that example by their spirit of contentiousness. Peter and John, who should properly have served as hosts, were reclining. Did they present the customary basin of water for cleaning the feet of the others as they entered the room that evening? Their Master had emptied Himself of the prerogatives of the deity and taken the form of a slave in order to serve human-kind.[2] He would teach them that "true greatness is in service not in rank."

But He further tenderly reminds them that despite their con-tentiousness, they are the ones who have stuck[3] by Him through His trials. Once more He asserts His confidence in them. As the Father had permanently assigned to Him the royal power of the Kingdom, so He now assigns to them the right of eating and drink-ing at His table in His Kingdom, and of sitting on thrones judg-ing the twelve tribes of Israel. But these would not be temporal thrones.[4] This He made plain to them.

6. The lesson in humble service reenforced and exemplified in the footwashing (Jno. 13:1-20).

While they were partaking of the paschal meal beginning at sunset or shortly after, Jesus exemplified in parabolic act a great fundamental lesson on humility and service, to illustrate the spirit which must characterize His apostles as they went forth to the Kingdom campaign. He performed this symbolic act in the full consciousness that He was shortly to be offered up in sacrifice, fulfilling the Passover type. It was with peculiar tenderness for His disciples that He approached that hour. He turned His eyes from Calvary to these who were His best friends and filled His heart with loving expressions for them, "loving them to the end." His life was a fight to the finish; but toward His disciples it was "love to the finish."[5]

It was "during the supper"[6] that Jesus performed the remark-able act which was to exemplify to His apostolic group the spirit which would win the world. He was conscious of the fact that the devil had gotten permanent possession[7] of the heart of Judas, having already (ede) cast the seed purpose[8] into that heart to betray Him. The Saviour was also fully conscious[9] of His divine

---

1 Personal pronouns in place of emphasis.   2 Phil. 2:5-11.
3 Diamemenekotes, perfect participle bearing the idea of permanence, reenforced with the preposition intensifying the meaning.
4 Epi with the genitive, place denoting contact.   5 Eis, telos, to complete or to end.
6 Idou genomenou, present middle participle, the supper was in progress.
7 Beblekotos, perfect participle denoting permanence.
8 Purpose clause with hina and second aorist subjunctive.
9 Eidos, absolute knowledge, not mere knowledge of experience.

origin, nature, and mission, which entitled Him to the highest honors, yet performs the menial act of washing the feet of the disciples.

a. Details of the foot-washing (vv 5-11).

The foot-washing came after the initiation of the paschal meal which ran after the following routine: (1) a benediction, (2) cup of wine, (3) the hands of the company washed, the master of the feast passing the basin while reciting a prayer, (4) bitter herbs dipped in sauce and eaten, (5) the lamb brought in with other portions of the meal, (6) a benediction and second eating of bitter herbs, (7) a second cup of wine with questions and answers as to the origin of the feast, (8) singing of the first part of the Hallel (Pss. 113, 114) followed by a benediction, (9) the master of the feast washes his hands and makes a sop by wrapping a bit of lamb with unleavened bread in bitter herbs and dipping it in the sauce, for each one present in turn, (10) each eats as much as he likes, finishing with a piece of lamb, (11) a third cup of wine after washing hands, (12) singing of second part of the Hallel (Pss. 115-118) in conclusion, (13) a fourth cup of wine.[1]

It was after the initiation of this routine of a highly specialized symbolism, and probably when the first benediction and first cup of wine had been disposed of, that Jesus substituted in the place of the washing of hands—for the purpose of teaching a special lesson—the symbolic act of the foot-washing. This customary act of feasts had probably been neglected on their entrance. Peter and John, thinking that the time of the establishment of the Kingdom was near—for had not Jesus just said so?[2]—did not wish to take the menial part of servants, and hastened with the others to occupy the chief couches at the table. Such conduct seems almost puerile, if we did not reflect that it has been repeatedly exemplified in history in those who are among the chief apostles. Jesus administered a rebuke in act rather than in words —something that would burn its way into their memory forever. They were aware of His deity and Messianic dignity; but now behold the marvelous spectacle—Jesus washing their feet!

He rises[3] from the supper, lays aside His cape,[4] and taking a towel girds Himself. Then He pours water into a basin and begins to wash[5] their feet, and to dry them with the towel with which He was girded. At first they were amazed and looked on speechlessly as He went from one to another. It was a long jump of their imagination, from the highest places in the Kingdom to this low menial service! It took some moments for them to realize what was happening.

---

1 Philip Vollmer, Life of Christ, p 237.   2 Luke 22.29, 30.   3 Vivid present.
4 Himation, a kind of sleeveless overcoat or cape.   5 Ingressive aorist middle.

Jesus comes[1] to Simon Peter, who by this time has collected his wits. "Lord, washest thou my feet?" Instinctively, but reverently, he rebelled. "What I do you do not understand now," Jesus observed, "you will learn by experience later on after these things." Peter's aversion to his Master's humiliation in such a menial service quickly found vehement expression: "You will never wash my feet, never!![2]" he exclaimed. His protest now passed to what amounted to refusal, as he drew his feet back[3] and left the Master standing, basin in hand. Jesus met this act with a loving but firm reply: "If I wash you not," He said gravely, "you have no part with me." Peter had not understood all that was involved. He had not reflected that to deny Jesus the right to wash his feet was to contradict the whole principle of the self-emptying[4] life of the Master in the incarnation. Peter thought such menial service degrading and incompatible with the Messianic dignity. He must learn that the very basis of all the power of Jesus to wash away the sin-stains from the soul of man depended on His humiliation to the point of dying on the cross. Simon had assumed again the attitude of superior knowledge which brought from the Master, once before, the painful words: "You are not thinking about these things as God thinks but as men think." He had judged that the Messiah ought not to suffer and die;[5] he refused now, in his impetuous but unthinking love, to accept with reverent submission the humble service expressive of the Christ-mission[6] Simon must be willing to let his Lord descend to the lowest depth of humiliation in order to *serve*, and must recognize that such humiliation was not incompatible with sublime Messianic dignity. He must also learn that the first condition of discipleship is self-surrender.[7] That disciple saw now that the deeper mystic fellowship between the Sanctifier and the sanctified, between the Master and the disciple, depended on self-surrender in the disciple. Alarmed by the warning, he now springs to the other extreme: "Lord, then wash not only my feet but my hands and my head," he suggested. How characteristic of Peter—impulsive and unstable. But some day he will be a rock! Jesus assures him that he has not failed to the extent of forfeiting his discipleship, (as Judas would do). His purpose was correct and his motive was good. Jesus would have to correct his impulses and judgment.[8]

The Teacher dealt patiently with His disciple, who loved Him much. The custom of washing the feet of the incoming guests now

1 Dramatic present.   2 Strong double negative, Weymouth's Translation, with first aorist active subjunctive.   3 Bernard and Dods.   4 Phil. 2:5-11.   5 Matt. 16:22.
6 Bruce's Training of the Twelve, p. 346-7.   7 Wescott, com, on John, in loco
8 Studies in the Inner Life of Jesus, A. E. Garvie, pp. 365ff.

served Him for illustration. His deeper meaning Peter would readily grasp. "He who has bathed needs only to have his feet washed; he is clean all over." One who has once been purged in the "laver of regeneration" only needs after that to wash off daily "the soil of the way." Then Jesus adds, remembering that not all the apostles were complete in this deeper sense: "And you are clean, but not all of you." John explains the reason for this parenthesis—the traitor was there.

b. Jesus explains His act (vv 12-20).

After finishing the foot-washing, Jesus took His cape and assumed His place on the couch. "Do you recognize," He said, "what I have done[1] to you?" Did they understand the meaning of His act? "You call me Teacher and Lord, and you say well, for that is what I am. If[2] I, then, have given you the example, being your final and authoritative Teacher and your rightful owner, you also ought to follow my example and wash one another's feet." He thus presents Himself to them as an example "under their very eyes."[3] It was His purpose that they should follow this example.[4] In support of this He adds: "Verily, verily I say to you, The servant is not greater than his Lord; neither is the apostle greater than the one sending him. If[5] you know these things—as you surely do— you are to be congratulated if you do them habitually."[3] Such progressive activity in humble service of the Lord's Kingdom and their fellow-disciples would bring happiness, and more important still, their Lord's approval.

Again He reminds them—He is not saying that all of them understand these things. Obedience is the organ of spiritual vision, and spiritual understanding comes through experience. Just knowing does not bring happiness nor are we to be congratulated when we occasionally do our duty, but when right action is habitual with us. Jesus was fully conscious of the fact that when He chose the Twelve, one of them did not fully demonstrate right character and obedient disposition. The divine purpose set forth in the Scriptures was to be fulfilled through Judas, who used his power of free choice wrongly. Even now, as the traitor sat at the table with Jesus, he was seeking in his heart to trip Him up,[7] like a wrestler taking advantage in a wrestling match. He was in a mortal grip with Jesus, to throw Him down into the power and grasp of His enemies. His close companionship made worse his sin of faithlessness.[8] Even a wily Arab robber would honorably

1 Perfect active indicative with humin.   2 Condition of the first class assumed to be true.   3 Hupodeigma, shown under, i.e., under the very eyes.
4 Hina with subjunctive in purpose clause.   5 Condition of the first class followed by another clause with third class condition.   Present subjunctive in third class condition.   7 The metaphor is that of kicking or tripping with the heel, Robertson's Word Pictures.   8 A. E. Garvie, Studies in the Inner Life of Jesus.

guard the law of hospitality; not to sit down to eat bread with anyone and immediately afterwards betray him. Judas must have felt
condemned by these searching words. Jesus was warning his disciples now before the betrayal took place, in order that[1] they
might believe whenever it did come to pass, and have an unshaken faith in Him. He again identifies Himself with His apostles
for their assurance in this crisis. In the campaign of the Kingdom,
anyone who received at any time His messenger, would be blessed
as one receiving Him personally; and such a host would be receiving God as his guest.

Thus Jesus sets forth, in His explanation of the meaning of
His act in washing the disciples' feet, the ideal of humility in service as the real road to true greatness and pre-eminence. The disciples had been contending for the chief places in the supper and in
the Kingdom; they were to learn that the greatest in the Kingdom
must be the servant of all.

7. Jesus openly declares Judas as the traitor (Mark 14:18-21;
Matt. 26:21-25; Luke 22:21-23; Jno. 13:21-30).

After the washing of the hands, for which in this case the foot-
washing was substituted, came the fourth step in the routine of the
meal—the eating of bitter herbs, dipped with bread in sauce
and made into sop. Suddenly Jesus paused, greatly agitated in
spirit.[2] In His hand He held the bitter herbs, symbol of the bitterness of bondage in Egypt. He now startled the disciples with
sad words, solemnly pronounced:

"Truly, truly, I tell you, one of you will betray me. Even one
of you now sitting at the table and eating with me is already engaged[3] in plans to betray me." A deep and sorrowful silence fell
upon them. They began to look[4] around at one another with anxious
and suspicious looks. "The Son of Man," added Jesus. "is moving
on toward the horizon of His destiny, but woe to that man who is
to be the agent in His betrayal!" Then the disciples began to try
to find out among themselves who might be the one about to do
such a thing. Sad and perplexed, but unable to find out who the
traitor was, they were filled with sorrow and began to say unto
Him one by one: "Is it I? Is it I, Lord?" "It is one of the twelve"
replied Jesus, "one that dippeth[5] with me in the dish shall betray
me. The Son of Man must go, according to the predetermined
counsels of God, but the man by whom He is to be betrayed would
better never have been born."[6] Then Judas, stirred by these terrible words of warning, being near the Lord to catch every word,
nervously whispered: "Is it I, Rabbi?" Jesus replied also in a low
voice: "Thou hast said."

1 Hina with the subjunctive in a purpose clause.   2 Locative of sphere.
3 Progressive present (Luke 22:21).   4 Incohative imperfect.
5 They all dipped into the dish with their hands having no knives, forks or spoons.
6 Second class condition contrary to fact.

Reclining on the couch[1] to the right of the Master was John, the disciple most intimate and most loved by the Master. Peter nodded to him saying: "Tell us whom He means." That disciple leaning back thus on the bosom of Jesus, whispered to Him: "Lord who is it?" Jesus replies: "That is he to whom I shall give the sop after dipping it." By Oriental custom it was a special honor for the host to offer anyone a tid-bit and indicate that he was considered a favoured guest. Jesus used kindness toward Judas to the last, even in the hour of betrayal. Then Jesus took bread and having dipped it gave it to Judas. But when Judas took the bread, at that same moment Satan took complete possession of him. He became furious because he had been discovered and exposed. Therefore Jesus said to him: "What you are doing,[2] do more quickly."[3] No man at the table knew why Jesus spoke this to him. Some thought naturally that, since he was the treasurer of the apostolic group and carried the money bag, Jesus had told him to buy what was needed for the festival or perhaps to give something to the poor. So Judas went out immediately, and it was night. Alas! such a night for him! It was dark and his errand was one of darkness. And it was also a dark night for Jesus and for his disciples too!

8. After Judas departs, Jesus initiates His final discourses and warns the disciples against desertion, while all protest their loyalty (Mark 14:27-31; Matt. 26:31-35; Luke 22:31-38; Jno. 13: 31-38).

They were yet in the midst of the supper, when the sad interruption, the revelation of the traitor, came. Jesus felt relieved when Judas was gone. He could henceforth speak freely to the faithful eleven. "Now the Son of Man is glorified[4] and God is glorified in him," He exclaimed. The traitor was on his way to carry out his conspiracy with the enemies for the arrest. Jesus had crossed the Rubicon and felt a sense of exultation. "God will glorify him in himself[5] and he will glorify him immediately." It was a matter of hours now until He would have passed successfully the experience of the cross and that would be followed soon by the Ascension.

As they went on eating the paschal lamb—which must be totally consumed[6]—Jesus talked to them in familiar homily about the hours out just ahead. He initiates in informal conversational style His last great discourse to the disciples. "My own little children,"[7] He began tenderly, "I am to be with you only a little

1 Periphrastic imperfect, protracted and progressive action.
2 Present progressive, linear action.   3 Tachion, comparative degree.
4 Aorist an accomplished fact.   5 Reflective pronoun.
6 Robertson's Word Pictures.   7 Diminutive, technia.

longer; then you will look for me, and as I told the Jewish leaders I tell you now, where I go you cannot come. I give you a new command—to love one another:[1] as I loved you, you are to love one another."[2] His was a great sacrificial love. Their real brotherly love would be the primary basis for the revelation of Him to the world. "But where art thou going, Master?" said Peter. "I am going where you cannot follow at present," replied Jesus; "Later on you shall follow me." "Lord," said Peter, "why cannot I follow thee right now? I will lay down my life for thee. I am ready to accompany thee both to prison and to death." "Will *you* lay down your life for *me*?" replied the Master. "Truly, truly I tell you, before the cock crows, you will have denied me three times over."[3] Then Jesus, addressing the impulsive Peter and calling him by his old name, said: "Simon, Simon, behold Satan asked to have thee that he might sift thee as wheat; but I made supplication for thee that thy faith may not fail; and do thou, when thou hast turned again, establish thy brethren." But Peter protested to the last: "If I must die with thee I will in no wise deny thee." And so did all the others. But Jesus startled them with the repeated warning: "All of you shall stumble at me in the course of this night." Furthermore, He bases His affirmation on the Scripture: "I will smite the shepherd and the sheep shall be scattered abroad."[4]

The disciples would need a long period of discipline before coming to maturity. The example of Peter was typical. It was dealt with frankly and prophetically by Jesus that all might get the benefit. Satan would pass him through a sieve of temptations, but through the intercession of Jesus the chaff would be separated from the wheat. Peter would deny his Lord but he would repent and come back, an humbler and wiser man. He would later become a great under-shepherd of the Lord's flock and follow his Master through a martyr's death on a cross to celestial glory. He would follow Him to prison and to death after his recovery.

Jesus pauses to remind the eleven of the seriousness of changed conditions since they went out to the campaign in Galilee. They needed to remember now how He stood by them in that campaign.[5] "When I sent you forth with neither purse nor wallet, nor sandals, did you want for anything?" The answer was obviously "No!"[6] Now the conditions are changed. They must be on the alert and make use of every resource. They are not to repel force by violence, but be ready to defend the cause at every

1 Present tense linear action, keep on loving.   2 See Wemouth's version.
3 Future middle indicative. Peter would do this of his own accord.   4 Zech. 13:7.
5 Matt. 10:10; Luke 10:4; 12:33.   6 Me, expects negative answer.

cost. "Now, he that hath a purse let him take it up, and likewise a wallet; and he that hath no purse let him sell his cape and buy a short-sword.[1] For I tell you that this that hath been written must be fulfilled in me 'And with transgressors he was reckoned';[2] for what concerneth me is having its fulfillment."[3] The disciples took His words literally. "Lord, see, here are two swords," they said. Peter used one of those short-swords a little later and would have cut off the head of Malchus, probably, if he had not made a miscalculated stroke. But Jesus rebuked him sternly at that hour and, healing the severed ear of Malchus, told Simon to put his sword in the sheath, declaring that those who took up the sword would die by the sword. At this present moment with sad irony Jesus simply dismissed the subject: "It is sufficient," He declared. Poor, faithful, dull disciples; when will they rise above bald literalism! Jesus never had such a conception of His ministry. Never once did He manifest the slightest tendency to use armed force to establish a Kingdom. He several times, and particularly when He fed the five thousand, refused armed support for His Messianic campaign.[4]

9. Jesus institutes the memorial Supper (Mark 14:22-25; Matt. 26:26-29; Luke 22:17-20; I Cor. 11:23-26).

The paschal meal was far advanced.[5] For a second time the bitter herbs had been eaten, preceded by giving of thanks. The paschal lamb had also been consumed when Jesus, making use of the part in the program where explanation of the origin of the feast was in order, instituted the Memorial Supper, which was a near symbol of the great anti-type corresponding to the Passover. As they were eating, He took a loaf and giving thanks, broke it and gave it to them and said: "Take ye, eat it, this is my body which is given for you; do this in remembrance of me." Then later on after the meal He took a little cup[6] of wine which was handed to Him[7] and again giving thanks said: "Take this and divide it among yourselves, for I say unto you, I will not drink henceforth of the fruit of the vine[8] until the Kingdom of God is come." Then He added in explanation: "This is my blood of the new covenant. It is poured out for you and for many unto the remission of sins (Ex. 24:8; Lev. 4:18-20; Jer. 31:31; Zech. 9:11). This do as oft as ye drink it in remembrance of me. For as often as ye eat of this bread and drink the cup, ye proclaim the Lord's death till He come."

1 Machaira, short sword used in hand to hand fighting in ancient warfare.
2 Isaiah 53:12.   3 Present indicative, action in progress.   4 The mission and
    Message of Jesus by H. D. A. Major, T. W. Manson, C. J. Wright, p. 286 (1938)
5 David Smith, In the Days of His Flesh.   6 Potarion, diminutive.
7 Luke 22:17, four cups passed.   8 The word "wine" is not used in the Gospels, but
    "fruit of the vine."

The Supper was a new institution. It, like baptism, is symbolic of the life in Jesus. Christ left us only two church ordinances; but the two cover symbolically the whole Christian life. Baptism stands at the beginning and symbolizes the spiritual transformation which takes place in the new birth—the death to sin and resurrection to a new life. The Memorial Supper represents the means of a continuation of the disciple's life through the continuous assimilation of Christ who is our bread of life—our Passover. The Supper commemorates the atoning death of Jesus, but at the same time symbolizes the life—flesh and blood—which must be eaten[1] by the disciple for the sustenance of his spiritual life. The life of Jesus—His example, personality, ideals, teachings—must be appropriated by the believer in a constant process. The Supper is a memorial of the redemptive death which sums up and consummates the sacrificial life of Jesus. The testator of the new covenant or testament died. In His blood is to be found the new covenant. "Fix your eyes on Calvary," Jesus would say to His disciples, "for it is in the atoning power of the blood that you are to have remission of sins." His death procures the vital benefit of forgiveness for the believer. The Supper commemorates the death, for this reason. It is not the mere pardon of sin, but forgiveness of the sinner and his reception into the social bonds of the family of God. The death of Jesus was therefore a sin-offering, atoning for guilt, and was not just for the Jews but "for the many," including all people who believe on Him.[2]

Much has been written and said about the meaning and character of the Supper. Theological controversy as always found here a favorite battle-ground. But in this ordinance, as in that of baptism, it is necessary to adhere simply to the fact that they are symbols. There is no spiritual grace conferred in either. It is in the atoning blood of Jesus that the power for the remission of sins resides. The bread does not become the body of Christ in the Supper, much less His soul and divinity.[3] In no sense is the bread changed in nature. The fruit of the vine—probably grape-juice—was in no sense changed in nature by its use in the Supper. It symbolized the blood to be shed on Calvary. The purpose of the shedding of that blood was the remission of sins.[4] When sins are removed or remitted, forgiveness is involved. It is only sin that separates from God. The believer who sits down at God's table has entered into the sphere of forgiveness or restored fellowship. The new testament or *will* about which Jeremiah spoke so elo-

1 I Cor. 11:23-26. The account of Paul 56 A. D. is followed by that of Luke, 58 A. D. Luke must have had Paul's narrative in his hands when he wrote. Matthew followed Mark more closely. 2 Bruce's Training of the Twelve. 3 Decrees of the Council of Trent in loco. 4 Eis with the accusative case. The death on the cross was the basis for forgiveness of sins.

quently, has been established. (Jer. 31:31-34). The cup symbolized the blood of Jesus, in the sphere of which the new will or testament is set up (Heb. 8:8-12). The Super-symbol looks to the great reality prophesied by Jeremiah: "For this is my covenant which I will make with the house of Israel: I will put my laws into their mind and on their hearts will I write them; and I will be to them a God and they shall be to me a people. For I will be merciful to their unrighteousness and their sins will I remember no more." This is the prophecy that Matthew had in mind, doubtless, when he spoke of the remission of sins. The Jewish passover commemorated the exodus from the bondage of Egypt; Jesus, our Passover, symbolized in the memorial supper, points to a greater deliverance—the redemption of mankind from the bondage of sin. The ancient covenant was ratified with the blood of animals; the new in the blood of Jesus. As often as we partake of this memorial supper we bring to memory and interpret to the world the atoning death, as a means of forgiveness of sin and entrance into the fellowship of a new life, into which all may come through faith. In this new ordinance, substituted in the place of the old Paschal Meal, is a glorious picture of the new spiritual life in Jesus — the everlasting life.

10. After the institution of the Supper, Jesus continues His discourse in the Upper Room (Jno. 14).

In His introduction to the familiar dialogue-discourse, preceding the institution of the memorial supper, the Master had prepared the disciples for His separation from them (Jno. 13:31-38). He exulted in the victory which He foresaw in His death just ahead (vv. 31, 32) and affectionately addressed them in an appeal, that they should love one another even as He had loved them (vv 33-37). By the bond of brotherly love they would be known as His disciples. He insists that they have a long way to travel before reaching the goal of such a brotherhood and warns them against over-confidence in their own fidelity. Even their out-spoken and self-confident leader, Simon Peter, would soon ingloriously deny Him—even that very night—in spite of his protest of faithfulness unto death (vv 36-38). He tells them that His hope for the future of the Kingdom centers in them. They face the supreme test now and He seeks to prepare them for it.[1] His dying counsel to them is that they should love one another in His absence even as He had loved them.[2]

The memorial supper being finished, the Master continues His homily by explaining the goal and purpose of His departure (vv 1-4), and clearing up some difficulties raised by two apos-

1 Robertson, The Divinity of Christ.   2 Bruce, Training of the Twelve, p. 380.

tles, Thomas and Philip (vv 5-7; 8-11).[1] This first part of the
discourse stresses the necessity of their accepting Jesus as the
unique representative of the Father for all mankind (Carver).

With infinite tenderness Jesus turns now to minister comfort
to their hearts, made desolate by the revelation of His near departure. Like a dying parent to His little children, soon to be
left alone in the world, He pours out His heart in consolation and
reassurance.[2]

"Let not your heart be troubled," He began, "ye believe in
God, believe also in me."[3] Jesus pleads for the same faith in Himself that they have in God, thus putting Himself on a par with the
Deity. True, His departure was near. But He was going ahead
as a forerunner to prepare lodging-places in the heavenly home for
them. One of the novelties of the new covenant is that Jesus is our
High Priest who goes before us into the Most Holy Place, not as a
substitute, but as a forerunner whom we are to follow. In that
home of His Father there were many abodes. If this were not so
He would have told them.[4] He gives them His promise to return
and receive them personally into that eternal home of heavenly
fellowship. He will come again to earth in the second advent but
He comes also to each disciple at the hour of death. "And where I
am going away ye know the way," He adds. Jesus had just told
Simon Peter that He could not follow Him in that way now, but
would follow later. Peter had seemed to understand then where
Jesus was going.[5]

But Thomas, the twin,[6] takes up the declaration of Jesus about
"knowing the way," for he was puzzled about the way to the
Father's house (vv 4b-7). He was of a doubting disposition like
many moderns. Science has minimized the personal and fastened
the eyes of mankind too much on the material. "Lord, we do not
know where thou art going, and how do we know the way?" he
asked despondently. Neither the goal nor the way was clear to
him. Jesus replies: "I am the way, the truth and the life." It is
Jesus who brings God into the vision of man, so that he can follow
and understand and live. He is the way to God who is the Goal.
In His incarnation Jesus revealed the goal; and He is both the
way of God and the way to God.[7] The kind of life Jesus lived—
His kind of character and conduct—is the way. He is also the personification and incarnation of *truth*, which is correspondence with
reality. God is reality and Jesus incarnated, *the* truth. All the
real questions and problems of mankind are resolved in the per-

1 Mission and Message of Jesus; Major, Manson, and Wright; and Wescott Com.
  in loco.
2 David Smith, In the Days of His Flesh, p. 448.
3 Indicative followed by imperative, present in both cases.
4 Suppressed condition of second class.   5 Jno. 13:36.   6 Didimus.
7 W. O. Carver, The Self-Interpretation of Jesus, p. 146.

son, example and teachings of Jesus. He is the truth about God, man, and the universe. Browning was right when he said:[1]

"I say the acknowledgment of God in Christ,
Accepted by thy reason, solves for thee
All questions in the earth and out of it."

For one to know the truth he must cultivate the consciousness of Jesus: His God-consciousness, man-consciousness and world-consciousness.[2] Jesus is also the life—the eternal life—life in its essence. He is not life as mere physical or durational existence, but He incarnated the Father's life. He claims to be the exclusive representative in knowing and revealing the Father—the sole agent of man's salvation. No man comes to the Father-goal and has a mansion in the heavenly home except through the agency[3] of Jesus. He is the way for sinful men to come to God, and only through Him can man come. If they had known Him—and they certainly did[4] in a way, but not perfectly—they would have known His Father also. "From now you begin[5] and will go on knowing Him in experience progressively, and you have perceived Him[6] and so have a permanent but imperfect knowledge of Him," He explained.

At this juncture, Philip breaks in with still another problem. He recalled the theophany of the Old Testament perhaps (Ex. 33:17ff and Isa. 40:5). Philip longed for an objective manifestation of God. He had not recognized that Jesus was Himself that objective manifestation, graciously granted to blind humanity. Disappointed that Philip and the others had failed to recognize this, Jesus exclaimed: "Have I been for so long a time[7] with you and you have not recognized me, Philip? The one perceiving me has perceived the Father." His very being, all of His words and works, were expressive of the Father. Jesus always longs for a faith that identifies Him in character with the Father.[8] It was almost unbelievable that Philip was so dense as not to see the correspondence in nature between Him and the Father. He and the Father had been inseparable in all His words and works. His character and works had exemplified before their eyes constantly for three years the nature and works of the Father. He appeals to them again: "Believe me," He says, "that I am in the Father and the Father in me." If they could not take His bare affirmation, let them bolster up their faith by a close observation of His works. God alone could do such works as that of raising a man four days in the grave to life again.

1 Quoted from The Mission and Message of Jesus (cf Browning, A Death in the Desert).
2 Carver, Self-Interpretation of Jesus.
3 Dia with genitive of agency.   4 First class condition showing that they knew him in a way.   5 Inchoactive present active indicative.
6 They had seen Jesus. This is a claim of deity.   7 Accusative of duration of time.
8 Carver, Self-Interpretation of Jesus.

In the second part of His discourse, Jesus proceeds to discuss the place of the believer in His great work and world-plan (vv 12-21). The disciples are to go forward with the work. His departure, far from being a calamity, will enable them through His intercession to do greater works than He had done for the glory of the Father in the Son (vv 12-14).[1] "Verily, verily I tell you, the one who goes on believing in me shall do the same kind of works that I am doing in quality but greater in quantity, because I am going back to the Father." In the presence and fellowship of the Father, as their great High Priest, through His intercession, He will release new divine powers for the carrying out of the mission He had begun. This power will operate through the disciples. The releasing of these new energies was to be linked up with their prayers (vv 13, 14). Whatsoever they might ask in His name— the open sesame to the Father's will—He will do, in order that the Father may be glorified in the Son. They will have direct access to Him in prayer. That was a great assurance to them as He was on the eve of His departure. His name was the key to open the door to the Father's heart. Their greater works would depend on true, constant, and faithful effort in prayer.[2] They were to pray in the name of Jesus; but what did that mean? There is no *magic* power in the name of Jesus. To pray in His name is to identify one's self with Him. His name stood for His character, which was one of complete trust and obedience. Jesus taught us how to pray. He dwelt in the fellowship of the Father, full of humility, trust, forgiveness, passionate longing for the eternal well-being of men, consecration and devotion to God's Kingdom. Prayer took Jesus to the cross; it cost much. We must be willing to follow Him to the cross if we would be powerful with God in prayer.

Jesus will go on working for His disciples after He is gone. He will send them another Helper (Paraclete). But He expects their cooperation in loving obedience, that this action may be efficient (vv 15-17). Their love for Him was the secret of prevailing prayer and the test of that love was obedience to His commands. Jesus would pray the Father and He would send them another Helper.[3] The purpose of the Spirit's coming was in order that He might be with them forever. His name is the Spirit of Truth. He is a Helper who will exhort, encourage, stimulate, arouse, challenge, and comfort. He is a person, the third person of the Trinity. He was sent by the Father and also by Jesus. The world cannot receive Him because it does not see Him, neither knows Him by experience. But the disciples go on knowing Him

1 Wescott, Com. on John in loco.   2 Jno. 14:14. Third class condition, success in
   prayer depends upon the one praying.
3 Comforter, Paraclete, One who may be called or One whose function is to call.

progressively through their experience with Him, because He remains with them, in their fellowship. He is among them in His
mighty works and shall dwell in their hearts.

Jesus consoles them further by assuring them that He will
come and makes His person more real to them than ever, though
invisible to their eyes (vv 18-21). Again He speaks to them in tender words: "I will not leave you orphans"—as little children bereft of parents, helpless, and abandoned in the world. "I will
come to you. Yet a little while and the world will see me no
longer but you will go on seeing me.[1] Because I go on living, after
death you shall live also." The continued life of Jesus after death
is a guarantee of our immortality. In that day—probably the day
of Pentecost and following times—they would know by their own
experience and for themselves[2] that His present declaration about
His unity with the Father and His divine Sonship were verities, as
well as His continued unity and intimate relationship with the
disciples. They would experience these relationships as real
through the indwelling Spirit. These blessed realities could not be
experienced apart from loving loyalty and loyal love toward Him,
manifested in keeping His commands. Where there should be a
fulfillment of these conditions in the believer, Jesus promised a
loving relationship between the believer and the Father, and also
with the Son, who would in appropriate but real ways manifest
Himself to the disciple. The building up of this vital fellowship
and unity with the Father and the Son was a fundamental and
primal necessity for the greater works and the far-reaching influence of the individual believer. A vital love for Christ is the
first step—such a love as would follow Him to the cross. The disciples are not to lose the help of His presence. He will make Himself nearer to them than ever. They will not lose His leadership
in the greater tasks of the Kingdom out just ahead, because the
Holy Spirit will come to be their universally present and powerful Helper and leader. What more could they ask? But this was
all so new and strange that they could not grasp it yet.

Judas Thaddeus next raises a question about the special, intimate manifestation of Jesus to the disciples. In their dullness of
comprehension they continued to cling to their traditional Jewish
expectation, that Jesus would yet display His power and glory to
an astonished world. Judas (not Iscariot) was the third to interrupt the sermon with a question (vv 22-24). Surprised at the
idea of an exclusive manifestation to the disciples, he asked:
"Lord, what has happened that thou art about to manifest thyself unto us, and not unto the world?" How was such a manifesta-

1 Present tense progressive linear action.
2 See future middle of ginosko, force of middle voice.

tion possible and what was the reason for it? Judas was perplexed. The disciples could not give up the hope of the coming of the Kingdom in glory and power, visible to the eyes of all men. They had accepted possibly the idea of His exodus by death but had He not said He would rise again? Would not His resurrection be like that of Lazarus, visible to all? Jesus did not try to explain the invisibility of the spiritual manifestation but points them rather to the nature and conditions of His revelation to them. If anyone would fulfill the conditions of spiritual love[1] toward Him, he would keep the words or teachings of Jesus. The result which would flow out of this was the reciprocal love of the Father and the consequent coming of the Father and Son to him,[2] accompanied by the setting up of their abode[3] with him. The disciple must "keep on loving Jesus—progressively and habitually." This is the key to the special, constant, and progressive revelation of the Father and Son in his experience. The heart of the believer is the temple of the Holy Spirit (I Cor. 3:16f) and must be a fit dwelling place for the Father and Son. The heart includes the realm of the thoughts, feelings, and volitions. The one who does not love Jesus progressively[4] will not be keeping the teachings of Jesus and thus shuts himself out from the invisible but real manifestation of the Father and Son and their eternal fellowship. Thus Jesus, by indirect ways, explains the invisible but real character of His revelation, possible to the understanding of true believers but incomprehensible to the world.

Jesus brings this first of the last discourses to a close realizing doubtless that the disciples had not grasped all of its meaning (vv 25, 26). In a little while Iscariot would come with armed forces to take him. He must leave the further revelation of these great truths to the Helper, the Spirit of Truth, who would be sent shortly in His name to teach them the fullness of these things and make all the things He said to them real in their memory and experience. The Holy Spirit would stimulate their memories with respect to all the things He had been saying to them day after day. But He had spoken these deep things to them which they were to keep as a permanent possession.[5]

He bequeaths to them now a precious legacy, different from anything the world could give, and which the world could not take away from them—His peace (vv 27, 28). It was a peace

---

1 Condition of third class, fulfillment dependent on meeting conditions of a sacrificial spiritual love.   2 Into his fellowship-presence.
3 Progressive future middle, the Father and Son will for themselves come and make their abode with him.   4 Present participle, linear action.
5 Perfect indicative active, denoting a complete message which was permanent in its continuing state. See Perfect Tense, Dana and Mantey, Greek Grammar.

THE CHRIST OF THE GOSPELS

such as comes through spiritual insight and discernment. The
shalom of the Orient was for greeting or parting. It was used by
Jesus after His resurrection (Jno. 20:19, 21, 26); but here Jesus
gives spiritual peace, such as He alone can give. It is the kind
of peace that made Him calm in the midst of all His persecuted
life. It is not a delusive sense of security, nor is it a Stoic acceptance of the inevitable with calm indifference or a security
built up by human barriers; but an inward possession. He commands them now: "Stop letting your heart be troubled!" They
should stop all nervous fluttering from fear (v. 27),[1] as of one
already condemned to death. There was no need for them to be
troubled or fearful. If they loved Him with a perfect love they
would rejoice that He was going to the Father, who is greater
than the Son—superior in rank, as every father. He had taken
upon Himself the limitations of the incarnation and must pass
through the way of death; but the way led home to the Father
and to the heavenly abode. They should rejoice in that fact.

Jesus closes the discourse, impressing upon them the solemn
reality of the situation and victorious outcome (vv 29-31). He has
told them already of the coming separation and so they cannot
be taken unaware. They are prepared thus to meet the shock of
the tragic hours just ahead. He would not have opportunity to
speak with them much more, because the prince of the world,
Satan, was already marshaling the powers of darkness for the
final attack. But Satan would not succeed because there was
no unrighteousness in Jesus; the darkness of Satan would not
master the light of Him. But He wished that the world of humanity might know that His loyalty and love for the Father remained
unbroken and that He fulfilled the commandment of the Father
in the manner of His death, demonstrating obedience to the divine
will. He would voluntarily submit to the death-penalty for sin.
Such was to be the victorious end of His career on earth, through
voluntary submission to a cruel death at the hands of His enemies.
On the cross His love for the Father and for mankind would shine
out as a rainbow of grace on the dark cloud of the devil's hatred
and cunning and man's cruelty and sin.

"Arise and let us go hence," He said. And when they had sung
the Hallel, they went down from the Upper Room[2] into the deserted street below, into which the full Passover moon poured a
flood of radiance.

---

1 Mede deiliato, neither let it be timid or fearful.
2 The second part of the Hallel (Pss. 115-118) was always sung at the close of the Paschal
 Meal. Cf. Robertson's Word Pictures on Matt. 26:30. They went out from the upper
 room after singing (Jno. 14:31).

CHAPTER XXXI

FINAL CHARGES TO HIS DISCIPLES

(Harm. §§ 150, 151)

Jesus had much to say to His apostles yet, but to remain in the Upper Room longer would likely mean intrusion of the traitor with the Sanhedrin's emissaries.[1] He must seek another retreat. After midnight the gates of the Temple were thrown open. It would be a natural desire of Jesus to pass that way and the Temple would be one of the safest places for Him at that hour. The future of His Kingdom work was uppermost in His thought as He passed through the deserted streets at midnight. He was wending His way toward the eastern gate of the city near the Temple going toward Gethsemane. He wished to turn the minds of His disciples from sad reflections on His near departure and separation from them to the great work they must do as His friends and representatives in the world. He recognized that He was dependent upon them for the successful carrying forward of His mission.[2]

On the way to Gethsemane He takes up further the subject of the great world-movement of His kingdom and the relation of His disciples to it, and discusses it under the figure of the Vine and Branches (Chapter 15), following that with an exposition of their work with the Holy Spirit, their Helper, and their relation to that Helper in the great Kingdom campaign (Chapter 16). Concluded His final charge to them, He lifts them in a great high-priestly prayer with Him to the heavens, in intercession for Himself in the present crisis, for them in this crucial hour and especially in the hard days out ahead, and for the disciples of future generations; that all may be united, preserved, and guided in carrying on the world-movement[2] of His Kingdom successfully to the final victory (Chapter 17).

In His discourse in the Upper Room, Jesus had pointed out, first, the necessity and issues of His separation from them (13:31-38); second, the fact that He was the unique and divine representative of the Father and would lead them to the heavenly home (14:1-11); third, the intimate and continued relationship between Himself and the disciples in the "greater works" they were to do through the presence and direction of the great Helper, the Holy Spirit (14:12-21); and fourth, the manner of God's inward and invisible revelation of Himself to them, making them effective in the greater works and giving them peace in the midst of the persecutions and struggles (14:22-31).

The metaphor of the true or genuine vine — the Messianic

---

1 David Smith, In the Days of His Flesh, p. 452.   2 Carver's Self Interpretation of Jesus.

Vine—and the Branches was suggested to Jesus on this night perhaps by the vines seen in the moonlight around the house of the
"goodman" where the paschal meal was eaten; or else on the way as
they went through the streets lit up by the radiance of the full
moon, when passing in front of the Temple gates on which was to
be seen a bronze vine, symbol of the True Israel[1] (Jer.
2:21); or
in passing by the vineyards outside the city toward Gethsemane.
The vine had appeared on the Maccabean coins as an emblem
of the nation. Israel had degenerated as a vine, bringing forth
wild grapes (Isa. 5:1). Jesus presented Himself as the true —
the genuine Messianic-Vine, just as He had referred to Himself
as the light (Jno. 8:12), the door (Jno. 10:7), and the good
shepherd (Jno. 10:11). No mere man could have made such
claims and sustained them successfully. Jesus was the true vine
planted by God in the deep soil of eternity and His abundant
fruitage down through the centuries sustains every syllable of
His claim to be the genuine Messianic Vine (v. 1).

1. The necessity and consequences of a vital union between
Jesus and the disciples (vv 1-10). A parable is difficult to interpret
unless one remembers that there is only one main point of illustration, and that allegorical interpretation of details in support
of favorite ecclesiastical theories must be excluded. The main point
of illustration in this parable is the necessity of vital union between Christ and the disciple looking to fruit-bearing, which is
the principal means to the glory of God — the main issue of life.
To arrive at the real meaning of the words of Jesus, we must know
the circumstances under which they were spoken. Due regard
must be had for the grammatical construction of each sentence,
and interpretation must be made in the light of the context and
Scriptures as a whole. On these principles we may arrive at the
mind of the Master.

Jesus points out that spiritual vitality—real life—is in the incarnate Son, and human beings must be in vital connection to fulfill the purpose of God in the race[2] (v. 1, 2). There are two kinds
of connection with Christ: a mere cosmic relation which bears no
fruit, and a genuine spiritual connection which brings forth fruitage in spiritual life. Jesus was probably thinking of Judas, who
professed to have a spiritual connection but was only connected
cosmically (Bernard). He had just been eliminated by the prun-
ing hand of God, the great Vine-dresser. Jesus would call the attention of the eleven to the necesstiy of the cleansing effect of
severe trials in order that they might go on bearing more and
more fruit.[3]

1 Josephus Ant. 15:11:3.
2 The Mission and Message of Jesus, p. 889.
3 Hina with present subjunctive expressing the purpose of God.

The Master brings home the application of this great doctrine to the apostolic group (vv. 3-6). "Already ye are clean on account of the word which I have spoken to you." He had said "they were clean but not all," when the betrayer was yet among them. Now they are clean potentially, due to the doctrine He had given them as a permanent possession.[1] Judas is gone and Satan will sift the rest of them. They are commanded[2] to abide, remain, continue in the sphere of His example, life, and doctrine. Their wills must cooperate with His will in maintaining the vital flow of life from His to them. Real religion is a personal and mutual relationship of cooperation. The disciples must appropriate the life in Christ if they are to bear fruit. Unless they keep on abiding in Him they cannot bear fruit. He reiterates the fact that He is the vine and they are the branches. A vital spiritual relationship is necessary; a mere cosmic relationship is not sufficient. The apparent life in a Judas, who was never vitally connected, would dry up and wither away like the disconnected branch. "If anyone may not remain in me he is cast forth[3] as a useless shoot-branch, and is withered away and they gather them up and cast them into the fire and they are burned." The figure of the burning of the prunage in the vineyards of the Kedron valley was vivid in the minds and even now before the eyes, of the disciples.[4] This was a warning to them against presumption and a stimulation to activity in fruit-bearing. Were they really vitally united or were they like Judas, destined to be severed from the apostolic company which was the true vine of Israel?

Jesus points them to a way to put the reality of the spiritual connection to the test (vv 7, 8). Real union is evident by prayer fulfilled and fruit borne. The real prayer of a true believer, who identifies himself with the name and character of Jesus in his petition, is always answered. "If you remain in me and my words remain in you, then ask[5] whatsoever you wish and it shall come to pass."[6] This is the acid test of true and complete discipleship. The condition is such intimate unity and harmony with Christ and the Father that nothing will be asked which is not in accord with the will of God. It is by and in the sphere if this intimate communion and vital connection leading to much fruit-bearing — the purpose of Christ in them—that the Father is glorified.[7] It is thus also that they may hope to "go on becoming"[8] more and more His disciples, learning from Him. This was one of the blessings of the intimate union to be progressively realized in their lives.

1 Perfect tense denoting permance of His message (15:3).
3 Timeless or gnomic first aorist passive of ballo.   4 Cf. Matt. 13:41ff.
5 Aorist middle imperative, in which they are active agents asking for themselves;
    cf. force of middle voice, Dana nad Mantey, Greek Grammar.
6 Future middle of ginomai.   7 Gnomic timeless aorist.
8 Future middle indicative of ginomai.

The fundamental condition of this union, Jesus reveals, was to be in love of the Father for Him and His love for them. They are enjoined to continue and abide[1] in the sphere[2] of "the love He had for them." Our love for Christ is grounded in His love for us and in the Father's love for the world.[3] Again, the acid test and best evidence of their love was their obedience to His commands. That is also the way they are to preserve themselves permanently in His love—the same way He had ever continued[4] the Beloved of His Father.

2. In the second division of His discussion of the living union of the disciple with his Lord, the Master points out the two results of the union (vv 11-16). The first is the production of Christian joy in them and the filling out to the full of their joy. He wanted them to have the Christian joy—the kind of joy He had—and that it might not be half-hearted but complete. That was the reason for His giving them His final and permanent word[5] on this subject. Their joy depended on being fruitful and holding to the only true objective in life—the glory of God. The joy of the unfruitful disciple is precarious and fitful. Joy in the highest sense is the reward of complete obedience to the Father, and if the disciples obey, they will love one another with the sacrificial love He had demonstrated in laying down His life for[6] them. Self-sacrifice is the high-water mark of love (Dods).

The relation which ought to exist between Master and disciple was one of love and friendship. The proof of their true friendship for Him would be their continued and persevering obedience. "You are my friends if you go on doing[7] what I command you." The inevitable prerequisite to discipleship and fellowship is obedience to Christ's commands.[8] Paul was glad to be called a bond-servant or slave of Christ and spoke to himself as such constantly. But Jesus deals with His disciples not as slaves, but as His friends. Abraham was called "the friend of God." As His friends, we should be faithful and always loyal to Him, as our rightful Lord. It is the highest honor we could receive, to be called His friends. The privilege of such a friendship is the intimate fellowship in the revelation to us of all that He has received from the Father. The most precious fact of all about this friendship is that Jesus took the initiative Himself in its establishment. He chose the disciples. They were vessels of His election. He placed them in the apostolate and His purpose was that they should keep on bearing fruit in a permanent growth and fruitage. If they should fulfill these conditions, then they might ask the Father anything they wished in His name and Jesus Himself would give it.[1] He undertakes personally the advocacy of the disciples' requests to the Father.

3. The great Teacher concludes His discussion of the union between Himself and His disciples by pointing out the result of the union in their relationship to the outside world (vv 17-27). They would be hated by the world and would need all the more to go on loving[2] one another (vv 17-21). Hatred is hard to bear, and the desire to escape it is one of the principal causes for unfaithfulness and fruitlessness. Jesus would fortify His disciples for endurance of wrongs before they came upon them and be caused to stumble. They would be outlawed, religiously and socially. The reason for their being hated by the world was obvious.[3] The character and work of the disciples correspond to those of their Lord. Such character is contrary to the darkness and evil of the world. There is always an inevitable antagonism between the light and the darkness. Jesus was for this reason even now suffering the permanent[4] hatred of the world, which would soon sweep Him away in an early death. The disciples should not wonder if they had to suffer; their Lord had to suffer before them. If they were of the world they would not suffer, but they were not.[5] He called to their memory what He had said before: "The slave is not greater than his Master." If they had persecuted Him—as they certainly had[6]—they would persecute His disciples also. A second reason why the men of the world would persecute the disciples was because they did not know God who sent Jesus. This classified His enemies, at least. That this hatred of the world toward them had no justification, Jesus made it plain (vv 22-25). The word written in the Scriptures: "They hated me without a cause,"[7] was having its fulfillment in Him even now. He came and revealed the Father, but His revelation only served to arouse to fury and hatred against Him and against the Father, the evil that was in those men, and made it yet more pronounced. The teaching of Jesus had this effect on many evil men. And His works, which were far beyond anything the world had ever seen, had the same effect. The works revealed not only the real character of the Son but also the Father. Even that only served to fan the flame of their hatred into a conflagration. These hard-hearted, blind, incredulous enemies

---

1 Nestle's text, Jno. 15:16.   2 Hina with present subjunctive active; His purpose was that they go on loving one another.
3 Condition of first class; the world certainly does hate the disciple of Jesus.
4 Perfect tense, v. 18.   5 Condition of second class, contrary to fact; Dana and Mantey, Greek Grammar.   6 Condition of the first class.
7 Pss. 35:19; 69:4.

had no excuse for their opposition. Their hatred for Him was *gratuitous*—the kind of hatred found in hell.[1]

If Jesus Himself had failed with these hard sinners, should His disciples hope to succeed? This question would naturally rise in their minds. He hates to remind them of His previous promise to send the Spirit (vv 26, 27). Before the Helper, this hatred of men will be powerless because He is the Spirit of Truth. They were to go forward[2] fearlessly, giving their testimony along with that of this unfailing Guide and invincible Leader. They had the facts about His ministry from its beginning and possessed the message of His life also, for they had been with Him. Theirs was to serve as witnesses. The Spirit would also bear witness, but in His own way. He is a person, though invisible, and was sent by the Father and Son for a special mission.

4. The relation of the Spirit or Helper to the world of sinful men (Jno. 16:1-11). The discussion of the relation of the disciples to Christ had led naturally to their work after the crucifixion and their relationship to the Holy Spirit sent by Jesus from the Father to take up His work in the world and carry it forward through the disciples. The Master explains first of all, however, the work of the Spirit in the hearts of unbelieving men. He had just revealed to them the hatred of the world and consequent religious and social persecutions they would have to undergo, even to suffering ostracism and death. He carried forward this topic further and tells them why He had spoken thus painfully (vv 1-4). It was a dark and gloomy picture. He had painted of their future, and they sank into a silence which betokened sorrowful hearts. It is no wonder, for Jesus had announced definite persecutions just ahead — a storm which their ship was destined soon to enter. Blind religious fanaticism, motivated by a feeling of religious zeal, brings on the bitterest persecution with death to the heretic considered the best worship-service.[3] Ignorance of God and Christ on the part of the persecutors was the adequate explanation for such irrational persecution. Forewarned is forearmed, and Jesus had given them the warning. He had not revealed the definite persecution to them earlier because He had been with them to help them sustain any sudden shock at any time. Now that He is going away what are they do to?

Overcome with grief and submerged in the first waves of this approaching flood of sorrow, the disciples appeared stunned (vv 4b-7). They no longer asked Him questions about the future. Filled with amazement, they knew not what to expect. He was

1 The Mission and Message of Jesus, in loco.
2 Present active indicative or imperative, rendering may be either in exposition.
3 Jno. 16:2, Nestle's text of Greek New Testament.

going away! They may have had many questions in their minds but dared not ask them now. The thought which would be uppermost with all of them was the wonder that He should go away and leave them in the midst of such a crisis. He now calls their thought away from their own grief by telling them it is expedient that He go away even now in spite of the impending crisis which they were facing. Their work as apostles of His Kingdom would be helped forward by His going away, because He would send the Comforter and with His coming they would be rendered effective. The Spirit was to operate in their preaching, making them efficient, and in the hearts of unbelievers, opening their hearts to the message.

He now tells them plainly how the Spirit is to work in the hearts of unbelievers (vv 8-11). He will convict the world of ungodly men with respect to three things: sin, righteousness, and judgment. The Spirit puts the truth about these things in a clear light before the worldly man. The application of the truth thus revealed comes in condemnation of the one who rejects it. The Spirit is to be Christ's Advocate in the law-court trial of the world of sinners. Wicked men would, in a few hours, hail Jesus before their illegal court, and the high priest himself would serve as advocate in the prosecution in a farcical trial. But the truth was that these Sanhedrists were the culprits and the Holy Spirit would prosecute them before the jury of their own consciences until they should tremble and cry out in their guilt. And all the world of sinners would be convinced and convicted by the great Advocate: (1) In respect of sin, as missing the mark or goal of life and wronging God and man. Sinful men must be convicted of the reality of sin—the sin of putting self above Christ in their intellectual pride. To believe in Christ is to surrender the lordship to Him and take the place of trusting dependence under Him. Unbelief toward Christ is the tap-root of all sins. (2) He would convict them with respect to righteousness, the righteousness of Christ, who was altogether right and never wrong. This righteous character of Jesus—the sinlessness which He claimed—was proven to be real when He rose from the dead and ascended on high. The Spirit brings conviction about the necessity of standards. (3) He convicts of judgment, because the prince of this world stands[1] judged. Satan was already as good as judged and decisively defeated. On the morrow he would be thus overcome at the cross, when Jesus would meet curse with blessing, and cruelty with eternal kindness.

1 Perfect acitve indicative, completed action and continued state.

5. The office of the Spirit with relation to the disciples is made plain to their understanding (vv 12-15). Jesus must go away and cannot continue His teaching longer. The untaught disciples could not grasp now all the truths they will need to receive shortly, even if He had the time to teach them. Some of the main redemptive facts were to be those of His death and resurrection. The disciples were not able to bear the revelation of those facts in all their tragic character at one time. He points them to the coming of the Spirit of Truth, who will be their teacher henceforth. "He will guide you into the way to the full truth," He said. Christ was the Way and the Truth. The Spirit would interpret for them the redemptive facts about Christ, even those yet to come into their experience. He leads those who are seeking the truth into the fuller understanding of the truth. This He would do for the apostles, to the end and purpose of their enlightment and sanctification. In this work, the Spirit is not alone and does not speak from His own authority independently, but whatever He "goes on hearing" in the counsels of the Godhead He will speak, and declare the things of the Kingdom out ahead. They will be able to depend on the Spirit's[1] leadership in these things. Their future Helper is completely one with Him and will go on glorifying[2] Him, because He would receive directly from Christ and would announce the message of the person and work of Jesus in gradual revelation to them. The Spirit would draw from the full common store of Father and Son in His work of teaching the future apostles of the Kingdom. Such an assurance ought to comfort and strengthen them in the crisis just ahead and all the disciples and apostles of the Kingdom in future generations. The search for truth is the human condition for the reception of truth and for guidance from above. Truth was completely enfolded in Jesus like the bloom in the bud; but its revelation is progressive in our experience through the ministry of the Spirit. He takes the things of Christ and shows them unto the truth-seeker. The glorious facts of Christian history must ever be reinterpreted and progressively comprehended in the stream of the living present. The apostles under the guidance of the Spirit would be able to understand and preach the Christian message.

6. Their sorrow will be turned into joy (16:16-24). The Master had declared that His going away was expedient for them. He now reveals more clearly how this is to be. His disappearance from their physical sight would enhance their spiritual vision. He was to disappear in a little while from their presence; in another brief space He would reappear and be seen by them for moments, that

---

1 Present tense, linear progressive action.   2 Future active indicative, linear action.

their physical sight might be transformed into spiritual insight. Then He would disappear again and they would have to rely solely on spiritual vision and insight.[1] This was hard for them to understand. They passed whispered remarks around among themselves about these enigmatical and paradoxical words of the Master, confessing their inability to understand. But they did not ask Him any question.

Jesus knew by their looks that they wanted to ask Him about His puzzling expression. He did not explain the paradox but gave them to understand that they would weep and mourn in the dark hours just ahead, while the world would rejoice. But they must not despair in that hour because their grief would be changed into joy (vv 19, 20). He adds an illustration out of the intimate experience of a mother, who is filled with the anguish of pain and uncertainty when she is to give birth. Immediately after the birth she no longer remembers the affliction, because of her joy that a man is born into the world. When Jesus came forth from the grave after the crucifixion, the disciples were beside themselves with joy. Jesus tells them now that He will see them after His death and resurrection and that their hearts will be filled with a joy which cannot be taken away from them. His eyes would be upon them constantly[3] in the future. This ought to be a great comfort to them. Their joy could now be permanent and stable.[4] When this joy should come to its complete fulfillment, they would ask no more questions of the kind they had been asking. They had asked questions out of their immaturity and doubt hitherto. And their petitions had been selfish and short-sighted. With the new enlightenment, accompanied by greater faith and understanding, they will enter shortly upon a new and longer sphere of discipleship, and thus no longer need to ask childish questions.[5]

"Truly, truly I tell you," He says, "Whatsoever you shall ask the Father He will give it to you, in my name," Their desires and prayers had been petty, as those of most disciples always, even in this day of enlightenment. Now He urges them to longer vision and greater desires and requests for the Kingdom.

"Ask and you shall receive, in order that your joy may go on being more and more full." Large requests of an enlarged faith bring fullness of Christian joy.

7. In conclusion of His last discourse and charge to the future apostles of His world-movement (vv 25-33), Jesus reminds them that His teaching has been in parables and way-side sayings.[6]

---

1 Historic present of theoreo, to see or perceive with the eyes.
2 Imperfect of repeated action.   3 Future active indicative, linear action.
4 Idem, v. 22.   5 Bruce, The Training of the Twelve.   6 Paroimiais, locative or instrumental of means.

In spite of the imperfect means, His message was a permanent one.[1] The hour comes when He will no longer speak to them in proverbs and enigmas, but tell them plainly concerning the Father. After the ascension He could speak more clearly of the hidden mysteries. In that coming time just ahead of them they shall need to pray more than ever. Let them be assured that their prayers will be heard. He will be in the presence of the Father, but it will not be necessary for Him to intercede on their behalf, since the Father Himself loves them warmly as friends who have loved His Son and are still loving Him[2] and have expressed a firm faith in Him as the One who came out from God on a divine mission. This faith the apostolic group had expressed at Caesarea-Philippi and also at other places more recently. They were firm in this expressed belief, though they might not understand all it meant. In order to put His seal and approval on that incipient and not too stable faith, Jesus restates explicitly His mission in the incarnation, in a more complete way. "I came forth from the Father and am come[3] into the world. Again I leave the world and go to the Father." The incarnation is a permanent fact. It was once a mere hope; now it is a reality. This the disciples might now fully comprehend. What they did not understand fully yet was His voluntary return or exodus to the Father, about which some of them should have learned at the Transfiguration.

The disciples were helped by this explanation now and thought they understood at last (vv 29-30). "Behold now thou art speaking openly and no proverb. Now we are sure that thou knowest all things and dost not need that anyone should ask thee any question." They had penetrated to the fact that He understood their thoughts. From that they reasoned that they need not ask any further question. This implied their belief in His deity and His divine mission. Their faith in His divine origin rested in their comprehension of His supernatural insight. But they did not comprehend fully that the coming of Jesus from the Father implied a going thither again. They would not comprehend this fully until the Lord should take His departure and send the Spirit to interpret the fact of the ascension to them.

That their faith was imperfect and would not carry them through the dark hours of the crucifixion, Jesus was aware. To prepare them better for the shock, He raises the question of the character of their faith. Their belief in Christ was genuine as far as it went, but peril awaited them.

"Do you believe now?" He asked with a rising inflection in His voice. "See, the hour is coming and is already here, when you

---

1 Perfect indicative active. 2 Perfect active indicative, permanence.
3 Perfect active indicative, permanent fact—the incarnation.

shall be scattered every man to his own, and shall leave me alone."
He reminds them that for His personal peace He is resting in the
assurance of the continuous fellowship of the Father, whose will
is His peace. All that He had spoken was meant to lead *them also*
to such a peace. He points the way for them. In the world they
might expect to meet with tribulation, confusion, hatred, and
strife. In His final word He commands them: "Be of good courage!"
Danger is ahead and they will need courage to face it. But He had
gone through with all the trials and come out victorious; He had
conquered sin and temptations of all kinds as their representative.
They could conquer also, in His name, and of that He assures them.
"I have overcome the world!" This was a high note of victory; for
Him a realized one; for them one assured.

8. The intercessory prayer of Jesus was offered at the close of
His last discourse and charge to the apostles (Jno. 17:1-26). The
place must have been somewhere between the upper room where
they had celebrated the passover, and the Garden of Gethsemane
where He was later arrested. It might have been before the
Temple, as they paused for a few moments to contemplate its
beauty lighted up by the radiance of the Passover moon; or in
the heights of the Mount of Olives overlooking Jerusalem, or
perhaps at the gate of the Garden of Gethsemane. It must have
been with all the eleven present. The prayer was not offered
mentally or in private, but for the benefit of the apostles. It reflected much of the thought and needs referred to in the discourse
that preceded it. It is therefore highly beneficial and challenges our
most careful consideration. We tread on holy ground as we seek
to understand and interpret it.

Jesus prayed for three things in this great high-priestly
prayer. First, He prayed for Himself (vv 1-8), then for His intimate disciples around Him (vv 9-19), and finally for the disciples of future generations (vv 20-26). His prayer for Himself was
that He might seal the successful work of His life with such a
testimony in His death as would glorify both Son and Father. His
death on the cross, resurrection, and ascension would complete
the work of His mission in the incarnation. The aim had been to
bring eternal life to men through revealing God to them in all
His holiness and grace. He now asks that He be restored to His
position and character in the glory of heaven. His prayer for His
genuine disciples around Him, whom He was to leave in a few
hours, was that they might be protected and kept in the midst of
the bitter trials through which they must pass, and sanctified
through His word, becoming thus positive forces in the work of
the Kingdom. For the disciples of Christianity, down through the

centuries to come, He prayed that they might be united by mutual confidence and faith in carrying on the work of the Kingdom to glorious success and final victory.

(1) The Son's prayer to the Father for Himself (vv 1-8). Finished the discourse, spoken on the way to Gethsemane, Jesus lifted up His eyes to heaven and said: "Father, the hour is come; glorify thy Son that thy Son may glorify thee." This was the simple twofold petition. The hour had come indeed! The bitter struggle of Gethsemane, the arrest, trials, and crucifixion were to begin now! But the presence and fellowship of the Father were so real in these moments that a note of hope, joy, and victory rings out clear in this prayer. He wished to die such a death, that His own nature and character would shine forth clearly and cast a sheen of glory upon the Father whom He came to represent. The Father had given Him power, as His special messenger, over all humanity, both Jew and Gentile, that He might bring to them eternal life. This had been the end and purpose of His whole mission.[1] His prayer was for strength to meet the cross successfully and overcome death in a glorious resurrection and ascension. He had come to the world to bring salvation (eternal life) to all those whom the Father had given Him. He describes eternal life as the continued knowledge[2] of God and Jesus Christ, His messenger. He is conscious of having finished this work successfully and now He prays for restoration of the glory He had in the fellowship of the Father in His preincarnate state. He does not face death as a disappointed man but with a sense of victory. His permanent task, entrusted by the Father, had been accomplished.[3] He had made eternal life a reality to a small group of the God-chosen ones. He had made manifest the name (character) of the Father to the men given Him out of the world. Their acceptance of the doctrine[4] was not merely apparent but permanent and real. The confession of belief in His divine origin and mission, based on the observation of His works and reception of His message, was clear and unmistakable. They had proclaimed Him the Messiah and Son of God. He describes the disciples as good men, God-elected and God-given. They were true believers; not just head but heart-believers. Their faith was not superficial but deep and abiding. Thus, glory for the Father and eternal life for men through His successful death, together with a restoration of His state of preexistent glory after completing the plan of redemption, constitute the burden of His prayer for Himself as the Christ.

1 Hina with present subjunctive, purpose in a progressive and unceasing process, life increases as knowledge increases.
2 Present tense, go on knowing, keep on knowing God the Father and Jesus Christ His messenger.   3 Aorist participle, His work was looked upon as finished already.
4 Logon.

(2)   In the second part of the prayer, Jesus concentrates on the disciple band around Him (vv 9-19). Here is exclusion of the world for the present moments, with a view to inclusion in the future. The disciples are the sole objects of His prayer now, that they may be His missionaries to the world in the years ahead. In placing the emphasis thus, Jesus was not indifferent to the current needs of the outside world. In the intimacy of the fellowship between the Father and the Son, the disciples are a common interest of equal import to both. He pleads for the Father's interest. "And I am glorified in them," He said. Such words, spoken by the Master in spite of all the shortcomings of the disciples, should be a source of comfort to them, leading to humble self-examination. With infinite tenderness the Master continued: "No longer am I in the world, but these are to continue in the world, and I am coming to thee. Holy Father, keep[1] them in the sphere of thy name (character) in order that they may be one[2] as we are one." He yearns for unity of mind and spirit for them, such a unity as that exemplified between the Father and Son. Here are the two things He most desires for them: first, preservation in the character of God-like holiness and separation from the world, and second, spiritual unity in the brotherhood. "I continued to keep them in your kind of holy character while I was with them," He pled. He had been successful in His guard over them in spite of the fact that Judas, 'the son of perdition,' was lost. This was not Jesus' fault. He had known that Judas was wrong in character from their first contacts in the beginning of His ministry. It was in accord with the Scriptures and eternal counsels of God that he was lost.

His prayer is that the disciples may keep on having[3] His kind of joy realized in their hearts to fulness and completion. He had given them the heavenly teaching and the world hated them because they had His mind and spirit which was essentially in antagonism to that of the world. But joy in the disciple's heart is founded in the sacrifice and service of the Kingdom.

"I ask not that thou shouldest take them out of the world," He continues, "but that thou shouldest keep them from the evil one." He explains that they have His, not the worldly character "Sanctify them in the truth," He earnestly pleads, "thy word is truth." The disciples must remain in the corrupt and hostile world in contact with worldly society, that they may be a purifying influence. They are to be in the world but not of the world. They must not get their spirit, standards, and message from the

---

1 Constative aorist active imperative urgency.   2 Present indicative, active, keep on being one as we.   3 Imperfect indicative active, indicating habitual, repeated, and continuous keeping on the part of Jesus.

worldly society about them. He prays for their sanctification—
that they may go on in growth and perseverance to maturity. To
do this they must continue to dwell in the realm of truth. The
ultimate purpose and concern of Jesus in all His petition for them
is that they may go forth prepared, as the missionaries or apostles
of the Kingdom campaign—the great world movement which He
has initiated. It is to that end that He sets Himself apart in a
sacrificial death, that they may also be set apart and made holy
for their great world-mission. He is sending them out on the
identical mission that the Father had given Him to accomplish
in the world. His great concern now is that they should be fitted
to carry that mission forward.

(3) Jesus does not pray for the intimate group of disciples
around Him alone. He also prays for the disciples who will be
converted through the conversations and preaching of the present
group (vv 20-26). The thing He longs for, on behalf of the future
Kingdom workers and learners, is that they might be one in spirit
and purpose. He would have them go on being unified and keep on
believing in the divine origin and mission of their Lord. He had
just prayed for unity among the eleven (17:11), who had shown
a lack of love just a few hours before at the paschal meal. Jesus
is not thinking primarily of organic union for the future church,
though that would likely be a logical outgrowth of spiritual unity,
in the end. They had organic unity when the prayer was offered
and would have for a long time to come. The most important question is not organic union for denominations, but spiritual unity
for local churches and larger bodies too. Organic union of denominations, without spiritual unity, would be a disaster. Jesus had
imparted to the disciples the glory of the Incarnate Word. This
glory the Son had received from the Father and by self-revelation
had imparted to them. The purpose of his self-revelation was that
they might be one, as He and the Father were one. Schism would
not be possible with such a unity. This unity should embrace the
disciples with the Father and Son, leading to full growth and
efficiency in the promotion of the Kingdom. Lack of spiritual
unity in a church destroys its ability to make the world see the
divine mission of Jesus and the love of the Father for Him and
for them. The Master's great wish for the disciples as He comes
to the close of His prayer is that they should be with Him in order
that they might see His glory, the preexistent glory which the
Father had given Him before the foundation of the world. He
was conscious now of that glory.

He concludes by praying that the Kingdom forces may be
triumphant. "Righteous Father, the world did not know thee,

though I knew thee and these knew that thou didst send me. And I made known thy name (character) and will make it known, that the love with which thou lovest me may continue in them, and I in them." This was to be the secret of the greater and final success—the spiritual unity of the Christian brotherhood founded in love.

CHAPTER XXXII

THE ARREST AND TRIALS OF JESUS

(Harm. §§ 152-161)

Whether the final charge of Jesus to the disciples was given in the upper room or within the Temple enclosure, we are not able to determine. We do know that when He had finished His charge and consecration prayer, He went forth with His disciples from the city to go to Gethsemane, an enclosed place or garden not far from the Stephen's gate.

1. Jesus suffers agony in Gethsemane. (Mark 24:26, 32-42; Matt. 26:30, 36-46; John 18:1).

Descending from this city gate, the group of twelve passed down into the deep gorge and over the little bridge that spanned the brook of the Cedars (Kedron), swollen at this time of the year into a winter torrent[1] and tinged black with the constant stream of blood from the altar of the Temple. Silently they made their way, a spirit of awe upon the disciples, until they arrived at the gate of the well-known enclosure, where Jesus had been accustomed to repair often with the twelve for rest and communion. The present Gethsemane, an enclosed summer-retreat, a garden about seventy paces square containing eight stubby, gnarled, and very ancient olive trees, is pointed out to travelers as the identical garden where Jesus suffered. Even the olive trees are indicated as the very ones, in the moonlit shadows of which Jesus passed the bitter hours of struggle. This is not possible, as we are told by Josephus that the Romans under Titus destroyed all the trees around the city in the siege of 70 A. D. Then too, the long period of two thousand years far surpasses the usual age of such trees. The probable site of the garden would be higher upon the side of the mountain, though the present Gethsemane agrees with the Gospel records, and is much like the original site must have been.

Less than a half-mile walk, in silence from the Stephen's gate and they paused at the garden entrance. "Sit ye here while I go yonder and pray," He said, pointing to a place a little further on in the dense shadows of the olive grove.[2] Eight of the eleven He left at the gate of the enclosure to serve as guard, that He might not be taken by surprise. To them, He gives a parting counsel: "Keep on praying not to enter[3] even once into temptation." Then, taking Peter, James, and John, that they might share with Him the agony of soul and give Him some human sym-

---

1 Edersheim, Life and Times of Jesus, in loco. 2 The garden was well known, and probably belonged to John Mark's mother or some other friend or acquaintance of Jesus.
3 Ingressive aorist infinitive, Robertson. This was a real temptation to evil, not just a trial. cf. Mar. 6:13.

pathy, He began to be amazed and bewildered as the long foreseen passion drew nearer. He became greatly agitated and overcome by a feeling of terrified surprise. Deep sorrow crept over
His soul, and He was troubled. The Gospels use three different
words to describe the state of anguish which submerged Him at
this midnight hour in the garden.

"My soul is exceeding sorrowful, even unto death," He
groaned. "Abide here and watch[1] with me," He entreated the
three. Going forward about a stone's throw, He knelt in prayer.
Moments passed as the three disciples watched Him kneeling
there. He began to pray[2] that this hour might pass away from Him.
Some words of this prayer they overheard: "Abba, Father," He said
"All things are possible unto thee; howbeit, not what I will, but
what thou wilt." Moments passed in silence, and then they saw
Him falling to the ground, and remaining for a long time prostrate
on His face. Then His earnest words broke the silence of the
midnight hour in a cry of anguish: "O my Father, if it be possible, let this cup pass away from me." Then, after a moment, He
added: "Nevertheless, not as I will but as thou wilt." It was the
cup of death—of spiritual death and temporarily severed fellowship with the Father—that Jesus would escape if possible. He
did not shrink from the physical death, but from the hiding of
the Father's face when He "was made a curse for us." Another
period of silence, longer than the first, and again they heard His
voice: "Father, if thou be willing, remove this cup from me;
nevertheless, not my will, but thine be done." Silence again fell
on the scene, and the tired apostles sank down on the ground.
Exhausted and overcome with weariness and sorrow, they soon
fell into a heavy sleep.

> *"Tis midnight, and on Olive's brow*
> *The star is dimmed that lately shone.*
> *Tis midnight in the garden now*
> *The suffering Saviour prays alone."*

He was alone now, humanly speaking. Suddenly a light shone
out from the deep shades of the olive trees, above the brightness of
the full moon. Once before, when Jesus was sorely tried in the
desert, exhausted with the struggle of forty days, He was aided
by angelic visitation. Now, again, an angel appeared unto Him
from heaven and strengthened Him. Being in the dire struggle with
Satan, He prayed yet more earnestly; His sweat became, as it
were, great drops of clotted blood, falling down upon the ground.
It was in such a conflict as this that He conquered Satan in the
desert temptations, and now again He wins a victory over His
arch-enemy, which will give Him confidence and calmness hours

1 Keep awake, gregoreite, present imperative.　　2 Inchoactive imperfect, indicative.

later when He must face His enemies in trial, and on the morrow, when He will have to meet the tragic hour of the cross.

Arising from His posture of prayer, He comes to the disciples and finds them sleeping — sad spectacle of human weakness. "Simon," He called in grieved tones of disappointment, "are you asleep? Did you not have strength enough to keep awake with me one hour?" "Wake up and pray," He adds to the three, "that ye may not enter into temptation." The spiritual nature is ready enough but the flesh is infirm. Again He appeals to them: "Why do you sleep? Rise and pray that ye enter not into temptation." Once more He went away and prayed, saying: "O my Father, if it is not possible[1] that this cup pass away except I drink it, thy will be done." In this second prayer He was more resigned, seeing now more clearly His Father's will.

Again returning, He found them sleeping, for their eyes continued to be weighted[2] down with sleep, and were very heavy. They were extremely embarrassed, and did not know what to answer Him. Both their shame and their drowsiness made them dumb. Again He left them, and prayed the third time, using the same words. Returning, He said with sadness: "Are you still sleeping and taking your rest? It is enough: the hour has come." Seeing the lights of the approaching cohort, and their armor glistening in the light of the moon, He exclaimed: Look! the Son of Man is already betrayed[3] into the hands of sinners. Arise! let us be going! See, the one betraying us is already here."

2. Jesus is betrayed, arrested, and forsaken. (Mark 14:43-52; Matt. 26:47-56; Luke 22:47-53; John 18:2-12).

Judas knew the habit of Jesus of repairing to the garden of Gethsemane frequently to spend an hour in communion or sometimes a night in the open air with His disciples. Acquainted with this custom, he had deliberately planned with the Sanhedrists to arrest Him in this place in the dead hours of the night and thus avoid a popular tumult. It was the very spirit of the devil in him that would make him stoop so low as to arrest his defenseless Teacher, and that in His place of secret prayer.[4] Judas doubtless led the arresting party first to the house of John Mark's mother, where the paschal meal had been eaten hours before. We know that a young man, probably John Mark himself, followed the band of soldiers to Gethsemane, and, when apprehended as a suspicious character, left the linen wrap which he had hastily thrown around him and fled, naked. The Gospel of Mark alone mentions this fact and without giving the name.[5]

1 First class condition, determined as fulfilled.
2 Past perfect passive indicative periphrastic.   3 Perfect indicative, active stands betrayed.   4 Robertson's Word Pictures. (Jno. 18:2).   5 Mark 14:51, 52.

The arrest of Jesus was effected by the Sanhedrists through the Temple police, accompanied by a part of the cohort of Roman soldiers from the tower of Antonia. This cohort of some five hundred soldiers was kept in the tower to quell any tumult among the people and act as an emergency police force. It is possible that these soldiers were granted the Sanhedrists by Pilate, in order to effect the arrest without a tumult among the people. The arrangement of this matter would account for the delay in the coming of Judas and the armed force to Gethsemane until after midnight. The Temple police were under direct orders as servant-officers from the chief priests and Pharisees. The party came armed with short-swords and staves or clubs, and brought torches and lanterns fastened on the top of the poles.

Judas came a little in advance and entered the garden gate. He had combined with the police, before arriving at Gethsemane, on a secret sign by which they might identify Jesus. There was a great mob of the street rabble who followed the soldiers, perhaps largely through curiosity. The officers likely supposed that their intended prisoner might seek to escape into the midst of the crowd, or hide in some dark corner of the garden, and so evade arrest. The sign by which they were to identify Jesus was the friendly salutation of a kiss bestowed by Judas in this dastardly act of treason.

He had instructed the police to seize the one thus indicated and lead Him away safely. Immediately, on entering the gate, and perceiving Jesus with the eleven, he drew near to kiss Him. Stepping forward, he said: "Rabbi!" and kissed Him effusively.[1] Jesus consciously permitted the contemptible desecration of the friendly salutation but did not allow it to go unchallenged. "Judas," He exclaimed, "betrayest thou the Son of Man with a kiss?" He reminded him that it was the Son of Man, the Messiah, whom he was betraying, and that his act of treachery was known. He exposes the attempted parade of affection as a despicable act of treason. "Comrade," He said, "do your errand!" Thus He reprimanded the disloyalty of one who had been harbored for three years as a comrade and friend, and at the same time prompted him to finish with his fiendish task. Then, brushing the traitor to one side, and conscious of all the plans of His enemies and of the inevitable suffering ahead, He stepped forth into the clear radiance of the full moon and asked the captains of the Temple police: "Whom seek ye?" They answered, abashed "Jesus the Nazarene." He said: "I am He."

1 Katafilein, intensive force of kata, warmly, intensely.

A strange thing happened when He thus announced His identity. In fear, perhaps, of some miracle of power which this great Wonder-Worker might produce against them, or in sheer fright before the awfulness of His majesty as He stood before them in the weird light, they went backward and fell to the ground. He advanced nearer to them and asked again: "Whom seek ye?" and they answered: "Jesus the Nazarene," He repeated: "I told you that I am He. If therefore ye seek me, permit these to go their way," He added, pointing to the eleven disciples. Thus He voluntarily surrendered Himself, and, solicitous for His disciples, begged that they be permitted to retire unmolested. This was that His word in the great high-priestly prayer should be fulfilled: "Of those whom thou gavest me, I lost not one."[1]

Then the police, when they saw that He was giving Himself up voluntarily, without any show of resistance, came forward and laid hands on Him. When His disciples saw the cruel treatment and death which would follow, they said: "Lord, shall we smite with the sword?" They had only two short-swords, used probably in the preparation of the Passover lamb. But before the question had scarcely been uttered, impulsive Peter drew his sword and struck at the nearest assailant of His master, never stopping for a moment to consider the consequences. He loved his Lord, and was willing to lose his life for Him, if need be. He doubtless meant to make an end of Malchus, the servant of the high priest, but he missed his head, and only took off his ear. John preserves for us the record of this act of uncalculating bravery, years afterwards. It was an act that would have brought death to its perpetrator, had it not been for the immediate action of Jesus.

Calling Simon Peter, He said: "Put up thy sword in thy sheath; for all they that take the sword shall perish with the sword." Then addressing Himself quickly to the police who were holding Him, He said: "Give me leave just thus far," and, stepping forward, He touched the severed ear of Malchus and healed it.

Again turning to His devoted disciple band, He pleads: "The cup which the Father hath given me, shall I not drink it?" He had shown by His ready use of the healing power in benefit of an enemy that He was not divested of that power which they feared but now. But He would not make use of that power except for others. He reminds the disciples at the same time that He must follow the divine plan for His life, and drink the cup of suffering and death to the dregs. He neither claimed nor expected any protection from them in this hour. "Thinkest thou," He added, "that I cannot beseech my Father and He will send even now twelve legions of angels?" If one angel slew in a single night a hundred and eighty-

1 Jno. 17:12.

five thousand of Sennacherib's army, what would this handful of police and soldiers be in the face of an angelic army of seventy-two thousands? But "how then would the Scriptures be fulfilled that thus it must be?" Elisha's man at Dothan had his eyes opened, and saw the hosts of angelic defenders encamped about the prophet. Jesus did not need human defenders. He had won the victory in Gethsemane and now faces His destiny unflinchingly.

But He did not leave the forces of darkness unreproved. He reminded them with biting irony that they were treating Him as if He were a violent bandit-robber[1] like Barabbas. "They had come out against Him with short-swords and with clubs." With keen satire, He reproached them. "Day by day, I was in the Temple teaching, and ye did not arrest me." He made them understand that this was a clear exhibition of errant cowardice. Such reproachful and cutting words directed against the bigoted priests and their servant-officers would only provoke them to violence. The disciples were filled with fear. They were not permitted by their Master to interfere. He had given them to understand that this was the "hour of the power of darkness." Though He rebuked the Jewish rulers for their secret and violent mode of arrest, the disciples must submit to the divine will as the ultimate cause.

The best thing was to withdraw. "They left Him and fled." Only one sympathetic bystander lingered. He had overheard something of the conversation of the Paschal Supper in the upper room, and, after the apostles had withdrawn with Jesus, he had lain awake, thinking of some impending peril for the great Rabbi who had celebrated the Passover in his mother's home. Far into the night, Judas had appeared at the door, inquiring of the whereabouts of Jesus. The young man, prompted by curiosity, had arisen hastily and throwing a linen cloth, perhaps a sheet, about him, had plunged out into the street and followed at a distance the soldier band until they had come to Gethsemane. Then he had been a too-interested observer of all until all the disciples had fled. He was noticed and as quickly seized, but escaped from the hands of the police with the loss of the linen cloth, and tradition adds, with the loss of the fingers of one hand, severed by a soldier's stroke.[2] This striking incident was written down by the "stub-fingered" writer of the earliest of the gospels. None of the other writers were eye-witnesses to this young disciple's early devotion, except himself.

1 Lestes, a robber that uses violence in his theft
2 David Smith, In the Days of His Flesh.

3. The preliminary examination by Annas, the Ex-High-Priest. (Jno. 18:12-14, 19-23).

The Roman officer (chiliarch) was with the Temple police and took part in the arrest. They seized Jesus and tied His hands behind Him. He was led away, first to Annas, who had served as high-priest from 6 to 15 A. D., and, through astute politics, had succeeded in securing from the Romans the succession of this office to his five sons, and now his son-in-law Caiaphas, who was the present occupant of the high-priesthood. Annas owned the famous Bazaars of Annas, which ran a monopoly on the sale of animals for the sacrifices and the stalls of the money-changers. It was the vested interests of this monopoly that Jesus had assailed in the first and second cleansing of the Temple. From the day of the first cleansing of the Temple, the young Rabbi had incurred the eternal enmity of this astute old politician and his ring of coadjutors. Various times the representatives of this clique had assailed the Messianic authority of Jesus, assumed on that occasion. They had dogged His steps with their emissaries everywhere He went, seeking to entrap Him in some word or work. Now at last they have Him in their power. One of His own disciples had betrayed Him, and He is led before this arch-enemy for a preliminary hearing, in preparation for the mock trial which is to follow as soon as the Sanhedrin can be aroused and brought together.

Caiaphas, the high priest (18-36 A. D.) and his son-in-law, was thoroughly lined up with Annas in all that he might perpetrate against the hated Nazarene. Weeks ago, he had suggested in a secret session of the Sanhedrists, when plotting the ruin of the "pretender-Messiah," that it was very convenient that one man die for the people rather than that the whole nation perish. It was to the interest of the people that Jesus should die. By interests, Caiaphas doubtless meant the personal and vested interests of the Bazaars, as well as the political interests of the leaders. The Talmud pronounces a curse on the family of Hanan (Annas) and their serpent-hissings.[1] They made the Temple a "market-house" and a "den of robbers."

The preliminary examination before Annas and the later hearing before Caiaphas during the hours of the night took place in the palace of the high-priest, in which Annas also seems to have resided. The palace of Caiaphas probably stood on the southern slope of the western hill, a short distance outside of the present city wall, but in what was then the finest part of the city. Annas was the high-priest emeritus at this time, and, as such, retained a large place of influence and prerogative in the pro-

1 Pesach 57:1.

ceedings of the Sanhedrin. To him was the task assigned of the preliminary hearing of the urgent case under consideration. This preliminary hearing took place in one of the apartments of the high priest's palace, a large building surrounding a central court, designated for the uses of Annas, whose residence was in another part of the city, between the Tyropoean valley and the upper city. Jesus was conducted around the northern wall of the city to the palace of Caiaphas. This was the best road to avoid a popular tumult.

Annas questioned Jesus on two counts: first, as to His disciples, and second, as to His doctrines. His desire was to find out how extensive the following of Jesus had become. Probably he thought that Jesus had some such organization as the Order of the Essenes, yet undiscovered to the outside world. He might have desired to prepare the way for the extirpation of the hated movement by harrying the followers with persecution. Incidentally, he might desire to know how extensive Jesus' influence had become in the higher circles of Jerusalem society. At least two members of the Sanhedrin had been infected with His doctrines. Others might have suffered the same contagion. But to this astute and crafty old politician, Jesus gave no word of information about His disciples. The whole proceeding of this examination was illegal, both as to time and place. With calmness Jesus maintained a dignified and justified silence, asserting His legal rights as a prisoner.

Annas, perceiving the impossibility of going further into this question, turned to the examination of His doctrines. To his questions on this count, Jesus protested that He had no secret doctrine. "I have spoken openly to the world, I ever taught[1] in the synagogues and in the Temple, where all the Jews customarily congregate. In secret, I spoke nothing." These facts were beyond discussion and known to all. The inquiry about His disciples got no answer from Him; the one about His doctrine was needless, He asserts: "Why askest thou me? ask them that have heard[2] me, what I spake unto them." Such a clear statement at once made ridiculous the shallowness of the present examination, and, at the same time, incriminated the illegal "secret" procedure of the designing Hanan in such a night trial, which should have been conducted, if at all, in the Temple. But when the argument is at an end violence begins with such rulers, and one of the servile attendants of the nefarious judge, seeing Annas worsted in argument, struck Jesus an insulting blow in the face with his hand, saying: "Answerest thou the high priest thus?"

1 Constative aorist, edidaxa, gives a summary of His methods in the ministry.
2 PPerfect active indicative, His message was permanent in the minds of the hearers.

In a hall of judgment, such an act of violence was an outrage upon common decency. Jesus did not turn the other cheek literally, but with quiet dignity protested: "If I have spoken evil, bear wit· ness to the evil; but if well, why smitest thou me?" Such a violent turn with the silent approval of Annas, met by such a calm and dignified reply, terminated the examination. It was evident that the prisoner got the best of the argument. But He was sent, bound, to Caiaphas, who had meanwhile summoned those Sanhedrists who would best serve his ends.[1] Jesus had meekly required a legal procedure with the summoning of witnesses. Such a requirement could not be refused. But Annas, the chief conspirator, though baffled and defeated in his first hearing, will be a secret but prime mover in the subsequent trials.

4. The first trial before Caiaphas and the Sanhedrin. (Mark 14:53, 55-65; Matt. 26:57, 59-68; Luke 22:54, 63-65; Jno. 18:24).

The regular place for the meeting of the Sanhedrin was in the Temple, but they led Jesus away to the house of the high-priest Caiaphas, situated in a place just outside the present wall of the city, where all the chief priests and elders and scribes had been summoned to meet. Nor was the legal hour of meeting for trials in the night. Other features in the illegality practised in the trials of Jesus were: undue haste, seeking or bribing witnesses, neglecting to warn the witnesses solemnly before they should give evidence, forcing the accused to testify against Himself, judicial use of the prisoner's confession, and failure to release the prisoner when there was failure of agreement between wit-nesses.

Caiaphas, who had been high priest for a number of years, was a Sadducee and a crafty and hard individual, tied up with all the corruption of the Annas Bazaars and their intriguing poli-tics. Aided and abetted now by Annas with the chief priests and whole council, he made diligent search[2] to secure false witnesses to testify against Jesus with the express purpose[3] of putting Him to death. Many false witnesses came and gave their testimony but no agreement was found. According to the code of the Jews, the testimony of at least two witnesses must be identical or in harmony (Deut. 19:15). They had a difficult time finding any two that were equal.

Finally, two stood up and made an attempt to bear false witness against Him, saying: "We have heard Him say, I will destroy this temple that is made with hands and, in three days, I will rebuild it without hands." This was evidently a perversion

1 It seems that Nicodemus and Joseph of Aramathea were not present.
2 Imperfect tense, ezetoun, repeated and protracted search.
3 Hina with aorist subjunctive in purpose clause.

of the words of Jesus, uttered in connection with the first cleansing of the Temple (Jno. 19:12). Jesus had said: "Destroy this temple, and I will build it up again in three days," referring to the temple of His body, an enigmatic answer to the demand of the Annas Bazaar leaders, who challenged His Messianic authority, for a sign. Mark's account of the false testimonies in the trial is slightly different. "This man said, I will destroy the temple of God and build it again in three days." But these witnesses did not agree, and they could make out no definite charge to lay before the Roman authorities to secure His death sentence. All efforts seemed to no avail. In the midst of all, Jesus maintained a dignified silence.[1]

The high priest, incensed by failure to secure adequate testimony for conviction, and stung by the calm and composed attitude of the accused, stepped forth, and facing the prisoner who stood guarded by soldiers, he demanded in impatient and provoking tones: "Answerest thou nothing? What is it that these are testifying against thee?" But to his haughty, rasping, and repeated demands, Jesus maintained a calm silence.

Then the astute and wily high-priest resorted to an unjust legal trick: "I put thee on oath," he said. "By the living God, are you the Messiah, the Son of God?"

The hour has now come for the declaration Jesus had avoided making to the general public through the three years of His ministry. If He had so declared Himself, it would have led to open and disastrous revolt against the Roman government, under His forced leadership, or to His condemnation before the Jews if He had refused them their wishes. He was not the kind of Messiah the Jews were expecting—a temporal king. He could easily have evaded the issue through rabbinical casuistry, but He chose deliberately not to do so, but voluntarily deliver Himself into their hands to be condemned. To claim divine sonship or equality with God was blasphemy and subject to the death penalty. Jesus was fully conscious of this. Silence fell on the court as, with intensity, all awaited His answer.

His words, pronounced with majestic calm, in tones of unmistakable conviction, ring down through the centuries until now: "Thou hast said I am," and He added, "from now on, ye shall see the Son of Man sitting at the right hand of power and coming on the clouds of heaven." To His declaration of what He claimed to be, Jesus added predictive words of what God would show Him to be in His resurrection, ascension, and second advent. In the last-mentioned event, the tables would be turned, and they

1 Imperfect tense of continued action·

would appear in judgment before Him, the Messianic judge, when He should come upon the clouds of heaven. This prophecy was partly fulfilled in that generation and is being fulfilled progressively in history.

Jesus was not their kind of Messiah. He was not seeking an earthly throne. But He claimed to be the Messiah, and they would make use of His confession to secure His condemnation of treason before the Roman court. Before the Jews, He would stand condemned for blasphemy. To have remained silent would have amounted to denial of His Messianic claims. He could not do that. So Caiaphas had gained his end, as he thought, by a smart trick of the law. In reality, Jesus had voluntarily chosen to meet then and there the issue of His atoning death. With a great show of horror, the high-priest rent his upper and outer garments, saying: "He hath spoken blasphemy. What further need have we of witnesses? Ye have heard the blasphemy. What think ye?" And they all of one accord condemned Him to be liable to death.[1] The vote was taken and, with but two exceptions, was unanimous. Joseph of Arimathea and Nicodemus were probably absent, not being invited to the session because they were under suspicion of secret attachment to Jesus (Luke 23:51). But the sentence was not pronounced. This was impossible, since the sentence of blasphemy would not serve as an accusation before Pilate, and the Sanhedrin had no power to pass sentence of treason against the Roman government involving the death penalty.

Following the vote of the Sanhedrists, which to all intents sealed the doom of the prisoner—the sentence awaiting the mere formal ratification in the legal session at sunrise—ensued one of the most disgraceful scenes recorded in the annals of the human race. With uncontrolled glee and abandon, like a lot of hoodlums, these doctors of divinity insulted Jesus. They actually spat in His face, beat Him on the neck with their fists, struck Him in the face with the palms of their hands, giving vent to their spite and hatred. This was the hour of the power of darkness indeed![2] The soldiers and the Temple servant-officers of the high priests who were holding Him, blindfolded Him, and striking Him with rods, said: "Prophesy unto us, thou Christ, who it is that struck thee?" Luke adds: "Many other things spoke they against Him, reviling Him." Such a scene of vulgar brutality, enacted by and with the approval of the dignified Sanhedrin, was worthy of the lowest criminals of the underworld. It left upon that august court a blot which was mainly the cause of its extinc-

1 Lev. 24:15.   2 Robertson's Word Pictures, Matt. 26:68.

tion a few years later. Well might the Jews wish to obliterate this
smirch on the national garment in generations to come, but it
remains an indelible record in the annals of the Jewish race.
And, too, He was "the glory of His people Israel."

5. Peter three times denies His Lord. (Mark 14:54, 66-72;
Matt. 26:58, 69:75; Luke 22:54-62; Jno. 18:15-27.)

All the Gospels give the sad account of the denials of Peter,
but in varying order. The denials cover some time, more than an
hour at least during the illegal and informal ecclesiastical trials
before Annas and Caiaphas. They took place in the official residence of the high priest Caiaphas, where Annas had retained lodging apartments on one side of the large open court of that com-
modious building.

After the panic, in which all the eleven had left Jesus to His
enemies in Gethsemane, two had gained courage enough to turn
back and follow the arresting party as it was leading Jesus away
to the palace of the high priest on the west side of the city. John,
whose name is not revealed, came up with the band and entered
in immediately on arrival, being a personal acquaintance of the
high priest, probably through business relationships when he was
in the fishing firm in Capernaum. Peter, in spite of his previous
boast that he would follow Him even to death and his reckless
assault on Malchus, servant of the high priest, in the hour of arrest, "was following the party now afar off." There were others
of the twelve who did not follow at all, but went and hid themselves for fear of the officers. Peter was a leader and bore a
greater responsibility. Though he was filled with dread and fear
at this hour, he yet loved his Master. He did not press up in the
crowd with John, for fear of identification after the tragic attempt
in Gethsemane. Coming finally to the palace of the high priest,
he stationed himself just outside the door of the inner court where
John had passed with the soldiers and police leading Jesus. When
John, who had doubtless caught sight of his fellow-disciple following afar off, saw that he had not entered with them, he came
back and spoke to the porter-maid[1] and brought Peter on the
inside.

The maid suspected Peter, doubtless from his distressed looks,
and asked him. "And you are not one of the disciples of this
man, are you?" Her question was formed to expect a negative
answer,[2] but her attitude obviously betrayed her suspicion. Peter
was caught off guard, and awkwardly yielded to his impulse and

1 Feminine form of article te, with thuroro, porter; also paidiske, feminine.
2 Me expects negative answer.

replied: "I am not." But his whole attitude revealed the fact he had not spoken the truth. Meantime, Jesus had passed through the first examination before Annas.

Admitted to the open court by the door of the archway, Peter took his place among the officers, sitting around the coal fire which they had kindled in an iron container in the open court. It was a chilly night, and Peter, unabashed by his lie, joined himself to the group and stood in the light of the fire. While he was warming himself[1] the inevitable porter-maid, relieved at her post of duty, came into the group, and, with her unallayed suspicion, fixing her eyes upon him said: "Thou wast with the Galilean." Peter tried this time to pass the matter over lightly. "I know not what thou sayest," he declared. But her curiosity was unabated and his affected innocence confirmed her suspicions. With furtive glances at the shrinking figure of Peter, she passed in and out, and imparted to the officers her misgivings: "This man was also with Him," she said, pointing to him. "Woman, I know Him not," affirmed the evidently disturbed stranger. Others of the party continued to probe him with the same question: "Art thou also one of His disciples?" To which he returned the same affirmation: "I am not."

Pursued further by the mischievous porter-maid, he denied any knowledge at all of what she was asking, and quietly passed out of the group into the porch, to escape, if possible, further notice. Then the cock crew and Peter remembered what Jesus had said. Years later, he related to Mark the pang of conscience at the signal, recalling the warning words of Jesus. He could not escape even here the sharp eyes of the suspicious porter-maid. She had doubtless informed her substitute at the gate to keep a sharp lookout for this suspect. So when he sought temporary concealment on the porch, this other portress saw him and reported his whereabouts. Leading the officers to him, she said: "This man was also with Jesus the Nazarene." Again Peter denied it, and this time with an oath, "I know not the man."

An hour dragged by as Peter nervously waited outside on the porch. Jesus was now before Caiaphas. The false witnesses were giving their testimony. Peter had become more desperate by this time and returned once again to the group by the fire. John was in the quadrangle-hall where they were trying Jesus. One after another, men and maids charged Peter with being a Galilean, as evidenced by his provincial pronunciation.[2] Finally, the sharp question of a kinsman of Malchus: "Did I not see thee in the garden with Him?", revealed the deception of Peter, who

1 Periphrastic present, vivid picture of continued action.   2 Matt. 26:73.

was thrown completely off his balance, and, losing his temper, fell into bitter curses, invoking the sacred oath to prove his ignorance and lack of acquaintance with Jesus. Just at this juncture, the cock crew the second time, and Peter again remembered with a pang of conscience the words of the Master: "Before the cock crows twice, thou shalt deny me thrice."

Just at this juncture, Jesus, who had been condemned already by the adroit but illegal trickery of the high priest, turned His eyes in one understanding sad look at Peter, who had failed Him in this tragic hour; and that disciple, pierced to the heart, went out to weep alone in bitter and agonizing repentance. How it must have hurt the heart of Jesus that Simon, His trusted lieutenant, had failed Him. The devil was sifting this poor disciple, who loved his Lord but who through weakness had failed Him in this tragic hour. It was the prayer and love-look of Jesus that saved Simon then and gave to the world Peter, in the years to come.

6. After dawn, Jesus is formally condemned by the Sanhedrin. (Mark 15:1; Matt. 27:1; Luke 22:66-71.)

The trial before Caiaphas during the night finished, Jesus was subjected to the unrestrained insults, taunts, and brutality of the Temple police, the servant-officers of the high priest under the vengeful patronage of Annas and Caiaphas. It had been only three days since Jesus had dared to cleanse the Temple of their nefarious traffic and scandalous robbery. Their hour of vengeance had come and they made use of it, filling every moment with insults and injuries.

In order to give a legal sanction to their notoriously illegal proceeding, the elders of the people were assembled immediately at the dawn of day, including both the Sadducean chief priests and Pharisaic scribes, for consultation against Jesus, for the express purpose[1] of putting Him to death. A court is founded for meting out justice; and not to purposely work injustice. Before the sun had risen, they came, leading Jesus into their Sanhedrin council chamber, the Hall of Hewn Stone within the Temple area. They led Him to the Temple before the city was astir.

"Tell us,"[2] they demanded roughly, "If you are the Messiah." This trial was for mere ratification of what had been decided during the night. They would brook no hesitation. There was no time to be lost. All justice was disregarded in this session, as in the illegal night session which preceded. The reply of Jesus was against the injustice of their whole proceeding: "If I tell you that I am the Messiah, ye will assuredly not believe; and if I question you,

1 Hoste with aorist infinitive, to put Him to death quickly.
2 Second aorist imperative, a quick reply was expected.

and try to discuss the matter with you, ye will not answer my questions. But from now on, the Son of Man shall be seated on the right hand of the power of God." This declaration they rapidly recognized as a declaration of the Messianic Psalm, a claim to Messiahship, and to the prophecy of Daniel, a claim to divinity.[1] "Art thou then the Son of God?" they all asked in a chorus of disorder. "Ye say that I am," He replied calmly. He had clearly claimed to be the Messiah and the Son of God, to be the human and divine Messiah, to be man and God. "What further need of witnesses have we?" they declared with vehemence. "For we ourselves also have heard from his own mouth." In accusing Him to Pilate, they said nothing of this charge of blasphemy, the ground of His condemnation before the Sanhedrin.

7. The remorse and suicide of Judas the Betrayer. (Matt. 27: 3-10; Acts 1:18, 19.)

Judas was stricken in his conscience deeply in the garden when he saw Jesus roughly bound by the soldiers and led away to His trial. Through the succeeding hours, it is likely that he followed closely every tragic step of the mock trials until the final condemnation before the Sanhedrin. When they led Him away to Pilate, Judas knew the doom of the prisoner.

Filled with remorse, and realizing that every hope was lost, he hastened ere the Sanhedrists had dispersed, and came to the high priest and elders with his belated confession, returning the thirty pieces of silver. This they disdainfully rejected "I betrayed innocent blood," he protested. "What is that to us," they sneered, "You will see to that." To be rid of this despicable nuisance, these hypocritical rulers retired into the holy place. Thither Judas might not penetrate. So, coming to the door, he cast the silver shekels on the pavement of the floor at their feet and left. Judas had a deep sorrow in his heart, unconfessed to God, that led him to his death. Peter sinned, and filled with sorrow, came back to Christ. Judas sinned, and filled with remorse, sought death at his own hands as refuge.[2] Going out, he hanged himself. This was a tragic obituary, the inevitable end of a traitor's career.

The vile priests, no better than the betrayer, were left with the blood money lying scattered at their feet. What use could these pious hypocrites make of it? They might not defile the treasury with it. They cast about to find a fitting use and soon bethought them of the potter's field, a useless clay-bed outside the city walls, which they purchased to use as a burial place for the "Gentile dogs" who might perchance die in the holy city of Jerusalem. This was an ancient prophecy fulfilled: "And the thirty pieces of

1 Ps. 110:1; Daniel 7:13.   2 Direct middle voice.

silver, the price of him that was priced, whom certain of the children of Israel did price, he gave them for the potter's field, as the Lord appointed me." (Zech. 11:13; Jer. 18:2; 32:6-15.) In the Acts of the Apostles,[1] Luke refers to the potter's field, Alcedama, the field of blood. It seems that in the primitive church, there was a belief that Judas hanged himself there and his swollen and putrefying body fell headlong and burst asunder. Such a loathesome tale has come down through the centuries, a monument to the crime and terrible end of the traitor, who is burned in effigy in thousands of towns and hamlets where the story of his treason has penetrated. But the Field of Blood has remained a monument also to the crime of the Sanhedrists, who were worse if possible than the traitor, whom they depised. The price of the blood of Jesus was cast as garbage to the poor Gentile dogs, a prophecy of the near rejection of the Jews and grafting of the Gentile races.

8. First appearance before Pilate. (Mark 15:1-5; Matt. 27:2, 11-14; Luke 23:1-5; Jno. 18:28-38).

The civil trial could not be held before sunrise. The term "early" usually meant the fourth watch, from three to six A. M. The whole Sanhedrin,[2] with the probable exception of Nicodemus and Joseph of Arimathea, rose up, and brought Jesus bound from the Temple to the Praetorium built by Herod on the western hill of the city. Since it was yet "early" when they came, the second "religious trial" before Caiaphas, must have been as technically illegal as was the first; for it was illegal to condemn a prisoner to death during the night. The main purpose of the Sanhedrists was to get the sanction of the Roman government to their sentence, so that the execution might take place early in the day, and be out of the way before the Sabbath, which began at six P. M. They also feared a revolt among the people and wished to get the civil sanction before the city was astir.

Pontius Pilate was the Roman Procurator from 26 to 36 A. D. He resided ordinarily in Cesarea, but during the feasts was accustomed to be present in Jerusalem, so as to quickly suppress any disorder. He was born in Seville, Spain, was twice married, having abandoned his first wife to marry Claudia, the daughter of Julia, the prostitute daughter of the Emperor Augustas. After a checkered political career as procurator, he was banished by Caligula on account of his cruelty and inability to maintain order, to Vienne, Gaul, and at Mount Pilatus he ended his life by suicide. He was a typical Roman—stern and practical. He had a contempt

1 Acts 1:18, 19.   2 Luke 23:1.

for religious superstitions and traditions, and an imperious desire to rule with a high hand, compelling obedience. He had not tactfully managed his government, and soon became odious to the Jews and Romans. He planted his standards on the citadel on his first entry to the city, regardless of the religious feeling of the people, prohibiting all images. The people were greatly incensed at the standards, bearing the Emperor's image, and requested their removal. Pilate at first scorned their request, and threatened them later with violence; but, with extreme persistence, the Jews won out and the Governor submitted. Later, when he would have constructed an aqueduct for supplying the city with water, he made the serious blunder of defraying the cost from the Temple treasury. When the people revolted, he suppressed the tumult with great cruelty. Just a short while before the trial of Jesus, he had suppressed a popular uprising among the people by falling on a company of Galileans in the Temple court and mingling their blood with their sacrifices, a thing which sent a shudder of religious superstition and horror through the whole nation. Other tactless measures and acts of atrocity had so disposed the rulers of the Jews, that they were ready to withstand his rulings and make demands at his hands, with the conviction that with persistence they would force him to yield to their desires. They were also acquainted with the fact that the Roman Emperor followed the policy of sustaining the governor of a province only so long as he could succeed in raising successfully the imperial taxes and maintaining peace and order in the land. To this hated and despised governor, who resided in the magnificent palace erected by Herod the Great, the whole company of the Sanhedrin brought their prisoner to secure the civil sanction to their judicial murder. They would not enter the palace under the pretext of religious scruples. They would, by entering a Gentile house, incur a ceremonial pollution which would debar them from taking part in any festal solemnities. They were not scrupulous about the cruel and bloody deed they were enacting in bringing an innocent man to his death. This is an illustration of much unrighteousness in some who profess to be religious. It was part of their policy, in dealing with the vacillating Pilate, to sting him with a refusal to enter his palace, on the ground of defilement by his Gentile-contact.

They came demanding his unqualified approval of their death sentence, already deliberated by the Sanhedrin. They did not wish that he should even examine the case at all. Pilate surprises them with a bold demand that they should state the terms and grounds of accusation. "What accusation do you bring against this man?" They answer that he need not make this inquiry or reopen the case. "Had he not been an evil doer, we would not have handed him over to thee." They intimated that they would suffer no delay or interference.

Pilate had suffered their effrontery in their refusal to enter the Praetorium and had come on the outside to hear their accusation against the prisoner. When they demanded his sanction without stating their accusation, he replied with Roman hauteur: "Take[1] him right now and judge him according to *your* law." But this procedure had been of the form of criminal investigation and had been in private. The Roman law, to the contrary, demanded public proceedings and definite accusations.[2] While they attempted to evade and intimidate in their peremptory reply, they had to recognize that Pilate had Roman law clearly on his side in this instance, and they had to yield. But in yielding, they made known to him that their august Sanhedrin had judged Him worthy of death, and such a verdict was not to be passed over lightly. "We may not put anyone to death," they reminded him. They had come to have their sentence confirmed and to get the death warrant.

They would not be defeated in their aim. They had foreseen that they might not obtain his sanction to their accusation of blasphemy, through mere intimidation. So they pretend compromise and offer an accusation of *treason* on three counts: (1) They charged Him with plotting sedition. "We found this fellow perverting our nation," they declared. The way the Jewish enemies of Jesus shifted their ground from a political to a religious charge was a piece of chicanery, born of subtle malignity. Of course, the charge of fomenting sedition was the furthest thing conceivable from the whole character of Jesus. (2) The second item in the charge was that He forbade paying tribute to Caesar. This was a deliberate falsehood. On the previous Tuesday, Jesus had said to the Herodians: "Render unto Caesar the things which are Caesar's," thus inculcating loyalty to the government as due from every citizen. (3) The third count of the charge was that He claimed to be the Messiah, a King. Of course Jesus did not claim to be a temporal king. It was such a kingship that He had refused to accept constantly. It was these same accusers of Jesus who were secretly nourishing in their hearts the desire for a temporal Messiah, a king who would throw off the yoke of Roman bondage.

When Pilate had received the accusation of sedition, he entered again into the Praetorium, where Jesus had remained, and made a personal examination of the accused. He called Jesus and had Him come and stand before him. "Thou," he said respectfully, "art thou

---

1 Second aorist, prompt action.   2 Edersheim, *Life and Times of Jesus.*

the King of the Jews?" There were many pretenders to kingship
in those times, but Jesus did not impress Pilate as such. Still,
he could not ignore the accusation brought against Jesus without
himself being accused of disloyalty to Caesar. Before the multitude and leaders, Jesus had maintained a dignified silence; now
when alone with Pilate, He speaks freely. Jesus judged that
Pilate was not hardened beyond appeal, so, in reply, He said:
"Sayest thou this of thyself, or did others tell thee about me?"
He sought thus to enlist the personal interest of Pilate, and interpret to him the falsity of the charge of the accusers. Did Pilate
have a personal interest in His claims or merely official concern?
To this question, the governor quickly replied disowning any personal interest.[1] "Am I a Jew? Thy nation handed thee over to me.
What didst thou do?" There was a tinge of proud Roman scorn in
these words of Pilate. He did not deign to have a personal interest
in any prisoner, much less a Jew. His sole interest was to learn
the truth or falsity of the accusation. Jesus gives him a clear
statement of the facts in the case: "My kingdom is not of this
world," He declared, "Had my kingdom been of this world,[2] my
servants would have been striving that I might not be handed
over to the rulers. But, as it is, my kingdom is not from hence."

At once, Pilate was more interested. "Then thou art a King?"
he exclaimed.

"Thou sayest, because a King I am," was the clear reply.
"To this end, I have been born, and for this purpose came I
into this world, in order that I might bear witness to the truth.
The one who is of the truth goes on hearing my voice." Thus
Jesus explained that His kingdom was not secular, as the Sanhedrin accused, but spiritual, a Kingdom not of outward force,
territory, law and order, but of inward convictions and sentiments,
a Kingdom of the heart, a Kingdom of truth.

Pilate was convinced that Jesus was a religious enthusiast
and visionary philosopher. There could be no danger to the Roman
government from such a person; of that he was quite sure. Jesus
had spoken of the Kingdom of truth in order to awaken in Pilate,
if possible, some personal interest in spiritual and moral realities
in the spiritual kingdom. "What is truth?" Pilate asked. But he
did not wait for the reply. He went out again to the waiting
rulers and announced: "I find no fault in him." Such was his
verdict. He should have set Jesus free at once.

But it was not so to be. The enemies of Jesus turned loose a
deluge of venomous accusations, and kept up a clamor. But
Jesus maintained a calm and dignified silence, insomuch that the

1 Edersheim, Life and Times of Jesus. 2 Second class condition, contrary to fact.

governor was impressed, and asked: "Hearest thou not how many things they witness against thee? Answerest thou nothing?" But Jesus held His peace, and Pilate greatly marvelled. In the midst of the pandemonium, some shouted out repeatedly: "He stirreth up the people, teaching throughout all Judea, beginning from Galilee even unto this place." Pilate caught the word "Galilee," and bethought him of a device to rid himself of the responsibility of this troublesome case. Herod Antipas was on a visit to Jerusalem during the Feast. Jesus came from Galilee. He could turn the case over to Herod; and he did.

9.   Jesus before Herod Antipas, the Tetrarch (Luke 26:6-12).

Luke probably had the report of the appearance of Jesus before Herod Antipas from Joanna, the wife of Chuza, Herod's steward. Pilate was glad to find a loophole, to escape, if possible, the responsibility for the death of Jesus. When he heard about His being a Galilean, he made inquiry and secured more complete information concerning His coming under Herod's jurisdiction. It seems that there had been some dispute between these two rulers as to their respective rights; and here was a case in point. It furnished a fine pretext for Pilate to recognize formally the full rights of Antipas and incidentally escape the difficult situation in which he found himself. So he sent Jesus to Herod, doubtless with a flattering letter of recognition of Herod's rights in this case.

It had been Herod's desire for a long time to see Jesus. He had heard of the many wonderful miracles performed by Him, and had felt that possibly it was John the Baptist come back to life again. He had beheaded John to please the wicked Herodias, to whom he was married unlawfully, and to satisfy a whim of Salome, the daughter of Herodias, in payment for a lewd dance in the entertainment of his drunken guests at an anniversary banquet. His conscience since that time had given him no peace, and he was glad to have his doubts about the identity resolved favorably when he saw Jesus, who was so different in appearance from the stern wilderness prophet. Herod had hoped to see some miracle by Jesus, much as one would hope for a magic performance of some sleight-of-hand trickster. He plied Him with questions.[1] But Jesus maintained a dignified silence. Not one word did He condescend to speak to the murderer of His great forerunner. Whereupon the priests and scribes, who were present in a body, "broke forth with their accusations, like a pack of hounds in a well tuned chorus." They were well trained for their part.

1 Imperfect of repeated action.

Herod could get nothing out of Jesus. For his baffled curiosity he would take revenge at least. He did not wish to condemn Him to death. His experience with John had taught him the penalty of such a death. He would treat Him as a mere religious enthusiast, with utter contempt — as a nobody. So he had some of his body-guards array Jesus in a bright-colored robe in mockery, and sent Him, possibly with a letter of bland flattery, to Pilate. So the old feud was settled. Herod had been the slicker of the two in escaping the responsibility for the death of Jesus.

10. Jesus the second time before Pliate. (Mark 15:6-15; Matt. 27:15-26; Luke 23:13-25; Jno. 18:39 — 19:16).

It was now near sunrise on Friday. The Jewish rulers were impatient to extract from the Roman governor his legal sanction to the Sanhedrin vote, and his death-warrant for the crucifixion. Pilate, convinced thoroughly of the innocence of Jesus, and the envious motive of His enemies, came forth and took his seat on the Bema, or golden throne, placed on an elevated pavement of vari-colored marble. With a confident air, he summoned[1] the Sanhedrin and the people before him to deliver his verdict. "Ye brought unto me this man," he began, "and behold I have examined him thoroughly before you, and found no fault in him touching those things whereof you accuse him.[2] No, nor yet Herod, for he sent him back unto us; and behold, nothing worthy of death hath been done by him.[3] His habitual conduct is contrary to the charge and sentence."[4]

As he spoke, a murmur of disapproval ran through the crowd, and the vacillating Roman governor read in the faces and scowls of the Jewish leaders their determination not to submit to his verdict. Wavering for a moment, he bethought him of an alternative which might placate their ire and soften their hearts. So he added in foolish compromise of his just decision, "I will chastise him, and release him." (Luke 23:13-16). But they were not satisfied.

The idea of setting the prisoner free brought to memory another suggestion which might relieve the tensity of the situation. Luckily just at that juncture, a crowd came up for the very purpose of asking the governor to grant unto them the release of a prisoner whom they should choose, according to the time-honored custom of the Roman government to pardon one prisoner at the time of the Passover each year. It was a strange coincidence. The idea had just come to him and in it he saw his opportunity. If Pilate should offer to release unto them Jesus on this

1 First aorist middle participle, he hoped Jesus had some friends in the crowd.
2 He summarized the three charges in one: Jesus is a rival of Caesar.
3 Periphrastic present.   4 Periphrastic perfect passive.

ground of custom, he would thus escape the necessity of making of no effect the death sentence which doubtless he knew the Sanhedrin had passed on Jesus, though they had purposely not referred to it in their accusation. This seemed to be a tactful policy. But then he remembered that the Jewish rulers would never accept Jesus as the one to be released.

Casting about in his mind for some way to thwart his opponents, he recalled the name of a notorious bandit-robber, who had led a bloody insurretcion in the hill-country of Judea at a recent date, and, caught red-handed, lay in prison, awaiting the execution of the death sentence. His name was Barabbas, "son of the father." In order that it might be difficult for the people to choose some other prisoner and easier for them to select Jesus in spite of the Sanhedrist influence, he put the choice in the form of an alternative: "Whom do you wish that I release unto you?" he asked, "Barabbas or Jesus, who is called Christ?" In referring so to Jesus, he gave them to understand that the mere appellation given to Jesus, the Messiah, was a matter of no consequence politically. He was a mere religious enthusiast, and there was no fear of His usurpation of the Roman power. Their accusation of treason had been ill-founded. He thus declared that Jesus was innocent of any such charge. In an effort to placate their ill-will, he adds with a contemptuous sneer for any such supposed assumption of power on the part of Jesus: "Shall I release unto you the King of the Jews?"

While he was seeking to lead the people thus to sanction his own intention of releasing Jesus, there came a brief interruption, which gave the wicked Sanhedrists chance to get possession of their wits, and organize concerted action. A messenger came from Pilate's wife saying: "Have thou nothing to do with that righteous man; for I have suffered many things this day in a dream because of him."[1] Pilate had already been deeply impressed by the whole hearing of this extraordinary prisoner, and especially with His words about the Kingdom and about His coming to testify to the truth. This added warning, and this time from the dream-world, played upon the superstitious nature of the Roman governor who believed in omens and dreams. It was a brief interruption, but the Jewish rulers were alert always. They had meantime stirred up to the very depths[2] the mob, to ask for Barabbas in preference to Jesus. When Pilate put the alternative again "Whether of the twain will ye that I release unto you?" they came out in a deafening and rasping chorus: "Barabbas! Not this man, but Barabbas! Away with this man, and release unto us

1 Matt. 27:19. Claudia, in spite of bad ancestry, seems to have been a woman of noble impulse.   2 Aneseisan, shake up like an earthquake.

Barabbas." Such was the choice of the rabble, many of whom were doubtless brought here at this early morning hour by the Sanhedrists for the purpose of helping to extract from the governor by pressure the desired verdict. The sad commentary which the evangelist John, author of the fourth gospel, makes on the choice is: "Now Barabbas was a bandit-robber."

It seems that Pilate had exhausted every way to escape the pronouncing of the death sentence, all but the right way of a firm decision, backed up by the courageous act of liberating the prisoner, whom he had already declared innocent. He now carries out the plan suggested earlier, that of scourging Jesus. Perhaps the severity of the Roman scourge would soften the hard hearts of some at least of the rulers, and elicit the sympathy of the popular crowd. And well it might, for its extreme cruelty and barbarity. It was customary to scourge the prisoner, sentenced to be crucified, just before the crucifixion. Pilate proceeded, with the scourging — a wholly unjust act, if Jesus were innocent, as Pilate had declared—his motive being to get the sympathy of the crowd for Jesus. Thus he revealed his weakness again, in a case that called for strength and firmness of decision. This had been his proverbial failing, and at once revealed to his enemies the weakness of Pilate's determination. He had by this act made a concession that would lead his antagonists on to victory in the contest. This was past history being repeated, and the Jews knew that with persistence they would secure the death warrant they desired.

So the soldiers took Jesus away and scourged Him. The scourge was a whip with several thongs, each loaded with acorn-shaped balls of lead, or sharp pieces of bone or spikes. Stripped of His clothes, His hands tied to a column or stake with His back bent, the victim was lashed with the flagels by six lictors, who plied these instruments of torture with severity almost to the point of the death of the prisoner. Each stroke cut into the quivering flesh, until the veins and sometimes the entrails were laid bare. Often the scourge struck the face and knocked out the eyes and teeth. Scourging almost always ended in fainting and sometimes even in death.

In the case of Jesus, it was made all the worse by the period of mockery which followed. Over His lacerated body, they cast a purple robe — provided by Herod — and pressed down on His head a plaited crown of thorns. In His right hand, they placed a reed for a sceptre, and then made Him the subject of jesting, striking Him insultingly with rods on His thorn-crowned head, and with the palms of their hands in His face, and on His lacerated body.

Kneeling down to Him, they exclaimed in derision: "Hail, King of the Jews." Most nauseating of all the insulting treatment, they repeatedly spat in His face.

Pilate had an object in allowing the utmost barbarity to be used in His scourging. Going out now with Jesus, before the impatient and infuriated mob in front of the Praetorium, he exclaimed: "See! I am bringing him out to you that ye may know that I find no fault in him." One look at the pale bleeding form, fainting almost from exhaustion, arrayed in a clownish garb as a mock-king, should convince all of the mob of the utter folly of the accusation of treason and dispel any suspicion of intentions of usurpation of the Roman throne, by any such person. "Look at the man," he said in an appeal to their compassion. "What shall I do with this so-called Christ?" The people were doubtless touched by so sorrowful a sight, but the cruel priests and Temple officers led again in a chorus of denunciation, calling for His death. "Let him be crucified," they said. "Why? What evil hath he done?" asked the exasperated governor.

Stimulated now by the chief priests and officers, the mob raises a hubbub of yells: "Crucify him, crucify him!" "Take him yourselves and crucify him, for I find no fault in him," retorted Pilate. "We have a law," they said with a threat, "and by that law he ought to die, because he made himself the Son of God." At last, the leaders had revealed the real cause for their partisanship. But the unreasoning mob kept up the cry: "Crucify him, crucify him."

Once again, Pilate was stricken to the heart with a superstitious fear. His enemies had said that "Jesus made himself the Son of God." If Pilate was afraid when he received the message of his wife's dream, he was more afraid still now when he heard that Christ claimed divine origin. The majesty of the personality of his prisoner had profoundly impressed this haughty Roman governor.

He entered into the Praetorium again, and approaching Jesus, respectfully asked: "Whence art thou?" But Jesus made no reply, using this dignified method of dealing with his pusillanimous, compromising, unjust ruler, to show His disapproval of such conduct. Pilate was stung by this attitude of dignified silence. "Speakest thou not to me? Knowest thou not that I have the authority to release thee, and," he added significantly, "to crucify thee?" Jesus answered him calmly, pitying his lack of insight. "Thou wouldest have no power against me, except it were given thee from above; therefore, he that delivered me unto thee hath greater sin." Here was something Pilate had never heard of before. Even the Roman could not claim absolute power of life and death over Him. Pilate welcomed, at least, the declaration that the Jewish leaders had the great responsibility, and consequent guilt, in the condemnation of the prisoner. All real authority had its source in God; Pilate must recognize that the abuse of his power as a Roman governor would incur for him guilt and the inevitable consequences of his sin.

Pilate, himself, had already felt that, for he made renewed efforts to release Jesus. But his efforts were antagonized by the Jewish rulers with threats and intimations: "If thou release this man, thou are not Caesar's friend." When they said this, they used their most telling argument. He did not want the Emperor Tiberius, now on the island of Capri ill with loathsome diseases, filled with suspicions and full of ill-will and revenge, to hear that he had sided with a prisoner in a case of *laese majestas*. The punishment meted out for any officer of the Empire on such a charge was confiscation of property, removal from office, torture by banishment, or something even worse. Pilate was sure that the Jewish Sanhedrin would like to send such a report to the Caesar. He quailed before the clear threat.

But he would make one last appeal in favor of justice and the release of the prisoner. Again, he brought Jesus out before them. He now took his seat on the judgment throne for the pronunciation of the final verdict, for it was already about the sixth hour, the hour of sunrise. A few moments more might bring a great concourse of the people and possibly the violence of a tumult. He says, turning to the Jews in a final appeal: "Behold your king!" The sad spectacle of the exhausted, bedraggled, and suffering prisoner made ridiculous any pretention on His part to the imperial throne. Again the rulers raise the cry: "Away with him! Away with him!" Pilate asked: "Shall I crucify your King?" Like the crack of a whip came the sharp reply from the Sadducean leaders: "We have no king but Caesar." Thus they could carry their point against Jesus, and secure His condemnation by denouncing their theocratic ideal and sealing the doom of the nation. And the Pharisees gave their silent approval.

Pilate finally gave up hope. He realized that the crowd was unanimous against Jesus. He feared a tumult.[1] Just now, the clamor rose again like a swelling tide. Louder and fiercer was the cry of the mob demanding His crucifixion. Seeing that he prevailed nothing, Pilate took a basin of water and washed his hands before the multitudes saying: "I am innocent of the blood of this righteous man; see ye to it." But Pilate could not escape the sense of his

1 Jos. War 14:8, 9; 5:11.

responsibility. There was a custom among the Greeks, Jews, and Romans of that time that when a man shed blood, he would wash his hands, thus symbolically cleansing away the stain. Pilate felt that he was a murderer. The tragic reply came back like an echo of a groan from future generations: "His blood be on us and on our children." Thirty years later, on this very spot, judgment was pronounced against some of the best citizens of Jerusalem. Of the 3,600 victims of the governor's fury, not a few were scourged and crucified! Judas died in a loathsome suicide, the house of Annas was destroyed some years later, Caiaphas was deposed a year after the crucifixion, and Pilate was soon after banished to Gaul and there died in suicide. When Jerusalem fell, her wretched citizens were crucified around her walls until, in the historian's grim language, "space was wanting for the crosses, and crosses for the bodies." The horrors of the siege of Jerusalem are unparalleled in history.

So Pilate, wishing to content the multitude, released unto them Barabbas, the public enemy, bandit-robber, murderer, and leader of insurrection, and delivered Jesus up to their will to be crucified.

CHAPTER XXXIII
THE CRUCIFIXION
(Harm. §§ 162-168)

Sometime between six and nine o'clock the final sentence was pronounced by Pilate and Jesus was turned over to the Roman soldiers to be crucified. These soldiers of the governor belonged to a cohort made up of Syrians, or more probably Germans. They led Jesus into the open court of the governor's palace and after calling the rest of the cohort together to take part in the cruel sport, they stripped off His garments and put on Him a short red cloak—worn by military and civil officers, this one probably an old one discarded by Pilate—as a kind of substitute in mockery of a king's purple robe. It soon became tinged purple-scarlet[1] by the blood from His lascerated body. Then they plaited a garland of the flexible boughs of the Arab *nubk*, a bush filled with long sharp thorns, and placed it on His already bruised head. For a mock-scepter they thrust a reed of the common cane-grass in His right hand and, imitating the Sanhedrists, crowded around Him in cruel mockery, striking Him insultingly with the palms of their hands and with rods. The Sanhedrists had derided Him as the prophet, bidding Him, blindfolded, to prophesy who it was that struck Him; these hard-hearted soldiers mocked Him as King, saying: "Hail, King of Israel!" Repeated indignities[2] they heaped upon Him during the time allotted for this barbarous scourging before the crucifixion. This hectic experience, following the vexatious betrayal and trials of the previous night, constituted a terrible prelude to the more horrible hours on the cross (Mark 15:16-19; Matt. 27:27-31).

1. Jesus on the way to the cross on Golgotha (Mark 15:20-23; Matt. 27:31-34; Luke 23:26-33; Jno. 19:16, 17).

Three times Jesus had run the gauntlet of mockery: once by the Sanhedrin and their servant-officers, then by Herod's body-guard, and lastly by the Roman cohort. The purple-scarlet robe was now removed and His own garments put on Him again. Then they led Him away to crucify Him, obliging Him to bear (for Himself) His own[3] cross, according to the custom for criminals who were to be crucified.

The procession was composed of a great multitude, embracing the High Priests and their servants, who would want to witness the end of their enemy and victim; the crowd of the street rabble and the merely curious spectators; the two malefactors, also

---

1 Mark 15:17; Matt. 27:28.   2 Imperfect tenses, prosekunoun, etupton, and eneptuon.
3 Reflexive pronoun, houtoi in dative of personal interest.

bearing their crosses; all preceded by the centurion in charge of the bloody business, with four soldier-guards detached for each prisoner. None of the disciples were present except John, who records the fact that Jesus started out on the Via Dolorosa to Golgotha "bearing the cross for Himself."[1]

The destination was Golgotha, the place of the skull, situated, not within the city walls according to the tradition which would locate it at the place of the Church of the Holy Sepulchre, but a knoll without the walls to the north of the city, being a part of the Temple ridge. This was the usual place of execution and has the appearance of a skull, whence it must have derived its name. It was near the northern highway and in the proximity of gardens, where rock-hewn sepulchres of dates from that period have been discovered. The knoll was a weird, dreary, rock elevation which meets with the description in the evangelical narratives.

When they were coming out, leading Him away to the place of execution, Jesus was unable to bear His cross from sheer exhaustion, due to the intense strain of the previous week, the excessive excitement of the trials, and the brutality of the scourging and mockery through which He had been passing. Tradition says that He fell under the weight of the heavy beam which He bore on shoulders lacerated by the fearful scourge. Happily they met a man coming in from the country—a man of Cyrene—Simon, the father of Alexander and Rufus, of subsequent apostolic history. Cyrene was a city of north Africa where there was a large colony of Jews. Simon might have been a Jewish proselyte going up to the Feast. Him they compelled to render the service of bearing the cross of Jesus, who went before, aided[2] by the soldiers. It is likely from the place his sons occupied in subsequent evangelical history[3] that Simon was brought, through this service he was made to render, to personal knowledge of the Saviour.

There is one incident recorded of what happened as the procession wended its way through the streets, thronged with curious spectators. Women beholding the melancholy procession broke out in lamentations, beating their breasts and bewailing His sad end. But Jesus, turning to them, said: "Daughters of Jerusalem, stop weeping[4] for me. Weep for yourselves and for your children! For behold the days are coming in which they shall say, 'Blessed are the barren and the wombs that never bore, and the breast that never gave suck.'" Just a few years ahead, barrenness, which was now considered a curse, would be coveted as a blessing. That time did come within a generation at the fall of Jerusalem in

1 Middle voice, subject of verb actively participates.
2 Mark 15:22, ferousin auton, they bear Him, probably aiding Him in walking ahead of Simon who followed with the Cross.   3 Romans 16:13.
4 Present active imperative with me.

70 A. D.[1] Continuing His warning He added: "Then shall they
begin to say to the mountains, 'Fall on us'; and to the hills,
'Cover us.' " They shall seek refuge from their misery in death.
He assigns next a reason for predicting such things.[2] "For if
they do these things in the green (moist) tree, what shall be done
in the dry?" If the Romans dealt with Jesus thus, whom they considered innocent, how much worse will they deal with the guilty
and rebellious ones in the time of the future war. And so it was
later when more than a million Jews perished in Jerusalem in a few
days' time. Or from another and more fundamental view, historically, and correct interpretation, grammatically: if the leaders
of Israel now do these things, such as deliver up their Divine
King, in the early stages of Israel's history, thus setting a flame
to her green tree; how terrible will become the judgment of
God in the dry wood of an apostate and rebellious people in future years.[3]

Luke adds that along with Jesus, who had taken the place
of Barabbas, the murderer, two others, malefactors,[4] were being
led out by the halter of death. When they came to the rock-strewn
skull-shaped knoll, which a fanciful tradition says was the place
of the death and burial of Adam[5]—a place called Golgotha[6]—
they offered Jesus wine flavored with myrrh and gall; but when
He had tasted it He would not drink it. He preferred to drink to
the bitter dregs the cup which His Father had given Him, and
remain in full possession of all His powers through it all. The nar-
cotics, prepared possibly by the charitable hands of the women
of Jerusalem were to alleviate the sufferings of the victims of
this horrible death by deadening the senses. Jesus would not receive them though offered repeatedly[7] and by humane hearts.

2. The first three hours on the cross (Mark 15:24-32; Matt. 27
35-44; Luke 23:33-43; Jno. 19:18-27).

During the first three hours on the cross, from 9 A. M. until
noon, on Friday, there were a number of things that transpired:
three sayings of Jesus, the soldiers' gambling for the garments,
the inscription nailed to the cross, the scoffing of the multitude
and the Sanhedrists, the derision of the soldiers and of the two
robbers on each side of Christ, and the repentance and salvation
of the penitent one.

The cross was the most disgraceful and one of the cruelest
instruments of death ever invented. The Romans, who borrowed it
from the Carthaginians, would not allow a Roman citizen to be

1 Jos. War 6:3, 4.   2 Plummer on Luke in loco.   3 Edersheim, Life and Times
of Jesus.   4 Evil doers, Kakourgoi.   5 Origen and Chrysostom.
6 In Aramaic, Gulgatha, In Hebrew, Gulgoleth, In Latin, Vulgate Calvariae locus. There is
a rock eminence just outside the Damascus gate, known as Jeremiah's Grotto, which
satisfies all the requirements of the Evangelical records for the place of crucifixion.
(Robert and David Smith.)
7 Imperfect indicative active, repeated action.

crucified; but reserved crucifixion for slaves and foreigners or provincials. The Jews customarily used stoning and never crucifixion. It was not only the death of greatest ignominy but of the most extreme anguish and suffering. There were five forms of the cross used for this ghastly punishment: a plain stake to which the victim was nailed; the *Tau* cross with the transom below the top—the traditional type on which Jesus was crucified; the *crux commissa*, or Greek cross, with four arms of equal length; and St. Andrew's cross, consisting of two beams obliquely crossed. The cross of Jesus was probably slightly higher than the traditional type, in the use of which the feet of the crucified were only a foot or two from the ground. The victim was usually first stripped naked, the garments falling to the lot of the executioners; but in the crucifixion of Jesus, tradition says that a loincloth was used.[1] First the upright was planted firmly in the ground and then the victim was laid down with arms extended on the crossbar to which they were fastened by cords and afterwards by nails through the palms. Then the transom was raised to its position on the upright and nailed while the body was left to swing or its weight rested on an iron saddle peg driven into the upright. Following this the feet were nailed either through the instep separately, or both together with a single iron spike.[2] There the body was left to hang in agony sometimes two or three days, until death from pain and starvation ensued.

It was the third hour of the day, by Jewish time (9 A. M.), when they nailed Jesus to the cross placing above Him the superscription variously reported in part by the evangelists: "This is Jesus of Nazareth, the King of the Jews." It was intended doubtless by Pilate as a revenge on the haughty priests, who had triumphed over him. They had retired to the Temple for services after their apparent victory in the trial and when they heard of the words of the superscription, highly insulted, returned to the Praetorium, and demanded that it be changed. "Write not," they suggested, "the King of the Jews, but that He said, 'I am the King of the Jews.' " But Pilate laconically replied: "What I have written[3] I have written." The placard was borne customarily before the victim on the way to the crucifixion as an announcement of the cause or criminal charge. Sometimes it was hung by a cord around the victim's neck as he marched to the place of execution.

As they were driving the spikes through Jesus' hands and feet, He prayed for His tormentors and enemies around the cross, saying: "Father, forgive them for they know not what they do."

1 Gospel of Nicodemus 10.   2 Plummer on Luke, 23:33.
3 Perfect tense denoting complete action and permanent continuing state.

This was in striking contrast to the way many victims of crucifixion were accustomed to act. Instead of prayers for the tormentors, they would beg, shriek, curse, and even spit at the spectators. But no evil word escaped the lips of Jesus, nor any entreaty to spare Him. He prayed not just for the rude pagan soldiers who despised all Jews; who went about their cruel work as professional executioners and did not know Him personally. To them He was just one more rebel Jew who had earned His just reward, like the two robber-thieves hanging one on either side of Jesus, who had followed Barabbas to their destruction. They might be more in His thought as He uttered the words "for they know not what they do," but His great heart of love took in His worst enemies also. Even the hateful Sanhedrists knew not what they were doing when they crucified the Lord of Glory. In this prayer Jesus gave expression to the unconquerable spirit that gained moral victory over Satan and sin—the decisive victory of the great conflict of the ages between the forces of darkness and the forces of light. This was the great victory of the cross, where love overcame hate and opened a door of redemption for the sin-enslaved race. This was the first expression on the cross revealing the inner conflict in the heart of the Saviour of mankind.

Finished their cruel job, the four soldiers cast lots for His garments: the turban, cape, girdle, sandals, and the under-garment. The last named was seamless, woven all in one piece, probably by His mother. There was one article for each of the four, aside from the seamless tunic, and they decided to cast lots to see which would have that—an unconscious fulfillment of the Scripture: "They parted my garments among themselves and upon my vesture did they cast lots." John observed this terrible scene which recalled the dark picture of the Messianic Psalm of which it was the fulfillment.[1] These things the soldiers did and then sitting down they remained watching Jesus on the cross.

The place of the crucifixion was near to the city and very near the highway, going out from the Damascus gate to the city of that name to the north. The three crosses, that of Jesus a little higher than the other two, attracted a crowd of curious spectators, who stood gazing[2] on the sad spectacle silently. The Synoptics mention three other kinds of ill-treatment which Jesus suffered as He hung in an agony of suffering on the cross. The rulers of the Jews, with unutterable abasement, fearing lest the significant words of the inscription on the cross might unduly influence some of the Galilean friends of Jesus, hastened to Calvary, where they mingled with the crowd, inciting it to jeers and mockery. They

---

1 Ps. 22:18.   2 Present active participle.

led the unthinking rabble and passers-by in piteous derision. Passing around among the spectators, they turned up their noses at Him[1] saying contemptuously: "He saved others, let Him save Himself, if this (fellow)[2] is the Christ (Messiah) of God, His chosen." Unintentionally they uttered a great truth, fundamental in the whole plan of vicarious redemption, through the life of Jesus as well as that of His disciples. One who saves others must give Himself vicariously in order to do so. If Jesus had saved His physical life by coming down from the cross, He could not have become the Saviour of mankind. These blinded rulers were committing and leading Israel to commit moral suicide with regard to the Messianic hope. They would not recognize that Jesus was God's *Chosen One.* These chief priests, Annas and Caiaphas and others of the Sadducean party, with the Scribes of the Pharisees and the elders, went about repeating this jeer with variations: "He saved others by professed miracles of cure; His own physical being He cannot save from the cross." In derision they add: "He is the King of Israel; let Him now come down from the cross and we will believe on Him." With a shake of the head those hypocritical wiseacres could with complacency remind the people, who had known of the claims of Jesus, that now on the cross He could not sustain them. To them all His claims to kingship were thus proven false. Their declaration that they would believe on Him if He should descend from the cross was wholly false, and contrary to their previous actions. They became more contemptuous, almost blasphemous, and said: "He trusteth on God; let him now deliver him if he desireth him: for he said, 'I am the Son of God.'" They were referring in this, to the confession Jesus made before the Sanhedrin when put on oath and asked if He were the Son of God. They were there to lead the people in this mockery and had organized their group in this spiteful work.[3] They added, to the much repeated declaration about His saving others and not being able to save Himself, the challenges cast in derision in His teeth as He hung on the cross dying for them: "Let the Christ (Messiah), the King of Israel, now come down from the cross, that we may believe on him." Thus they would seek to deceive the people and make them believe in their own sincerity, as their leaders.

The unthinking multitude is easily led into mob-action, and copying their long-bearded, hypocritical leaders, they passed by on the highway near, wagging their heads in derision and saying: "Thou that destroyest the Temple and buildest it in three days,

1 Exmuktarizon, imperfect active indicative of repeated action, scoffed.
2 Houtos, demonstrative pronoun, used to express contempt.
3 Mark 15:31.

save thyself, if thou art the Son of God, and come down from the cross." The rulers were responsible for leading the crowd in all this derision and hateful raillery.

The soldiers also took up the words of the Sanhedrists, and in brutal jest, coming near to the agonized Sufferer, lifted their wine cups, offering Him of their sour wine, and drank to Him in their heartless glee, saying in blasphemous words: "If[1] thou art the King of the Jews, save[2] thyself quickly." This was a reenforced reflection of the words of the Jewish leaders, but with a fling at the Jews themselves whom they looked upon as dogs.

The two robber-thieves, especially one of them, next took up the jeer of the Sanhedrists repeatedly and cast in His teeth this bitter taunt: "Art thou not the Christ? Save thyself and us." This blasphemous expression was drummed into the ears of Jesus in monotonous repetition through one hour. The other remained silent for the most part with but an occasional expression, perhaps with a misery-filled look of hope toward Him whom his companion so loudly reviled. An hour of hopeless torment had dragged slowly away while the impenitent thief, with shattered nerves, kept up his reproaches. The other, who at first had thought to gain some consideration from his tormentors by joining in the raillery, had later reflected on the prayer of Jesus for those who had crucified Him and relented, seeing the wonderful patience and calmness of the one upon whom the rulers and others heaped their mocking jests. Moved at length to reflect on his own life and lost estate and hearing in the taunts and jests about the claims of Jesus to be the Messiah, the King of Israel and Son of God, resentment of the tormentors coupled with admiration for Jesus elicited from him a protest and rebuke to his impenitent and reviling companion: "Dost thou not even fear God, seeing thou art in the same condemnation?" Then further including himself he added: "And *we* indeed[3] justly for we are receiving the due reward of our deeds; but this man hath done nothing amiss." Such a noble expression and under such circumstances shows that the crucial hour of suffering had brought this poor man of violence and blood, to catch, through the thick fog of his ignorance and sin, a gleam of the brightness of the Son of God, who hung near him on the same kind of ghastly instrument of torture and death, with never a word of complaint. The meaning of the words of the superscription, as well as of those spoken by the rulers in derision, assumed now for him a new meaning. His whole life of utter loss in sin stood out in a panorama to the dying man. Reaching out his

1 First class condition, the soldiers would not deny the fact, but is was a jeer at the Jews and a jest about the King, a crucified King.   2 Aorist imperative urgency.
3 Emphatically, position of emphasis, with the Greek particle men.

groping hand of faith in the blackness of the night of his utter
desolation, he turned to Jesus and said: "Jesus (Saviour), remember me when thou comest into Thy Kingdom." Where did he
derive the idea of the spiritual and everlasting Kingdom which is
not of this world? He may have had some previous knowledge
of Jesus and His claims, even through Barabbas; he could have
gathered, from the very denunciations of the rulers at the foot of
the cross, and pieced together enough to understand that the
Kingdom was not a material one. He had heard also on the way
to Golgotha the words spoken to the women. The response of
Jesus to the brief but earnest plea of this blood-stained but now
penitent bandit-thief has inspired hope in the despairing and
left potent the fact that there is hope for every man, however
deeply immersed in sin, if he will but turn to Jesus. Clear and
strong came the frank words of acceptance of the repentant one
into the fold of eternal salvation: "Today shalt thou be with me
in Paradise." It took a great faith to believe in one who was
crucified with him, and a great leap of the imagination from a
cross to a crown, from a felon's death to eternal life. Such a faith
was instantly rewarded with a happy assurance of a new and unending life in the wonderful fellowship of Jesus, to be instituted
now and more fully known within a few fleeting moments in
Paradise, a beautiful park-like place beyond the tomb. There
he was to have conscious and happy existence immediately after
death. Luke, who was alone in giving this incident, would take
interest, because he wrote to the Gentiles and about the universal
salvation.[1]

Besides the four soldiers, who had been the instruments of
the cruel work of the crucifixion, was another group, four women
who appear with John, the disciple whom Jesus loved. That disciple had remained until after the crucifixion, standing bravely
by in mute sympathy, and then hastened away to bring the mother
of Jesus and a few sorrowing relatives, that they might show their
love to the last toward Him whom they adored. Along with the
mother of Jesus, who was John's aunt, came Salome, her sister
and John's mother, Mary, the wife or widow of Clophas who was
probably the brother of Joseph, and Mary of Magdala, greatest
trophy of the ministry of Jesus among the outcast classes and
one of the brightest jewels of His Kingdom. At the foot of the
cross they took up their station in the ministry of waiting love.
Here was the courage of abandon, and devotion stronger than
death! They came to minister to Him in His dying hour. This was
a scene to move the hardest heart to tears and repentance.

1 The Mission and Message of Jesus, Major, Manson and Wright.

No physical anguish was too extreme to hold the attention of the "strong Son of God" away from the needs of the loving mother-heart in this hour. With infinite tenderness He addresses Himself to His mother and to John the Beloved, and commits to the strong and manly care of that disciple, her whom he had personally counseled and sustained through many years in the Nazareth home. "Woman," He said tenderly to Mary, "behold thy son!" Then He said to John, His cousin in the flesh, "Behold thy mother!" His relationship to Mary had been that of an obedient son. He would be faithful to the uttermost in providing for her material well-being and peace of mind. The unbelieving half-brothers were not present at the crucifixion and could not sustain her in this bitter grief, anyway. John accepted the sacred charge and "from that hour took her to his own home" probably in Jerusalem. Tenderly he led her from the scene of horror to that home, where she dwelt the rest of her life sustained in affection and honour.[1]

3. The three hours of darkness from noon to 3 P.M. (Mark 15: 33-37; Matt. 27:45-50; Luke 23:44-46; Jno. 19:28-30).

It was noon and the brightness of the Syrian sun should have been at its intensest. But a strange, weird haze had settled down over the world, obscuring the sun until it could be seen no more. The darkness was not due to an eclipse because it was the time of the full moon of Passover week. The sun failing, a peculiar supernatural darkness came over the whole land until the ninth hour or 3 P.M. Darkness sometimes precedes earthquakes, as in Syria when the sirocco comes up from the desert. A smoky haze obscures the sun and gives the impression of the close of day, as in total eclipse of the sun. But this was not a simple phenomenon. While the Gospel records do not speak of it as a miracle, the simplest explanation is that it was a supernatural manifestation in nature, embracing Palestine and the surrounding regions, in sympathy with the crucial experience through which nature's Maker was passing during those three hours.

When the darkness, like a heavy curtain, fell over the scene of the tragedy, silence reigned and a feeling of awe and horror crept over all. For the three portentous hours of darkness Jesus hung on the cross in silence. It was doubtless a period during which He suffered extreme anguish of spirit and physical pain. The increasing nameless agonies of the crucifixion were deepening more and more with every moment into death. He was forsaken almost wholly by men and felt the sense of a desolate isolation and loneliness.

1 David Smith. In the Days of His Flesh.

Almost at the close of the three hours of darkness, feeling Himself also God-forsaken, He cried out words of anguish in the awful stillness of the darkness; words which have echoed through eternity and reverberated down the centuries of time: "Eloi, Eloi, lama sabachthani[1]? which interpreted from the Aramaic is: "My God, my God, why hast thou forsaken me?" It was a bitter cry rung from His lips by suffering far greater than that of the mere physical pain of crucifixion. A crushing grief, even greater than that which He had felt in Gethsemane, was expressed in these words of desolation. Of course the Son was never more well-pleasing to the Father than in this hour when He was voluntarily laying down His life for the redemption of the human race. Of this we can feel wholly assured by all the teachings of the Scriptures. But we must remember that here we deal with a human soul, having human limitations in a human body, and now under the conditions of extreme physical pain and mental anguish. The best that we can offer in the way of explanation is that, in these distressing words, we face an inscrutable mystery beyond our human ability to understand. It was not mere human weakness nor yet any failure of His faith in God. The word "forsaken" gives the impression that Jesus felt the Father was not present in the sense in which He had always been. He seems to express the desolation of the feeling of temporarily broken fellowship.

These words mark the climax of the suffering of Christ for a lost world. Here He drank to the dregs the cup of sorrow, grief, and pain on our behalf. In these hours when the sun refused to shine upon suffering deity, Jesus found fitting expression to His feeling of desolation in the words of the Psalmist.[2] Isaiah had given a vivid portrayal of the suffering Servant who was to be "wounded for our transgressions."[3] John the Baptist pointed to Jesus as "the Lamb of God that taketh away the collective sin of a world of sinners."[4] Christ gave Himself a "ransom for many."[5] Him who knew no sin God "made sin"[6] for us. On the cross Christ became a "curse for us"[7] and so redeemed us from the curse of the law. We are "redeemed by the precious blood of Christ"[8] shed on Calvary. He gave Himself a "ransom for all."[9] The writers of the Gospels make it plain that Jesus "had a baptism to be baptised with" and a "cup to drink." Paul and other writers of the epistles lay out clearly the same plan of redemption. Jesus had to pay the price alone and tasted death—spiritual death—for every man.[10] Spiritual death is broken communion.

1 More likely spoken in Aramaic according to the Marcan record than in Hebrew of Matt. 27:46.   2 Ps. 22:1.   3 Isa. 53.   4 Jno. 1:29.   5 Matt. 20.28.
6 II Cor. 5:21.   7 Gal. 3:13.   8 I Pet. 1:19.   9 Antilutron huper panton. I Tim. 2:6.   10 Hebrews 2.

Jesus had a taste of such a broken communion, the first and last He ever experienced—in those desolate hours when darkness lay upon the earth and upon His soul. That is the reason He used the words of distressed astonishment: Eloi, Eloi, lama sabachthani (Hebrew)—"my God, my God, to what end or purpose hast thou forsaken me?" Jesus was our forerunner in every kind of experience, even to the feeling of God's frown of disapproval on sin, that He might become our High Priest, understanding all our infirmities and being tempted in all points like as we, apart from sin. He felt the way a lost sinner feels, without Himself having sinned.

They who stood within earshot of the cross were deeply impressed with these words of Jesus. The provincial soldiers, some of whom were doubtless foreigners, would not understand the words, and thought He was calling someone to His aid. The mocking Jews suggested scornfully that He was calling for Elijah, the prophet, who was expected to return as the forerunner of the Messiah.

John, the beloved disciple, had returned after conducting Mary to his home and was standing with the women in the distance. Hearing the sounds of utter desolation, he came to the cross, arriving in time to catch Jesus' words of failing senses: "I thirst." Even the cruel soldier's heart was moved by a feeling of sympathy and one immediately ran to the vessel of *posca* and took a sponge, and putting it on a short[1] caper-reed (hyssop), filled it with vinegar and gave Him to drink. Jesus refused the drugged wine at the beginning, but this vinegar-wine was a mild stimulant which would revive His failing senses momentarily. John found in this incident a fulfillment of Scriptures.[2] Others interrupted this sympathetic ministration. "Hold," they cried, "let us see if Elijah will come and take him down."

Jesus received the vinegar for a purpose. His parched lips and throat would not render clear articulation until thus moistened. His senses now revived, He uttered the final redemptive words: "It is finished!" The work of redemption, which was the object of His earthly life, had been completed and the plan of salvation established.[3] The prophecy with reference to the Messiah had been realized and the last suffering for sin endured. Nothing had been left undone or unborne.[4] It was a shout of triumph. He cried with a loud voice, not the weakened utterance of one dying from physical exhaustion but of a Conqueror in the full flush of strength and victory. His task was complete.

1 The hyssop grew to be three or four feet high.   2 Ps. 69:21.
3 Cf. Moulton's Winer, p. 356 n. 3.   4 Perfect tense denoting completed action and continued state of redemptional work.

"Father," He said, lifting His face in glorious contemplation toward the heavens, "into thy hands I commend my spirit."[1] Fellowship was fully restored. He had finished the work which the Father had given Him to do, and having said this, He bowed His head and willed to give up His spirit,[2] sending it back[3] to the Father.

4. The phenomena accompanying the death of Christ (Mark 15:38-41; Matt. 27:51-56; Luke 23:45, 47-49).

A number of supernatural portents followed immediately the death of Jesus. The first, which was recorded by all three of the Synoptics, was the rending of the veil in the Temple from top to bottom. This veil, which was the thickness of a palm breadth, was sixty feet long and thirty broad, and separated the Holy and Most Holy Places. Various attempts have been made to explain this strange phenomenon on naturalistic grounds, such as the earthquake, or as Jerome's comment on the Gospel according to the Hebrews, by the fall of the huge lintel of the Temple broken by the earthquake. But this veil was of such tough fabric and so woven that it could not have been rent in twain by an earthquake or the falling of a lintel. Matthew connects the phenomenon directly with the death of Jesus, calling attention to the fact that it was rent "from top to bottom" by God's hand, throwing open thus the Most Holy Place to all men. Previously only the High Priest entered the Most Holy Place, and that once a year on the day of the Atonement, to offer on behalf of himself and the people. Early evangelical tradition held to this supernatural interpretation which is confirmed for us by the Hebrew epistle.[4] This significant portent was doubtless the explanation for the fact that a great number of priests became Christians in early apostolic times.[5] The way is open now for all men to come boldly to the throne of grace through the atoning death.

Following the rending of the veil came the supernatural earthquake. It is true that Palestine has experienced down through history various seismic disturbances. In 31 B. C. there was such an earthquake, and several thousands of people in densely populated districts of Judea were buried beneath the ruins of their own houses. But the exact coincidence of the earthquake with the death of Jesus is hardly conceivable on mere naturalistic grounds. God's hand was evidently in the earthquake as it was in the supernatural phenomena accompanying the birth of Jesus, and why should we not give credence to this as readily as to those?

---

1 Wescott, Jno. 19:30.   2 Ps. 31:5.   3 Jno. 19:30.   4 Heb. 9:3, 10:19.
5 Acts 6:7.

Other tokens accompanied the earthquake. The rocks were rent and the rock-hewn tombs were shaken open at the hour of His death. Saints of Jesus who had believed on Him and fallen asleep in death before His crucifixion were raised from the dead and appeared unto many of the disciples after the resurrection three days later. Such a miracle of God's grace would be useful, to show the disciples that the resurrection of Jesus was not an isolated phenomenon, but that He was only the first-fruits of the victory over death.[1]

These portents impressed deeply not only the disciples, but many others. The Centurion, who had doubtless had charge of the soldiers who arrested Jesus and served as guards through the trials, scourging, and crucifixion, had heard the testimony of Jesus when He claimed to be the Son of God in the presence of the Sanhedrin. He was standing near the cross on which Jesus hung and observed all that occurred during the six hours. Other soldiers also were with him and agreed to his testimony. The earthquake and the darkness were interpreted by them as being supernatural. They were filled with an exceeding great fear. The centurion expressed their conclusion: "Truly this was the Son of God." They might have a heathen conception of what a Son of God was, but they were convinced that He was a righteous man, and the Centurion glorified God with a frank and fearless testimony. It is probable that it was from him that Luke had the intimate account of three of the seven sayings recorded solely by him, as well as the other facts of the crucifixion related by his gospel alone.

A group of the faithful, both women and men, beholding from the distance, were deeply grieved and sorrowful. They had been accustomed to minister to Him and the apostles. Among those devoted women who had come up to this Feast with Him were, His own mother—not present at the crucifixion in the later hours, having been taken to John's home by that disciple—Mary Magdalene, out of whom Jesus had cast seven devils; Mary, the mother of James and Joses; and Salome, the mother of John and sister of Jesus' mother. With them, besides John, were others of His acquaintance.

There were literally multitudes of people who witnessed the crucifixion. The supernatural portents swelled the numbers rapidly as they came running "to this sight." When they beheld all these things—the cruelty of the soldiers, the vengeful and spiteful things done by the enemies, the words from the cross— they returned to the city full of remorse, smiting their breasts in token of their sorrow and awe.

1 I Cor. 15:20.

5. The meaning and message of the cross.

The significance of the death of Jesus has ever been but poorly comprehended even by many who count themselves among the disciples. A brief statement in summary as to its meaning may throw some light on the crucifixion. There are just two spheres in which God operates for the salvation of lost humanity: revelation and redemption.[1]

The cross is the core and marks the climax of revelation. "God in ancient times, having spoken unto the fathers in the prophets by divers portions and in divers manners, hath at the end of these days spoken unto us by His Son" (Heb. 1:1). Revelation was progressive until it reached its completion in Christ. The victorious death of Jesus sums up His sacrificial life.

At the cross sin and Satan were revealed as never before or since, in all the blackness of their real character. Sin in men was seen in the trials, scourgings, and at the foot of the cross, when He was mocked, derided, and crucified. The Jewish rulers exhausted their resources in injustices and cruelty. The Roman soldiers employed their utmost in coarse brutality. The very bandits who were crucified with Him heaped on Him vile epithets and insults. The people who passed on the nearby road reviled and derided Him, "wagging their heads."

The cross revealed God as He was never revealed before or since—in all His exacting holiness and righteousness on the one hand, and in the fulness of His wonderful redemptive love on the other. We understand now, since the only-begotten Son hung on the cross, how God hates sin. He suffered His own Son to be despised and rejected by men and hung on the cross of shame and suffering; nay, He even "made Him sin" that He might eradicate sin forever from the human race. On the background of the black cloud of God's hatred for sin shines out the rainbow of His redemptive love and grace. "God so loved the world of wicked men that He gave His only begotten Son to hang on the cross and die for them." Such love the world never saw before or since—the love of the Father and the Son at the cross.

The cross is central in redemption. It was God's eternal purpose and plan to redeem mankind, and the cross was the method He chose to do it. Christ was the Lamb of God that taketh away the collective sin of the world.

The cross marked the decisive victory of Christ over Satan and sin. At the cross was fought out to the finish the decisive battle between the forces of darkness and the forces of light. At the cross "when He was reviled He reviled not again" but rather prayed

---

1 The Hebrew Epistle sustains this thesis; cf. Bruce, Wescott and others.

for His tormentors. This unparalleled conduct at Calvary conquered sin and defeated Satan. Jesus could say, looking forward to that hour: "Be of good cheer. I have overcome the world." He broke the power of Satan who wielded the power of sin and death.

At the cross Jesus paid the price of our redemption and "bought us up" from the bondage of sin to set us at liberty and make us free. All mankind was involved in this state of slavery from the beginning, when sin entered into the world through Adam, the progenitor of the race. At the cross Jesus brought about reconciliation between men and God. Man sinned against God and departed voluntarily from the fellowship of His Creator. Jesus became a curse for us and wrought out a work of substitution which opened the way to justification and consequent peace, restored fellowship, and fulness of joy by means of faith in Jesus.

The crucified One is the object of vital and vivifying faith, which is the direct cause of the new birth or regeneration. The cross is the mainspring of repentance, which is the sorrow for sin and change of mind and purpose in relation to sin. In the cross is the strength of sanctification for the individual life and the dynamic for the compaign of world evangelization leading to a new social order in a Kingdom of the heavens.

CHAPTER XXXIV

THE RESURRECTION

(Harm. §§ 169-184)

The resurrection of Jesus is the keystone to the arch of Christianity. It is the seal of all His claims to the Messiahship and Divine Sonship. Without the resurrection, He could not be the Saviour of mankind. Through His resurrection, He reached the reality of the life beyond the tomb and substantiated His claim to be the giver of life and the judge of mankind. By His resurrection, He became the first fruits of the eternal life which He guarantees to His true disciples.

The resurrection of the body of Jesus is the best attested fact of the evangelical records. On the basis of its historic validity rests the whole fabric of His supernatural birth, sinless life, miracles, and vicarious death. His whole life from the cradle to the grave is unified by the glorious resurrection from the dead.

The history of Christianity finds its source and final authority and power in the resurrection. When Jesus was laid in the tomb, the disciples were overwhelmed with grief and loss. They had thought that it was He "who should have redeemed Israel." They could not get away from the traditonal conception of the Jews relative to the Messiah. The apostolic group fled and hid themselves, for the most part, at the hour of the arrest in Gethsemane. They would soon disperse, and the interest created by the ministry of their Itinerant-Teacher was in a way to evaporate soon. They did not seem to grasp the idea of the resurrection, reiterated to them on various occasions. Soon the apostles would go back to their native places and resume their chosen occupations. Vast multitudes had thronged Him for times, and many thought He might be the long-expected Messiah. But He had flatly refused any offer or suggestion of an earthly Kingdom. Abject weakness now possessed and held the small band of followers who had been loyal to Him. The crucifixion had disillusioned them. To the world, they now appeared the dupes of delusion.

But a vast change came in one day. They had a faith in Jesus as the Messiah which still inspired some kind of hope in them. His vicarious death was a climax and a fitting close to His earthly life. This they could not but observe. He had long foretold what kind of treatment He would receive at the last, and accurately described, months before it happened, the character of His death. They were in the darkness of confusion and overcome by grief and fearful forebodings. The resurrection came as the one thing needful to clarify the atmosphere and explain the necessity of

His sufferings and death. It eradicated fear and uncertainty. It opened up the world task of Christianity and revealed the power for its accomplishment. A dead Christ could mean nothing to a lost race; but a living Christ became at once the motive power in a movement which has swept the world with an irresistible dynamic. It is no wonder then that the resurrection was the most fundamental note of apostolic preaching. In the language of Paul: "If there be no resurrection of the dead then is Christ not risen: and if Christ be not risen, then is our preaching vain, and your faith is also vain . . . ye are yet in your sins." With this preliminary word as to the significance of the resurrection, we are now prepared to examine the historical facts which reveal it.

1. The visit of the women to the tomb of Jesus late Saturday afternoon (Mark 16:1; Matt. 28:1).

There is difficulty in harmonizing all the details of the gospel records of the resurrection. This arises from no contradiction between the four gospel accounts, but is due to the fact that no one of them gives a complete report of all the appearances. The manifestations of Christ during the first week all occurred in and around Jerusalem. Those during the rest of the forty-day period were in Galilee, where most of His active ministry had taken place.

One of the most wonderful phases of the dark picture of the crucifixion and desolate hours when He was in the tomb was the loyalty of the noble women whom His ministry had won. A small group, names of only a few of whom have been preserved for us, constituted the main factor in the constant financial and spiritual support of the great Teacher and the group of twelve. They provided the means and had followed Him with their prayers and sympathetic help through the three years. In this, they became typical of similar small groups of the faithful women down through the centuries, who have, through their devotion to the Master, sustained His cause of world-evangelization with an incomparable zeal. A few of these devoted women had come up from Galilee with Him and the Twelve, at this Feast.

When the Master arrived in Bethany, two women, devoted sisters, Martha and Mary, led in giving Him a royal reception in the home of Simon, whom Jesus had months before cured of the leprosy. In the home of these sisters and Lazarus, Jesus found a haven at night, during the stormy days which followed in the week of the Passion, just preceding the tragic end. When He needed a place for celebrating His last Passover with the Twelve, it was probably the hands of the mother of John Mark that ministered so wonderfully in preparing the upper room in her house, for that memorable night when the Lord's Supper was instituted. When Jesus was passing through the streets, bearing the heavy cross-beam of His own cross, it was the women on the way that broke out in lamentations of extreme grief and sympathy. It was their hands that sadly prepared the anaesthetic potion to help mitigate the horrors of the cross, which Jesus thankfully declined to take, that He might drink of that other cup of salvation of mankind to the bitter dregs. When He was hanging on the cross, four of these devoted women braved every peril and risk of insult from the rude soldiers and hateful enemies of their Master, and came to minister to Him of their tender sympathy in that crucial hour. When the darkness spread over the land and John had thankfully received the honor of taking the mother of the Lord into the protection of his own home, a group of the women yet remained, looking on the terrible scene from a distance. Two of them, Mary of Magdala and Mary the mother of Joses, had remained untiringly at their post through the six hours of the crucifixion, and then continued later in the afternoon that they might see what would be done with His body. When Joseph of Arimethea and Nicodemus took the body to Joseph's new tomb in the garden, these two women were still there, and came and sat over against the sepulcher, venturing nearer at last to the open door to get a glimpse, to see "how the body was laid." When Joseph and Nicodemus came out and rolled the cylindrical rock door into its place, these women returned to their homes to prepare spices and ointments, that they might supplement the hurried work of the two men who had embalmed His body just before sundown, the beginning of the Sabbath. It was a grateful work that the two men had done, but these deft-handed women wanted to add anything that might have been overlooked by the two men in the necessary hurry of the hour just preceding the Sabbath. It was the same devotion to Jesus that led the women to observe the true Sabbath law the next day, though their hearts were oppressed. But in the late afternoon, they came eagerly to the place of the tomb again to see if all was as they had left it the day before. This was just at the "dawn."[1] or "the beginning of the first day of the week," which began at sunset. When the Sabbath was past, they went on to buy spices, preparatory to the work of anointing His body the next morning. Such has been the devotion of woman to her Lord!

2. The earthquake and rolling away of the stone by the angel, and the fright of the Roman guard (Matt. 28:2-4).

The supernatural was as much an order of the resurrection

---

1 Matthew was speaking of sunset. Mark refers to the early hour of dawn as Sunday morning, the resurrection morning.

as it had been that of the birth and infancy of Jesus. Before sunrise on Sunday, there was "a great earthquake." Matthew gives us to understand that the earthquake happened before sunrise, when the women made their next visit, and that it was connected directly with the appearance of the angel at the tomb, who rolled the stone away from the mouth of the sepulcher and sat upon it. An angel of the Lord had announced the birth of Jesus. Why should he not minister at the resurrection? Some of the soldiers of the guard must have been converted to discipleship in the extraordinary experience of that night. Their report of the angelic visitation would be vivid enough. To them, he appeared "as lightning, and his raiment to be as white as snow." No wonder the soldier-guards quaked with fear and fell to the earth as dead men before this terrible sight. They probably lost little time in getting away from that place when the angel disappeared, and so were not at the tomb when the warden came at sunrise.

3. The visit of the women at the tomb at sunrise on Sunday morning (Mark 16:2-8; Matt. 28:5-8; Luke 24:1-8; Jno. 20:1).

Jesus was buried shortly before sunset on Friday afternoon, lay in the grave through Saturday, and rose from the dead sometime before sunrise on Sunday morning. The Gospels record seven times that He had said He would rise from the dead "on the third day." This could not mean after seventy-two hours. The method of calculating time among the Jews, Greeks, and Romans would make the "three days in the tomb" mean one whole central day and any part of each of the two other days.

Luke gives us the most complete account of the Resurrection Day. For three days after the burial, the Jews had the custom of visiting the sepulcher to see if the soul—which, by popular tradition hovered about the sepulcher—had returned to the body. But the apostles wisely avoided visiting the tomb of Jesus and uselessly exposing themselves to the suspicion and fury of the determined and triumphant rulers of the Jews, who would be glad to do to them what they had done to Jesus. It was not the right time or place for them to suffer martyrdom yet.

The order of the events of this memorable Sunday, the resurrection day, are probably as follows: the earthquake, followed by the descent of the angel, the opening of the tomb, and the resurrection (Matt. 28:2-4). The group of women came together and started for the tomb at the "very early" hour of "deep dawn," while it was yet dark. Mary Magdalene being a nimble young woman, eagerly ran ahead and came first to the tomb, finding it open. Immediately she ran back by the nearest way to inform

Peter and John of this fact (Jno. 20:1). The other women completed their two miles' walk from Bethany to the sepulcher, arriving a little after the rising of the sun (Mark 16:2). An angel suddenly appeared to them and gave them an urgent message to the disciples (Matt. 28:5; Mark 16:5f). Another party of women come a little later, and see "two young men" dressed in white at the tomb, and receive words of comfort and instruction (Luke 24: 4). About 6:30 A. M. Peter and John arrive, John running ahead (Jno. 20:3-10). Mary Magdalene coming a little later saw two angels (Jno. 20:11-13). The other women had returned to bear the message to the other apostles (Luke 24:10). About 7 A. M. Jesus first revealed Himself to Mary of Magdala (Jno. 20:14-18; Mark 16:9). A little later, He appeared to the company of women returning to the sepulcher, and sent them with the charge to the brethren to go to Galilee (Matt. 28:9f). About 4 P. M. He appeared to Simon Peter (Luke 24:34; I Cor. 15:5), and from 4-6 P. M. to Cleophas and his companion on the way to Emmaus. Finally, in the evening, probably about 8 P. M., He appeared to the eleven, (ten) and others in the room with barred doors. (Luke 24:36f; Mark 16:14; Jno. 29:19f).[1] Surely this was a never-to-be-forgotten day for the disciples. It made a new world for them, and for His disciples of all subsequent times.

Mary Magdalene, who had waited at the tomb on Friday until Jesus' body was laid away in the sepulcher, and who restlessly returned that way on the afternoon of the Sabbath, was the first to arrive at the tomb on Sunday morning, probably running ahead of the others in her eagerness. Seeing that the great cylindrical stone, covering the door of the sepulcher, had been removed, and concluding that the body had been taken way, she did not wait for the other women to arrive, but ran back by another way to report this urgent fact to Peter and John.

The other women came on in the way, discussing who would roll away the stone from the door of the tomb for them. They were ignorant of the fact that the Jewish rulers had appealed to Pilate and secured from him authority to seal and guard the tomb, in view of the prophecy of Jesus that He would rise from the dead on the third day. Approaching the place, they looked up and saw that the great stone had been removed already. Having no memory for His prophecies concerning His resurrection and suspecting nothing, they entered into the sepulcher[2] and found that the body of their Lord was gone. This fact threw them into a state of great agitation, and they were greatly perplexed as to what had become of the body. Suddenly two bright shining figures

---

Wescott, Com. on John for order of appearances.   2 Eis with accusative, inside the sepulcher.

in dazzling apparel stepped forward, and the women exceedingly amazed and terribly frightened, prostrated themselves on their faces on the ground.

"Be not amazed," said the angel, "ye seek Jesus the Nazarene, which hath been crucified. Why seek ye the living among the dead? He is not here he is risen. Come hither and see the place where they laid him. He lay *there*, but he is now risen from the dead. Remember the words he spake unto you while he was yet in Galilee, saying that the Son of Man must be delivered up into the hands of sinful men and be crucified, and on the third day rise again." Yes, they remembered now what Jesus had said. How dull they had been to forget so quickly. The other angelic being added: "Lo, I have told you." Then with urgency the other angel commanded them: "Go, tell his disciples and Peter,[1] he goes before you into Galilee; there ye shall see him as he said unto you."

No wonder these timid women whose nerves were already at a great tension, were held spell-bound[2] with trembling and astonishment at this strange and most remarkable angelic appearance. They got out as quickly from the tomb as possible, and fled with fear and great joy, to bring their marvelous message to the disciples. They did not stop by the way to impart the joyful news to anyone. They were too afraid and were beside themselves with joy.[3]

4. Mary Magdalene and the other women report to the apostles, and Peter and John visit the empty tomb (Luke 24:9-12; Jno. 20:2-10).

Mary of Magdala had returned hastily on first seeing the open sepulcher, before the other women with whom she started out to the tomb had arrived. With the same eagerness and devotion, she ran back to the lodging places[4] of Peter and John, and reported to them: "They have taken away the Lord out of the tomb, and we know not where they have laid him."

Electrified with the report and thinking like she that the enemies probably had removed the body, they started running together,[5] but John being a younger man, ran ahead more rapidly. Arriving at the tomb first, he stooped down and looked into the sepulcher timidly. Reverence prevented his drawing near to examine the grave clothes, which he saw[6] in the niche where the body had been lying.

But when his more impulsive companion came up, he at once

1 Peter remembered gratefully this special message.
2 Eichen from echo, have or hold.   3 Vivid dramatic present, trechei.
4 Their lodging places were probably separate, but near together, cf. repetition of the preposition pros.
5 Imperfect active of trecho, they were running together, homou, together.
6 Blepei, sees, to see.

entered into the tomb and examined everything more closely.[1] With keen discernment, he noticed how the napkin, with which the head was bound, was lying in a separate place, doubtless where the head of Jesus had been. All the cloths, with which the body had been wrapped, were lying there in order. The napkin was rolled up. Evidently, here was no work of grave-robbers, as Mary had surmised. There had not dawned on Mary, and until now on them, any idea of the resurrection. They face a puzzling situation. If His enemies or even His friends had removed the body, they would not have left the grave cloths at all, much less in this orderly state. It remained for John, who had followed Peter down to the lower level of the niches of the tomb, to grasp the meaning of all the combined circumstances. They were so submerged with sorrow that they had forgotten all about what Jesus had told them about rising from the dead. John, with his rare insight, began now in his heart to catch a glimpse of the great fact of the resurrection. He afterwards confessed that "he knew not the Scriptures," which pointed out the necessity of His rising from the dead(Ps. 16:10). But for the time, he kept the matter in his heart, awaiting further light, and the two wended their way thoughtfully homeward, John doubtless to convey to Mary, the mother of Jesus, his yet undivulged hope. But Peter came away "wondering to himself, at what had come to pass."

Meantime, the other women had returned, and with ecstatic joy, narrated the experience they had on their early arrival at the tomb. They had found the great stone rolled away, and when they came near, had seen the two angelic figures, who said that Jesus had risen from the dead, and had bidden them return and tell the disciples. But the nine apostles received this report as the wild talk of those who were half hysterical. The women were worked up too much, these men thought. It was a mere fancy. It could not be true. So they kept on distrusting and would not believe the report.

5. The appearance to Mary of Magdala, and the message to the disciples (Jno. 20:11-18).

Five appearances are given by the Gospels as occurring during the day of the resurrection, and five more during the forty days that Jesus remained on earth. The five during the resurrection-Sunday were: first, to Mary Magdalene (Mark 16:9-11; Jno. 20:11-18), then to the other women (Matt. 28:9, 10), and to the two disciples going to Emmaus (Mark 16:12, 13; Luke 24:13-32), to Simon Peter (Luke 24:34), and finally to ten apostles and others (Mark 16:14; Luke 24:36-43; Jno. 20:19-25).

1 Theorei, he sees intently.

The honor of being the first to see Jesus after His resurrection was given to Mary of Magdala, out of whom Jesus had cast seven devils. Peter and John had visited the tomb and gone away before Mary Magdalene returned. They did not see the angels, for reasons we do not know. When she arrived, she stood weeping on the outside of the tomb, and as she was weeping she stooped and looked intently into the door of the sepulcher and saw the two angels, clothed in white, sitting one at the head and the other at the foot, where the body of Jesus had lain. "Woman," they asked, "why weepest thou?" Blinded by her tears, and overcome in her anxiety, she did not grasp at first the character of the two figures dressed in white. With a sobbing outburst of her grief, she replied: "Because they have taken away my Lord, and I know not where they have laid Him."

Suddenly she became conscious that someone was entering the sepulcher door behind her, and turning, she saw but did not recognize in the dim light of the sepulcher and being blinded by tears, that it was Jesus. "Woman, why weepest thou? Whom seekest thou?" He asked tenderly. Supposing it to be the keeper of Joseph's garden, she replied with a sob of anguish: "Sir, if thou didst carry[1] him off, tell me where thou didst put him, and I will carry him away." "Mary," He said in the old familiar tone and accent. "Rabboni,"[2] she cried, and embraced His feet. Moments of silent adoration passed. She had her Lord back.

"Do not cling to me," He admonished tenderly, "for I am not yet ascended unto the Father; but go unto my brethren, and say to them, 'I ascend to my Father and your Father, and to my God and your God.'" With these kindly words, He reminded her that He had not come back to resume the identical relationship He had sustained to the disciples before His death. The previous fellowship of sight, sound, and touch no longer existed, and His final state of glory was not yet begun (Robertson). The present state was a gap between the period of the incarnation and the future glorious reign upon the throne of the universe. These days were to be used for reassurance, consolation, preparation, and teaching of the disciples.

Then, suddenly, He vanished out of her sight and she hastened back to bear the thrilling message to the disciples that she had seen the Lord, and the things He had said to her. When she burst upon them with her glad news, she found them mourning and weeping. They had refused to believe the other women, nor would they believe her. The idea of His being alive! It was nonsense, they thought. They did not remember that He said He

1 Condition of the first class, she was convinced he had done so.
2 Teacher, such a teacher as was outstanding.

would rise on the third day. They had never gotten away from the current idea of the Jewish Messiah. With His death, their hope had vanished. They were in the depths of despair.

6. The appearance of Jesus to the other women (Matt. 28:9, 10). The testimony of Mary of Magdala was soon to be re-enforced by that of a group of the other women. They had already left the group of apostles—who did not dare venture forth to the tomb, knowing that they would thus uselessly expose themselves to imprisonment and possibly death—before the appearance there of Mary with her wonderful news. The women would not be readily suspected of evil intentions, and thus their visits to the tomb could be easily disregarded by the Roman officials and Jewish rulers. On the way back to the sepulcher, they were discussing the experience they had earlier in the day when they saw the angels, and how their message had been disregarded by the apostles as "idle talk," when suddenly they came face to face with Jesus.

"All hail," He saluted, with His old time geniality. Filled with joy and awe, they fell down at His feet and embraced them in reverent worship. This customary greeting bore with it this time a wonderful cause of rejoicing[1] indeed. They were overcome by this extraordinary experience of the supernatural, and who would not be? He calmed their excitement and gave them a message for the brethren. "Stop being afraid," He admonished them, "go tell my brethren that they are to depart into Galilee, and there they shall see me." This was a great message of reassurance for the apostles and other disciples who were in imminent peril while they remained in Jerusalem. They were to see the Lord! That gave a new horizon to their troubled lives.

7. Some of the guard report to the Jewish rulers. (Matt. 28:11-15).

The account of the report of the Roman guard to the Jewish rulers is an interesting episode, recorded by Matthew alone, but meriting all our credence as any other part of the evangelical narrative—the critics to the contrary. When the guards fled from fright to the Jewish rulers, from whom they had their secret commission, they were in fear for their lives. They told the story frankly, of all that had happened, but these Sanhedrists who had crucified Christ refused to accept this information and make an investigation. Such a method of procedure would not be in accord with their purpose. They therefore bribed the soldiers to put out a false report that the disciples had come and stolen the body of Jesus from the tomb while the guard slept. Even the rude soldiers knew that such a report would incriminate them-

[1] Chairete.

selves, for it meant death to a Roman soldier to fail at his post of duty. But the Sanhedrists assured the soldiers that if this report should come to the ears of the governor, they would persuade him and rid them of their punishment. The report did actually go forth among the Jews. From the time of Justin Martyr, this has been the explanation of the empty tomb. The base calumny was repeated and amplified twelve centuries later in Toldoth Jeshu.[1] It was substituted in modern Jewish writings by the Vision-hypothesis, which is that the disciples were self-deluded into believing in the resurrection by their conviction that Christ must rise from the dead, which produced in their over-excited imagination ecstatic visions. But the fact is that the disciples, far from having that conviction to begin with, were with great difficulty brought to believe, until they had many infallible proofs, that Jesus had risen. Some of the guard must have given the truth out about the report, and Matthew recorded it. It is reasonable to suppose that some of the soldiers were converted through the wonderful experiences of that night.

8. The appearance to the two disciples on the way to Emmaus (Mark 16:12, 13; Luke 24:13-32).

The third appearance of Jesus and the first to a man was to Simon Peter; the fourth, to the two disciples, Cleophas and another—whose name is not recorded—on the way to Emmaus, on the afternoon of the resurrection day, and manifestly in the act of giving thanks at the supper-table that night. These men, who were not apostles, but disciples from the rank and file, were leaving Jerusalem in a state of despondency and foreboding.

On their way to Emmaus, modern El Kubeibeh—a town seven miles northwest of Jerusalem—they were discussing all the things that had taken place relative to Jesus during those days. Being probably men of different dispositions, their discussion was warmly contested. It was natural that a passer-by, with Oriental liberty, should draw near and listen in on their conversation as they walked together, without attracting their attention away from the matter under discussion. Their conversation took the form of cross-questioning each other, and the unrecognized stranger drew near and became a participant in the homily as they went along the way. "What was all the discussion about between you as you were coming along the way?" He asked, as He noted a lull in the conversation when He came up with them. Surprised, they stopped still, looking sad. One of them, named Cleophas, was the first to speak, in half-reproachful words, saying: "Are you a lone stranger living aside to yourself in Jerusalem that you do not know what has been happening there?"

[1] Farrar's Life of Christ, in loco.

"What was that?" the stranger solicited with lively interest.

Then both of them, judging Him friendly, began to summarize for Him, "those things." "All about Jesus the Nazarene," they confided, "who got to be a prophet, powerful in work and word before God and all the people. How the high priests and rulers turned him over to the Romans for a death judgment and crucified him." They recognized that the Jews had the greater responsibility for His death. "We had hoped," they went on, "that it was even He who was about to liberate Israel." Evidently, they held to the characteristic traditional belief in a temporal Messiah and nothing more. With the death of Jesus, this hope had vanished, so far as He was concerned, for they added: "Besides all this, it is the third day since these things happened." There was no hope that His soul would return to His body, after three days, according to the Jewish conception. "In spite of all this disappointment," they add, "certain of our own women, who had been early at the tomb, astounded us with the report that they had not found his body, but had seen a vision of angels, who declared that he is alive!" Some of our company[1] went off immediately to the tomb, and found that it was just as the women had reported; "but," they added doubtfully, "they did not see him."

Now, the divinely disguised Jesus took up the conversation: "O senseless men," He said with sadness, "and dull and slow of heart to believe all the things the prophets have spoken! Was it not necessary for Christ (Messiah) to suffer these things and enter into his glory?" Then beginning with Moses, He interpreted passage after passage which referred to the Messiah, from all the prophets and all the Scriptures. What an exposition of passages on the sufferings and death of Christ that must have been, and by the prince of all expositors! No wonder their hearts burned within them.

Then they came to the forks of the road near the village, destination of Cleophas and his companion. The stranger turned to leave them and go on His separate way. But they constrained Him with their insistent invitation, saying: "Stay over with us. It is already growing late!" So He went in to be their guest. The simple evening meal was soon spread, and they were ranged around, reclining on their couches at the table.

A strange thing now happened. Jesus was invited to take the place of host at the table, a mark of their appreciation; and in His characteristic way, taking the bread He gave thanks, and breaking the loaf distributed it among them. Nobody could perform that customary, familiar, Jewish service with the fine delicacy and reverence which characterized the Master. Their eyes which

1 They were careful not to expose the names of Peter and John who went.

had been blinded with unbelief and darkened with faithless pessimism, were suddenly opened, and they recognized their Lord. His purpose had been accomplished and He immediately vanished out of their sight. With glad surprise, they turned to one another and said: "Were not our hearts burning[1] within us, as He was talking to us in the way, and was opening up unto us the Scriptures?"

The risen Christ was revealed, in this incident, to the disciples who represented the rank and file of the early church. They were in utter bewilderment and had not come to comprehend the true character of the Messiah. Least of all did they understand the character of the resurrection, about which Jesus had told them. Disintegration had already set in, and the group of apostles and disciples were leaving Jerusalem and seeking safety elsewhere. They had no conception whatever of the purpose of Jesus for world evangelization, because they had not grasped the real character and mission of their great Teacher. Their hope of the Kingdom's realization through Jesus had been blasted by His death. These two had left the group before Mary Magdalene and the other women brought back their report of having seen the Master. But now it was different with them, and with hearts thrilled they can return and make known their conversation with the risen Lord.

9. The report of the two disciples, and the news of the appearance to Simon Peter (Luke 24:33-35; cf. I Cor. 15:5).

Eager to get back to report to their fellow-disciples in Jerusalem, they arose at that same hour[2] and hastened back over the seven miles, a new hope and thrilling wonder filling their souls. They arrived after dusk, and made their way quietly to the rendezvous of the disciples, finding them now gathered in a group. They had not dared to be found in group meetings for fear of exposure to the Jewish rulers. Even now, they had barricaded the doors and were careful not to admit any stranger into their group.

Cleophas and his companion were admitted and found the eleven, minus Thomas the Twin, and others with them, engaged in cautious but glad and animated conversation about the many glorious revelations of the day. Already three times Jesus had appeared to different members of the group. They had to acknowledge with shame that they had not given credence to the report of the first appearance to the women and Mary of Magdala. But

---

1 Periphrastic imperfect middle.   2 Locative case, expressing the point of time.

Jesus had appeared to Simon Peter, who might least expect such an honor, because he had denied his Lord. At least that was the way the others thought about it. But Jesus had honored Simon, whose real friendship and love He recognized, and would yet make of him, Peter, a foundation stone in the Kingdom. They really[1] believed that Jesus was alive, now that Simon Peter had seen Him. How little they had understood, much less believed, what Jesus had so many times told them about rising on the third day. It was too good to be true!

Cleophas and his companion received this joyous chorus of blessed experiences of the women, and Simon Peter's account of the gracious manifestation of his Lord to him, impatient for an opportunity to narrate their own story. When they got their turn, they rehearsed their experiences with the stranger on the way in detail and how He was made known finally to them by His manner of breaking the bread and giving thanks at the table. Their eyes were beholden in the way. He had seemed not altogether a stranger, but His appearance was somehow different. And so they were going on with their explanation when suddenly they became conscious of another presence.

10.   The appearance to the astonished disciples (minus Thomas) with a Commission (Mark 16:14; Luke 24:36-43; Jno. 20:19-25).

Cleophas and his companion had been admitted while the disciples were partaking of a simple and hurried repast. They had finished eating before the story of the Emmaus appearance was rehearsed. The news of the open tomb had spread like wildfire over the city. It was the talk of the town, and the Jewish leaders had already put out the base calumny laying the blame of the tomb robbery to the charge of the disciples. It is no wonder that the disciples were in a high state of nervous tension, and that they had both shut and barred the doors securely for fear of the Jews. All of the eleven were present except Thomas, called Didimus or the Twin. They were all intent on the story of the appearance in Emmaus when Jesus Himself suddenly appeared, standing in their midst. He had not knocked or entered by the doors. They had been discussing the possibilities of spectral appearance. True it was that Simon Peter had been with Jesus. Still His appearance was so sudden that they were thrown into a state of nervous terror and fright.

Jesus saluted them in the old way. "Peace be unto you," He said. But they continued to think[2] they were looking upon a spirit. They believed Peter's reports that Jesus was risen from the dead, but they had not conceived the idea of the resurrection of

---

1 Outos, indeed, really.   2 Imperfect indicative active, characteristic continued action.

His body, though they had heard the report of the women and of Simon Peter. Jesus knew all about their unbelief and their hardness of heart and refusal to believe or give credence to the reports of their fellow-disciples. This must have been a surprising revelation to them. He had been able to discern their thoughts when He was with them. He had the same ability to read their minds now as ever.

But He saw their half-convinced and troubled look at incredulity and uncertainty. They needed to be convinced of the reality of His bodily presence. "Why do you continue to be troubled," He asked kindly, "and why do your reasonings continue to rise in your hearts?" When He said this, He showed them His hands and His side and His feet also, that they might see that His body was identical with the one which was hung upon the cross. Knowing their inmost thought, that He might be a spirit-apparition from heaven, He said: "See my hands and my feet, that it is I myself; handle me, and see; for a spirit hath not flesh and bones, as ye behold me having." This ought to have been sufficient to convince the most incredulous that this was His real body, and that they were not looking at a spirit.

They were indeed hard to convince, and their minds were yet full of questionings as to His real character after rising from the dead. They were gradually becoming convinced, but it was still just too good to be true. From sheer joy and wonder, they could not yet fully accept the resurrection as a reality. The Master would leave no stone unturned to convince them: "Have ye here anything to eat?" He asked. This was a welcome suggestion. If He could eat they would be convinced of the reality of His body. They gave Him a part of a broiled fish, and He, taking it, really ate it in their presence. What more could they desire? They were glad when they were convinced at last that this was really their Lord.

Convinced now of His real bodily presence, the disciples were prepared to hear the plans of the Master. "Peace be unto you." His salutation this second time would remind them that He was satisfied they were fully convinced of His resurrection. In simple words, He sets before them their commission. Many times He had spoken of His being sent on a mission into the world. Now it would be theirs to take up the same commission and carry it out to the ends of the earth. His own personal mission was completed. The tremendous responsibility rested upon this small disciple band to evangelize the whole world. Of this, they would hear more later.

To be able to undertake this staggering task, they would need adequate power. Jesus did not ignore this important fact.

Breathing upon them symbolically, He added: "Begin now to receive[1] the Holy Spirit." He was giving them a foretoken of the power of Pentecost. They would receive that Power in greater measure in days to come. Power for their task depended on the taking it. They were to take this power themselves as they needed it. The power-resources were unlimited. The amount each one should have would depend upon the special need and their appropriation of it for their use in the Kingdom work.

Their authoritative function had been explained to them already, just after the great confession at Cesarea Philippi: "If the sins of any ye may forgive,[2] they have been forgiven and stand forgiven unto them, if any ye may retain, they stand retained." The right to forgive sins in the absolute sense belongs to God alone (Mark 2:5-7). Jesus forgave sins in virtue of the fact that He was the Son of God. He commits to His disciples everywhere the prerogative of handling the Gospel, the keys of the Kingdom, and correctly announcing the terms of forgiveness. There is no actual proof that He transferred to the apostles or their successors the power, of themselves, to forgive sins.[3] The Rabbis spoke of binding and loosing by proclaiming and teaching. Any believer can open the door of the Kingdom to those outside by telling the story of Christ's love and the condition of salvation by acceptance of Him through faith. There is no power of absolution from sin given to the disciples.

Perhaps it was Thomas' sole fault that he was not with the group of disciples when Jesus appeared. He was pessimistic by disposition, as it seems. But he was courageous when convinced, though he found difficulty in getting convinced. The other disciples found him and told him of their glorious experience of the night before. "We have seen the Lord," they enthusiastically declared. But he was not so easily convinced. "Except I shall see in his hands the print of the nails," he exclaimed dogmatically, "and put my finger into the print of the nails, and my hand into his side, I will not believe." This he said in spite of their repeated[4] testimony as to the resurrection. If Thomas could be convinced, all the world would believe.[5] He was one of the strongest arguments ever after for the reality of Jesus' resurrection.

11. The appearance to the disciples on the following Sunday night, with Thomas (Jno. 20:26-31; I Cor. 15:5).

Just a week later, in the same lodging place in Jerusalem, under the same circumstances except that Thomas was this time present with the group of apostles and that the disciples now

---

1 Ingressive aorist imperative.   2 Condition of third class with an instead of ean.
3 Cf. Matt. 16:19; 18:18.   4 Imperfect indicative active, repeated and continued action.
5 Present middle imperative.

were not so afraid of the enemies and were in a hopeful frame
of mind instead of despair, Jesus again comes, and, taking His
position in their midst, once more salutes them. "Peace be unto
you," He said, and immediately without further ado, He addresses
Himself to Thomas personally: "Reach hither thy finger, Thomas,
and see my hands and extend thy hand and thrust it into my
side, and stop becoming faithless but believing." Jesus taught
Thomas that his disbelieving condition depended on him, and
that there was no virtue in being a doubter. It is no mark of
superior intelligence to doubt. Skeptics sometimes pose as persons of unusual mentality, which does not follow.

Thomas yielded at once when granted the sensuous evidence.
"My Lord and my God," he exclaimed, addressing Jesus as deity.
His confession is no sooner made than accepted. "Because thou
hast seen, thou hast believed," said Jesus. "Blessed are they that
have not seen, and yet have believed." The highest form of faith,
Thomas had missed: that not based on the evidence of the senses.

"Many other signs therefore," concludes[1] John, the author of
the fourth gospel, "did Jesus in the presence of the disciples,
which are not written[2] in this book." "But," he adds, defining
the purpose of his writing it, "these are written that ye may
believe[3] that Jesus is the Christ, the Son of God, and that believing, ye may have life in his name."

12. Appearance to seven disciples beside the Sea of Galilee.
The marvelous draught of fishes (Jno. 21:1-25).

Five times Jesus appeared to different disciples within the
first eight days after the resurrection in Jerusalem. Five times
He would appear to them in Galilee, where He had done most of
His mighty works. The first time was by the Sea of Galilee, which
from the capital of the tetrarchy, Tiberias, is sometimes called
the sea of Tiberias.

The account of this appearance is recorded in the epilogue
to the fourth gospel, which was added to that greatest of all books
after it was completed, probably to correct an impression prevalent in the early church that John, the author of the Gospel, would
continue to live until the Master's return to the world in His second
advent. The misinterpretation of a saying of Jesus, in His private
conversation with Peter and John after the appearance to the seven
together, gave rise to that impression. There is given first the
account of His dealing with the seven, recalling them to their
sacred task and mission. He would guard the disciples against

1 John may have intended to stop here but afterwards added the epilogue.
2 Periphrastic perfect passive indicative of grapho, do not stand described.
3 Hina with the present subjunctive, that ye may keep on believing.

drifting away from the work which awaited them, and lead them to consecrate their attention on the task of fishers of men and not that of mere fishermen. If they would do that, and lead the others to do so, He would provide for their daily sustenance and they could depend on Him to do that (vv 12-14). Then He singled out Peter, who was to be the outstanding leader of the evangelical movement, due to his superior gifts of leadership and his ardent love, even in spite of his past failures and blunders, for which he was truly repentant. In the presence of the other disciples, Jesus examines him searchingly, rebukes him tactfully and tenderly, and reinstates him fully in his apostolic work of the Kingdom (vv 15-19). In the remaining part of the epilogue, John refers to the saying of Jesus about himself, correcting the false report that had gone out (vv 20-23) and concludes with a fitting expression about the great works of Jesus and the few illustrations that could be even mentioned in his short Gospel.

Seven disciples—Simon Peter, Thomas the Twin, Nathanael, James and John the sons of Zebedee, and two other disciples whose names are not given—were gathered in Peter's home in Capernaum. Some days had passed, doubtless, and Peter, a man of activity, would naturally grow impatient and want to be at something. Waiting was a real test to this man of work. One evening, when the sun was setting behind the Horns of Hattin, casting its last rays upon the blue waters of Galilee, the desire for the old occupation and ventures of the fisherman's life swept over Simon Peter, and he enthusiastically announced to his companions: "I am off to fish tonight." The others bethought them for a moment. Why not go out for their livelihood while they were waiting for Jesus? This met with their unanimous approval. "We are going with you," they exclaimed.

So they went out and embarked, doubtless in one of the boats belonging to the fishing firm of which Peter had once been the head. With all the old enthusiasm, they were off for the night's ventures in the old haunts of other days. But luck was against them that night. They caught nothing.

When it was approaching daylight, and the first streaks of the dawn were deepening into red, they descried through the dim light a figure on the beach a hundred yards away. They could not see by the insufficient light who it was, and so did not recognize Jesus. He called to them across the stillness of the waters, broken only by the lapping of the wavelets on the beach at His feet and the occasional remarks of the fishermen as they commented about their failure of the night or as they gave direction to their work.

"Lads," He said, using the customary language of the fishermen, "have you anything to eat?" He might be a fish merchant,
who would do business with them, they thought. "No," they said,
in tones of disappointment. "Cast the net on the right side of the
boat and you will make a haul," the stranger suggested. Perhaps
this man might have experience as a fisherman; perhaps He knew
nothing at all about it. But a fisherman is always ready to make
one more attempt and so out they flung the net. In a few moments
it enclosed such a multitude of fish that they could not draw it.

As they tugged at the net, suddenly John remembered another
experience three years before, when he and James were beckoned
to by Peter to help him and Andrew manage their net, over-full
with a large catch. Quick as a flash, he turned to Peter. "It is
the Lord," he exclaimed joyfully. In an instant, Simon snatched
his fisher coat on, and tucking it under the belt of his loin cloth
in his eagerness, sprang into the sea and swam to the shore. The
others hastily followed him, dragging the net with their boat in
the direction of the shore about a hundred yards away.

When they got out of their boat and came out on the land,
they saw a fire of coals with fish broiling on it. Jesus said to them:
"Bring some of the fish you caught just now." Simon Peter
quickly waded out into the shallow water and drew the net with
a hundred and fifty-three large fish to the land. Even so, he did
not tear the net, being an experienced fisherman.

Jesus said to them: "Come on now and eat breakfast." No
one dared ask him: "Who are you?" knowing that it was the
Lord. Jesus next comes, and, taking the place of the host, proceeds to pronounce the blessing and break and distribute the bread
and fish, as they had seen Him do so many times. Again they were
eating with their Lord, who had been crucified and had risen from
the dead. How wonderful it all was, how incomprehensible to
them, but how glorious! And best of all, this renewed fellowship
was going on further and further. Already He had been with
groups of the apostles and disciples three times—not to mention
His appearances to individuals and the group of women — since
He rose from the dead. During this early morning meal, He had
reminded them doubtless of their first call to exclusive discipleship, when they made a great catch, recalling vividly in detail the
circumstances to their memory, and impressing upon them the
unbroken relation He sustained to them in that call even now.
They were to pursue that great task, after a few more days of
instruction and preparation, when He should go up to the Father
and send the Holy Spirit upon them, and then they must give
themselves to that work solely. Three years ago, He had given

them the call; He now recalls these fishermen to the exclusive work of fishers of men. To their better preparation for this task, He would give Himself yet a few days.

When they had finished breakfast, He turned to Simon Peter. Here was the man who was to be His foremost leader in the initial movement of the Kingdom. John might claim the distinction of being the disciple whom Jesus loved, but Peter would be used at Pentecost and in the leadership of the first months of the Kingdom movement, in a way far excelling any other apostle. Jesus says to him, using his old name as a reminder: "Simon, son of John, do you love[1] me more than these?" Thus, He probes the inmost recesses of Peter's heart to secure the humility necessary for service.[2] Peter remembered very well his boast "that all others might leave Him, but he would follow Him to death." He knew that Jesus was referring to that boast, by the words "more than these." Did Peter have that devoted love and did he have a love superior to that of his fellow disciples? Peter was humiliated by his failure, and had repented bitterly in his heart, even the same night of the denial. Jesus had forgiven him even then and had honored him with being the first of the disciples to be visited by Him after the resurrection. What passed in that first intimate meeting between Him and Peter, nobody knows. We may well imagine that there was full confession and blessed forgiveness and restoration to fellowship with the Lord in that sacred hour.

In his reply to the question, Simon left out the reference to the "love superior to that of his fellow disciples." That was a delicate point and he felt that comparisons were not needed now that he had failed so miserably. Nor did he trust himself to assume to love with a high devotion which would go "even unto death" for the Master. Such a love Jesus had asked about and summoned him to rise and attain in His appeal. But Simon did love the Master, and Jesus knew it. "Yes, Lord, thou knowest that I love thee." Peter replied. It was enough to be called by the name Simon, the old preconversion name, and not Peter, the name Jesus had given him. His heart was grieved by the question.

Jesus did not leave him thus, but did what above all was welcome to that sorely vexed and humiliated soul. He restored him to the fellowship of the Kingdom work. "Provide food for my lambs," said the great Shepherd of the sheep. A profound silence held the group of disciples as they tried to grasp the meaning of these amazing words of the Lord.

Once again, He accosted Simon: "Simon, son of John, do you love me?" This time the Master used the same name Simon, but

---

1 Jesus uses the word agapa, high spiritual love, which serves at the cost of sacrifice.
2 Robertson, Word Pictures.

followed Simon in leaving out the reference to the "love superior to that of the other disciples." He also held to the word (agapas), calling for the high love of devotion and sacrifice. This time, Simon replied in the same words as before: "Yes, Lord, thou knowest that I love thee." He would not venture to assume his ability to live up to the love that might lead him to death for the Master. But he was certain of the real attachment he had for Jesus in his heart. He would undertake to stand by Him as a friend.[1] Had he not attempted that in Gethsemane? Jesus knew that his ardent disciple was His friend, though He might have failed Him once. He also knew that none other except John had stood by Him that night, and even John had withdrawn in Gethsemane.

Greater assurance Jesus brings to Simon Peter in his second assignment of work, in the renewed fellowship: Shepherd my little sheep," He charged him firmly. Here was an advance in the difficulty of the task. It is difficult enough to minister instruction to the new converts and thus feed the little lambs, but is is more difficult to minister individual pastoral care to the older members of the flock of the great Shepherd. A pastor must be a leader, and Simon is thus called to a high leadership. The group sat spellbound, listening intently to every word. Did Simon grasp the meaning of this high commission? He was to be a pastor to the individual members of the flock.

Again, the third time, Jesus addresses him, still using his old name: "Simon, son of John, do you love me?" This time, Jesus descends to the level of Simon's word "friendship," and questions Simon as to whether he really felt that he could attempt to live up to the standard of a true friendship for the Master. No wonder Peter was cut to the heart when this question was repeated the third time. All the disciples had dwelt in repeated discussions on the fact that he had denied his Lord *three times*. This was a sore point, and humiliated almost beyond endurance, he submitted: "Lord, you are omniscient in your understanding of the human heart; you recognize[2] that I love you."

"Provide food for my sheep," commanded the Lord. This was the hardest task of the Kingdom, the feeding of the sheep. It is harder to adapt one's religious ministrations in teaching to the older sheep of the flock than to the younger ones who are more open minded and ready to receive them.

Jesus brings His "re-signing" of Peter's call to apostleship to a conclusion, by pointing out to him the way to martyrdom for the Kingdom and bidding him follow his Master in it. When Peter was younger, he was accustomed to go forth[3] more in his own

1 Philein, to be a friend, to love as a friend.
2 Ginoskeis, you know from your experience and divine understanding.
3 Imperfect of customary action.

strength and following in his own impulses and judgment. Jesus points out now that when he shall be older in the service, he shall stretch forth his hands in dependence and the weakness of old age and another shall gird him with divine strength and lead him in Kingdom bondage into a death he would not naturally choose. Tradition says that Peter glorified God in a martyr's death by crucifixion, and that, feeling himself unworthy to die as Jesus had died, made a special request that he be permitted to be crucified with his head downward. He is called upon now to follow Jesus not in the mere abandonment of the previous occupation of a fisherman to become a fisher of men, but in the participation of disgrace, peril, and a martyr's death. But the command was positive: "Begin now and go on following me[1] in this course of life." Peter had followed Jesus better than any of the group except John. The others had all fled and hid out until the storm had passed over, sweeping their Lord with it, into a violent death on the cross. Peter had also fled, but had turned and followed afar off. He got into trouble by this half-way profession of faith, but that was better than completely abandoning the Lord. All the others present in the group of seven, except John, must have felt the sting of the rebuke to themselves. They were humiliated, recognizing their crime against the Lord, worse than that of Peter, and prepared now to accept not merely Peter's restoration to fellowship, but his call to leadership as well.

When Jesus commanded Peter to follow Him, He seems to have gradually drawn apart from the group. Peter literally obeyed and followed the departing Lord. John was also following. Peter turning[2] and seeing John coming behind him, knowing that John had held the distinction of being "the disciple whom Jesus loved," wondered if he also would be called upon to follow to a martyr's death. "Lord," he cried out to the receding form of the Master, "but what about this man?" He and John had walked in intimate fellowship and he was concerned to know if they would suffer together at the last. The reply of Jesus pointed to the individual offices and responsibilities of the disciples. "If I may wish him to remain while I am coming, what is that to thee?" Christ is sovereign in the disciple's life. The disciple's service is personal and individual. John calls attention to the fact that the misinterpretation of this saying of Jesus gave rise to the idea that he himself would continue in life until the second advent of his Lord. The tradition that John was sleeping in his grave at Ephesus and that the moving dust witnesses to the breathing of the saint be-

1 Present active imperative, progressive action, to go on continually.
2 Ingressive second aorist, passive participle, suddenly turning around.

neath, survived for a long time. It had its origin in the false interpretation of this saying of Jesus.

Thus, the curtain falls on the private interview of Peter and John with Jesus. He had led them apart, perhaps into one of the sacred haunts[1] of prayer and communion of those hallowed days of the ministry in Galilee. They were to be His leaders in days out ahead and each would have his individual part in the heroic drama and together they would face the issues of the early struggles of apostolic Christianity. They needed this wonderful hour with the Master alone in preparation for the great tasks of the Kingdom just ahead of them.

13. The appearance to above five hundred on an appointed mountain in Galilee and the Great Commission (Mark 16:15-18); Matt. 28:16-20; I Cor. 15:6).

The eleven apostles went into Galilee to the definite mountain, where Jesus had signified He would meet them. They probably went immediately after the sixth appearance to the eleven in a lodging place in Jerusalem. At this time, He met with over five hundred brethren, as Paul testifies in his letter to the Corinthians written within the time of that generation. The greater part of the five hundred remained alive even at the time Paul wrote that letter. It would be wonderful to talk to eyewitnesses about that glorious appearance. We do not know where it occurred, but the Mount of the Beatitudes would lend itself to such an occasion beautifully, and might have been the place.

At first some of the rank and file of the disciples—not the eleven—doubted that it was Jesus when He appeared in the distance, perhaps in the mountain heights. But as He came nearer, most of the large congregation bowed in reverent worship,[2] recognizing that it was the risen Lord. They, like Thomas, were ready to accept Him as their divine Lord, their God. This was the most important appearance up to the present, because it embraced the masses of the rank and file of His followers. They were to be witnesses and His it is to prepare them for their important task.

Jesus now assigns to His disciples of all time the great task of the Kingdom, that of world evangelization. He had already definitely pointed out to the Eleven their Commission, which was to go forth as apostles, do the same kind of work and carry out the same program that Jesus had begun in His ministry. As a preface to the great commission, the Magna Charta of Christianity, which He now entrusts to His larger body of disciples, He makes an astounding claim: "All authority[4] in heaven and upon earth

1 David Smith, In the Days of His Flesh.   2 Prosekunesan, bow the knee in worship.
3 Jno. 20:21-28.   4 Exousian, authority, power.

was definitely given[1] me." His power and authority now is far beyond that of His earthly life. It is boundless, including heaven and earth. Here then is the great authority, above that of all earthly kings and potentates. The disciples are to remember that no earthly power has the right to countermand the order or impede the carrying out of the commission He assigns His Kingdom forces.

The commission or mission to which He sends them is now made plain: "Go ye therefore and make disciples of all the nations, baptizing them in the name of the Father, and of the Son, and of the Holy Ghost, teaching them to observe all things whatsoever I have commanded you." A dead Christ could never have sustained a commission like that. Jesus spoke "as one already in heaven, with a world-wide outlook and with the resources of heaven at His command." All the nations, Jew and Gentile, Greek and Barbarian, were to be evangelized.[2] Here then was a dynamic faith. Christ sends His band of men and women out to evangelize the whole world. They are to make disciples or learners of all the nations. Evangelism is not limited to mere conversion. The whole life individually and socially of the people must be changed by the power of the gospel. As many as accept the message of the glad tidings, they are to immerse, not with true immersion, but in the name or character of the triune God: Father, Son and Holy Ghost. The program of the commission does not stop with baptism, which is but the door into the activities of the church. It includes teaching along all the lines exemplified in the ministry of Jesus. Religious and Christian education have a vast field and scope for their activities.

Great authority, sending the disciples out as apostles to a great task, called also for a great assurance and personal help from the Divine Lord. He did not fail His disciples in giving this assurance. "Behold," He says, calling their attention sharply, "I am with you all the days, even until the consummation of the age." He would be with them in all sorts of days and all kinds of experiences until the goal of the Kingdom should have been reached out in the future. This was a definite program, with all the authority of heaven behind it, and all the dynamic of the living Christ in it. While the task seemed impossible, the resources for its accomplishment were absolutely unlimited. Mark adds some details in the program, which are little more than a repitition of instructions[3] given to the apostles and disciples, when sent out to the evangelistic campaigns in Galilee and Judea during His ministry, and they fall within a passage which textual criticism has called in question.[4]

1 Timeless aorist.   2 Mark 16:15, another report of the Missionary Magna Charta.
3 Cf. Luke 10:19; Acts 28:3.   4 Robertson, Word Pictures.

14. The appearance to the disciples with another commission
(Luke 24:44-49; Acts 1:3-8).

Jesus appeared to James,[1] one of His half-brothers, who had
been converted after the resurrection. We do not know the circumstances of his converison, but apostolic history reveals the
fact that he became a great worker and afterwards served as
pastor of the church in Jerusalem. The account of the appearance to James given in the apocryphal gospel to the Hebrews is
not historical.[2] This manifestation preceded immediately another
appearance in Jerusalem to the eleven disciples, probably with
some others. It was the final manifestation to the apostolic group
just preceding the farewell meeting on the Mount of Olives and
the ascension.[3] The forty-day period of instruction came to an
end with this final group-meeting, perhaps at night and in the
same lodging place where they had met before. Jesus now commanded them to remain in Jerusalem; previously, He had instructed them to go to Galilee. He now repeated for them some
of the same messages which He had spoken to them during His
earthly ministry, together with a condensation, perhaps, of the
instructions He had given during the forty-day period. He continues His method used during the forty days, illustrated in the
case of the two disciples who walked with Him on the way to
Emmaus, of explaining the word. He opened up their understanding and showed "how things written in the law of Moses,
the Prophets and Psalms"—the customary tripartate division covering the Old Testament—"concerning Himself must be fulfilled."
There was continuity of thought from the days of His earthly
ministry with the experience after the resurrection. In this last
meeting, He covers adequately the whole field of canonical revelation. He had breathed upon them the Holy Spirit in the first
meeting, that they might be illumined to understand. The same
Spirit must illumine now, as then, and always.

He sums up the message of the Scriptures concerning the
Messiah in a very brief statement: "Thus it is written (Hosea 6:2)
that the Christ should suffer, and rise from the dead the third
day; and that repentance and remission of sins should be preached
in his name unto all nations, beginning at Jerusalem." This
was to be the core of the Gospel message to the world.

The Risen Christ could point out to His disciples the prophecy
of the beginning, in the Law, about the bruising of the serpent's
head by the seed of the woman (Gen. 3:15), God's plan in the
call of Abraham (Gen. 12:1-3) and the prophetic ideal of Israel
(Ex. 19:1-6) as being fulfilled in Him. Passing to the prophets,

1 David Smith, In the Days of His Flesh.   2 I Cor. 15:7.
3 Robertson's Harmony of the Gospels.

He could show the "purpose of God in calling, saving, and preserving His people, that they might be witnesses in the presence
of all the nations to the fact that He (the Messiah) alone, is
God and Saviour"[1] (Isa. 42-43). The same mission was set forth
in Amos, Micah, Jeremiah, and Zechariah. By the passages about
the Suffering Servant (Isa. 49, 53), He would explain His death
and resurrection. By Isaiah, Daniel, and Ezekiel, He would prove
to them that the disciples were linked up with the Redeemer in
the great redemptive work. Many of the Psalms, as He showed,
set forth the universalism of the Messianic Reign, as well as the
sufferings and dedication of the Messiah.

The Resurrection had sealed the book of Scriptural testimony
and gave to the disciples the completed Gospel message. That
message revealed the eternal life of Jesus. He brought life and
immortality to light. Old Testament saints had but a hazy understanding of the future life. He was the Columbus-like discoverer
of a new world, a new life beyond the ocean-like abyss of death
and the grave. The Resurrection message therefore revealed the
eternal nature of Jesus. Moreover, His resurrection-life was one of
activity and fellowship with His disciples. His workers were to
experience this presence and continued fellowship with Him, as
they have ever since. He is the powerful living Christ, continuing
His activities, as always for the Kingdom. His resurrection sealed
all the claims of Jesus to His Divine Sonship and His saving mission. He had just claimed to have all power in heaven and upon
earth. He had commissioned the small disciple-band of some five
hundred, to undertake the evangelization of the whole world. The
resurrection gave Him authority to send them out to this seemingly impossible task and the power to stand behind them in it.
The sinless life, the suffering on the cross, the declaration that
the work of redemption was finished, all were substantiated by the
resurrection from the dead.

The resurrection message related also to the salvation of
mankind. It assumed the reality of sin, which is missing the mark[2]
or goal of life, to which God destined every human being. Sin
is abnormal in human life and must be extirpated. It is calamitous
and ruinous, resulting in death both spiritual and physical. The
remedy for sin is to be found in repentance unto remission. At the
name of Jesus there is remission, removal or forgiveness of sin.
Jesus set forth perfectly the standard of human life which God
requires. His life was sinless. All men sin and come short of the
glory of God. Through the atoning death and glorious resurrection, Jesus provided the way for pardon and forgiveness of sin

---

1 Carver's Self-Interpretation af Jesus.   2 Hamartia, missing the mark, sin.

for everyone who will accept Him. Repentance is holy sorrow for sin and a deliberate turning away from it. This naturally must be accompanied by trust in Jesus. The death on the cross and resurrection revealed a God of love, giving His only-begotten Son to suffer, that sin might have an adequate remedy. The resurrection reveals also a judgment to come. Sin is to be punished. Jesus paid the price for forgiveness and provided the way of escape for the repentant sinner. Self-substitution was the way He paid the price of the sinner's redemption. God offers amnesty, free pardon, and eternal forgiveness to everyone who will lay down the arms of rebellion and come back in loyalty to His Kingdom rule.

Jesus spoke many times concerning the Kingdom of God during the forty-day period. He also charged the disciples that they must not depart from Jerusalem but wait for the promise of the Father, which He had told them about. They had been baptized by John with water, but they were to be baptized with the Holy Spirit not many days hence.

The disciples yet clung to the old traditional idea of a temporal King and Kingdom. They therefore raise the question: "Lord, dost thou at this time restore the Kingdom of Israel?" His reply was absolute, complete, and final: "It is not for you to know the times and seasons which the Father hath set within his own authority." The main issue for them was to carry out the program of the commission given them on the Mount of Galilee. For that purpose, they would have need of power. So He adds: "But ye shall receive power, when the Holy Ghost has come upon you." The end or purpose of the power was to make their witnessing efficient. When they should be clothed with power from on high, they would be prepared to witness. "Ye are witnesses of these things," He declared. "Ye shall be my witnesses both in Jerusalem and in Judea, and Samaria, and unto the utmost parts of the earth."

He points out to His disciples in these words the fact that they are and are to continue to be[1] His witnesses. But they must first be equipped with the power to make their witnessing effective. To that end, He commands them to remain in Jerusalem until they shall be clothed or endued with power from on high. All the disciples were to be witnesses. In apostolic times, they "all went everywhere preaching the word," just as we find in mission fields today in many places. The disciples are to be communicative, and constantly testify to their faith, in aggressive, personal evangelism. Witness-bearing is the narrating in a positive way of the things that are real, which we have experienced in our religion,

1 Present tense of progressive, continued and habitual action.

that others may be convinced of their truth, and, accepting them personally, be saved. The disciples could witness through preaching by narrating to others their personal experience of salvation through faith in Christ, and especially by their manner of life. Their testimony written or verbal, to the sinless life, the wonderful teachings, the atoning death, and the bodily resurrection of Jesus, together with their simple explanation of the conditions of salvation through repentance and faith in Jesus, was their obligation[1] to the Saviour and a lost world. They were Jesus' own witnesses. He has bought them as slaves from the market-place, with the price of His own blood.

The witness of the disciples was to begin in Jerusalem. There He had suffered at the hands of cruel enemies. His prayer was offered for them on the cross, and now He sends His disciples to bear to them the message of free pardon and forgiveness. Oh infinite grace! Evangelization must begin at home. They must next go to the surrounding regions of Judea. The Samaritans, that hybrid race, as despised by the Jews as the very scavenger dogs of the streets, were to be ministered the heavenly bounties of the Gospel feast. All the nations to the ends of the earth, the most ignorant and degenerate tribes of heathendom, the haughtiest and most cruel of pride-filled peoples, and the most cruel, ignorant and sinful of the earth, were to be evangelized at the cost of millions of consecrated and devoted lives and untold material wealth.

This huge, this unlimited task, called for a special equipment. They must be clothed with *power* else they would fail. So they were to wait in Jerusalem for the "promise of the Father." After the Ascension, Jesus would send the Holy Spirit upon them. The Spirit would be the agent of that power, to convict the world of sinners of their sin of unbelief; of Jesus' righteousness, set forth in a sinless life, vicarious death, glorious resurrection, and especially the ascension to the Father; and of the judgment to come, because Satan was defeated and judged at the cross and so all sinners will be judged. He would illumine, inspire, and lead the disciples in their work for the Kingdom. He would go before the messenger and prepare the hearts of the hearers for the reception of the message. The disciples must have faith to remain in Jerusalem at the peril of their lives and, in trust and consecration, receive the Holy Spirit. They were to go forth everywhere witnessing boldly and faithfully in His name.

15. The last appearance and Ascension. (Mark 16:19, 20; Luke 24:50-53; Acts 1:9-12.)

1 Shall be my witnesses.

The Ascension is recorded twice in the Gospels and in the Acts. It took place on the Mount of Olives in sight of Bethany, and near the place where Jesus pronounced His prophetic sermon. When Jesus finished His last instruction to them in their meeting place in Jerusalem, He led them forth to the high point on the Mount of Olives, a Sabbath day's journey or two thousand cubits from the city, and there "lifted up His hands and blessed them." Then suddenly, while He was blessing them, and they were looking steadfastly at Him, they saw that His feet were no longer touching the ground. They were held spellbound with wondering awe, as He floated up and up until He was enveloped in a cloud and disappeared.

For moments, they remained in worship, gazing at the vacant sky. Suddenly, they were aware of the presence of two shining figures, who said: "Ye men of Galilee, why stand ye looking into heaven? This Jesus, which was received up from you into heaven, shall so come in like manner as ye beheld him going into heaven." The angels had answered the last question the disciples had asked Jesus about "the restoration of the Kingdom." He would return to earth as He had gone away, "upon the clouds," and then with a great host of angels in great power and glory.

This message made them glad, and they returned to Jerusalem with joyful hearts and were continually in the Temple blessing God. Jesus had ascended on high to sit on the right hand of God. Soon He would send the Holy Spirit at Pentecost and then they would go forth and preach everywhere, with the approval and blessing of heaven upon them. The same note of joy and victory has continued to be the keynote of Christianity throughout the ages, and shall be until He shall return in the final great victory of all time, when the "Kingdom of the world shall become the Kingdom of our Lord and His Christ."

A Selected Bibliography

A SELECTED BIBLIOGRAPHY

Acknowledgments: In dealing with the order and arrangement, A. T. Robertson's *Harmony of the Gospels* constituted the foundation guide. The Greek text of Nestle, with occasional references to Westcott and Hort, furnished the order by paragraphs for the contextual exposition.

The procedure employed was as follows: (1) careful grammatical study of each individual unit paragraph, employing grammars, lexicons and "word pictures" of the best authors, including Robertson, Dana and Mantey, Vincent, Thayer, and others; (2) examination of the best commentaries on the Greek text on difficult points came next; (3) following this the use of many Lives of Christ, and general treatises covering a wide range and authorship. The general reading was done during some thirty years of the life of the author, with the assimilation which comes through much teaching of the subject to classes of students in theological seminaries.

A complete bibliography would be too extensive to record in the precious space of a one-volume work such as this. The writer gives hearty thanks to all who have contributed to his clearer and better understanding of the narratives of the Gospel in the Greek language, which has been the primary and by far the greatest source of material and expositions in this volume.

I. *Grammars and Lexicons on New Testament (Koine) Greek*
Blass, F., *Grammar of New Testament Greek,* 1911.
Burton, E. D., *New Testament Moods and Tenses,* 1893.
Buttmann, A., *A Grammar of the New Testament Greek,* 1895.
Dana, H. E., and Mantey, J. R., *A Manual Grammar of the Greek New Testament,* 1936.
Moulton, J. H., *A Grammar of New Testament Greek,* 1906.
Robertson, A. T., *A Grammar of the Greek New Testament in the Light of Historical Research,* 1914.
Robertson, A. T., and Davis, W. H., *A Short Grammar of the Greek Testament,* 1931.
Thayer, J. H., *A Greek-English Lexicon of the New Testament,* 1889.
Winer, G. B., *A Grammar of the Idiom of the New Testament,* 1897.

II. *Texts*
Nestle, E. *Novum Testamentum Graece,* revised edition, 1927
Westcott, B. F., and Hort, F. J. A., *The New Testament in Original Greek,* revised edition, 1936.

III. *Versions*
English: Authorized King James, American Revised, Moffatt, Twentieth Century, Montgomery, Weymouth, Williams.
Latin Vulgate, Vatican Edition, 1892.

BIBLIOGRAPHY *(Continued)*

IV. *Harmonies of the Gospels*
Broadus, J. A., *A Harmony of the Gospels*, 1910.
Robertson, A. T., *A Harmony of the Gospels*, 1922.

V. *Word Pictures*
Robertson, A. T., *Word Pictures in the New Testament*, Vols. I, II, and V, 1930.
Vincent, M. R., *Word Studies in the New Testament*, Vols. I and II, 1924.

VI. *Commentaries Based on the Greek Texts*
Broadus, J. A., *Commentary on the Gospel of Matthew* in *An American Commentary on the New Testament*, 1885.
Bruce, A. B., *The Synoptic Gospels* in *The Expositor's Greek Testament*, 1897.
Dods, Marcus, *The Gospel of St. John* in *The Expositor's Greek Testament*, 1897.
Hovey, Alvah, *Commentary on the Gospel of John* in *An American Commentary on the New Testament*, 1885.
Plummer, Alfred, *The Gospel According to St. Luke* in *The International Critical Commentary*, 1907.
Westcott, B. F., *Commentary on the Gospel of John*, 1908.

VII. *Introduction to the Gospels*
Angus, S., *The Environment of Early Christianity*, 1915.
Bacon, B. W., *An Introduction to the New Testament*, 1900.
Bissell, E. C., *Biblical Antiquities*, 1893.
Dalman, G., *The Words of Jesus*, 1902.
Dana, H. E., *The New Testament World*, 1937.
Deismann, A., *Light from the Ancient East*, 1911.
Dods, Marcus, *Introduction to the New Testament*, 1892.
Enslin, M. S., *Christian Beginnings*, 1938.
Farrar, F. W., *The Early Days of Christianity*, 1882.
Josephus, Flavius, *The Life of Flavius Josephus.*
——————————, *Antiquities of the Jews.*
——————————, *Wars of the Jews.*
Maclear, G. F., *Class Book of New Testament History*, 1890.
McCoun, T., *The Holy Land in Geography and History*, 1897.
Moffatt, James, *An Introduction to the Literature of the New Testament*, 1911.
Moore, G. F., *Judaism in the First Centuries of the Christian Era*, 1927.
Morton, H. V., *In the Steps of the Master*, 1934.
Robertson, A. T., *An Introduction to the Textual Criticism of the New Testament*, 1925.
Sanday, W., *The Criticism of the Fourth Gospel*, 1905.
Schürer, Emil, *The Jewish People in the Time of Christ*, 5 volumes, 1891.
Streeter, B. H., *The Four Gospels*, 1924.
Thomson, W. M., *The Land and the Book*, 1868.
Westcott, B. F., *Introduction to the Study of the Gospels*, 1902.

VIII. *Lives of Christ*
Anderson, F. L., *The Man of Nazareth*, 1916.
Andrews, S. J., *The Life of Our Lord*, 1899.

Davis, Noah, K., *The Story of the Nazarene,* 1903.
Dawson, W. J., *The Life of Christ,* 1901.
DeMent, B. H., *The Bible Reader's Life of Christ,* 1928.
Edersheim, Alfred, *The Life and Times of Jesus,* 2 volumes, 1886.
Farrar, F. W., *The Life of Christ,* 2 volumes, 1874.
Geikie, C., *The Life and Words of Christ,* 1922.
Kent, C. F., *The Life and Teachings of Jesus,* 1913.
Klausner, Joseph, *Jesus of Nazareth,* 1926.
Papini, G., *Life of Christ,* 1923.
Robertson, A. T., *Epochs in the Life of Jesus,* 1923.
Rhees, Rush, *The Life of Jesus of Nazareth,* 1915.
Sanday, W., *Outlines of the Life of Christ,* 1908.
Smith, David, *In the Days of His Flesh,* 1915.
Stalker, James, *The Life of Jesus Christ,* 1891.
Vollmer, Philip, *The Life of Christ,* 1912.

IX *General Works*

Bacon, B. W., *Jesus the Son of God,* 1911.
Baillie, John, *The Place of Jesus Christ in Modern Christianity,* 1930.
Best, J. H., *The Miracles of Christ,* 1937.
Briggs, C. A., *The Incarnation of Our Lord,* 1902.
_____, *New Light on the Life of Jesus,* 1904.
Bruce, A. B., *The Galilean Gospel,* 1893.
_____, *The Parabolic Teaching of Jesus,* 1892.
Bruce, A. B., *The Training of the Twelve,* 1894.
Buttrick, G. A., *Jesus Came Preaching,* 1931.
_____, *The Parables of Jesus,* 1929.
Cadoux, C. J., *The Historic Mission of Jesus.*
Carver, W. O., *The Self-Interpretation of Jesus,* 1936.
Champion, J. B., *The Living Atonement,* 1910.
Clow, W. M., *Jesus Christ and the Social Order,* 1913.
Conybeare, W. J., *The Historic Jesus,* 1914.
Denney, James, *Jesus and the Gospel,* 1908.
_____, *The Death of Christ,* 1904.
Dods, Marcus, *The Parables of Our Lord,* 1895.
Fairbairn, A. M., *The Place of Christ in Modern Theology,* 1908.
Forrest, D. W., *The Christ of History and Experience,* 1897.
Forsythe, P. T., *The Cruciality of the Cross.*
_____, *The Person and Place of Jesus Christ,* 1909.
Garvie, A. E., *Studies in the Inner Life of Jesus,* 1907.
Glover, T. R., *The Jesus of History,* 1917.
Gordon, S. D., *Quiet Talks on John's Gospel,* 1915.
Gore, Charles, *The Incarnation of the Son of God,* 1898.
Horne, H. H., *Jesus as a Philosopher,* 1927.
Jefferson, C. E., *The Character of Jesus,* 1908.
Mabie, H. C., *The Meaning and Message of the Cross,* 1906.
Mackintosh, H. R., *The Doctrine of the Person of Jesus Christ,* 1912.
Mathews, Shailer, *The Social Teachings of Jesus,* 1897.
Meyer, F. B., *Christ in Isaiah,* 1895.
Morgan, G. C., *The Great Physician,* 1937.
Peabody, F. G., *Jesus Christ and the Social Question,* 1915.
_____, *Jesus Christ and the Christian Character,* 1905.
Robertson, A. T., *John the Loyal,* 1911.
_____, *The Christ of the Logia,* 1924.
_____, *The Divinity of Christ in the Fourth Gospel,* 1914.

BIBLIOGRAPHY *(Continued)*

..............................., *The Pharisees and Jesus*, 1920.
Robson, John, *The Resurrection Gospel*, 1908.
Sanday, W., *Christologies Ancient and Modern*, 1910.
Schweitzer, Albert, *The Quest of the Historical Christ*, 1910.
Simpson, P. C., *The Fact of Christ*, 1900.
Smith, B. T. D., *The Parables of the Synoptic Gospels*, 1937.
Speer, Robert E., *The Man Christ Jesus*, 1896.
..............................., *The Finality of Christ*, 1933.
..............................., *The Principles of Jesus*, 1902.
Stevens, G. B., *The Johannine Theology*, 1900.
Taylor, W. M., *The Miracles of Our Saviour*, 1912.
..............................., *The Parables of Our Saviour*, 1912.
Trench, R. C., *The Parables and Miracles*. 2 vols. 1902.

INDEX

INDEX

MATTHEW

INDEX *(Continued)*